Black Man vs. The World

Jack Johnson's Trials, Tribulations, and Triumphs

Adam J. Pollack

Win By KO Publications
Iowa City

Black Man vs. The World:
Jack Johnson's Trials, Tribulations, and Triumphs

Adam J. Pollack

(ISBN-13): 978-1-949783-00-1

(softcover: 50# acid-free alkaline paper)

Includes footnotes and index.

© 2018 by Adam J. Pollack. All Rights Reserved.

No part of this book may be reproduced, or transmitted in any form or by any means, graphic, electronic or mechanical, including photocopying, recording, taping, or by any information storage retrieval system without the written permission of Adam J. Pollack.

Cover design by Adam J. Pollack and Gwyn Snider ©

Manufactured in the United States of America.

Win By KO Publications
Iowa City, Iowa
winbykopublications.com

Contents

Preface: An Unusual First	5
1. From the Shadows of Poverty	8
2. Texas vs. Jack Johnson	22
3. A Cautious Approach	26
4. California Notice	30
5. Jim Jeffries and the Color Line	32
6. Ascendance	39
7. Colored Champion and More	45
8. Testing the East	55
9. Up Against the Color Line	59
10. Nitpicking Backlash	69
11. The Color Line, Regardless of Performance	84
12. The Set-Up For A White Challenger	99
13. A Matter of Perspective	108
14. Passed Over Again	118
15. The Color Line In the West	129
16. Black East	132
17. A New Champion	137
18. Continuing Proof	140
19. Coasting While Waiting	149
20. Australia	162
21. A Big Name Finally Crosses the Line	170
22. Convincing San Francisco	180
23. Chasing the Champ	187
24. Promoting the Absolute World's Boxing Championship	201
25. A True World Championship	210
26. Racial Implications: The White Hope Era Begins	233
27. The Return	246

28. A Trick or a Treat?	258
29. Big Talk	273
30. Scouting the Champ	275
31. Better Than We Thought	281
32. Fighting for the Films	292
33. The Future Welfare of His People	319
34. A National Obsession	333
35. Battle of the Races	363
36. A Nation's (and the World's) True Colors Revealed	402
37. Revisionism	443
38. Reverberations of the Big Fight	448
39. The British Empire's Color Line	460
40. Best White Hope	479
41. Under Siege	501
42. The United States vs. John Arthur Johnson	536
43. Escape	564
44. The French Dispute	573
45. Prejudice Pervades the Record	585
46. Reversal of Opinion	592
47. Something More	611
48. After the Crown	641
Acknowledgments	648
Index	649

An Unusual First

During the era of racial segregation, when the color line, or separation of the races, was the norm, legally and socially, Jack Johnson was the first black fighter to challenge for and win the world heavyweight boxing championship under modern-day Marquis of Queensberry rules. This is the story of Johnson's battles with the white world, inside and outside of the ring, his rise as a contender, his struggle to obtain a championship match owing to his race, the analysis of him as a fighter and person by the press, both black and white, his symbolic value and impact as champion, and the many legal battles and struggles he faced.

Racial bias impacted how reporters wrote about and interpreted Johnson's actions, his performances, or scouted upcoming bouts. Very few writers could escape the impact of the colored lenses of the racially biased world from which they emerged and took part. His story is as much the story of the press, and how race affects perception in reporting.

Early gloved boxing thrived at a time when the general white population abhorred the idea of mixed-race competition in any area of life. Reflective of the social mores of the late 19th and early 20th centuries, many top white fighters refused to compete against black fighters, particularly when it came to financially lucrative championship matches. Usually black fighters were not paid as well as whites for the few big fights that they did have.

This is not to say that top black fighters did not earn more money than the average citizen. Boxing could be a financially lucrative profession for all races, which in part explains why it flourished. The public loved watching good fights, regardless of race. Many racial minorities, including Blacks, Italians, Jews, and the Irish, whose economic opportunities were limited severely by racism, saw boxing as a way to earn money.

Although segregation existed in many areas of life, often mandated by law, it did not always exist in various sports, including boxing, track and field, horse racing, football, and bicycle racing, with blacks Isaac Murphy and Major Taylor respectively having obtained fame in the latter two sports in the late 1800s and early 1900s. In the bareknuckle boxing era, particularly in the early 1800s, several former slaves, like Tom Molineaux and Bill Richmond, traveled to England to fight white champions. Sports oscillated at times in the degree in which integration was allowed, or which segregation was required. While most sports eventually became totally segregated, the sport of boxing did not always follow the general social rule, making boxing the most racially progressive of all sports. Ironically, this in part was because boxing was considered to be an utterly morally depraved sport, so depraved that normal social conventions did not necessarily or always apply. Fighters purportedly had no social standing, and therefore were not always expected to follow standard social norms. Hence, there was somewhat of a greater tradition of fairness in sport, but particularly so in the sport of boxing. Actually, non-title-fight mixed-race bouts took place more often than some realize.

Many fair-minded sportswriters and sportsmen supported fair competition for all, and wanted to see the best fight the best, regardless of race. Economics, sportsmanship, and press support helped obtain mixed-race fights for many black fighters.

However, as the sport's participants obtained popularity, economic power, and prestige, and boxing champions to some degree became social, national, and racial symbols, greater opposition to mixed-race bouts arose. Many fight folks wanted to elevate the sport to a higher social level, and minimize legal opposition, which meant avoidance of black champions.

Yet, many fair-minded sportsmen felt that there was no color line in boxing, and did not have a problem with mixed-race bouts. Some only objected to mixed-race *championship* fights, which had the greatest symbolic importance. And still others were not opposed to racially mixed championship bouts, some even advocating for equal opportunity, until there were black champions, and then their deep-seated feelings of displeasure emerged. The theory of equality was one thing; its actual application was quite another.

Regardless of the fairness of many writers, they still were a product of their times, and many could not help, either consciously or subconsciously, allowing racial biases or stereotypes to influence their analysis of a fight or fighter. Sometimes, rather than laud a black contender for his performance, the writer would denigrate his defeated opponent as not being very good. Or the writer might find ways to criticize the performance of a black fighter even in victory.

Owing to the color line, it required many years for Jack Johnson to obtain a title shot. One could argue that he was the world's best heavyweight and de facto champion much sooner than when he was able to win the championship. Without the color line, or if Jack Johnson had been a white fighter, it certainly is possible that he could have begun his reign as many as five years sooner, and been champion for several more years. This is speculation for the ages.

Jack Johnson's story is amazing in part because he rose to prominence and became champion during a time when blacks rarely were allowed to achieve the top rung of anything in life. He did it during a time when blacks were persecuted in every way, had limited recognition of their legal or human rights, and lynchings and mob violence were regular occurrences. Hence, in order to appreciate his significance, one must understand the context of his times and the struggles that blacks in general faced. Jack Johnson is the ultimate underdog story.

Once he became champion, the response to Johnson's status as the world heavyweight champion further revealed the tremendous importance of racial symbolism to the world. The hunt for a "White Hope" to dethrone him was quite overt. Rather than being mere boxing contests, his fights and his status as champion had larger racial implications, particularly in a world where race determined caste in the power structure. Many were determined to undermine him in any way they could, even outside the ring.

As world champion, the significant racial meaning of his fights and personal choices outside the ring was not limited only to the United States, but had world-wide implications. In a world where white nations conquered non-white nations, a black heavyweight champion had racial and political implications which many nations had to consider.

Furthermore, Johnson's story also reveals the world's problem with the issue of miscegenation. He dated and married white women in an era when such was social taboo, and often illegal. These issues affected the treatment he received, including by the public, press, police, prosecutors, and in the courts.

Jack Johnson continues to be a hot-button topic of debate as much today as he was back then. Issues of race and analysis of black athletes have historical underpinnings that go all the way back to Jack Johnson. Some might argue that the remnants of the issues revealed during his era still remain today.

CHAPTER 1

From the Shadows of Poverty

To understand the perception of and reporting about Jack Johnson and other black fighters, and to grasp fully Johnson's struggle, impact, and historic relevance, one must understand the times from which he emerged.

Jack Johnson's parents, Henry and Tina "Tiny" Johnson, both grew up as slaves in the United States. Slaves were seen as less than or not even human, but rather as wild beasts which needed to be controlled and tamed, and therefore entitled to no rights whatsoever. It was the psychological justification used for the assertion of dominion over an entire race. Such a perception had to be perpetuated in order to continue slavery and the imbalance of power.

Slavery of blacks had existed in colonial America at least since the 1600s, so for hundreds of years it was part of the fabric of American life. Therefore, beliefs about blacks as property and as being inferior to whites were ingrained deeply into the psyche of Americans. However, over time, increasingly many came to believe that although blacks were inferior, and not entitled to the same rights as whites, slavery was morally wrong.

Concerned that Republican United States President Abraham Lincoln and Congressmen from Northern states might gradually limit or even eliminate slavery in the South, or prevent its expansion into new territories, in late 1860 and early 1861 the South seceded from the Union. This led to the U.S. Civil War, the most costly war in terms of casualties in U.S. history, with well over half a million dead from various causes associated with the War.

During the Civil War, on September 22, 1862 and January 1, 1863, President Abraham Lincoln issued emancipation proclamations abolishing slavery in the Southern states which had seceded, but not in those which did not, because the proclamations were issued under and limited by the president's war-powers authority to suppress rebellion. Slavery was officially legally abolished in December 1865, after the Civil War was over, with the ratification of the 13th Amendment to the U.S. Constitution, which abolished slavery and involuntary servitude except as punishment for crime. The passage of this amendment did not come without debate and resistance.

Although slavery had ended, its abolition did not mean that blacks would have the same rights as whites. Far from it. It just meant that they no longer were slaves.

Even though the Civil War's warfield battles technically had ended, the battle over race and power shifted into a phase in which the United States had its own form of internal social war. Slavery had ended only as a result of force and violence, not as a result of folks being convinced that it was wrong. On April 15, 1865, Abraham Lincoln became the first U.S. president to be assassinated, the motive being Southern revenge.

Southerners, including those who had not been slaveholders, were very concerned about what impact freed blacks would have on their post-Civil War society. Blacks technically might have been freed, but the South was adamant and unwavering in its efforts to ensure that it ended there, that black rights would be limited and circumscribed severely. Many were determined to make sure that freed blacks knew their place, which was subjugated to and separated from the white race - socially, economically, and politically. Many laws were designed to ensure that blacks de facto remained slaves, or as close to it as possible.

Since the 13th amendment did not bar slavery as punishment for crime, many laws were designed to criminalize blacks, who would be arrested by white police, and the courts would sentence them harshly, so they could be used as cheap labor through a convict leasing system in which the state prison hired out convicts for labor. Hence the incentive was to arrest as many as possible. Because of the reliance on convict leasing, Southern states did not build any prisons until the late 1800s.

Black Codes often restricted black people's right to own property, conduct business, buy and lease land, and move freely through public spaces. Black employment opportunities were severely circumscribed, often only allowing them to work for meager wages for their former slavemasters. Vagrancy laws criminalized those who were unemployed or not working at jobs whites recognized for them. Those arrested for vagrancy then were forced to work under the convict leasing system, or "slavery by another name," as it has been called.

Even many Northerners who believed that slavery was wrong did not necessarily believe that freed blacks should have the same rights as whites, or that they should be treated in the same way. They just thought that blacks should not be enslaved.

During the decade following the Civil War, known as Reconstruction, several constitutional amendments and laws were passed, recognizing black civil rights. However, as time passed, a significant number of Northern whites in positions of political power decided that they did not care for the ascendance of black economic or political power either, and those Northern whites who were tired of the race issue, and who wanted to gain Southern support in the 1877 presidential election, made a compromise by agreeing to withdraw troops from the South, which had ensured some degree of recognition of black civil rights. The advances of Reconstruction gradually were eliminated, interpreted in a limited way, or ignored.

The state governments that emerged following the troop withdrawal from the South passed legislation known as Jim Crow laws, which mandated segregation of blacks from whites. A caste system based on race was created via law and by custom. Enacted laws made voter registration and elections more restrictive, so as to eliminate the black vote and black political power. Poll taxes, literacy and comprehension tests, and residency and record-keeping requirements limiting the ability to vote effectively disenfranchised large portions of the population that were poor or illiterate. Public accommodations for blacks invariably were underfunded, inferior, and fewer. Hence, political, economic, educational, and social disadvantages for blacks predominated, and were perpetuated and ingrained into the society. Mob violence and intimidation did whatever the law did not.

On March 31, 1878 in Galveston, Texas, thirteen years after the U.S. Civil War ended, and one year after the Union withdrew its troops from the South, Jack Johnson was born, either as John Arthur Johnson or Arthur John Johnson. Galveston was a southern Texas coastal town on the Gulf of Mexico, about 50 miles southeast of Houston. The town had a thriving port, and a population of about 25,000. Texas had been a slave-holding state and was part of the Confederacy that had seceded from the Union (voting 166-8 to secede), fighting for the South in the Civil War. Johnson claimed that his father had fought in the Civil War. In 1860, about 30% of the state's total population of 640,000 were slaves.

Henry Johnson and Tina, also known as "Tiny," who was 19 years younger than Henry, to support their family, worked very low-paying blue-collar jobs, the only employment available to recently freed slaves. Henry worked as a manual laborer, woodcutter, and saloon porter. In 1888 he became the Galveston, Texas school district janitor/cleaning man.

They had Lucy, Jennie, Arthur, Henry, Fannie, and Charles. Three other girls died at birth. All of the Johnson children learned to read and write. Jack possibly had some half-brothers and sisters as well. They were members of either the Baptist or the Methodist church.

In 1888, when Johnson was 10 years old, U.S. Senator John Ingalls (from Kansas), who the previous year had been elected President pro tempore of the U.S. Senate, said he feared that the black population might one day outnumber whites. "He fears negro supremacy." However, the *San Francisco Chronicle* responded,

> Neither the country nor the South is in any such danger. ... Instead of a gloomy view, we think the future full of hope and promise. This fine country was not conquered from the red man for the black; it will never cease to be a white man's country, unless all history is false, and the superior race shall yield to the inferior.[1]

Another San Francisco newspaper noted,

> Ingalls has sounded the keynote in declaring that there is an ethnological bar to the two races dwelling together upon terms of political equality. ...
>
> They [blacks] must demonstrate their fitness for the duties of citizenship. Then that fitness is not yet demonstrated, and yet the

---

[1] *San Francisco Chronicle,* December 24, 1888.

> denial of rights which it is confessed they are not yet proved fit to exercise is ascribed to "prejudice." ...
>
> A white minority, anywhere on earth, finally conquers a colored majority...
>
> But we need not discuss the matter. It is getting discussion enough by the men who rightly believed that the negro did not deserve slavery, and who now confess that they were so right in that proposition that they made the mistake of omitting to see that he also did not deserve citizenship.[2]

Jack Johnson was part of a new generation of blacks born free. The *Houston Free South* wrote, "[T]he young negroes – who are termed 'coons' and never knew what slavery was, are a nuisance – a curse to the South."[3]

Racism and separation of the races did not just exist in the South. In 1889, the *Times-Democrat* alleged that color prejudice actually was stronger in the North, but hypocrisy tried to conceal it. Northern merchants would not hire blacks as clerks and salespersons, no matter how deserving. White Northern mechanics refused to work with negroes. In New Jersey, blacks were not allowed to bathe in the ocean at the same time as whites. Northerners were upset that some blacks had been recruited in the South as postmasters.

> There is nothing extraordinary about this particular manifestation of the color prejudice. There are other exhibitions of the same feeling, in the North as well as in the South, which are even more remarkable....
>
> While such things are true at the North, it is arrant hypocrisy for Northerners to prate about the "insane prejudice" of Southerners against the negro. The truth is that this color prejudice is entertained by most white people – by a great many who concede that it seems unreasonable, and yet who confess that they cannot get over it.[4]

The grade-school-aged Johnson was a timid youngster who at first was a mark for the bullying boys at school, and received many a bad beating. His mother claimed that his older sister had to do some fighting for him. Enraged at this, when he was a young teen, his mom told him to fight his own battles, to fight the bullies back and beat them, or else she would give him a worse whipping when he returned home. She wanted her son to stand up for himself. One time, after he was beaten in a fight, his mother gave him a sound thrashing for having lost. She told him that she would administer the same every time he allowed anyone to whip him. Thereafter, Johnson showed courage, fought back hard, and won.

---

[2] *Daily Alta California*, January 4, 1889.
[3] *Times-Democrat*, July 1889; *Clarion-Ledger*, July 18, 1889, quoting *Houston Free South* and *Williamsburg Journal*.
[4] *Times-Democrat*, July 22, 1889.

Johnson was forced to leave school at about age 13 in order to help earn money for his financially struggling family. This was not atypical for poor black families; doing their best to survive in post-Civil War America.[5]

Johnson's various jobs in Galveston included helping his father with the cleaning business by sweeping up with a broom, assisting a milkman by taking care of his horse and delivering milk bottles up and down staircases, for which he earned 10 cents a week, and working on the docks as a stevedore, loading and unloading ships. Other odd jobs throughout his early life included horse trainer, bread baker's assistant, porter, and barber's assistant. Johnson also was a talented bass violin player. Life was not easy in Galveston, and Johnson said the days when his stomach went empty were more numerous than the feast days. He often suffered from hunger.

In early 1892, a black lawyer said, "[W]hite people fear the negro. They are afraid to give him a fair chance in life. ... They show their cowardice by claiming his utter inferiority, and at the same time placing every conceivable barrier across his pathway."[6]

The year 1892 saw a U.S. national record 161 black lynchings (since record-keeping began in 1882). Lynching was a way to ensure that blacks knew their place and remained fearful of attempting to defy the social or economic order. It could be used as a form of vigilante justice, without trial or due process, to punish blacks publicly for alleged crimes. It also was used as a way to intimidate blacks from voting or asserting any political power.[7]

Johnson said he began getting into fights with fellow Galveston dockworkers at about age 13, in the early 1890s. He fought bigger and older youths and suffered many beatings from the bullies, but was capable of withstanding much punishment. A fellow dockworker named Ed Harrison gave Johnson some valuable fight lessons so he could better defend himself. A thankful Johnson told him that if he ever became wealthy that he would buy him some fancy clothes. Years later, he would fulfill his promise.

One time, Johnson fell into the water at the docks, and almost drowned, for he was sucked under a vessel. However, a man named Cafferty Williams dove in and saved him.

At some point, his father arranged for a young Johnson to get on a train and travel either to Houston or Dallas, where he became a painter's apprentice, painting houses, carriages, and wagons.

It turned out that his boss was a professor in the art of self-defense, and gave the featherweight-sized Johnson boxing lessons. They sparred together. Johnson enjoyed boxing a lot more than he liked painting. Eventually, after about six months to a year, he returned to Galveston.[8]

Johnson said he never sought a fight, but he never avoided one either. He took up boxing in order to be able to compete with the boys, and

---

[5] *San Francisco Chronicle,* July 10, 1910; *Nevada State Journal, San Francisco Call,* July 8, 1910. *Freeman,* July 9, 1910; *San Francisco Evening Post,* July 7, 1910.
[6] *New York Sun,* February 14, 1892.
[7] Robert L. Zangrando, *About Lynching,* excerpt from article in *The Reader's Companion to American History,* Editors Eric Foner and John A. Garraty. Houghton Mifflin Co., 1991.
[8] *Richmond Planet,* January 9, 1909; *New York Herald,* December 28, 1908.

eventually he attained a bit of a reputation. Jack had a street fight with a black boy named Jackie Morris, the neighborhood tyrant and reigning bully of the docks. Johnson, a previous Morris victim, got his revenge. He later said, "Fights between kids give them self-confidence and are the first lesson in the struggle for survival."

Over the next several years, Johnson engaged in a number of trades. He improved the most, though, in fighting, which the neighborhood boys soon found out. He no longer was an easy mark, but became the top dog of his gang, and eventually was known as the best fighter of all the local gangs. Johnson was a prominent member of a local gang of poor white and black boys that roamed the docks. Johnson said he hung around the docks and in the streets, watching big boys throw dice.

At 16, Arthur Johnson had a street fight with a local colored tough named Dave Pierson, a grown man who was older, heavier, and more experienced, yet Johnson defeated him. People asked, "Did you hear what 'Lil Arthur did?" That was how his first nickname, "Lil' Artha," was generated. Eventually, Johnson would become known by his now well-known alias, Jack Johnson, derived from 'Black Jack.'

In a 4-round amateur boxing bout, Johnson defeated a negro boy of his own weight with a 3rd round knockout. He received $1, of which he gave his manager 25 cents. He used the remaining 75 cents to purchase a batch of pies, which he divided amongst his crowd of admirers. The fight fever had caught him.

Johnson was quite successful in his fights, and his reputation grew. He was an amateur middleweight champion, weighing about 156 pounds. He became popular amongst local blacks and commanded a large following.

Jack said he once stayed 4 rounds with a heavyweight boxer named Bob Thompson, who offered $25 to anyone who could last 4 rounds with him. The smaller Johnson barely made it, having been beaten badly, but he lasted the 4 rounds and earned what for a poor young man was very good money. Most black folk didn't earn that much in a week; some not even in months.

Young Johnson liked to ride the rails to other cities, leaving home at frequent intervals, roaming around the country, taking odd jobs as a laborer or as a sparring partner for top boxers, or both. If he could get paid something to fight, he fought as well. He typically traveled as a stowaway.

At one point, Johnson was a stowaway on a steamer that took him to Key West, Florida, and then to Boston. He had a number of quarrels and fights in Boston, but after the boys saw that he could hold his own, they left him alone. In Boston, he took a job working in the horse stables. He also became a sparring partner for fellow black and future world welterweight champion Joe Walcott, the Barbados Demon (born in British Guiana). Jack returned to Galveston, but eventually ventured forth to New York, Connecticut, and Chicago.

For a couple years, Johnson was a stable boy, jockey, and horse trainer. Sometimes he provided assistance in collecting bets that were made and owed. He also was a porter at a gambling parlor.[9]

Johnson occasionally fought in battles royal. A battle royal was a fight in which several boxers all fought each other at the same time in one ring, and the last man standing won the money. Whites were amused by watching black boys fight one another in this fashion.

Boxing in Texas technically was illegal, so generally the fights were underground occurrences without much news coverage or advertising, lest they would obtain too much notice from politicians or law enforcement. The degree to which law enforcement cracked down on boxing bouts depended on the local jurisdiction, the time, and the particular fight. The greater attention a bout received, the more likely that politicians would compel law enforcement to become involved. Sometimes, for lower-profile bouts, they let it slide, and the fights were sold as mere exhibitions of skill without a formal decision. Often they called the combatants professors who were just giving the audience lessons about boxing. It all was done with a wink.

In order to box and train there, Johnson began cleaning the Galveston Athletic Club, a local gym run by Herman Bernau.

Johnson claimed that his first legitimate bout fought for money was in Galveston when he was only 17 years old (about 1895) against John Lee, a skillful colored veteran boxer who weighed about 185 pounds, while Johnson only weighed 158 pounds. Because of legal concerns, they traveled 14 miles into the country and held the fight in an open field, where the ring was pitched. Under the broiling sun, Johnson knocked out Lee in the 17th round. He said this fight was the hardest he ever had.

Johnson earned decent money from the fight, and it gave him ideas. "After the fight I concluded that there was more money for me in the prize ring than in anything else I could do, and I resolved to stick to it. For a year or two I was the stalking horse in the training camps of various fighters."

Often, Johnson climbed into the ring without having eaten a thing for a full day, or without anything in his stomach other than a bit of bread and buttermilk. Poverty was the norm for him. It kept him very thin.[10]

In 1895, 17-year-old Johnson traveled to the East Coast, fought in some underground smokers, and acted as a sparring partner for better-known fighters, working for meager pay.

Professor James De Forest, a veteran boxing instructor, claimed that he had taught Johnson to box in New York, when Jack was a porter at the

---

[9] *My Life and Battles* by Jack Johnson, translated and edited from the 1911 and 1914 French versions by Christopher Rivers, Praeger Publishers, Westport, CT, 2007, 1-19; *Papa Jack: Jack Johnson and the Era of White Hopes*, by Randy Roberts, The Free Press, NY, 1983, 2-6; *Jack Johnson: Rebel Sojourner*, by Theresa Runstedtler, University of California Press, 2012, 13; Geoffrey C. Ward, *Unforgivable Blackness* (Alfred A. Knopf, New York, 2004), 13; Jack Johnson, *In the Ring and Out*, (National Spots Publishing Co., Chicago, 1927), 32-36.
[10] *San Francisco Bulletin*, July 27, 1910; *San Francisco Chronicle*, July 10, 1910.

Lenox Athletic Club. Jack was used as a punching bag there by Joe Walcott, Bob Armstrong, and others, but improved rapidly.[11]

Johnson eventually returned to Galveston, and claimed that he was elected president of the Republican Club in his neighborhood.[12]

In 1896, when Johnson was 18 years old, the Supreme Court of the United States, in deciding *Plessy v. Ferguson*, 163 U.S. 537 (1896), ruled that laws mandating separate but equal accommodations based upon race did not violate the U.S. Constitution's 14th amendment's equal protection clause, which required that no state deny persons within its jurisdiction equal protection of the law. The Court said,

Joe Walcott

> Laws permitting, and even requiring, their separation, in places where they are liable to be brought into contact, do not necessarily imply the inferiority of either race to the other, and have been generally, if not universally, recognized as within the competency of the state legislatures in the exercise of their police power. The most common instance of this is connected with the establishment of separate schools for white and colored children, which have been held to be a valid exercise of the legislative power even by courts of states where the political rights of the colored race have been longest and most earnestly enforced....

In his lone dissent, Justice John Harlan (a Kentucky lawyer) wrote:

> The white race deems itself to be the dominant race in this country. And so it is, in prestige, in achievements, in education, in wealth, and in power. So, I doubt not, it will continue to be for all time, if it remains true to its great heritage, and holds fast to the principles of constitutional liberty. But in view of the constitution, in the eye of the law, there is in this country no superior, dominant, ruling class of citizens. There is no caste here. Our constitution is color-blind, and neither knows nor tolerates classes among citizens. In respect of civil rights, all citizens are equal before the law....

> It is therefore to be regretted that this high tribunal, the final expositor of the fundamental law of the land, has reached the conclusion that it is competent for a state to regulate the enjoyment by citizens of their civil rights solely upon the basis of race. ...

> Sixty millions of whites are in no danger from the presence here of eight millions of blacks. The destinies of the two races in this country

---

[11] *New York Sun*, May 23, 1909. Many years later, New Jersey's Arnold Cream, a future heavyweight champion, took the fighting name "Jersey" Joe Walcott, an homage to the original Joe Walcott.
[12] *My Life and Battles* at 26.

are indissolubly linked together, and the interests of both require that the common government of all shall not permit the seeds of race hate to be planted under the sanction of law. What can more certainly arouse race hate, what more certainly create and perpetuate a feeling of distrust between these races, than state enactments which, in fact, proceed on the ground that colored citizens are so inferior and degraded that they cannot be allowed to sit in public coaches occupied by white citizens? That, as all will admit, is the real meaning of such legislation as was enacted in Louisiana. ...

State enactments regulating the enjoyment of civil rights upon the basis of race, and cunningly devised to defeat legitimate results of the war under the pretence of recognizing equality of rights, can have no other result than to render permanent peace impossible and to keep alive a conflict of races the continuance of which must do harm to all concerned. ...

[C]itizens of the black race in Louisiana, many of whom, perhaps, risked their lives for the preservation of the Union, ... who have all the legal rights that belong to white citizens, are yet declared to be criminals, liable to imprisonment, if they ride in a public coach occupied by citizens of the white race. ...

If evils will result from the commingling of the two races upon public highways established for the benefit of all, they will be infinitely less than those that will surely come from state legislation regulating the enjoyment of civil rights upon the basis of race. We boast of the freedom enjoyed by our people above all other peoples. But it is difficult to reconcile that boast with a state of the law which, practically, puts the brand of servitude and degradation upon a large class of our fellow citizens, our equals before the law. The thin disguise of "equal" accommodations for passengers in railroad coaches will not mislead anyone, nor atone for the wrong this day done.

Although technically boxing was illegal in Texas, in late 1897, a boxing enthusiast who read the law had figured out that the anti-boxing act was not violated by a glove contest to which no admission fee was charged. Friends of the fight-game exploited the legal loophole. Instead of charging money for the fight, they charged money for a vaudeville show, and then added on a boxing exhibition in which "a couple of 'athletes' will get up and try to hammer the stuffing out of each other."

On November 1, 1897 at Professor Bernau's gymnasium in Galveston, in a contest for the Texas middleweight championship, local 19-year-old Arthur John Johnson knocked out fellow black Charles Brooks in the 2nd round.

The middleweight-sized Johnson also scored a November 20, 1897 KO5 over fellow black Ed Johnson for the "championship of Texas."[13]

Over the next couple of years, Jack Johnson primarily was a local fighter, mostly boxing in obscure and unknown bouts, unrecorded and unremembered, even by Johnson himself.

Sometime during 1898, Johnson allegedly married a black woman named Mary Austin.

In March 1898, the U.S. under President William McKinley issued an ultimatum to Spain to end its presence in Cuba. Spain refused, and on April 20, 1898, Congress declared war, starting the Spanish-American War. Eventually, Lt. Col. Theodore Roosevelt's Rough Riders were victorious in Cuba. Spain also was defeated in the Philippines. A peace protocol ended hostilities on August 12, 1898. Under the subsequent peace treaty signed in Paris on December 10, 1898, Spain relinquished title to Cuba, which became independent, and ceded Puerto Rico, Guam, and the Philippines to the United States. The U.S. also took Hawaii.

On November 10, 1898, Wilmington, North Carolina exploded in the first major race riot since Reconstruction. A large white mob killed and wounded scores of blacks and burned down the office and printing press of the local black newspaper, the *Daily Record*. The local white mayor and biracial city council were forced to resign, and the mob installed its own Democrat white supremacist leaders. Despite pleas for assistance, U.S. President William McKinley did not respond. More than 2,000 blacks were forced to leave the city, turning it from a black majority into a white majority city. Soon thereafter, North Carolina began passing laws that mandated segregation and restricted the ability of blacks to vote.

In February 1899, British author Rudyard Kipling's poem, "The White Man's Burden," published at the start of the Philippine-American War, urged white Americans to join Europeans in the work of empire building. It became a catchphrase, calling upon a collective white moral responsibility to civilize the world's "savage" people of color (whom he called "half-devil and half-child") in part by conquering them. This poem became the mantra of those who supported colonialism and imperialism.

During early 1899, Jack Johnson left Galveston and traveled to Illinois.

On Wednesday April 19, 1899 in Springfield, Illinois, before a crowd of 500, 21-year-old 154-pound Jack Johnson won a battle royal and earned $5. He said that he had prior experience in battles royal, having won them all.[14]

On May 6, 1899 in Chicago, Jack Johnson fought top local black 21-year-old Klondike John Haines, one of the best black fighters in the country. At first, Johnson did well, and even dropped Klondike in the 2nd round. However, after the 3rd round, Jack grew quite fatigued and held incessantly, until eventually in the 5th round, at the request of the police, the referee stopped the bout.[15]

---

[13] *Galveston Daily News*, November 2, 21, 1897.
[14] *Daily Illinois State Register*, Springfield, April 19, 20, 1899; *Springfield Journal*, April 20, 1899.
[15] *Daily Inter Ocean, Chicago Chronicle, Chicago Times-Herald, Chicago Tribune*, May 7, 1899.

Although he showed early flashes of his ability and talent, his lack of weight, inadequate nutrition, and lack of proper training had led to early fatigue. Johnson was very thin and malnourished, for being poor; he struggled to earn enough money to eat well. As he obtained more money, he ate better and put on weight. Years later, Lou Houseman said, "Johnson was starved." As a result, he was besting Klondike, but grew weak and faint.[16]

In order to earn money, Johnson trained and sparred with several top pros, including whites Dan Creedon and Tom Tracy. Although top whites often were reluctant to fight blacks, they liked to use them as sparring partners. Blacks like Johnson earned what little they could.[17]

In May 1899, Johnson served as a sparring partner for top black fighter Frank Childs, a strong puncher who at various times claimed the colored heavyweight championship. Given that white champions refused to defend their titles against blacks, drawing the color line, black fighters often fought for "colored" crowns.[18]

Johnson recalled that Childs treated him poorly. "Childs wasn't on the square with me, and I would have starved to death for all he cared."[19]

Johnson lived with Childs while he was his sparring partner, for he did not have enough money to rent a room. One night, when Childs' wife came home, Frank forced Jack to leave, and gave him no money. He had to roam the cold rainy streets that night, because he was so poor that he could not even afford to pay for a five-cent bed.

Sometime during 1899, 21-year-old middleweight Jack Johnson was hiking along the roads of New Haven, Connecticut without a single cent in his pockets. He landed a job as a janitor at Becky Stanford's cigar store. For several months, he swept the store and cleaned up the poolroom. He also practiced boxing, sparring with white lightweight Kid Conroy. Jack lived with the Kid at Conroy's mother's house in New Haven.[20]

Referee Billy Roche was running a boxing club near Boston. Roche said that one night, a lean, hungry-looking negro asked to be put on as a substitute if any fighter failed to show. His clothes were in tatters and he had the appearance of being half-starved. Roche gave him a chance by putting him in with a hard-hitting give-and-take white slugger. Johnson won the fight and became a regular at the club. Roche said Jack usually lost most of his money playing craps games. Jack liked to gamble to try to generate more money, but more often than not he just lost it.[21]

Johnson mostly was operating quietly and somewhat anonymously in the shadows, learning his craft, earning meager pay as a sparring partner, and

---

[16] *San Francisco Bulletin,* November 5, 1903.
[17] Johnson, *In the Ring and Out,* at 40.
[18] *Police Gazette,* September 2, 1899.
[19] *San Francisco Bulletin,* July 27, 1910.
[20] *My Life and Battles* at 19-22; Ward at 30. Johnson defeated a fighter by the name of Dan Murphy via KO10 at Waterbury, Connecticut, just north of New Haven.
[21] *San Francisco Evening Post,* July 27, 1910; *Freeman,* August 6, 1910; Boxrec.com.

taking occasional lesser bouts. He was poor and had to take low-paying odd jobs between fights.

In early 1900, Johnson returned to Galveston.

On Wednesday March 21, 1900 at the Galveston Athletic Club, Arthur Johnson fought white Joe McCormick to a competitive and entertaining 15-round no-decision. By the end, Johnson's mouth was bloody, while McCormick had a bloody nose and a closed left eye.[22]

Two days later, in a March 23, 1900 speech before the U.S. Senate, Senator Benjamin "Pitchfork" Tillman of South Carolina, also a former governor of that state, defended the actions of his white constituents in using violence against blacks. A fellow senator had said that since the late 1870s, blacks had their rights taken away from them, in particular by the use of violence to influence elections. Tillman proudly admitted it.

> It was the riots before the elections precipitated by [blacks'] own hot-headedness in attempting to hold the government, that brought on conflicts between the races and caused the shotgun to be used. That is what I meant by saying we used the shotgun.
>
> I want to call the Senator's attention to one fact. He said that the Republican party gave the negroes the ballot in order to protect themselves against the indignities and wrongs that were attempted to be heaped upon them by the enactment of the black code. I say it was because the Republicans of that day…wanted to put white necks under black heels and to get revenge. …
>
> I want to ask the Senator this proposition in arithmetic: In my State there were 135,000 negro voters, or negroes of voting age, and some 90,000 or 95,000 white voters. General Canby set up a carpetbag government there and turned our State over to this majority. Now, I want to ask you, with a free vote and a fair count, how are you going to beat 135,000 by 95,000? How are you going to do it? You had set us an impossible task. You had handcuffed us and thrown away the key, and you propped your carpetbag negro government with bayonets. Whenever it was necessary to sustain the government you held it up by the Army. …
>
> We were sorry we had the necessity forced upon us, but we could not help it, and as white men we are not sorry for it, and we do not propose to apologize for anything we have done in connection with it. We took the government away from them in 1876. We did take it.
> …
>
> We did not disfranchise the negroes until 1895. Then we had a constitutional convention convened which took the matter up calmly, deliberately, and avowedly with the purpose of disfranchising as many of them as we could under the fourteenth and fifteenth amendments. We adopted the educational qualification as the only means left to us,

---

[22] *Galveston Daily News*, March 22, 1900.

and the negro is as contented and as prosperous and as well protected in South Carolina to-day as in any State of the Union south of the Potomac. He is not meddling with politics, for he found that the more he meddled with them the worse off he got. As to his "rights" - I will not discuss them now. We of the South have never recognized the right of the negro to govern white men, and we never will. We have never believed him to be equal to the white man, and we will not submit to his gratifying his lust on our wives and daughters without lynching him. I would to God the last one of them was in Africa and that none of them had ever been brought to our shores.[23]

Tillman took part in the July 8, 1876 Hamburg Riot, which was marked by the murder of a number of black militiamen who, much to the chagrin of Southern whites, were stationed in South Carolina. Tillman boasted that leading white men decided to provoke a riot so that whites could kill as many blacks as possible. Tillman used his participation to fuel his successful 1890 campaign for governor. He was South Carolina's governor for four years, from 1890 to 1894, and was elected to the U.S. Senate in 1894, where he served for the next 24 years. His open racism helped him secure consistent re-election.

On Monday April 9, 1900, the Galveston Athletic Club's exhibition show included an entertaining 4-round no-decision bout between Arthur Johnson and William McNeill, "two heavyweight colored boxers of note." After the bout concluded, the pleased spectators threw a shower of coins into the ring, which kept the colored boxers sliding on the sandy ground for several minutes collecting the contributions. This was the humble state of Jack Johnson's early career.

On April 20, 1900 at the Galveston Athletic Club, 168-pound Arthur Johnson defeated white 175-pound John Heimann, alias "Texas Jack McCormack," when in the 6th round the clearly outpointed McCormack was disqualified for a foul (likely a low blow).

On June 25, 1900 at the Galveston Athletic Club, in a rematch, 22-year-old "Jack Johnson" fought Chicago's 22-year-old Klondike John Haines to a dull 20-round draw, but in doing so earned an even split of the purse.[24]

On September 8, 1900, a massive hurricane hit Galveston. The powerful wind and torrential rain flooded and destroyed most of the town. The estimated death toll was about 8,000 people, making it the deadliest natural disaster ever to hit the United States. Johnson later claimed to have saved several lives, rescuing those who were standing on their roofs when their homes were under water. He piloted them to safety on a boat.[25]

While the town was being rebuilt, Johnson temporarily took his fight career on the road again, boxing in the South.

---

[23] "Speech of Senator Benjamin R. Tillman, March 23, 1900," Congressional Record, 56th Congress, 1st Session, 3223–3224. Reprinted in Richard Purday, ed., Document Sets for the South in U. S. History (Lexington, MA.: D.C. Heath and Company, 1991), 147.

[24] *Galveston Daily News*, April 10, 21, 1900, June 26, 1900.

[25] *Sydney Daily Telegraph*, January 25, 1907; *Referee*, January 30, 1907; Johnson, *In the Ring and Out*, at 240-241.

On November 28, 1900 in Memphis, Tennessee, after 170-pound Jack Johnson badly beat and decked several times 170-pound black Josh Mills, forcing Mills to retire and refuse to start the 7th round, the local press called Johnson "a threat against any negro heavyweight in the country."[26]

On December 27, 1900, again in Memphis, in a third match against fellow black fighter Klondike Haines, Johnson jabbed away, closed Klondike's left eye completely, and swelled up his face, forcing Haines to retire in his corner and refuse to start the 14th round. The local *Memphis Commercial Appeal* wrote, "Johnson is likely to become the best colored heavy-weight in the country. For a negro he has an intelligent face."

Klondike John Haines

Doc Hottum had refereed the bout in a pleasing and satisfactory manner. "It is hard to handle negro fighters, as they are easily rattled and disobedient." That said, "The men fought prettily and observed the injunctions of the referee to the letter."[27]

Jack Johnson had shown that he was a fighter who improved with time and experience. He had done better in each of his three bouts with the respected Klondike, going from a loss to a draw to a victory. More importantly, the money he was earning was enabling him to eat better, though he still was just a super-middleweight by today's standards.

Returning to Galveston, on January 14, 1901, against the far more experienced over 30-fight veteran 26-year-old white Jim Scanlan, the clearly superior Johnson was faster and more accurate, landing quite often, with his straight left raising a bump on Scanlan's face and causing blood to flow from his nose. As a result, Scanlan clinched often, held and hit, refused to break, and hit on the breaks. Johnson responded in kind. The frustrated referee was unsuccessful in his attempts to check such practices, and as a result, in the 7th round, he stopped the fight. He subsequently declared it a draw, which helped the white Scanlan avoid a loss.[28]

---

[26] *Memphis Commercial Appeal*, November 26, 29, 1900. It was around this time that Johnson scored a KO10 over George Lawler (or Jack Lawlor) in Hot Springs, Arkansas. He also defeated Howard Pollar.
[27] *Memphis Commercial Appeal*, December 28, 1900.
[28] *Galveston Daily News*, January 15, 1901.

CHAPTER 2

Texas vs. Jack Johnson

On February 25, 1901 in Galveston, Texas, 22-year-old Jack Johnson took on the 32-year-old vastly more experienced 50-fight veteran 170-pound "Jewish" Joe Choynski, who had fought nearly every top contender for over a decade, including three future heavyweight champions – James J. Corbett (1889 LKOby27), Bob Fitzsimmons (1894 LKOby5 – police stoppage; both men had been down), and James J. Jeffries (1897 D20 – hitting Jeff so hard his lips were wedged between his teeth). Choynski did not draw the color line, and held knockout victories over several top black fighters, including Frank Childs and George Godfrey. Johnson had been Choynski's sparring partner for a brief period of time back in October 1897.

Joe Choynski

After a lively, spirited, and competitive first two rounds, the 3rd round barely had begun when Choynski feinted with his left and then landed a lightning-fast right to the jaw. Johnson fell forward into Choynski's arms and gradually sank to the floor, face downward, out for the count of ten. The still-learning and growing 170-pound Johnson had met a far more experienced hard-punching veteran, got caught, and knocked out.

Making matters worse, as if being knocked out wasn't bad enough, while Johnson was laying prostrate on the canvas, out cold, Captain Brooks appeared and announced that he was a State Ranger and was placing the boxers under arrest in the good name of the State of Texas and Governor Joseph Sayers. Four rangers accompanied Brooks, and he produced warrants calling for the boxers' arrest.

Two rangers placed Choynski under arrest and took him away.

Two other rangers "stood guard over Johnson, who lay in the middle of the ring unconscious of the new show. He awakened from a deep sleep," and when his brain cleared, learned that he was under arrest.

Both Choynski and Johnson were accused of violating the state law against prizefighting, which carried a penalty of 2 to 5 years in the penitentiary at hard labor.

Both boxers were transported to the county jail and held there. Prosecutor Colonel John Lovejoy requested that bail be fixed at a whopping $5,000 each, which request was granted. Naturally, neither boxer could pay. Hence, they remained in jail.

Lovejoy told a reporter that Governor Joseph Sayers was determined to stop all boxing matches, no matter what the cost.[29]

Politicians often cracked down on high-profile fights, using anti-boxing fervor to get their names in the newspapers, enjoying the cheap notoriety that they obtained when they attacked boxing, as if they had nothing better to do. Johnson had been making a name for himself on the local Galveston scene. When a really big-name world-class fighter like Choynski was brought in to box him, the contest was elevated to a higher level. Choynski was too big of a name for word not to spread, and politicians took note.

A young and still developing Jack Johnson

It is likely that some of the ill-will regarding the bout might have been influenced by the fact that it was a mixed-race fight, of which the Southern state of Texas did not approve. At that time, Texas legislators had just introduced a bill to have separate rooms for white and negro jurors.

The same day that the Johnson-Choynski fight report was issued, the *Louisville Courier-Journal* published an article criticizing the book *Uncle Tom's Cabin*, saying,

> [The book is] a false statement of the social conditions of the South previous to the war. It was a crime on the negroes to free them. If it had to come, it should have been gradual. 'Uncle Tom's Cabin' largely aided in bringing about this terrible injury to the negroes by falsely representing the conditions of slavery.[30]

---

[29] *Galveston Daily News*, February 26, 1901; *New York Clipper*, March 16, 1901; *National Police Gazette*, March 23, 30, April 13, 27, 1901.
[30] *Louisville Courier-Journal*, February 26, 1901.

Many Southernors argued that blacks were better off when they were slaves than they were since being granted freedom.

Because their pre-trial bonds were so massive, and neither could pay, both Johnson and Choynski remained incarcerated for several weeks, simply for having engaged in a consensual boxing match, the kind which local police had been allowing for years, which may or may not have been illegal.

Joe Choynski and Jack Johnson behind bars

While in jail, Choynski gave Johnson boxing lessons, teaching Jack many of the sport's finer points. The local jailers, who had no objection to the sport, provided them with gloves, and derived entertainment from watching them spar in the jail yard. Johnson credited Choynski with teaching him more about boxing than he had learned in his entire career before then. Jack turned a negative into a positive.[31]

Governor Sayers was persistent in his efforts to punish Choynski and Johnson. When the local Galveston Grand Jury failed to indict them, instead of respecting its decision, the governor immediately telegraphed Captain Brooks, asking him to keep the boxers in jail until another Grand Jury could be empanelled and the case again considered.

The *National Police Gazette* noted that Texas had a new way of dealing with boxing, as illustrated by the Choynski-Johnson situation. Rather than prevent the bout, they simply allowed the fighters to fight and then arrested and held them afterwards. "The mere matter of arrest will serve as a salutary warning to all fighters that they are not wanted in Texas. Thus will the object be served, and the end justify the means."[32]

Having been arrested on the evening of February 25, Choynski and Johnson were not released from jail until 2 p.m. on March 22, when the Court of Criminal Appeals mandated that they be released on bonds of

---

[31] *San Francisco Chronicle*, July 10, 1910; *My Life and Battles* at 32.
[32] *New York Clipper*, March 16, 1901; *National Police Gazette*, March 23, 30, April 13, 27, 1901.

$1,000 each. Bondsmen, who asked that their names not be made public, paid the money, and the boxers were set free. Before he left, Choynski said,

> Prison life is especially irksome to an active man, and a fellow, after being in prison 24 days, feels like a 2-year-old on a fast track when given his liberty. A man who has never been detained against his will don't know the value of freedom.[33]

Eventually, the second grand jury also refused to indict the boxers, feeling "that the moral and religious element in the State has been unduly excited by sensational and exaggerated enlargement of what otherwise, to this Grand Jury, appears to be a small affair with no motive, intent or fact to show a violation of the law." The law had not been violated, but nevertheless, Choynski and Johnson had lost nearly a month of their lives.[34]

---

[33] *Galveston Daily News*, March 23, 1901.
[34] *New York Clipper*, March 16, 1901; *National Police Gazette*, March 23, 30, April 13, 27, 1901.

CHAPTER 3

A Cautious Approach

In late April 1901, 23-year-old Jack Johnson was in Denver, Colorado, acting as a sparring for former world-title challenger "Sailor" Tom Sharkey (1899 L25 to then world heavyweight champion James J. Jeffries). Johnson later called Sharkey "one of the ring's greatest fighters, though he never held a championship."[35]

Although Sharkey drew the color line and would not fight black fighters, like other top whites, he often paid black boxers to be his sparring partners. Bob Armstrong, a large and clever black fighter who once lost a 10-round decision to Jim Jeffries, was Sharkey's chief sparring partner, and he, along with Johnson, alternated in boxing with Sharkey.

Johnson was scheduled to box 29-year-old Billy Stift, a thickly built, strong, respected veteran of nearly 40 fights, who was expected to defeat the black man. The *Denver Post* said, "Billy will surely try to land one of his famous 'haymakers' on Johnson. If he does – well, goodby coon."

Sharkey spars Armstrong

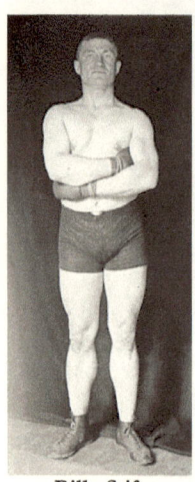

Billy Stift

Stift and Johnson had agreed to make their fight winner-take-all. Therefore, both fighters would have a big incentive to do their utmost to win, or at least not lose. In the event of a draw, the purse would be split.[36]

On April 26, 1901 in Denver, Colorado, Jack Johnson fought Billy Stift 10 rounds to what the local press called a slow, tiresome, and "very tame draw." Both weighed about 170 pounds.[37]

Johnson claimed to have eaten nothing but bread and water while in jail, so he was not at his strongest or most fit. It also is likely that coming off a knockout loss, he had become more inclined to be cautious, focus on defense, and not take chances. Also, keeping it close and fighting to a draw meant that the two combatants would split the purse. The poor Johnson probably was taking no chances of coming away with no money.

---

[35] Johnson, *In the Ring and Out*, at 44-45.
[36] *Denver Post*, April 23-26, 1901. *Denver Daily News*, April 26, 1901.
[37] *Denver Daily News*, *Denver Post*, *Denver Times*, April 27, 1901.

Johnson resumed his sparring and exhibiting with Tom Sharkey, "and the men go at it so rough that one would almost think they were engaged in a real contest."

On May 3, 1901 in Denver, a 5'8 ½" 192-pound Tom Sharkey scored a KO4 over 6'4" 205-pound Fred Russell.

On May 7, 1901 in Cripple Creek, Johnson boxed 4 tame but clever exhibition rounds with the 6'3" or 6'4" nearly 200-pound Bob Armstrong.

In the main event, after knocking down "Mexican" Pete Everett in the 1st round, while he was down, Tom Sharkey struck Everett with a right to the jaw that knocked Pete out, and the referee disqualified Sharkey.

Sharkey left Colorado, but Johnson remained and gave exhibitions for a while, until eventually he was matched to fight a 20-round bout with "Mexican" Pete Everett.[38]

On August 1, 1901 in Baltimore, Maryland, the Democratic state convention that met there "declared that the purpose of the party, if successful in the election, is to eliminate the negro from politics in Maryland, if such a thing be possible under the constitution of the state." The Democratic party recognized that the "peace, good order, personal safety and proper development of our material interests depend upon the control of the commonwealth by its intelligent white residents. Without the aid of the 60,000 colored voters, the Republican party in Maryland would be a hopeless minority." They wanted to prevent the control of the government "from passing into the hands of those who have neither the ability nor the interest to manage public affairs wisely and well."

A week later, the Western Negro Press Association met and made several resolutions. They wanted people to be judged not by their race or the color of their skin but by the right and wrong of their acts. "Democrats in Maryland in attempting to disfranchise the negro are unwise, unpatriotic and un-American." They also criticized Senator Tillman's claims that all men were not created free and equal, that education was not good for blacks, and that black folk were not fit to vote.[39]

Colorado native 26-year-old 6' 190-pound Pete Everett had a nearly 40-bout career, and for the past two years had fought solely in his home state, so he was the popular local man and betting favorite against the lesser-known and less experienced 20 pounds smaller-sized Johnson.

On August 14, 1901 in Victor, Colorado, Jack Johnson and "Mexican" Pete Everett boxed to a 20-round draw that was called a "very tame affair" and a "hugging match."[40]

However, a special to the nearby *Colorado Springs Gazette* said,

> It was plainly evident that the match was fixed and it was very tame throughout. The house was worth about $500 to the fighters and management. Everett was very slow, while Johnson proved himself

---

[38] *Denver Post*, April 29, 30, 1901; *Denver Daily News*, May 1-6, 1901; *Cripple Creek Evening Star, Denver Daily News, Denver Post*, May 6-10, 1901; *Denver Daily News*, August 14, 1901.
[39] *Colorado Springs Gazette*, August 2, 8, 1901. Article on the 2nd entitled, "The Negro As An Issue."
[40] *Denver Daily News, Denver Post*, August 11, 12, 15, 1901.

to be a good man and could at any stage of the game have put the Mexican out. The sports were disgusted and were not slow to let the fighters know that they were so.[41]

Though it is possible that Johnson simply had become more of a cautious combatant, clearly some believed the fight was a hippodrome/fake/fix in which the poor Johnson, in need of funds, in order to earn a payday had agreed to carry and work with Everett and keep it even, or at least not try to stop him. Johnson might not have cared if it was a draw, because he would be paid, which was better than not fighting at all. The question then is whether he recently did the same with Billy Stift. Regardless of whether the fix theory was true, many believed that Johnson was better and could have won by knockout if he had not held back. The suspicion was that he was working with Everett, who was the better known name fighter who could generate the revenue, and hence would have the ability to induce a lesser known, poorer, and financially needy Johnson to hold back against him in order to earn money.

Unlike white prospects, black fighters rarely had managers who looked out for them, and often had to take fights against bigger men with more experience who were expected to defeat them. Often they had to agree to smaller purses, and sometimes, in order to get fights, even had to agree to work with a white house fighter, at least to some degree.

The next day, Johnson's first wife, a black woman named Mary Austin, briefly left him. Johnson returned to Denver and reunited with her, for the time being. However, their relationship was in distress, and in December 1901, they split permanently.[42]

On August 19, 1901, white residents of Peirce City, Missouri (spelling changed to "Pierce" in the early 1920s), a town 30 miles from Joplin, ignited a rampage. An approximately one-thousand-member white lynch mob assembled in response to the day-before discovery in the woods of a dead white woman whose throat had been cut. The mob went to the jail where a black suspect was held, dragged him outside, and hanged him. Although the evidence against him was circumstantial, early newspaper reports deemed the evidence "conclusive." Unsatisfied, the mob shot at the body swinging from a local hotel. A stray bullet killed a white boy in the audience.

The mob next descended upon the town's colored section, where it engaged in a firefight with and shot and killed two black males. Their bodies later were burned.

Subsequently, there was a call to "run the niggers out of town." The rioters broke into the Missouri National Guard armory, stole the weapons, and began shooting at the town's black community in general - men, women, and children. They also torched the houses in that area. Essentially, the mob violently banished the town's 200 - 300 black residents, who fled in fear for their lives.

---

[41] *Colorado Springs Gazette*, August 15, 1901.
[42] Johnson, *In the Ring and Out*, at 45, 72.

This incident later prompted Mark Twain to write the essay *The United States of Lyncherdom*. To this day, Pierce City is 96% white.[43]

On September 6, 1901 at the Pan-American Exhibition in Buffalo, New York, U.S. President William McKinley was shot by Leon Czolgoz, a socialist-anarchist who believed the President was the working people's enemy, and that the government fostered great injustice and inequality allowing the rich to exploit the poor. On September 14, McKinley died of his wounds, and that day, Theodore Roosevelt was sworn in as president.

October 16, 1901 was the first time that a U.S. President, Theodore Roosevelt, dined in the White House with a black man – Booker T. Washington, a famous black leader, teacher, college principal, and writer. The action aroused much criticism and indignation, especially in the South. The New Orleans *Times-Democrat* wrote, "The negro is not the social equal of the white man. Mr. Roosevelt might as well attempt to rub the stars out of the firmament as to try to erase that conviction from the heart and brain of the American people." The New Orleans *Daily States* called Roosevelt's action an insult to the South. The Memphis *Scimitar* said it was a "damnable outrage" for the President to invite a "nigger" to dine with him. The Memphis *Commercial Appeal* said, "This is a white man's country. It will continue to be such as long as clean blood flows through the veins of white people. ... [R]ace supremacy precludes social equality." Another editorial said Roosevelt had committed a blunder worse than a crime. The *Augusta Chronicle* said the act would antagonize the South and "meet the disapproval of good Anglo-Saxon sentiment in all latitudes." Georgia Governor Allen Candler said, "No self-respecting white man can ally himself with the President after what has occurred. ... As a matter of fact, Northern people do not understand the negro. They see the best types and judge the remainder by them."[44]

When giving a lecture on the race question at a Presbyterian Church, the U.S. Senator from South Carolina, Ben Tillman, said, "Democracy means white people in the South. In my state the negroes are in subjection; we expect to keep them that way. Of course, you people in the North do not see the race matter in our light. We invite you to come down. ... You will feel this matter some day." Senator Tillman also allegedly said, "The action of President Roosevelt in entertaining that nigger will necessitate our killing a thousand niggers in the South before they learn their place again."[45]

---

[43] *Encyclopedia of American Race Riots*, Edited by Walter Rucker, Jr. and James Nathaniel Upton, Greenwood Publishing Group, 2006; Kimberly Harper, *White Man's Heaven: The Lynching and Expulsions of Blacks in the Southern Ozarks, 1894 – 1909*, University of Arkansas Press, 2012.

[44] *Evening Times*, Washington, D.C., October 19, 1901.

[45] *Guthrie Daily Leader*, October 29, 1901; Kantrowitz, Stephen, *Ben Tillman & the Reconstruction of White Supremacy*, University of North Carolina Press, 2009, page 259.

CHAPTER 4

California Notice

Hank Griffin

In October 1901, Bakersfield's Frank Carrillo became Jack Johnson's manager. Carillo matched 23-year-old Johnson against a well-respected 31-year-old black fighter named Hank Griffin, who stood about 6'2" or 6'3", weighed in the 180-pound range, and had a very long reach of 81 ½ inches. Griffin was one of the best black fighters in the country, with about 30 known bouts to his name. Somewhere between 1893 and 1895, future champion James J. Jeffries in his pro debut knocked out Griffin in the 14th or 15th round. However, prior to being knocked out, Griffin was way ahead on points, clearly outboxing the much larger and stronger 200-plus-pound man. In addition to the experience advantage, Griffin would have slight height, reach, and weight advantages over Johnson.[46]

On November 4, 1901 in Bakersfield, California, Jack Johnson lost a very close, highly entertaining, competitive, hard-fought 20-round decision to Hank Griffn. Many questioned the referee's verdict, feeling that it should have been a draw. Regardless, the bout had been exciting enough such that fans and promoters wanted to see Jack back in action again.[47]

On November 20, 1901, the front page of the *Anadarko Daily Democrat*, based in Oklahoma, reported,

> Councilman Robinson took three shots at a nigger last night. The nigger had gone into the Cow Boy saloon and asked for a drink.
>
> Mr. Robinson informed him that niggers all drank at the end of the bar and that he would have to move down apiece. The nigger answered with an oath and called Robinson a vile name. Robinson

---

[46] *San Francisco Evening Post*, July 21, 1902; Cyberboxingzone.com; Boxrec.com. *Los Angeles Express*, September 17, 1901; *National Police Gazette*, November 1, 1902; *Los Angeles Daily Times, Los Angeles Express, Los Angeles Herald, San Francisco Call*, September 12-19, 1901; *Los Angeles Express*, October 24, 1901. On September 17, 1901 in Los Angeles, the strong and shifty Griffin boxed a 4-round exhibition with world heavyweight champion Jim Jeffries, managing to last the distance despite going down several times. Two weeks later, on October 2, 1901 in Los Angeles, fellow black "Denver" Ed Martin knocked out Hank Griffin in the 7th round. The impressive victory catapulted Martin's career, leading the *National Police Gazette* to call Martin the colored heavyweight champion. *National Police Gazette*, October 26, November 16, 1901.

[47] *Bakersfield Daily Californian*, November 5, 1901.

promptly reached for his revolver and as the nigger ran he fired three shots after him. At the second shot the nigger fell, but quickly rose again, so that Robinson could not tell whether he hit him or not. Robinson is a man of courage and action, and he voices the sentiments of a large percent of the citizens when he says: "There should not be a nigger in the city."

On December 15, 1901, Jack Johnson was in the San Francisco bay area, acting as a sparring partner for the highly regarded, tough, and exciting 50-fight veteran white light-heavyweight Edward "Kid" Carter. They really went at it fast and hard, hammering away in lively fashion. Carter tried to hurt Johnson, but instead, Johnson's blows snapped the Kid's head back, and the Kid was groggy when Promoter Coffroth stopped their sparring.[48]

On December 18, 1901 at Fort Erie, Ontario, Canada, Johnson's former employer Joe Walcott won the world welterweight championship when he knocked out James Rube Ferns in the 5th round. Walcott was only the second black world champion of the gloved era, with black Canadian featherweight George Dixon being the first, in the early 1890s.

Johnson's impressive work as Kid Carter's sparring partner got him noticed, and resulted in a rematch with Hank Griffin being made.[49]

Jack said that when he was in jail for a month with Choynski, they were fed bread and water. Since then, whenever he entered a new town, it was his habit to ask what the Sheriff fed his guests at the County jail. Johnson was called a happy-go-lucky fellow who liked to tell jokes.

The day of the fight, Griffin was the betting favorite, though Johnson, who was "supposed to be a wonder," did not lack for support.[50]

On December 27, 1901, a packed Oakland Reliance Athletic Club saw Pacific Coast heavyweight champion Hank Griffin and Jack Johnson fight a hotly contested, fast, hard, exciting, hammer-and-tongs rematch to a 15-round draw. They engaged in fierce infighting, but Johnson was cleverer and a "wonder" on the inside. The more aggressive Griffin had done the leading throughout, though most of his leads missed, for his shifty "dusky rival" had the superior defense. Johnson countered well, with telling effect, and also landed more blows. Griffin's superior aggressiveness was the only reason why he was able to secure a draw. "When it came to leading, Hank had it all his own way, that being the only thing that kept him within the money." Other than that, Johnson had been superior. "Hank Griffin found a match in Johnson."[51]

---

[48] *San Francisco Evening Post*, December 14, 17, 1901; Dorgan, Tad, writing in Johnson, Jack, *In the Ring and Out* at 11.
[49] *San Francisco Evening Post*, December 19, 1901; *San Francisco Call*, December 21, 26, 1901; *San Francisco Bulletin*, December 26, 1901; *Oakland Tribune*, December 24, 27, 1901; *Oakland Enquirer*, December 26, 1901. Griffin knocked out Con Sheehan, pride of the British navy, in 7 rounds on November 22, 1901.
[50] *San Francisco Examiner, San Francisco Bulletin*, December 27, 1901.
[51] *Oakland Tribune, Oakland Times, San Francisco Examiner, San Francisco Evening Post, San Francisco Bulletin, San Francisco Call*, December 28, 1901.

CHAPTER 5

Jim Jeffries and the Color Line

In order to challenge for the world heavyweight championship one day, not only would Jack Johnson have to prove himself inside the ring, but he would need to overcome the color-line barrier. World heavyweight champion James J. Jeffries drew the color line on Denver Ed Martin, who held a 7th round knockout victory over Hank Griffin. Since his last loss, Martin had gone undefeated in eleven straight bouts, eight by knockout.

> When Jeff was asked the other day if he would fight Martin…[Jeffries' manager] Delaney chimed in by saying, "No, we won't fight a negro for the championship. … Suppose he were to fight Martin and be defeated, which does not seem possible. America would have to bow to a negro champion."[52]

Bill Delaney did not want to allow such a bout to take place, even though he thought Jeff likely would win. Even the possibility that a black man might win and become champion was too much of a risk to take.

Still, many boxing writers, particularly those from the popular *National Police Gazette*, argued for equal opportunity to compete when it came to boxing, a sport which did not always honor the color line.[53]

When Martin had challenged Tom Sharkey in late 1900, Sharkey responded that he had "never barred nobody outside of a nigger. I will not fight no nigger. I did not get my reputation fighting niggers and I will not fight a nigger. Outside of niggers, I will fight any man living." Of course, Sharkey and other white fighters like Jeffries had no problem using black men as sparring partners.[54]

The *Police Gazette* mentioned Martin as an up-and-coming fighter who could be a possible title challenger. "As I said several weeks ago, of all the men now looming up on the pugilistic horizon not one has better qualifications for usurping the title than he. … The next champion will be a black man, mark the prediction."[55]

Jeffries said he would ignore Martin's challenges. "While Jeffries does not draw the color line strictly, yet he refuses to box a negro for the championship." Bill Delaney insisted that Jeffries would not fight Martin or

---

[52] *National Police Gazette*, December 7, 1901.
[53] *Cincinnati Enquirer*, January 15, 1901; *San Francisco Chronicle*, June 7, 1899; *National Police Gazette*, June 24, 1899, January 5, 1901.
[54] *National Police Gazette*, September 28, 1901; *San Francisco Call*, September 16, 1901; *Oakland Tribune*, September 17, 18, 20, 1901; *San Francisco Call*, November 6, 1901; *San Francisco Examiner*, November 7, 13, 1901; *San Francisco Evening Post*, November 6, 1901.
[55] *San Francisco Evening Post*, November 27, 1901.

any other black fighter. The heavyweight championship was a whites-only position, for which only whites could apply.[56]

Denver Ed Martin

The Jeffries/Delaney color-line position had some historic precedence and support when it came to world heavyweight championship contests fought during the modern gloved Queensberry rules era, although such a stance also had its critics, owing to the fact that bareknuckle champions had not drawn the color line. Former world heavyweight champion John L. Sullivan, who in the early 1880s had popularized gloved boxing and made it a lucrative money-making sport, drew the color line. On the whole, the press did not care too much about the fact that Sullivan drew the color line, until the late 1880s, when Australia's Peter Jackson, a highly respected, admired, and well-liked black fighter emerged. Australians did not draw the color line in boxing, and Jackson had won the Australian heavyweight championship before traveling to the United States.

After first seeing Jackson in action, the local *San Francisco Examiner* said, "Fear alone…will prevent Sullivan from meeting him. … The white fighters will draw the color line tighter than ever, now."[57]

Regarding then colored champion George Godfrey, in 1888, the *Examiner* noted that "those who are recognized as the champions do not care particularly to face him, not because he has not backing enough, but because he is a man of color."[58]

Eventually, on August 24, 1888 in San Francisco, Peter Jackson defeated George Godfrey in 19 rounds to become the colored world champion.

When it was trying to get white California champion Joe McAuliffe to fight Peter Jackson, the *San Francisco Examiner* called the color line in boxing

---

[56] *San Francisco Examiner*, December 28, 1901; *National Police Gazette*, February 1, 1902.
[57] *San Francisco Daily Examiner*, June 5, 1888.
[58] *San Francisco Daily Examiner*, August 25, 1888.

a subterfuge and virtual acknowledgment of fear of the black fighter. "I suppose the excuse is as good as another to avoid a dangerous man." However, some believed the color line was "a remnant of the feeling that once existed between master and slave." Many felt that McAuliffe would "degrade himself by fighting the dusky Australian."[59]

Australians criticized the American color line. The Sydney *Referee* wrote,

> The painful part of all this is that the Americans make his colour a bar to fighting him, a thing that should never have obtained in any country, least of all in the land whose sons actually went to war with their own brothers for the emancipation of these very negroes, whose descendants they now refuse to box with, eat with, or sit beside. ... It is only these windbags, these men who don't want to meet men who mean real fight, that raise this black shield between them and the chance of defeat at the hands of a coloured antagonist.[60]

Eventually on December 28, 1888 in San Francisco, Peter Jackson knocked out Joe McAuliffe in the 24th round. San Francisco's black population celebrated the victory:

> The colored population of San Francisco have not had such a jubilee since Mr. Lincoln signed the Emancipation proclamation.... Every one of them had money on Jackson, but deeper even than the pleasure of winning was their joy at the victory of race.... Every one that had bet jingled coin in his pocket, and for once was disposed to dispute the superiority of any other race than his own.

Clearly, boxing had potentially powerful symbolic racial and social implications, which explains why the color line was so important to much of the white population. Such results and their interpretation could threaten the social order. As a result, many felt that Jackson's victory was not good for boxing. "Many regret that Jackson won, on the ground that no first-class Eastern pugilist will care to fight a colored man, and they think it will have a tendency to lessen the regard of outsiders for boxing if a black man demands the championship."[61]

Despite the fact that the general social norm was towards separation of the races, many believed that boxing tradition differed:

> A champion of the prize ring must meet all comers. He wouldn't be any kind of a champion if he didn't, and the rules bearing upon fistic encounters, whether of the bare knuckles or of gloves, do not in the remotest way recognize color. The history of the ring shows this conclusively. England's phenomenal fighters and champions met all blacks that challenged them. ... [Tom] Molineaux was never objected

---

[59] *San Francisco Daily Examiner*, June 12, 1888.
[60] *Referee* (Sydney), August 2, 1888.
[61] *San Francisco Daily Examiner*, December 30, 1888.

to because of his Ethiopian skin, and he was black as the ace of spades.[62]

The New York correspondent of the *London Sporting Life* criticized champion Sullivan's drawing of the color line:

> Sullivan has already put himself on record as refusing to meet a negro, and he now says that under no consideration will he meet Jackson. Many sporting men construe this as an acknowledgement of Jackson's great fighting powers. ... Would it not be a curious thing if Sullivan was whipped by a nigger, and a British subject at that?[63]

After defeating Jake Kilrain on July 8, 1889 after 75 rounds of London Prize Ring Rules bareknuckle fighting that lasted 2 hours 15 minutes, for the next three years, John L. Sullivan was inactive. He refused to fight Peter Jackson, "for the simple reason that he considered it entirely too degrading for a white man to place himself on an equality with a negro."[64]

On May 21, 1891 in San Francisco, in a fight to the finish, James J. Corbett fought Peter Jackson in a 61-round no-contest, the ruling made by the referee when he felt that neither fighter would be able to knock out the other, and that neither was trying to do so at that point. The fight had lasted 4 hours. It instantly catapulted Corbett's career.

In June 1891, when asked about Peter Jackson, Sullivan said, "He is a nigger, and that settles it with me. God did not intend him to be as good as a white man or he would have changed his color, see?"[65]

Later that year, the *Referee* quoted Sullivan as saying,

> I vowed before the public years ago that I would never fight a colored man, because I thought, and still think, that a white man is lowering himself too much when he faces a nigger. Why, God had a view in making them black, and I earnestly believe it was because they were always doomed to be our inferiors.[66]

In Sullivan's eventual March 1892 public challenge, he stated, "But in this challenge I include all fighters, first come first served - who are white. I will not fight a negro. I never have; I never shall."[67]

Despite some criticism, many praised Sullivan for his color-line stance, particularly in the South. New Orleans, Louisiana's *Daily Picayune* wrote, "I think that the fact that he has faithfully kept his word by not fighting a colored man makes him deserving of much admiration."[68]

On September 7, 1892 in New Orleans, Louisiana, James J. Corbett knocked out John L. Sullivan in the 21st round to win the world heavyweight championship.

---

[62] *Daily Alta California*, January 14, 1889.
[63] *Referee* (Sydney), February 27, 1889, quoting *London Sporting Life*.
[64] *New York Daily Tribune*, July 10, 1889; *Boston Daily Globe*, July 9, 1889.
[65] *San Francisco Chronicle*, June 27, 1891.
[66] *Referee* (Sydney), September 9, 1891.
[67] *Philadelphia Inquirer*, March 6, 1892.
[68] *Daily Picayune*, September 4, 1892.

Immediately after defeating Sullivan, Jim Corbett's trainer/manager Bill Delaney, a staunch color-line supporter, said,

> You can say that I am in a position to announce that Corbett will not meet Jackson again. He is averse to meeting a negro on principle; besides, all of his friends in the South do not want him to again face the black man. Jim is anxious to please them in everything, as they have proven true to him.[69]

However, lower-weight-class championships found occasional rare exceptions. Canadian-born black George Dixon had won the world featherweight championship in 1890, becoming the first black man to win a world boxing championship. The day before Corbett defeated Sullivan, Dixon, who was the first and only black world champion at the time, defeated a white fighter named Jack Skelly in New Orleans. Blacks were so enthusiastic over the victory,

> [T]hey are loudly proclaiming the superiority of their race, to the great scandal of the whites, who declare that they should not be encouraged to entertain even feelings of equality, much less of superiority. The Olympic Club management have about decided not to hold any more colored contests.

In New York, it was said that the hosting of a mixed-race bout had caused "sharp criticism and much indignation." It was opined that "if a white man puts himself on a level with a negro in a pugilistic contest he deserves to be thoroughly and completely thumped." Folks were upset even at the mere act of a white man entering the ring to fight a black man, regardless of the result. The mere act of fighting a black person was in and of itself an attack on the racial and social hierarchy, because competing with a black fighter was to concede that he had the right to compete on the same level. Hence, some thought it disgraceful for a white man to compete against black man.

Some argued that although mixed-race contests could take place in the North, "where there are very few negroes," such contests in the South would only "arouse a bitter feeling between the races which will lead to bloody affrays."[70]

The New Orleans-based *Times-Democrat* said that hosting a mixed-race bout had been a serious mistake; one that it hoped would not be repeated. Although there had been fair play, "it was a disagreeable duty to all Southern men present." It was concerned about the social message that such bouts conveyed:

> It was a mistake to match a negro and a white man, a mistake to bring the races together on any terms of equality, even in the prize ring...for, among the ignorant negroes the idea has naturally been created that it was a test of the strength and fighting powers of

---

[69] *New York Sun*, September 9, 1892.
[70] *New York Herald*, September 8, 1892.

Caucasian and African. ... [T]he colored population of this city...because of [Dixon's] victory...are far more confident than they ever were before of the equality of the races, and disposed to claim more for themselves than we intend to concede. ... We of the South who know the fallacy and danger of this doctrine of race equality, who are opposed to placing the negro on any terms of equality, who have insisted on a separation of the races in church, hotel, car, saloon and theatre; who believe that the law ought to step in and forever forbid the idea of equality by making marriages between them illegal, are heartily opposed to any arrangement encouraging this equality, which give negroes false ideas and dangerous beliefs. ... Some may argue that there is no race question in the prize ring. We think differently. ...

Mr. John L. Sullivan has set a good example in this matter. ... [H]e has persistently refused to meet a negro in the ring. No one can believe that he has done this for any other reasons than his confidence that such contests place the races more or less on terms of equality.[71]

The color line was about power. Allowing blacks to compete with whites would convey the idea to blacks that they could have the opportunity to advance themselves to the level of whites, or even above them. That was seen as a dangerous threat to the caste system. Hence, boxing and social politics were intertwined.

In 1894, while in the U.S., even English-born and New Zealand-and-Australian-trained world middleweight champion Bob Fitzsimmons, who had fought blacks in Australia, and even had received instruction from Peter Jackson while there, said that if he won the heavyweight championship, he would draw the color line. "I will fight anybody except Jackson, whom I would not meet because he is a colored man."[72]

In 1895, former champion John L. Sullivan said, "No man of principle...will fight in a ring with a colored man. No man can say I ever refused to fight when the time came for a fight, but I never would fight with a nigger."[73]

On March 17, 1897 in Carson City, Nevada, former world middleweight champion Bob Fitzsimmons won the world heavyweight championship when in the 14th round he knocked out James J. Corbett with a left hook to the body.

Fitzsimmons did not defend the title for two years, until June 9, 1899 in New York, when in only his 13th professional contest, 24-year-old James J. Jeffries won the world heavyweight championship by knocking out 36-year-old Bob Fitzsimmons in the 11th round.

---

[71] *Times-Democrat*, September 8, 1892.
[72] *New York Sun,* October 2, 1894; *National Police Gazette*, October 20, 1894; *San Francisco Chronicle*, November 14, 1896.
[73] *Brooklyn Daily Eagle*, December 10, 1895.

James J. Jeffries

Although Jeffries had boxed black men in non-title bouts, defeating Hank Griffin (KO14), Peter Jackson (KO3)(1898), and Bob Armstrong (W10)(1898), Jeffries openly drew the color line when it came to world title fights. Hence, as had been the tradition in the gloved era, the heavyweight championship remained a prize for which only whites could apply. The heavyweight champion was boxing's top dog, considered to be the best fighter in the world, and there was great symbolic power in having that representative remain a white man.[74]

This was the state of affairs in the boxing world that Jack Johnson and other black fighters entered, endured, and would have to overcome in order to become champion.

In the meantime, following his draw with Hank Griffin, in January 1902 in San Francisco, Jack Johnson sparred and trained with highly regarded white Jack Root, the undefeated 38-0-1 fast and clever boxer-puncher.[75]

Top whites might not have been willing to fight blacks, but they were willing to pay them small amounts to be their sparring partners. Johnson consistently proved that he was willing to spar with anyone, which helped develop his skills. It also made him a little money, and kept his name in the minds of the local managers, promoters, and press. He showed them that he could hold his own with anyone.

On February 24, 1902 in Chicago, Denver Ed Martin won a 6-round decision over then recognized "colored heavyweight champion" Frank Childs. As a result, many began calling Martin the colored heavyweight champion of the world. However, others said the bout was too short to determine who the better man was, for typically championships were won and lost in bouts scheduled for 20 rounds or more.[76]

---

[74] *National Police Gazette*, December 7, 1901.
[75] On January 31, 1902 in San Francisco, Jack Root defeated George Gardner via DQ7.
[76] *Chicago Tribune*, February 25, 1902.

CHAPTER 6

Ascendance

Oakland's Reliance Club was impressed sufficiently with Jack Johnson's performance in his recent draw with Hank Griffin such that in early March 1902 they brought him back for a scheduled 15-round bout against white Joe Kennedy. The 32-year-old 6'2" 220-225-pound Kennedy would have a 50-pound weight advantage over the 23-year-old 172-pound Johnson. Hence, Kennedy believed that he would knock out the much smaller man.[77]

Nevertheless, Johnson was so confident of success that he was "like a boy," and had a joke for everyone.

When Bill Delaney asked Johnson if he would meet champion Jeffries in a 4-round exhibition bout, Johnson quickly replied, "Yes, and I'll outpoint him, too."

The *San Francisco Chronicle* said Johnson was "considered by many as a possible candidate for championship honors." He had impressed observers with his local sparring performances, fights, and hard training. The *Oakland Tribune* said Johnson "severely punished" Hank Griffin.

The *Chronicle* said Johnson "thus far has not developed the 'yellow streak' which has stopped many a likely member of his race from becoming a top-notcher." The allusion

Joe Kennedy

to the "yellow streak" of blacks was one of the era's racial stereotypes; that blacks had no heart or courage. Another racial belief was that blacks could not take body punches.

At that time, Oakland's population was 75,400. A letter carrier's annual salary was $850. As of the 1900 census, San Francisco, the city across the bay from Oakland, had a population of 342,782, making it the ninth most populous city in the U.S.[78]

---

[77] Kennedy had some quality results, including 1899 W20 Gus Ruhlin and D6 Frank Childs; 1901 D20 Hank Griffin (twice), and LKOby2 James J. Jeffries in an exciting and fast-paced, albeit short war. Jeffries called Kennedy big, strong, willing, and hard-hitting. *National Police Gazette*, November 4, 1899; *Los Angeles Daily Times, Los Angeles Express*, September 24, 1901; *Louisville Courier-Journal*, June 25, 1899; *New York Clipper*, July 1, 1899: Boxrec.com; *Oakland Tribune, Oakland Enquirer, San Francisco Call*, September 25, 1901; *My Life and Battles* at 44.
[78] *Oakland Tribune*, March 1, 5, 7, 1902; *San Francisco Chronicle, San Francisco Bulletin, Oakland Enquirer*, March 5, 1902; *Oakland Tribune*, March 4, 8, 1902.

MR. JOHN JOHNSON, WHO WILL MEET MR. JOSEPH KENNEDY AT THE RELIANCE CLUB FUNCTION TO-MORROW EVENING.

San Francisco Bulletin, **March 6, 1902**

On March 7, 1902 at Oakland's Reliance Athletic Club, a large crowd witnessed the contest for the Pacific Coast heavyweight championship, in which Jack Johnson scored a 4th round knockout over the much bigger Joe Kennedy, the knockout blow coming from a straight right.

The newsmen called "Mr. Johnsing" a "hard-hitting and scientific boxer," a "fast man on his feet and wicked at infighting." Johnson had been the 10 to 7 underdog, but he didn't fight like it, pummeling the larger man.[79]

Tom McCarey of the Century Athletic Club in Los Angeles offered Johnson a contest against Jack Jeffries, brother of world heavyweight champion James Jeffries, if Johnson would accept a smaller division of the purse than Jeffries, who was the bigger drawing card owing to his name. Los Angeles was the Jeffries brothers' hometown. Johnson agreed.[80]

25-year-old 185-pound Jack Jeffries immediately began training and sparring with his 225-pound champion brother, James J. Jeffries. Jack Jeffries primarily had earned his living as his brother's sparring partner. Despite the fact that Johnson had more actual fight experience, the contest was an even-money proposition in the wagering. Justified or not, the Jeffries name brought with it an aura of ability and credibility.[81]

Nevertheless, "Ebon-hued giant" Johnson was "supremely confident, and says the white man will never have a chance from the start."

It was said that like most colored gents, Johnson was a great admirer of fine clothing, and "he shows rather more taste than do most of his race in the selection of their apparel. He wears better clothing than three-fourths of

---

[79] *Oakland Tribune, Oakland Enquirer, Oakland Times, San Francisco Chronicle, San Francisco Examiner, San Francisco Call, San Francisco Bulletin,* March 8, 1902.
[80] *Los Angeles Herald,* May 1, 1902; *San Francisco Call,* May 2, 1902.
[81] *Los Angeles Herald,* May 6, 10, 12, 16, 1902. Jack Jeffries' record included a 1900 10-round draw with Billy Stift.

the people on the streets, and is proud of his clothes." Johnson had been earning good money recently, and he liked to spend most of it on clothing.[82]

On May 12, 1902 at Fort Erie, Ontario, Canada, black Joe Gans won the world lightweight championship by knocking out Frank Erne in the 1st round. He became the third black fighter to win a world championship, joining George Dixon and Joe Walcott. However, Gans was the first U.S.-born black fighter to become a champion. Dixon was Canadian and Walcott was from Guyana and Barbados.

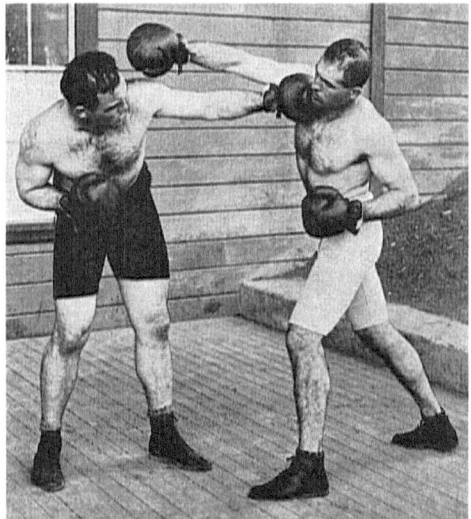

Champion James J. Jeffries (left) spars with brother Jack Jeffries (right)

The *Los Angeles Times* noted that the upcoming card featured white men fighting blacks. "If there is a favorite, the white man is it. [Jeffries] certainly has a host of well-wishers here, and his would be a popular victory."[83]

The *Los Angeles Herald* said, "Opinion is in favor of Jeffries if the bout be prolonged. There is a suspicion that the negro will not stand up to his work under punishment, though his record in the past has been that of a game man." The suspicion that blacks would not stand up to punishment was a typical claim based on racial bias.[84]

On May 16, 1902 at Hazard's Pavilion in Los Angeles, Jack Johnson fought Jack Jeffries in front of the largest crowd ever seen at a local boxing contest, with just over 4,000 packing the rafters and balcony, wedged in like sardines. The ground-floor seats were selling for $3.

At 10:30 p.m., Johnson entered the ring first, wearing a most amazing pair of pink pajamas, which excited a fair amount of merriment and gasps of astonishment. The *Times* said, "It wasn't an ordinary, inoffensive kind of pink. It was one of those screaming, caterwauling, belligerent pinks." It called "Bold Mistah Johnsing's pajamas cruel." Johnson remained cool as the fans laughed. He sat in his corner "half asleep and yawning like a big cat." With him was his manager Frank Carrillo, who had bet $100 on Johnson, whom he believed was underrated.

There was a fever of excitement and great cheering when Jack Jeffries entered the pavilion with his champion brother James. Referee Harry Stuart introduced the champion of the world, and James J. bowed to the roaring crowd which yelled madly for him.

---

[82] *Los Angeles Herald*, May 11, 1902.
[83] *Los Angeles Times*, May 16, 1902.
[84] *Los Angeles Herald*, May 16, 1902.

The *Times* claimed that in his corner, Johnson looked at the champion, the great hulk of a man, "the way a little mangy dog with a lame leg stops in the road and looks up at a St. Bernard."

Johnson fought confidently and aggressively, dominating the fight, drawing blood from Jeffries' nose, rocking his head with rights to the jaw, and landing stiff body blows. They clinched often and worked hard on the inside. In the 5th round, Johnson landed a powerful right cross to the jaw that sent Jeffries down to the floor with a thud. Referee Harry Stuart counted to ten. "This was a useless formality, however, for half a minute would have done Jack Jeffries little good." After the count concluded, Johnson lifted Jeffries up in his arms like a bag of wheat and handed him to his seconds, which included the world champion.

Afterwards, a mob of colored gentlemen swooped into Johnson's dressing room, anxious to congratulate the winner. Grinning broadly with two rows of ivories that strongly contrasted with his black skin, Johnson said, "Dat was a bad punch, sure 'nuff. Huh, jes like findin' money."

The *Los Angeles Times* said, "Jack Jeffries lasted just five rounds in front of a good-natured black animal named Johnsing." Johnson had eyes "that glared like a wild beast's." He was "too much color" for "Brother Jack."

The *Times* further said that from appearances, Jack Jeffries ought to have won. He had a body like a Greek god, muscles glistening with health. Conversely, "Mistah Johnsing is a long, lean, bullet-headed, flat-chested 'coon.' ... [who] straddles out like a sick chicken." However, the *Times* did acknowledge that Johnson "goes into the ranks of the candidates for the first class of pugilism."[85]

Los Angeles was being noticed as an emerging hotbed of boxing. Still, it had less than one-third the population of San Francisco, with a mere 102,479 people as of the 1900 census.

Los Angeles promoter Tom McCarey arranged a third fight between 24-year-old Johnson and 32-year-old Hank Griffin.[86]

The *Express* noted that the upcoming card featured all black fighters, something the club never before had offered. The *Herald* called the all-black competition "black night" and "dark night."

The *Express* said that Griffin was game, skilled, experienced, tough, and could punch, having scored many knockouts. Both would weigh in the neighborhood of 182 pounds.

Proving that he was durable, Griffin had been sparring up north with the hard-hitting former champion Bob Fitzsimmons, who was preparing for his championship rematch against James Jeffries.

The *Herald* said they were well-matched. Although Johnson obtained a draw in their last fight, "if Billy Delaney and William Lavigne are good authority, Johnson had all the best of the last rounds."[87]

---

[85] *Los Angeles Herald, Los Angeles Times*, May 17, 1902.
[86] *Los Angeles Express*, May 27, 1902; *Los Angeles Herald*, June 15, 1902.
[87] *Los Angeles Express, Los Angeles Herald*, June 20, 1902.

On June 20, 1902, fighting for a packed house at Hazard's Pavilion in Los Angeles, the third Jack Johnson versus Hank Griffin contest resulted in a 20-round draw. In the 1st round, Johnson split open Griffin's nose, and it bled nonstop. They went at it hammer and tongs, giving and taking back-and-forth throughout. Although aggressive at times, Johnson relied more on counterpunching. In the 18th round, Johnson landed a succession of short-arm blows which clearly dazed and hurt Griffin for a good minute, the only time in the fight that a knockout seemed possible.

After Referee Harry Stuart's draw ruling, Bakersfield's Frank Carrillo, Johnson's manager, protested quite fiercely. "You never will referee another fight for me. My man did all the fighting and you have robbed him." Stuart retorted, "You are lucky to get a draw, and Griffin was the aggressor."

The local newspapers agreed with the draw decision, calling it a very competitive, even contest in which the progress of the rounds was see-saw. "Griffin would have the shade in one, and a hard wallop by the other man would give him the best of the next round." They fought neck-and-neck throughout. "Hank's nose emitted all the gore produced during the mill."

Given the high quality of opponent, the *Los Angeles Herald* was impressed with Johnson, and saw his potential. Its writer appreciated the subtle effectiveness of his work, saying that although cautious about taking chances, Johnson had a good punch, excellent footwork, superb blocking, and never was hurt. He landed some powerful blows in the clinches that nearly ended matters. "Johnson's infighting was effective, but not many in the house appreciated it at its true value." He was not showy, but utilized "short uppercuts and piston rod jolts that sting wherever they strike."

In his dressing room, "Johnsing" was gloomy. He and his seconds strongly disagreed with the referee's decision. "Ise jes been robbed," Jack said as he carefully folded his pink pajamas. "Everybody knows dat Hank was licked." Johnson explained some of the fine points which he felt that the spectators and referee had overlooked. Clearly, the draw result did not affect Johnson's confidence or belief in himself.[88]

On July 25, 1902 in San Francisco, sparring partner Hank Griffin was amongst Bob Fitzsimmons' cornermen in Bob's attempt to regain the heavyweight championship crown from James J. Jeffries. Despite 185-pound Fitzsimmons' excellent performance, boxing well and cutting up the champion, 218-pound Jeffries took all that Fitz had to offer, and with his non-stop pressure and body punching, eventually wore down Fitz and knocked him out in the 8th round. It had been a wonderful championship contest. A crowd of 7,000 spectators paid $31,880 to witness the bout.[89]

On September 13, 1902 in Los Angeles, in a fight between 185-pound Hank Griffin and 6'3 ½" 210-pound white fighter Fred Russell, in the 14th round, the hard-punching Russell, who was behind on points, finally knocked Griffin down. While Hank was down, Russell deliberately fouled by hitting Griffin with an uppercut. Instead of disqualifying Russell as he

---

[88] *Los Angeles Express, Los Angeles Herald, Los Angeles Times,* June 21, 1902.
[89] *National Police Gazette,* September 13, 1902; *Daily Inter Ocean,* August 19, 1902.

should have done, Referee Tom Darmody counted out Griffin and awarded the victory to the white offender. The *Los Angeles Express* believed that Darmody either was ignorant or deliberately biased against the black man.

> To strike a man when he is down never has been considered anything but unfair, no matter in what grade of society it may be, and in boxing contests it is looked upon as more than a disgrace. It is a heinous offense and is punishable by the loss of the fight, according to the rules governing boxing contests.

Before the fight, Jack Johnson, who was present, announced that he wanted to meet the winner.[90]

---

[90] *Los Angeles Express*, September 13, 1902; *Los Angeles Herald*, September 8, 13, 1902.

CHAPTER 7

Colored Champion and More

24-year-old Jack Johnson's next bout, a scheduled 20-round contest set for late October 1902 in Los Angeles, was of great significance. It was for a claim to the world's colored heavyweight championship.

35-year-old 5'9 ½" 190-pound Frank Childs was a very experienced veteran, with over 50 career fights. He held knockout victories over Bob Armstrong (KO2, KO6), Klondike Haines (KO6, KO4, KO3), and George Byers (KO17), obtaining undisputed recognition as colored heavyweight champion. A 1902 6-round decision loss to Denver Ed Martin caused some to call Martin the new champion, though others

FRANK CHILDS

disputed the claim owing to the fact that it was only a short rounds victory.

Johnson had been a Childs sparring partner back in 1899 in Chicago. Upset at the poor treatment and lack of payment that he received from Childs, Johnson wanted payback.

Childs, "a fighter of wide reputation," was the strong 2 to 1 favorite. He had the superior experience, a long history of success, was known as an aggressive two-fisted puncher and finisher, and had the reputation for being a dead game fighter. Once again, manager Frank Carrillo wagered heavily on his 180-pound underdog, Johnson.[91]

On October 21, 1902 at Hazard's Pavilion in Los Angeles, before one of the largest crowds ever seen there, against colored champion Frank Childs, Jack Johnson was careful, but punched Childs often, knocked his head back with jabs, puffed up his face, winded him with stiff body punches, and cleverly evaded Childs' occasional powerful attempts. By the 11th round, Childs was spitting blood and had one eye closed. In the 12th round, "it was noticed that Childs's right arm was hanging limp. Johnson saw it, too, and rushed him savagely to the ropes, beating him about the face." At that point, a Childs second rolled a sponge into the middle of the ring to retire his man, and the bout was stopped. Childs claimed to have injured his arm in sparring, and to have re-injured it during the fight.

---

[91] *Los Angeles Express, Los Angeles Times, Los Angeles Herald,* October 18, 20, 21, 1902. To prepare for the Johnson bout, Childs sparred with Hank Griffin, against whom he previously had fought to a 20-round draw.

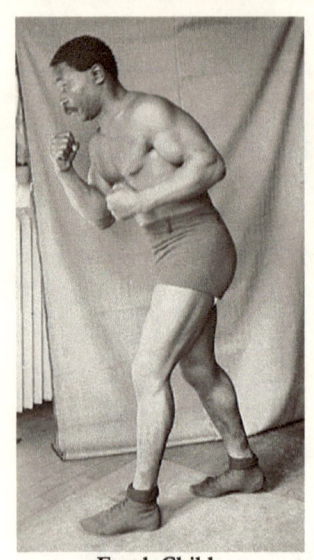

Frank Childs

The *Los Angeles Times* said the "colored champion of the world," "a big, gobby coon named Frank Childs," was licked by "the Johnson Giant," "the new champion of coon pugs." While Childs was waiting for one big punch, Johnson punched him all over the ring. "The new champion is a big, lean grinning negro named Jack Johnson." The *Los Angeles Herald* said, "Johnson's stock went up 100 per cent last night."

However, the *Los Angeles Express* said the patrons were disgusted, exclaiming, "Fake! Take 'em away! How much money will be spent in coontown tonight?" They were convinced that Childs never tried, and demanded an investigation. At least $20,000 changed hands locally as a result of the wagering. The Childs bettors were quite upset.

Childs, like many gamblers, had underestimated Johnson, failing to realize how much Jack had improved since they had sparred back in 1899.[92]

Years later, Johnson said the fight was personal. "I thought of all the mean things he had done to me and I gave him the slamming of his life."[93]

Johnson's next fight would be against George Gardner, whom Alex Greggains managed and promoted; the fight set to be held in San Francisco on October 31, a mere ten days after the Childs fight.[94]

Top light heavyweight George Gardner was an elite white fighter with at least 32 victories to his credit and only 3 losses, all avenged. Gardner had

---

[92] *Los Angeles Times, Los Angeles Herald, Los Angeles Express,* October 22, 1902.
[93] *San Francisco Bulletin,* July 27, 1910.
[94] *San Francisco Bulletin,* October 24, 1902.

beaten fast, strong, and clever fighters in George Byers (WDQ14), Kid Carter (KO18, KO8), Joe Walcott (W20), and Jack Root (KO17). He was 25 years of age, one year older than Johnson.

Despite Johnson's advantages in height (6'1 ½" vs. 5'11 ½"), reach, and weight (182 vs. 172), the oddsmakers had Johnson as the 2 to 1 *underdog* against the experienced well-known Gardner. Most believed that Gardner would win handily, via knockout.[95]

Jack Johnson, the Shortender in Tomorrow Night's Fight.

On October 31, 1902 in San Francisco, the Jack Johnson vs. George Gardner fight resulted in a clear 20-round decision for Johnson, who dominated. All of his punches hurt, whether they were straight left jabs or short inside jolts. Gardner clinched and hung on repeatedly. Johnson scored several knockdowns, in the 4th, 8th, and twice in the 14th round, ripping in his short-arm right. Conversely, Johnson successfully blocked or eluded all of Gardner's blows. The confused Gardner "scarcely laid a glove on the big black man." Johnson fought in spurts, each time after decking or hurting Gardner, backing off and playing defense again, fighting cautiously, pacing himself, remaining in control to the end.

All of the local newspapers believed that Johnson could have stopped Gardner had he fought harder and cut loose more consistently. He seemed happy and content to do what he was doing, laughing throughout.[96]

The *San Francisco Bulletin* said the result was the biggest surprise in recent memory, for most had expected Gardner to win with ease.

Johnson was jubilant. He said that he was ready to fight champion Jim Jeffries, Bob Fitzsimmons, Jack Root, Kid McCoy, or any of the big guns. His manager Frank Carrillo said he would back Johnson against any man in the world, and would wager up to $2,000 on him. Carrillo had been earning very good money betting on Johnson in all of his recent contests.[97]

---

[95] *San Francisco Bulletin*, October 27, 29, 1902.
[96] *San Francisco Examiner, San Francisco Chronicle, San Francisco Call*, November 1, 1902.
[97] *San Francisco Bulletin*, November 1, 1902.

San Francisco Bulletin, **November 1, 1902**

That evening, Carrillo was relieved of a revolver, and later was arrested and charged with carrying a concealed pistol, despite the fact that he had a permit from Bakersfield. He was released on bail.[98]

Carrillo said his arrest was the result of joking remarks he had made:

> I said yesterday in a josh to some fellows that if that nigger tried to lay down I'd see that he stayed down with the weight of a little lead. I may have said the same thing about the referee if his decision wasn't on the square, but I didn't mean it. I had a wad of money up on Johnson because he looked good to me and I didn't want the double cross worked on me. It was all a josh and someone, I guess, took it the other way.

---

[98] *San Francisco Call,* November 1, 1902.

Gardner and Johnson each took 50% of the 50% fighter's share of the gross receipts, evenly splitting the fighter's share regardless of result. The white Gardner had earned just as much as Johnson, which was $354.25. Either way, it was good money for a man who came from poverty.[99]

Tom McCarey offered a $10,000 purse for a James J. Corbett vs. Denver Ed Martin fight, with the winner potentially to meet Jeffries the following year. However, Corbett did not fight at all in 1901 or 1902, and eventually was able to obtain the title fight without having any interim matches.[100]

On November 14, 1902 in Baltimore, Maryland, world lightweight champion Joe Gans knocked out white challenger Charles Seiger in the 15th round.

> Believing that the exhibition of the negro pugilist, Joe Gans, mauling and drawing the blood of a white fighter or boxer, has an unwholesome effect upon the rough negro element, tending to make it more disorderly, the police authorities are considering the possibility of refusing to issue permits for contests between white and colored boxers. ... For several years Baltimore has been a haven for pugilists and their exhibitions, but for the above reasons the authorities may decide to put a stop to such contests altogether.[101]

As this reveals, the long tradition of legal limitations and impediments upon the sport of boxing is in part based upon race. Writers, police, and politicians were fully cognizant of boxing's racial implications.

Jack Johnson's next fight was against white 24-year-old Fred Russell, a big and powerful 6'4" 215-219-pound 25-fight veteran. Russell would have significant height, reach, and weight advantages over the 180-185-pound Johnson.[102]

Russell was coming off a 5th round knockout loss to big black Sam McVey, so he would be motivated, because if "he takes two successive beatings from negroes he will draw nothing but flies hereafter."

The *Los Angeles Express* predicted, "Russell should win the battle inside of six rounds if he rushes things from the start." Russell's supporters asserted that Johnson did not like

Fred Russell

---

[99] *San Francisco Bulletin,* November 1, 2, 1902.
[100] *San Francisco Chronicle,* November 2, 1902.
[101] *Philadelphia Record,* November 19, 1902.
[102] *Los Angeles Herald,* December 1, 1902; *Los Angeles Express,* December 3, 1902. Russell was known as a foul fighter, having been disqualified against Joe Choynski (flagrantly hitting after the 4th round bell) and Denver Ed Martin (engaging in deliberate foul kicks to the shins in the 10th round after having taken a beating). Johnson had seen Tom Sharkey knock out Russell in 4 rounds. Russell held a KO3 victory over Klondike and KO14 over Hank Griffin, though most thought Russell should have been disqualified for hitting Griffin while he was down.

to get hit, that the much bigger Russell could punch, and therefore Jack would "stop like a clock if things do not go his way."[103]

On December 4, 1902 in Los Angeles, an immense crowd packed Hazard's Pavilion to watch Jack Johnson vs. Fred Russell. Johnson entered the ring led by manager Frank Carrillo, "a fat Mexican with a frightful scar on his face." Russell was a big, hulking fellow, with chrysanthemum hair and blue eyes.

Despite his smaller size, Johnson controlled the fight from start to finish. The contest featured terrible infighting – clinching, pounding, and occasional flurrying. In the 3rd round, Johnson landed a vicious left to Russell's right eye, cutting it badly, causing the blood to spurt and drip gore all over, onto both fighters and the referee, creating a horrific, ghastly spectacle. Referee Harry Stuart's blood-stained shirt made him look like a butcher as he wrenched apart the sweating, blood-covered bodies.

In the 7th round, Russell was weakening. The *Los Angeles Times* said,

> He was writhing under the awful beating. But the coon was as jolly and as good-natured as though it were just a little appetizer. He grinned like a china exhibit every time he was hit. He was generous in the clinches and many times raised his arms straight up in the air like a man in a hold-up to show it was not he who was doing the hugging.

In the 8th round, Russell stooped down and landed three furious flagrantly low blows in a row. Johnson dropped and rolled over on the floor several times in agony, holding his hands clasped to the "unmentionable delicate part of the body." The crowd went wild, enraged by Russell's obviously intentional actions. Eventually, after thinking about it, Referee Harry Stuart awarded the contest to Johnson via disqualification.

The *Los Angeles Express* said those who thought Russell would give Johnson all he could handle were sorely mistaken. "Johnson had his opponent at his mercy throughout the battle." The *Times* agreed: "Johnson just waded into him and battered him into a pulp." Russell's face was cut to ribbons. "That hunky coon Johnson would reach out and grasp the white man in a loving embrace and send a rain of frightful short-arm blows to his bleeding body. They didn't seem to be so very hard, but there was a crash and a groan to every one."

Regarding the ending, the *Times* said, "Russell was getting terribly licked by a good-natured grinning coon…and [in the 8th round] committed three deliberate fouls of a particularly atrocious character to save himself." The *Herald* agreed that the whipped Russell, maddened and frustrated by his inability to hit Johnson with anything tangible, was not game enough to take a beating, so he deliberately fouled in disgraceful fashion.[104]

On December 20, 1902 in Butte, Montana, James J. Jeffries boxed a 4-round exhibition with 200-pound miner Jack Munroe. Press releases had varying facts and levels of veracity regarding what happened. However,

---

[103] *Los Angeles Express, Los Angeles Herald,* December 4, 1902.
[104] *Los Angeles Herald, Los Angeles Express, Los Angeles Times,* December 5, 1902.

many newspapers throughout the nation ran a story saying that Munroe did very well with Jeffries. Some even claimed that Munroe dropped the champion and outpointed him. This story was used to catapult his career, and Munroe and his press agent repeated it quite often. Jeffries continually disputed the truth of the stories, and was extremely irked by them. Jeffries insisted that he had carried Munroe for 2 rounds, slipped down when missing a punch, and had decked Munroe several times. His version was closer to the truth. However, over time, the white Munroe was sold to the public as a legitimate threat to Jeffries.

In late December 1902, the *Butte Intermountain* reported, "Big Jack Johnson of San Francisco now wants to fight any of them. Johnson, himself as black as Erebus, says he bars no color. Mars Johnson is a humorist as well as a fighter."[105]

At that time, U.S. Senator John Morgan of Alabama, a former Confederate general and advocate for racial segregation and limitation of black rights, proposed a plan for colonizing the negroes of the United States in the Philippines and other foreign places "when their numbers increased to an extent that would make emigration necessary." Some said the plan was good in theory but unfeasible because it would require oppressive taxes (not that it was wrong because blacks were citizens).[106]

"DENVER ED" MARTIN.

In the meantime, the *Butte Miner* argued that neither Denver Ed Martin nor Jack Johnson would have clear title as colored heavyweight champion until he whipped the other. The Martin-Johnson fight would determine the undisputed colored heavyweight championship and the man most entitled to a world championship challenge. It was the fight that fans wanted.[107]

21-year-old Denver Ed Martin stood at least 6'4" tall and weighed "considerably over 200 pounds, not an ounce of it superfluous." "Being a colored man, it is needless to say he had sporting proclivities." "Since the start of his career, Martin's strongest card has been his cleverness. ... Endowed to an unusual extent by nature in respect to size and strength, he is also one of the most skilled men in the profession, big or little." He had defeated Hank Griffin (KO7), Bob Armstrong (W15), and Frank Childs (W6).[108]

Many reporters had hyped Martin as a potential world title challenger, causing Bill Delaney and Jim Jeffries to state expressly that they would not allow a colored man to challenge for the championship.

---

[105] *Butte Intermountain*, December 23, 1902.
[106] *Billings Gazette*, December 23, 1902.
[107] *Butte Miner* December 26, 1902.
[108] *Los Angeles Herald*, January 28, 1903.

General opinion favored Martin, for he had defeated Griffin decisively, and would have significant physical advantages of height, reach, and weight. He also had the bigger reputation.[109]

On February 5, 1903 in Los Angeles, Jack Johnson fought Denver Ed Martin for the undisputed colored heavyweight championship. A crowd of well over 4,000 packed Hazard's Pavilion, the largest local fight crowd ever seen, breaking all previous records. Patrons willingly paid higher prices to ticket speculators.

Before the fight, Martin said to Johnson, "I do regret having to knock down such a cute and charming little thing as yourself."

Throughout, Johnson boxed cautiously, counterpunching, particularly to the body, carefully winning most of the rounds. The 11th round proved to be the most exciting of the contest, for Johnson decked Martin three times, the first time with a counter right as Martin jabbed. Martin was all but out, weak and groggy, staggering about, clinching, and dropping until the gong saved him. The audience was wild with delight. Martin recovered, and thereafter, Johnson coasted to the end, fighting the same cautious but clever fight. Some believed that he could have finished Martin, but played it safe rather than attack hard and risk getting caught himself. Johnson said he was not taking unnecessary chances with his backers' money.

At the conclusion of the 20 rounds, Referee Harry Stuart awarded Johnson the "well-earned" decision, and the verdict for the underdog was met with roaring audience approval and applause. Jack Johnson was the undisputed "heavyweight colored champion of the world."[110]

On the heels of this significant financially lucrative victory, Johnson was scheduled to make his first defense of the undisputed colored crown a mere three weeks later.

Oxnard's 19-year-old Sam McVey, another highly touted up-and-comer, was the "pride of Beetville," for Oxnard was where they grew sugar beets. Hank Griffin was his trainer. The 210-pound "wonder" had a great physique and was a "quick, handy boxer for a man of his tremendous size." Most importantly, McVey was a knockout artist, undefeated in 14 bouts, with all 14 contests won by knockout within 7 rounds. Even big men could not take his punch. McVey knocked out 6'4" 215-pound Fred Russell in the 5th round with a right to the jaw. After knocking out 240-pound Toothpick Kelly in the 4th round, it required an hour to restore the Toothpick to full consciousness. The *Herald* said, "There is a general love for the punch among the public, and McVey is credited with it to a remarkable degree."

One report said that when striking the punching machines that registered the force of a blow, McVey's punch registered 1,270 pounds of force. Striking the same machine, Jeffries had registered 1,100 pounds and Fitzsimmons 1,070.

---

[109] *Los Angeles Herald*, February 3, 5, 1903.
[110] *Los Angeles Herald, Los Angeles Times, Los Angeles Express*, February 6, 1903.

McVey would have a 25-pound weight advantage over Johnson, and the ability to knock him out with a single blow. Fight fans were excited.[111]

The *Los Angeles Herald* wrote, "There has been a saying that two black men do not make a good contest to look upon, but the Griffin-Martin and Johnson-Martin battles give ample guaranty that a meeting between McVey and Johnson will be worth watching."

McVey was sparring with Hank Griffin, who reported that he could not last 4 rounds against his own protégé, "which is fair dope in itself."[112]

Sam McVey

On February 26, 1903 at Hazard's Pavilion in Los Angeles, more than 3,000 spectators paid to see Jack Johnson fight Sam McVey.

Throughout the 20 rounds, Johnson easily outclassed and handled the "Oxnard Wonder" in dominant fashion. McVey "was beaten and pounded and slammed around and punched and jabbed." Johnson's powerful blows made "the Oxnarder's bullet-like brain-box rattle like a dried walnut." The punishment McVey absorbed "would have whipped half a dozen ordinary men." Conversely, McVey could not hit the clever Johnson, whose blocking was splendid. Johnson earned referee Harry Stuart's 20-round decision with ease. The *Los Angeles Times* said,

> They don't arrange these coon fights right. The afternoon before the fight they ought to run the fighters through a steam carpet-cleaning machine, and set a pair of men pounding them a while with meat cleavers. A little thing like twenty rounds of punching can't worry a coon like McVey much. He could stand up for twenty rounds lashed to a post and let the other man take an ax.
>
> Any man who can stand up twenty rounds before McVey's face, however, and not run howling through the ropes for help, deserves a great reputation for bravery. McVey has a countenance that would scare back the rising moon. When you see his face peeking over his two gigantic fists, and realize that it is you he is after, it's enough to throw a man into fits.

---

[111] *Los Angeles Herald*, November 10, 1902, January 7, 1903, February 1, 7, 8, 12, 20, 1903; *Oxnard Courier*, March 29, 1902, October 25, 1902, November 8, 15, 1902, January 10, 17, 1903, February 14, 21, 1903.
[112] *Los Angeles Herald*, February 20, 1903; *Los Angeles Express*, February 26, 1903.

Referee Harry Stuart said Johnson was a brilliant and powerful boxer. "There is no colored heavyweight in the world today who is likely to wrest the title from Johnson while he retains his present form."[113]

Afterwards, the confident Johnson said, "I am by rights the next man that Jeffries ought to meet, and if the mill comes off I will give the crowd plenty of fun for their money.[114]

Jim Jeffries was scheduled to engage in a lucrative payday against former champion James J. Corbett, who had given him a tough title defense back in 1900, with Jeffries coming from behind on points to deck him in the 19th round and knock him out in the 23rd round. However, leading up to the rematch, Jim Corbett had not fought in 3 years.

Regardless, Johnson would have to deal with the color line, which Jeffries already had drawn unequivocally. Fair-minded members of the press and sporting fraternity, combined with economics, would need to convince Jeffries to take on Johnson, if such could be done.

In other news, a Los Angeles Methodist bishop declared that he was not opposed to interracial marriage and miscegenation. This "stirred up a violent controversy among the Methodists of the city." The bishop knew that most folks naturally would shudder at the idea. His "startling admissions" drew expressions of surprise and wonder.[115]

[113] *Los Angeles Times, Los Angeles Herald, Los Angeles Express* February 27, 1903;
[114] *Police Gazette*, March 21, 1903.
[115] *Los Angeles Herald*, February 28, 1903.

CHAPTER 8

Testing the East

Owing to his burgeoning national reputation, Jack Johnson finally obtained a meaningful fight back East, this time in Boston, Massachusetts. The *Boston Post* said, "Johnson is really a big attraction...and a real candidate for the world's championship." He was scheduled to fight the local man, John "Sandy" Ferguson, a 23-year-old white boxer from Chelsea (less than 4 miles from Boston) who took on all-comers and did not draw the color line. Ferguson, who had over 30 fights of experience, weighed in the neighborhood of 220 to 225 pounds and stood 6'3". Hence, he would have significant height, reach, and weight advantages over Johnson.[116]

On April 16, 1903 in Boston, the scheduled 10-round Jack Johnson vs. Sandy Ferguson bout took place.

Johnson made a big hit when he entered the ring "gayly gowned and dolled in pink pajamas, and wearing a highly checked gold cap." With Jack was welterweight champ Joe Walcott, who was resplendent in diamonds and smoking a long black cigar. They formed a visual combination hard to beat.

Sandy Ferguson

From the start, Johnson did all the forcing, leading, and landing. "Johnson was the aggressor all though the contest, and he landed many a hard left and right on Sandy's stomach and face." Johnson's blows worried Sandy, who appeared afraid, fighting cautiously. He stalled, broke ground, blocked, and clinched, landing few punches. Johnson clearly earned the 10-round decision.

Yet, both the *Boston Herald* and *Boston Globe* criticized the performance, saying Johnson was content to do just enough to win a decision, while Ferguson was content to last without getting hurt.

The *Boston Post* was much higher on Johnson, saying he verified all that had been said about his ability as a boxer.[117]

The day before Johnson-Ferguson, on April 15, 1903 in Joplin, Missouri, a black man named Thomas Gilyard was taken into custody for the murder of a policeman. In less than an hour, the Joplin streets filled with 2,000

---

[116] *Boston Post*, April 16, 1903.
[117] *Boston Herald, Boston Globe, Boston Post*, April 17, 1903.

angry white men. The mob soon demanded that Gilyard be surrendered to "justice," which to them meant a lynching without a fair trial. The mob got its way and hung him.

After the lynching, the mob drove all of the black citizens from the streets into the northern "colored" part of town. The mob then set fire to the houses there, and simultaneously prevented the Fire Department from extinguishing the flames.

The Joplin lynching was national news not for the lynching, which was nothing out of the ordinary, but for the subsequent riot aimed at eliminating the town's black population.

This began the history of Joplin being all-white. Joplin was just 30 miles from Peirce City, another all-white town that had used mob violence to force out all of the black people. To this day, Joplin is 87% white.[118]

On April 27, 1903, W. E. B. Du Bois' book, *The Souls of Black Folk*, was published. Regarding the topic of blacks obtaining civil rights, Du Bois rejected Booker T. Washington's philosophy of education and entrepreneurship combined with conciliation and accommodation when it came to segregation and disfranchisement laws, and instead called for agitation, protestation, and insistence upon recognition of black rights. Years later, Jack Johnson also rejected Washington's philosophy, stating,

> White people often point to the writings of Booker T. Washington as the best example of a desirable attitude on the part of the colored population. I have never been able to agree with the point of view of Washington, because he has to my mind not been altogether frank in the statement of the problem or courageous in the formulation in his solutions to them.[119]

Joe Butler

On May 11, 1903 in Philadelphia, Jack Johnson fought fellow black Joe Butler in a scheduled 6-round no-decision bout (all that was allowed there). The 6-foot 36-year-old Butler had nearly 60 known bouts under his belt. The *Philadelphia Inquirer* said Butler would be meeting "one of the cleverest men today in the ring, not excepting Jim Corbett. Johnson has a remarkable record of victories and is a candidate for the crown of champion Jim Jeffries." The *Philadelphia Evening Bulletin* said Johnson was credited with being second only to Jim Jeffries.[120]

During the tame first two rounds, Johnson toyed with Butler as a cat does with a mouse, blocking blows with ease, fooling around and barely trying, causing some to think the fight was friendly. "Mr. Johnsing fondled Joe in a patronizing manner."

---

[118] Joplin was the city famously destroyed by a tornado in 2011.
[119] Johnson, *In the Ring and Out* at 239.
[120] *Philadelphia Inquirer, Philadelphia Evening Bulletin*, May 11, 1903.

The 3rd round began in brotherly fashion as well, but after the spectators strongly voiced their disapproval of matters, Butler cut loose. In response, Jack's good nature disappeared, and he "showed just how good a fighter he is," landing a short right to the jaw that sent Butler down and out, laying motionless for several minutes.

On his way back to the dressing room, a crowd gathered around Johnson, giving him accolades. While Jack was shaking hands with his admirers, Harry Burke, a local white lightweight boxer, smashed a bottle on top of Johnson's shaved head, and Jack sank to his knees. A long gash was cut in his scalp, from which he bled profusely. The police immediately arrested Burke. Jack was taken to the hospital to have his wound dressed.

Johnson said he did not know who busted a bottle on his "crust," for his back was turned, and he knew of no reason for being assaulted. The cut left a scar on his "dome of thought."

Allegedly, the trouble started in the dressing room before the fight. Burke asked Johnson for the use of a towel, but Jack refused to loan it to him, saying that he never would lend a white fighter a towel, for the reason that no white pugilist would do him the same favor. Burke insisted and came at Johnson, who slapped his face, knocking him down. Burke grabbed a bottle, but was persuaded not to use it. He instead found his opportunity to do so in cowardly fashion after the fight.

Another newspaper reported a rumor that Johnson was told to carry Butler the full 6 rounds, and was warned that if he knocked him out, he would be assaulted. He tried to carry him, but when Butler attacked hard, he was compelled to retaliate. Hence, Johnson was punished for disobeying.[121]

At that time, Johnson was dating two colored women, one named Etta Reynolds, and another named Clara Kerr. Johnson became infatuated with Kerr. An attachment grew between them which lasted for a while. However, eventually Kerr left him for another man, who had been Johnson's friend and had lived with them out of Jack's generosity. They took his clothes and property of value. Johnson later found her and reconciled with Kerr. However, she again took his possessions and money and left him a second time. Johnson was despondent. The two black loves of his life had broken his heart. He later wrote, "The heartaches which Mary Austin and Clara Kerr had caused me, led me to forswear colored women and to determine that my lot henceforth would be cast only with white women." That wasn't entirely true. Johnson continued to date women of both races. Many years later, after Johnson learned that Kerr had been imprisoned on a charge of murdering her brother, he paid for lawyers to help get her acquitted, and also helped her acquire a small hotel.[122]

On July 4, 1903 in Fort Erie, Ontario, Canada, George Gardner solidified his claim to the world light heavyweight championship with a KO12 over title-claimant Jack Root, who had defeated Kid McCoy.

---

[121] *Philadelphia Record, Philadelphia Inquirer, Philadelphia Press, Philadelphia Evening Bulletin*, May 12, 1903.
[122] Johnson at 72-76.

Naturally, Gardner's success made Johnson's clear victory over him garner him more credit.

The Philly folks arranged a Johnson rematch with Sandy Ferguson, who recently had fought Gus Ruhlin to a 15-round draw. This was significant, because after being stopped by Jeffries via retirement after the 5th round in late 1901, Ruhlin's recent results included knockout victories over Peter Maher (KO2), Tom Sharkey (KO11) and Mexican Pete Everett (KO2). Many believed that "Chelsea Strong Boy" Ferguson had outpointed Ruhlin, who only managed a draw by forcing matters more.[123]

The *Philadelphia Evening Bulletin* said Sandy's performance against Ruhlin put him in line to meet the winner of the upcoming Jeffries-Corbett fight. "Johnson is a fighting marvel and if Ferguson can get away with him he is indeed a wonder."[124]

On July 31, 1903 in Philadelphia, Jack Johnson fought Sandy Ferguson in a 6-round no-decision bout. Johnson wore a particularly broad grin throughout the contest, a "smile that would not come off." Ferguson "gave no evidence of his ability to cope successfully with a boxer of Johnson's undoubted ability." That Ferguson stayed the full 6 rounds appeared to be due to Johnson's "gentlemanly forbearance." Whenever Johnson cut loose, he had Ferguson visibly worried. But then he would back off and coast. In the 6th round, Sandy was very tired, despite Johnson's "evident consideration for Ferguson." Ferguson clinched quite often, particularly during the last 3 rounds. Johnson did not seem to mind, and appeared to be carrying Sandy. "In fact the black seemed to content himself by suggesting to the spectators what he might do if he felt inclined that way, without actually trying to do it." "Johnson was by far the cleverer boxer."

There was suspicion that Johnson had a habit of carrying his opponents, doing so in order to induce them and others to fight him so he could earn. Others thought it simply was a matter of Johnson's natural caution, content to win decisions rather than try to win by knockout but increase the risk of getting caught or fatigued himself. As long as his foes didn't try too hard to beat him, he was content to lay back and win decision victories.[125]

---

[123] *Police Gazette*, June 13, 1903.
[124] *Philadelphia Evening Bulletin*, July 31, 1903.
[125] *Philadelphia Record, Philadelphia Inquirer, Philadelphia Press*, August 1, 1903.

CHAPTER 9

Up Against the Color Line

During July 1903, Jim Nell offered $2,500 to bind a match between Jack Johnson and Bob Fitzsimmons. However, Fitzsimmons said he was drawing the color line. The *National Police Gazette* noted that Johnson had been unsuccessful in his attempts to arrange matches with some of the best white fighters.[126]

On August 14, 1903 in San Francisco, 28-year-old 225-pound heavyweight champion James J. Jeffries defended his title in a rematch against 36-year-old 190-pound James J. Corbett. Before the fight, announcer Billy Jordan read off challenges to the winner from Jack Munroe and Jack Johnson. Munroe's challenge received jeers, but the crowd applauded Johnson's challenge. Jeffries told manager Bill Delaney that he would not fight a colored man, but would meet Munroe.

Jeffries knocked out Corbett in the 10th round, hurting him in the 2nd, dropping him in the 4th and 6th rounds, and twice in the 10th. They fought before a crowd of 10,669 which generated $62,340 in gate receipts, breaking all of the state's attendance and gate receipt records.

Jeffries was being called the greatest heavyweight champion ever.

> Jeffries now fears there is no pugilist on earth capable of giving him a battle. He laughs at Jack Monroe and smiles when Jack Johnson is mentioned. The negro may be a good, clever fellow, but he would be outclassed worse than Corbett was. He has a soft punch, and could not hurt the big gladiator in a month.
>
> There is one man who might have a faint chance of success, and that is Sam McVey, the Oxnard giant. He weighs in excess of 200 pounds, and has a very hard wallop. He is the only kind of a man of whom the champion would stand in the least bit of danger.[127]

Jack Johnson replied,

> They say there's only two men left who have a chance [with Jeffries]; that's Sam McVey and myself. Well, I have beaten this Mr. McVey once and can do it again any time he gets a side bet ready. ... My man now is Jeffries. I'm big enough, weigh near 200, and I'll tell you the fight won't be one-sided. He can't touch a man with his right, and I'm sure I could take care of that left and slip him a few on the side.[128]

---

[126] *National Police Gazette*, August 1, 8, 1903.
[127] *San Francisco Evening Post*, August 17, 1903.
[128] *San Francisco Bulletin*, August 18, 1903.

San Francisco Bulletin, **August 27, 1903, referring to Johnson, Martin, and McVey as "dark clouds."**

Jim Jeffries continually insisted, "I will fight any white man in the world, but will not fight a negro." The *San Francisco Bulletin* said "there is no chance of his ever crawling through the ropes with a coon."[129]

Race was a factor in boxing for writers, fans, fighters, and promoters alike:

> It is amusing to note the way in which the crowd at a ringside receives the different nationalities of fighter. There is always a hearty cheer and earnest backing for the Irishman; grins and good-humored tolerance for the German, and virulent hostility to the Italian and the negro.[130]

Nevertheless, the *Police Gazette* said the next title holder might be a black man. Experts had noted the emergence of colored champion Jack Johnson as a potential test for Jeffries. Johnson "threatens to provide a choice package of assorted trouble for the heavyweight champion at some time not distantly remote." The *Police Gazette* never supported the color line in boxing, so the champion's stance generated some criticism, as well as instant support for Johnson:

> Jeff knows him, and has followed his career with no little interest ever since he burst upon the scene as an eligible opponent for titular honors. George Gardiner, the present light heavyweight champion, who believes he can whip Fitzsimmons, proved to be little more than a plaything for this burly black fellow, and the latter did awful things to 'Sandy' Ferguson, a second-rate heavyweight fighter who knocked out Bob Armstrong in one round the other night. Johnson likewise put a terrific crimp in the championship aspirations of Denver Ed Martin, the giant black whom we all thought a year or two ago was the legitimate successor to the title. Just because he happens to be black, Sharkey, Ruhlin, Corbett and Fitzsimmons can't see him when he assumes a fighting attitude, and now Jeffries has found his eyesight so acute that he can differentiate between colors, and draws the line, although he was, perhaps, afflicted with a peculiar sense of blindness when he fought Peter Jackson, Bob Armstrong and Hank Griffin.
>
> Notwithstanding the prevailing objection to color, just keep your eyes on this black fellow.

---

[129] *San Francisco Bulletin*, August 24, 27, 1903.
[130] *Police Gazette*, August 22, September 5, 1903.

In subsequent issues, the *Police Gazette* continued voicing its support for Johnson, who was campaigning for a shot at Jeffries.

> While Jeffries continues to reiterate that he will not fight a black man for the title of heavyweight champion of the world, the curtain-colored individual whom he believes to be the only menacing factor to his remaining in undisputed possession of that title has started on a campaign of fistic engagements which he hopes will in time justify the support of public opinion in his demands upon Jeffries for a fight. That person is Jack Johnson, who is now the recognized colored champion heavyweight.[131]

Sam McVey, the Oxnard Giant.

Johnson signed to box a rematch with Sam McVey in Los Angeles for the colored championship, for which "McVey is considered the most promising aspirant."

McVey had impressed Los Angelinos, knocking out Kid Carter in the 11th round, significant because Carter held a knockout victory over Choynski. More importantly, on September 15, 1903 in Los Angeles, Sam McVey knocked out Denver Ed Martin in the 1st round. That caused sportsmen to want to see a Johnson-McVey rematch.:

> Among sporting men here who have followed both, much doubt is expressed as to Johnson's ability to repeat the dose. McVey is now larger and stronger as well as faster, and he has improved considerably in ring skill since the previous meeting, as shown by his quick disposal of 'Denver Ed' Martin. The Oxnard man is not yet 20 years old and many ring followers think they see in him a black Jeffries.[132]

Back East, the *Detroit Free Press* wrote,

> It really looks as if Jeffries will have to fight a black man or quit the game. McVey's easy victory over Ed Martin has boomed the first named's stock at the coast, and a battle between McVey and Jack Johnson should now be a big drawing card. With this over, there would be nothing further to consider but a match between the winner and Jeffries. The champion is doubtless right in his contention that a black champion would be repugnant to most sport followers. Still, we have a few of them now, with Gans at the top of the lightweight division and Walcott the leader of the welters. Their accessions to

---

[131] *Police Gazette*, September 5, 26, 1903.
[132] *Los Angeles Times*, September 19, 1903.

their respective thrones did not result in civil war. Dixon was the boss of his class for years, and was popular, though never so great an idol as he would have been had his skin been white. It is possibly up to Jeffries to show us that in some of the divisions that white talent is better than black. And defeat of Jeffries would merely result in greater activity in the heavyweight class, in the effort to bring to light a white man capable of recovering the lost laurels.[133]

Jack began calling himself "J. Arthur Johnson." The *Los Angeles Times* said the local betting fraternity always would refer to "the big dingy" and "big coon" lovingly as "Black Jack" Johnson. The colored champion also was called the "Black Fitzsimmons" and "Mistah Johnsing."[134]

In mid-October 1903, Jim Jeffries said, "I am still in the game, and will fight any white man they can trot out, but I draw the line on colored men. Not that I am afraid of the dark skinned fighters, but if I am booked for a licking I want a white man to do the trick." Jeffries also said, "When there are no more white men to fight I shall quit the game." However, "There are no men for me to fight in America except negroes, and I don't intend to fight colored men."[135]

McVey's wealthy manager Billy Roche was so confident in his fighter that he paid $250 to have a diamond-and-gold belt made, which would be given to the winner of the colored championship fight. No one thought Roche would do so unless he was sure that his man would be victorious. "Besides, Jack has all the diamonds he can pay interest on right now. They keep him poor. If he should ever fall into the water with his entire collection of rocks on his person he would be sure to drown."[136]

Johnson did not care about the belt, allegedly saying,

> Ah allus weahs suspenders. Nevah could get use' ter a belt. No swell dressers wears 'em, nohow. No, suh, Sam kin hev th' belt ef he wants it – jess' lemme win that fight an' Ah shorely meks a liberal prescription todes buyin' him all the belts he kin weah.

---

[133] *Detroit Free Press*, September 20, 1903.
[134] *Los Angeles Times*, September 30, 1903.
[135] *Chicago Tribune*, October 17, 18, 1903; *Los Angeles Times*, October 21, 22, 1903.
[136] *Los Angeles Herald*, October 21, 1903; *Oxnard Courier*, October 23, 1903.

The local *Los Angeles Herald* said "the coming mill will be the biggest drawing card ever pulled off in Los Angeles and the man who gets a pass to it had better take it home and frame it as a souvenir."[137]

Despite having lost to Johnson the first time, McVey had become the 10 to 8 betting *favorite*. Apparently, either Johnson was being overlooked and underestimated, or fans were very impressed by Sam's appearance in training, as well as his recent performances.[138]

McVey's admirers said the force of his blows was so terrific that it was impossible for any man to stand up when hit. Sooner or later McVey would land one. "One will be enough."

Regardless of the odds, Johnson was totally confident. "If you look up Jack Johnson he will tell you that this Oxnard man will be like eating chicken for him – chicken and watermelon."[139]

Not only did Johnson love jewelry, but he also had a great appreciation for fine clothes. When he came to town, it was wise to place one's order quickly, for he could keep tailors booked for many a day.

Johnson previously had mentioned to promoter Tom McCarey that he was thinking of having a suit made. McCarey told him that he knew a good tailor, and directed him across the street. "Go over there and turn in your order. ... If the man wants any references you tell him I will stand good." Jack went away, and ten minutes later, a fat tailor appeared in the doorway, cocking one eyebrow at McCarey. Tom nodded his head, and the tailor went away satisfied.

Several moons later, the tailor appeared before McCarey, saying, "I've got that bill for Johnson's clothes here, and Jack says it will be all right after his next fight." McCarey replied, "Oh, that's all right. Just give it to me and I'll settle." Tom expected something really large, like $30. Well, continuing the story, McCarey said,

> And what do you think that bill called for? Honest, you couldn't guess it in a thousand years! F-O-U-R H-U-N-D-R-E-D A-N-D E-I-G-H-T-Y D-O-L-L-A-R-S! Say, I nearly dropped dead! And what do you think that fellow had ordered? Three suits at about $80 a throw, a swell new top blanket, twenty-five waistcoats of every conceivable pattern and shade, and fifteen pairs of pants!

However, McCarey paid the tailor's bill, because Johnson generated a great deal of money for him.

When interviewed about his clothing supply, Johnson said, "Yassir, Ah allus 'lowed to carry a few extra clothes. Ah has only twenty-two suits jus' now, but Ah'm thinkin' of fattenin' up mah wardrobe some – not much, jes' half a dozen suits or somefin' lahk dat." Johnson had a taste for the good life, wearing nice clothes and jewelry, but he had to keep winning in order to continue enjoying it.[140]

---

[137] *Los Angeles Herald*, October 21, 1903.
[138] *Oxnard Courier*, October 23, 1903.
[139] *Los Angeles Herald*, October 26, 23, 1903.
[140] *Los Angeles Herald*, October 24, 1903.

The *Express* said Johnson weighed around 190 pounds, while McVey weighed about 206 pounds. It listed McVey's record as 18-1 with 18 knockouts.[141]

Tickets were sold out well before the day of the fight, despite the fact that McCarey had the pavilion's seating capacity expanded, for "no house in Los Angeles will begin to hold the crowd that wants to get in."[142]

The *Detroit Free Press* said of the fight's prospective winner, "Were he white he might demand a meeting with the champion."[143]

The *Los Angeles Times* said whoever won would be the next real aspirant for championship honors for the title held by local native Jeffries.

Johnson's current manager Zick or Zeke Abrams said, "I regard Johnson as the most scientific heavyweight in the world today. You understand me? In the world. I look for him to outclass McVey and take a decision."[144]

On October 27, 1903 in Los Angeles, Hazard's Pavilion was packed with the biggest crowd in its history for the Johnson-McVey rematch.

The cool and calm Johnson watched the first preliminary, clad in a swell bobtailed top blanket, a cloth cap, and a four-pound diamond stud. One report said, "He wore his best smile and three of his finest diamonds." The *Police Gazette* responded humorously, "Positively indecent. Where was the police?"[145]

When he approached the ring, Johnson wore a brand new bathrobe, "the most amazing garment ever aired in public." It was covered with large red roses the size of young cabbages. He looked like a "colonial wall paper design." Jack enjoyed being a fashion trail-blazer.

---

[141] *Los Angeles Express*, October 24, 1903. McVey had been brutalizing and knocking down Denver Ed Martin in sparring.
[142] *Los Angeles Herald*, October 21, 25, 26, 1903.
[143] *Detroit Free Press*, October 26, 1903.
[144] *Los Angeles Times, Los Angeles Herald*, October 27, 1903.
[145] *Police Gazette*, December 12, 1903.

Once again, Johnson dominated McVey, decking the "Senegambian" for the first time in his life, in the 1st, 6th, and 18th rounds, with well-timed rights and right uppercuts. Johnson hit McVey with every punch in the book, either cleverly timing and beating the rushing McVey to the punch, or countering him with lightning-fast crushing blows, without giving any indication of what blow he would deliver. His feints rattled and confused McVey. His powerful blows stopped McVey in his tracks, and the body blows doubled him up. Both inside and outside, Johnson was in total control. He could lift, shove, or move the larger McVey around as if he was a lightweight.

JACK JOHNSON, WHO WILL MEET WITH M'VEY TONIGHT.

Johnson's defense was perfect; exhibiting ghastly, marvelous cleverness, seeming to know whatever McVey was going to throw, often picking off blows before they were ripe, and "not once did the shifty fellow miscall the turn." He blocked, smothered, ducked, side-stepped, or slid or danced nimbly out of the way with his customary smile. "Nothing so much discourages a fighter as being totally unable to hit his opponent."

McVey was hammered so badly that his face looked as though a goat had chewed it, having the consistency of a pounded beefsteak. He bled freely from his nose, lips, and mouth. His left cheek badly swelled up, giving him the appearance of an "over-ripe tomato," the swelling closing one eye, while contusions damaged the other. His swollen lips made his mouth look like a balloon. His face had been pounded to a pulp.

At the bout's 20-round conclusion, Referee Charles Eyton promptly lifted Jack's arm in the air to signify his decision in Johnson's favor. Thousands chirped their unanimous approval, many climbing on their chairs. It had been a dominant victory over the Oxnard Wonder, who courageously bore in like a bull, but took a fearful amount of punishment. The *Times* said it was the worst hell ever inflicted upon a heavyweight in Los Angeles. Any other man would have been knocked out. As usual, Johnson emerged unharmed, without a scratch.

In sportsmanlike fashion, Johnson said McVey was a terrific hitter who would make his mark against anyone else. He was correct.

San Francisco experts "put Johnson in the championship class and say that he would whip Fitz and would give Jeff the battle of his life." Spider

Kelly declared, "Johnson would whip Jeff, as he would wear the champion out in futile rushes and then punish him as Corbett did John L."[146]

Tom McCarey said all four of his biggest houses featured Johnson as a contestant, proving that he was a drawing card. The Jack Jeffries fight generated a then-record $4,000. The first Johnson-McVey bout generated $4,100. The Ed Martin fight set yet another record at $4,200, until this most recent McVey bout outdid them all by far. The $7,600 generated nearly doubled the previous Los Angeles box-office record. The fighters' share was 60%, which was split 60% to the winner and 40% to the loser. Johnson made $2,796, McVey $1,864, and the club earned $2,940.

The Johnson-McVey fight also was the greatest betting bout ever in Los Angeles, for it was estimated that at least $30,000 had been wagered. Johnson won a bet on himself, cashing in over $600. His current managers, T. C. Lynch and Zick Abrams, each cleaned up handsomely. Will Tufts was so pleased with his winnings that he presented Johnson with the gift of a fine shotgun. There was "nothing Little Arthur loves better to do than bowl over jackrabbits on the run near his place in Bakersfield."

Advocating for a Johnson title shot, the *Los Angeles Times* headline said, "It's 'Up to You,' Champion Jeffries." It wrote that Jack Johnson was the champion's logical opponent; easily the master of his race, and possessor of undeniable ability both in giving and escaping punishment. He was "a better man than Jeffries has yet met, barring possibly Bob Fitzsimmons."

> The color line gag does not go now. It is 'pay or play' in the fighting business. Johnson has met all comers in his class; has defeated each and every one. Now he stands ready to box for the world's championship. He is a man who would wear that honor with decent grace if it fell on his shoulders, and Jeffries's solicitude for the future of the game is needless – that is safe in the hands and hearts of the sporting writers of the United States.
>
> Jeffries thus far has met all comers. Will he turn down this one? … The public, through the daily newspapers, demands a fight for the championship in behalf of Jack Johnson. Jeffries must heed the call. … Johnson is the man who will give him a chance to show the best that is in him. If he can beat the negro, Jeff need never fight again.
>
> When they meet, the world will see a battle before which the gladiatorial combats of ancient Rome pale into childish insignificance. And meet they some day will. It is up to Jeffries to say when.[147]

The *Los Angeles Herald* agreed. Clearly at this point, Johnson was seen as the top contender to the crown and most deserving of a title shot.

Two days after the fight, on October 29, 1903, Johnson's former manager Frank Carrillo took Johnson's current manager Zick Abrams to court on a suit filed in order to collect on a $297.25 note signed by Johnson.

---

[146] *Los Angeles Herald, Los Angeles Times, Los Angeles Express*, October 28, 1903.
[147] *Los Angeles Times*, October 29, 1903.

Carrillo had wanted to garnish Johnson's share of the receipts from the McVey fight to cover the outstanding debt. However, when a constable went to the Century Club to collect, Al Levy, the club's treasurer, told him that Johnson's share already had been paid over to Abrams. So Carrillo took Abrams to court to get his share of Johnson's money, which was owed.

On the witness stand, when asked if he had any of Johnson's money from the fight, Abrams coolly testified, "Johnson didn't have a cent coming. That money I got from Levy was mine, not Johnson's." Attorney Dwyer responded, "What? Didn't Johnson get any money out of that fight at all?" "Nope. Not a bean." Abrams said that he had been advancing money to Johnson, so Jack owed *him* money. He then pulled out of his wallet a note signed by Johnson for $3,500. The *Herald* writer jokingly commented, "Johnson's notes must be good. Everybody seems to have them." Johnson was tied up to Abrams for one year by an ironclad contract.

When asked what Johnson did with the money that was loaned to him, Abrams responded, "He bought his wife a nice sealskin cloak. ... Then he went up against other propositions with it." Dwyer asked, "How does he live?" Abrams replied, "Well, I'll tell you. He's a witty sort of fellow and he just lives by his wits." Dwyer: "But I understand that he rides about in a carriage." Abrams: "Does he? Well, that's more than his manager does. But, then, Jack's awfully clever on the touch. You ought to handle him for a week and see." Dwyer asked, "Johnson cannot have dissipated all the money he has made. What does he do with it?" Abrams responded, "Do with it? Why he shoots craps with it. You know how that is. Every nigger has to shoot craps." The attorney replied, "I used to shoot craps when I was young, but 15 cents was my limit." Abrams: "Oh you was just a piker, that's all." Trying to get in a final jab, Dwyer asked, "You've got a pretty good thing, haven't you?" Abrams: "A good thing? I know it. He's a puddin', that's what he is; a puddin'. I only wish I had four more like him. You understand?" Ultimately, Carrillo could not collect through Abrams, who had the winning hand in this case, which Justice Young dismissed.[148]

The *Police Gazette* discussed Jeffries' conundrum. He did not have a challenger who could give him a real fight unless he took on a black fighter, but he refused to give blacks an opportunity. It appeared that Jeff would lay back for a while and await the emergence of a white contender who hopefully would impress the public enough to justify a title shot.[149]

Kidding around, Johnson said of Jeffries, "He says he won't fight me because my skin is black. I can't change the color of my skin, for it won't fade." Johnson said he would be willing to take on Jeff in a horse race instead. In Texas, Jack used to ride horses, and was adept at it.[150]

Jeffries was consistent in his drawing of the color line against all black contenders. He turned down the Colma Athletic Club's offer of a $20,000

---

[148] *Los Angeles Herald*, October 30, 1903; *Los Angeles Express*, October 29, 1903.
[149] *Police Gazette*, October 31, 1903.
[150] *San Francisco Bulletin*, November 5, 1903.

purse for a Jeffries-McVey bout. Jeff replied, "I have made up my mind never to fight a negro again as long as there are white men in the field."[151]

Jeffries was not willing to fight Martin, McVey, or Johnson. The reason was race, not economics, ability, or style.

Figuring that he could beat him, the confident Johnson was determined to obtain a match with Jeffries. He said, "I will fight him under any conditions he imposes. He can dictate all the terms. The only thing I will insist upon is that the contest shall be for the championship of the world." Jack argued that Jeffries never had fought anyone as good as himself. Jeff was strong, but McVey was a marvel of strength too. "I know I can punch hard, and I am sure that I will hurt Jeffries if ever we get together."[152]

Jeffries and Delaney were firm in their insistence that he would not defend the title against a black man. Yet, Johnson and some members of the press seemed to think or hope that eventually Jeffries could be convinced or compelled to change his mind. Still, others were not thrilled with the idea of a black man challenging for the championship, and sought to curtail Johnson's momentum.

---

[151] *San Francisco Call*, November 5, 1903.
[152] *Detroit Free Press*, November 8, 1903, from a San Francisco dispatch.

CHAPTER 10

Nitpicking Backlash

Zeke Abrams negotiated another match for Johnson with Sandy Ferguson, to be held at Colma, California in December 1903. Abrams said,

> Ferguson is not going to beat Johnson. Now, listen to me. There isn't a man living who can get a decision over that coon, and this doesn't bar Jeffries. ... Jack can beat Jeff as sure as you are sitting in that chair, or I am no judge. I'll tell you, he is another Peter Jackson.[153]

Johnson told the *Police Gazette*, "I feel that notwithstanding the heroic efforts of Mr. Jeffries to erect the color barricade, I will yet get in the square with him, in the event of which I promise a good account of myself." The *Police Gazette* said quite a few people agreed:

> It is to be regretted that Jeffries, just at this time, when a huge, black cloud comes to obscure the pugilistic sky, found it convenient to draw the color line. If he had not previously fought Peter Jackson and Bob Armstrong and established a convincing precedent that he felt no race prejudice, it would have been quite consistent for him to decline the opportunity to meet the big, sturdy black man who now menaces his championship glory; but having engaged in contests with the two men above named, it seems as if he can hardly evade a meeting with Johnson, especially in view of what the latter has done to establish his prestige as a fighter.
>
> ... Jeffries himself says: ...
>
> "I am ready to meet any fighter in the world, if he is a white man, and as far as a licking is concerned, I don't fear any black man, but if such a thing should happen that I was to be beaten, I would rather give up my title to a white man."
>
> Of course he would, but if, as he says, there are no white men left to fight him, why he has only one alternative left, and that is to become color blind.[154]

However, there were other alternatives for Jeffries. He either could wait until a marketable white fighter emerged, or he could retire.[155]

On November 25, 1903 in San Francisco, at age 40, former world middleweight and heavyweight champion Bob Fitzsimmons won the world light-heavyweight championship with a 20-round decision victory over 26-

---

[153] *San Francisco Bulletin*, November 18, 1903.
[154] *Police Gazette*, November 21, 1903.
[155] *San Francisco Call*, November 24, 1903.

69

year-old George Gardner. Both men weighed in at 168 pounds. Fitz dropped Gardner in the 4th, 5th, 13th, and 14th rounds. Despite the clear victory, the *Chronicle* believed that this version of Fitzsimmons could not land on Jack Johnson, who was in attendance.[156]

Jack Johnson, Who Has Challenged the Winner of the Gardner-Fitzsimmons Fight for a $1,000 Side Bet.

Johnson noted that neither Gardner nor Fitzsimmons would accept his challenge to fight, which was backed by a $1,000 side wager.[157]

Speaking of Jeff's refusal to fight Johnson, Jeff's manager Bill Delaney said, "If ever a colored man should happen to win the championship the white people would have to move out of San Francisco." The *Police Gazette* responded humorously, "Please, Mister Johnsing, don't do anything that would lead up to such an awful calamity!"[158]

Johnson finished 1903 with a third match against John H. "Sandy" Ferguson, who was 24 years old, stood 6'3", and weighed about 225 pounds, which "makes him a bigger chunk of humanity than the present champion, who is no Lilliputian." Sandy was so strong that he played with 500-pound iron dumb-bells with ease. Ferguson said he had learned from their two prior encounters, and promised to knock out Johnson this time.

Johnson was confident not only of victory, but was willing to bet that Sandy would not hit him on the nose even once. "I don't think I am going to let Ferguson get away with this mill when upon it hinges a meeting with Jeffries for the world's championship."

The *Police Gazette* felt that Johnson might be growing overconfident, recently displaying symptoms of a swelled head. "This suggests a characteristic weakness of the negro race."[159]

San Francisco promoter James Coffroth said he would try to get Jim Jeffries to sign for a bout with Johnson, given that the prevailing opinion was that Johnson was the best qualified challenger.[160]

---

[156] *San Francisco Chronicle, Examiner, Bulletin, Call,* November 26, 27, 1903.
[157] *San Francisco Bulletin,* November 27, 1903.
[158] *Police Gazette,* November 28, 1903.
[159] *Police Gazette,* September 26, December 5, 1903; *San Francisco Evening Post,* December 1, 1903.
[160] *San Francisco Evening Post,* December 3, 1903.

From West Oakland, Johnson said,

I have an ambition to meet James J. Jeffries for the championship. I have fought myself into a position where he can't avoid a meeting with me. When Jeffries and I have signed articles then my ambition will have been satisfied. ... If he won't meet me, then I am open to fight with any other heavy-weight in the world. I'll agree to stop Gardner in ten rounds.

Despite his confidence, Johnson respected Ferguson, whom he said was the fastest big man on his feet since Corbett. He was quick, strong, and had a dangerous punch. Jack would not take foolish risks against such a man, and anticipated winning a decision.[161]

On December 8, 1903, Norfolk, Virginia was the scene of a small riot when the streets filled with a mob of 300 white Democrats armed with shotguns, rifles, and clubs, who forcibly opposed the voter registration of negro voters.[162]

A headline in the *Examiner* announced, "Ferguson Says 'Nigger' Don't Hit Hard Enough To Hurt." Sandy also said, "I will have a better chance of getting on with Jeffries as he won't object to my color."[163]

On December 11, 1903 at Colma, California, in the San Mateo County pavilion, 2,000 spectators watched Jack Johnson fight Sandy Ferguson for the third time.

Johnson came down the aisle to a ragtime melody, looking like a "colored Santa Claus." His bathrobe would "make any member of his race turn green with envy. It was a creation. Pink and blue roses on a black background, and a pink girdle set off the robe. Johnson's black face and

---

[161] *San Francisco Examiner*, December 9, 1903; *San Francisco Call*, December 10, 1903.
[162] *San Francisco Call, Boston Post*, December 9, 1903.
[163] *San Francisco Examiner*, December 10, 1903.

gold teeth shone beneath the big hood that covered his shiny head." Johnson's sensational robe garnered great laughter.

Throughout the contest, Johnson cautiously but clearly outboxed Ferguson, remaining in control. He displayed his usual clever defense, snapped Ferguson's head back with left jabs, and also landed thudding body shots. Occasionally in short spurts Jack attacked with powerful blows, but then backed off again and fired lighter punches.

In both the 4th and 17th rounds, the momentum of Johnson's rush and punches sent the off-balance Ferguson through the ropes and out of the ring. In the 16th round, Johnson crossed him with a right and Ferguson went down to his knee. Sandy rose at two, clinched, and was very defensive.

Overall, Ferguson mostly kept out of range, fighting very passively and defensively. The pace was slow, and the fighters cautious. The spectators jeered and hooted what they felt was a lack of action.

Often the men smiled, laughed, and spoke with one another, making the fight seem like a joke or a "burlesque." At one point, Ferguson turned to the crowd and called out, "Not a nigger in the world can beat me." Later, while being rushed from pillar to post, Ferguson shouted, "You see this fellow can't hit." Yet, Sandy moved, clinched, and refused to punch much. The crowd hooted. Ferguson was listless, while Johnson seemed to be taking it easy, content to earn a decision.

When the bell rang ending the 20-round contest, Referee Jack Welch declared Johnson the winner. In response, Ferguson said, "The coon had to fight to win." There was renewed hooting.

All of the local newspapers were fairly hard on both Johnson and Ferguson. Although Johnson had won clearly, the local writers were not impressed, and said the victory lowered the colored champion's stock. The *Examiner's* W. W. Naughton said the spiritless boxing disgusted the spectators, who jeered, hooted, and urged them to fight.

The *Evening Post* said that despite his cleverness, Johnson was too small and too soft a tapper to make any impression on a man like Jeffries. "He will have to retire to the woods and look for bouts with dubs or men of his own race. He does not show the quality to entitle him to a battle with the champion of the world." Some said that Jeffries, by drawing the color line, was cheating himself out of a chance to earn thousands of dollars.

Others thought that Johnson was carrying Ferguson, possibly for gamblers who had wagered that he would last the distance. "Johnson was the aggressor, in a mild sort of way, at all times, but there was something lacking. He could not make the spectators believe he was in earnest." Naughton said, "They say he ripped out a half dozen of McVey's teeth with a crack of the right in the southern country. Last night his right would not have mashed a house fly." Many times when Ferguson had his back to the ropes, with his hands down, Johnson still didn't hit him. "It looked as though all Johnson required last night was a small amount of fighting blood to encompass Ferguson's downfall a dozen times." The *Evening Post* said Johnson won 20 harmless rounds of sparring. "Occasionally his target slipped to the mat, but he quickly regained his feet and roughly pressed in, knowing that the negro was considerate enough not to hurt him."

However, some said it was "simply Ferguson's natural awkwardness that bothered the negro and kept him from showing to advantage." The *Call* said Sandy refused to do anything, uwilling to take a chance, for invariably he was on the receiving end of a punch whenever he did try. The *Chronicle* also realized that it was a bad style matchup. "One clever big black, who couldn't hit hard enough to put his man away, and one awkward, big, alleged fighter who wouldn't fight tells the whole story of the unpleasantness." Ferguson's style was "so miserably bad as to completely overshadow all of Jack Johnson's cleverness."[164]

Despite the criticisms of Johnson's power, clearly he hit hard enough to knock down Ferguson and make him very cautious, and this was a bigger man who had done well with big strong men like Ruhlin and Armstrong. Yet several local writers failed to give Johnson credit for causing the much bigger man's extremely ineffective caution. Perhaps it was a bit of a backlash to all of the good publicity that the black man had been receiving.

Jack Johnson won without taking too many chances. After all, he was the one who would have to suffer the consequences of a loss. He had gone undefeated in seven fights in 1903 alone.

A couple days later, W. W. Naughton said, "Johnson will be heard from again, but not as a world's championship candidate."

The *Examiner* printed a poem, which certainly gave the impression that racial animus had at least something to do with the criticism of Johnson:

> Sing a song o' Colma, pockets full o' "rhi,"
> Four an' twenty uppercuts, wouldn't hurt a fly.
> When the round was over, nigger outer breff - -
> Isn't he a gally coon to talk o' fightin' Jeff?
> "Club" was in the box office countin' up the money,
> Gods were in the gallery bawlin' "Soak him, honey,"
> Two big dubs a-gigglin', everybody sore,
> Crowd hotfootin' to the train yellin' "Nevermore."[165]

Because he was black, even if Johnson had stopped Ferguson, Jim Jeffries was not going to fight him. Jeffries said,

> If the public demands that I should fight Johnson I will surely have to decline. ... If I am defeated, the championship will go to a white man, for I will not fight a colored one. Now mind you, I am not shirking from this match because I am afraid of Johnson, for I think I could lick him as easily as I have the rest, but I simply will not fight a colored man for the championship. The only regret I feel is that Sandy Ferguson did not whip Johnson. I would have willingly given

---

[164] *San Francisco Evening Post, San Francisco Call, San Francisco Examiner, San Francisco Chronicle*, December 12, 1903.
[165] *San Francisco Examiner*, December 13, 1903.

Ferguson a match – I was anxious that he should win in order that I might do so.[166]

Jim Corbett said a Jeffries-Johnson championship fight "would be no attraction, and there would be nothing but Jeffries to it." Corbett "did not blame Jeffries for drawing the color line, and thought that Johnson should meet such men as Ruhlin, Munroe, Hart and one or two others before going after the world's champion." However, all of those men drew the color line on Johnson. Ironically, Corbett obtained his recent title shot without having fought anyone in three years.[167]

On December 15, 1903 in Boston, 200-pound Jack Munroe stopped 6'4" 220-pound Al Limerick in the 4th round. One reporter said, "He has gone up another rung of the pugilistic ladder, and has stronger claims than ever for a match with Jeffries." The *Boston Post*'s Rob Roy said, "Munroe stands today before the sporting world the one and only legitimate rival that Champion Jim Jeffries has." Many in the press were boosting the white Munroe as much as possible, despite the fact that his quality of opposition and depth of resume was nowhere near what Jack Johnson's was.[168]

On December 17, 1903 at Kitty Hawk, North Carolina, Wilbur and Orville Wright became the first persons to invent and successfully fly a motorized airplane.

1903 also was the year that Henry Ford started his auto company, which by October 1908 began mass-producing automobiles (the Model T) and making them more affordable. Jack Johnson would become a huge fan of the automobile, purchasing many during his lifetime.

Some thought Jack Johnson's performance in the Ferguson fight might do him some good, because it might make more top fighters willing to take him on. The only white boxer to fight Johnson in the past year, since Fred Russell in December 1902, was Sandy Ferguson. No white fighter other than Ferguson would step into the ring with Johnson until 1905. Hence, despite the criticisms, top white heavyweights were none too eager to enter the ring with Jack Johnson. Their inaction spoke louder than words.

In early 1904, Jim Jeffries said, "I don't think the public wants me to defend my title against any one but a white man. Don't think I am afraid of a negro. I'm not. They can be licked just as easily as anybody else." Bill Delaney said Jeff would fight neither Johnson nor any other colored man, if he had any say in the matter.[169]

In his early 1904 inaugural address, Mississippi Governor James K. Vardaman, a Democrat, said that education had no deterrent influence upon the black race in the commission of crime, and the Negro grew more criminal as he became more intelligent. He felt that education harmed the black race more than it helped it. Vardaman was a pro-slavery advocate who

---

[166] *Boston Globe*, December 14, 1903.
[167] *Boston Herald*, December 15, 1903.
[168] *Boston Post, Boston Globe, Boston Herald*, December 16, 17, 1903.
[169] *Detroit Free Press*, January 31, 1904; *Philadelphia Inquirer*, February 6, 1904; *Philadelphia Press*, February 7, 1904.

believed that negroes were less than human, unworthy of consideration, and had no rights which whites need respect. By obtaining his goal of limiting educational opportunities for blacks, the governor would not only limit them economically but also could limit their right to vote.[170]

On February 6, 1904, at a boxing card in Philadelphia, Jack Johnson was in attendance as a spectator. When the main event fell through, National Athletic Club manager Jack McGuigan asked Johnson to box with Sandy Ferguson, and vice versa. Johnson and Ferguson got together and talked it over. "Such easy money! How could they help it?" Jack and Sandy agreed.

Freeman, January 2, 1904

Johnson and Ferguson proceeded to box in their impromptu bout, but just went through the motions, barely trying. After warning and threatening them, and without improvement in their work, Manager McGuigan, who had been acting as referee, decided that they were trying to obtain money without doing much, so he terminated the bout in the 5th round and left the ring, ruling it a no contest.

The *Philadelphia Inquirer* called it a "raw fake." "There is not the slightest doubt that Johnson was bound to not hurt or stop Ferguson; there would have been no way of pulling the latter into the ring with the big black if the bout had been on the level."[171]

Hurt by the accusations, Johnson called the *Philadelphia Record* to defend himself, saying he did the best he could under the circumstances, given that he had not planned to box that evening, and was doing the management a big favor to prevent the show's cancellation. He did not fake or stall, but had done all of the leading and forcing of the pace.

> I never faked a fight in my life, and have no cause to do so here, as I have had lots of chances to fake in California, where I was a 10 to 4 favorite, and where I could have made a lot of money by throwing a fight for the gamblers, who will offer lots of inducements out there to men who can be bought. … Ferguson is a big, husky fellow and

---

[170] *Colored American*, January 30, 1904; *Seattle Republican*, April 8, 1904; *Muskogee Cimeter*, August 11, 1904.
[171] *Philadelphia Inquirer*, February 8, 1904.

Gus Ruhlin could not stop him in 15 rounds, and I have previously tried to stop him...but failed to do so.[172]

Johnson kept lobbying for a title shot, saying, "Unless Jeffries consents to withdraw his color-line declaration and fight me, I shall claim the world's championship. It was not my fault that I was born black, and Jeffries will have to meet me in three months or drop the championship title."[173]

Johnson remained in demand. On February 15, 1904 in Philadelphia, before a crowded house, he fought Black Bill (whose real name was Claude Brooks), who had been fighting since 1897, stood 6' tall, was 26 years old, and only weighed slightly less than the champion. Johnson decked Bill twice in the 4th round, once in the 5th, and kept pounding on him in the 6th and final round. Black Bill clinched and hugged often enough to survive.[174]

Black Bill

Despite the dominant performance, some Philadelphians still were not sold on the colored champ, and remained critical. The *Philadelphia Record* wrote,

If any of the lovers of boxing were really worried over the idea that the championship of the world was likely to fall to a colored man they can cease their lamentations for a while at least. ... One thing is an almost absolute certainty. If the championship ever goes to a colored man his name is not Jack Johnson.

The *Record* argued that Johnson either lacked a punch or the ability to finish, saying that "it is hard to see why any one should worry over any possibility of Johnson ever becoming heavy-weight champion of the world."[175]

The criticism was harsh and unfair, given that Johnson had dominated and almost knocked out Bill in a short bout, dropping him three times in only 6 rounds, and Bill had survived by clinching often. Still, many writers often criticized or belittled Johnson even when he won clearly. It seems that this was a recent theme that writers had caught onto and perpetuated.

Once again, these criticisms appear to be a backlash to all of the previously positive publicity that Johnson had been receiving, in order to curtail the momentum for his challenge to Jeffries. After all, there were those who did not like the idea of a black man challenging for what they felt a white man should own. At the very least, these critics were not satisfied easily, wanting an exciting dominant performance terminating with a knockout before they would give any credit. That was not always easily done against solid experienced pros, particularly ones who knew how to survive. The irony is that sometimes when Johnson did knock out his foe,

---

[172] *Philadelphia Record, Philadelphia Evening Bulletin,* February 8, 1904.
[173] *Philadelphia Record, Detroit Free Press,* February 8, 1904.
[174] *Philadelphia Record, Philadelphia Evening Bulletin,* February 16, 1904.
[175] *Philadelphia Record,* February 28, 1904.

instead of giving him full credit, some members of the press chose to denigrate his opponent.

On February 27, 1904 in Philadelphia, 196-pound 27-year-old Jack Munroe "won" a 6-round no-decision bout against 182-pound 30-year-old Tom Sharkey. Both went down in the 1st round, first Sharkey, then Munroe, who rose and dominated thereafter, both outboxing and outslugging Sharkey. The performance made believers out of many skeptics.

Although he only had a few decent wins, primarily built his record on nobodies or has-beens in short bouts, and did not have anywhere near the experience against tough opposition that Johnson did, Jack Munroe's championship challenge was boosted, and he did not have to endure the level of criticism that Jack Johnson did. But he was white, so he was perfect, for Jeffries was willing to fight him, and they arranged a contest.[176]

Although Johnson agreed to forfeit his stipulated share of the purse if he failed to stop white John Willie within 6 rounds in their upcoming March 11 bout in Chicago, someone tried to change the bout's terms to make it more of a hippodrome/fake. Johnson would not agree, so the bout was called off:

> Johnson says he was asked to permit Willie to stay the limit and also to accept a knockdown, which he refused, so the management declared the match off. Johnson is without doubt the most scientific colored heavyweight in the world. He is making Chicago his home, and says he does not care to get mixed up in any shady fight transactions. He might have failed in stopping Willie, as the latter is a tough proposition to down for the count, but he showed his willingness to try at the expense of his reputation.[177]

In April 1904, Johnson returned to San Francisco for a third bout with Sam McVey. The press hyped the contest as a meeting of "the two greatest colored men." "It is now generally thought that if Jeffries defeats Monroe he will withdraw his refusal to meet a colored man and take on the winner of this month's bout." Of course, that might have been wishful thinking, or a way to promote the upcoming contest.

---

[176] *Police Gazette*, March 12, 1904; *Boston Post*, February 28, 1904.
[177] *Chicago Daily Tribune*, March 11, 1904.

Jim Coffroth noted how the two boxers had filled the house in Los Angeles, drawing the largest crowd ever known in that town. Dollars make sense to promoters, which explains why he made the match.

Coffroth was hoping to convince Jeffries to remove the color line and fight the winner, "for the sake of the money, if nothing else."[178]

The *San Francisco Bulletin* described Johnson as a "showy colored man," who wore good clothes and "makes some pretensions to being a beau among the gentle sex of Colordom."

Johnson said McVey was the toughest and hardest hitter in the business, "but I shall see that he don't hit me."

Estimates of their weights were 190s for Johnson, and 215 for McVey.

Johnson opened as only the slight 10 to 8 favorite. McVey manager Billy Roche said McVey was faster than ever, had been suffering from gastritis in their last fight, and this time the ring would be smaller, so Johnson could not escape. Roche was betting $2,000 on McVey, showing his confidence.

Harry Corbett said McVey was a wonder, the strongest and most wiry man he had ever seen, and would give Johnson a beating. "If he wins on Friday night I shall never quit trying until I succeed in matching him with the winner of the Jeffries-Munroe battle."

Except for height, the "Herculean" McVey was bigger than Johnson in every way. He even had a longer reach by one inch. "With all his size he is quick as a cat on his feet and moves about in a lithe, graceful way." Although built like a professional strong man, Sam was not muscle-bound.

Famous referee Harry Stuart had seen the two prior fights between Johnson and McVey, and yet he still felt that McVey would win this time.[179]

Johnson said,

> I hear every one saying what a 'wonder' this McVey is. Didn't I trim him twice? That's just the way it was in Los Angeles the last time we fought. Every one picked McVey, although I had a decision over him. I fooled them then and will fool them again.[180]

The *Chronicle* said most fans and experts preferred McVey's bull-like aggressive puncher's style, and that affected their judgment. Most white fans wanted to see the Oxnard giant win, although Johnson was "the pride and the terror of Pacific street and a favorite with his colored confreres."[181]

The *San Francisco Bulletin* said, "There does not appear to be a ringman in all the wide area where pugilism holds sway with sufficient inches and heft to meet the world's champion after Munroe than one of tonight's fighters."[182]

On April 22, 1904, at the Mechanics' Pavilion in San Francisco, Jack Johnson fought Sam McVey for the third time. Eddie Graney refereed.

---

[178] *San Francisco Chronicle*, April 8, 10, 1904.
[179] *San Francisco Bulletin*, April 16, 19, 1904; *San Francisco Evening Post, San Francisco Bulletin*, April 15, 20, 1904; *San Francisco Call*, April 21, 1904; *San Francisco Examiner*, April 22, 1904.
[180] *San Francisco Bulletin, San Francisco Evening Post*, April 21, 1904.
[181] *San Francisco Chronicle*, April 22, 1904.
[182] *San Francisco Bulletin*, April 22, 1904.

Once again, Johnson dominated McVey, landing with great regularity and avoiding most of what McVey threw. Johnson scored knockdowns in the 1st and 10th rounds, and staggered him in the 6th, 9th, and 12th rounds. When hurt, McVey managed to recover by clinching and wrestling.

McVey hit hard enough such that Johnson was cautious, not taking too many chances, owing to his concern that he might run into something powerful. Much to the crowd's chagrin, the pace slowed from the 13th through 18th rounds, for the fire had left McVey, and Johnson simply sparred. Someone at ringside sarcastically remarked, "Cease this brutality," causing great laughter. The hooting crowd later appealed, "Fight! Fight!" and even "Fake! Fake!" Some yelled, "Throw them out." Johnson was coasting to victory, although he landed enough punches to knock the sense out of anyone, and McVey was growing weaker. Sam's left eye was closed and his lips were puffed out prominently.

In the 19th round, Johnson finally took a chance again and staggered McVey with blows to the head and body.

In the 20th round, Johnson kept up his attack, repeatedly landing throughout the round. Near the end of the round, with only about 20-30 seconds left in the fight, after a break, quick as a flash, Johnson landed a left and right flush on the jaw, which turned McVey completely around; and he fell in a huge limp mass, face downward on the paddock floor with a thump. He laid there breathing heavily, out cold as Referee Eddie Graney counted him out.

When he awoke, "Mr. Sambo McVey," as the *Bulletin* called him, asked Spider Kelly, "Was it a draw?" The Spider amusingly answered either, "It should have been, but they robbed you," or "Yes, and they robbed us." Later, Sam learned that he had been "caught napping on the mat." It was his first knockout loss. Johnson had been the only man to defeat him.

Despite the dominant performance, three knockdowns and a knockout, the local newspapers called it the poorest local fight in years. McVey was no match in either strength or skill. "He stood to be pecked to pieces last night and by the time shifty Mr. Johnson got through with him his right eye resembled a buttonhole, and his lips were badly puffed." Some found it hard to imagine that McVey had defeated Ed Martin and Kid Carter. The press overlooked or failed to concede that it simply was great Johnson.

The *Examiner's* W. W. Naughton said the crowd wondered what was the matter with Johnson:

> He is cleverness personified, but the fighting spirit seems to flare in flashes with him. He loafs along grinning and at peace with himself and the other fellow while his seconds are bawling themselves red in the face in their attempts to get him to go in and mix it.
>
> He showed before last night's fight was ten minutes old that he had McVey thoroughly at his mercy, yet he played with the beet field warrior as a cat plays with a mouse. His tactics were such that the gallery became frantic with chagrin and disgust.

The *San Francisco Evening Post* said the city's sports were tired of Johnson's cleverness. He landed at will, but only lightly. "Occasionally, when spurred on by the hoots of the gallery, he put force behind his delivery, and on such occasions demonstrated that he has a knockout punch, but is afraid to use it, apparently fearing that his rival would come back with as good as was sent."

In fairer and perhaps more insightful fashion, the *San Francisco Bulletin* said Johnson had beaten McVey throughout, "but it was like hammering a carcass of beef hung in a butcher shop." The tough McVey could absorb punishment. "McVey stood a horrible walloping, and it was only his great strength and endurance that kept him from meeting his fate earlier in the fight. When pressed too hard, McVey found his way into clinches and wrestled around in Johnson's arms, waiting for a return of his wind." It was not easy to stop a tough man who knew how to survive. Yet most of the local press and the spectators overlooked these facts.[183]

Instead of lauding his brilliant skill for winning in dominant fashion via knockout over a big, strong, dangerous puncher who never before had been knocked out, Johnson garnered little appreciation. McVey would not be stopped again until 1909, five years later, and even then, it was only via retirement after 49 rounds of fighting against another black fighter - Joe Jeannette. Quite simply, Jack Johnson was underappreciated.

---

[183] *San Francisco Call, San Francisco Examiner, San Francisco Chronicle, San Francisco Bulletin, San Francisco Evening Post*, April 23, 1904.

While watching the fight, when asked whether there was any chance for Jeffries to fight the winner, Jeff's manager Bill Delaney responded,

> Not the least. Jeff recognizes that Johnson, who looks like the winner, is a good man, and may be the best heavyweight aspiring to be champion, but he has thoroughly made up his mind never to fight a colored man again. He is determined upon this, and no argument or persuasion can change his course. When Jeff has his mind set once, you don't know how hard it is to change it. Yes, my advice to him will be to fight a couple more battles and then retire, the undefeated champion of the world, and I think the greatest champion in the history of the prize-ring. Jeff has enough money whereby he doesn't have to stay at the game.[184]

The *Police Gazette* said that by defeating McVey, Johnson, "the dusky hero of a score of fights, has placed himself in a position to legitimately claim a fight with Jim Jeffries for the championship of the world."[185]

However, in San Francisco, the calls for Jeffries to face Johnson were diminishing. The *Chronicle* said,

> When Johnson clamors again for Jeffries to drop the color line his desire should be granted, and he should be allowed to meet the big fellow, if for nothing else than to get his block knocked off. ... Johnson would die of fright before the first gong were he to meet Jeffries. It is a safe gamble, too, that the champion could take the pair of them in one night and send them both to sleep in ten rounds.[186]

The *Evening Post* said San Francisco wanted negro boxers and their style of fighting to move on. Johnson had "furnished all of this sort of sport this metropolis can stand for months to come."

When speaking with promoter James Coffroth, Jeffries said,

> I suppose I will now be relieved of any further talk of a match with Johnson, after the miserable showing the colored champion made with Sam McVey. That battle proves one thing decisively and that is that a pugilist must have the willingness to fight as well as the ability.[187]

Johnson offered to fight and attempt to beat both Jack Root and George Gardner on the same night.[188] Neither accepted.

On June 2, 1904 in Chicago, in a scheduled 6-round contest, Jack Johnson fought a rematch against former colored champion Frank Childs. Johnson was supremely confident. "In fact, he thinks there is no man in the world, not even excepting Champion Jeffries, that can beat him." Still, Johnson knew that Childs had a terrific punch.[189]

---

[184] *San Francisco Bulletin*, April 23, 1904.
[185] *Police Gazette*, May 14, 1904.
[186] *San Francisco Chronicle*, April 24, 1904.
[187] *San Francisco Evening Post*, April 25, 1904.
[188] *Police Gazette*, April 30, 1904.
[189] *Chicago Chronicle*, May 29, 1904; *Daily Inter Ocean*, June 1, 1904.

There was an extreme diversity of perspective regarding what happened. The next-day *Chicago Record-Herald* said that after a cautious feel-out 1st round, in the 2nd round Johnson cut loose, hammered Childs all over, and dropped him with a right to the jaw. The rest of the bout was more of the same. Childs was so far outclassed that he rarely could land a blow or block any of Johnson's punches. He was chopped up terribly, and went down five times in all, though he gamely lasted to the end. The referee's 6-round decision for Johnson was quite clear.

However, the local *Daily Inter Ocean* said the contest was slow, and although Johnson scored two knockdowns, "as a general proposition the fight had a bad odor." This writer thought that Johnson had carried Childs.

The *Chicago Tribune's* George Siler agreed, saying Johnson had won a slow and unsatisfactory fight that was "too much on the brotherly love order to satisfy the spectators. Johnson did not come up to expectations, and Frank, although he tried, could do nothing with the champion."[190]

Once again, Johnson had won clearly against an experienced hard-punching veteran, dropping him several times in only 6 rounds, and yet found it difficult to find respect and accolades.

One has to wonder whether race played a part in some of these tough perspectives. Many wanted to curtail the momentum for Johnson's title challenges. Or perhaps it was lack of appreciation for Johnson's style. One thing that does emerge from the accounts is that often for Johnson bouts, there could be several different perspectives. Clearly, some continued to underestimate Johnson and failed to give his clear victories due credit.[191]

The black-owned popular Indianapolis-based *Freeman*, "America's greatest colored newspaper," which had a national distribution of over 500,000 readers and subscribers, and was sold as far west as San Francisco, where boxing was hot, hoped that colored fighters could obtain something more than simply prominence as sparring partners to white fighters whom they could whip. Many blacks were relegated to sparring-partner status in order to make money. Few had good managers who cared for them.

The *Freeman* also wrote that "the history of important colored men, of a race very meanly represented to this country by newspapers, is kept very

---

[190] *Chicago Record-Herald, Daily Inter Ocean, Chicago Tribune,* June 3, 1904.
[191] *Chicago Daily News,* June 1, 1904; *Daily Inter Ocean,* June 2, 1904; *Police Gazette,* June 18, 1904.

shady." Hence, this newspaper often highlighted the differences in perspectives between black-owned newspapers and white-owned newspapers, even when it came to boxing.[192]

Regarding the color-line in boxing, the *Freeman* wrote,

> All prize fighters who draw the color line are curs and cowards. All white heavyweight champions of the past, including John L. Sullivan and James J. Jeffries, can not go down in history as fighters with honorable records. They were cowards who were afraid of a black fighter, for good reasons. They dishonor the country and indicate the cowardice of white men in all other walks of life. For instance, no white man's newspaper will dare to be brave enough to publish my assertions. ... What kind of men do Edgren, Naughton and other sporting writers call themselves, to stand for a 'bluff' that the public does not like.... What do respectable people care about whether fighting champions are red or green since they have no social standing. What we need next is a good heavyweight champion who is not a coward or afraid of a colored man. Every time the 'white feather' cry goes up, the Negro race is flattered.[193]

The *Freeman* believed that famous writers like Robert Edgren and W. W. Naughton had more than a modicum of racial animus in their boxing analysis and perspectives. Hence it was and is always important to consider potential source biases.

Apparently, some folks on the West Coast were under the impression that rising contender Marvin Hart was black. Correcting the error, Jack McCormick, Hart's manager, told newsmen, "Hart is a white man who does not fight negroes, and has drawn the color line on two different occasions when challenged. He refused Joe Walcott and Jack Johnson for this reason. ... Hoping you will let the people know that Hart is white." Hart wanted to fight Jeffries after Jeff was through with Munroe.[194]

The *Freeman* noted that Jimmy Britt, James Jeffries, and Marvin Hart had promised not to take any chance of being whipped by a Negro. It believed that if they fought Joe Gans, Joe Walcott, or Jack Johnson, "they will surely go home in deep disgrace."[195]

---

[192] *Freeman*, July 9, 1904. A one-year subscription to the weekly *Freeman*, sent to any address in the U.S., cost only $1. *Freeman*, December 19, 1908.
[193] *Freeman*, July 16, 1904.
[194] *San Francisco Evening Post*, July 18, 1904.
[195] *San Francisco Evening Post*, July 22, 1904; *Freeman*, July 30, 1904.

CHAPTER 11

The Color Line, Regardless of Performance

Jack Johnson said he would be on hand at the Jeffries-Munroe championship fight to challenge Jeffries, notwithstanding the champion's color-line declarations. Jack said, "I think I'm entitled to a fight with him. I believe he would have given me a chance before this, but Billy Delaney stands in the way." Johnson picked Jeff to defeat Munroe.

The *Bulletin* said, "Mistah Johnson can go some himself, and many look upon him as the only pugilist in the game who would stand a good chance to wrest the title from Jeffries. He is young, strong and willing, and has a punch that kicks in like a mule with his mad up."[196]

Jack Munroe on left shakes hands with James J. Jeffries

On August 26, 1904 in San Francisco, 29-year-old 225-230-pound James J. Jeffries successfully defended his world heavyweight championship by knocking out 210-220-pound Jack Munroe in the 2nd round. Jeffries easily blew through him, dropping Munroe three times in the 1st round before finishing him early in the 2nd.

Reporters and observers agreed that Jeffries was the wonder of the age whom no one could defeat. They called him the best fighter in the world by

---

[196] *San Francisco Bulletin, San Francisco Examiner, San Francisco Call,* August 25, 26, 1904.

far, "the greatest champion the world has ever seen," and said he would remain champion until he was an old man, for at least another ten years.[197]

Bill Delaney wanted Jeffries to retire rather than go stale waiting for a viable white challenger to emerge.[198]

Jack Johnson was present at the Munroe fight, and tried to enter the ring to challenge Jeffries, but the management refused to allow him to do so.

Zeke Abrams said he and Johnson were willing to bet Jeffries $10,000, and even would make their fight winner-take-all, they were so confident. The *Bulletin* said, "Johnson is the only heavyweight in sight who has the size, cleverness and punching ability to make the champion get busy in order to win."

A Black Cloud in Sight.

Jeffries offered economic rather than merely racial reasons for refusing to fight Johnson, saying, "We wouldn't draw. ... Johnson hasn't any reputation. What's he ever done, and besides he has a shady record aside from being shady in color."

The *Bulletin* believed or hoped that if the public demanded the fight, and no white challenger loomed up in the near future, that Jeff might brush aside the color line. Johnson could garner momentum and public demand on his behalf if he sufficiently proved himself, because most boxing followers had no prejudice about mixed-race boxing matches. "It matters little to the average ring-goer whether the fighters be white or black as long as the sport is of a high order and the best man wins. And Jeffries' popularity would not suffer a particle if he fought Johnson, for some of the best liked pugilists the world knows never drew the color line."[199]

Still, Jeffries said he would hold firm on his color line stance, regardless of economics. When Tim McGrath told Jeff that he would have to fight Johnson, Jeffries responded, "Well, you might as well forget that, because I'll never fight a nigger. I could put him away in less time than I did Munroe, but I'll never fight a nigger."[200] The *Police Gazette* quoted Jeffries as saying, "I have no desire to see a colored man even get a chance to win the world's championship, and I will never meet one."[201] Jeffries further said,

> Jack Johnson is a fair fighter, but he is black, and for that reason I will never fight him. If I were not the champion I would as soon

---

[197] *San Francisco Call, Evening Post, Bulletin, Examiner,* and *Chronicle,* all August 27, 1904; and *National Police Gazette,* September 3, 10, 1904.
[198] *San Francisco Call,* August 31, 1904.
[199] *San Francisco Bulletin,* August 28, 1904.
[200] *San Francisco Evening Post,* August 29, 1904.
[201] *Police Gazette,* September 17, 1904.

meet a negro as any other man, but the title will never go to a black man if I can help it. I do not think this fellow has anything on a lot of heavies that I have licked. He's a good man, but not as good as Fitz and Sharkey. He is an in-and-outer, and has some queer fights in his record. But the only thing that makes a fight with him impossible is that he is a negro.[202]

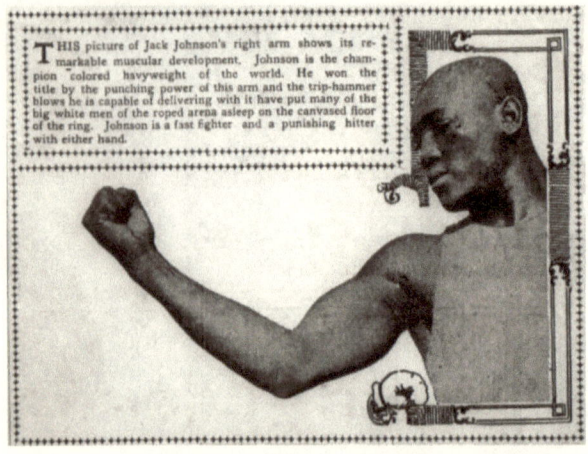

THIS picture of Jack Johnson's right arm shows its remarkable muscular development. Johnson is the champion colored hsvyweight of the world. He won the title by the punching power of this arm and the trip-hammer blows he is capable of delivering with it have put many of the big white men of the roped arena asleep on the canvased floor of the ring. Johnson is a fast fighter and a punishing hitter with either hand.

Jack Johnson had done no worse than a draw in any fight for almost three years, over the course of at least eighteen contests. He had fought a high caliber of opponent, particularly from the black community, and he fought often and ducked no one, whereas most top white fighters drew the color line against him.[203]

Next up for Johnson was a rematch with Denver Ed Martin in Los Angeles. Recently, in August 1904 in Los Angeles, Martin defeated Sam McVey via 10-round decision, outpointing him throughout, demonstrating all of his cleverness and speed. Los Angelinos liked the 23-year-old Martin, and wanted to see him in the ring with Johnson again.[204]

The *Los Angeles Examiner* said Jack Johnson was not a tough interview. He usually was full of talk, and enjoyed sharing his opinions. "Jack always has a great deal of surplus language." Johnson said,

> Nevah felt mo' like winning in mah life! Youall knows Ah ain't been fightin' much East. Gotter win something so's Ah kin pervide mahse'f with that new fall wardrobe. Gotter have some of them brown weskits an' some of them tan suits. When Jack Johnson gits trimmed down so's he's only got 'leven suits what he kin allow himse'f to wear, something's got to be doing right presently. …

> Suah, there's a fat chance fo' me to fight Jeff. Afteh this fight Ah'm going' afteh him an' deman' a scrap. How kin he be champion of the worl' if he don' meet all comers? Britt's goin' wipe up de color line an' tackle Gans, an' the public will expec' Jeff to meet me. Guess Ah'm de onliest heavyweight what wants a chance an' if Ah cain't stall along longer than Munroe Ah don' want a cent fo' mah services.

---

[202] *Police Gazette*, October 8, 1904.
[203] *Freeman*, October 1, 1904. During September 1904 in Los Angeles, Jack Johnson was a sparring partner for Jack "Twin" Sullivan.
[204] *Los Angeles Examiner*, October 8, 1904.

The *Examiner* agreed that Johnson was the only one who really deserved a fight with Jeffries. Johnson hoped to dispose of Martin in quick time in order to force Jeffries to pay attention to him.[205]

The "giant mulatto" Martin responded that he might be the one challenging Jeffries, not Johnson. "Ah cain't see where Johnson has got it on me foh clevahness, on me whatevah, and Ah guess Ah can git away from that punch. Mebbe Ah can punch mahse'f."

The local press said Martin was in great shape, his muscles like steel, his wind perfect, his speed remarkable for a man so large, and his eye for distance as good as ever. He was pounding on his black sparring partners daily, "confident that he will be the dingy heavyweight champion" once again.[206]

MARTIN ADVISES JOHNSON TO DELAY CHALLENGE TO JEFF

"DENVER ED" MARTIN AND HIS POWERFUL RIGHT, WITH WHICH HE EXPECTS TO PUT A STOP TO JACK JOHNSON'S ASPIRATIONS FOR CHAMPIONSHIP HONORS

At that time, the *Seattle Republican* printed an article by Clifton Johnson that was written for the *Springfield Republican* (in Massachusetts), which offered some insights regarding the feelings of whites towards blacks:

> One of the oddest impressions that a northern person gets in the South is that there are no colored people or Negroes there, but only "niggers." The term is recognized as opprobrious. It is like calling an Irishman a "paddy," an Italian a "dago," or a farmer a "hayseed." It is equivalent to a kick, yet there is a superstition that it is not only the Negroes' due, but that it is necessary to administer these verbal kicks in order to avoid the possibility of their forgetting their inferiority. Besides, it is affirmed that the Negroes will not work unless one is rough and vigorous with them. "If you want anything done, you must say, 'Come here, nigger!' Why, if you was to say, 'Come here, Mr. Jones,' they wouldn't do nothin' for you."
>
> "A nigger is all right in his place," the whites explain, but add emphatically that his place is very lowly and that he must not step out of it. If he fails to keep "his place" of his own volition, they will go to any length of force or subterfuge to compel him to do so. ...

---

[205] *Los Angeles Examiner*, October 11, 1904.
[206] *Los Angeles Herald*, October 14, 1904; *Los Angeles Examiner*, October 12, 15, 16, 1904.

The intolerance with which the Negro is regarded is a natural outcome of the former relations of master and slave; but it is depressing to find that in all the years since the war, so little progress has been made. Men of intelligence will soberly argue with you that "niggers" are not wholly human, that they are more akin to beasts and should be dealt with accordingly. "If anything would make me kill my children," declared one woman, "it would be the possibility that niggers might sometime eat at the same table and associate with them as equals. That's the way we feel about it, and you might as well root up that big tree in front of the house and stand it the other way up and expect it to grow, as to think we can feel any different."

I was solemnly assured that for a southern white man to invite a Negro, however accomplished, into his house as his guest, would mean that white man's social ruin. "It's like this," one informant remarked — "equality ain't safe. Now I've got a servant that was raised with me. He loves me and I love him. He'd do anything for me, and I've remembered him in my will. But if I was to take him into my family and treat him like a white man, he'd murder me in three days. They always do jus' thataway when you go to favoring 'em."

"And yet the president of the United States has had a nigger to dine with him! The South never got a worse shock than that. Up to then we'd thought a heap of Roosevelt down hyar. Why, we'd named all our dogs after him and members of his family; but we've changed those dogs' names since that dinner."

In one town I heard a tale of a colored army officer who attempted to attend a white folks' church and sit in a pew among his white skinned brethren. To them this was intolerable. They compelled him to get out, and he barely escaped the worst scouring he ever had in his life. ...

Whatever tends to lift the Negro out of a position of servility is regarded with suspicion and irritation. ... "You northern people don't understand this matter. If you would come down here and live six months you'd see it just as we do."

Their view is that a Negro must constantly in word and action acknowledge the whites' superiority. He must be respectful to them on all occasions, while it is optional with them whether they shall be respectful in return. Hence they have a decided preference for the older Negroes who began life as slaves and have had the right sort of training to make them humble. ...

The sentiments of the whites being such as they are and their pride in their superiority so keen and belligerent, it is no wonder that the lynch spirit is often aroused. Unquestionably there are Negroes who are to be feared, and they are a good deal of a nightmare to the southern household. The whites all have guns in their houses ready, for black depredators. ... Very little provocation is required from a Negro to make a white man get out his gun, and bullets and lynch law are not by any means reserved for the more serious crimes. ...

I do not wish to infer that sympathy is entirely lacking between southern whites and blacks. In most ways there is no friction, and as a rule the whites are considerate and kindly. ...

But after the war there was chaos. "The niggers were turned loose just like a herd of cattle," an Alabamian enlightened me. "There never was a more fatal mistake. Not one in a thousand knew beef from a side of sole leather. We've got an ole nigger still living in this town who come clost to getting into the United States Senate, and he's only a common brick mason. I bet he couldn't tell in three guesses how much seven and six is."

The situation was intolerable, and the whites felt they must by fair means or foul disfranchise the blacks. ...

It is recognized that the colored people must feel chafed by southern conditions, and yet it is argued that they are better off than they would be in the North. A story told for my benefit was that, "There was a Mississippi nigger who had been sent to the penitentiary, and the governor of the state give him his choice between bein' set free and goin' to Massachusetts, and he said he'd rather go back to the penitentiary."

The joke perhaps travesties Massachusetts, yet our treatment of the Negroes is scarcely angelic. We have the same feeling of superiority that exists in the South. This is characteristic of the Anglo-Saxon race in its relations with all other races, and very likely the North would discriminate against the blacks more if they were with us in greater numbers. Nor is the southern antipathy without any reasonable foundation. A colored preacher recently declared: "The only way to get rid of the 'Jim Crow' car is to get rid of the 'Jim Crow' Negro. If I could use 200 bars of soap on the unwashed Negroes that travel on trains and hang around depots I would solve the Negro problem about 20 per cent."

There is a vast deal of slovenly poverty and thriftlessness, easy morals and lack of ideals among the Negroes, and the leaven that works for better things is entirely inadequate. The chance of their being vouchsafed any but the most meager political rights for a long time to come is very small; and it would seem as if their especial need was to strive quietly and steadily for better homes, for better and more general education, and for the ownership of property. They are a race apart, and must learn self-reliance and build up a worthy social life in their own ranks.

It is often claimed by southern men that the Negroes were better off as slaves than they are now, with regard to physical comfort and all essential needs, but this view finds no indorsement among the Negroes themselves; and even the whites are agreed that for the owners and the South itself slavery was a curse.[207]

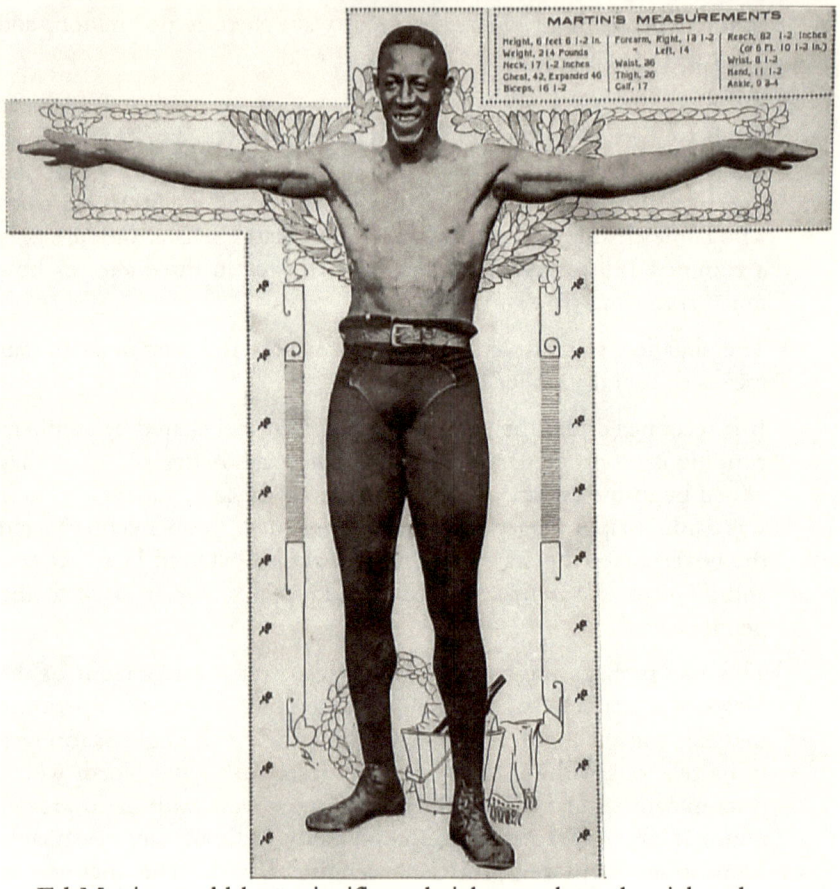

Ed Martin would have significant height, reach, and weight advantages over Jack Johnson. He was at least 22 pounds bigger, if not more. The day before the bout, allegedly he weighed in at 205 pounds (though some said he was closer to 214), while Johnson allegedly scaled 183 pounds, though he too might have been bigger than that.

Tom McCarey promised the combatants that if their fight was up to expectations, he would do everything in his power to match the winner with Champion Jeffries.[208]

The *Los Angeles Times* said Johnson had announced his intention to tear right in this time, hoping to win so decisively that Jeffries would be forced to fight him. The *Times* was doubtful, saying, "For verily it is easier for a leopard to change his spots than for a fighter to change his style." Johnson

---

[207] *Seattle Republican*, October 14, 1904.
[208] *Los Angeles Herald*, October 18, 1904.

had strength, speed, power, endurance, and skill, but often was content to fight cautiously on the outside and win decisions.

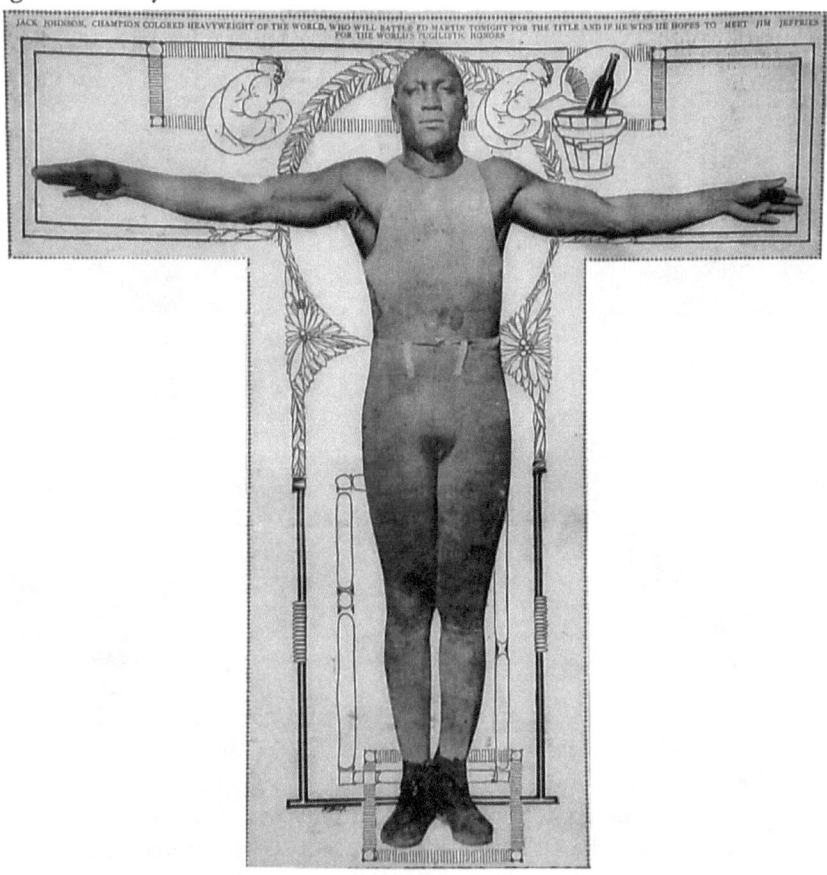

However, given that both fighters knew that a fight with Jeffries might be made if they performed well, in exciting fashion, such incentive might motivate them to make a hot fight of it rather than box cautiously. Or so the press hoped.[209]

On October 18, 1904 at Hazard's Pavilion in Los Angeles, the Jack Johnson vs. Denver Ed Martin rematch took place. The 26-year-old Johnson approached the ring first, wearing a suit of pink pajamas which put the crowd in good humor. Upon seeing Jack's apparel, a black man in the audience who was wearing a black check suit arose and exclaimed, "My King! Looka dat niggah!" The *Examiner* said, "We have seen Kid McCoy's fighting trousers and Twin Sullivan's green belt; we have seen Jim Jeffries and his red, white and blue sash, and we have seen S. McVey and his face, but Jack Johnson's pink pajamas win by miles and miles." The crowd cheered the "dream of pink splendor" and "champion mandolin player."

The next "dark cloud" to enter was Ed Martin, along with a troop of "black-face minstrels." Referee Charles Eyton wore a soft white shirt.

---

[209] *Los Angeles Times*, October 18, 1904.

Observing Johnson, Eyton, and Martin together, local baseball manager James Morely said the three men looked like a checker board. Some pressmen called Martin and Johnson two "Black Diamond express trains."

This time, Johnson utterly dominated from the start, attacking with vicious body blows, his "thick, muscular arms like the legs of a horse in their sleek but massive symmetry, shot in and out as the rods of some great steam engine." Johnson continually decked Martin with short rights to the heart, three times in the 1st round. Many did not see the punches, they were so short and fast, but the effects were obvious, for Martin staggered about. One black spectator asked, "Whaffo that coon up dar? Dem feet uh his am better adapted foh restauran' wuk dan foh sprintin' roun' dis enclosure."

In the 2nd round, the "big mulatto" Martin mixed it up, but again Johnson's body blows with both left and right decked Martin four times. Finally, Johnson landed his right to the solar plexus and immediately followed with a vicious, tearing left hook flush onto the point of the jaw, and Martin shivered, then toppled like a tree, falling face forward onto the canvas floor with a crash.

Martin tried to respond to the count, drawing his knees up under him, but it was as if his head was tied to the floor, and he could not raise it. He went limp, sliding down onto the canvas, out cold. His seconds had to carry his body to the corner, and it took ten minutes before he recovered full consciousness.

This time, Johnson gave the fans an exciting, quick, decisive knockout. The question was whether the critics would give him full credit.

Instead of lauding Johnson's dominant performance, the *Los Angeles Herald* instead chose to denigrate his opponent. It harshly said that Martin was a disappointment, the talk about him being in the pink of condition was a "con," and he no longer would be a drawing card.

Unlike the *Herald*, the *Los Angeles Times* praised Johnson, who had shown class, aggressively forcing the pace and using effective body punching to defeat Martin impressively; quickly and decisively. Burly "Black Jack" was bigger, stronger, and faster than ever before; a truly wonderful man with a magnificent physique and the ability to finish.

> Nor would a match between Martin's conqueror and the White King be any Jeffries-Munroe affair. In Johnson, the champion will meet the toughest game of his career – a man who not only can box with the best, but whose blows travel with the speed of a shot and the smash of a pile-driver. No fool is this man; instead he is a cool, level-headed ring general equal to any, and up to all the veteran's tricks.

Jack Johnson was "one that other heavyweights had best sidestep from now on, always the White King excepted."

Johnson deserved a title shot. "No longer can Champion Jeffries urge lack of class in answer to Johnson's insistent demands for a chance at the title." Until Jeffries abandoned his "untenable position on the color line and sets himself right with the world that loves fair play, Johnson's admirers will be just as incessant in their nagging as the black fellow himself has been."

Johnson said, "I want Mr. Jeffries next. I think I am entitled to a fight with him and it was to prove that I am right that I went in this way tonight. I am faster than ever and bigger, and stronger. I'll be no Jack Munroe and I guess everybody knows it."

The *Los Angeles Examiner* said Martin fought "a different Jack Johnson than we have ever seen before." The suddenness of it all had surprised the crowd. "Johnson's blows had been delivered so quickly and at such close range that not half the people in the house saw them go home, but the effect was plain to all."[210]

The next day, Martin said,

> Yo' tells 'em Denver Ed done receive HIS las' night – yo' tell 'em he got it GOOD. Tell 'em dat Johnsing pahty is one gran' fighting man – aw, tell 'em any ole thing you wanter – ah knows yo' will anyhow!

> How does it happen? Sufferin' Moses in de bullrushers! How yo' 'spect dat ah'm gwineter know? Sposin' yo' backs inter a buzz saw, yo' gwine say 'Dis yere's de tooth whut cotch me?[211]

Johnson said Jeffries was sidestepping behind the color line in order to avoid the one man who could make him extend himself. "I will not rest until public opinion forces Jeffries to recognize my claim for a fight with him. His drawing the color line is all bosh." Jack believed that Jeff was not entitled to draw the color line, for he had fought negroes before. Johnson

---

[210] *Los Angeles Herald, Los Angeles Times, Los Angeles Examiner,* October 19, 1904. Of the $3,885 generated, Johnson earned $1,165.50, and Martin $777. Tom McCarey offered Jeffries $15,000 to fight Johnson.
[211] *Los Angeles Examiner,* October 20, 1904.

called the color-line a time-worn, old, cowardly, four-flusher's means to side-step a top opponent.[212]

The *Los Angeles Examiner* said Johnson was "a very much tickled coon" and was "crazy about himself," saying that he would give Jeffries no rest until he consented to a meeting. "There are many who believe that Jeff will make the Galveston gentleman jump out of the ring, but Johnson is not among them." It quoted Johnson as saying,

> Jess what Ah tol' you – jess what Ah tol' yo'. Ain' Ah good, bo? ... [N]ow Ah'm after dat man Jeffries. ... Yo' kin say foh Jack Johnson dat he's goin' to git er fight wit' Jeff one way or another, an' when he does, yo' string a pinch of change on dat short end, yo' hyar me, bo?

Zick Abrams, Johnson's manager, said,

> I believe this big black chap of mine has shown championship timber. ... I think public opinion will force this fight on Jeff. You remember how it used to be with John L., don't you? Every time he appeared on the stage somebody in the gallery was sure to yell, "Why don't you fight Peter Jackson?" ... I feel that he has earned it, earned it twice over, you understand me? ... I see that the Eastern sporting papers are all for it strong. The Munroe business left a bad taste. Let Jeff fight a real man. I'll guarantee that Johnson will make a good showing and the champion won't have any cinch with him.[213]

Despite the fact that he clearly deserved a title shot, once again Jeffries declined to consider a Johnson match. It did not matter how good Johnson looked in the ring, nor what style he used to win, for Jack was black, and that automatically disqualified him. Jeffries said,

> I do not care whether Johnson licks the Japanese army. I have repeatedly declared that as long as I am in the fighting business I will never make a match with a black man. The negroes may come and the negroes may go, and some of the negroes may be excellent fighters. Just tell the public that James J. Jeffries has made up his mind that he will never put on boxing gloves to give battle to an Ethiopian.

> I might have admired Jack Johnson's prowess as a pugilist had I been at the ringside Tuesday night. I will even go so far as to state that I think he would be able to give a pretty good account of himself were he in the ring with a man many points better than the fellow he whipped last night. But when Johnson applies to me for an engagement I will tell him in direct language to look for some one of his own color and class to give him a fight.

> I am against boxing black men first, last and all the time.[214]

---

[212] *National Police Gazette*, November 5, 1904; *Utica-Herald Dispatch*, October 19, 1904.
[213] *Los Angeles Examiner*, October 20, 1904.
[214] *Los Angeles Examiner*, October 21, 1904.

Los Angeles Examiner, October 23, 1904

What Credit Is It For An Elephant To Crush An Infant.

Freeman cartoon

On October 29, 1904, the *St. Paul Appeal* reported that South Carolina Senator "Pitchfork" Ben Tillman, upon hearing the statement of someone who suggested that the race question could be settled by education, replied,

> "Educate niggers?" repeated the senator, and then he laughed. "Say, there is only one nigger in 100 that can stand an education. The first thing that an educated nigger wants to do is to preach the gospel. If not that he wants to practice law or teach school. Somebody has got to pound it into their heads that they were put on earth to pick cotton and that's what they'll have to do in the South. You certainly have made a mess of the nigger in the North. It's mighty seldom that a nigger becomes educated. He gets a sort of veneering and wants to associate with white people, and when he learns that he can't he drops the veneering and becomes just a plain nigger. A nigger is a nigger and you can't make anything else out of him. It will come mighty near being war if the fifteenth amendment [granting voting rights regardless of race] is not repealed."

On October 31, 1904 in San Francisco, Jack Johnson was present and introduced at the Jimmy Britt vs. Joe Gans world lightweight championship fight, won by Gans via disqualification in the 5th round when the thoroughly beaten white Britt struck the black Gans while he was down. The fight generated a whopping $31,790. The fighters evenly split the 70% fighters' share, so each came away with about $11,123. Mixed-race bouts could generate a lot of money. Johnson was hoping that public pressure and economics would cause Jeffries to withdraw the color line.[215]

Jeffries and Delaney saw a difference between fighting a black man in a championship bout and one in which the championship was not involved. The symbolic racial and social impact was much different. Jeffries did not want to give a black man even the chance to win the championship. Still, the *Police Gazette* said, "Many people say Armstrong was the cause of Jeff's drawing the color line, because he broke his arm on Armstrong's head."[216]

The *Police Gazette* said the manner which Johnson whipped Martin, showing wonderful class, qualified him for a title shot. "Private advices say that Johnson looked every bit a whirlwind heavy of the kind that would make Jeffries fight for his life." This magazine's writers continued supporting Johnson's challenges to Jeffries:

> Jeff does not seem to care one bit how many people may knock him and even accuse him of cowardice in warding off Johnson with the old-time color line dodge. He won't budge from his position, notwithstanding the public clamor that he fight the negro champion.
>
> Jack Johnson's record entitles him to a match with Jeffries and he is the only man now in sight who would seem to have a chance with the hitherto invincible rivet driver. …

---

[215] *San Francisco Call*, November 1, 1904.
[216] *Police Gazette*, November 5, 1904, December 3, 1904.

> Ordinarily fighters don't make much of a hit when they draw the color line. The fighting game is not a calling that permits of such finely drawn social distinctions. The public does not care whether the champion in a certain class is black or white or green as long as he's a good, game fighter and willing to fight any deserving aspirant for his title without surrounding his championship pedestal with a lot of impossible and unreasonable conditions.
>
> When a fighter draws the color line it is usually not far to seek for the "nigger in the woodpile." A few years back many a first-class featherweight drew the color line on George Dixon. It's pretty safe to say that Tommy Ryan's principal reason for the color line was Joe Walcott. Even old John L. Sullivan had a bad case of the color line bugaboo. Peter Jackson was in his prime in those days. ...
>
> So, taken on the whole, the color line is looked upon as a pretty shallow excuse for a good fighter to use in side-tracking a good match. There are but few who think Jeffries has any fear of Jack Johnson, but he, nevertheless, lays himself open to an accusation of cowardice in refusing to meet the husky negro.
>
> Jeffries has a strong hold on the American people. He is a most popular champion. But a fighter is expected to fight, not rest on his laurels, while there is a man in sight who has a possible chance for the title. Jeff's most partisan admirer must admit that Johnson has a chance. ...
>
> The fight loving public wants to see Jeffries fight and fight soon. Jack Johnson stands ready. It's up to Jeffries to forget the color line until he has rubbed this big black speck off his title.[217]

Providing a black perspective, the *Freeman* wrote that Jeffries was a coward who had disgraced the country:

> The color line, as everybody knows, is out of date but comes in session only in social circles and is there only because the newspapers and the second degree of rich remind us of the fact. ... This is not a social question; no, it's a cowardly slugger's cry and yet some reporters don't seem to have sense enough to know that this nuisance has come to a place where the laugh is on the white man. ... Any fighter who is small enough to incite race prejudice in this new age simply to evade a Negro fighter for fear of defeat should retire from the business as quick as possible and so prevent a general white skin disgrace. ...
>
> Many big, strong fighters like Johnson would resent Jeffries' continual insults by publicly slapping his face and make him fight any how or shut his mouth forever. But I would not advise Johnson to slap Jeffries' face while he has his pants on for fear that the big

---

[217] *Police Gazette*, December 3, 1904.

coward would draw his revolver and shoot him dead. In such a case Jeffries could call it an accident and poor Johnson would be out of the way.[218]

Jeffries was "in a peculiar position. He is a pugilist who wants to fight but cannot secure a logical opponent to meet him. ... Rather than swap punches with a negro Jeffries says he will go without an engagement and retire from the ring."[219]

Omaha sports-writer Sandy Griswold criticized Jeff's color-line stance, though he did not believe it had anything to do with fear of Johnson.

> Not that I think for a moment that Jeff has the slightest apprehension as to the outcome with Johnson, for I believe he would be as easy as Jack Munroe, but his lofty stand is ridiculous to the extreme. ... He took down $12,000 for making a holy show out of that big Montana booby, and owing to the peculiar condition of things just now, I think he would double this sum by showing up the coon.[220]

On December 24, Jeffries said,

> I have nothing against the colored fighter himself, but his followers. ... I have seen times, and from what Delaney tells me, when [Peter] Jackson was in his prime in San Francisco the colored element were almost unbearable. They were insulting and insolent and every time an argument came up about fighting they would insult all the white people within their hearing. I therefore came to the conclusion that I would not be instrumental in any manner, no matter how remote, of reviving that state of affairs on the coast.[221]

The *Examiner's* W. W. Naughton said given Jeffries' unwavering declaration that he would retire from the ring before exchanging blows with a negro, the prospect for a Jeffries-Johnson fight was slim. Jeffries likely had fought his last championship battle, and would retire, because there was no white contender in sight good enough to test him and garner public interest. Like Sullivan vs. Jackson, it appeared that the public would be deprived of Jeffries vs. Johnson. There was nothing that Jack Johnson could do about it.[222]

---

[218] *Freeman*, December 3, 1904.
[219] *Police Gazette*, December 10, 1904.
[220] *Police Gazette*, December 10, 17, 1904.
[221] *Pittsburgh Press*, December 24, 1904.
[222] *San Francisco Examiner*, January 1, 4, 1905.

CHAPTER 12

The Set-Up For A White Challenger

In late 1904, rising white heavyweight contender Marvin Hart came to San Francisco and proclaimed that he wanted to fight Jeffries. The *Police Gazette* said,

> If Hart expects to succeed Jeffries as champion when the boilermaker retires, he can show his prowess in no better way than by tackling Johnson. By whipping the black man he would at one bound take second place in the line, with no one ahead of him but the unbeatable champion.[223]

"Marvelous" Marvin was a Southerner from Louisville, Kentucky, and was concerned about taking heat from his hometown fans if he crossed the color line. Hence, he never had fought a black man. However, he knew that beating Johnson would put him in line to fight Jeffries, or for a vacant title if Jeff retired.[224]

When Jack Johnson appeared at the San Francisco Club, heavyweight Jim Casey whispered to someone, "I'd like to get the big nayger." After being told what he said, Johnson responded, "I'll fight him for $4. Clear away the chairs in the back room." However, there were no hostilities. "This was a matchmaking party."[225]

Despite Hart's concern about violating the color line, ultimately promoter Alex Greggains convinced Hart to fight Johnson. On December 27, the 20-round Johnson-Hart fight was signed, initially set to be held on January 27, 1905. The parties agreed to use Greggains as the referee.[226]

Marvin Hart was a very strong and exciting fighter who could take any amount of punishment and always come forward throwing nonstop power punches with both hands. He had excellent conditioning and recuperative powers. He generally won his bouts by knockout, and even when his fights went the distance, Marvin usually managed to hurt or deck his opponent at some point in the bout. He was known to have all-out wars, forcing his opponents to duke it out with him, making him a fan favorite. The 5'11 ½" 195-pound Hart's record consisted of at least 35 fights: 24 wins, 3 losses, 3 draws, and 5 no-decision bouts, with 19 knockouts.[227]

---

[223] *Police Gazette*, December 24, 31, 1904.
[224] *San Francisco Call*, December 26, 1904.
[225] *San Francisco Chronicle*, January 7, 1905.
[226] *San Francisco Call*, December 28, 1904.
[227] Significant Marvin Hart bouts included: 1902 KO3 Billy Stift, KO9 Kid Carter, W6 Stift, L6 Jack Root, and DND6 Jack O'Brien; 1903 DND6 Jack O'Brien (although outpointed early, Hart decked and

On the East Coast, the *Police Gazette* reported that Johnson had agreed to stop Hart within 20 rounds or lose the fight. Hart might have agreed to cross the color line and take the bout because Johnson had agreed to the handicap. Jack was not known as a knockout artist, while Hart was known for his toughness and durability.

> Johnson has agreed to stop the Southern man within twenty rounds, and Alex Greggains…has arranged everything. The two big men are to divide the proceeds on a sixty and forty per cent basis, and if Johnson does not put Hart away before the end of the bout he is to get the short end, regardless of what he shows as a clever boxer. In agreeing to knockout so tough a fellow as Marvin Hart Johnson has undertaken no easy task. Hart has been hailed as a comer by Eastern sporting critics for the past year or more. He is a big, tough boy, not overly clever, but with more than an ordinary amount of endurance. While he may not be able to reach Johnson with a knockout punch, it is certain that the colored champion will have to go some to put him away.[228]

The fact that the bout was taking place in San Francisco was no coincidence. "At present 'Frisco is the only centre where championship contests of at least twenty rounds can be had with the assurance of a large crowd." Only eighteen states allowed boxing, and most of them had many restrictions.[229]

However, boxing was coming under attack even in California. State Senator William Ralston introduced a bill to stop prize fighting. He said the state had attained a dignity equal to the East, but because prize fighting was allowed, California still had the reputation of being the "wild and wooly West." The only way to destroy that impression was to destroy the game. He also said boxing needed to be banned because of all the crookedness, fakes, and fixed fights that had been perpetrated.

The proposed bill created a panic amongst boxing lovers. The two legislative houses appeared to be about evenly divided. Even those in favor of boxing were reluctant to speak up in its defense too much, for fear of incurring the wrath of their church-going constituents.[230]

The Johnson-Hart contest was derailed temporarily. Various theories circulated. The *Police Gazette* offered its interesting insights, saying,

> The limelight of publicity has been turned upon an inside view of boxing affairs as they exist in San Francisco and the disclosures are of such a manifestly rotten character that an announcement from the

---

badly hurt O'Brien late in both no-decision bouts), LTKOby12 George Gardner (retirement owing to broken right hand), DND6 Joe Choynski, and KO15 Kid Carter; 1904 D15 George Gardner (vast majority felt that Hart won), W20 Sandy Ferguson (most felt Sandy deserved a draw), and WND6 and D12 Gus Ruhlin, managing to deck Ruhlin in both contests. Hart "has a pile driving wallop that can do a heap of damage if it lands."
[228] *Police Gazette*, January 14, 1905.
[229] *Police Gazette*, January 21, 1905.
[230] *San Francisco Examiner*, January 5, 6, 1905.

authorities that no more contests would be permitted would not be surprising. Jealousy among the managers, brutal rivalry between the fighters, fakes, frame ups and crooked decisions have brought matters to a crisis. One of the first suspicious events was the cancelling of the supposedly on the level Marvin Hart-Jack Johnson fight, that was to have been held on Jan. 27. Rumors at once flew in all directions as to the cause of the cancelling.

It is now asserted that the affair was booked as a frame up for Hart to win under all circumstances, so that he would be a logical opponent for Jeffries in March, because it was feared that if Johnson won, Jeff would still refuse to withdraw the color line.

So strong did this rumor become that the management called the fight off altogether.[231]

This rumor lent credence to the prior report that Johnson could not win in any way other than via knockout. The feeling was that all Hart had to do was last the distance and he would win, so that a Jeffries-Hart bout could be arranged. There was no money in it for promoters if Johnson won, because Jeff was not going to fight him, no matter what. Hence, unless Johnson knocked out Hart, he was going to lose. Or so the rumors and reports went.

If the fix rumor was true, then it made sense to call off the bout temporarily until the legal issues surrounding the sport were handled first. A fight with any form of crookedness taking place before the vote on the anti-prize-fight bill would hurt boxing's chances to remain afloat.[232]

In response to Jeffries' declaration that it would lower the pugilistic game should a black man become champion, former colored pugilist Allen Johnson said Jeffries had to be slightly afraid of losing to Johnson. He disagreed that having a black champion would ruin the game. "The American public is fair minded enough to give fair play to any champion, no matter what his color or creed may be." Allen also heard that Jeff declared that he did not want to fight blacks because their heads were too hard. "I can say that it does not take a harder blow to knock out a Negro than a white man."[233]

In late February, Alex Greggains once again announced the Hart-Johnson fight, set to be held in late March, *after* the vote would be held on the Ralston anti-prize-fight bill. The fight was back on. "Greggains figures that the winner of this bout will be pitted against Jeffries, but the sporting public in general is rather doubtful of this fact."[234]

The *Oakland Tribune* said his name was John James Arthur Johnson. He had a shiny head "that is shaped like a chocolate drop. When he smiles he shows a clean set of ivories and a lot of good nature." "In his manners he is quite gentlemanly, like Peter Jackson, and he knows that his color entitles

---

[231] *Police Gazette*, February 11, 1905.
[232] *Oakland Tribune*, March 22, 1905.
[233] *Freeman*, February 25, 18, 1905.
[234] *San Francisco Call*, February 28, 1905.

him to a back seat when everything shows white in front of him. He never fights outside the ring. He likes money, and spends much of it for clothes." He also liked jewelry and adornments such as a watch, cane, diamonds on his shirt and tie, and a diamond ring on his finger. "That's Jack Johnson as he is today. What would he look like should he become the champion of both the white and black class?"

JACK JOHNSON, THE COLORED BOXER, WHO WILL MEET MARVIN HART.

On March 9, 1905 in Sacramento, the Ralston anti-prize-fight bill was defeated narrowly in the assembly by a vote of 35 Noes to 33 Ayes.

James J. Jeffries predicted that Johnson would win a points decision, although he granted that Hart was capable of scoring a knockout. "Will I fight the winner? Well, no, not if it comes out the way I anticipate. My ideas are too well known."[235]

Johnson was known as a "shifty smoke," while Hart bore in continually and never broke ground. However, Jack said he would make Marvin back up. He was not afraid to fight on the inside, and Hart could not set too fast a pace for him. He was betting some of his own money on a knockout.

A good fight was expected not only because of the possibility of fighting Jeffries, but because Hart "has as much regard for a colored man as most Southerners have." Racial animus and the desire not to lose to a black man would be additional motivation for Hart.[236]

> He is a Kentuckian, born and bred, and has the Kentuckian's race prejudice. It took an even two months to convince him that it was to his best interests to meet a colored boxer, even though Johnson was colored heavyweight champion of the world. Nothing short of his desire to get at Jeffries by using Jack as a stepping stone brought about the change of sentiment. The fact that he does not care to be put on an equality with a negro will only add fuel to the flame next Tuesday night. A Kentuckian is going to take a world of beating before he will succumb to a man of Johnson's color.[237]

When interviewed, Hart said, "One punch is all I want to land on the nigger, and I'll do that before the fight is half over. I don't care how fast the man is, he'll go down for the count if I land on him, and I'm not afraid to take a few to get mine in."[238] Another writer quoted Hart as saying,

---

[235] *Oakland Tribune*, March 3, 9, 18, 1905.
[236] *San Francisco Call*, March 19, 1905; *San Francisco Bulletin*, *San Francisco Evening Post*, March 20, 1905; *San Francisco Chronicle*, March 21, 1905.
[237] *San Francisco Bulletin*, March 22, 1905.
[238] *San Francisco Bulletin*, March 24, 1905.

I tell you right here that this coon will have to go some to beat me. He won't beat me. ... I realize that this coon Johnson is a clever fellow. I am not a clever fellow except in my own peculiar way, but I have got the wallop that will win. ... I am a knockout fighter. He is a clever boxer. One punch will be all that's necessary for him.[239]

As the fight approached, the Hart team would not agree to any referee other than Alex Greggains, who had made the match. Johnson suggested Eddie Graney or Jack Welch, both of whom had sterling reputations. Hart's manager Jim McCormick insisted that there would be no fight unless Greggains refereed. He did not say why the other named referees, who had more experience, would not be fair. Perhaps he was concerned that they *would* be fair. Regardless, Johnson's manager Zeke Abrams was comfortable with Greggains. Therefore, Greggains was chosen to referee the bout.[240]

San Francisco Bulletin, **March 21, 1905**

Many were picking Hart to win. Jimmy Britt said, "I can't see anybody but Hart. The coon might make him look cheap for the first few rounds, but Hart has the stamina and will finish strong." Tom Dillon said, "I like the coon to get the decision." Dave Barry said, "Hart for mine. Any man that puts Jack O'Brien to the floor six times in a six-round bout will have no trouble in reaching Johnson." Billy Wilson picked Hart. "He'll have a task on his hands with the clever smoke, but he's beaten fast fighters before." Harry Corbett said it was an even match.[241]

---

[239] *San Francisco Chronicle*, March 24, 1905.
[240] *Oakland Tribune*, March 25, 1905.
[241] *San Francisco Bulletin*, March 26, 1905.

There was some discussion and concern regarding Johnson's tendency to give dull, albeit winning performances, which could hurt ticket sales. The press raised this concern with Greggains. "It was suggested to him that the public should be assured that Johnson intends to fight from the first gong, and not to loaf along through…twenty rounds to a decision." The *San Francisco Chronicle* said, "Now if [Greggains] he will give 'Mistah' Johnson to understand that no money will be forthcoming if the big 'dinge' does not get busy, he will have the eternal gratitude of those who intend to occupy chairs." Greggains responded by saying,

> I have notified Johnson that he must fight all the time or the fight will be called 'no contest.' I don't expect any difficulty on that score. Johnson's manager, Zick Abrams, has also told him that he must win in a hurry. "If you stay twenty rounds for a decision," Abrams told him, "we will run you out of town."[242]

Hence, both the promoter (who was the referee) and Johnson's own manager were putting a great deal of pressure on Johnson to try to win by knockout rather than attempt to win a decision by cautiously outboxing his opponent. The local press had a hand in this pressure as well. Indeed, Johnson was being pre-judged heading into this fight.

If Johnson had been white, the prejudice against his style would not have been as great. Jack O'Brien and Jim Corbett were cautious defensive boxers, yet they were hailed as brilliant and intelligent.[243]

The *Chronicle* did not think Johnson would be able to coast or loaf against Hart, owing to the latter's ripping, smashing, nonstop style.

W. W. Naughton said, "If Hart should down Johnson in a fair fight the rest will be easy. Marvin will be the sensation of the hour." "The champion has already said that he will not hesitate about giving Hart a match, if Hart disposes of the colored heavyweight."

But first, Hart needed an impressive and clear victory in order to garner sufficient public demand and press clamor for a Jeffries-Hart bout, which was necessary for the fight to be lucrative financially for Jeffries. Jeff was ready to retire, and was willing to box again only if the bout with Hart would yield a big payday. Jeffries said he hoped Hart would win decisively so that he could draw fans and a big gate.

However, if Johnson won, Jeffries insisted that he would refuse to withdraw his color-line objection. "Up to date neither criticism nor cajolery has caused Jeffries to waver in his determination never to fight a negro." When asked if he would meet Johnson if he defeated Hart, Jeff said:

> No; I'm not fighting skunks as yet, not while there are white men in the field. I'm not going to discuss Johnson's abilities as a boxer. He may be a wonder and all that, but if any one is to take my title I want that man to be of my own color.

---

[242] *San Francisco Chronicle*, March 25, 1905.
[243] *San Francisco Chronicle*, March 26, 1905.

If Hart wins I will cheerfully give him a fight. I suppose it will be up to me to do so. He's a young fellow, and they say he has physique, too. I hope he will draw, though, for I'm not going to be drawn into another Jack Munroe farce.[244]

San Francisco Chronicle, **March 26, 1905**

Regarding the feelings towards blacks at that time, in the local news the day before the fight, a Boston correspondent to the *San Francisco Call* wrote:

> Our great duty toward the negro is in protecting him against himself. We must govern him according to what he needs, and not according to what we think he needs. There isn't a negro who is fit to legislate for a cat. It is a degradation of white citizenship to elect one to office, and nobody knows that better than a negro.[245]

The night before the fight, from New York, Bill Delaney said,

> Should Hart beat Johnson tomorrow night Jeffries will fight Hart, but if the negro wins there is nothing doing. In June 1905, Jeff will arrive in California, and by that time, if there is no white man ready to make a match with him, Jeffries will forever retire from the ring.[246]

Johnson said, "Hart may be a big strong boy, but I've met and defeated his kind before. It's up to 'Jeff' to cut out that color line for I'm the man he will have to meet."[247]

---

[244] *Oakland Tribune*, March 27, 1905.
[245] *San Francisco Call*, March 27, 1905.
[246] *Washington Post*, March 28, 1905.
[247] *San Francisco Evening Post*, March 28, 1905.

The morning of the fight, the *San Francisco Examiner* said,

> Tonight's fight looks to be the first good heavyweight match that has been carded for two years. Aside from this, general interest is being manifested because of the probability of a match with Jeffries, should Hart be returned the winner. Jeffries has, of course, persistently declared his determination to draw the color line.

The *San Francisco Chronicle* reported,

> As a special inducement to the two men to go in and make a rattling fight of it, Greggains has practically promised a match with Jeffries to the winner – in case the winner should be Hart. If Johnson wins, matters will not be altered so far as an opponent for Jeff is concerned, since the Hairy One has not withdrawn the color line and has no intention of doing so. If Hart wins, however, and brings about his victory in a way that looks good to the sporting public, he will be next in line for the champion of champions.

The *San Francisco Call* said,

> If Hart wins the battle and makes any kind of a showing it is about settled he will be matched with Jeffries. … He is anxious to get after the big fellow and for that reason he will probably put up the fight of his life when he steps into the ring to-night.

The *San Francisco Bulletin* said the time-honored custom of shaking hands would be eliminated from the proceedings, owing to race. "A natural hatred seems to exist between the two, and every blow struck, besides bringing the smiter that much nearer the long end of the purse, will carry more than the ordinary sting on account of the clashing of the two ever warring races."[248]

Those on the East Coast wondered whether the fight or its decision would be on the level. Some thought the fight was fixed for Hart, given that Jeffries utterly refused to fight Johnson. The *Trenton Times* wrote,

> The bout has a peculiar looking angle to it, for the reason that Hart has repeatedly declared that he would not enter the ring with a negro. He once announced in Boston after winning a bout from Kid Carter that he was a Southerner and would not insult his friends by fighting a colored man. For this reason sporting men are somewhat skeptical about the genuineness of the fight, some hinting that Johnson is certain to lose in order that Hart may force Jeffries to a meeting, the latter having refused many times to fight Johnson.
>
> … Many good judges say that Johnson would give Jeffries the hardest fight of his life.[249]

---

[248] *San Francisco Examiner, San Francisco Chronicle, San Francisco Call, San Francisco Bulletin*, March 28, 1905.
[249] *Trenton Times*, March 28, 1905.

The fear was that a points decision surely would go to Hart no matter what, so that a Hart-Jeffries bout could be made. A Johnson-Jeffries fight would be more lucrative, but because of Jeffries' color-line stance, that fight could not be made even if Johnson won. Hence, the sense was that Greggains would be more inclined to award the decision to Hart if he wanted to promote a heavyweight championship fight. There was no money in it for Greggains if he awarded the contest to Johnson.

Further, the fact that previously Hart had drawn the color line consistently, but now was willing to fight Johnson, made some think that he had been told that he would be given the decision if it went the distance. Perhaps this is why the Hart side had insisted on Greggains as the referee and would not accept anyone else, including reputable men. Plus, there had been some pre-fight news reports on the East Coast that Johnson could win only via knockout.

Hart explained that he was fighting Johnson only because no one else would fight him. Marvin said, "This is the first colored man I ever fought and it will be the last, win or lose. Fighting is my business, and I am just forced to fight Johnson, as he is the only man that will fight me."[250]

However, in Hart's hometown of Louisville, the day of the fight it was reported, "Johnson must knock Hart out to win." The *Louisville Times* quoted Hart as saying, "Johnson has to knock me out in twenty rounds to get the big end of the money, and this fact will work to my advantage, as it will cause him to attempt to carry the fight to me."[251]

---

[250] *Louisville Courier-Journal*, March 30, 1905.
[251] *Louisville Times*, March 28, 1905.

CHAPTER 13

A Matter of Perspective

On March 28, 1905 at Woodward's Pavilion in San Francisco, 26-year-old (just three days shy of 27) Jack Johnson fought 28-year-old Marvin Hart. Because it was a heavyweight bout, no official weigh-in was required, but it was estimated that on fight-night the two pugilists weighed somewhere between 193 and 198 pounds.

From the start, and throughout the contest, Hart attacked ferociously with hard punches in nonstop fashion. He wanted to get to the inside and fire away at both the head and body, particularly focusing on the body. It immediately was apparent that it would be a rough and tumble fight, primarily on the inside, owing to Hart's constant attacking and rushing tactics. Johnson landed many jabs from the outside. They exchanged and clinched, and worked in the clinches. Johnson liked to block and counter, and he laughed at the busier Hart's efforts to land. Hart was the more active, but Johnson was much cleverer, landing more cleanly and more often, and defending well, as usual.

Intermittently Johnson would spurt with vicious offense, knocking Hart backwards to the ropes with volleys of blows, proving his assertion that he would make Hart retreat. However, throughout the fight, every time that Johnson sent him back, Jack would back off, and Marvin would attack again. Jack liked to jab and play defense, but whenever Hart landed, Johnson always made him pay for it, showing his tendency to fire back hard and attack ferociously whenever his opponent landed a good one. When Jack mixed it up, he clearly had the best of matters. But then he played defense again and jabbed the aggressive Hart. Johnson drew blood from Hart's nostrils, and his nose bled badly throughout the fight. Marvin's left eye also swelled and puffed up from the repeated jabs.

In the 9th round, Johnson attacked ferociously and landed repeatedly, backing Hart against the ropes. "Hart was beaten here had the negro followed up his advantage. He was bleeding badly and his eye was all but closed. Johnson let up, however, and Hart's trouble was over." Marvin bled profusely from his nose and mouth.

Although Hart rushed continually, Johnson kept administering punishment, landing jabs, hooks, and uppercuts. However, Hart kept trying and punching all the time, making the careful Johnson more defensive. The *Examiner* said that in between frequent clinches, Hart's face was battered. Though Marvin kept pressing and constantly kept after the cautious Johnson, his blows did little damage. It was only when "the coon was riled that he got to fighting hard. He landed time and time again on Hart's bad face, but the Louisville gent seemed satisfied to take all that was coming." The *Chronicle* said, "The coon had all the better of the infighting, landing short arm hooks on Marvin's face at will. Hart kept plowing into the stomach, but with very little effect." Hart kept attacking, being the busier and more active fighter, but absorbing considerable punishment.

The crowd chanted Hart's name and cheered his nonstop efforts, appreciating his unflinching gameness and constant aggression regardless of how hard or often he was hit. He waded in with blows, but Johnson eluded or blocked and hit Hart, mostly with jabs. Johnson played defense, while his cornermen begged him to hit back more often. In the final round, Johnson held a fair amount, and the house was in a wild uproar, the spectators on their feet cheering for Hart and yelling for him to knock out Johnson.

Referee Alex Greggains immediately pointed to Hart and declared him the winner of the 20-round decision. The applause which greeted the decision lasted for several minutes. The white crowd was quite pleased.

In explaining his verdict, various local newspapers quoted Referee Alex Greggains as saying,

> I gave the decision to Hart because he was the aggressor throughout and carried the fighting all the way. ... I always give the gamest and most aggressive man the decision. Johnson, in my opinion, dogged it. He held at all times in the clinches.
>
> Before the men entered the ring I warned them that if the fight went the limit the aggressor would get the decision. This was in order to make Johnson fight. Hart forced the fighting every step of the way, and, in view of my warning to them, no other decision was possible. I believe Hart won and I believe that he won all the way. It was a good

fight to look at, but Hart did the work, and he properly received the decision. Under the same circumstances I would give the same decision at any time.

Hart said, "Johnson is a big, clever nigger with a long left arm, and that is why I wear this battered face. Outside of his straight left jabs he had no punch. ... I did all the leading ...."

The marked-up Hart looked like the loser. His "face was very much warped on the left side. His left cheek and the left side of his lips were badly puffed." Johnson showed no marks.

Jack Johnson strongly denounced the decision:

> All I can say is that I was robbed. That is all there is to it. After fighting until I reached the top, I have been thrown down by an unfair ruling. I fought a good fight and am satisfied with the showing I made. I got the worst of it. Had I had my way I would never have stood for Greggains at any stage, but it was all Abrams' say and I have to suffer.... I put up the best fight I knew how and was satisfied that I was a winner at every stage.

The local sports-writers had mixed opinions. Some felt that Johnson deserved the victory, or at least no worse than a draw. Some explicitly stated that race prejudice probably influenced the crowd and the referee's decision. Certainly a prejudice in favor of Hart's more aggressive style disposed referee Greggains in his favor. Most agreed that Johnson was the more scientific, having shown better defense, landing more blows, and leaving the ring without a scratch, whereas Hart's face was puffy and bleeding. Still, several others wholeheartedly applauded the decision. Of course, the writers all were white, and some of them had their own biases, as reflected by a liberal use of the word "coon." If that was what they were willing to put in print, just imagine what they were saying and thinking outside of the newspapers. The decision garnered a great deal of subsequent discussion and debate, and was considered controversial.

The local *San Francisco Examiner*'s W. W. Naughton said Hart's pluck, awkwardness, aggression, and gameness were better than Johnson's mixture of cleverness and cowardice. Hart's face was puffed up from Johnson's jabs, but he never faltered, constantly pressing forward except when carried backwards by the force of Johnson's blows. Johnson fought in spurts, whenever he felt like it.

> The indifference to punishment and great pluck displayed by the white man seemed to discourage the negro. Johnson beyond a doubt showed that he lacks that essential fighting qualification – grit.

> It would be ridiculous to say that Hart is a better ringster than Johnson. If Johnson were only as stout-hearted as the man from Louisville the chances are the negro would dispose of his opponent of last night in ten rounds. ...

There was a sameness between the rounds from the tenth onward. Johnson spurted occasionally and hammered Hart to the ropes. Then Marvin would pull himself together and force the big negro back across the ring. Johnson's seconds seemed to be in despair. They leaned in through the ropes and railed at the weak-hearted colored champion.

Still, even Naughton said the decision was in doubt. "From the manner in which the Louisville heavyweight skipped around it almost seemed as if he had not expected more than a draw."

Like the *Examiner*, the *San Francisco Call* agreed with the decision, saying that Johnson counterattacked very well, but would not follow up. "Had Johnson a small part of the aggressiveness shown by Hart there would have been nothing to the fight." The *Oakland Times* and *Oakland Enquirer* agreed, feeling that Hart beat the "coon," though they noted that plenty of folks thought it should have been a draw.

The *Oakland Tribune* said the decision was based on the fact that Hart was the aggressor nearly all the time, except when sent back by Johnson's blows. Johnson was clever and strong on points, but not willing to attack as often, lacking Hart's aggressive grittiness. "Had the decision been given on points scored by clean hitting, blocking and punishment administered, then Johnson would have won by a country mile." Essentially, Johnson would have won by any standard other than pure aggressiveness and work rate.

Despite frequently calling Johnson a "coon" in its fight description, the *San Francisco Chronicle* did not agree with the verdict, recognizing that race played a part in the result. The decision was "immensely popular" with the white crowd, which during the fight yelled Hart's name and cheered when he landed, but remained silent when Johnson did so.

> In all this enthusiasm there was doubtless a great deal of racial prejudice. ... Throughout the entire battle the spirit was manifest. Johnson's clean hitting, his cleverness at blocking and his work all through was allowed to pass with scarcely a murmur, while every blow landed by the white man was cheered to the echo. This blinded the judgment of many, beyond a doubt. ...
>
> Those who did not agree with Greggains last night based their argument on the assertion that Johnson had shown pronounced superiority over Hart at all stages: that, if there was nothing else, his clean hitting should have entitled him to the verdict. The Hart faction answered this with the statement that Hart had forced the fighting all the way, and that if he had not done this there would have been no fighting to speak of. ...
>
> Johnson did more actual fighting last night than he has done in all his other fights in San Francisco put together. ... Marvin Hart rushed him all the time, kept lunging at him, kept on top of him all the time, and Johnson was forced to retaliate. When he did retaliate it was much to Hart's discomfort, for the black man had everything in the

way of cleverness, and the white man had little or nothing beyond his indomitable grit and his infinite willingness.

To put the thing briefly the way it appeared to a man who had no interest one way or the other – only a desire to see fair play and to have the better fighter win – on the score of aggressiveness Hart was entitled to the verdict. On any other score Johnson should have been the favored one. This is a thing that will be argued on the street corners for days.

The fight had been decided on style, entertainment value, gameness, and toughness rather than number of scoring blows landed, defense, ring generalship, or effectiveness.

The *San Francisco Evening Post* said that although Hart had put up a gritty fight, his only redeeming quality as a fighter was that he was a glutton for punishment, coming on for more no matter how hard he was walloped. Hart fought hard all the time, whereas Johnson only opened up in spots, showing flashes of offensive brilliance, followed by long periods of defensiveness, cautiousness, and clinching, and that cost him.

The *San Francisco Bulletin* strongly disagreed with the decision. It too believed that race prejudice was a factor. Johnson had a decided lead on points and cleverness. He beat and pounded on Hart, who demonstrated remarkable recuperative powers.

> [Johnson] landed so often on the face of the Blue Grass State's aspirant for championship honors that the right side wouldn't recognize the left side if they should perchance gaze upon each other in a looking glass. Hart's left eye was put very much to the bad in the early stage of the contest, and his face began to puff out like a toy balloon. …

> Naturally, the house was with Hart, not only because he was the short-ender, but also owing to racial prejudices. Whenever the Kentuckian landed a blow, no matter whether it was a love tap or a hard body punch, the gallery would howl with delight, and long before the final rounds cries of "Hart! Hart! Hart!" rang through the pavilion. So, when Referee Greggains pointed to Hart as the winner at the end of the contest, pandemonium reigned supreme throughout the auditorium, but if a person looked at the contest from an unbiased standpoint and carefully weighed everything in the balance, he would be compelled to acknowledge that the worst Johnson should have received was a draw. Looking at it from a scientific angle, the colored man should have been declared the victor. It is true that Hart did all the forcing and was ever on the aggressive, but his blows rarely landed on a vulnerable spot, and he never had his opponent in distress. On the other hand, Johnson outpointed and outboxed him from start to finish, and on several occasions forced the white man to break ground with such alacrity that the ropes alone saved him from going into the audience.

The *Bulletin* felt that race prejudice not only was behind the fan support for Hart, but the referee's decision. It contrasted this decision with the one given in the Battling Nelson vs. Jimmy Britt fight. There, although Nelson was the aggressor like Hart, and Britt was content to block and retaliate with jabs and uppercuts like Johnson, Britt still won the decision, although with a different referee – Billy Roche. Plus, Britt was white. In that instance, in a bout between two white men, superior cleverness won the day.

> Of course, Greggains took the stand that he told both men that he would give the fight to the man who did the fighting, and on this score gave the decision to Hart. But this was not justice to the betting public who wagered their money on the merits of the two men as fighters and not simply on a man's bulldog tenacity and ability to assimilate punishment. … The general public was extremely pleased over the decision, but if Johnson was a few shades lighter and had no trace of negro blood in his veins there would have been a different story to tell.

Hence, this writer explicitly stated his belief that if Johnson was white, he would have been awarded the decision.

The ticket sales yielded $6,200, of which the club retained 40%, or $2,480, with $3,720 to be divided equally between Hart and Johnson, or $1,860 each. Apparently they had agreed to divide the fighters' share evenly, regardless of result.[252]

Wire dispatches allowed newspapers throughout the country to report on the fight. The *Los Angeles Daily Times* said Hart appeared to be the beaten man, for his face resembled a swollen "large raw steak," with his left eye completely closed. Conversely, Johnson did not have a mark, and "did not even appear to be tired, and yet he had fought as nobody had ever seen him fight before in California."

> Hart's gameness was what won the fight. … In point of cleverness and point of blows landed, Johnson led all the way. At times, he placed as many as a half a dozen short-arm uppercuts upon his opponent without return. In the mixing, he also landed oftenest; … From the ninth round on, Hart was bleeding from the nose continuously, and it seemed at many times during the rough infighting that he could not see his opponent at all. But he lasted out, and fought and tugged like a demon all the time. Often during the twenty rounds he was borne to the ropes and received full-arm uppercuts. Throughout the last five rounds he had the crowd shouting wildly for him. The Kentuckian's gameness won nearly every man in the house. Color certainly figured to some extent in this support of a practical stranger.

---

[252] *San Francisco Examiner, San Francisco Call, San Francisco Chronicle, San Francisco Evening Post, San Francisco Bulletin, Oakland Times, Oakland Enquirer, Oakland Tribune*, March 29, 1905.

Johnson was a badly disappointed man. He considered he had landed two blows to every one that his opponent gave him, and he believed that he had led fully as often as the Kentuckian.

The Associated Press similarly reported,

Hart was far from demonstrating that he is qualified to meet Jim Jeffries. Hart was as badly punished a man as has been seen in the ring for a long time, but he was game to the core, and kept boring into the big colored man all through the fight.

... The sympathies of the large crowd present were openly with Hart...and every lead he made at Johnson, whether he landed or not, was greeted with yells of joy.

On the East coast, the *Newark Evening News* and the *Trenton Times* said:

Hart was the worst punished of the two, and had the negro fought a fight which he showed himself at times capable of he would have won handily. ... The spectators were wholly of the opinion that Johnson was suffering from a streak of bright yellow. Whenever he did fight, he made Hart look like an amateur. The Louisville man's aggressiveness seemed to rattle Johnson and his courage would ooze.

Interestingly, the *Philadelphia Evening Bulletin* said:

Hart's victory puts him in line for a fight with Jeffries, the champion sending a wire to the club last night to the effect that he would meet the winner, provided it was Hart. The latter's form was not good enough to warrant him being dangerous against Jeffries, but as he is the best man in sight local clubs will try to land the match.

The size of the crowd was disappointing, the general impression being that the fight was fixed for Hart to win and thus secure a match with Jeffries.[253]

The *National Police Gazette* questioned the legitimacy of Hart's victory, saying, "He did not have the better of the going and a draw would have been a present to him."[254]

Most fair-minded writers believed that Johnson deserved the verdict, or no worse than a draw.

Alex Greggains was not the most neutral unbiased arbiter. Greggains was a promoter. Promoters needed to fill seats in order to make money, and therefore Greggains was concerned with fan opinion, for the fans generated dollars. The white fans liked Hart, not the black Johnson.

If Greggains had said that if there was no knockout, he was going to award the fight to the man who was the most aggressive, that gave Hart a distinct advantage in the scoring because there wasn't a fighter alive who was more aggressive than him. Everyone knew going into the fight that

---

[253] *Los Angeles Daily Times, Newark Evening News, Trenton Times, Philadelphia Evening Bulletin,* March 29, 1905.
[254] *Police Gazette,* April 15, 1905.

Hart was more aggressive than Johnson. Hence, Greggains was biased against Johnson's style even before the bout began, essentially formulating his scoring criteria in a way that assured Hart of victory in the event of a points decision. This also showed his promoter's bias, specifically saying that his scoring criterion was designed "to make Johnson fight."

In fact, most of the pre-fight talk from Greggains centered on his statement that if Johnson did not fight he would declare it a no-contest. Yet, everyone agreed that Johnson had fought hard, harder than he had in all of his previous local bouts.

Greggains had to be influenced and biased by economics. Awarding Johnson the decision did nothing for Greggains, because Jeffries would refuse to fight Johnson. A Hart victory would be more popular with the white paying public and might lead to a big payday with a Jeffries-Hart promotion. Hence, Greggains, a promoter and referee, had a clear interest in having Hart win. He wanted to promote a Jeffries-Hart fight, the only one that Jeffries might accept. Therefore, he naturally would have more of an inclination and incentive to award the bout to Hart.

One also has to consider all of the pre-fight talk that either the fight was fixed for Hart to win if it went the distance, or that Johnson had agreed to knock him out or lose. Even Hart said so, being quoted accordingly by his hometown newspapers. Combine this with the fact that the Hart faction insisted on Greggains, and would accept no other referee, even ones considered wise and fair. Some writers believed that Greggains' assurances to Hart of victory explained why Hart had crossed the color line. They also believed that explained why the fight was postponed until after the Ralston bill vote. A crooked decision occurring before the vote could have hurt boxing's chances to remain afloat.

Ultimately, several writers agreed that if Johnson was white, he would have won the decision or at least been awarded a draw. This viewpoint gained more momentum as time passed. The only ones who said Hart won said he won because he was more aggressive. However, no one said his aggressiveness was more effective. Over time, more and more writers and experts believed that Johnson had been robbed.

Johnson was broken up over the decision, and disputed Greggains' claim that he told the boxers before the fight that he would give the decision to the most aggressive fighter. Greggains might have made such a claim to the newsmen in order to justify his decision, but Johnson said Greggains never said that to the fighters. "I want to say that he never did any such thing. ... I did not want Alec to referee, but Hart would not take Welch or Graney, whom I mentioned. Hart said it was Greggains or nobody."[255] Perhaps it is telling that Greggains would not referee again for the next five years.

James J. Jeffries was happy that the white man had won:

---

[255] *San Francisco Bulletin*, March 31, 1905.

> I am glad Marvin Hart won over Johnson last night. Not that it means a prospective candidate for my title, but it places the negro out of the running. If Johnson had won he would never have fought me. My decision never to meet a negro while I am champion would have been faithfully kept.
>
> I don't want the public to think that I'm looking for easy game, and if the press and public decide that Hart is a suitable opponent for me I will gladly meet him this Fall. I have defended the title against all white aspirants and stand ready to meet the popular choice, whoever he may be. If Hart is considered out of my class, I will retire from the ring this year forever.[256]

Jeff said he would fight Hart only if the public demanded it. He was sorry that Hart had not knocked out Johnson.[257]

It turned out that there was not much demand for a Hart-Jeffries contest, because Hart had neither clearly nor impressively defeated Johnson (and many questioned whether he really had won), nor showed the qualifications to defeat Jeffries.[258]

W. W. Naughton said it would be inhuman to put Hart in the ring with the champion. "Hart would be candy for Jeff."

> Just at present, Hart's principal fighting qualifications – pluck and endurance – are the very things that would place him in a serious predicament were he left alone in a Queensberry enclosure with the modern pine-bender, big Jim Jeffries. ...
>
> The Kentuckian's grit and powers of assimilation would only serve to prolong the agony.[259]

Hart's defense was criticized: "The only redeeming qualities he possesses is rare gameness and a willingness to force matters. But if he should run into one of Jeffries' pile-driving solar plexus punches with the frequency that he displayed last evening in stopping Johnson's wallops it would be 'curtains' for the Kentuckian in short order."

Two weeks after the fight, the *Police Gazette* was tough on Hart, and again questioned the decision, saying,

> As the critical public was not favorably impressed by the manner in which Hart won from Jack Johnson...there will hardly be any crying demand for such an unequal match [with Jeffries]. ... Hart did not prove himself a first-class pugilist. The only thing that he showed in the scrap was that he was capable of taking a lot of punishment. Johnson's defeat was as big a surprise to Hart as it was to the negro, and although the crowd as a body upheld Referee Greggains, he

---

[256] *Trenton Times*, March 29, 1905; *Philadelphia Press*, March 30, 1905.
[257] *Washington Post*, March 30, 1905.
[258] *Trenton Times, Newark Evening News*, March 30, 1905.
[259] *San Francisco Examiner*, March 30, 1905.

could only find one favorable thing to say in Hart's favor, and that was that he forced the fighting.

At the end of the bout Hart was the worse scarred of the two. His face was so puffed and bruised that one could hardly recognize him. On the other hand Johnson was unmarked.

Bob Fitzsimmons said, "It looks like Johnson received a bad deal, but I'm willing to fight [Hart] if he wants to make the match."

Yet, another week later, another reporter was giving Hart more of a chance against Jeffries, or at least to make a good showing. "It is true that Johnson is not one-third the hitter that Jeffries is, but it must be admitted that the champion is not as clever as Johnson. The deduction is, it seems at this stage, that Hart has a fair chance of making a good fight."

However, another reporter said, "Marvin Hart is now considered the next best man to Jeffries, but to borrow an expression from another game, there is a broad streak of daylight between Jeffries and Hart."

The upset Johnson attempted to secure a rematch with Hart. "Johnson has been saying some sassy things about the Louisville idol." However, Hart insisted that never again would he fight a colored man.[260]

In 1910, when discussing Johnson's abilities and responding to Jack's critics, Battling Nelson said,

> A number of scribes lay particular stress on the Johnson-Hart battle held in San Francisco, at which I was a ringside spectator and on which I had $40 bet on Hart against $100 on Johnson. The only reason I bet on Hart was that I was figuring that the promoters were laying plans for a championship battle between Hart and Jeffries, and that if there was anything crooked the white man would win, which he did through the referee, and only through the referee.
>
> After the twentieth round was about one minute old I offered to sell my bet [on Hart], which would amount to $140 if I won, all for a five-dollar note, to Billy Benner, with whom I had made the bet. He said: "No. If you want $5 I will give it to you, but I wouldn't buy the bet." The next thing we knew the referee held Hart's hand aloft, signifying he was the winner. If that's what they call quitting or laying down on Johnson's part I am willing to string with the quitters all the time.[261]

Nelson and Benner both believed that Johnson had won clearly.

---

[260] *Police Gazette*, April 15, 22, 29, 1905, May 13, 1905.
[261] *San Francisco Evening Post*, June 27, 1910.

CHAPTER 14

Passed Over Again

Following his controversial decision loss to Marvin Hart, which he and others hotly disputed, Jack Johnson got away from the West Coast and primarily fought in the East.

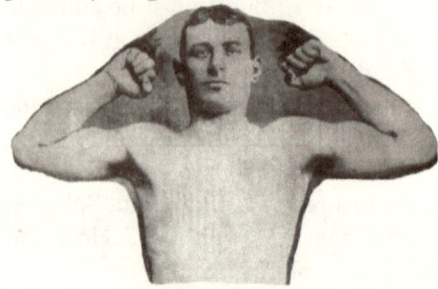
Jim Jeffords

Just under a month after the Hart fight, on April 25, 1905 in Philadelphia, against 24-year-old 6'4" over 200-pound white Jim Jeffords, who had over 30 fights of experience, the "dusky" Johnson was in control throughout, punishing the head and body, bloodying his nose, decking the much larger man in the 3rd round with a right to the jaw, and in the 4th round knocking out Jeffords with a vicious left uppercut into the solar plexus.[262]

The hard-hitting Johnson made a splendid impression. "Cool and clever, without any fancy movements, Johnson calmly followed Jeffords around the ring and made nearly every one of his leads count." Conversely, Jack evaded Jeffords' blows with ease.

One writer suggested that at times, "joker" Johnson appeared to be carrying Jeffords, playing with him, engaging in "phony tactics." "He simply stalled with Jeffords, and but for the latter's thoughtless punch in the last round the chances are that Johnson would have permitted the bout to have gone the limit."

Johnson's performance "strengthened the belief of the spectators that he was robbed of the decision in his recent battle with Marvin Hart in San Francisco or that the latter battle was not on the level." Jack said he could beat Hart every morning before breakfast. Hart's refusal to rematch him helped bolster Jack's claims of robbery.[263]

Hart responded, saying, "That coon has enough yellow in him to paint the City Hall. It cropped out in his fight with me so plainly that his own seconds noticed it. ... Johnson is a fancy boxer, but when he gets stung he is strictly a 'tin-canner and staller.' I'll never fight another negro."[264]

---

[262] In 1898, Jeffords had boxed a 4-round exhibition with James Jeffries. He scored an 1899 KO4 over a shot Peter Jackson in Pete's last fight. Jeffords had suffered a knockout loss to Gus Ruhlin, but also held a 6-round no decision victory over Ruhlin. Jeffords was 5-1-2 in his last eight bouts, which took place over the last five months, so he was fight-sharp.
[263] *Philadelphia Inquirer, Public Ledger, Record, Press, Evening Bulletin*, April 26, 1905.
[264] *Police Gazette*, May 13, 1905.

A week later, on May 2, 1905 in Philadelphia, in a rematch with Black Bill, the biggest crowd of the season saw Johnson dominate, decking Bill in the 3rd and 4th rounds four or five times with hooks and uppercuts, until a series of body blows in the 4th round sent him down for the full count.[265]

The *Philadelphia Inquirer* said Bill had endured a fierce grueling from "Jack Johnsing." The *Philadelphia Press* said Bill's lips were puffed to twice their size and his nose was swollen.[266]

That same day, it was reported that James J. Jeffries would be retiring. Jeffries said he was retiring because there was no big money fight on the horizon. He even went so far as to say that pugilism did not pay. However, if he had remained a boilermaker, his first profession, "he would probably have still been working 10 hours or more a day for the munificent sum of about $18 or $20 a week." Jeffries was rich, and no longer needed to box.[267]

At that time, Marvin Hart arrived in Philadelphia to box John Willie. He and Johnson were in the same town at the same time. Marvin refused to box Jack again while there, although Johnson was willing to box Hart. The impression was growing that Hart had not truly earned the decision over Johnson, and the verdict was the result of something nefarious. The *Philadelphia Record* said,

> The match between Jack Johnson and Marvin Hart, as well as the result of the same, seems to have been cleverly planned, but, according to the old Scotch saying, "the best-laid plans of mice and men aft gang aglee," the public appears to have gotten wise, and there is little demand for a fight between Hart and Jeffries, for which all the fine work was done. It may be easy to fool some of the people, but you can't fool them all the time.
>
> Johnson is still in Philadelphia, and he has shown by the way in which he so quickly disposed of Jeffords and Black Bill that he can punch considerably. Hart is still of the notion that he will not fight a colored man again. Hence, there is no chance to see Johnson and Marvin in a bout in this city, although such a contest would draw a big house. Hart probably knows his own business best, but a demonstration of the way he says he made a punching-bag and a foot racer of Johnson in California would be more convincing to the sporting men of this city than any mere recitation of his recollection of what took place in the ring in San Francisco.[268]

Continuing his weekly fighting clip in Philadelphia, on May 9, 1905, Jack Johnson took on 25-year-old Joe Jeannette and 28-year-old Walter Johnson, both black, each in scheduled 3-round bouts on the same night.

---

[265] Since nearly being stopped by Johnson in a February 1904 6-round no-decision bout, Black Bill had boxed Joe Walcott in a 6-round no-decision which some said Bill had won, while others said it was a draw. Other results included a 1904 D15 Young Peter Jackson and a 1905 KO2 Joe Jeannette.
[266] *Philadelphia Inquirer, Philadelphia Press, Philadelphia Record, Philadelphia Evening Bulletin*, May 3, 1905.
[267] *Philadelphia Record, Seattle Post Intelligencer*, May 3, 1902; *Philadelphia Record*, May 7, 1905.
[268] *Philadelphia Record*, May 7, 1905.

Joe Jeannette

Despite the game Jeannette's aggression throughout the 3 rounds, Johnson hurt and decked him at least once in each round, and "it was easily seen that Johnson was his master as a boxer."

After a minute of rest, next up was Walter Johnson, who had been a professional for 10 years.[269]

Johnson hammered Walter unmercifully, drawing blood from his mouth and punishing his body. In the 3rd round, Jack feinted with his left and then sprang forward with a whipping right to the jaw that sent Walter down and out.[270]

On May 13, 1905, James J. Jeffries officially retired at age 30. Apparently, owing to the fact that most knew or strongly suspected that Marvin Hart had not actually defeated Johnson, there was insufficient public demand and therefore insufficient financial incentive for Jeffries to fight Hart. Therefore, without a viable white foe, Jeff decided to retire. Most white folk said that Jeffries was the greatest pugilist who ever lived.[271]

Regarding which contenders were most viable or deserving to fight for the vacant title, the *Police Gazette* said, "Hart looms up as the most eligible because of his victory over Jack Johnson, a win that has been questioned in many quarters." Despite the questionable victory over Johnson, no black fighter was mentioned as amongst the strongest aspirants for the title, for it was understood that only white men could or would be allowed to fight for Jeff's vacant crown.[272]

Ultimately, promoters Al Livingston and Dan Egan matched Mavin Hart to fight former light heavyweight champion Jack Root in a fight to the finish, to be held in Reno, Nevada on July 2 for a guaranteed purse of $5,000. Eventually, the promoters paid Jeffries a hefty sum to convince him to referee the bout and declare the winner the new champion.

Johnson was hurt and frustrated by the fact that he was not one of the combatants in the title bout. He felt that he had defeated Hart, who then drew the color line and refused a rematch. Johnson had sparred with Root, who then refused to fight him. Root had been knocked out twice by George Gardner, whom Johnson had decked several times and defeated with ease. But Root was white, which meant that Hart was willing to fight him. So Jack Johnson had to wait while others obtained an opportunity which he had earned, but for his race.

---

[269] Walter Johnson's record included: 1895 D10 Bob Armstrong; 1896 KO17 Willie Lewis; 1899 LKOby7 Ed Martin; 1902 L6 Frank Childs and D6 Klondike; and 1904 LKOby2 and KO4 Bob Armstrong.
[270] *Philadelphia Inquirer, Philadelphia Press, Philadelphia Record, Philadelphia Evening Bulletin*, May 10, 1905.
[271] *Chicago Tribune*, May 14, 1905; *Police Gazette*, May 20, 1905.
[272] *Police Gazette*, June 10, 1905.

Regardless of the color line, Johnson wanted to fight the winner of Hart-Root. "Jack Johnson threatens to retire from the roped arena if he does not succeed in getting a match with the winner of the Jack Root and Marvin Hart battle."[273]

Freeman, June 10, 1905

On June 26, 1905 in Philadelphia, Jack Johnson fought Jack Munroe in a scheduled 6-round no-decision bout. Munroe had beaten Tom Sharkey, but was stopped in 2 rounds by Jeffries. The 5'11 ½" 28-year-old Munroe was muscular, thickly built, and weighed about 220 pounds.

Despite weighing much less, Johnson outclassed Munroe throughout. Munroe tried to rough it and work at close quarters, attacking the body, but he could not land cleanly, and he left himself open to counters to the head and body, often walking right into the well-timed punches. Johnson alternated between pummeling him with ferocious blows, staggering and badly hurting Munroe, but then boxing cautiously. Whenever Munroe attacked and picked up the pace, Johnson fought hard and staggered him. This caused some to think Johnson was carrying him, for when Munroe backed off, he backed off too.

Jack Munroe

---

[273] *Police Gazette,* July 1, 1905; *Philadelphia Record,* May 28, June 21, 1905.

Nevertheless, in the 2nd round, Johnson decked Munroe with a right jolt to the chin. In the 3rd round, a right uppercut drew blood from the miner's mouth. In the 5th round, a Johnson right uppercut opened a cut over Munroe's left eye. In the 6th and final round, Munroe rallied, and as a result, Johnson punished him. A vicious right opened an ugly gash on the miner's cheek-bone near the eye. Another blow further opened the cut over his left eye, turning it into a large gash. The cuts bled freely and almost blinded Munroe. Johnson hammered away, wobbling Munroe, who at every opportunity clinched and wrestled in order to survive. His legs were unsteady, and he was lucky to hear the final bell.

Johnson had dominated and pummeled Munroe at will, dropped him, cut him up, and had him hurt and hanging on often in order to survive.

However, rather than laud Johnson's performance, several members of the press denigrated Munroe and criticized Johnson as not being dominant enough, having failed to win by knockout. Some believed that Johnson was under a pull, for several times it appeared that he could have stopped him. Regardless, the *Philadelphia Press* unfairly said Johnson "failed miserably" to impress anyone that he could be champion.[274]

A *Police Gazette* writer said Johnson battered Munroe so badly that afterwards he was "almost unrecognizable by his friends." Still, Jim Jeffries had blown through Munroe so quickly and easily that this writer felt that Johnson's performance did not add to his reputation.

Some of the white press never overlooked an opportunity to criticize the black Johnson's dominant performances as not being dominant enough.

> [T]he "Coon" must have left his alleged knowledge of the scientific art of scrapping in his dressing room. It was a roughhouse battle, devoid of science on one side and almost everything else on the other. Jeff need not have drawn the color line, for he could have met both of these men in the same ring simultaneously, so far as their ability to do him is concerned.[275]

One week later, on July 3, 1905 under the hot, over 100-degree Reno, Nevada sun, in a fight to the finish refereed by retired champion Jim Jeffries, 28-year-old 195-pound Marvin Hart knocked out 29-year-old 170-pound Jack Root in the 12th round with a single right to the body to win the vacant world's heavyweight championship. Root outboxed Hart early, and brutally dropped him with a right to the jaw at the end of the 7th round. However, Hart showed his usual ability to absorb punishment and recover, as well as his knockout power.[276]

Although Johnson challenged Hart, the new champion openly drew the color line, saying, "I will fight any heavy-weight in the world except niggers." He also said,

---

[274] *Philadelphia Record, Public Ledger, Inquirer, Press, Evening Bulletin,* June 27, 1905.
[275] *Police Gazette,* July 15, 1905.
[276] *San Francisco Call, Examiner, Evening Post, Bulletin, Chronicle,* July 4-5, 1905.

> I am now ready to meet anybody in the world, except a negro. I fought Johnson because he was said to be the next best man to Jeffries. I will not fight another negro. When I fought Johnson it was very much against my will, but as I had defeated all the big ones outside of Jeffries I was obliged to take on Johnson.

The *San Francisco Evening Post* criticized Hart for drawing the color line, especially given his questionable decision over Johnson:

> At the end of the twenty rounds, with rings boxed all around him, the referee practically made him a present of the contest. A draw would not have been giving Johnson the best of it.

> With Root's scalp hanging to his belt the first statement uttered by Hart was to the effect that he was ready to fight any man in the world, barring a colored man (meaning, of course, Johnson). In other words, Hart is not particularly anxious for Arthur's game, and the only way to side step is to draw the color line.

Although famous referee George Siler recognized Hart as the new champion, he said,

> Undoubtedly the best big man in the business at present is Jack Johnson, the colored heavyweight champion, and Hart shows excellent judgment in drawing the color line.

> It is the opinion of all fair-minded witnesses that Johnson beat Hart in their recent fight at San Francisco, and undoubtedly can repeat the trick, so it probably is better for the game that Hart drew the color line. We have never had a colored heavyweight champion and it is too late to change the order of things.

The *Police Gazette* said Hart's fight with Johnson was an "alleged fake fight," for Hart could not lick Johnson "on the level," and that was why he drew the color line; to avoid another meeting.[277]

The *San Francisco Evening Post* said Hart needed to beat Johnson in order to obtain clear fully earned recognition as champion:

> The memory of the recent Hart-Johnson fight, when nearly every report was that Hart was rushing and was being cut to pieces with jabs and hooks...does not linger pleasantly. ... Nobody is especially anxious to see Johnson beat Hart. At the same time, the fact that Hart has drawn the color line will certainly not boost him. Johnson is one of the cleverest big men that ever stepped into a ring. ...

> Johnson will be the 'yellow peril' to be avoided for a long time. He showed this by the way he pranced around 'Miner' Jack Munroe, outclassing him and punching him at will.

---

[277] *Reno Evening Gazette*, July 3, 1905; *San Francisco Chronicle*, July 4, 5, 1905; *San Francisco Evening Post*, July 5, 1905; *Philadelphia Inquirer*, July 9, 1905; *Police Gazette*, July 29, 1905.

Hart is the heavyweight champion as long as Jeffries is out of the ring. ... The best way for Hart to try to earn Jeffries' crown is to wipe out the smudge left on his record by Jack Johnson, for, though Hart did receive the decision it was anything but a clean one.[278]

Gus Ruhlin said Hart should fight himself or Jack Johnson. Gus never had fought a colored man, and did not intend to start now (though he didn't mind using blacks like Ed Martin as sparring partners). However, he admired Johnson, saying,

> Don't think that I'm underrating this man Johnson. Outside of Jeffries, I think that this fellow Johnson can trim the world. Yes, Fitzsimmons and the whole bunch of them. I only saw him in one fight, but he's a marvel. ... The way he handles himself is great, surely. Why, he has a chance even with Jeff, in my mind. Jeff was a bit leary of him, too. I'm not saying that Jim was afraid of him, you know, but he didn't want any of it if he could get out of it. You know he drew the color line on Johnson, and he had met four coons before that time. I guess he knew a little about Johnson.[279]

Morris Harris

On July 13, 1905 in Philadelphia, Jack Johnson again took on two black men in one night in scheduled 3-round bouts: Morris Harris and Black Bill.[280]

Johnson went at Harris like a whirlwind, decking him four times in the 1st round until the referee stopped the bout. It was Harris' first knockout loss.

The *Philadelphia Record* was impressed, saying, "Harris was a mere plaything in his hands and it showed clearly that there was something wrong with the victory of Marvin Hart over Johnson in California."

The *Philadelphia Press* said the next man, Black Bill, stayed the 3 rounds with Johnson, but was beaten badly, mostly hanging on to save himself.

Conversely, the *Philadelphia Record* and *Philadelphia Evening Bulletin* believed that Johnson could have stopped Bill if he had tried, but he allowed him to last, obviously holding back, demonstrating kind-hearted generosity. Johnson "faked" and feinted, laughing at Bill's efforts to hit him, while not really trying to hit him back much. Bill was Johnson's "old friend," so he "just missed him" for old times' sake. Jack said the reason he did not stop Bill was because he had a sore hand after stopping Harris.[281]

---

[278] *San Francisco Evening Post*, July 13, 1905.
[279] *Philadelphia Inquirer*, July 9, 1905; *Louisville Courier-Journal*, July 11, 1905; *San Francisco Evening Post*, July 17, 1905.
[280] Morris Harris' record contained at least 19 known bouts that dated back to 1903. He held two 6-round no-decision victories over Joe Jeannette, in 1904 and 1905.
[281] *Philadelphia Press, Philadelphia Record, Philadelphia Evening Bulletin*, July 14, 1905.

27-year-old 190-pound Johnson fought again a mere five days later, on July 18, 1905 in Chelsea, Massachusetts, for a fifth bout with 25-year-old 210-pound Sandy Ferguson, the local Chelsea resident who was bigger, taller, and had a longer reach. Ferguson was such a huge local hero that he actually was the 3 to 1 betting favorite.

The *Boston Globe* said if Ferguson beat Johnson, he would be first in line to fight Hart for the title. Hence, he was highly motivated.[282]

The *Boston Post* said 4,000 people tried to cram into the Pythian rink, a place where 2,000 could not have been accommodated comfortably. As high as $10 was offered for tickets, and thousands had to be turned away.

Ventilation inside the rink was poor, which made the environment even hotter on this already hot summer day. The closely-wedged-together mob sweltered and perspired freely, the beads of sweat rolling off in large drops to the floor in the oppressive environment. Hundreds smoked cigars, adding to the heat.

Johnson had Joe Walcott in his corner. Ferguson had manager Alec McLean and Bob Armstrong. At 9:30 p.m., the fight was on.

Ferguson started off as the aggressor, winning the first two rounds with his left jab to the face and right to the body, fighting furiously, even landing a couple rights to the jaw. Johnson started off cautiously and conservatively, but in each round gradually increased his pace, while Sandy started showing the effects of the heat and his own fast pace. In the 2nd round, Jack drew blood from Sandy's nose with a jab. They kept exchanging in exciting fashion. As the rounds progressed, though fighting hard, Ferguson was being worn down. He began clinching and holding on more, but whenever he did, Johnson freed his hands and worked.

By the 7th round, despite Sandy's fierce rushes and aggression, Johnson was outgeneraling him and viciously hitting the body in the clinches. The red-headed Ferguson roughed matters, wrestling and forcing Johnson back by sheer strength. But Johnson was a master at infighting, and smashed

---

[282] *Boston Post*, July 17, 18, 1905.; *Boston Globe*, July 18, 1905. Ferguson's recent results included a 1904 20-round decision loss to Marvin Hart, which many thought Ferguson won or at least earned a draw. Sandy had nearly 50 fights of experience to that point.

blow after blow into his body. Ferguson called to the referee, "Make him stop." The *Boston Post* asked, "Was Sandy beginning to quit? He was yelling for no good reason."

While still entangled in each other's grasp, frenzied by the body punches that Johnson sent in, Ferguson's face turned purple with rage and he lost his head completely. In the "rawest manner ever seen in New England," while holding onto Johnson, three times Ferguson deliberately fouled by violently smashing his knees one at a time into Johnson's groin with great force, first the left knee, then right knee, and then left knee again.

Johnson reeled and went down to the floor in a heap, badly disabled and writhing in great pain, amid the groans, howls, shouts, and hisses of the immense gathering which had seen the fouls and were disgusted by Ferguson's horrific breaches of the rules. Referee Bill Crowley disqualified Ferguson, which was "the only thing he could do." "Crowley was right. ... Johnson had been fouled and fouled in a most vicious manner."

The local papers agreed that the pair had fought a rattling good contest full of action, but Ferguson spoiled it with deliberate fouls. The *Boston Post* believed that Ferguson wanted to lose on a foul, because he made his intentional fouling quite obvious to everyone. Some thought Ferguson was afraid of losing on the merits, sensed that the tide of the fight was shifting, regardless of his best efforts, and he grew frustrated. Many called Ferguson a coward and a quitter.[283]

Joe Grim, the Marvel of the Ring.

On July 24, 1905, just six days later, returning to Philadelphia again, Johnson took on Italian Joe Grim. Born Saverio Giannone, the durable 24-year-old Grim was famous for his ability to last the distance, including against the hard-punching Bob Fitzsimmons. Hence, when a fighter was called a "Joe Grim," it meant he could take a licking and keep on ticking.

5,000 people jammed the arena to a point of suffocation, for every seat was taken. Hundreds were turned away, unable to gain admission, and thousands of Italians blocked the street outside, waiting to hear the result.

The *Press* said Grim would be dropped nine times in 6 rounds. The *Public Ledger* said Grim was down twice in the 2nd round, once in the 4th, five times in the 5th round, and eight times in the 6th round. The *Philadelphia Evening Bulletin* said Johnson dropped the blood-bespattered Grim to the floor eighteen times.

With just a few seconds left in the 6th and final round, Johnson decked Grim with a clean straight right. He was out cold on his back, but at the count of two, the referee stopped counting, for Grim was saved by the bell; the only reason he was not officially recorded as a knockout victim. In

---

[283] *Boston Globe, Boston Herald, Boston Post,* July 19, 1905; *San Francisco Evening Post,* July 24, 26, 1905.

reality, though, Johnson had knocked him out, and for the first time ever, Joe Grim had to be carried to his corner at the end of a contest.[284]

The *Police Gazette* reported that Grim bled so much that the ring was slippery from his blood. He was out cold for five minutes.[285]

In late July, the black-owned *Topeka Plaindealer* asked whether the white man was civilized, and answered the question in the negative. As soon as a white man learned that someone had colored blood, he looked about with dread, uneasiness, and hysteria. The white man tried in every conceivable way to close all avenues for negro livelihood, even importing foreigners to take his place in all classes of labor. Then, as a result, "because his castaway sits idle, he is called immoral, unfit for society of a white man, worthless."

Often, when a white woman was engaging in a consensual relationship with a black man, if she feared detection, "the old cry of rape or assault goes out from the lips of this virtuous white lady, and a poor Negro is lynched for daring to be near the premises of one of the best families of the South. Then come the yellow journals with a photo of a maiden of brave and pure blood, exonerated of all guilt." When blacks were lynched, the perpetrators of the lynching never were found or prosecuted.

> The white man's histories are false, even their holy book, teaching only the servility of the darker races and the superiority of the whites, from time 'immemorial' – base lies. His Christianity has long since failed as the above conditions show. He is more dishonest than any other race. His declaration of independence is a farce. His municipal governments are a fraud. He is the most envious, egotistic and jealous of human beings and has really grown to believe that this world was made for him to govern and for white men only.[286]

In August 1905, the *Police Gazette* reported, "Marvin Hart says positively that he will never meet Jack Johnson in the ring again." The *Police Gazette* felt that such a declaration put Hart's title claims on the ropes.

> A black man, in my esteem, is entitled to just the same rights and prerogatives, as long as he is cleanly and decent, upright, capable and honest. Both Jeffries and Hart have fought niggers, as they style their colored rivals, before, and why not fight again? .... [W]hen he barred colored men he was thinking of no one on earth but Mr. Johnson.... Mr. Hart knows, as well as he knows that he is alive, that Jack Johnson was entitled to that fight out in San Francisco, and he also knows, I'll bet my boots, that Mr. Johnson can lick him every day in the week, not even barring Sunday.[287]

The *Police Gazette* continually criticized Hart's color line stance:

---

[284] *Philadelphia Press, Philadelphia Public Ledger, Philadelphia Inquirer, Philadelphia Evening Bulletin, Philadelphia Record*, July 25, 1905.
[285] *Police Gazette*, August 12, 19, 1905.
[286] *Topeka Plaindealer*, July 28, 1905.
[287] *Police Gazette*, August 12, September 23, 1905.

Marvin Hart...will probably never know what a peaceful moment is until he fights Jack Johnson, the negro premier, again...

Johnson is a slugger and boxer of no mean ability; in fact, he is one of the best big men in the ring. But Johnson is colored, and the color line has been drawn by Hart, who, following in the footsteps of his predecessor, Jeffries, who so graciously donated the heavyweight championship to the Kentuckian, declares that as long as he is on top, no negro will get the chance of becoming the star of the fistic firmament. This was to be expected. Hart being a Southerner, he would be inviting trouble to fight a negro, so he says. Association between colored men and whites is not countenanced in the South, which fact is well established, and while Hart, for this reason, may have a good excuse for not fighting Johnson, he is not consistent. He once fought him and beat him. That was when Johnson was not what he is today, and no one can blame the negro for pressing his claims for another fight. Hart will find less worthy opponents than the colored man, but, then, race prejudice is a barrier to one of the best boxing cards that could be arranged. It's an unsatisfactory state of affairs that exists in the heavyweight and lightweight classes.[288]

---

[288] *Police Gazette*, August 19, 1905.

CHAPTER 15

The Color Line in the West

In August 1905, Jack Johnson was back in San Francisco, hoping to obtain a fight there. However, no one wanted to fight him. Several openly drew the color line.[289]

Although not coming out of retirement, Jim Jeffries said, "I am not bragging when I say that I could beat all four of them in one night. I mean Hart, Johnson, Ruhlin and McCormick. That Hart-Johnson mill was one of the saddest sketches ever perpetrated on an unsuspecting public." George Siler replied, "To my mind Jeffries is today really more afraid of Johnson than any other man in the ring."[290]

In early September 1905, the Russo-Japanese War ended with Japan having defeated Russia. This unexpected major military victory shocked the West, for the fact that a non-white Asian power had defeated a white European nation challenged racial beliefs about white superiority.

The *Topeka Plaindealer* said the recent brutal burning of another Texas Negro in broad daylight by a mob of over 500 white barbarians who took the law into their own hands for the "old 'chestnut' charge of outraging a white woman," the second time in two months, should be the keynote for blacks of that state to fight back. It said that more often than not, the white woman was having a consensual relationship with a black man, and to save herself, she squealed on him and claimed rape, or to save her black sweetheart and herself, raised the alarm, and the first Negro that was brought to her, she laid the crime on him. "I for one, knowing the condition in the South as I do, do not believe the threadbare lies coming from that or any other section when it is charged that Negroes commit assaults upon the person of white women unwillingly. It is a lie, and a barefaced one at that."

Many newspapers fostered race prejudice. "The reporters of the Associated Press herald their falsehoods to the world and the world becomes prejudiced against the most humble and pathetic people on earth." This writer asked whether Negroes would submit forever to such indignities. The passing of resolutions would do no good. Negroes needed to fight back, defend themselves, and apply the torch in lawless communities that permitted innocent persons to be burned at the stake to satisfy the mob's mad bloodlust. "The Italian way of taking revenge must be the Negro's watchword."[291]

---

[289] *Police Gazette*, September 9, 1905.
[290] *Freeman*, September 9, 1905; *Police Gazette*, September 16, 1905.
[291] *Topeka Plaindealer*, September 15, 1905.

Those same Associated Press reporters often wrote about boxing too. Hence, the sources needed to be considered when evaluating their critiques about black fighters.

Marvin Hart once again said, "What I have said heretofore about fighting negroes goes for all time. I am a Southerner, and do not like them. I was forced to fight Jack Johnson in San Francisco, and I beat him."[292]

The *Police Gazette* again addressed Hart's inconsistency regarding the color line. "Like all Southerners he has inherited a prejudice against the colored race." Marvin previously had refused to fight Joe Walcott, saying, "I am a Southerner and my folks would disown me if I fought you. ... I could not go back to Kentucky again." Yet, Hart had fought Johnson. So his moral stance was not as fixed as he claimed.[293]

Promising 19-year-old heavyweight "wonder" Al Kaufman said he too would draw the color line, no matter how long his career might be.[294]

On October 2, 1905, in Harrison, Arkansas, a white mob stormed the jail and took two black prisoners, one of whom had been charged two days earlier with breaking into a doctor's residence, and transported them outside city limits. After whipping their captives, they ordered them to leave town.

Not fully satisfied, the thirty-member mob returned to town and expanded their rampage through Harrison's black community. They burned down homes, shot out windows, and ordered all black folk to vacate the town. Many fled. Those who remained experienced attacks and harassment.

During early October 1905 in Los Angeles, Jack Johnson was a sparring partner for top middleweight Jack "Twin" Sullivan, who was preparing for a rematch against Tommy Burns, against whom he had fought a March 1905 20-round draw. On October 17, 1905, Sullivan won a 20-round decision over Burns in a lucrative fan-friendly middleweight fight.

Johnson proposed an interesting challenge to Jeffries. The *Times* said,

> The defi of Jack Johnson to go into a real dark room with Jeffries and let the first one who comes out be declared the winner, should contribute largely to the joyfulness of the summer hours. While he is a good fighter he would probably be on the short end of a 4 to 1 bet on the winner. Johnson is probably making his talk because he knows that Jeffries has retired from the game and wouldn't fight him if he was still in it.[295]

In mid-October 1905, Marvin Hart said, "I do not mind what Johnson says. I was forced into fighting him once, but I will not do so again. I am not side-stepping him, but it is against my principles to fight a negro."[296]

The *Topeka Plaindealer* lamented the fact that the white man's policy to belittle the black man stood as a barrier against his progress. "There is a

---

[292] *San Francisco Evening Post*, September 13, 1905.
[293] *Police Gazette*, September 16, 1905.
[294] *Los Angeles Herald*, October 11, 1905.
[295] *Los Angeles Times*, October 13, 1905. This report is interesting because Jeffries later claimed that *he* made this proposal to Johnson, who turned him down.
[296] *Los Angeles Examiner*, October 15, 1905.

disposition in this country to undervalue all that the Negro has done since and before the war to increase the wealth of the nation, and it seems to be the policy of the white man to count for naught the labor of the Negro in bearing the white man's burden for 240 years." Blacks had cleared the forests, built homes, churches, and school houses, and had fought in every war. Yet, he was denied the most common rights of a free man, and the same government "now absolutely refuses to protect him" in the exercise of what rights he did have, for "thousands and thousands of black men have been murdered in this country." Because "God made them black the Negroes are condemned by the whites, and no doubt many have condemned God for making a black man." Despite all the obstacles and condemnation that blacks had to endure, "the Negro is not allowed to hold office in many parts of this country for fear of political domination. ... and all manner of hellish schemes are devised and practiced by the whites to check and retard the progress of the Negro."[297]

George Siler said colored boxers were in poor circumstances. Black fighters were not being given the chance to prove themselves, for white fighters were "greedy" and fearful that they would not get all of the money were they to fight blacks. Hence they drew the color line. "It is not a case of qualification but it is greed. For if any thing the colored 'pug' is altogether too powerful in science and muscle – his ability to stand punishment and his knowledge of delivering punishment is too great." Men like Marvin Hart "should be laughed at whenever they speak of barring colored fighters." Because of prejudice, blacks had to accept uneven challenges and give whites the best of the financial arrangements in order to obtain bouts.[298]

Jack Johnson said he would allow Marvin Hart to dictate the terms of a rematch between them, for he only wanted to get him into the ring again.

Police Gazette writer Sam Austin wanted another battle to take place between Hart and Johnson, to "prove the black man to be all that I have claimed for him."[299]

Not only was Johnson not successful at getting Hart to fight him again, he was not able to get anyone to fight him on the West Coast at all.

---

[297] *Topeka Plaindealer*, October 27, 1905.
[298] *Freeman*, November 25, 1905.
[299] *Police Gazette*, December 2, 1905.

CHAPTER 16

Black East

Having been unsuccessful at obtaining any bout during the several months that he was out West, Jack Johnson returned to the East Coast, where he would fight other black boxers; the only ones willing to face him.

On November 25, 1905 in Philadelphia, Jack Johnson boxed Joe Jeannette for the second time. The local *Philadelphia Public Ledger* said Johnson outclassed Jeannette for a round and a half, thumping him in lively fashion, but then during the 2nd round, Jack was disqualified as the result of an "alleged foul." This writer saw Johnson land a ripping right to the jaw and Joe drop to the floor, writhing in agony, claiming to have been struck a foul blow. He was taken to the dressing room, where the club physician substantiated the claim, and the referee promptly disqualified Johnson. Unsure abou the legitimacy of it all, "It is understood that the police proposed to keep Johnson, Jeannette and the club official under surveillance."[300]

Philadelphia Inquirer,
November 27, 1905

The *Police Gazette* reported that in the 2nd round, Johnson "rushed madly at Joe and swinging a wicked left it landed low on the New Yorker, who dropped to the floor, where he lay writhing in agony for some time, until he was carried to his dressing room."[301]

Ultimately, the foul, if there was one, was regarded as an accident, and the bout did not tarnish Johnson's status as the world's elite colored heavyweight. In fact, the fight did not garner a great deal of attention. Besides, Johnson and Jeannette would fight again a mere week later to settle matters.

Some children sued the Asheville, North Carolina Board of Education for refusing to allow them into a white public school. The children contended that they had no negro blood in their veins, but instead their ancestor was of Portuguese ancestry. In late November, a jury found in the children's favor, so they could attend the white schools.[302]

Just six days after the Jeannette bout, on December 1, 1905 in Baltimore, Jack Johnson took on local black fighter Young Peter Jackson in a scheduled 12-round no-decision bout. Although much smaller than

---

[300] *Philadelphia Public Ledger,* November 26, 1905.
[301] *Police Gazette,* December 9, 1905.
[302] *Baltimore Sun,* November 26, 1905.

Johnson, the sturdily built 5'6" middleweight Jackson had over 100 fights of experience, far more than Johnson, and still was only 28 years old. The well-respected veteran's results included KO13 Jack O'Brien, KO4 Joe Walcott, and D15 Sam Langford.

Because Johnson was anxious to obtain a match, he agreed to stop Jackson in 12 rounds or accept the small end of the boxers' share of the receipts. The confident Jackson laughed, for he had been stopped only twice in his career, and not since 1900, five years ago.[303]

Throughout, Johnson did the work, while Jackson mostly played defense, ducking, covering, clinching, and moving, fighting only to survive, rarely throwing punches. Johnson decked him twice in the 6th, once in the 8th (going through the ropes from a body blow), twice in the 9th (again going through the ropes), and twice in the 10th round (rights to the jaw). Johnson punished him as much

Young Peter Jackson

as he could, and tried to stop him, but the purely defensive Jackson used every survival tactic in the book in order to last the full 12 rounds.

The local newspapers agreed that Johnson was by far the more expert boxer, and had been superior throughout, dropping Jackson seven times. Owing to their pre-fight agreement, for going the distance, Jackson earned 75% of the fighter's share of the purse to Johnson's 25%.[304]

The next day, on December 2, 1905, Jack was back in Philadelphia again to face Joe Jeannette, only seven days after he had been disqualified for an accidental low blow against Jeannette.

The *Philadelphia Public Ledger* reported that Johnson defeated Jeannette over 6 fast rounds, repeatedly catching the plucky and aggressive Jeannette with counters, dropping him once in the 5th round, and thrice more in the 6th round.[305]

The *Philadelphia Inquirer* said "Jack Johnsing" vindicated himself, proving "he is the New Yorker's master."

Joe Jeannette

Regardless, despite scoring four knockdowns, some unfairly questioned Johnson's punching power, simply because he had failed to win by knockout. They still were not sure about Johnson, for "his hitting ability and his gameness are yet to be demonstrated here." "Taking him all in all, he is the hardest fighter to get a straight line on that has appeared in this section of the country for years."[306]

---

[303] *Baltimore Sun*, November 26, 1905.
[304] *Baltimore Sun, Baltimore American*, December 2, 1905.
[305] *Philadelphia Public Ledger* December 3, 1905.
[306] *Philadelphia Inquirer,* December 4, 1905.

One *Police Gazette* report was critical as well, feeling that he should have stopped Jeannette. "Somebody ought to tell Jack Johnson that being fancy and 'gallus' don't get a 'coon' anything in the fighting game."[307]

Jack Johnson had fought thirteen times in 1905.

In the winter's biggest fight, on December 20, 1905 in San Francisco, 8,000 fans saw 28-year-old Philadelphia Jack O'Brien win the world light-heavyweight championship by defeating 42-year-old Bob Fitzsimmons, who retired following the conclusion the 13th round. O'Brien had dropped Fitz in the 3rd and 8th rounds en route to the victory.

Zeke Abrams posted $2,500 as a side bet in a challenge from Jack Johnson to fight Jack O'Brien. He noted that Young Peter Jackson had defeated O'Brien once, and Johnson had handled Jackson with ease. He was certain that Johnson could whip O'Brien.

However, "O'Brien refuses absolutely to fight Jack Johnson at any time. He says Johnson would not be a drawing card, and besides he has drawn the color line." Yet, O'Brien had fought other black boxers.

Johnson told the *Police Gazette* that he "doesn't understand why O'Brien should draw the color line since…he fought George Cole, Black Bill and many other colored aspirants within the past five years."[308]

O'Brien's color-line stance was inconsistent and selective. He once had drawn the color-line against Joe Walcott. The *Police Gazette* had then said, "The Philadelphian bases his refusal on Walcott's color, but he probably has another reason."[309] O'Brien eventually fought Walcott (1902 ND6).

At that time, a 1905 popular novel entitled *The Clansman: An Historical Romance of the Ku Klux Klan*, by Thomas Dixon, Jr., a Baptist minister and former North Carolina state legislator, had been converted into a play, and was set to start performances in New York on January 9, 1906. *The Clansman* was influential in promoting the ideology that helped support the Klan. It portrayed blacks as inferior to whites, and advocated to Northerners to maintain racial segregation; the point being that when blacks were freed, they turned savage and robbed and plundered from whites, and when allowed to hold public office, they over-taxed the people and enacted laws that encouraged interracial marriage. The Klan needed to be organized to overthrow Republicans, restore white supremacy, and ensure that blacks be kept separate from whites. It was predicated upon the theory that the Negro was unfit for citizenship. Both the book and the play were so popular that they later inspired D. W. Griffith's 1915 film, *The Birth of a Nation*. Many whites declared the play to be a true epic of the South. However, it aroused a storm of protests from blacks, who attacked it as ridiculously false and dangerous.

The *Freeman* concluded that Dixon, Jr. was using the play to argue that "neither religion or education, or both combined, can make men of that part of the human family which God made black instead of white."

---

[307] *Police Gazette*, December 23, 1905.
[308] *Los Angeles Times*, January 3, 1906; *Los Angeles Herald*, January 7, 1906; *Police Gazette*, January 27, 1906.
[309] *National Police Gazette*, October 19, 1901.

Although Dixon was a minister who preached the gospel, his play was inflaming "the passions of the white race to murder the black people."[310]

On January 15, 1906 in Butte, Montana, after Marvin Hart had been dropped in the 1st round en route to scoring a KO2 over Pat Callahan in an exhibition bout, the local press said fans "no longer doubt but that Jack Johnson and Jack Root both had him jabbed to death as was reported when he fought those men, and that it was only his ability to stand punishment that enabled him to defeat them."[311]

Hart was scheduled to defend his heavyweight crown against Tommy Burns, whose original name was Noah Brusso. Burns was coming off a 20-round decision loss to Jack Sullivan at middleweight, but claimed the reason for the loss was that he was weight drained. Burns was a gate draw, so promoter Tom McCarey made a title fight with him as the challenger. Hart probably took the fight because he figured that a man whose last bout was fought at 158 pounds was too small to defeat him.[312]

So, once again, instead of being given his rightfully earned opportunity at the crown, Jack Johnson had to sit by as a former middleweight who was coming off a loss in a 158-pound bout was granted a world heavyweight title shot. Imagine the frustration.

On January 16, 1906 in New York, Jack Johnson again met Joe Jeannette, this time in a 3-round no-decision bout. At that time, New York was allowing only very short 3- or 4-round no-decision bouts.[313]

The *New York World* reported that Johnson vs. Jeannette was a very close 3-round bout, but Johnson seemed to have the edge. Honors were even in the first two rounds. Jeannette was the aggressor, landing stiff jabs to the face and body blows, but Johnson countered hard with left swings to the face and stiff uppercuts to the body. In the last round, Johnson had the best of the fighting, landing many hard smashes to the face and wind at close quarters.[314]

---

[310] *Freeman*, January 6, 1906; *Topeka Plaindealer*, March 2, 1906.
[311] *Butte Intermountain*, January 16, 1906.
[312] *Police Gazette*, February 3, 1906.
[313] *Police Gazette*, January 13, 1906. Since last fighting Johnson in December, that same month Jeannette had stopped black middleweight Sam Langford, who retired after the 8th round. To that point, Langford had nearly 50 bouts of experience, so it was a quality victory for Jeannette.
[314] *New York World*, January 16, 17, 1906.

KEEPING HIM PLUMP.

Freeman, December 2, 1905

THE WAYS OF THE HEATHERN.

"WHATSOEVER YE WOULD THAT MEN DO UNTO YOU, DO YE EVEN SO UNTO THEM."

Is this the way for Christian Nations to aid in bringing---"Peace on Earth, Good Will to Men?"

Freeman, December 23, 1905

CHAPTER 17

A New Champion

On February 23, 1906 in Los Angeles, before a crowd of 5,000, 175-pound Tommy Burns won the world heavyweight championship when he won a clear 20-round decision over 195-pound Marvin Hart.

According to the *Los Angeles Express*, Hart, the "so called heavyweight champion," made a "wretched showing." Burns used straight lefts to the face and then bore into repeated clinches. He "stepped in and out at will, sending lefts to the big fellow's nose, eyes and jaw and he hugged his way into the clinches, danced tantalizingly before the helpless bulk in front of him and grinned at his seconds." Hart had a cut, swollen, and bleeding face, and "he spit blood from the bruises on his lips." Burns was unmarked and unhurt. There was no doubt about the decision.

The *Los Angeles Times* harshly called Hart a "monumental dub" and a "big stiff." Conversely, Burns was "quick, active, strong, confident and courageous." "It was a battle of a big man against a little one who jumped in and jabbed and then jumped away or hugged himself safe into a clinch."

The *Los Angeles Examiner* said, "Burns is a quick, shifty fellow, who can hit and go away or hit and go in as suits his pleasure. ... He could hit Hart wherever and whenever he pleased." "He went in and fought, and when fighting seemed to him too hazardous, he grappled and ducked. ... It was hit and hug with Burns through the long, dreary twenty rounds." Another *Examiner* reporter harshly said, "The reign of the Pretender is over. If Marvin Hart ever had the slightest claim on the heavyweight title, he lost it last night." "Burns fought a great defensive fight. He took no chances. It was jab and clinch, jab and clinch, and Referee Eyton wore himself out tearing Burns away from his victim."

W. W. Naughton said Hart was very willing, slugging and cuffing, but failed to accomplish anything. "About the only thing accomplished was to show that Marvin Hart is a poor apology as a world's champion."[315]

The *Los Angeles Herald* said Burns outpointed, outfought, and outgeneraled Hart in every round to earn a decisive victory in a pretty exhibition. "Those who accepted Hart as champion must also accept Burns as the new champion."[316]

Jack Johnson was irked. He felt that he had defeated Hart clearly, yet Hart obtained the decision and the title shot, and then refused to face him again owing to his color. Then a former middleweight who had lost his previous bout at middleweight secured a heavyweight title shot and now

---

[315] *Los Angeles Express, Los Angeles Daily Times, Los Angeles Examiner*, February 24, 1906.
[316] *Los Angeles Herald*, February 24, 25, 1906.

was world champion, winning by using similar tactics that Johnson had used against Hart; but receiving plaudits and the decision.

Even the *San Francisco Bulletin* said the San Francisco public had been unable to forget Hart's bout with Jack Johnson, who "outpointed him," despite the referee's decision. "That one fight cooked Hart's goose with local fight fans as far as taking him seriously as a champion."

Initially, Tommy Burns did not overtly draw the color line. He said,

> I do not draw the color line. If Jack Johnson, Jack O'Brien or any other fighter in the world wants to meet me I will be ready to talk business in a couple weeks. Heretofore I have gone out of my class and weakened myself fighting at the middleweight limit. I was twenty pounds heavier tonight and fought stronger than ever before.[317]

However, despite what he said, Burns did not make a match with Johnson, and was not anxious to do so.

In subsequent days and weeks, Johnson vainly attempted to obtain matches with any of the top white heavyweights. None would fight him. Once again, the decision in the Johnson-Hart bout was acknowledged to have been a "raw bit of work. Johnson won a block."

The fight that the white press and white public most wanted to see, and which would generate a great deal of revenue, was Tommy Burns vs. Jack O'Brien. Like Burns, O'Brien was another white light-heavyweight-sized heavyweight. Not a fan of a black challenger to the crown, the *Los Angeles Herald* wrote, "If Burns meets and defeats O'Brien he will have a clear and undisputed right to the title." Negotiations would be ongoing for several months. Once again, the big black Jack Johnson was left on the outside looking in.[318]

---

[317] *San Francisco Bulletin*, February 24, 1906.
[318] *Los Angeles Herald*, March 25, 27, 1906.

Tommy Burns

CHAPTER 18

Continuing Proof

Frozen out of the heavyweight championship title picture, Jack Johnson scheduled a 15-round bout to be held in mid-March 1906 in Baltimore against Joe Jeannette. Joe had been having the same trouble as Johnson in obtaining matches with top white fighters. "The old cry of the color line has been the howl raised every time." Jeannette instilled enough fear into white heavyweights such that they had to use the color line to avoid meeting him. Hence, to earn money, he and Johnson were fighting each other yet again.

The *Baltimore Sun* said, "Everything that Johnson does in the ring is noted all over the country, because he is believed by many to be the only possible successor to Champion James Jeffries at this stage of affairs."

> Johnson is well known the country over as one of the best colored heavyweights who ever stepped between the ropes. His color has been a serious handicap against him, and he has had great trouble in arranging matches. ... Jeffries would not grant Johnson a match, although the followers of the sport were anxious for it.

Johnson was listed as 28 years old, 205 pounds, and 6'1" tall, with a reach of 74 ¾". Jeannette was listed as 24 years old (actually he was 26), 185 pounds, 6-feet tall, with a 79-inch reach.[319]

On March 14, 1906 in Baltimore, a big crowd watched Jack Johnson and Joe Jeannette box for the fifth time. The *Baltimore American* said Jeannette put up a stiff argument and was eager to mix, but Johnson was the cleverer boxer and landed more often, outpointing Jeannette and winning the 15-round decision. They fought at a fast clip, but neither one did any harm.[320]

The *Baltimore Sun* writer believed Johnson had carried Jeannette, boxing prettily, doing just enough to remain in the lead and earn the decision without taking any risks, nor really trying to hurt his foe.

> Neither man was hurt or took a chance of being hurt unless he was crossed, and there was an absence of crossing.
>
> The exhibition of boxing was, however, a good one. ...
>
> It looked as if Johnson should have stopped or put out his man in quick order. He looked to be able to do this, but there was no occasion for him to do it. He got the decision at the end of the fifteenth round and had not distressed his man. Johnson was

---

[319] *Baltimore American, Baltimore Sun,* March 12 - 14, 1906.
[320] *Baltimore American,* March 15, 1906.

considerate. Jeannette has to make a living and Johnson and he can double up and give nice exhibitions, such as they gave last night.[321]

On March 28, 1906 in San Diego, California, heavyweight champion Tommy Burns fought two men in one night, scoring 1st round knockouts over both 190-pound Jim O'Brien and 180-pound James Walker.[322]

The *Topeka Plaindealer* was advising blacks to leave Texas, where Jack Johnson grew up, for it was no place for decent people to reside. "The Negro must go to places where he will be recognized as a man, but as Texas is so close to hell, we advise the Negro to stay away."[323]

Actually, lynchings were frequent throughout the South. During Easter weekend, on April 14, 1906 in Springfield, Missouri, a white mob broke into the jail, seized three black men and lynched them in the public square. It all began when a white woman and her male friend alleged that they had been assaulted and the woman raped by two black men on Good Friday evening.

Despite the fact that the men allegedly wore masks, so there wasn't much of a description, the police found two black men and arrested them. Their foreman gave them an alibi and vouched for them, saying that they had been loading freight all night long and had been with him, so it could not have been them. They were released.

However, a few hours later, the men were re-arrested, supposedly for their own "protection," as rumors grew that a lynch mob was forming. Eventually, the mob descended upon and broke into the jail, took the suspects, and hung them from the Gottfried Tower in the Park Central Square, which ironically had a replica of the Statue of Liberty atop it. The men then were burned and dismembered by the mob, who took body parts as souvenirs.

Later, the mob took a third black man who was in the jail being held as a suspect on a murder charge (who claimed that he was innocent and named the man who actually committed the crime), and lynched him as well.

Ironically, in the process, owing to the fact that the mob so badly wrecked the jail, 14 prisoners escaped.

The next day was Easter Sunday. The Missouri governor sent in troops from the state militia to prevent further violence.[324]

On April 21, 1906, the Missouri-based *Sedalia Weekly Conservator* quoted the *Kansas City Journal*, discussing what was called the "Bad Nigger."

> "Bad niggers," are only children in morals and intellect, but all that is brutal and cruel development to adult standard. It is the "bad nigger" that is responsible for most of the prejudice against the race. He is usually addicted to cocaine or whiskey, or both. He insists upon taking advantage of every opportunity to annoy a white man or woman if he thinks he can do so safely. ... [T]he "bad nigger" has not ordinary sense. ... The "bad nigger" is more of an enemy to the

---

[321] *Baltimore Sun*, March 15, 1906.
[322] *Police Gazette*, May 12, 1906.
[323] *Topeka Plaindealer*, March 30, 1906.
[324] *New York Times*, April 16, 1906.

Negroes than the whites, as intolerable as he is to the latter. Race wars are started by the "bad nigger," and many innocent colored men and women are made to suffer through the conduct of one such specimen. The three men lynched by the Springfield mob were probably innocent of the specific crime for which they paid the penalty, yet they were all known as "bad niggers," and it was apparently the mob's conclusion that if they were not guilty of the specified crime they should be killed on general principles. ... The Negroes themselves should take every reasonable precaution to allay feeling against them. They should do every thing possible to subdue the "bad nigger" who seeks to stir up strife. If the "bad nigger" were eliminated from the race problem there would be few lynchings and far less prejudice against the blacks.

As It Appears.

The People of Danville, Va. Took the Matter in Hand and Found that the. "Transgressors Were but a Handful of Young Men Who Took it Upon Themselves to Regulate the Community."—*Indianapolis News.*

Freeman, April 21, 1906

In another editorial, the white-owned *Kansas City Journal* did not blame the white mob for its lawlessness, but instead blamed the town's Negro residents.

> The Negroes, as a race, must shoulder their share of the responsibility for the crimes that led to the Springfield riot, because they are too tender with the lawless element of their own race. ... If they wish to win the respect of the white race they must show they are worthy by frowning down crime and ostracizing the criminals who disgrace them. Instead, too often the tendency is to defend the bad Negro, and to shield them from punishment.

In its scathing response, the black-owned *Topeka Plaindealer* said the *Kansas City Journal* not only was unfair, but created prejudice instead of quieting it. The one-sided views of white newspapers were responsible for the deaths of many blacks. There was an utter failure to blame the vigilante white offenders who broke the law in several ways. Law-abiding Negroes were not responsible for the alleged crimes committed by low Negroes any more than the respectable class of whites was responsible for the crimes committed by their worthless class.

> In reference to the colored people wishing to win the respect of the white race, we wish to inform you that if the respect of that class of white people that lynched these men of Springfield, is the standard to which you wish the black people to rise, you may as well stop wishing, for we are far superior to them and do not wish respect or anything else from such a class of thugs and hoodlums. Respectability is due any man who respects himself and the rights of others. ... It is an injustice to charge every crime that is committed to the bad colored people, and have it go down in history as sanctioned by the whole race. ...
>
> This lynching and burning is due, to a certain extent, to the white newspapers, who aid and abet this class of lawless white men who commit these offenses, as well as give encouragement to the officers who are lax in their duties. The white newspapers are responsible for the majority of the lynching and burning in this country, and until they change their attitude toward those who are only accused of committing these offenses, the colored people must get their Winchesters, put them in their homes and be prepared for the emergency in all cases as they arise.[325]

About a month later, a special grand jury found that the victims of the Springfield mob had not been guilty of any crimes. The Negroes that were hung were innocent; and no assault upon the white woman ever was committed. Further, it found that the sheriff, his deputies, and the police department were negligent in the performance of their duties. There even was testimony that the police officers and the city marshal stood on the

---

[325] *Topeka Plaindealer*, April 27, 1906.

corner of the street and square, laughing and talking while the mob was conducting its final lynching.[326]

Eventually, 18 men were indicted for the lynchings, but none were convicted.

Fearing for their safety, blacks left the town in droves, dropping the black population of Springfield, Missouri from 20% to 2%. The desired effect was achieved. To this day, even over a century later, there are relatively few blacks in Springfield, Missouri, at about 4% of the population.

APPARENT CO-OPERATION.

The Most Lynchings Occur After the Accused Is Under the "Protection" of the Law.
Freeman, September 1, 1906

---

[326] *Topeka Plaindealer,* May 25, 1906.

Some white wirters who did not want to see a black man become heavyweight champion occasionally criticized Jack Johnson. The *Los Angeles Herald* unfairly said, "Johnson has never shown anything that would entitle him to the slightest consideration as an opponent of Jeff. Jeff would make him jump out of the ring inside of two rounds."[327]

On April 16, 1906, near Pittston, Pennsylvania, just outside of Wilkes-Barre, Jack Johnson fought Black Bill for the fourth time, clearly outclassing and knocking Bill down and out for the full count in the 7th round. Johnson was "in a class entirely by himself." Bill did not land ten blows. "Johnson showed himself to be one of the cleverest men in the ring today and has a punch in either hand that will bring home the money almost every time."[328]

On April 18, 1906, a huge, approximately 7.9 earthquake rocked San Francisco, and that, along with the resulting fires, destroyed nearly two-thirds of the city and left it in ruins. At least 3,000 people were killed, and 300,000 were left homeless. Losses were estimated at $500 million dollars.

Most elite white boxers had drawn the color line on top middleweight Sam Langford. "As there are no colored boxers of his weight worthy of a chance against him, he was asked if he would meet Johnson." Despite Johnson's size advantages, Langford, who was "boxing in great form," agreed, confident that he would win.[329]

Boxing as a professional since 1902, the very talented 20-23-year-old Langford had over 50 known pro bouts of experience. Although relatively short at only 5'7", the powerful Langford had long arms.[330]

On April 5, 1906 in Chelsea, Langford avenged a prior loss to Joe Jeannette by winning a 15-round decision over him, punishing the 30-pounds larger man and even scoring a 7th round knockdown with a right. The victory showed that Langford could beat heavyweights, for he was skillful, powerful, experienced, and gifted.[331]

Sam Langford

---

[327] *Los Angeles Herald*, April 2, 1906.
[328] *Wilkes-Barre Times, Scranton Republican*, April 17, 1906. Since last boxing Johnson, Bill's career had included: 1905 LKOby7 and D6 Joe Jeannette; and 1906 LND6 Morris Harris.
[329] *Boston Globe*, April 16, 1906.
[330] Langford's career included: 1903 W15 Joe Gans (world lightweight champion, 120 victories to his credit) and D12 Jack Blackburn (who later became Joe Louis' trainer); 1904 KO2 George McFadden (over 70 fights of experience), D15 Joe Walcott (reigning world welterweight champion, who defeated Choynski and had 88 victories); 1905 W15 (twice) Young Peter Jackson (Langford 155-pounds, Jackson over 100 fights of experience); and 1906 KO15 Larry Temple.
[331] *Police Gazette*, April 21, 1906.

The *Boston Herald* said, "In the past when two colored boxers have been the main attraction, they have not drawn very well, but the chances are that there will be a large crowd present at this bout."[332]

Amongst the local colored population, Langford was the star and favorite. Debates about their relative merits got heated. Several sports "had their hands full quieting the Darktown brigade, and yet the interest in the show is at fever heat owing to these clashes."[333]

On April 26, 1906 in Chelsea, Massachusetts, just outside of Boston, Langford's hometown, Jack Johnson fought Sam Langford.

During the first five rounds, Johnson used his left jab in a wonderful manner, occasionally hooking his left to the body and swinging his right and left wickedly to the head, carefully outboxing Sam. A wallop on Sam's left eye closed it and bothered him considerably for the rest of the bout.

The contest virtually was decided in the 6th round, when Johnson twice decked Langford with vicious rights, hooks, and body blows (though one local source claimed Langford actually went down three times). Each time, Langford appeared all but out, barely rising at the count of nine. Johnson rushed him all over the ring, but Sam stalled, hugged, and survived.

Thereafter, it became a question of how long Sam could stay, and how much punishment he could stand. "After the sixth it ceased to be a contest." Still, "Langford never once showed signs of flinching, even though blows were being handed to him hot and fast."

The local press unanimously agreed that although the game Langford tried and fought back as best he could, flashed occasionally, and lasted the full 15 rounds, he was beaten badly. Johnson left the ring without a mark, while Langford's face was a sight. Johnson clearly earned the referee's 15-round decision. The *Boston Globe* said, "It was a wonder that he could stand the beating that Johnson handed him. ... It was too one-sided to be interesting. ... Johnson didn't try very hard. His superiority was evident from the outset, and he didn't have to." The *Boston Herald* said, "Langford was hammered as no fighter ever has been hammered in the same number of rounds." He suffered a "wicked," "one-sided," awful beating. Johnson closed Langford's eye and "gave him the worst licking a man ever took in the Chelsea ring." The *Boston Journal* echoed, "Johnson was too clever, too fast, too heavy, too strong and too powerful in punching for him. ... It was a one-sided fight. It was all Johnson all the way." Some wondered whether the licking he received would affect Langford's future health.

Regardless, Johnson endured criticism for weighing 195 pounds and not stopping a middleweight. The *Globe* said Johnson would have stopped Langford "if he was made of championship timber." Even the *Journal* said Johnson's challenges to Jeffries were "preposterous," for he would have been an easy mark for the champion. However, the future would show that

---

[332] *Boston Herald*, April 23, 1906.
[333] *Boston Post*, April 24, 25, 1906; *Boston Globe*, April 25, 1906. Joe Walcott, who had fought Langford to a 15-round draw, was acting as a trainer and sparring partner for Johnson.

the very tough Langford was one of the best fighters in the world, regardless of weight.[334]

Two days later, on April 28, 1906 in Boston, a vaudeville entertainment and boxing exhibition was given for the benefit of the San Francisco earthquake sufferers. Between $500 and $600 was raised for the relief fund. Jack Johnson boxed 3 friendly rounds with Langford.[335]

During April 1906, it was announced that after a hiatus of several years, and after recently only allowing 3- and 4-round bouts, New York soon would allow up to a maximum of 10 rounds in no-decision boxing bouts.[336]

On June 18, 1906 in Gloucester, Massachusetts, against Lowell's Charles Haghey, a white veteran with over 40 fights,[337] Jack Johnson scored a quick 1st round knockout, landing a series of rapid blows to the head and body, finishing with a left swing to the wind which sent Haghey through the ropes. He laid there while counted out.[338]

On August 13, 1906, near Brownsville, Texas, whites who were upset by the placement of black troops at a fort in their area decided to blame the troops for a melee that led to the death of a bartender and a seriously wounded police officer. Commanding officers insisted that the 12 suspected black soldiers had been in the barracks the entire night. When the soldiers refused to confess or point their fingers at fellow soldiers, asserting that they had no idea who committed the shootings, all 167 members of the troop were recommended for discharge without honor on the basis of lack of cooperation and insubordination. No formal charges ever were brought, and no trial was held. The soldiers received no due process.

Cleverly waiting to make the final decision until after the Congressional election, so the black vote would not be lost, on November 9, 1906, President Theodore Roosevelt signed all 167 discharges. Many blacks were upset at Roosevelt and the Republican party, for the general belief was that the soldiers were framed and that evidence of empty Army shell casings were planted to implicate the soldiers. Many soldiers had been in the military for over 20 years, had sterling records, were close to retirement, and lost their pensions as a result. In 1972, after a renewed investigation exonerated the soldiers, Republican President Richard Nixon signed a bill correcting the soldiers' records to read "honorable discharge."

In September 1906, the *Freeman* called U.S. Senator Benjamin Tillman a "self-confessed murderer" who without provocation had assailed the country's Negroes. In his August address, Tillman said, "There are enough Negroes in the South to outvote the whites on any question if they were allowed to vote." However, he declared that there were enough shotguns in the South to carry the election for the Democrats. "In behalf of the white

---

[334] *Boston Post, Boston Globe, Boston Herald, Boston Journal,* April 27, 1906.
[335] *Boston Herald, Boston Post,* April 29, 1906.
[336] *Wilkes-Barre Record,* April 19, 1906.
[337] Significant Haghey results included: 1903 W10 Jack McCormick and LND6 Hank Griffin; 1904 LKOby1 Sandy Ferguson; and 1906 LKOby4 Bob Fitzsimmons.
[338] *Gloucester Daily Times, New York World,* June 19, 1906; *Police Gazette,* July 7, 1906. In order to give the fans their money's worth, the considerate Johnson also boxed a lively 5-round exhibition with his lightweight sparring partner, Jimmy Murray.

people of the South I say to you that as long as I live, we will see them (referring to the Negroes) in hell before we will let them have their way." He further said, "I am glad that slavery was dead and gone, but I wish that the Negroes in this country were also dead and gone."

It was the "shot-gun policy" of folks like Tillman which demonstrated that the constitutional amendments written to protect blacks and ensure their voting rights in fact were not worth the paper upon which they were printed. "The history of the South since the Civil War has been an epoch of unremitting terrorism. Lynching, Whitecapism, incendiarism, kukluxing, intimidation and various other forms of outrage and crime have so permeated that section of the United States that it seems to be are established institution for the depraved." The *Freeman* called men such as Tillman and Thomas Dixon, Jr. satanic devils who supported the killing of Negroes.[339] However, Tillman was popular enough to be elected and re-elected several times, and Dixon's book and play, *The Clansman*, were hits, both in the North and South.

Industrialist steel magnate Andrew Carnegie of New York, one of the world's richest men, wrote an article in which he made the case that the Anglo-Saxon race was destined to rule and monopolize the entire earth.[340]

---

[339] *Freeman*, September 1, 1906.
[340] *Bangor News*, September 4, 1906.

CHAPTER 19

Coasting While Waiting

On September 3, 1906 in Goldfield, Nevada, in a mixed-race world lightweight championship fight to the finish promoted by Tex Rickard, Joe Gans defeated Battling Nelson in the 42nd round, when referee George Siler disqualified Nelson for low blows. U.S. President Theodore Roosevelt's son Kermit was in attendance. Champion Gans earned $11,000, while white challenger Nelson earned $22,500, the amount negotiated for the fight, win or lose. The bout once again demonstrated boxing's popularity and ability to generate huge revenue, as well as the superior negotiating power of top white fighters. The fight was filmed, and the films would generate a great deal of additional revenue. Mixed-race championship fights were financially lucrative.

Joe Gans

That same day, which was Labor Day, September 3, 1906, in Millinocket, Maine, Jack Johnson boxed relatively unknown and inexperienced "Sawmill Champ" Billy Dunning, a local firefighter for the town company, the Great Northern Paper Co., to a 10-round draw. The bout was interesting and satisfying, "though some thought there was a spark of tender heartedness in the burley darkey." Apparently Johnson had carried Dunning, the local white fighter.[341]

The bout garnered little to no attention or discussion, in part because it was held on the same day as the very big Nelson-Gans fight, and probably also because folks likely knew or strongly suspected that Johnson took it easy on the local man in order to earn some money. Johnson later told a reporter that the police had warned him not to knock out Dunning. Hence, he carried him. Johnson probably did not care, as long as he got paid and did not lose.[342]

Heavyweight champion Tommy Burns claimed,

> I will defend my title as heavyweight champion of the world against all comers, none barred. By this I mean white, black, Mexican, Indian or any other nationality without regard to color, size or nativity. I propose to be the champion of the world, not the white or the Canadian or the American or any other limited degree of champion.

---

[341] *Bangor Daily News*, September 4, 1906.
[342] *Bangor Daily News*, November 27, 2010. In 1910, Dunning died after suffering a 5th round knockout loss to Jack Leon.

If I am not the best man in the heavyweight division I don't want to hold the title.[343]

Yet, he was not negotiating with Johnson.

On September 20, 1906 in Philadelphia, Jack Johnson once again boxed Joe Jeannette in a 6-round no-decision contest. Jeannette was the aggressor, but Johnson usually timed and met him with punches. In the 3rd round, Jack partially closed Joe's left eye.

Although the tough Jeannette was able to hold his own, cleverly cover up, and withstand punishment, Johnson "had a shade" on him. Jack did little forcing, taking no chances, mostly hitting lightly, which disappointed the crowd. The colored champ "earned the decision, but without displaying too much of his real fighting quality."[344]

Two days later, Atlanta, Georgia was home to one of the worst race riots since the Civil War. During the summer of 1906, white fears regarding increasing negro economic and political power, heightened by sensationalized rhetoric from unscrupulous white politicians who advocated for the disfranchisement of blacks, combined with unsubstantiated and inflammatory news stories claiming several rumored assaults and rapes by black men upon white women, created a powder keg of racial tension in Atlanta.

That racial tension exploded on Saturday, September 22, 1906, later known as "Blood Saturday." White mobs numbering in the thousands, which included law enforcement and military members, attacked, injured, and murdered blacks, and looted and destroyed their homes and businesses. Many yelled, "Kill the Niggers!" In response, blacks fought back and killed and injured many whites. One police officer was killed. Many blacks were arrested merely for arming themselves in self-defense.

The race war continued for at least four days, not ending until September 25, although minor skirmishes continued for a couple days after that. Hundreds were injured on both sides. Reports of the number of deaths vary widely, but supposedly anywhere from 10 to 25 blacks were killed (though some say 25 - 40) and allegedly only 1 or 2 whites were killed. However, some said many more whites actually were killed, closer to the numbers of blacks, but the real numbers were suppressed so as not to give blacks any ideas that their fighting back was or could be successful. Hundreds of blacks were arrested and thousands more fled the city.

It later was said that false newspaper reports about an alleged "carnival of rapes" had started the riots. The *Atlanta Evening News* was blamed for seeking to precipitate a race war. Its editor had championed the reorganization of the Ku Klux Klan, and allegedly had offered a reward to lynchers of alleged black rapists. The editor of the *Georgian* also was blamed for stirring racial passions with race-baiting and inflammatory editorials.

---

[343] *National Police Gazette*, September 22, 1906.
[344] *Philadelphia Inquirer, Philadelphia Record, Philadelphia Evening Bulletin*, September 21, 1906; *Police Gazette*, October 6, 13, 1906.

The local *Voice of the Negro*'s exposure of the true causes of the riot led to its editor, Jesse Max Barber, being forced to leave the city, which caused the previously successful black newspaper's demise. Barber charged that if the Atlanta mobs were a pyramid, "we would find hoodlums at the base, but white politicians and newspaper editors at the apex."

The *Freeman* published a letter from a Georgia reverend who said,

The Criminal Class, whether Black or White, should be Punished according to the law, but the Innocent should be protected if not Allowed to Protect Themselves.

Freeman, October 6, 1906

Various reasons have been given as being the cause leading up to the trouble, but people here on the ground know. ... Georgia had been swept from side to side with a flood of oratory defaming the Negro and demanding the election of Hoke Smith for Governor on the proposition to disfranchise the Negro. The vices and imagined and trumped-up vices of the Negro had been held up on every cross-road. ... Daily, weekly and monthly newspapers, ministers...and heads of families at their firesides had cursed and abused the Negro...to such an extent that the whole state was in a foment of excitement.

Negroes were pictured as being hideous monsters, lying in wait to catch, ravish and kill white women and children. Just two days before the state primary, trumped-up charges of rape were announced as having been committed in great numbers.

The *Atlanta News*, an evening daily, had been openly demanding the lynching of Negroes and the reorganization of the Ku-Klux-Klan.

Hoke Smith, on his campaign trail for governor, had fanned the flames of racial hatred. Smith was a lawyer, former Secretary of the Interior under President Grover Cleveland's second administration, and the former publisher of the *Atlanta Journal*. He overwhelmingly won the governorship on a platform advocating black disfranchisement.

White women were so worked up to a state of excitement, fear, and nervousness that even upon encountering a black man, the women would become frightened and make an outcry that he intended to assault her, or that he had raped her. Having read flaming headlines in the local papers, white mobs formed, swearing vengeance. Blacks were chased, shot, and clubbed like beasts. Eventually, many blacks fought back in self-defense.

> [T]here were as many wounded and bleeding white men as there were Negroes. The papers and news distributors would not say so, for fear that it would both embolden the Negroes and inflame the whites. I have learned from the most truthful and conservative sources that what is said above about the wounded is true about the dead. The number was very nearly equal between the two races. ... I personally conversed with a doctor who examined nine dead white men. ... The grand jury, in session, condemned the *Atlanta News* for its incendiary editorials, and held it responsible in a large measure for the mob that swept over Atlanta.[345]

Around that time, in October 1906, Mississippi Governor James K. Vardaman argued that Negroes should not be considered citizens, were mere chattel, and once again should be enslaved. He also advocated repeal of the 15th amendment, which gave blacks the right to vote.[346]

In sports, it was announced that Australian Sam Fitzpatrick had taken Jack Johnson under his managerial wing. The well-known and respected Fitzpatrick had managed Peter Jackson, among other top fighters.[347]

Fitzpatrick said that all of the best white fighters were avoiding Johnson:

> I have been watching Johnson's work for a long time, and I think he is the best colored heavyweight since the days of Peter Jackson. He never was given a chance at Jeffries, Jack O'Brien, Bob Fitzsimmons, Kid McCoy, Jim Corbett or Tom Sharkey, but was forced to meet the men with smaller reputations, but who were strong and dangerous just the same.

Fitzpatrick was willing to match Johnson against Tommy Burns, Jack O'Brien, Al Kaufman, Sam Berger, Mike Schreck, Gus Ruhlin, Bob Fitzsimmons, Marvin Hart, Bill Squires, Jack Sullivan, or any other top heavyweight. He would accept any reasonable terms. Nobody seemed interested, either because they were afraid of losing, because they did not want to fight a black man, or both.

The *Los Angeles Express* said that during the past several years, all those who had tried to defeat Johnson had failed, while the others had drawn the color line. Few truly believed that Hart had defeated him.

However, not everyone was as high on Johnson. The *Los Angeles Examiner* believed that Johnson had "a yellow streak a foot wide," and if he ever fought Jeffries, they could not "build a fence high enough to keep the black-and-tan champion from climbing over and taking to the woods."[348]

Of course, the claim that Johnson was yellow was a laughable statement, given that he was willing to fight anyone, had boxed seven times in 1903,

---

[345] *Freeman*, October 6, 1906.
[346] *Seattle Republican*, October 26, 1906; *Hawaiian Star*, October 31, 1906.
[347] *Freeman*, October 6, 1906.
[348] *Los Angeles Express*, September 26, 1906; *Los Angeles Examiner*, September 28, 1906.

five times in 1904, and thirteen times in 1905. He would wind up boxing eleven times in 1906. In two years, from 1905 - 1906, he would box more often than Jim Jeffries had in his entire career.

The *Police Gazette* believed that Johnson, not Burns or O'Brien, was the best heavyweight in the world outside of Jeffries:

> The trouble is that most of the leading heavyweights have carefully avoided getting in a bout with the negro. ... Like Gans, he has probably been compelled to hide his real punching powers a bit in order to get contests. Johnson is a fighter of the Gans ilk. That is to say, he has everything a successful pugilist should have, including remarkable skill, endurance and the power to inflict punishment. ...
>
> Jack Jeffries was an easy mark for Johnson. He gave him a terrible beating, and knocked him out cleanly in the fifth round. It was thought then that Jeffries would seek revenge, but Johnson's ability has evidently made a deep impression on his mind, for he never said a word about fighting the black, and drew the color line harder than ever.
>
> A meeting between Jeffries and Johnson would certainly be the greatest attraction possible in the ring today. ... Johnson is the only man with the right to face Jeffries today.[349]

A *Freeman* writer said there was not the least doubt that Johnson would "be successful in beating the boiler-maker clear out of the ring."[350]

On October 2, 1906 in Los Angeles, in a highly entertaining hard-fought battle, heavyweight champion Tommy Burns scored a KO15 over "Fireman" Jim Flynn. Burns combined science with power to wear down the strong and aggressive Flynn, outboxing and outfighting him both on the inside and outside.

Shortly thereafter, Burns signed to meet Philadelphia Jack O'Brien for a $12,000 purse. The big fight was scheduled to be held in late November.

Jack Johnson said he would fight Burns, O'Brien, Berger, or Kaufman, winner take all, if they wanted. Kaufman openly drew the color line.

The *Police Gazette* reported that colored boxers of the highest order gradually were becoming scarce, for white boxers were drawing the color line, and club managers did not care to match black and white. Of course, this overlooked the fact that many black boxers were fighting each other.[351]

In Australia, the *Referee*, quoting the *New York Evening Mail* of October 20, reported that all top American heavyweights had side-stepped Johnson:

> While Sam Fitzpatrick is wilting away collars in the rush to get somebody with nerve enough to fight Johnson, the big smoke is not worrying at all. He struts around Philadelphia togged out simply gorgeous, and rather seems to enjoy the prestige he gets from not

---

[349] *Police Gazette*, October 13, 1906.
[350] *Freeman*, October 20, 1906.
[351] *Police Gazette*, October 27, November 3, 1906.

being able to get a fight through fear on the part of possible opponents. Johnson really does seem to be in hard luck. Few men of his weight want any of his game.[352]

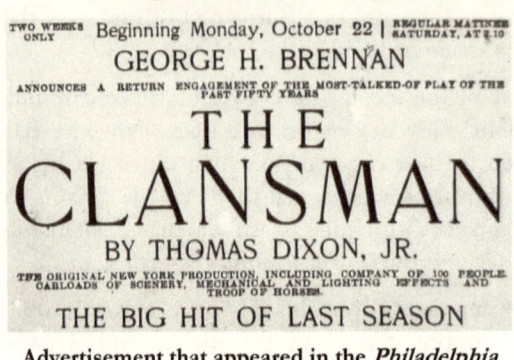

Advertisement that appeared in the *Philadelphia Record*, October 21, 1906

During October 1906, *The Clansman* was being performed in Philadelphia, where Jack Johnson then was residing.

On October 31, 1906 in San Francisco, Al Kaufman scored a KO10 over the highly touted rising heavyweight contender, former 1904 Olympic champion Sam Berger. Still, the *Police Gazette* said Kaufman did not have the right to fight for the title until he defeated Jack Johnson.[353]

Johnson even offered to contract to knock out Kaufman in 20 rounds or not take a cent of the receipts, but Al refused.

As a result of their refusal to face Johnson, the *Police Gazette* called the current crop of white heavyweights "yellow." It said Johnson had the would-be champions such as O'Brien, Berger, and Kaufman on the run with fear, for all of them had drawn the color line on him.

Some suggested that Johnson was receiving more ink and praise than his performances warranted, simply because of the fact that white heavyweights were refusing to face him. "In spite of all the boosting that Johnson has accumulated, much of it in these columns, there is no doubt a lot of sympathetic sentiment attached to it. We are prone to overrate the big negro out of sympathy for him in his loneliness." Certainly though, something about Johnson had made top whites afraid, and the press did not believe that it simply was a matter of race pride.

Matches had been arranged for Johnson with Jim Jeffords and Joe Jeannette, but "doubtless there is some kind of an insurance clause in the articles in order to make this pair sign."[354]

Australians, aware of Johnson's struggles with the color line, sympathized with him, for they remembered how their champion Peter Jackson had endured the same obstacles. The National Sporting Club of Sydney, New South Wales, made an offer for Johnson to fight there, guaranteeing $1,500 for each of two matches, as well as transportation for two. "Johnson will probably accept the offer. He has about given up hope of getting any of the present crop of American heavyweights into the ring."

---

[352] *Referee*, December 12, 1906, quoting *New York Evening Mail*, October 20, 1906.
[353] *Police Gazette*, November 17, 1906.
[354] *Police Gazette*, December 8, 1906; *Philadelphia Record*, November 10, 1906.

The thinking was that Johnson would fight Bill Squires and Peter Felix, the best heavies in Australia. Co-manager Alex McLean felt certain that eventually the best American heavyweights would have to accept a challenge from Johnson, including for the title.[355]

Alex Greggains, perturbed by all of the criticism he endured for his Johnson-Hart decision, said the "big coon" Johnson had a "yellow streak," mostly jabbing and holding Hart on the inside, despite the fact that Hart "didn't know enough about fighting or boxing to cut any ice." He claimed that Hart's rushes "scared him half to death," causing him to hold a lot. "So when I was breaking them I said: 'Get in and fight, you big dubs. What are you stalling around like this for?' 'Why, I's a-fightin', Mr. Greggains,' says Johnson. 'I'se a-fightin' scientific.'"[356]

The *Lancaster Daily Intelligencer* said, "While there is much discussion about the championship between Kaufman, Burns and O'Brien, the truth is that all of them are afraid of Jack Johnson." It quoted the *New York World*:

> All the present day champions draw the colored line, and will not agree to fight Johnson. And there is method in their madness. Johnson is undoubtedly cleverer, faster and a heavier puncher than any of the men whom he is trying to get a match with. The only man in the ring today who would be able to make a creditable showing against Johnson is Jack O'Brien, and the Quaker is far too shrewd to risk losing what prestige he has gained after beating a long list of easy ones. O'Brien won't fight the colored man, as the chances are even he would meet with defeat. All the other heavy weights fear him. But that word 'colored' gives them all a chance to escape without admitting their fear. When Johnson challenges they pay no attention to his challenges and seek safety behind the color line.[357]

On November 8, 1906 in Lancaster, Pennsylvania, in a 6-round no-decision rematch with 26-year-old 6'4" 200-plus-pound Jim Jeffords, Jack Johnson outclassed him, landing two blows to one, of the "clean-cut, sledgehammer type." Several times the aggressive Johnson had Jeffords on the ropes, and he closed his left eye. The local newswriter said,

Jim Jeffords

> While the big coon had the best of it, Jeffords deserves the greatest amount of credit for staying the limit, despite the vigorous efforts of Johnson to put him out. He took an awful lacing, but came back every time, and he was the favorite with the audience, even if he did get the worst of the match. There are a

---

[355] *Philadelphia Record*, November 7, 8, 1906.
[356] *New York World*, November 2, 1906.
[357] *Lancaster Daily Intelligencer*, November 5, 1906.

dozen other big men in this country who would not have stayed, for as Jeffords said after the match, he was never hit so hard before.[358]

Joe Choynski had told the Australians to bring Johnson there to fight their champion, Bill Squires. Joe said, "They are all afraid of him here. ... He is a fine fellow, and can be got reasonably."

On November 8, boxing manager Sig Hart wrote to an Australian,

> Jack Johnson...is going to Australia to fight someone. Now, if he lands on your side I want to tell you that he will beat any man you have there, for he can beat anyone we have here. He is better than Peter Jackson was in his palmiest days. He is clever, can hit hard, and can stand the gaff. Not one of our heavies here would box him. Be sure you have a bet on him if ever he comes to your town to fight, for, as I said before, he is the best big man in the world today, and I don't bar anyone. By the way, your old townie, Sam Fitzpatrick, is looking after him now, and Sam knows a thing or two about the fighters.[359]

Fearing prejudice, many fighters changed their names to conceal their racial ancestry or national origins. Italians often changed their names to Irish-sounding ones. Hugo Kelly was an Italian, born Ugo Micheli. Joe Grim was born Saverio Giannone. Jim Flynn, who was of Irish-Italian heritage, had changed his name from Andrew Schreiglione. Tony Ross was born Antonio Rossilano. Tommy Ryan was Jewish, despite his repeated denials. They were trying to minimize racial prejudice.[360]

The *Daily Eastern Argus*, which was based in Portland, Maine, where Jack Johnson would fight next, argued that the Caucasian and the Negro fundamentally were extreme opposites in evolution.

> The Caucasian, and more particularly the Anglo-Saxon, is dominant and domineering and possessed primarily with determination, will power, self control, self government and all the attributes of the subjective self, with a high development of the ethical and aesthetic faculties and great reasoning powers. The negro is in direct contrast by reason of a certain lack of these powers, and a great development of the objective qualities. The negro is primarily affectionate, immensely emotional, then sensual, and, under provocation, passionate. There is love of outward show, of ostentation, of approbation. He loves melody and a rude kind of poetry and sonorous language. There is undeveloped artistic power and taste – negroes make good artisans and handicraftsmen. They are deficient in judgment, in the formation of new ideas from existing facts, in devising hypotheses and in making deductions in general. They are imitative rather than original, inventive or constructive. There is

---

[358] *Lancaster Daily Intelligencer, Philadelphia Public Ledger, Philadelphia Press,* November 9, 1906. Previously, Johnson had stopped Jeffords in the 4th round of their 1905 meeting.
[359] *Referee,* December 19, 1906.
[360] *Hawaiian Star,* November 9, 1906.

instability of character incident to lack of self control, especially in connection with the sexual relation, and there is a lack of orientation or recognition of position and condition of self and environment. ...

The white and the black races are antipodal, then, in cardinal points. The one has a large frontal region of the brain, the other a larger region behind; ... the one a great reasoner, the other pre-eminently emotional; the one domineering, but having great self control, the other meek and submissive, but violent and lacking self control when the passions are aroused; the one a very advanced race, the other a very backward one. The Caucasian and the negro are fundamentally opposite extremes in evolution.[361]

Such views were common. A black man being the central figure in boxing and the best fighter in the business could serve to contradict such notions.

Next up for Jack Johnson was a seventh bout with Joe Jeannette. The local *Daily Eastern Argus* said, "Johnson is without doubt the most prominent star in the heavyweight class in the squared circle today and in spite of open defies to all the best men in the business, the alleged title holders as well as promising aspirants of the honor have sidestepped a meeting with the giant." Top white fighters had "conveniently drawn the color line when Johnson sought a match, which is a polite way of saying 'cold feet.'" Therefore, Johnson was forced to go to foreign countries to do business. Since he was headed to Australia, this would be the last opportunity to see him box in the U.S. for a while.

The "great" and "famous" Jeannette was the only good man not afraid of an encounter with the "world famous" Johnson. He was expected to put up a stiff argument, as he had in their previous six contests.[362]

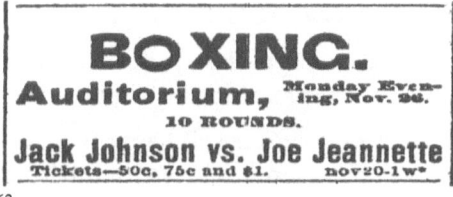

On November 26, 1906 at the Portland, Maine Auditorium, a large and enthusiastic crowd of 1,200 to 1,500 people saw Jack Johnson fight Joe Jeannette in a scheduled 10-round no-decision contest.

Johnson climbed through the ropes first. "All who looked upon the powerful negro understood why so many heavyweights have been sidestepping a meeting with him." The smaller Jeannette followed, receiving great applause. The crowd sympathized with and cheered for him.

The contest featured lively exchanges throughout. Usually Joe threw and then clinched around the waist to prevent Johnson from countering him. Johnson often wrestled himself free from clinches and hit the body. Jack was calm and collected all the time. Jeannette landed a number of left stabs to the face, while Johnson sent in a whirlwind of slashing uppercuts and hooks, though Joe covered and guarded his face fairly well. By the 7th

---

[361] *Daily Eastern Argus*, November 9, 1906.
[362] *Daily Eastern Argus*, November 16, 20-23, 1906.

round, Jeannette was bleeding, but he kept rushing in and working the body. They mixed it up in a slashing manner.

Near the conclusion of the 10th round, Johnson landed a left hook to the jaw and Jeannette went down to his knee. When the referee counted to five, with Jeannette still down, the gong sounded ending the bout.

The local paper said Johnson and Jeannette boxed 10 fast rounds in a "corking good main event." The perfectly satisfied crowd had "seen one of the best heavyweights in the business and another boxer possibly not in Johnson's class, but who is fast coming to the front."

Although no formal decision was rendered in the no-decision bout, "we are inclined to believe that, though slightly outclassed by a man who had a marked advantage in weight, height and reach, Joe Jeannette fairly earned a draw by his clever exhibition." This writer also said, "Both men were strong at the finish and while Johnson showed himself the cleverer boxer and ring general Jeannette certainly deserved a draw for his work. No decisions are given, however, and it is only a matter of opinion at best." So the local paper half-heartedly called it a draw, though it also said that Jeannette was outclassed slightly by Johnson, who was the cleverer boxer and ring general. Johnson had drawn blood and had scored the only knockdown.[363]

The "black and tan champion of the world" wanted to fight the winner of the upcoming Burns-O'Brien championship contest, but not everyone supported his title challenges. The *Los Angeles Examiner* said Johnson had a "canary streak," and that "so long as the memory of his orange stripe lingers Jack Johnson will be a beggar for matches. That is where he figures."[364]

The *Examiner*'s C. E. Van Loan questioned Johnson's gameness, saying,

> If he disposes of Jack O'Brien there is no man in the country who will have the right to dispute Burns' claim to the championship.
>
> Jack Johnson still lingers about the scene and every little while he emits a small yellow growl, but Jack deserves his fate. He might have been a top-notch fighter, but he was cursed with a great display of citrus fruit and every time he got in a pinch he showed the lemon color. The championship lies between Burns and O'Brien, and by this time next week it is hoped that one man will have a clear title to Jeff's cast-off shoes.[365]

Several writers often had a twinge of racial animus towards Johnson, as well as dislike of his style, referring to him as yellow or cowardly for having defensive inclinations, even though the white Burns and O'Brien often had fought quite defensively themselves, yet received heaps of praise.

On November 27, 1906 in Chicago, U.S. Senator Ben Tillman, in his address for the benefit of the Union Hospital, talked about the race question in a manner which "shocked some and delighted the majority of 3,000 listeners." He said a "black curse" hung over every Southern home.

---

[363] *Daily Eastern Argus*, November 26, 27, 1906.
[364] *Los Angeles Examiner*, November 28, 1906.
[365] *Los Angeles Examiner*, November 22, 1906.

When discussing the 15th amendment, which gave blacks the right to vote, Tillman said, "If this law was enforced it would result in two states at least being dominated absolutely by Negroes, while four other states would be so near being governed by the Negro that there would practically be an equal division of offices." When someone asked, "What about the law?" Tillman

WHY TILLMAN DISCUSSES THE NEGRO

Could He Get Into the Senate by Advocating Any Other Question?

Freeman, December 15, 1906

responded, "To hell with the law!" Tillman discussed how the negro was prevented from casting the ballot in the South. He said the white race never would allow itself to be dominated by the Negro, that before any such thing took place in South Carolina, "we will make it red before we make it black."

Pointing to a black man in the audience, Tillman said, "Look at that nigger down there. He's as black as the ace of spades. Don't tell me you haven't got niggers up here." Continuing, Tillman said, "The negro must be kept in subjection. He is not capable of ruling a white population. ... I want to be fair with the negro, but we must protect ourselves first." He also said,

> God Almighty made the Caucasian of better clay than the Mongolian or the African or any other race. The Ethiopian is a burden carrier. He has done absolutely nothing for history, nor has he ever achieved anything of any great importance. There are no great men among the race. Yet this people has been picked out by the fanatics of the North and lifted up to the equality of citizenship and to the rights of suffrage. No doubt many of you have listened to the oratory of the greatest colored man of this country – Booker Washington. He had a white father, however, and his brains and his character he has inherited from that father.

Tillman further spoke of the alleged attacks upon white women by Negroes in the South.[366]

On November 28, 1906 in Los Angeles, before a crowd of over 10,000 spectators, former champion James J. Jeffries, acting as referee, ruled the Tommy Burns vs. Jack O'Brien heavyweight championship bout a 20-round

---

[366] *New York World, New York Tribune*, November 28, 1906.

draw, although most observers thought Burns had won clearly. 168-174-pound Burns attacked throughout, throwing the harder punches, while 163-170-pound O'Brien moved incessantly and threw few punches, which though not very powerful, were quick, and he clinched whenever Burns drew close. Burns pummeled his body on the inside and broke O'Brien's nose with a right. O'Brien closed Tommy's left eye with his stabbing jab.

Johnson said he would fight either O'Brien or Burns winner-take-all, or split the purse evenly. He even was willing to agree that if he failed to score a knockout within 20 rounds that he would forfeit his share. The *New York Sun* said, "Johnson has a big following in his attempt to force these alleged heavyweight champions to fight or run." If Johnson could beat both, then Jeffries might be forced to fight him.[367]

Johnson said he was so certain of victory over Jeffries that he would split the purse any way Jeffries wanted, and also would bet another $10,000 on the result. He had a burning desire to fight him.[368]

Jack also said that O'Brien, Burns, Kaufman, or Berger had to fight him or ring in a cowardly excuse.[369]

Sam Fitzpatrick no longer was worrying about Johnson's future:

> He sees the public clamoring more and more every day for the white heavies to try the chocolate colored heavyweight out, and knows that they cannot ignore Johnson much longer.
>
> In fairness to Burns, it must be said he has never said anything about drawing the color line, and it may be that he will be willing to meet Johnson.[370]

Tommy Burns had not specifically drawn the color line, but eventually he did, at least temporarily. In December 1906, Burns said,

> I wish someone would put an end to these stories that I ever intended meeting Jack Johnson. I am having a hard time with my wife now, as she wants me to cut out this business. I don't know what she would do if she heard I fought a negro. She's a southerner and I guess you know what southern folks think of negroes. They may say I am afraid of Johnson and anything else they want to, but I am never going to fight a negro. I have fought them, but am drawing the line now.[371]

The *Police Gazette* responded, "As was expected, Tommy Burns has drawn the color line in the direction of Jack Johnson."

Burns was making a great deal of money already, which made it less likely that he would want to fight Johnson. The Burns-O'Brien fight drew over $26,500 in gate receipts. A rematch with O'Brien would be another big payday against a man he was more certain of defeating. On December 22,

---

[367] *New York Sun,* December 9, 10, 1906.
[368] *Referee,* February 20, 1907.
[369] *Freeman,* December 22, 1906.
[370] *Police Gazette,* December 22, 1906.
[371] *Los Angeles Herald,* December 13, 1906.

Tom McCarey secured the Burns-O'Brien rematch for an alleged purse of $30,000.[372]

The *Police Gazette* lobbied,

> Johnson is as much entitled to consideration as any of the others. Many an expert is of the opinion that he is the greatest fighter of his race since the days of Peter Jackson, and there hardly is any question on that score. But Johnson has been sidetracked by all the white heavies because of his color, they claim. As a matter of fact, they are afraid of him if they only would acknowledge the corn. Johnson has as much right to fight for the title as any of the prominent men, and if he is treated fairly he will be given a chance. Barring him will not settle the much-twisted heavyweight situation.[373]

There were some negotiations for a match between Jeffries and rising Australian star Bill Squires, but Jeff wanted $25,000 guaranteed, win, lose, or draw. He turned down a $20,000 guarantee. The Rhyolite club representative in Nevada said Jeff's demands were unreasonable:

> He should understand that this fight will not be a great drawing card compared to a fight with Johnson. ... He can pretty nearly name his own purse if he will fight Johnson, but when he refuses to fight the only man for whom there is a really national demand, he cannot expect to get a gold mine for fighting someone else.[374]

CREEPING

Prejudice Against the Dark Races Seems to be Assuming a World-wide Scope

Freeman, February 2, 1907

---

[372] *Police Gazette*, December 29, 1906.
[373] *Police Gazette*, December 29, 1906.
[374] *Philadelphia Inquirer*, January 4, 1907.

CHAPTER 20

Australia

In late December 1906, Jack Johnson and co-manager Alec McLean left San Francisco on the *Sonoma*, heading for Sydney, Australia.

Australia advertised Johnson as the cleverest and most dangerous aspirant for the world's crown; the man whom Jeffries and all top white fighters in the U.S. refused to box. "Jeffries and others have refused to meet him, alleging as an excuse that they 'have no use for colored men.'"

The question was whether Australian champion Bill Squires would look for an excuse to duck Johnson as well, given Jack's big reputation.

The *Sydney Bulletin* said, "It is just possible that Johnson may be overrated – Amurkan papers have been known occasionally to exaggerate." Australians were about to find out.[375]

On January 24, 1907, after nearly a month at sea, a 211-pound Jack Johnson arrived in Sydney. He quietly but confidently said,

> I am here to make as much money as I can, and add to my reputation if possible. I heard of your champion, Bill Squires…and I have travelled a long way mainly to meet and beat him, provided I get the chance.
>
> I am the colored champion of the world, and I am proud of the fact, for there are more colored than white boxers where I come from. I was born in Galveston, Texas, 28 years ago, and I have had 65 battles during my career. … I tried hard indeed to meet Jeffries before he left off fighting, but he drew the color line on me, despite that he had already fought other colored men in the persons of Hank Griffin (twice), Bob Armstrong, and Peter Jackson.

The local writers were impressed. "Johnson is a bright-looking fellow, able to talk very intelligently, and entirely free of the mannerisms and style of speaking so pronounced in the music-hall negro." Clearly, Johnson spoke a lot better than several white newsmen in the U.S. admitted or reported. Another said, "A little chat discovered Johnson a bright, brainy fellow, able to talk intelligently, and as one who knew his subjects well, of American fighting and fighters, and the country's resources generally. … Johnson spoke modestly and to the point." There was a "lurking suspicion that Johnson is a better fighter than either O'Brien or Burns."

A telegram was read which said that Bill Squires' manager John Wren intended to take him to America. Johnson responded,

---

[375] *Referee*, January 9, 23, 1907; *Sydney Daily Telegraph*, January 21, 1907; *Sydney Bulletin*, January 24, 1907.

Say, here's a nice thing. I've journeyed thousands of miles to hear that your champion, who advertised himself ready to meet anyone in the world, is going to side-step me directly I set foot on Australian soil. Is this the guy that pretended such great anxiety to shape up to Jeffries? Let him go to America. I'll bet his cake'll be dough when he gets there.

Johnson's manager Alec McLean added that Burns and O'Brien would be fighting a rematch of their draw in May, and therefore Squires would not be able to fight either one before then. Hence, he questioned why Squires was so eager to leave Australia just when Johnson had arrived.

From Melbourne, Squires read Johnson's remarks implying that Bill was afraid to meet him, and became so angered at Jack's rudeness that he said he would fight Johnson if the money was right. However, Bill also said that he was under a management contract to John Wren, and would do as he said. Wren thought they could make more money in the U.S., but also claimed that he would make the Johnson match for 1,000 pounds.

BILL SQUIRES—Australia.   JACK JOHNSON—America.
When they meet who will win?

Johnson's manager said they came 12,000 miles to fight, and he was willing to back his protégé for any amount from 1,000 pounds upwards, and the gate or purse could be divided however Squires pleased. "Mr. McLean further stated that if Squires defeated Johnson he could very justly claim the championship of the world, as he reckoned neither Tommy Burns nor Jack O'Brien, between whom the title now rested, would have a chance with Johnson."[376]

Starting on January 28, 1907, to packed houses at Sydney's Queen's Hall, Johnson began giving daily sparring exhibitions with local Australian heavyweights. "The visitor showed much cleverness, and created a favourable impression." "Johnson is evidently a more skillful boxer than any we have seen here for many a year; he uses a clever left effectively and

---

[376] *Sydney Daily Telegraph,* January 25, 28, 1907; *Referee,* January 30, 1907.

accurately, and is as nimble as a cat on his feet." He moved in and out and side-stepped "with the rapidity of a lightning flash."[377]

Australia Regrets They Will Not Meet.

JACK JOHNSON.   BILL SQUIRES.

Ultimately, John Wren said Squires would not fight Johnson. It appeared that Wren's 'thousand' side-wager offer had been a big bluff. The *Sydney Bulletin* said Squires obviously was afraid, but tried to bluff the public into thinking otherwise by making an offer that they never intended or wanted "the nigger" to accept. They had no intention of fighting Johnson. "Does he expect darkie Johnson to go back to America in pursuit of him?" Clearly, Wren thought he was going to obtain a bigger purse for Squires in the U.S., and the potential to win the championship, and the truth was that he did not want to imperil a trip to the United States with a potential loss. "They have no time for beaten men in the States." "Squires persists that he is going to America, is in a great hurry to gather in scalps, has no time for Johnson's scalp."[378]

James Brennan instead matched Australian black Peter Felix to box Johnson for the colored heavyweight championship of the world.[379]

The *Sydney Daily Telegraph* said Johnson was rangy, quick, and knew all the tricks of the game. *Referee* editor W. F. Corbett said Johnson was cool and intelligent:

> Johnson is a great boxer, and a fine fellow, and one only has to see him going to understand why Jim Jeffries sheltered behind that cowardly protection, the color-line, and also why the admitted cleverest boxer in the world this moment had to come all the way to Australia.[380]

The *Referee* scouted the upcoming bout. Johnson and Felix both stood over six feet, weighed about the same, and "both are first-class boxers." "The visitor is, as was Peter Jackson, essentially a jabbing, and consequently safe, fighter, so that even if he does triumph over Felix – a happening which certainly cannot be written sure – there'll be some time of good boxing, and, in my opinion, great excitement, before the referee is called upon to

---

[377] *Sydney Morning Herald*, January 29, 1907; *Referee*, January 30, 1907.
[378] *Referee*, January 30, 1907; *Sydney Bulletin*, January 31, 1907, February 7, 14, 1907.
[379] *Sydney Daily Telegraph*, January 31, 1907.
[380] *Sydney Daily Telegraph*, February 2, 1907.

make his announcement." The *Sydney Morning Herald* said Felix "is one of our cleverest boxers, and the contest to-night should be as skillful as one could wish to see." Felix had about 40 fights of experience.[381]

On February 19, 1907 in Sydney, Jack Johnson had his first formal fight in Australia, defending his colored heavyweight crown against Peter Felix.

Although both were well received by the large crowd, Felix was the more popular, "for the Australian ring-sider is patriotic even with his black man when the opponent is a foreign colored man."

Physically, they seemed well matched; both looking quite muscular. The *Bulletin* said, "Felix is, as everybody knows, as black as a parson's new hat, while Johnson is merely brown, and of a build which suggests that somewhere in the generations a-rear was a white ancestor."

Peter Felix

Felix started very cautiously, evading some blows, while Jack smiled, showing his gold-encased ivories. Felix half-heartedly poked out a left, which Johnson easily evaded and immediately countered with a left hook into the stomach, and Felix went down to the boards face first.

---

[381] *Referee*, February 6, 1907; *Sydney Morning Herald*, February 19, 1907.

After rising, Felix used his his long reach, but only succeeded in barely tapping Johnson's chest and gloves in a feeble manner. As Johnson closed in, he landed "a playful right" that sent Felix down again.

Felix rose, stepped in and tapped Johnson on the forehead with the tip of his glove, and the smiling "brown man" fired a counter uppercut that caught Felix on the point of the chin, and down he went, this time for the full ten-count. The surprised spectators were disappointed by the quick and easy 1st round knockout, and they hooted and jeered.

The *Sydney Bulletin* called it a shocking and awful fiasco. The *Referee* said that although many good judges were quite impressed with Johnson, highly rating him, "nothing that occurred last night justified such a rating, for Felix has never done his capabilities such scant justice."[382]

Bill Lang

Johnson traveled to Melbourne, Australia to give exhibitions there and to fight Bill Lang for a 500-pound purse ($2,500) offered by John Wren, to be split $1,750 to the winner and $750 to the loser. Of French-Italian descent, Lang's original name was Langfranchi. He had never been stopped, and twice had gone 20 rounds. The 6'1" 23-year-old weighed about 174 pounds. The *Referee* said Lang was ambitious, strong, and vimful. "He is not at all scared at Johnson's fine record."

American lightweight Dick Cullen advised Australians to bet on Johnson against any man, "for he is a great fighter, and will out-point any heavyweight in the world. Jack O'Brien and Jeffries know this, and that is why they bar him."[383]

Those who saw Johnson spar on February 28, 1907 at the Melbourne Cyclorama said he "made it very apparent that he is a man of unusual versatility." The *Melbourne Argus* said, "Jack Johnson as a scientific boxer stands today without an equal in the universe."

Another observer of his sparring exhibitions wrote, "Johnson is not only a master of the art of boxing, but the possessor of an immense reserve of strength. ... [N]one of our boys seem to be in the negro's class."[384]

On March 4, 1907 at the Richmond racecourse in Melbourne, the Jack Johnson vs. Bill Lang fight took place. Although the fight was held outdoors at night, the ring and grounds were lit brilliantly with electric light. A massive crowd of 15,000 to 20,000 men were in attendance. Unfortunately, torrents of rain fell, and the spectators were soaked.

Johnson appeared first. His entrance was "as theatrical as it was funny." A roar of laughter could be heard as an "elongated figure, attired in a duchesse robe, made of chintz or cretonne, besprinkled with damask roses

---

[382] *Sydney Daily Telegraph, Sydney Morning Herald, Referee*, February 20, 1907; *Sydney Bulletin*, February 28, 1907.
[383] *Referee*, February 27, 1907.
[384] *Melbourne Argus*, March 1, 1907; *Melbourne Age*, March 2, 1907.

and hlac sparys, with frills around the hem and a hood attachment similarly figured with flowers, stepped through the ropes." A humorist in the crowd yelled, "We don't want to see Mrs. Johnson. Go away woman, and send your husband; this is no place for ladies." The crowd laughed and chaffed Johnson unmercifully. Unruffled, Jack's white eyes peered out and he smiled. "At this stage it was hard to say whether Johnson looked most like a hoodoo man from the Congo or Red Riding Hood's grandmother."

When Jack stripped, he appeared to be a "beautiful physical specimen." He shaved his hair so closely that he appeared almost bald. He had a wide, constant smile, which displayed a gleaming mass of gold fillings.

Lang's entrance brought wild cheers and shouts from the white crowd. Johnson was an inch taller and the bigger man, by at least a stone (14 pounds) in weight. "His shaved shiny black head radiated the beams of the electric lights like a policeman's helmet."

Although Lang vigorously rushed in and attacked throughout, Johnson dominated and toyed with him, displaying his remarkable defensive skill, standing in a relaxed attitude, moving his head or blocking with his gloves or arms, foiling all of the attacks with ease. He smiled and said, "Oh! Dis is a joke." The *Argus* said, "The smile made the crowd very angry before the fight was over." Johnson retaliated only occasionally, apparently carrying Lang. However, when Jack did punch, he ripped in lightning-fast uppercuts and straight drives, shooting his long left out or up. In the 3rd round, he cut open a gash on Lang's forehead, and red rills of blood trickled down.

In the 7th round, Johnson dropped Lang with a left hook to the body, and a second time with a smashing blow on the jaw. "Johnson pranced across to his corner in a dancing cakewalk step." Upset by Jack's theatrical attitudes and obvious disregard for his opponent, the crowd hooted vigorously. Lang paid the penalty. Johnson brought him down over and over again, nearly a dozen times. Still, Bill kept rising and fighting gamely.

In the 8th round, Johnson backed off, appearing to be "in a lazy mood," although he still decked Lang once more. Bill's forehead was bleeding in two or three places as a result of the heavy uppercuts.

In the 9th round, Johnson swung left and right to the face and body, and Lang crumpled down in his own corner. His seconds threw in the towel.

Despite fighting with remarkable gameness and determination, Lang's assaults had been in vain, and he lasted 9 rounds only because Johnson had allowed him to do so. "He could not have held himself more in reserve had he guaranteed to allow his opponent a few rounds of practice before going in to finish him." The fight was "farcical in its one-sidedness."[385]

Some criticized Johnson for failing to stop Lang sooner. Of course, most thought he could have stopped Lang more quickly had he tried. Further, when Johnson stopped Peter Felix quickly, in one round, the press criticized the opponent's performance and the fight. So this time Johnson gave them more rounds, but still suffered some criticism.

---

[385] *Melbourne Argus, Melbourne Age*, March 5, 1907.

The *Referee* reported that Johnson played with Lang, punching him whenever he pleased, "in a happy-go-lucky style."

> Johnson 'cake-walked' all over his opponent. His theatrical style did not please the crowd, which hissed him. This made Johnson angry, and he sent Lang down several times by way of getting even with the crowd. It is an open question whether Squires would have beaten the colored champion, and a good many people think that Bill was wise in getting away to America before his career was cut short.[386]

A week later, the *Referee* wrote, "Jack Johnson, who has made a splendid impression everywhere, both as a boxer and a man, desires me to tell the people of New South Wales and Victoria how highly he appreciates the many kindnesses extended him."

The Colored Progressive Association intended to tender Johnson a farewell before he left.[387]

However, Johnson did not leave Sydney as planned. Jack and his manager Alex McLean had a dispute that first would need to be dealt with in the local courts. On March 18, McLean, accompanied by the sheriff, served a writ upon Johnson, claiming that £112 was due him in accordance with an agreement signed before they sailed to Australia. After accepting the writ from the sheriff, words were exchanged with McLean, and Johnson punched his manager in the nose, breaking it and damaging McLean's face. The sheriff arrested Johnson, and Promoter James Brennan posted his bail.

The next day, in the Police Court, testimony revealed that McLean had called Johnson a vile name. The evidence of the abusive epithet caused the magistrate to be more more lenient, and Johnson only received a £5 fine.

Still, the *Referee* criticized Johnson, saying he lost many friends by acting like a brute and losing control.[388]

Back in the U.S., the *Freeman* said that colored fighters always had to give their white opponents the better of everything, including the purse. Some black fighters even had agreed to lay down, but fewer were doing so recently, finding that taking dives hurt them more in the long run than it helped them.

White fighters were so fearful of losing to colored fighters that they were drawing the color line more and more. "Afro-Americans are made of sterner stuff." Hence, several top black fighters were going overseas to find matches. This writer dreamed of blacks becoming champions in the welter, middle, and heavyweight divisions. "Wonder will that dream ever come true. We would like to see such be the case, as Negro pugilists have had a hard road to travel on."[389]

On March 31, 1907, Jack Johnson turned 29 years of age.

---

[386] *Referee*, March 6, 13, 20, 1907. *New York World*, November 25, 1908.
[387] *Referee*, March 13, 1907.
[388] *Referee*, March 20, 1907.
[389] *Freeman*, March 16, April 6, 1907.

On April 12, 1907, Johnson left Australia on the *Sonoma* and returned to the United States.[390]

The scuffle between Johnson and McLean led the *Sydney Bulletin* to say that "the departing nigger, whose refreshment bills here were very large, departed in a halo of recrimination."[391]

Some local experts debated just how good Johnson really was. Former fighter Mick Nathan said Johnson was a wonder, quick as lightning, as nimble as a cat, and probably better than all past Australian greats.

The *Referee*'s editor, "Amateur" W. F. Corbett, criticized Nathan's opinion. "Put a first-class boxer before Johnson, and I'll be bound he would be found very much wanting. ... I am satisfied from what little I have seen of Johnson...that he is a defensive boxer pure and simple, and by no means a top-notcher at that."[392]

Nathan noted that Corbett previously had spoken well of Johnson's exceptional merits. Hence, he asked, "Why this sudden change of front?" Perhaps it was personal, or racial, or simply a matter of national pride. In conclusion, Nathan said he would be pleased if an Australian boxer could beat Johnson, "but I am not going to allow my national pride to run away with my judgment."[393]

Freeman, April 4, 1908

---

[390] *Sydney Bulletin,* April 18, 1907; *Referee,* April 17, May 1, 1907.
[391] *Sydney Bulletin,* March 21, 1907.
[392] *Referee,* April 10, 1907.
[393] *Referee,* April 24, 1907.

CHAPTER 21

A Big Name Finally Crosses the Line

The *Freeman* said Jim Jeffries had drawn the color line because he was "afraid that if the doors are thrown wide open, the whites may not be able to retain the championship." Jeff said, "If I were not champion I would fight a Negro at any time. I would be specially willing to meet one were he the champion." He meant that he would want to recover the title for the white race, but would not risk losing the title to a black man. The *Freeman* responded, "Surely the white man's claim to superiority lacks ground to stand upon when those who are in a position to defend that claim are compelled to put up the bars to keep another race out of the charmed circle. Yet he has only confessed what others have felt all along."[394]

On May 8, 1907 in Los Angeles, before a crowd of 4,000, 178-pound Tommy Burns clearly won a 20-round decision over 170-pound Jack O'Brien in a championship rematch. O'Brien ran and grabbed and barely threw any punches, much to the crowd's chagrin, which hooted and taunted him, as did Burns. The gate receipts were just over $22,000.

There was a bit of a scandal when Burns subsequently revealed that O'Brien had refused to rematch him unless Tommy would agree to throw the fight. Burns indeed agreed to throw the contest, but then double-crossed O'Brien, who upon realizing it, fought purely to survive. Promoter Tom McCarey backed Burns' claims. Because of his prior knowledge, he told referee Charles Eyton to call off all bets just before the fight began, which he had done. At that point, O'Brien realized the game was up. James J. Jeffries further revealed that O'Brien once had offered him $80,000 to lie down to him. Burns' reputation took a hit for being involved in such a fiasco, though O'Brien's reputation took an even bigger blow.

Another story claimed that O'Brien once had been offered $42,000 to lay down to Joe Gans in Nevada, but O'Brien would not accept because "he did not want to stand the jibes of the world by losing in any way to a 'nigger,' according to his own alleged words." Many fighters drew the color line in part for fear that if they lost, they would be ridiculed and their reputations tarnished worse than if they had lost to a white boxer.[395]

Regardless of the scandal, San Francisco promoter James Coffroth offered Burns an $8,000 guarantee to fight Australian champion Bill Squires in a fight to be held on July 4, and Tommy accepted.

---

[394] *Freeman*, April 20, 1907.
[395] *Los Angeles Times*, May 12, 1907.

Jack Johnson was perturbed by the fact that Squires had avoided him in Australia, and now had obtained a title shot as his de facto reward.

> Jack Johnson is running around San Francisco in an effort to make disturbance directed at Sir William Squires. Not for a while, Jack. Tommy Burns may celebrate the national holiday by attending to Mr. Squires' downfall. But, Tommy, what if you win and Jeff says no? A certain big black shadow will be looming above Thomas. How about it, Tommy? Yes? No?[396]

Johnson made it clear that he wanted to fight Burns, and was not happy about his inability to obtain a title shot. Jack told Tommy so, in person. "When matters were clinched, Johnson spoke to Burns in reference to a match to follow the one with Squires, and hot words, which nearly brought about an impromptu scrap, were indulged in."[397]

In a letter to famed sportswriter Tad, one man from Missouri offered advice on how the press and promoters should treat black fighters. He said,

> If you editors would drop the name of Gans, or, if you did mention him, say that he is a faker, the public would soon forget him, the way they did that other black gent, Mr. Jack Johnson. Keep them in the background. That's the way to treat them, and after a while, if they do fight, they will be old and stale and will get their black blocks knocked off. ...
>
> The clubs are doing their part by not letting them fight, and if they do fight, they make them meet some man of their own color, and thereby keep them from getting any more championships. Now let the press do its work. Draw the color line on them. ... I am a Southern man, and believe that it is the place of the white man to beat the black man, and not the reverse.

Tad Dorgan responded,

> What is a champion, unless he can beat every man in the world of his weight, regardless of color? ... The trouble with the black men is that they are too good. If they were easy and lost every fight there would be no such thing as the color line. ... I don't like to see a black man wallop a white myself, but if they are in the game to show their skill it is coming to them.[398]

The *Freeman* agreed, saying, "Sport followers want to see the best fighters, be they black or white, given a chance and the white fake pugilist does not want to see it that way."[399]

On July 4, 1907 at Colma, California, in the San Francisco Bay area, before an estimated 9,000 spectators, 25-year-old 176-179-pound Tommy Burns scored a 1st round knockout over 28-year-old 182-185-pound Bill

---

[396] *Los Angeles Herald*, May 17, 1907.
[397] *San Francisco Examiner*, December 25, 1908.
[398] *Freeman*, June 8, 1907.
[399] *Freeman*, June 29, 1907.

Squires, dropping Squires three times in all. Observers said Burns was a shifty, intelligent fighter with good footwork, timing, and a terrific punch.

The gate receipts totaled $25,251.50. Burns earned his $8,000 guarantee, plus an alleged $5,000 side-bet.[400]

Freeman, June 8, 1907

Regardless of his impressive victory, Tommy Burns still struggled to obtain respect and full recognition as champion. The *San Francisco Call* said, "The status of Tommy Burns as the successor to Jim Jeffries has not been firmly fixed by his victory yesterday. It is conceded that no foreign boxer has a chance with him, but Jack Johnson is to be reckoned with in this country." Former lightweight champion Battling Nelson believed that Burns needed to defeat Johnson to clinch his claim to the world title:

> [H]e should take on the only real legitimate candidate for the championship honors, Jack Johnson. If Burns can defeat Johnson, the colored heavyweight champion, he will be proclaimed the undisputed heavyweight champion of the world beyond the question of a doubt, now that the only real heavyweight champion, James J. Jeffries, has retired.[401]

Jack Johnson, who was training for a scheduled mid-July 6-round fight in Philadelphia with former champion Bob Fitzsimmons, said,

> Didn't I tell you Squires was the biggest sucker that they ever sent over? ... He never did anything, never had anything and never will amount to anything. ... I will fight Burns any way he wants – clean break, straight rules, cut the purse or winner take all. He is not a champion until he beats me, and I am recognized as the best big man in America today.
>
> Fitzsimmons? Well, I'll put him away before the limit – you'll see.[402]

---

[400] *San Francisco Chronicle*, July 5, 1907.
[401] *San Francisco Call*, July 5, 1907.
[402] *San Francisco Call*, July 8, 1907.

When the press asked Burns about the possibility of fighting Johnson, Tommy said he was not sure whether he would be able to do so. He wanted to show the world that he was the "dusky" fellow's master, but his wife and family did not want him to engage in a mixed-race title fight.[403]

Jack Johnson's next fight was against a legend. 44-year-old Bob Fitzsimmons had been boxing longer than the 29-year-old Johnson had been alive. His amateur career dated back to the 1870s, and his professional career spanned over 27 years, since the early- to mid-1880s. Fitzsimmons had been world middleweight champion in 1891, world heavyweight champion in 1897, and world light heavyweight champion in 1903. He had over 80 pro fights, which included victories over Jack Dempsey[404], Joe Choynski, Peter Maher, Tom Sharkey, James J. Corbett, Gus Ruhlin, and George Gardner.

Bob Fitzsimmons feeds his pet lion

Although Fitzsimmons was old and inactive, he was a big-name fighter, one of the biggest in boxing, and still was highly respected. Bob had that special aura, charisma, and reputation that made fans want to see him no matter what; and suspend their disbelief about his age and inactivity, conceding the legendary Fitzsimmons a chance to defeat Johnson.

The confident Fitzsimmons said,

> I figure that Johnson, who has gained a lot of prominence in the ring because the white men have refused to meet him, will be so busy blocking that he won't be able to hit me. I may step in with a shift and land one of my 57 varieties. One, I think will be enough. I expect to win with a knockout.[405]

Robert Edgren said,

> Fitzsimmons surely has the courage of his convictions. His fight with Jack Johnson will squelch those howlers who claim white men fear the big smoke. Bob Fitzsimmons never feared any man. ... And when Jack sees the icy glint in Bob's blue eyes it's a good bet that he will feel less like fighting than like running a hundred yards in 9 3/5 seconds.

After all, Fitz was crazy enough to keep lions as pets. He feared no man.

---

[403] *San Francisco Evening Post*, July 9, 1907.
[404] The original "Nonpareil" Jack Dempsey, a welterweight and middleweight champion, later served as inspiration for William Harrison Dempsey, a future world heavyweight champion, to change his name to Jack Dempsey, in homage.
[405] *San Francisco Call*, July 8, 1907.

Speaking of Johnson, Dick Kain said, "If there is anything yellow about him Fitz will not be long in finding it out and then the way things will come to Johnson will be sure to surprise him."[406]

The gate receipts would be divided based on an agreed-upon percentage, regardless of result. Still, both were motivated to do well.

> A decided victory for either man will do him a lot of good. It would be a great feather in Fitzsimmons' cap to knock out the man whom all the other white heavies have been dodging. ... Johnson, by putting Fitz away in a decisive manner, can strengthen his claim for a fight with Burns or any other white heavyweight who claims the championship.[407]

Jim Corbett picked Fitzsimmons. He knew how Bob could punch, and "he also knows that the big negro heavyweight dislikes body blows."[408]

On July 17, 1907 in Philadelphia, Jack Johnson fought Bob Fitzsimmons. When Johnson skipped over the ropes, he received feeble and scarce applause. He was seconded by Sam Fitzpatrick, trainer Barney Furey, and Black Bill. Spectators amused themselves by throwing money at Bill, whom Morris Harris had knocked out in the 3rd round earlier that evening.

When Fitzsimmons came down the aisle, the house cheered so loudly for several minutes; it was deafening. When introduced, Bob received another rousing cheer. Johnson practically was ignored.

After a tame and cautious feel-out opening round, in the 2nd round Johnson was more determined. He rushed in and landed a right to the face and a hard left hook, followed by a twisting motion in the clinch, and Fitzsimmons went down to the floor.

Fitzsimmons seemed to be jarred and unnerved, and took his time in rising at the count of five. He still was full of fight, though, and went after Johnson hard. Bob landed a short left hook to the body, which Johnson returned in kind.

Johnson landed a right uppercut to the body and then a hard jolting right uppercut to the face and Fitzsimmons went down again, with a gash on his left cheek bone. Fitz tried to rise, getting up to one knee, but fell over sideways with his head landing on the mat. The referee counted him out.

The *Philadelphia Record* said, "The fight, if such it could be called, did not amount to much. Fitzsimmons, who is only a poor imitation of his former self, was no match for the big black, who could probably have stopped Bob in the first round had he gone at it with a little more determination." The *Philadelphia Public Ledger* and *Philadelphia Press* said it was a pitiful spectacle and nearly a fake, for Fitz put up no competition, and there was little action.

Johnson said that although the crowd wanted him to allow Fitz to last the 6 rounds, he wasn't taking any chances, and was not about to allow Bob

---

[406] *San Francisco Bulletin*, July 8, 1907.
[407] *Philadelphia Record*, July 16, 1907.
[408] *Philadelphia Public Ledger*, July 16, 1907.

to land a devastating blow, so he figured that getting him out as soon as possible was the best course of action.

Johnson showed no signs of exultation. "He seemed to feel as the crowd did - that he was viewing the wreck of the greatest fighter that the game ever saw." There were no cheers. It had the feel of a funeral. Tom O'Rourke said, "He was a kingpin in his day, but his days are over."[409]

Yet, there was some significance to the victory. It was the first time that a black man had defeated a former world heavyweight champion. Although Fitzsimmons was a shell of himself, as has proven to be the case in boxing, names sell tickets, and putting names with reputations on one's record helps build a fighter's reputation. Ironically, this victory actually helped boost Johnson's reputation a great deal further.

Years later, Johnson said he normally allowed fighters to last rounds in order to give the crowd their money's worth, but he could not afford to compromise his reputation, given Bob's age. Therefore he took him out quickly. Jack took little credit for beating a man so far past-it. However,

> The oddest thing about the entire affair was that this knockout earned me a huge leap in everyone's esteem. He knocked out Bob Fitzsimmons! This Johnson must be a real boxer! ... This goes to show how reputations are made. For years I had been fighting the best men who ever put on the gloves and all of those bouts put together did less for my reputation than knocking out poor old Bob Fitzsimmons![410]

Contender Mike Schreck's wife did not want him to fight Johnson. She said, "No, I do not approve of Mike fighting a colored man, unless he held the title. Then I would insist on Mike's fighting him. But there is no chance for Mike to meet Jack Johnson as long as Johnson is not the champion." So Schreck, who recently had defeated Marvin Hart (KO21), also drew the color line.[411]

In late August 1907, Tommy Burns told promoter Jim Coffroth that he would fight Johnson if offered $25,000. Burns said, "I am not afraid of Johnson, as so many people seem to think. While the husky Negro is clever, he has a streak of yellow in his makeup that will show itself in short order when he gets into the ring with me."

Sam McClintick, Dick Hyland's manager, said,

> Johnson is game enough. He has no yellow streak. The only trouble with him is that he isn't aggressive enough. He is too careful. He stalls along all through his fights, taking good care of his face and letting the other man do the work. It's almost impossible to reach him. He doesn't take any chances. He has faked a lot of fights. Perhaps that was because he couldn't get the matches without

---

[409] *Philadelphia Record, Philadelphia Inquirer, Philadelphia Public Ledger, Philadelphia Press,* July 18, 1907; *Freeman,* July 27, 1907.
[410] *My Life and Battles* at 60-61; *In the Ring and Out* at 55.
[411] *Freeman,* August 3, 1907.

promising to be good. Tommy Burns has faked a fight or two as well as Johnson. But neither Johnson nor Burns has ever 'laid down.'[412]

On August 28, 1907 at the Wilmington, Delaware Farmer's Fair, U.S. Senator Benjamin R. Tillman of South Carolina delivered an address to thousands of people who were on hand to hear him talk about "The Race Problem From a Southern Standpoint." Tillman said, "The race problem is threatening the civilization of the South." Tillman declared that the negro was a menace, and the problem that the negro created was greater now than at any time since the Civil War. He "dwelt upon the sad fact that the Civil War cost the nation a half million lives of the very flower of its manhood, yet, he asserted that the race question has to-day more aspects of danger than prior to the opening of the war."

Tillman declared emphatically that education would not solve the race question, and ridiculed that idea which black leader Booker T. Washington had advanced. Tillman declared that Washington's brains were due to the white blood in his veins. His father was white and his mother a negress. "There are 10,000,000 negroes in the country and one Booker T. Washington." He said that one of the worst things in connection with the race problem was the education of the negro, for it would lead to a dreadful war of the races. Tillman abhorred the idea of mixed-race schools, feeling that they would cause racial contamination.

Tillman said the negro vote was venal and purchasable, and was the controlling vote in many Northern States. "The worst of all creatures is the mean, low, white man who puts himself on the level with negroes in order to secure their votes and for political purposes. They are worse than the negroes themselves." Continuing, Tillman said, "I despise a man who for the sake of securing the franchise of negroes placed them on their level."

He said the 15th amendment had led to the pollution of the ballot. "The remedy and the solution of the question lies in the repeal of the Fifteenth Amendment. Unless this is done there will be a race war eventually, and what can now be settled by the ballot will be settled by the bullets."

Tillman related the experience of South Carolina and other Southern states during Reconstruction, when blacks had held political offices. "How would you like to be ruled by negroes?" In response, there were cries from the audience of, "No, no." He said that all acts designed to disenfranchise blacks were necessary in order to preserve civilization. Tillman further said,

> Therein lies the root of the trouble, the doctrine that a negro is as good as a white man. I make this prediction, that the time will come when the two races will be engaged in a deadly conflict. You will wake up some morning and read of the slaughter of whites and blacks, and a race war in all parts of the South. But we shall be able to take care of them. And I have no doubt that the white men of the North, even from Pennsylvania, would come to the help of the Caucasians of the South if their help were needed. But we want the

---
[412] *Freeman*, August 24, 31, 1907.

long-nosed Yankees to keep their hands out of it and let us settle the problem.

And the cause of this feeling between the races in the South? We have been spending our money to educate the negroes. We have been educating them so that many of them can read and write. ... But the fanatics and negroes of their North are sending down their papers to the South Carolina and other Southern negroes, and this incendiary stuff inflames them. They believed from reading it that they are oppressed and deprived of rights which they are told were given them as an outcome of the civil war. This flame of hatred fanned by the Northern fanatics will cause the outbreak that will bring bloodshed to the South and a war of the races.

The negro can never be the equal of the white man because he is by nature the inferior. You can't make a white man out of a negro by sending him to school. The negro race has not the necessary moral fibre in it.

After his speech, members of the Democratic League presented the senator with a handsome gold-headed ebony cane. "Tillman held the attention of the large crowd from beginning to the end of his speech, which was frequently interrupted by applause. Many of his hearers were women, who were particularly demonstrative when he made some of his most effective points."[413]

That same day, on August 28, 1907, in an open-air arena on the Atlantic League baseball grounds at Lauer's Park in Reading, Pennsylvania, Jack Johnson fought 23-year-old 197-pound 6' tall Charles "Kid" Cutler. Cutler had traveled with John L. Sullivan as his sparring partner in exhibitions. Recognized as one of the best wrestlers in the country, of the 215 wrestlers that he had met, only 5 were able to stay 15 minutes with him. As a boxer, Cutler held a KO3 over Jim Jeffords. Sullivan hailed Cutler as the coming champion. Johnson weighed 210 pounds.

According to the local *Reading Eagle*, in the 1st round, after carefully sparring and studying his opponent, suddenly Johnson landed a terrific uppercut on Cutler's jaw and he fell like a log, down and out for the full ten-count. The quick ending surprised the crowd. The fight had lasted only a minute. "People who saw how quickly [Johnson] disposed of Cutler think he would have a good chance with Champion Jeffries. Cutler is one of the best built fighters that ever donned fighting togs."[414]

Kid Cutler

Years later, Johnson explained that he had stopped Cutler quickly because John L. Sullivan had declared that Johnson

---

[413] *Philadelphia Press, Philadelphia Record*, August 29, 1907.
[414] *Reading Eagle*, August 28, 29, 1907; *New York World*, August 28, 1907.

didn't have a champion's punch. Jack wanted to demonstrate his punching power and see to it that Sullivan's protégé obtained little glory. "That was the last I ever heard of John L. Sullivan's opinions."[415]

The *Freeman* predicted, "Burns has no idea of taking on Johnson, and when he gets ready to fight again he will sidestep big Jack and take on one of the white men."[416]

On September 12, 1907 in Bridgeport, Connecticut, Jack Johnson boxed 165-pound 22-year-old white Sailor Burke in a 6-round no-decision bout. Burke had scored 9 knockouts in 17 wins. He had never been stopped.

5,500 people attended, including sporting men from all over the East Coast, packing the sold-out Smith's Opera-House to capacity. About 1,500 New Yorkers paid $2.30 each for railroad fare and from $2 to $5 for seats.

When Burke was a no-show for 30 minutes, the crowd wondered whether he had grown cold feet. His manager explained, "He can't get on his shoes." A spectator asked, "Are his feet frozen?" Nevertheless, when finally he appeared, Burke received a tremendous ovation.

The nearby *New Haven Evening Register* said the Sailor kept dropping down constantly from terrific body blows, several times in every round, taking nine-counts to survive. He also clinched incessantly, as often as he could, making it impossible for Johnson to stop him. The crowd hissed and yelled at Burke for his survival tactics. Jack smiled and said, "Stand up and fight; I can't knock you out when you are on the floor. Here, how do you like this one? Go ahead, shoot one at me; I want to see if I can catch it." Only Burke's clinching, dropping, and stalling kept him from being stopped. Afterwards, Johnson said, "I tried hard to get him, but he was there to stay and he did it. He just wouldn't stand up and fight."

The *Washington Times* reported that the Marine Burke went to his knees 17 times, often without being hit. Still, "he took a whaling that would have torn the heart out of an ordinary fighter." The *Day* said Burke hit the floor five times more often than his glove landed on any part of Johnson's anatomy.

However, Robert Edgren of the *New York World*, whom the *Freeman* had accused of being racially biased, and whose reports on Johnson's fights often contained some degree of racial prejudice, presented a totally opposite perspective. Edgren accused Johnson of holding back and carrying Burke, never having any intention whatsoever of putting him away. In his article, Edgren called Johnson the "dinge with a broad smile," the "cloud," and the "ink person." Johnson mostly slapped the body, and refused to hit the Sailor's jaw, for fear of knocking him out. "Johnson flapped and slapped Burke on the crossed wrists, but never, never risked hitting him on that open and exposed jaw." "It puzzled Johnson to think out some way of getting at him without hitting his jaw by accident. Burke's jaw was so near that it was always getting in the way. It was a nuisance." Burke swung and fell down when he missed. He rose in only four seconds, and Johnson said

---

[415] *My Life and Battles* at 61.
[416] *Freeman*, September 7, 1907.

in a jokingly reproachful way, "Aw, why didn't you take nine?" Johnson allegedly "urged the sailor in a soft whisper to stay down as long as he could," so he could kill the clock.[417]

SCENES AT RINGSIDE WHERE WOULD-BE 'CHAMP' WAS PRINCIPAL IN RAW FAKE

New York World cartoon by Robert Edgren, September 13, 1907

Jack O'Brien sat at ringside. He said, "I think Jack Johnson is a wonderful boxer, puncher and fighter. I believe he could whip Jeffries and I don't blame any of the big fighters for ducking him."[418]

In early October 1907, Tommy Burns confirmed that he would fight Johnson if he was paid a guaranteed $25,000. However, at that point, no promoter was willing to put up that much money for the fight.[419]

Burns decided to travel to England to fight British champion Gunner Moir. Burns was willing to fight the white Moir for less than a third of what he demanded to fight Johnson - a $5,000 purse and a $2,500 side wager.

---

[417] *New Haven Evening Register, New York World, Washington Times, Day*, September 13, 1907.
[418] *Freeman*, September 21, 1907.
[419] *Los Angeles Herald*, October 2, 6, 1907.

CHAPTER 22

Convincing San Francisco

In mid-October 1907, Jack Johnson arrived in San Francisco with manager Sam Fitzpatrick for a fight with "Fireman" Jim Flynn, whose 34-bout career included a LKOby15 to Tommy Burns in a heavyweight championship contest. Against Burns, Flynn fought a game, grueling, entertaining bout, so his stock rose even in defeat. Since then, Flynn had not lost a fight, defeating Jack "Twin" Sullivan, George Gardner, Dave Barry, and Tony Ross. Fans enjoyed his aggressive hard-punching style.

Flynn fought like Marvin Hart, and they were fighting in the San Francisco area, where Johnson felt he was robbed of the decision against Hart. This would be Johnson's first bout in San Francisco since that late March 1905 fight, two and a half years prior. To allay Johnson's concerns about an improper decision being rendered, they agreed to schedule the contest for 45 rounds, long enough such that Johnson would not have to worry too much about a bad decision. Someone likely was going to be stopped in that length of time.

They would fight for 55% of the receipts, to be divided 55% to the winner and 45% to the loser.

The local *Call* said Johnson would have to show gameness to win, instead of just coasting to a 20-round decision, for Flynn would be on top of him throughout the 45 rounds.[420]

The "big smoke" Johnson advertised a ladies' day at his training quarters. "The fair members of his race are expected to appear in numbers, as 'Arthur' is popular with his people." Jack had been seen on on the street with his bulldog and "his swaggering walk," totally confident of victory.

Impressed with Flynn's training, local reporters said, "Before making a bet on Johnson, it would be well worth while to look this fireman-fighter over." "As a gymnasium worker, Flynn is in a class by himself." "He is constantly on the move – he really works." Flynn was lively on his feet, could hit hard, and was extremely aggressive. He had the fighting spirit of a bundle of tiger cats.[421]

Before setting sail for England, Tommy Burns said he would fight Jack Johnson when he returned to the U.S. Burns said of Johnson, "I haven't much regard for him. He is big, but he isn't as big as he looks. ... His body isn't strong, and I'm satisfied that he has a yellow streak. ... I'll give Johnson a fight, but I'll make terms."[422]

---

[420] *San Francisco Call*, October 16, 17, 20, 1907.
[421] *San Francisco Call, San Francisco Evening Post*, October 22 - 25, 1907.
[422] *New York Evening Word*, October 24, 1907; *Call*, October 27, 1907.

Jack Johnson and sparring partner Denver Ed Martin

Fireman Flynn was absolutely certain that he would stop Johnson, whom he claimed had a weak heart.[423]

Flynn's trainer said Johnson had the newspaper reputation for being the man whom Jeffries and Burns were afraid to fight, "and this has given him a lot of prestige that he hasn't really earned."

Flynn's followers were so enthusiastic that they wanted to wager that Johnson would not last 10 rounds. They believed that Johnson would jump over the ropes in fear once Flynn started after him.[424]

Sports-writers were excited. "This mill is especially interesting to local fans, as it will give the patrons of the game the proper dope on the gameness of the negro, who has never been called upon to go above the twenty-round mark before a rough and hustling fighter of the Jim Flynn variety."

The unconcerned Johnson said, "I think about ten rounds at the outside will be enough for Flynn. I'm going to show the public that when it comes to rough work, I'm there. They tell me that Flynn will come to me in every round. That will make it still easier." Johnson walked around town featuring his confident "I should worry!" smile.[425]

---

[423] *San Francisco Call, San Francisco Evening Post*, October 31, 1907.
[424] *San Francisco Examiner, San Francisco Call*, November 1, 1907.
[425] *San Francisco Bulletin*, November 1, 1907.

San Francisco Examiner, November 2, 1907

The *Call* criticized Johnson for refusing to take chances in the ring, calling him faint-hearted. "Without the courage he would present the spectacle of a black man turning white if he ever faced Jeffries in the ring." The upcoming fight would show whether Johnson had heart or would quit under fire. However, Sam Fitzpatrick, "who knows a fighter when he sees one," smiled when broached on the subject of "Johnson's timidity." He said such a notion was false, and Jack would win by knockout.

The *San Francisco Chronicle* questioned whether it was right to attribute to Johnson the "so-called streak of yellow." Although he often took matters too leisurely, that did not mean he was not game. The aggressive Flynn would make Johnson fight. When Jim landed "his punches are going to hurt and the spectators will then have an opportunity to find just how much punishment Johnson will stand."

The *Examiner* said that Johnson, "who disputes Tommy Burns' right to call himself champion of the world," promised to create demand for a Burns match with his performance.

The day before the fight, on November 1, *after* their final training, 22-year-old 5'10 ½" Flynn weighed 174 ½ pounds, while 6'1" 29-year-old Johnson weighed 192, giving him the 17 ½-pound weight advantage.

Al Kaufman said he would challenge Flynn if he won, but was passing up Johnson. He continued to draw the color line.[426]

On November 2, 1907 at Jim Coffroth's Mission street outdoor arena in Colma, California, the Jack Johnson vs. Jim Flynn fight took place. It was a sunshiny day. The scheduled 45-round contest started at 3 p.m.

Johnson entered the ring first, with an air of confidence, smiling. After Flynn climbed through the ropes, Johnson put out his hand to shake, but Jim rudely thrust it to one side with a vicious scowl on his face. They later touched gloves at the behest of Referee Billy Roche.

Billy Jordan announced Johnson as the heavyweight champion of the world by default, and Flynn as the Colorado fireman and cyclone.

---

[426] *San Francisco Call, San Francisco Examiner, San Francisco Chronicle*, November 2, 1907.

Throughout the fight, the game Flynn constantly attacked, rushing in and firing vicious blows on the inside as much as possible, maintaining a fast pace. As usual, Johnson's defense held up very well, but every time Flynn forced him back or threw or  landed any kind of blow, whether solid or not, the crowd cheered wildly and urged him on. The boxers often clinched and wrestled. Johnson smiled and laughed at Flynn's efforts. Jack sometimes peppered him with long-range blows, and other times mixed it up in close, digging in body shots, hooks, and uppercuts. He was very cool, and stood his ground quite often. Johnson gradually picked him apart and landed effective punishing blows that wore down Flynn.

In the 1st round, the "big smoke" landed a vicious straight right just beneath the left eye, gashing the fireman's cheek and starting to raise a lump which gradually swelled and puffed up, assuming the size and color of a plum. Eventually Flynn could not see out of it at all.

In the 3rd round, as he was rushing, Flynn ran into a left jab and straight right to the jaw that sent him down to his knees, though he rose immediately and continued attacking.

In the 6th round, with a broad grin, Johnson goaded and taunted him, saying, "Come on, Flynn, come right in. They're asking you to do it. Step right in, my boy." As usual, Flynn rushed and charged in, smashing away, with the crowd cheering his efforts, but he ran into a shower of clean blows. Flynn's right ear commenced bleeding.

At the end of the 9th round, Johnson blocked a high right and then ripped a right uppercut into the stomach which brought Flynn to the floor on his hands and knees. A deathly pallor spread over his face. Flynn was saved by the ringing of the bell, and his seconds carried him to his corner.

In the 10th round, like a matador, Jack stepped aside from the blind attacking bull and laughed. In the clinches, Jack laughed over Jim's shoulder. The desperate Flynn butted Johnson severely with his head, drawing a warning from the referee. Johnson kept landing frequently. Flynn laughed and said, "Gee, but you're a tough nigger, ain't you?"

Before the 11th round, Flynn remarked, "I wish I was as clever as this coon." When the round began, Johnson yelled derisively, "Come on Flynn. They're telling you to." With his left eye closed tight, the savage Flynn rushed continually, while Johnson kept hitting him. Flynn shook his head and laughed, saying, "You're a clever big nigger. I wish I was as clever as you." Johnson replied, "That's what I am."

Flynn lowered his head and rushed in, firing an overhand left, and the next instant Johnson nailed him with a swift perfectly-timed counter right uppercut to the jaw that dropped Flynn.

After momentarily glancing nonchalantly at Flynn's prostrate body, Johnson walked leisurely to his corner, feeling sure that the blow had ended the fight. Flynn's cornermen agreed, for they jumped through the ropes to attend to him and carry Jim to his corner. Flynn remained out of it for several minutes, until finally he recovered and was able to leave the ring.

The local newspapers agreed that Flynn had been no match, for the colored man outboxed, outfought, outroughed, and outclassed the Coloradan throughout. Johnson finished him in the 11th round with "as neatly placed a right uppercut as ever crashed against the fighter's chin," landing with the speed of a sixteen-inch shell, exploding on the point of the jaw. "The wallop would have made a class A re-enforced concrete structure look displeased." "He told his friends he would accomplish his task in ten rounds and he made a fairly good forecast, for it took him about one minute longer." Flynn never could land his vaunted punch cleanly.

The *Chronicle* said Flynn was game to last as long as he did with "that big cannibal," but he had as much chance "as a Prohibition candidate in Kentucky." "Flynn did not land one punch that hurt the Ethiopian."

Johnson's impressive performance garnered him more momentum for his championship challenges. "That he must be reckoned with when the heavyweight championship is discussed Johnson proved to the satisfaction of the crowd that was present." No longer was "Little Arthur Johnson" a "dark joke." Jeffries was lucky to be retired. As for Burns, "he must come out of the cyclone cellar and take a look at this black cloud that is waiting for him. He must drop the festive stall and cease the airy bull and fight Little Arthur or forever hold his peace."

> If Johnson has any of that yellow streak, he left it at home yesterday or he must have thought that the ropes were too high to jump over. Those who expected him to bark or show other symptoms of the dog breed that is in him were disappointed. The gold mine he uses for teeth was flashing all the time as the fight went on, for the coon was grinning like a black Cheshire cat. Jack will never be broke as long as he retains his dentistry. There is enough of the root of all evil in his face to support him comfortably in his old age.
>
> After the battle everything black or tan adjourned to the Rue Pacific, where the countrymen of the winner indulged in the dances of their native jungles in sunny Africa. The attendance of the "cullud" population at the show was a large one, and very few of the chickens in the vicinity of Colma ventured out of their apartments until long after the backers of "Lil Arthur" were well on their way to the Rue Pacific.
>
> Tommy Burns, please write.

The delighted black crowd at the Rue Pacific sang songs and jingles in gleeful celebration of Johnson's victory.

According to the *San Francisco Call*, afterwards, Johnson said,

> Well, that yellow streak they have all been talking about has not shown in me yet, and I want to say right now there is not a man living who can bring it out. ...
>
> Now I will fight any of them. They can not bring them up too fast. Burns is my meat and I am going to keep after him until he consents

to meet me. He will have to fight me sooner or later, and when he does he will get the same as Mr. Flynn got this afternoon.

Jim Flynn said,

> I am the only one of these fellows who is game enough to take a chance with Johnson ... Just say for me that he is too much for any of the white fellows, bar none. I've tried them all, and I know that if Johnson can get me this way he can take care of any of them. ... They'll find out for themselves what I found out. I wish I was as clever as he is. ... Take it from me, Johnson is a wonder and the best of them all.[427]

Flynn told the *San Francisco Bulletin*, "Just let these other white fellows go up against that nigger, is the best compliment that I can pay him. I have met all of the top-notchers and have managed to hold my own with them."

The impressed *Bulletin* said, "Tommy Burns was wise in picking Gunner Moir for his next opponent for the probability is that if he had tackled Jack Johnson prior to taking on the Englishman, the trip to King Edward's country would have been indefinitely postponed." Johnson had shown that "he is in a class by himself so far as the heavyweights of the present day are concerned."[428]

Finally, even San Francisco was sold. Jack Johnson deserved a title shot. He had fought six times in 1907, and had been far superior to all of his opponents.

JACK JOHNSON, WHO KNOCKED OUT FLYNN

---

[427] *San Francisco Examiner, San Francisco Chronicle, San Francisco Call,* November 3, 1907.
[428] *San Francisco Bulletin,* November 4, 1907.

CHAPTER 23

Chasing the Champ

After knocking out Jim Flynn, Jack Johnson's chances of finding anyone willing to fight him were looking dim. Tommy Burns was fighting in England. Al Kaufman and others drew the color line. Therefore, according to the *San Francisco Bulletin*, "the husky negro will be obliged to await Burns' return from England. Even then it is no cinch that he will be able to get a match, as Burns doesn't appear very anxious to meet the 'ding.'"

Jim Ryan said, "Since his defeat of Jim Flynn, Jack Johnson's smoke has increased in volume and has received such recognition that the chances are Tommy Burns will be forced into a meeting with him when he returns from England." There likely would be a very good house, too. Therefore, unless affected by racial considerations, promoters probably could make the match. Burns believed that Johnson was overrated. Ryan agreed, feeling that Burns would stop the black champion in 15 rounds or less.

On December 2, 1907 in London, England, in his third title defense of the year, 171-pound Tommy Burns knocked out 182-pound British champion James "Gunner" Moir in the 10th round. As a result of beating title claimants Hart and O'Brien, Australian champion Squires, and British champion Moir, several newsmen said Burns had to be given firm recognition as the heavyweight champion of the world.

Still, some believed that Jack Johnson was the best heavyweight in the world, and Burns would not earn full undisputed recognition as champion until he defeated him. Tommy Ryan said, "Tommy Burns, a good fighter, is a joke for a champion. Really I must consider this fellow Johnson as a sure enough black peril. I doubt if there is a heavy today that can stand him off. He is getting better all the time, too."

Talk of a Burns vs. Johnson bout continued. "Burns is under promise to come back to the United States and give battle to the negro heavyweight. Johnson, who doesn't bank altogether on what Tommy has said in the connection, says he will be waiting at the dock."[429]

Jack O'Brien tentatively scheduled a match with Johnson, but then called it off with a hand injury claim. The *Freeman* said that like Burns, O'Brien would make any excuse not to fight him. "They all fear Johnson, because they are satisfied Johnson is the real superior of them all in the heavyweight division."[430]

Regardless of his claim that he would return to the U.S. to fight Johnson, Tommy Burns was not about to return to America or box

---

[429] *San Francisco Bulletin*, November 4, 1907; *Freeman*, November 23, 1907; *Los Angeles Herald*, December 8, 1907; *San Francisco Examiner*, December 3, 1907.
[430] *Freeman*, December 28, 1907, January 4, 1908.

Johnson any time soon. He was receiving too many lucrative offers to fight against lesser foes abroad. Burns was in the business to make as much money as possible, and the easier the better. Hence, he decided to remain overseas. From England, Burns wrote, "Yes, I'm getting the easy money and anybody who wouldn't take this easy money would be a fool." He would earn about $10,000 to fight Jack Palmer in London, and $8,500 to fight Irish champion Jem Roche in Dublin. "Don't blame me do you? This beats gold mining."[431]

From New York, Johnson said he intended to sail out to England to meet Burns. "I won't give him a chance to turn around again. ... I certainly am anxious to meet that man. ... I'll lick Burns in the same time that it took to trim Flynn. All I want is the chance. That's all, just the chance."[432]

On February 10, 1908 in London, Tommy Burns knocked out Jack Palmer in the 4th round.

W. W. Naughton wrote, "The American public will forgive Tommy for taking on these easy marks if he will keep his promise and come home within a reasonable time to fight Jack Johnson."[433]

The *New York World*'s Robert Edgren believed that despite their great difference in height and weight, "it is no cinch that the champion will turn his title over to the big smoke." Edgren called Johnson a faker.

Sam Fitzpatrick said Johnson was willing to fight Burns anywhere on Earth. He would accept any fair offer.[434]

The *New York Sun* said Burns had avoided Johnson by traveling abroad, and then remaining there. Many believed that "with the big negro Burns will have the fight of his life."

From England, Burns said,

> This fellow Jack Johnson is the first man I'll fight when I return to America, if shown the money, as he does not look any harder to beat than some of the fighters I've already defeated, such as Marvin Hart, who beat Johnson in San Francisco several months before I trimmed Hart.

Burns claimed that Johnson once offered to bet him $10,000 on a fight between them, which Burns accepted and immediately wrote out a check, but Johnson was not able to come up with the money.

> I then told him I would show the people present what kind he was. I asked him to step into a room, lock the door and fight me for nothing. But the big black was not game. I called him in a way that I wouldn't take from any man even if I knew I was going to be killed the next minute. All yellow fighters are alike. Give then an inch and

---

[431] *New York World*, January 10, 1908.
[432] *Freeman*, January 11, 1908.
[433] *San Francisco Examiner*, February 10, 11, 1908.
[434] *New York World*, February 11, 25, 1908.

they'll try to grab the whole world. I am going to force him to fight or crawl just as soon as I get back to the States.[435]

Johnson offered to fight Burns winner-take-all, and claimed that Burns was a liar who did not want to fight him. The war of words was on.[436]

Mrs. Burns said her husband "will make Johnson jump out of the ring before the fight is over." However, she didn't want him to fight a black man:

> He would never fight Johnson if I had a chance to decide it, for I don't like him to fight colored men, and he promised me when we married that he would never fight a Negro. But he's sore about what has been printed about him and Johnson, and I'm positive that he will have to sign up for the battle just as soon as he gets in America and leave the explanations with me later.

Johnson said he was willing to fight Burns for $5,000 cash as his end. He would accept whatever conditions Tommy wanted:

> Burns can make the ring ten feet square and select a private ring and throw the key out of the window if he dares. I know I can beat him and I think he knows it, too. If he backs down on the proposition, I will go over to London anyway and shame him out of King Edward's islands.
>
> When the offer was first cabled from the other side it seemed so unfair to me that I naturally balked. We could get more money in California, and money is what we are both after. But I am so anxious to get him into a ring that I will waive everything within reason to make the match. By betting the $5,000 I can double my end of the purse. ... If Burns can beat me, I am willing to quit the game. Any number of rounds will suit, from one to a thousand. ... Burns can name the terms.[437]

The *Freeman* believed that Johnson would be given fair treatment in England, for there was less race prejudice there. "Prejudice has grown so strong in this country that a majority of the sporting element can barely stand to see the black boy defeat the white."

On St. Patrick's Day, March 17, 1908 in Dublin, Ireland, 168-pound Tommy Burns scored a 1st round knockout against 177-pound Irish champion Jem Roche. The fight lasted only 88 seconds.

In early April 1908, Tommy Burns' manager Billy Neil said Burns would remain in Europe for several more months, for the money there was too good to turn down. Tommy already had made $53,125 in fight purses, side-bets, and theatrical engagements.

Neil said Burns would fight Johnson for any club that paid him $30,000 as his share of the prize money, regardless of the result. He also was willing

---

[435] *New York Sun*, March 1, 1908.
[436] *New York World*, March 2, 1908.
[437] *Freeman*, March 8, 1908.

to bet Johnson $5,000 that Jack could not stop him within 20 rounds, as he claimed he could do.[438]

The biggest impediment to a Johnson-Burns fight would be finding a promoter willing to pay the amounts demanded, and one willing to promote a mixed-race heavyweight championship, something which never had been done in the gloved era.

On April 18, 1908 in Paris, France, Tommy Burns stopped the husky 200-plus-pound Jewey Smith in the 5th round.

Parisians liked Sam McVey, who had scored knockouts in all of his fights there, and they wanted to see him fight Burns. Tommy said he would fight McVey *if* the money was right.[439]

Speaking of how badly he wanted to fight the champion, Johnson said,

> Say, there's one thing in this world I'm crazy for and that's fried chicken, with corn muffins on the side. Would you believe me if I told you that I'd fast for three days with that outside my window if I thought I could fight Burns the next day? Burns isn't treating me right, and I don't think he's treating himself right. Suppose he beat me – why, he could go round the world and be just twice as big a drawing card as he is. People think he is afraid to fight me, and is picking the quinces. Why, my golly, if he can beat me, why don't he come back and do it? He said that right after the Moir fight he was coming back to muss me up, but I see now that he has two more fights up. Well (sigh), everything comes to him who waits, they say.[440]

In late April, Jack Johnson and his manager Sam Fitzpatrick set sail for England, arriving in London on April 27, 1908. Johnson hoped that his presence there would help facilitate the Burns match being made in Europe, and make it harder for Burns to turn him down. However, neither the English nor the French were willing to meet Burns' financial demands for a Johnson fight.[441]

Fighter Willie Lewis offered his thoughts on Burns, Johnson, and McVey, saying,

> [Burns] played with [Jewey] Smith and he would occasionally drop over a left hook or a right cross, and down would go 200 pounds of English beef. Believe me, Burns is a terrific puncher. He dropped this fellow Smith with little hooks that didn't travel six inches. He's a corking good puncher, and the fastest big man I ever looked on. If you want my opinion, he'll whip Johnson to death certainly. Anyone who picks Burns for a sucker is a sucker himself for doing it. … He carries a sleep pill in either mitt, and fights with a crouch that makes it hard for an opponent to get to his jaw.

---

[438] *Los Angeles Herald*, April 11, 1908; *New York World*, April 11, 15, 1908.
[439] *New York Herald*, *New York Daily Tribune*, *San Francisco Chronicle*, all April 19, 1908.
[440] *New Zealand Truth*, April 25, 1908, quoting the *San Francisco Bulletin*.
[441] *New York World*, April 21, 27, 1908.

He is very short and put together compactly, but he's got an awful reach. That's the secret of his fighting. His reach is 74 ½ inches, about the same as Bob Fitzsimmons. He is a fast puncher, quick to take advantage of an opening, and he is the jollying kid in the ring, for while fighting Smith he kept encouraging the latter to fight by saying, "That's right, Jewey, keep coming," and "Oh, you forgot to block that one," and "That's right, put more steam in it." This got Smith's goat, and he had barrels of confidence when he entered the ring.

You may be surprised to know that Sam McVey, the big Los Angeles negro, is the Parisians' fighting idol, and as soon as Burns got to Paris he was pestered to death with challenges from McVey and his followers. They offered a purse of $20,000 for the match, and Burns said to me:

"I had made up my mind that I would fight only one negro – that's Johnson – but I hate like the deuce to let this money get away from me." At the fight Saturday McVey and his backers again challenged Burns, and Tommy replied:

"Give me a purse of $25,000, split $20,000 to the winner and $5,000 to the loser, and a side bet of $5,000, and I'll fight McVey here." If they fight the scrap will draw an awful mob. Everybody in this town is crazy over McVey. They never saw anything else as big and ugly. ... You ought to see that coon. He's got clothes that would make a Sixth avenue darkey dude look like a rag picker. Last time I saw him he wore a cream-colored suit that looked like silk – sort of a pajama rig. He goes to fights in a carriage with a dress suit on and a bouquet in his hand, and they say society has taken him up, and he is taken around to dinners in the swell houses, and let sit at the table without putting a muzzle or a chain on him.

The frogs will go crazy when Johnson comes home. And they will think we're a dingy nation for fair when those two big smokes go down the boulevard at the same time.[442]

Burns declined the National Sporting Club's offer of 2,500 pounds ($12,500) for a Johnson fight, insisting upon $30,000 guaranteed.[443]

Burns-McVey was not going to happen either, because French promoters were not willing to pay Burns what he demanded for that fight.

The British were upset by Burns' financial demands. "Burns is fast losing favor with the general public, owing to his excessive demands. Johnson has the general sympathy of the English sporting world, and many are already calling him the world's champion, saying that Burns has lost the title by default."[444]

---

[442] *Los Angeles Herald*, May 6, 1908.
[443] *Manchester Guardian*, May 6, 1908.
[444] *Freeman*, May 23, 1908.

Los Angeles Herald, June 7, 1908

The *New York World's* Robert Edgren believed that Burns would defeat Johnson, an opinion which he said was growing in favor. A few drives into Johnson's stomach and ribs would suffice to end matters. "No black fighter ever entered a ring who was game when he got a body lacing."[445]

Burns accepted an Australian offer to fight Bill Lang in Sydney during the visit of the American fleet. He would earn $10,000 for that fight, regardless of result, and possibly more for another fight.[446]

The *Los Angeles Herald* wrote, "Tommy Burns, of course, stands out as the leading light in the heavyweight class, though the dark cloud created by the appearance on his trail of Jack Johnson has somewhat dimmed his star. The title seems to lie between these two, however, and should be so confined for some time."[447]

While in England, Johnson engaged in several sparring exhibitions.

Sam Fitzpatrick wrote that he and Johnson had been in England for four weeks, doing their best to force Burns into a match. "The British public know full well that we have placed no obstacle whatever in the way of Burns." Burns was scheduled to rematch Squires in Paris, a man whom he had defeated already in a single round (and whom Jim Flynn had stopped after Johnson had stopped Flynn). Burns then would fight Lang in Australia, a man whom Johnson had handled and stopped easily. Fitzpatrick saw these bouts as a way to get Burns out of England, where he was taking criticism for his financial demands, and again avoid Johnson.

> In the face of all this, there is surely no question as to who is today the genuine champion of the world. Johnson is, as he has been all along, prepared to box, and Burns fails to come forward. There is, therefore, only one inference to be drawn, which is that Burns is afraid. From this date I therefore feel justified in claiming the championship for Jack Johnson, who, I may add, is ready to defend it at all times, and against all comers, giving Burns the first chance.

---

[445] *New York World*, May 12, 1908.
[446] *Los Angeles Herald*, May 24, 1908; *New York World*, May 28, 1908.
[447] *Los Angeles Herald*, June 7, 1908.

Tommy Burns said,

> Johnson strolled into the National Sporting Club yesterday, lording it in a disgusting way, and I turned him down cold – wouldn't shake hands with the big dub. I'll beat him just as sure as my name is Brusso – that is, if I can get him into a ring with me. ... I am going over to Paris to trim Squires. ... I have a tempting offer to run down to Australia, where I will find another lemon. I know I have been regarded as a joke during all my fighting career, but I am getting the money, so what's the difference? Thirty thousand for mine, though, don't forget that.

The Brits called Burns a bluffer. They believed that Tommy only wanted the easy money; scoffing at a real test.[448]

In the meantime, in his second fight in Paris, on June 13, 1908, in a rematch, Tommy Burns knocked out Bill Squires in the 8th round. Jack Johnson was sitting at ringside. The plan was not to allow Burns or the sporting public to forget about Johnson and his rightful challenges.

Within days of their rematch, it was announced that an Australian sporting syndicate had arranged a third bout between Burns and Squires for a quite large $15,000 purse.[449]

The *Los Angeles Herald* defended Burns, saying,

> Burns is the most pronounced globe-trotting champion the world ever knew. ...
>
> When he returns to America next fall he undoubtedly will be ready to take on Jack Johnson and all other fighters who want his game. Never lacking in cool courage, he is not afraid of any of them, and his good judgment in passing up the hard game for the soft money engagements should not be construed as cowardice on his part. It merely is an exhibition of good sense in taking easy money where no chance is involved, in preference to taking the same money where a materially greater chance of losing exists.[450]

Johnson wrote an article published in London entitled, "I Am Getting Very Tired." In it, he discussed his Tommy Burns hunt. He was convinced that Burns was anxious to avoid meeting him.

> [N]ot content with wriggling out of a match with me, he adds insult to injury by declaring that I have a 'yellow streak,' which, in everyday language, of course, means that I am afraid, or am not game, which, all things considered, seems hardly justified, since every sporting man in England knows that, for some time past, I have been chasing Burns half round the world in order to get a match with him.

---

[448] *Freeman*, June 20, 27, 1908.
[449] *New York World*, June 15, 1908; *Los Angeles Herald*, June 16, 1908.
[450] *Los Angeles Herald*, June 22, 1908.

Johnson noted that when he went East to try to get a match with either Burns, Kaufman, Berger, or O'Brien, all of them left and went West. When he went West, they all scattered about. Then he went to Australia to get a match with Squires, but then Bill sailed away to America. The "white fellows were beating it faster than ever to keep out of my way."[451]

On July 4, 1908 in Colma, California, Battling Nelson knocked out Joe Gans in the 17th round to win the world lightweight championship.

The *Los Angeles Herald* observed that the Negro fighter was passing away, and had been eliminated from championships. George Dixon, Joe Walcott, and Joe Gans all had been defeated and lost their world titles to whites, having fought once too often. "The negro of today in the ring occupies a decidedly less conspicuous position and will find it remarkably difficult to get engagements. Jack Johnson alone stands in a position to command the admiration of the fight world for his prowess, real or imaginary, as it may be."

There were many who did not want a mixed-race championship bout to happen. No American, English, or French promoter put up the money necessary to make the Burns-Johnson match, even though it was justified both from a financial and sporting perspective. Fewer and fewer were promoting mixed-race championship bouts in any weight class, at least not after whites had recovered the titles from black champions. Hence, it was not entirely clear whether any promoter would financially back a Burns-Johnson championship fight.[452]

Ben Taylor

On July 31, 1908 in Plymouth, England, Jack Johnson took on Big Ben Taylor, "the Woolwich Infant," who had engaged in about 40 fights.[453] Taylor was the only one willing to fight Johnson. Jack had not fought since early November 1907 - nearly nine months.

The *London Sporting Life*, which helped make the match, said Ben Taylor had been boxing for 7 to 8 years, was 28 years of age, stood 5'11 ½" and weighed about 14.5 stone (203 pounds) in his present top condition, although sometimes he fought as high as 252 pounds. In his last bout, with McVey (a.k.a. McVea), Ben was stopped in 11 rounds, but it was one of the finest contests ever seen in Paris. The Cosmopolitan Club agreed to pay the boxers 80% of the gate receipts for a 10-round contest of 2 minutes each, fought with 6-ounce gloves.

Both boxers received a warm welcome from the crowd of 3,000. Johnson bowed gracefully to the crowd. He was taller and slightly heavier than Taylor, who was a big man himself.

---

[451] *Penny Illustrated Paper and Illustrated Times* (London, England), June 27, 1908.
[452] *Los Angeles Herald*, July 6, 1908.
[453] Ben Taylor's record included: 1901 W5 Sandy Ferguson; 1902 L10 and D6 Sandy Ferguson; 1904 L10 Gunner Moir; 1907 LKOby3 Sam McVey; and 1908 LKOby11 Sam McVey.

As usual, Johnson dominated, smashing the body and head, while exhibiting his brilliant defense, smiling while parrying the blows with ease and nonchalance. He alternated between coasting and playing defense, then sailing in, staggering and sometimes decking the Englishman, and then stepping back and allowing him to recover, carrying him. At one point in the 3rd round, Johnson literally caught and held Taylor up, actually preventing him from falling. Taylor gamely took the blows and kept coming back for more, showing tremendous pluck.

Johnson drew blood from his mouth and dropped Taylor in the 2nd, 4th, 6th (twice), 7th (five times, twice through the ropes), and 8th (twice) rounds. Seeing that he had enough, the referee stopped the bout in the 8th round and declared Johnson the winner. Had the rounds been of regular three-minute duration instead of two minutes each, the fight would have been over much sooner.

The *Sporting Life* said, "Johnson's display was that of an accomplished boxer, and those critics who asserted that he was as clever as the late Peter Jackson were by no means wrong in their assertion." Johnson kindly paid tribute to Taylor, saying that he never met a gamer man.

The *New York Journal* reported that Johnson said he allowed Taylor to stay as long as he did just to give the spectators a run for their money.[454]

The National Sporting Club was looking for a white fighter who was both willing and able to face Johnson, for it "was not the desire of the club managers to put two black men into the ring." However, it was obvious that no white man in England could cope with Johnson. Those who had a chance to compete, like Mike Schreck, drew the color line.[455]

Robert Edgren described Tommy Burns as a white Sam Langford in build, "but twenty pounds heavier, twice as fast, twice as clever, fully as hard a hitter, and a man of keen active intelligence."[456]

Burns wrote to a Los Angeles reporter, "Give my regards to Spring street and tell the doubting ones to cage Johnson and hold him until I get back. I don't want this mess of gravy spilled before I return."[457]

On August 11, 1908, Burns arrived in Sydney, New South Wales, Australia. Promoter Hugh D. McIntosh said if Burns' bouts there were successful financially, his enterprise would make the Burns-Johnson fight.[458]

The black-owned *Washington Bee* noted that from 1906 to 1907, 122 negro lynchings had taken place under the supposed U.S. democracy, all in states under Democrat rule.[459]

Starting on August 14, 1908, in the Northern town of Springfield, Illinois, where Abraham Lincoln once had resided, a three-day riot took place, initiated by a white woman's claim that a negro had violated her

---

[454] *Sporting Chronicle*, July 31, 1908; *London Sporting Life*, *Manchester Courier*, *New York Journal*, August 1, 1908.
[455] *Freeman*, August 29, 1908; *New York World*, August 6, 1908.
[456] *New York World*, August 7, 11, 1908.
[457] *Los Angeles Herald*, August 5, 1908.
[458] *Sydney Daily Telegraph*, August 12, 1908.
[459] *Washington Bee*, October 17, 1908.

(which she later admitted was false). Inflamed by newspaper sensationalism, and fueled by mounting economic and racial tensions, crowds of whites gathered around the jail demanding that the arrested black man be lynched.

When the sheriff transferred the accused and another black man to a jail in a nearby town, white mobs instead headed for Springfield's Negro section and attacked and destroyed homes and businesses. Two blacks were lynched, while many others were dragged from their homes and streetcars and beaten.

By the time National Guardsmen reached the scene, seven persons were dead—five whites and two negroes. The Northern race riot shocked white liberals. By year end 1908, at least 89 black Americans would be lynched.

On August 24, 1908 at Rushcutters' Bay in Sydney, Australia, before a huge crowd of 15,000 to 18,000 spectators, Tommy Burns stopped Bill Squires in the 13th round. Australians were impressed. "Added to his scientific precision of boxing is a capacity for taking punishment which is almost superhuman. It may be possible to hurt Burns with a battle-axe, but most of those who witnessed his performance of yesterday would be inclined to doubt it." Burns proved to be a skilled boxer-puncher who could stick and move from the outside or rough it in the clinches on the inside. "This power Burns has of dealing terrific hits with either hand at a distance of about a foot, combined with his amazing footwork, make him the wonder he is." He was quick, powerful, well-conditioned, and calm under fire. The *Sydney Bulletin* did not believe anyone could beat Burns.[460]

Speaking of the reasons why Burns had not yet fought Jack Johnson, the *Sydney Bulletin* noted, "Racial pride counts for something in pugilism, and one great reason why Burns would not give Johnson a chance to wrest the championship of the world from him was a ferocious hatred of the idea of the negro being the bruising monarch of the earth." Although Australia had the reputation for being fair when it came to boxing, the country still had its own race issues.[461]

Racial prejudice aside, given that Burns had drawn a huge crowd for the Squires fight, and Australians had seen Jack Johnson defeat Peter Felix and Bill Lang the previous year and were well aware of his prowess, Hugh McIntosh likely would be able to meet Burns' financial demands for a Burns-Johnson title fight, if he wanted to do so.

From London, Johnson said his offer to stop Burns in 20 rounds still was good. He was willing to fight Burns anywhere in the world.

James Jeffries called Johnson's talk "guff" and a "feeble effort to talk big." Jeffries said Johnson "has no call to talk about knocking any clever man out. Not once in his career has he been guilty of such a thing." "As far as one may judge on form in boxing, Johnson should prove a certain victim for Burns." The frequently fighting Burns was improving with every fight, and would not be rusty, "while it is the other way about with Johnson." Continuing, Jeffries said,

---

[460] *Sydney Morning Herald*, August 25, 1908; *Sydney Bulletin*, August 27, 1908; *Referee*, August 26, 1908.
[461] *Sydney Bulletin*, August 27, 1908.

Tommy Burns will defeat Jack Johnson if they ever meet, provided Burns can get in a couple of good punches in the midsection of the Senegambian. ... Jack Johnson is the biggest quitter that ever entered a prize ring, and has a streak of yellow in his system as wide as a street. This is the kind of man who does lots of talking, but in actual work does nothing. I think Tommy Burns is as game as they make them, quick on his feet, clever, and able to stand a world of punishment. This last is what Jack Johnson cannot do. I think this talk about Burns being afraid of Johnson is more or less a fable. Burns is afraid of no man, white or black, and has taken chances that no other man in the world would have taken. He fought Marvin Hart when the latter was a 5 to 1 favorite over him, and has never balked at fighting any man. Tommy probably sees a chance to get a lot of Press agent matter out of this controversy, and is working both ends against the middle with good results.[462]

Increasingly the American press was warming up to Burns, and some writers, particularly those who didn't care for black boxers being champions, took his side against the fighters who were challenging him:

Jack Johnson is making a big noise about claiming the heavyweight championship from Tommy Burns, because Tommy deemed it his duty to keep his contracts with the Antipodean promoters to go to Australia and whip all the heavy crop in that neighborhood. These big blacks consider themselves of extreme and exclusive importance any time they desire to talk and evidently believe that because they are black they should have first call on any of the champions they desire to fight. ... It is a cinch that Burns and [middleweight champ] Ketchel will mop up with the fighters who are in line for their titles, as neither is afraid of any fighter in his class, black or white. ...

Those who are criticizing Burns for going to Australia to pick the lemon crop in that country are making an error that they readily will admit any time they think it over without prejudice. Burns has had a hard climb to the top rung. Easy money is the rule now, instead of small purses and hard fights, as he experienced in his climb up the ladder. Having attained that prominence that is the goal of all fighters ... he has the right to accept all the emoluments of his office, and a few easy scraps and big money are among them. Nobody ever has accused Tommy of being a coward, as he has accepted fights with bigger and heavier men and whipped them, and has done all that has been asked of him since he claimed the championship. ... He will return to America in November or December, and after he gets home there will be considerably less talk by fighters who now are seeking matches (in their minds) with him.[463]

---

[462] *Referee*, September 2, 1908.
[463] *Los Angeles Herald*, September 1, 1908.

Just ten days after the third Burns-Squires contest, on September 3, 1908 in Melbourne, Australia, before a crowd of 7,000 to 10,000 spectators, Tommy Burns took on current Australian heavyweight champion Bill Lang. Since his March 1907 9th round knockout loss to Jack Johnson in Melbourne, Lang had been undefeated for nearly two years, having won 13 fights in a row, including KO12 and KO7 Peter Felix (vacant Australian heavyweight title). The *Sydney Bulletin* said of Lang, "He was quite a novice, as he says, when he stood up against Johnson, the tall nigger whom Burns, thus far, has avoided." Lang had grown larger since the Johnson fight, and was weighing 186-189 pounds. Burns weighed 174 pounds.[464]

Although Lang decked Burns in the 2nd round with a powerful left hook, Burns rose and fought back well, hurting and dropping Lang several times throughout until he knocked him out in the 6th round.

The *Melbourne Age* said, "There is probably no boxer alive who has been more perfectly equipped by nature for the game he follows than Tommy Burns. He is a big man packed into the smallest possible space, and overflowing with strength and endurance." On the inside, "It was the force, the speed and the roughness of these close range attacks that wore Lang down." Burns was a "ring general and a brainy fighter." The *Referee* said, "I have seen all the best men Australia has known during the past quarter of a century, but I can't recall one who had the combative instinct so strongly prominent. Burns would beat a cleverer man." Pat O'Keefe said Burns had a great chin and never would be beaten until someone knocked him limp. "I don't think the man lives who has the necessary weight in his punch." The *Sydney Bulletin* said, "Tommy is a 'born fighter,' to be sure, and God gave him a stocky figure and a quick eye and more brains than most men in the stoushing business."[465]

The next day, Burns said of the Lang fight, "I had a lot of energy in reserve all the time, but I dare say I'll put it all into the Johnson encounter whether it is needed or not – that is, of course, if I have the good luck to meet him, and I hope to meet him here."[466]

The recent Burns-Squires fight drew 13,700 pounds, or $68,500, not including the motion picture rights. When Burns fought Lang, the gate was 4,400 pounds, or $22,000. Burns had generated $90,500 in two fights in ten days. He was a very big revenue generator in Australia, which meant that McIntosh could offer him what he wanted to fight Johnson.[467]

In America, there were rumors that Johnson and Burns had been signed to fight in Australia. The rumors were doubted, for,

> [I]t is the biggest sort of a cinch that if Johnson had been signed the big black would be making so much noise about it that the news would come by word of mouth from him in London, instead of by cable or telegraph. They may be matched, but if so, Burns has been

---

[464] *Sydney Bulletin*, August 20, 1908.
[465] *Melbourne Age*, September 4, 1908; *Referee*, September 9, 1908; *Sydney Bulletin*, September 10, 1908.
[466] *Melbourne Age*, September 5, 1908.
[467] *New York World*, November 25, 1908.

shown considerably more money than he could get in America or England for fighting Johnson. ... Burns is not afraid of Johnson, but he realizes that a match with the saffron streak would be worth more to him, financially, than any half a dozen fights in which he could engage, and he means to make the club that stages it stand a tap. And he is right as a fox, too.[468]

When interviewed, Burns said,

> Johnson has been running about England making a big boast of what he would do, and trying to make out that I was afraid of him. I never avoided Johnson, and he knows it; but he has religiously avoided me. I have always been ready to meet him, insisting, of course, that a certain amount would have to be guaranteed me, win or lose. I did not care what he made out of the encounter. ... He is a great bluff.

Burns said that Johnson's claims that he had placed wager deposits for a fight with him were false, for no money had been posted. "This is the way this fellow has been going on. He is simply living on my reputation."

> As a matter of fact, I don't think Johnson wants to be any closer to me than he need be. He knows how he fared at the hands of the game, gritty Marvin Hart, who is not clever, but certainly is courageous. Johnson doesn't like rough usage. ... I want to meet Johnson, firstly, to make it plain that I draw no color line, that I do not bar any man in the world; and secondly to establish my own opinion that I am Johnson's superior, and thirdly, to quit the game as champion of the world.[469]

The *Sydney Bulletin* supported Burns, saying that Tommy had proven himself to be a world-beater, unlike Johnson, whom it called a talkative "Galveston nigger." "If there is any loquacity about, Johnson, whom the British papers laud as a sort of ringside Crichton, is guilty of it."

The *Bulletin* said Johnson was backed by a section of the U.S. press that jeered at Burns for "running away" from Johnson, the "murky person" who recently described himself as champion of the world and accused Burns of "having fled from the glare of his countenance." The *Bulletin* believed that in fact, Johnson was reluctant to come to Australia and "get half-killed for £1000, when he can make twice as much by staying in Paris and keeping an undamaged countenance."[470]

Regardless of all the talk, on September 16, 1908, Jack Johnson and Tommy Burns signed articles of agreement with Hugh McIntosh to fight in Australia in late December for the championship. Burns would receive $30,000 guaranteed, and Johnson $5,000, a mere one-sixth of what Burns would make. The fight was on.

American newspapers wrote,

---

[468] *Los Angeles Herald*, September 3, 1908.
[469] *Melbourne Age*, September 7, 1908; *Referee*, September 9, 1908.
[470] *Sydney Bulletin*, September 10, 17, 1908.

> Johnson has practically chased Burns around the world in an effort to get a match. The champion has long evaded the negro, although he has frequently said he would fight him in good time when sufficient financial inducements were made. ...
>
> Where American and English sporting men have failed the New South Wales people have succeeded.

No American, English, or French promoter had been willing to back financially a mixed-race world heavyweight championship with the money required to make the fight. But Australia's Hugh McIntosh had done it.

Johnson booked passage on the steamer *Ortona* for Sydney.

> When the black man meets the Canadian-American in the ring there will be a battle for generations to remember, unless the general acceptance of the respective abilities of the two men is all wrong. ... All that those who follow the fighting game can see for either man is a knockout after a bruising, punishing fight.[471]

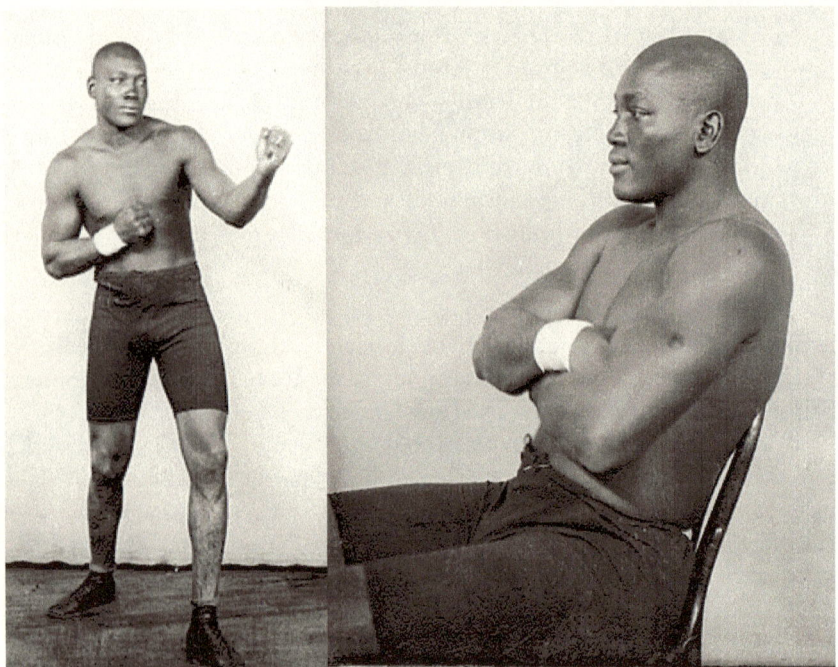

---

[471] *New York World, New York Tribune, Los Angeles Herald,* September 17, 1908.

CHAPTER 24

Promoting the Absolute World's Boxing Championship

Jay Davidson of the *Los Angeles Herald* predicted that Tommy Burns would knock out Jack Johnson:

> The big saffron streak will have the time of his life at knocking out the world champion, and I still am a Missourian on the subject. I rather prefer to predict that before the fight has gone twenty rounds the Antipodean sportsmen will witness a new kind of an airship, as a combination black-yellow streak makes an aerial flight out of the ring to escape annihilation. There is a vast difference between Burns and the mutts that Johnson has been putting away in his ring career.[472]

The *Herald* complimented Burns' business sense in holding out until he got the $30,000 that the match was worth, showing good, calm judgment, and also that he was not afraid of Johnson. "Burns is the only fighter with a title who will fight a negro nowadays, and after he whips Johnson, as he surely will, he probably will draw the color line, as his wife strenuously objects to her hubby fighting negroes."

The *Herald* further said, "Tommy may have had a few enemies in the world before this match was made, but practically every fight fan in the world will pull for him to win, as it will be a case of a game fighter against a big coward, and no fighter with the yellow label on ever had much of a following."

Jim Jeffries said, "I think that it will be a great fight, and I look to Burns being returned the winner. He is too clever, too strong, and too courageous for the black fellow. Burns is better than he is given credit for being."[473]

The confident Burns deposited a £1,000 wager that Johnson could not stop him in 20 rounds, as Johnson had boasted he could. Burns also deposited another like amount wagering that he would win the fight. Johnson just had to cover the bets.

Hugh McIntosh deposited with Sydney *Referee* sporting scribe W. F. Corbett "cheques" for £7,100, the stake for the Burns-Johnson fight, set to take place on Boxing Day, December 26.[474] Many boxing scribes looked at

---

[472] *Los Angeles Herald*, September 20, 1908.
[473] *Los Angeles Herald*, September 25, 1908; *New York World*, October 3, 1908.
[474] Boxing Day was not in honor of the sport. It was the day in which the English gave their servants presents, which came to be known as Christmas boxes. It was a legal holiday in Australia, which would allow the biggest attendance possible for the fight.

the huge checks "with watering mouths and wondered why their misguided parent hadn't brought them up to be world-famous bruisers."

Johnson would earn 1,000 pounds ($5,000) plus an extra 100 pounds ($500) for the motion picture rights, plus three round-trip tickets from London ($1,200 in expenses). Burns' guarantee was 6,000 pounds, which was about $30,000. He also would receive a motion picture film, valued at 350 pounds ($1,750), plus $1,000 in expenses.

The *Sydney Bulletin* said the underrated Burns would enter the fight with a personal feeling against his opponent, for Johnson had pursued him with irritating talk, sneering at Tom's reputation as a paper one.[475]

The *New York Sun* said Johnson had been trying to make a match with Burns for the past two years. At first Burns ignored him, then he drew the color line; until finally he said he would fight him for $30,000. Johnson had chased Burns out of both the U.S. and England, all the way to Australia.

> The negro is said by expert judges of pugilism to be the cleverest big man in the world today. He can punch, but whether he is dead game or not under grueling punishment remains to be seen. Few negro fighters as a rule relish a beating, and for that reason some wise men think that Burns, with his rushing tactics and heavy hitting, will take the heart out of Johnson.[476]

As a result of his talk, Johnson had been "held up to scorn, hatred, ridicule and contempt as a loud-mouthed braggart." Yet, such publicity had garnered sufficient momentum and financial interest to get the Burns fight made.

Upon his arrival in Australia, Johnson said had had chased the "'Liddle' chap from his nursery in 'Amurka'," followed his "'Liddle' footsteps" to Paris, all the way to Australia. Sam Fitzpatrick called Burns a bluffer. Johnson replied, "A bluffer he is, and yet that is the man who has called me quitter. He is the man who is going to play for my body all the time, and win out." Grinning, Johnson held his huge fists above his head and asked, "And am I going to keep my hands above my head, so, while Burns is playing for my body? No sir. I have been fighting for sixteen years now, and I reckon I know more about the game than any other man. I am a larger man than he, and I am cleverer."[477]

It was noted that Johnson had failed to cover Burns' wagers on the fight. "And all the killing of Burns with his mouth that has been accredited to Johnson does not make up for that little oversight." Of course, it is possible that Johnson did not have enough money to cover the wagers. However, some took his failure to cover the bets as a sign of who really had the confidence and who was just a talker.

---

[475] *Freeman*, October 31, 1908, November 7, 14, 1908.
[476] *New York Sun*, October 25, 1908.
[477] *Freeman*, December 19, 1908.

Jack was traveling with a white woman, and the press took note. "The colored man is accompanied by his wife, a white woman, somewhat addicted to jewellery."

Johnson trained before admiring crowds, including a fair sprinkling of females. "There is a touch of Louis XIV about Johnson, and as far as possible he lives in the glare of publicity." Jack liked attention.

The *Bulletin* questioned the logic of paying visiting pugs £6,000 when the country's own prime minister only earned £2,100 for an entire year's work. "Go into the ring, young man, go into the ring."[478]

Writing from Australia early in his training, Burns said,

> Johnson is as flash as ever and looks flash, and he sure is holding me cheap by his talk. That suits me fine, as those fellows are the kind I like to fight. ... I'll win this battle, unless I'm badly mistaken in Johnson's ability. ... The people sure are grand in this country.[479]

Bill Delaney picked Burns to defeat Johnson:

> [Johnson's] claim upon the consideration of other heavyweights is based upon the suspicion that seems generally held by the sporting public that he can do things that he never has done and that he will show class that no fight he ever put up really would justify. ...
>
> Johnson has not the class that is desired in a champion. He is accused on all sides, and not without justification, of being the possessor of a yellow streak. If he has that streak Burns will develop it.

Delaney felt that the game fighter usually won in a long fight, and Burns was much gamer than Johnson. "Burns has my best wishes for his success in the battle with Johnson because I want him to eliminate the negro from the contention. I do not believe in the recognition of the negro as a contender for any championship."[480]

The fight was set for 11 a.m. on December 26, but most New Yorkers would be able to learn about the result on the evening of the 25th, owing to the time difference of 14 hours and 40 minutes. "Most New Yorkers who follow the game think they know the ultimate result now – Burns will win."[481]

Speculators had purchased the Australian rights to the motion pictures for 4,000 pounds, or $20,000, equal to the cost to purchase the land and erect the arena. Seats were selling for £ 10, 5, 3, 2, 1, and 10s. That was $50, $25, $15, $10, $5, and $2.50, which was quite expensive for the era.

The fight was advertised in Sydney as Burns (World's Champion) vs. Johnson (Colored Champion) for the Absolute World's Boxing Championship, to be held at the Stadium at Rushcutter's Bay in Sydney, known popularly as The Stadium.[482]

---

[478] *Sydney Bulletin*, November 5, 12, 1908.
[479] *New York World*, December 22, 1908. It usually took a long while for letters from Australia to arrive.
[480] *Los Angeles Herald*, November 15, 1908.
[481] *New York World*, November 21, 1908.
[482] *New York Sun*, November 25, 1908; *San Francisco Chronicle*, December 6, 1908.

Sam Fitzpatrick had wanted to hold out for better financial terms, but he said, "Johnson was crazy to get at Burns and there was no holding him. ... Master Tommy is in for the whaling of his life."[483]

Jim Jeffries previously had said that if a black man won the championship, he would emerge from retirement to recover the title for the white race. Hence, Johnson said, "I don't wish to boast, but if my present feelings are any indication, I think you can announce to James J. Jeffries that he better get ready to come out of retirement."[484]

Although Johnson was the slight odds favorite in the U.S., in Australia, Burns was the strong betting odds favorite. Australians considered Burns to be invincible. The *Sydney Bulletin* argued that the white man would win as a result of his naturally superior brain.[485]

6,000 people paid to watch Burns train daily (making him even more money), demonstrating the remarkable interest in the fight.

Robert Edgren said Burns, the Rockefeller of fighters, had made a tremendous hit in Australia. "As a money-maker he is a marvel." If he "whips this big negro, who has been a bugaboo to all the heavyweights for a year past, he'll be as popular a champion as even the great John L. Sullivan."[486]

Burns wrote,

> There was never a champion before me who gave a Negro a chance to win the title, and I simply named a good stiff price for my end of the match. I am getting it, too. ...

---

[483] *San Francisco Examiner*, December 24, 1908.
[484] *Sydney Bulletin*, November 26, December 3, 1908.
[485] *Sydney Bulletin*, December 3, 1908.
[486] *New York World*, December 10, 1908.

> Those who said that I was a careful matchmaker want to remember that I am about the only world's champion who went clear around the world, meeting and beating my challengers in the countries they belong in.[487]

Predictions were that the world's record would be outdone. A $100,000 audience was expected.[488]

The local *Sydney Bulletin* noted an unfounded rumor that if Johnson won, he would draw the color line against whites. "And there is no earthly reason why he should not. If it is a fair and reasonable thing for a white fighter to refuse to allow a black or colored man to compete for the championship, a colored champion is quite within his rights in refusing to meet 'white trash.'"[489]

Despite Burns' reputation for being a dangerous infighter, Johnson said he would give Tommy every opportunity to get in his deadly work. He was willing to fight on the inside:

> I know that Burns expects me to fight at arm's length, keeping him off. He's going to get a surprise, good and early. I'm going to sail right in, and I will keep little Tommy real busy from the jump. Do I think I'll win? Well, in London, I offered to take absolutely nothing for my end of the purse if Burns was on his feet at the end of 20 rounds.[490]

John L. Sullivan was upset at Burns for crossing the color line, something no other reigning heavyweight champion of the gloved era had done in a championship contest. Excoriating him, Sullivan said of Burns,

> He is money mad. His every instinct is for the coin. He is shameless in his degradation of the great game of boxing in favor of the commercial side of it. ... Shame on the money-mad champion! Shame on the man who upsets good American precedents, because there are Dollars, Dollars, Dollars in it! Burns may lose his title to this black man. But I don't think he will. ... He is a 'sure thing' man, but I must say a better fighter than people give him credit for.[491]

The *Los Angeles Herald* agreed with Australians that Burns was the better man, calling him "the greatest heavyweight now in harness." "Johnson is accused, and very rightfully, of being a big yellow streak." In another article, the *Herald* said,

> [Johnson's] cardinal feature is of the yellow hue, and he will not take a beating. Burns' supporters refer to Johnson's yellow streak and his inclination to 'dog' it when pressed too hard as proof that they are correct in picking out Burns as the winner. They argue that Tommy

---

[487] *Freeman*, December 12, 1908.
[488] *Melbourne Age*, December 14, 1908.
[489] *Sydney Bulletin*, December 17, 1908.
[490] *Melbourne Age*, December 19, 1908.
[491] *Freeman*, December 19, 1908.

will go after the big black-and-yellow streak like a flash and fight him off his feet, giving Johnson little chance to do anything except defend himself. Owing to the difference in their height, Burns will find it easy to get to Johnson's vital spot, his stomach, and a brief pounding in that region should make Johnson 'dog' it until Burns puts over the dreamland wallop.[492]

Ultimately, the *Los Angeles Herald* said, "It will be quite disappointing to local fans if Burns fails to keep up his winning streak."[493]

On December 21, 1908 in San Francisco, Sam Langford, who weighed in the neighborhood of 168 pounds, knocked out Jim Flynn in the 1st round. A local writer said Langford had the strength of a gorilla and the intelligence of a human being. He was such a "bone breaker" that white fighters now would have reinforced concrete color lines.

Langford said he wanted to meet any man in the world, "bar Jack Johnson." Johnson was the only man whom Langford conceded was better than him. "Just tell them that I will fight any man in the business save Jack Johnson, and that I'll let Stanley Ketchel name the weight if he will only meet me." Langford's greatest desire was to fight Ketchel for the world middleweight championship, but Ketchel had drawn the color line.[494]

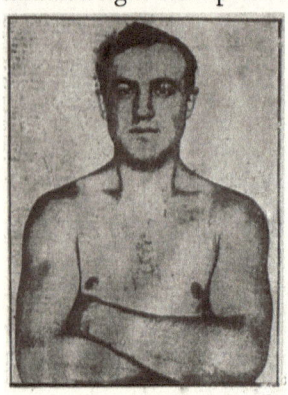
TOMMY BURNS.

Burns and Johnson met at McIntosh's office to decide the referee issue. The press did not reveal what happened in that meeting until several months later.

The fighters could not agree on a referee. Johnson said, "If I go into the ring I shall have one point the worst of it." The surly Burns growled, "Yes, they don't like niggers in this country, do they?" "What do you mean by nigger?" asked Johnson, objecting, though remaining cool. "O, niggers, that's all," Burns replied. McIntosh said, "It means a colored gentleman." Burns sneered, "You don't want to fight. You used to be a good fighter, but you are all shot now; you might as well take your medicine." Jack replied, "Well, is that so?"

Burns continued using racial epithets. There was a little girl in the office. Johnson said, "Take that kiddy out of the room. Burns, the newspapers are describing you as a gentleman, so be careful what you say. If you swear any more before this child, I shall give you a lacing right here. Now if you are chasing a fight. I'm ready."

The excitable Burns picked up a folding chair. "I'll slip it over on you," threatened Burns. Tom rushed at him, but McIntosh jumped between them and took the chair. Tom told Johnson, "I will kill you." Johnson replied, "I

---

[492] *Los Angeles Herald*, December 21, 1908.
[493] *Los Angeles Herald*, December 22, 1908.
[494] *New York World, San Francisco Examiner, San Francisco Chronicle*, December 22, 1908; *San Francisco Chronicle*, December 5, 1908.

will eat you up." Then Burns grabbed an inkwell and was about to hurl it at Johnson, but McIntosh again interceded and grabbed his arm. Burns appeared to be trembling. "You've spilled ink on your hand, haven't you, Tommy?" remarked Johnson, laughing.

Burns then put his hand in his hip pocket (which Johnson took as him implying that he was going to pull a gun) and again said, "I will kill you, nigger." "All this time Tommy was pouring out a line of abuse on Jack that would not look good in print." Johnson remained calm, and replied, "Tommy, you're a gentleman."

Burns kept going, and Mac held him back. Burns tried to instill fear in Johnson, telling him, "Regardless of whether you win or lose, that crowd will mob and kill you." Johnson responded, "I would just as soon die in Australia as anywhere else." Burns persisted that he would not get away alive. "Either I'm going to kill you or that crowd will."

Johnson finally coolly said: "Let him come, man. Don't interfere with him. Don't hold him, Mack; let us see what he will do. Let him loose. He's tame and harmless." However, McIntosh would not let go of Burns. Jack said to Tommy, "I'll remember this when I get you into the ring." McIntosh opened the door and got Tom out of there.[495]

Boxing Day was supposed to be the hottest day on the calendar in Australia, for the American winter was the Australian summer season. Hence, the fight would take place in the morning, before it got too hot. Plus, the filming processes required sunlight. Sam Fitzpatrick did not want Johnson working too long in the heat. "The big tar baby is watched like a hawk by his wise old owl manager, Sam Fitzpatrick."[496]

Some thought Johnson had not trained hard enough, but others said he had paid careful attention to his training. Jack's frequent motor car trips into the city caused some to wonder. However, "Johnson boasts that he has forgotten more than Burns ever knew."

Burns said he never felt better or fitter in his life. He would rely on infighting and his hitting powers. Johnson replied that it was foolish for Burns to let him know what methods he would use. In response, Burns said, "Johnson's answer has tickled me to death, for if he thinks I'm telling him how I'll fight, well, he's a 'huge guy.'"[497]

The *New York Sun* noted that public opinion had forced Burns to become the first heavyweight champion to meet a negro for the title. Johnson finally accepted the most unfair financial terms, just 1/6 of what Burns would earn, but he wanted the title so badly that he was willing to take the short end. He was tired of waiting for his chance at the title.

From Oakland, Burns' brother said if Tommy won, the champ would fight Stanley Ketchel next.[498]

---

[495] *Tacoma Times*, February 17, 1909; *New York Sun*, March 13, 1909; *New York World*, March 13, 1909; *In the Ring And Out* at 162.
[496] *Sydney Morning Herald, Daily Telegraph, San Francisco Examiner*, December 22, 23, 1908.
[497] *Melbourne Age*, December 24, 1908.
[498] *New York Sun*, December 23, 1908; *New York World*, December 24, 1908.

As of December 24, two days before the fight, no referee had been chosen. Without providing details, the local press simply said there had been some stormy meetings between McIntosh, Burns, and Johnson. "The colored pugilist is reported to be very obstinate."[499]

When Jim Jeffries was asked if Johnson won and challenged him, what he would do, Jeff said,

> If that coon comes around here and challenges me to fight him, if he wins from Burns, I'll grab him by the neck and run him out. ... I have repeatedly declared that the ring would never know me again, yet some simple-minded stiff in the east wired me today asking if I would meet Johnson in case the smoke won. I didn't take the trouble to answer, for every one knows that I have made up my mind.

Allegedly, on a previous occasion when Johnson challenged Jeffries, "Johnson was told that he could accompany Jeff into the cellar, lock the doors and let the best man come out when he was ready. This did not appeal to Jawn Arthur's heart, so there was no Jeffries-Johnson scrap to go down on the book."[500]

Jeffries was swamped constantly with nervous telegrams asking him whether or not he would box again if Johnson won. Jeff said, "In the event of the negro winning I realize full well that there will be a powerful demand, or rather series of demands, made upon me to meet Johnson and re-take the heavyweight title."[501]

The *Sydney Bulletin* said the air was full of disquieting rumors about Johnson's training, which allegedly consisted of champagne and female society, "interlineated with streaks of terrifically hard work."

Burns was very well trained and impressive. "Judging by the exhibitions given by both men, Burns is faster on his feet, and hits more quickly and with much more weight behind the blows. Johnson hits with his arm, Burns with his whole weight. The difference is tremendous." Burns' body appeared to be protected by a coat of thick, hardened muscle, while Johnson's midriff appeared vulnerable and soft-looking. Johnson's most effective blow would be the uppercut, but it would "probably be met on Burns' glove." And when Jack threw the uppercut, his body would be exposed. Ultimately, this writer believed that Burns would win the contest between the 9th and 13th rounds. "Barring the random swipe, Johnson, if he is to win, will have to show a degree of skill and speed not so far indicated in any of the exhibitions that he has given."[502]

After several days of wrangling, at the request of both fighters, promoter Hugh McIntosh finally agreed to be the referee and sole arbiter of the bout.

The *Chronicle* said Burns was a 10 to 7 favorite in Australia. Others said the odds had shifted to 2 to 1, with Burns the heavy favorite.[503]

---

[499] *Sydney Daily Telegraph*, December 24, 1908.
[500] *Los Angeles Herald*, December 24, 1908.
[501] *San Francisco Chronicle*, December 24, 1908.
[502] *Sydney Bulletin*, December 24, 1908.
[503] *New York Tribune, New York Sun, San Francisco Chronicle*, December 25, 1908.

In world heavyweight championship contests, Burns was undefeated, with a record of 13-0-1 with 11 KOs over course of the past three years.

Former champ Jim Corbett said, "I think that Burns will outgame the negro." "My sympathy is all with Burns, as it always has been where a white man has met a negro."

Marvin Hart, who had fought both, said Johnson would whip Burns.[504]

Burns wired, "Feeling confident will beat alligator. Am two-to-one favorite. Advance sale over ten thousand pounds."[505]

One writer noted the acute tension in the air, in part because of race. "There is bitter feeling between the principals. Public sympathy is almost wholly with Burns, owing to color prejudice. There is some fear of a row in the stadium, especially if Johnson should win. Consequently a big force of police has been ordered to be present."

The day before the big fight, on Friday December 25, Christmas Day, as Burns and his wife exited St. Mary's Cathedral, thousands congregated around the main entrance and cheered him.

The local churches drew the color line on Johnson.

Burns, as the white man, was the clear favorite, and the general desire was to see him emerge victorious. Even those who bet on Johnson said things like, "Well! I've backed the nigger, but I won't be sorry if I lose my money."

When not training, Tommy remained at home, living quietly. There was a "strong, almost unanimous prejudice in his favor," though "Johnson, as a matter of fact, has been quite as assiduous in his work as Burns." Some said that Johnson had been cutely "hiding his light under a bushel" so as to secure better betting odds.[506]

Finally, after being the top contender to the crown for six years, Jack Johnson was going to get his chance at boxing's top prize.

---

[504] *New York Herald*, December 25, 1908; *Melbourne Age*, December 26, 1905.
[505] *San Francisco Chronicle, San Francisco Examiner*, December 25, 1908.
[506] *Melbourne Age*, December 26, 1905.

CHAPTER 25

A True World Championship

On December 26, 1908 at the Stadium at Rushcutters' Bay, in Sydney, New South Wales, Australia, the Tommy Burns vs. Jack Johnson world heavyweight championship contest took place; the first mixed-race heavyweight championship of the gloved Queensberry rules era.[507]

No athletic event ever had taken place in Australia that caused anything like the excitement engendered by this fight. "Practically nothing else is talked about in the city." References to the battle were made in Christmas sermons. Even women seemed interested.[508]

The contest generated enormous world-wide telegraphic cable business. The U.S. Deputy Postmaster-General said 46,362 telegraphic wires passed over the lines from Sydney on the day of the fight.

Many of those who were interested in the result were not interested because they enjoyed boxing, but because of the bout's racial and social implications. The *Sydney Morning Herald* said,

> We should probably be right in saying, however, that that interest has not had its root exclusively in the love of a prize fight for its own sake. On the American side, for instance, there would be the 'colour' consideration – a consideration of tremendous import to many millions of Americans, both white and black, and one which would have held sway in any supreme encounter between a white man and a black, whether in a prize ring or on any other species of trying ground. In England the 'colour' question would not appeal in the same intense way.

Australians were biased towards the white man as well, but they could be generous and just to a black man, as had been the case with Peter Jackson.

Superintendent Mitchell was in charge of 250 policemen, including a force of mounted men, who positioned themselves around and throughout the Stadium to ensure order.

---

[507] *Sydney Daily Telegraph, Sydney Morning Herald, Melbourne Age,* all December 28, 1908; *Sydney Referee,* December 30, 1908; *Sydney Bulletin,* December 31, 1908.
[508] *Melbourne Age,* December 26, 1905.

FIGHT FOR THE WORLD'S CHAMPIONSHIP

TOMMY BURNS AND JACK JOHNSON

Over 20,000 people filled the stadium to the brim, making it an impressive sight. By fight time, there was not a vacant seat. Probably another 1,000 or so more than capacity were crowded into the arena. 5,000 were unable to obtain admission, even though the tier of benches went up to 20 feet off the ground. Another 15,000-20,000 just wanted to be in the vicinity of the arena, and they eagerly waited outside to hear any news.

At 10:40 a.m., a grinning Jack Johnson climbed into the ring with his attendants. The crowd faintly cheered him. Jack bowed and smiled - north, south, east, and west. "He didn't get much homage, but made a lot of what he did get." He then pirouetted around and finished by kissing his hand and waving it towards the cinematograph, which was inside a small shed atop a tall stand.

Jack created an impression of confidence and cheerfulness. "Perhaps the most prominent feature of the whole business was Johnson's smile. ... Johnson's smile made a tremendous impression. It fascinated and filled all beholders with amazement." He seemed unconcerned, "bored even." He took a seat in his corner, beaming.

A few minutes later, the thick-set Burns approached the ring. His appearance set the crowd alight, rising and showing their sympathies, hailing him with loud, roaring, invigorating applause and cheers. The sounds that thundered from the crash of applause and cheering mass of humanity made the earlier cheer for Johnson seem like a whisper by comparison. The local *Daily Telegraph* said, "Mainly it was White against Black with them, and they roared defiance to the 'coon', and frantically cheered Burns." The local *Bulletin* agreed, saying, "[T]hat huge crowd was aggressively white in its sympathy." They came not to see a fight, but to "witness a black aspirant for the championship of the world beaten to his knees and counted out."

However, Johnson was not worried, and acted unconcerned, maintaining his grin. Leaning over the ropes, he asked one of his attendants whether he had got "that bet on." Johnson seemed happy that he had.

Despite the cheers, Burns looked cross, and his smile was not really a friendly one as he acknowledged the crowd with bows. He looked game, determined, and anxious.

Tommy's looks were far less cordial when Johnson rose from his seat and crossed the ring from his corner smiling broadly, showing his gold-filled teeth as he approached and said, "Tahmy," holding out his hand to shake. Burns hesitated, looked his opponent up and down, then daintily just barely touched the big black hand with the tips of his fingers and let it drop, in sullen silence, in a "no-love-lost sort of fashion." He gazed at Johnson as he returned to his corner. Not disconcerted, Johnson smiled more pleasantly. The crowd sensed that razors would be in the air shortly.

Hugh D. McIntosh was introduced as the referee. The gloves were placed on the scales in the ring and declared to be the correct weight of four ounces each. They put on their gloves in the ring.

Final preparations were made. In Tom's corner were placed smelling salts and various chemicals, making it a small chemist's shop.

McIntosh brought them together to discuss the rules. They followed straight Queensberry rules, meaning that hitting in the clinches and on breaks was perfectly legal; hence they would protect themselves at all times.

Tom wore maroon-red trunks, an old-gold belt, and a Stars and Stripes American flag knotted at his hip. Johnson was attired in dark sky-blue trunks and was belted similarly with an American flag.

When Johnson objected to Burns wearing elastic rubber bandages on each of his elbows, refusing to fight unless they were removed, several spectators hooted and hissed, urging Burns not to give way to the "black cow" and other animals. Johnson insisted he would wait as long as it took, sat down, and grinned at the crowd. Larry Foley said custom dictated that Burns must remove the bandages. An annoyed Burns finally conceded the point and allowed his seconds to wrench off the offending elastic bands. There was some applause, cheers, and yells of "Good boy, Tommy." Conversely, "The colored man was soundly hooted."

It was announced to the crowd that if the police stopped the contest that McIntosh would declare the winner. McIntosh told the fighters to shake hands, and he had to drag their hands together to get them to do so.

Burns cast a look of hatred towards his towering opponent, showing his aversion to Johnson in every glance, wearing a heavy frown whenever he looked in Jack's direction. Conversely, Johnson simply wore an "ominous" smile. The excitement was intense.

The announced weights were Burns 12st. ½ lb.; (168 ½ pounds)(allegedly taken the day before), and Johnson 13 st. 10lb. (192 pounds), but "as neither was placed on the scales because there was no necessity for it, the information must be taken for what it is worth." No one really knew what they weighed. "The Ethiopian towered over the Canuck."

They returned to their corners to await the bell. "At last the two men who had lashed each other into a fury with stinging words across oceans and continents were going to have it out." The fight began at 11:05 a.m.

When the 1st round started, Johnson stood still near his corner, smiling with supreme confidence, and sneered, "Aal right, carm ahn, Tahmmy!"

Within the fist 15 seconds of the contest, while they were clinching and scuffling on the inside, like a flash, Johnson smote Burns on the chin with a tremendous right uppercut so heavily that he was lifted off the floor and fell hard to the canvas in a sitting posture. Johnson smirked and taunted him, saying, "What you want to lie down so soon for, Tommy?"

Burns rose after eight seconds. He immediately moved inside and attempted to work the body, but Johnson blocked nearly every effort, and the few punches that did land had no effect. Johnson either blocked, clinched, or pounded away.

As they broke from another clinch, Johnson crashed a heavy short right to the chin or ear and Burns went down again, the second knockdown of the round. Burns rose quickly and played defense up until the bell.

Local observers agreed that already it was evident that the very cool and methodical Johnson was too big and strong for Burns, who had no chance, despite the fact that he was full of fighting spirit. The *Bulletin* said Johnson uppercut him again and again. Tom tried to respond, but Johnson locked his arms. Johnson would push him off and smash him with grinding punches on the jaw. Jack had demonstrated that Tom's defence was useless against him, and that he was so much stronger that he could hold the champion helpless until he was ready to punch him.

In the corner, Tommy's attendants combed his hair.

Johnson sat coolly, laughing and talking. He asked for water. He gargled and spat it out, with a fair amount splashing over the furious pressmen.

In the 2nd round, Johnson became an orator and talked to Tommy, taunting him while grinning. Jack said in a soothing manner, "Come along, Tommy, my boy. Come right in here, and show the folks some of that infighting of yours! I want you, ma honey, an' I'll give you the best I've got! I've been keeping it so long, Tommy, an' I'm jest crazy ter hand it out to yer!" The crowd did not like it, and many rose and protested by jeering at Johnson. As Burns worked away like a bull terrier on the inside, an irate spectator remarked, "He'll knock the smile off you directly, you flash nigger." Johnson coolly turned and said, "Well! He's jes' doin' his little best, but I can't help smilin'. He's ticklin' me to death! Why, deary me, I thought he wuz de little man wat wuz goin' to make ma head swim!" He spoke to Tommy in a patronizing way throughout the fight, incessantly chaffing him and laughing over his shoulder. Jack passed the time of day to someone in the crowd he called "Patsy," and commented about the good weather.

Throught the fight, Johnson alternated between playing defense on the inside, smiling and talking to Tommy, and then blasting him with short jolting inside blows to the body, kidneys, and head.

Jack looked down at a photographer and asked, "Did you get that? Anyhow, I'll give you a good picture." Then he suddenly sprang in on Burns and smashed away.

The black man stood like a tower.

Often Johnson would hold Burns in a clinch, pause and kiss his mitten to the cinematograph. "This sort of thing soon made him unpopular, and he was subjected to a running fire of hoots and adverse comment, which, however, seemed to affect him as little as Burns's blows."

Johnson frequently held Burns against himself, helpless, while he exchanged gibes with the crowd, grinning as he did so. Then he would twist Burns into a position that he wanted so he could smite him.

Even when Burns landed lightly or partially, the crowd cheered him. "Good boy, Tommy!" But his blows had no effect other than to make Jack grin and make remarks, which he continued throughout the fight. Repeatedly, Jack brought down his right with an awful smash onto Tom's kidneys, then pushed him off and uppercut him on the jaw as he did so.

At the start of the 3rd round, Jack said, "Come on, leedle Tahmmy," as he laughed. Burns worked, but could not land cleanly or with any power. Johnson sneered, "Carm ahn." Burns landed his right to the ribs, but Johnson simply grinned "like a chimpanzee," showing his gold teeth.

When Burns clinched, Johnson showed his immense strength, moving freely in Tommy's grasp. "The grip of the white man was no more to him that the pressure of an ordinary elastic band would be about the arm of an average athlete. He simply changed his position at will and punished Burns every time he moved."

Johnson knocked Burns about with right uppercuts to the chin and hard lefts to the ribs, and then grinned at the plucky man who could not land. "A more one-sided struggle it would be impossible to imagine." Burns took his smashing heroically and came in again and again. His mouth was bleeding, his cheek beginning to swell, and his eyes growing puffy. He made no impression on Johnson, who occasionally stood still with his hands down, talking and jeering at Burns.

In the 4th round, addressing him as a mother would an impatient child, Johnson said, "Carm ahn, Tahmy! Come right here where I want you!" Folks in the crowd hollered in response, "Why don't you go on yourself?" When Burns tried an uppercut in a clinch, Jack replied, "No good, Tahmmy! I'll teach you!" A nasty powerful right uppercut nailed Burns on the chin. The round was a series of frequent clinches, with Johnson scoring heavily during the infighting, the solid blows sounding like the beating of a drum. Burns fought back, but his efforts were futile. His seconds started calling out numbers, secret codes for what punches Tom should throw.

In the 5th round, Johnson again taunted Tom with his usual sneering invitation, "Come right in, Tommy, and stay a while." His eyeballs rolled and his row of gold and white teeth shone. Johnson coaxed him to lead, saying, "Take a chance, Tahmy." Burns dashed madly to close quarters, where he met with a veritable storm of smashing blows.

Johnson fired his left and right to the ribs with considerable force, followed by a smashing hook to the chin and Burns went down, twisting his ankle on the way to the floor, spraining it. It was the third knockdown.

Burns rose and advanced. Johnson fired blows that went every which way - up, down, and across.

In a clinch, Burns said, "You are holding and hitting, you cur!" Tom then danced back out of range. Johnson replied, "Now, don't stand talking to the people, Tommy. Come back here till I finish."

Jack maintained his ever-ready grin regardless of whether Burns landed or missed. Tom's supporters would cry out, "Let him do the fighting, Tommy." Johnson wanted to wait, counter, and clinch. Tom said, "Why, you won't fight at all."

Burns came in like a shot, but Johnson dealt out heavy punishment. Jack would make remarks to the ringsiders and then punctuate his statements with powerful short jolts and jabs.

As the round finished, Burns landed a heavy overhand left to Johnson's right eye, but Jack merely shook his head and said, "Why! Durn you, Tommy, be careful!"

In the 6th round, as Burns attacked, Jack said, "Look! He's gaht me now." Johnson stood straight up and grinned while Tommy fired rights onto his ribs. Jack kept landing while smiling and talking. A right cross shook Burns, and a left to the neck sent him into the ropes. The plucky Burns went to his corner with his lips puffed and his right eye swollen.

In the 7th round, Burns showed an amazing capacity for absorbing punishment. Bleeding from the mouth and right eye, and with his eyes and cheek looking swollen, he still fought aggressively, with game courage. Yet, Johnson kept blocking, clinching, smiling, and pounding. Burns was tossed from side to side as Johnson's mighty fists thundered in on him, body and head, up, across, over and under.

When Tom's seconds called to him, "Get away from him, Tommy; get away from him!" Johnson drew Burns in close and remarked, "Now, look, see, I thought Tahmy was an in-fighter." When Burns clinched, the smiling Johnson said, "Look at him now," humorously appealing to the referee as he held his arms up, showing that Burns was the one who was holding. Jack said, "Why don't you fight, Tommy?"

After breaking, as Burns came in again, Johnson stepped in and sent in a left swing to the stomach and Tom fell to the floor for the fourth time.

Burns rose quickly and rushed in. Johnson landed his right uppercut and they clinched. Tom pumped his right to the ribs and Jack grinned as usual.

Despite the fact that Johnson had dealt out a great deal of punishment, some said he also intentionally backed off and carried Burns. "There was little doubt that Johnson had no desire to have the fight over too soon."

"He relinquished fighting for insult, and proceeded to taunt Burns afresh, and pass asides to the spectators."

In the 8th round, Johnson asked Burns, "Do you hear them telling you to come right along, Tom? Do as they tell you, Tahmy!" A ringsider said, "Stick to him, Tom. That yellow streak's there. You'll find it!" Johnson retorted, "You can't find it." After Johnson landed some effective body blows, he asked, "Aren't I clever? Yah!" The crowd replied by hooting vigorously. Between speeches, and sometimes accompanying them, Johnson administered terrific punishment, shaking up Burns badly. Johnson grinned and swapped remarks with the other corner, which he often did throughout the fight. While Burns was punching his ribs, the unphased Johnson asked, "Do you call this in-fighting?" "Are you having fun?"

When the bell rang, Johnson smiled and waved his hand at Burns as if to say "ta-ta." Some in the crowd responded, "The cur!" "The brute!" "Burns has no chance with the black fellow. He is simply playing with him."

In the 9th round, Johnson appeared to be resting again, allowing Burns to work. Tom said, "You're holding again, you cur! You're always holding." Jack said, "Come on, Tommy; swing your right!" Burns responded by calling him a "yellow dog." Burns kept working as best he could. The crowd called out, "Good boy, Tommy!" But he did no harm.

Johnson was content to put in an odd blow now and then and reflect on his adversary, replying to Tom's punches by saying, "He can't hurt, he can't hurt." In a tone of shocked pleasantry, Jack said, "Why, I thought you could hit, Tahmy." "What's that rib hit of yours, Thomas?"

In response to "Thirteen now, Tommy," from the champ's corner, Jack said, "Here's fourteen! Put that down." Or Johnson might respond with

"Look out, Tommy; here comes 24!" "[A]ll the strategy in the world was powerless against the irresistible battery of the giant negro."

While Tom was hammering away at his body, Jack coolly raised up his arms and intentionally allowed Burns to strike him, smiling and saying, "Find that yellow streak. You have had much to say about it; now uncover it." Jack nodded to acquaintances at ringside. He was showing everyone that he could take it to the body, something whites claimed black fighters could not do. Johnson literally invited Burns to hit him, saying, "Hit here, Tahmy," exposing the right side of his unprotected stomach, and when Burns struck, Johnson would neither wince nor cover up. He received the blows with a happy, careless smile directed at the spectators. Then he would turn the left side of his unprotected stomach towards him and say, "Now here, Tahmy." While Burns hit as directed Johnson would continue to grin and chuckle and smile his golden smile. Johnson then held Burns and posed and smiled at the cinematograph above.

On one occasion when Johnson threw Burns to the ropes, the camera resting at ringside had to be pulled back. Johnson looked down at the cameraman and asked, "Did you get it?"

In 10th round, Johnson kept talking and nailing Burns. Tommy said, "Say, you can't fight a lick!" Johnson ducked a right in time to allow the blow to go over his neck. As they crashed together, Jack gurgled, "Ah, that's what I like," and he smashed Burns heavily in the ribs with his right.

Johnson kept administering punishment, sending Burns to the ropes. Tommy was rattled and groggy when time was called. The *Daily Telegraph* said he was fortunate that the round ended when it did, for Burns appeared to be on the verge of going down. In the corner, one of his seconds combed Tommy's hair.

In the 11th and 12th rounds, Johnson continued joking and pounding away, though Burns kept fighting gamely. Tom's face puffed out on one side, his jaw hanging down as though it was broken, and the blood oozing from his battered mouth. "Outgeneralled, over-reached, overmatched in strength, insulted and treated like a helpless mouse by a great black cat, he came up heroically to take his punishment."

In the 13th round, Johnson fought fiercely, attempting to finish Burns with a quick succession of heavy punches. Tom's badly swollen face presented a sorry spectacle. His fighting instincts remained, but it seemed as if he was about to fall.

Between rounds, Police Superintendent Mitchell and Dr. Maitland consulted, and they remained close to the ring to monitor matters.

In the 14th round, Johnson quickly rushed in, making a genuine effort to end it. Jack hooked a right to the side of the head and followed it up with blows to either side of the face, making the blood spurt from the right eye.

Johnson was slaughtering him, landing his left hook, right uppercut, and left rip to the ribs. Burns was "too far gone, and could not guard. He was just a plaything in the hands of the negro, who was as fresh and strong as a horse." Burns "took his gruel with a courage that earned him the whole hearted admiration of everyone." Johnson followed up with ferocious rushes, serving out punishment at a fast rate and in heavy doses. Burns swayed like a drunk.

A hard right reached Tom's jaw. Johnson landed a heavy left to the body and then measured off his distance and landed a right cross to the chin that dropped Burns with such force that he rolled over twice.

Burns scrambled to his feet at the count of eight. Johnson bounded from his corner like a panther, sweeping down like a cyclone on the staggering champion. He smashed away with a fusillade of successive blows: rights, left hooks, and right uppercuts. Burns swayed to and fro, staggering.

At that point, Police Superintendent Mitchell entered the ring and waved his hands aloft, commanding a cessation of the bout. He had seen enough. McIntosh said, "Stop, Johnson!" McIntosh pointed to him and said, "I declare Johnson winner on points."

There was a new world heavyweight champion. Jack Johnson waved his hands to a crowd that did not cheer him, but rather remained silent. He went to the ropes, grinning, and said to the press, "What did I tell yar?" He had dominated Burns.

Regarding the finish, the *Morning Herald* said, "There was no need to continue. The fight was over, and nobody in the Stadium was sorry to see Superintendent Mitchell, who was in command of the police arrangements, scramble through the ropes, and wave the giant back to his corner." Burns had been down twice in the 1st, and again in the 5th, 7th, and 14th rounds. Everyone agreed that he had taken enough.

THE LAST FEW SECONDS OF THE FIGHT.

The spectators were not happy about the black man's victory, for Burns was the fan favorite. There was little cheering. Mostly there was sad silence. The heartbroken crowd quietly put on their hats and quickly streamed out. In twelve minutes, the stadium was empty. They had wanted Burns to win, but when it was over, they admitted that he never was in it.

The *Sydney Bulletin* said Johnson had won "from start to finish," and probably "could have knocked Burns out at any time after the seventh round." The *Sydney Daily Telegraph* said, "The contest was one-sided throughout." Ugly rumors about Johnson's inability to stay and his indifferent training were proven to be untrue.

Another *Daily Telegraph* writer said the scene provided a great human drama and stark contrast. Johnson was the black man full of humor, almost tickled to death with the situation. Burns was a sallow-looking, determined, steely-eyed white man. "It was a joke to one, a tragedy to the other." Johnson battered his way to the championship with a smile on his face and a joke on his lips, while Burns received terrible punishment with a sullen, stony silence that garnered the crowd's sympathy. Even when Burns struck "the nigger somewhat hard," his efforts were useless. Johnson would make speeches, hit Burns, and then they would clinch for long spells.

> But in these clinches there would be thud after thud, and the clicking sound of a man's teeth being rattled. The victim was Burns. ... So the contest went on, hopelessly for Burns, treated as a joke by Johnson. The champion was being slowly pounded. ... Game to the last, he poked his tongue out at the swarthy giant who was steadily teaching him to taste the bitterness of defeat by a process of battering that

only a brave-hearted man with a tremendous capacity for taking punishment could have withstood so long.

The *Morning Herald* said Johnson had carried and toyed with Burns. "Johnson was greatly the superior of Burns; in fact, it seemed possible that he could have beaten him in half the time had he so chosen." Spectators acknowledged that Johnson was the finest fighter they had ever seen, and possibly the best fighter of all time. "He has everything in his favour except his over-confidence; and unlike many of his race, is conscientious in his training." Although the lack of knockouts in his record had caused some to think he lacked hitting power, "the fallacy of such a theory required nothing beyond Saturday's performance to reveal it."

The *Melbourne Age*'s on-scene reporter said Johnson did just as he liked, in good humor, rubbing it in, "goading the white man on with sneering remarks, laughing at the hardest body blows, and replying with quick retort to the incessant comments and advice of the attendants in the Burns corner." All the pleasantry was with Johnson. He was cool, collected, and "determined to impress the fact on this crowd of white trash" that he was quite unruffled by anything Burns did. Johnson talked and joked at or about Burns with a tireless fluency. Jack inquired scornfully regarding all the talk about Tommy's infighting, of which he had heard so much. "I thought you called yourself an in-fighter, Tommy."

In between speeches, Johnson would alternate his flash remarks with awful wallops and grins. "The big negro distributed some sickening punches in the stomach. They sounded like a well-kicked football banging against a wall – whoomph. Then there would be a sharp, grinding click – that was the grinner sending his long, brawny arm jolting upwards to the Canadian's chin." "Human endurance has its limits, and Burns had to be beaten."

After every round, a Burns attendant combed his hair. "He might lose his championship, the supremacy of the white race might go to the Devil, Burns himself might be slowly battered to pieces or suddenly killed outright, but at least he should die with his hair properly parted."

The *Daily Telegraph* said Johnson became champion of the world "on an award of points which would have been quite unnecessary had the police held back another minute." But that was the point. They did not want to allow the black Johnson to knock out the white Burns.

Another writer said the sun mostly was behind the clouds, but it came out near the end. "With the sun came the end. It was the setting of the sun for the White man, and the rising for the Black."

The *Melbourne Age* said Johnson proved incorrect the assertions that he would show a yellow streak against Burns. "If Johnson has a 'yellow streak' he showed no evidence of it. He did not need to, as he was always safe."

Burns had been told that like all blacks, Johnson's weakness was his inability to take body punishment, but Johnson proved that he was just as strong as a bull about the body, for Burns' violent blows did no harm. Conversely, Johnson ripped in irresistible uppercuts, hooks, and crosses that buffeted Burns from side to side like a bundle of straw.

Johnson was such the master of the situation that he became "offensive and flash," taunting his game antagonist. He "might just as easily have accomplished his task without recourse to such an amount of quite unnecessary flashiness."

None of the local writers or fans appreciated Johnson's mouthiness, comedic though it was. The *Morning Herald* said that unfortunately, Johnson's "fine boxing was disfigured by a display of bombast that is happily seldom seen in any sporting arena." Its writer believed that Johnson's verbal taunts had robbed him of personal acclaim.

The *Bulletin* called Johnson's publication of delight during the fight a depressing feature. This writer said that had he been as flashy in America, he might have been killed, justifiably.

> Had his nods, becks, wreathed smiles, etc., occurred in America, a prominent citizen would inevitably have risen impressively somewhere about the close of the fourth round, and, amid encouraging cheers, have drawn a gun upon Johnson and shot that immense mass of black humanity dead. In the ensuing murder trial counsel for the defence would have put in the cinematograph film as his sole exhibit and evidence, and on its testimony alone secured a verdict of 'justifiable homicide.'

The *Daily Telegraph* said Johnson's grin was the most noticeable feature.

> The first thing that struck the huge assemblage about the big negro was his grin – an everlasting, confident, self-possessed, defiant grin. He took it into the ring with him, he carried it unimpaired through the fight, mixing it up occasionally with some terrific blows, and an almost ceaseless chatter of a deep, husky voice – and when the depressed crowd last saw him, he still had it; and there was something else with it – the triumphant gleam of the victor. It was not a savage, ferocious grin, but the simple, good old painstaking, faithful smirk of the negro that would not leave its native home. Times have been when the multitude has roared its sides out at that type of grin, but on Saturday morning it gave thousands the heartache. And Burns could not drive it away, and therein was the despondency of the people.

The *Morning Herald* said it was a pity that Johnson would not let his boxing do its own talking. "He is so fine a fighter that advertisement is unnecessary, and people who attend fights appreciate the points of the game without having their attention directed to them by their author." Instead, Johnson kept up a running fire of remarks that either directly insulted Burns or were intended to express indirect contempt.

The *Referee*'s W. F. Corbett also commented on Johnson's conduct:

> No man the world over has been a greater supporter than myself of the colored boxer's claims for consideration; but after last Saturday's happenings, and the subsequent exultation and gloating of the winner

over the fall of so brave a foeman, and such a clean-living fellow as Tommy Burns, I am satisfied there is a great deal more than most of us suspected behind America's prejudice against the black.

When an American previously had said that Johnson was "as flash as chain-lightning," the writer put it down to racial hatred existing throughout the U.S. "Johnson's actions and bearing on Saturday have, however, had such an effect upon me that I never want to see a white and a black man face each other in the ring again." Peter Jackson had suffered the same racial slurs and indignities, but conducted himself in a sportsmanlike, gentlemanly, modest, and chivalrous fashion nevertheless. Johnson was different. He grinned, bitterly taunted, and waved "ta-ta" to his opponent.

The local papers failed to note Burns' history of verbal taunts and insults directed toward Johnson (and others), either because they were unaware or because they did not care.

Whites throughout the world felt that blacks were required to endure insults and suffer indignity from whites with solemn silence and not retort. Yet, that was not Jack Johnson. He intended to get revenge, and he got it. Hence, the question was asked, "Who will dethrone him?"

Certainly, race factored into the feelings regarding Johnson, even in Australia. The *Bulletin* said, "But the victory, fairly won as it was, was wholly unpopular. That crowd was white to the core. It had given the brown man a fair deal, and didn't feel called upon to do more."

The *Daily Telegraph* said that although many were sympathetic to Johnson's struggles to obtain a title shot owing to his race, there remained strong race sympathy with the white man. Yet, the spectators were fair. "Jack Johnson, who was favorite with comparatively few, had an absolutely fair field on the color line. If the people did not rejoice in his systematic and regular punishment of the white man, they certainly did not manifest any resentment. But the crowd was sorry – it was sad."

The *Morning Herald* said the 20,000 fans were sadly disappointed, in part because for the first time in history, a black man was the world heavyweight champion.

The weekly *Referee* headline said the top notchers of the white and colored races had met. "The past must be dug very deeply into before an occasion may be discovered when accredited representatives of the Caucasian and colored peoples of the earth contended for anything approaching the distinction involved" in this fight.

The *Melbourne Age* also said the crowd was not happy, for racial reasons.

> A general feeling of antagonism to Johnson permeated the crowd inside and outside the Stadium. It was there, and there was no gainsaying it. Deep down beneath the spirit of fair play it made itself felt – people could not help manifesting it. The 'white Australia' color prejudice cropped up.

Hence, despite Australians' fairness regarding the color line in boxing, they still had their own racial prejudices and rooting interests. They wanted to see the white man win. And they did not want to see the black Johnson vengefully taunt the white man who had called him "yellow" and "nigger."

Some said that race prejudice against the colored fighter explained the odds which made Burns such a strong betting favorite in Australia.

The fight not only was memorable for the racial angle but also because the gate amounted to £26,200 ($131,000), easily a world's record. The previous best was Nelson-Gans, another interracial championship fight, at $69,715. The purses totaled £7,500, showing that McIntosh had made a wise investment, and that Burns' £6,000 ($30,000) demand was not unreasonable, something of which Johnson took note when it came to his own future purse negotiations. Johnson earned £1,500 ($7,500), including expense money.

McIntosh said he would offer £10,000 ($50,000) to Jeffries to fight Johnson. "Jeffries stated that he would re-enter the ring if a colored man or a foreigner won the championship. Now he is morally obliged to come back."

In his dressing room, the new world heavyweight champion said,

> I never had a doubt regarding the outcome of the battle since the match was made. Burns fought a better battle than I anticipated, and took a lot of punishment. He is a very plucky fellow. ...
>
> Some of them have been talking about me being yellow – having a yellow streak, and all that sort of thing. Well, he looked as 'yaller' as I did, I reckon. When I got him in the ring I made up my mind I'd not only win, but I'd give him a beating he'd remember into the bargain. I beat him proper, and I did it on purpose. I wanted to beat him down bit by bit, and show him and the public how much yellow there was in me. I could have won sooner, only I wanted to beat him so he'd remember me. ...
>
> I wanted to get even. He and those with him had spoken very slightingly of me, and I laid myself out to make the drubbing as severe as possible. Wonder if they think I have a yellow streak now.
>
> None of the blows delivered by Burns troubled me much, and I was not concerned at any stage of the fight. I just wanted to give it him in small doses, and he got it, and I'm satisfied.

A local writer said, "Johnson was inclined to exult over his victory at the expense of the defeated man, and said things which, it is to be hoped, he regrets today."

Johnson was willing to fight Bill Squires if Bill could come up with a £2,000 side bet ($10,000). Continuing, Jack chuckled, "That is, mind you, in case he still wants to."

The *Referee* said the fight neither proved nor disproved the assertion that Johnson had a yellow streak, because he was more or less the master of the situation throughout, and therefore he had not been put to the test.

Conversely, Burns had proven his grit because he took the pounding and kept fighting hard.

Burns said he had promised Johnson that he would fight him after all of the top-notch white fighters in sight were accommodated, and he had honored his promise. "I need not have done that. As you are aware, the color line was drawn very strongly by all modern champions who preceded me, and had I followed suit none could or would have raised the slightest objection." Still, Burns hoped that a white man would regain the title.[509]

Jack London (author of *The Call of the Wild* and *White Fang*), who was at ringside, famously reported back to America for the *New York Herald*. He wrote, "The fight! There was no fight. No Armenian massacre could compare with the hopeless slaughter that took place in the Sydney Stadium today. It was not a case of 'Too Much Johnson,' but of all Johnson. A golden smile tells the story, and a golden smile was Johnson's." London said it was a "playful Ethiopian" against a small and futile white man. Johnson cuffed him like a naughty child. When Johnson smiled, a "dazzling flash of gold filled the wide aperture between his open lips, and he smiled all the time. He had no trouble in the world." When the fight began, the monologue began. With an exaggerated English accent, Johnson said, "Tahmy," and he talked throughout the bout when he was not smiling.

It was a case of a plucky, determined fighter who tried hard but had no chance at any time.

> There was no fraction of a second in all the fourteen rounds that could be called Burns'. So far as damage is concerned Burns never landed a blow. He never phased the black man. ... Johnson was too big, too able, too clever, too superb. He was impregnable. ...
>
> As for Johnson, he did not have to extend. He cuffed and smiled and smiled and cuffed, and in the clinches whirled his opponent around so as to be able to assume beatific and angelic facial expressions for the benefit of the cinematograph machines.
>
> Not Burns, but Johnson, did the infighting. In fact, the major portion of the punishment he delivered was in clinches. At times he would hold up his arms to show that he was no party to the clinch. ... [B]ut principally in the clinches Johnson rested and smiled and dreamed. This dreaming expression was fascinating. It seemed almost a trance. It was certainly deceptive, for suddenly the lines of the face would harden, the eyes would glint viciously and Burns would be frightfully hooked, swung and uppercut for a bad half minute. Then the smile and the dreamy trance would return as Burns effected another clinch. ...

---

[509] *Sydney Daily Telegraph, Sydney Morning Herald, Melbourne Age*, all December 28, 1908; *Sydney Referee*, December 30, 1908; *Sydney Bulletin*, December 31, 1908.

> Johnson play-acted all the time, and he played with Burns from the gong of the opening round to the finish of the fight. Burns was a toy in his hands. ...
>
> But one thing remains. Jeffries must emerge from his alfalfa farm and remove that smile from Johnson's face. Jeff, it's up to you.[510]

However, Jeffries said he had no intention of coming back:

> I refused time and again to meet Johnson when I was in the ring and now I am out of it for good. ...
>
> Tommy Burns' mistake, the one big mistake of his career, was in letting Johnson have a chance to fight for the championship. When I was holding the title I refused to let him have a chance, although I knew I could defeat him. I surely would not return to the ring to fight a negro now. ...
>
> All night last night and all day today I was besieged with telegrams asking me if I would re-enter the ring. I answered them now as I have answered hundreds of times before. I have fought my last ring battle. I am through with the game.

Another paper quoted Jeffries, who previously had hinted that he might come back if necessary to prevent a negro from holding the championship, as saying that he would not come back unless and until there were no more qualified top white contenders with a good chance to dethrone Johnson, such as Al Kaufman and Jim Barry. "I don't expect to fight him until he has disposed of all the legitimate aspirants for the championship. ... [I]t is not for me to butt in when there are men who probably can defeat Johnson."

Jeffries criticized Burns for crossing the color line. "Burns had no right to fight Johnson for the heavyweight championship."

Burns' mother was gloomy. She said, "I didn't want him to fight Johnson, and his wife tried to persuade him not to fight a colored man."

Stanley Ketchel said he would challenge Johnson in order to recover the title for the white race. "Until now I have always said I would draw the color line. Now it is different. I had expected to meet Burns in San Francisco July 4th."[511]

Several American newspapers had same-day or next-day reports, based on cabled dispatches.[512]

The *New York Herald, New York Daily Tribune,* and *San Francisco Examiner* all said Johnson treated Burns as a joke. When Burns landed, Johnson would laugh outright in his adversary's face, make sarcastic remarks; and turn to his corner and wink. Johnson deliberately took some of Burns' best blows just to show the public that he was not yellow and that Burns could

---

[510] *New York Herald,* December 27, 1908.
[511] *Chicago Tribune,* December 26, 1908.
[512] *New York Herald, New York Daily Tribune,* December 26, 1908; *San Francisco Examiner,* December 26, 27, 28, 1908; *San Francisco Chronicle,* December 26, 27, 1908; *Los Angeles Times,* December 27, 28, 1908.

not hurt him. The *San Francisco Chronicle* said Burns had kept Johnson waiting for a long time, and he paid for it in the ring.

The next day, Johnson said, "I have forgotten more about fighting than Burns ever knew. I was sure I would win from the start."

Jim Coffroth wanted to promote a fight between Al Kaufman and Johnson. However, manager Bill Delaney declared that he never would let Al fight a colored man, and would draw the color line. Bill said, "When I managed Jeffries, I would not allow him to fight Johnson or any other negro, and the same holds good for Kaufman." However, some thought he might change his mind, given that he wanted Al to be champion.

Some were discussing the possibility of a Burns-Johnson rematch. The *Examiner* quoted Johnson as saying,

> I can lick Burns every day in the week and twice on Sunday. Of all the men I have ever met he is the easiest. I could have knocked him out much sooner had I wished. I wanted to take a good revenge and had my satisfaction. Fight him again? Well, count me in.
>
> Now that the shoe is on the other foot, I just want to hear that fellow come around whining for another chance. I'll give him a real live taste of my match-making genius. See how he will relish the chances of a beating for bare expenses. Ha! Ha!

Johnson was prepared to give Burns the same financial treatment that he had received.

Burns was cognizant of the racial implications of his loss, saying, "I feel the sting of defeat doubly because of the fact that my fall allowed a colored man to usurp the title for the first time in ring history."

W. W. Naughton said Jim Jeffries had made a big mistake by not fighting Johnson when he was at his best. It would be quite difficult for him to refuse to do so now. Given the powerful symbolic racial significance of the fact that the world heavyweight champion was a black man, a huge amount of public pressure would be placed upon him to recover the crown for the white race:

> My, what a jacketing is in store for big Jim Jeffries. He took time by the forelock to the extent of declaring ahead of things that no earthly consideration could induce him to give battle to Johnson, but if Jeff remains of that way of thinking in the face of the clamor that will arise and the pressure that will be brought to bear, he is more adamantine in his resolves than I have any suspicion of.
>
> And even those who are not hounding him to gird his loins and give the negro battle are blaming him for existing conditions.
>
> "Why did Jeffries refuse to fight this fellow when Jeffries was at his best," they are saying. "If he had done so Johnson would have been put aside for all time, and he wouldn't be going around, as he is now, saying, 'I licked Tommy Burns, and I can lick Jeffries, too.'"

And meanwhile, Johnson is the undisputed world's champion and fully entitled to the title, black skin or no black skin. He is of the world all right. If you prick him he will bleed, and if you hit him hard enough he will tumble. ...

Verily the negro is a power in pugilism at present. And it might have been worse. Had Johnson and Langford happened along when Dixon, Gans and Walcott were on top, championship row would have looked like a spade flush.

When told of the $50,000 offer to fight Johnson, Jim Jeffries said, "I have said that there was not one chance in ten million that I would ever fight again, and I meant it. Why can't the public take what I say as final and let it go at that?" Already Jeff was annoyed by the persistent attempts to get him to agree to fight Johnson.

The possibility of Jeffries coming out of retirement would be an omnipresent hot topic of discussion. Jeffries would be hounded to death by a white press and public which could not stand the idea of a black man holding the world's heavyweight championship.

Unlike whites, when they learned that a black man had become world heavyweight champion, most blacks were jubilant. Speaking about black folk in the "black belt" of Chicago, the *Chicago Tribune* wrote,

> Of course all wore expressions of unmixed joy, but there was a total lack of arrogance in their manner towards white men and many of them politely tried hard to conceal the delight they could not help showing.
>
> It was purely pride of race that made them joyful, for in the matter of betting not a single wager of any size, as far as could be ascertained, was made by them upon the fight.

Both the black-owned *Freeman* and the *Richmond Planet* offered black newspapers' perspectives. The *Freeman* wrote, "Dopesters who made the spread that Jack Johnson would show a yellow streak, lay down, and do a hundred other things to lose his fight with Tommy Burns are now speechless." The *Planet* said Burns believed Johnson would lose his courage if hit in the stomach, but Johnson had proven him wrong. Tom soon learned that Johnson was as stout-hearted as any elite fighter, and there was no quit in him. "The sports are beginning to see now why Burns held off Johnson so long before making a match with him."

Most top white fighters had used the silly color-line as a subterfuge to avoid meeting Johnson. There was nothing but admiration for Jack's patience in obtaining his title shot. Blacks were elated that Johnson was the first of his race to win boxing's top prize.

Jack Johnson had chased Tommy Burns around the world and had been forced to accept the vastly smaller end of the purse. However, it proved to be a wise business move. Now that he was champion and in a position of power, he would have no trouble obtaining good purses, and the money would not be split so unevenly. Now he had what everyone wanted. The man who for years had agreed to any financial terms, including ones unfair to himself in order to obtain fights, finally was in a position to do the dictating and make a fortune. Not bad for the poor son of former slaves.

The *Freeman* said Johnson's championship status would earn him very good money, for whites would pay a lot of money to see a white man recover the crown.

> Prejudice is so great against a black man holding the championship title that there are many right at this moment who would take a chance, be it ever so desperate, to grasp the title from Johnson because of his shady hue. Even Jeffries, who once declared he would never again fight a battle, is considering a go with Johnson. Prejudice, that's all. …
>
> Johnson deserves recognition and will get it. He is the most wonderful fighter of the day, regardless of what the gossipers say in reference to his being a second rater. He is a giant in size and in knowledge of the fistic art, as perfect as any.[513]

The *Richmond Planet* noted the joy of colored folk, which was the greatest since Emancipation. The result had great meaning to them:

> No event in forty years has given more genuine satisfaction to the colored people of this country than has the signal victory of Jack Johnson. … The cause of this is not to be found in the satisfaction of knowing that a colored man can whip a white one, for that species of superiority could be demonstrated in every day life, due primarily to the physical superiority of the average citizen of color, who is bent in the performance of his exacting duties, which tend to develop bone and muscle, but in the superior skill in training to that definite degree of excellence that caused the white referee to decide that Johnson, the Negro, won on points scored as well.
>
> The further cause for this satisfaction is the action of President Roosevelt and the War Department in black-listing 167 soldiers in the United States Army and of creating the impression that they were inefficient, lawless and a positive menace to the service. The report from the United States Military Academy at West Point, N.Y., coupled with this victory at Sydney, Australia will tend much to rehabilitate the race in the good opinion of the people of the world.[514]

Two days after the fight, on December 28 the fight films were shown on a big screen at the Stadium, and close to 8,000 people watched. The crowd cheered Burns and groaned at Johnson's every move and counter move.

---

[513] *Freeman*, January 2, 1909.
[514] *Richmond Planet*, January 9, 1909.

In the days following the fight, as Johnson whirled about Sydney in his motor car, he met with a mix of cheers and hoots.

Starting just two days after the fight, Jack began giving exhibitions before large Sydney crowds, which greeted him with both cheers and hisses. Jack laughed all the way to the bank. He would earn $1,750 per week on the vaudeville stage for five weeks in Australia, earning more in one week than most folks made in a year.[515]

The new champion felt that the newspapers were biased for Burns and had skewed their reports against him in Tom's favor. They mostly printed his taunts, but did not print what Burns had said to and about him.

> Johnson complains that he has not been treated fairly by some newspapers. They have, he says, been a little bit too one-sided, and language that Burns has used to him and about him has never been allowed to get out, while a few things he has said playfully have been made the most of, to make it appear as if he did not play the game fair.[516]

Johnson told the press about the incident in McIntosh's office. When told of what Johnson said, Burns replied, "Johnson said things to me that it would not do to print. He said something about my wife in the ring, and if the public had heard him they would have lynched him."

A New York correspondent said white Americans disliked Johnson's victory and were depressed by it, but negroes were greatly delighted and jubilant, welcoming the announcement with great enthusiasm.

American reporters were saying that the way Johnson had dominated proved that Burns had no right to be classed with the best champions of the past. Perhaps Johnson was just that good, as opposed to Burns being that bad. Race politics affected interpretation.[517]

The *Bulletin* felt that Burns had fought the wrong fight, for he should have played a waiting game and allowed Johnson to do the work, so that the "inky antagonist's" "moral fibre would crumple up" once he tired out.

Another *Sydney Bulletin* writer gave Johnson a lot more credit, saying,

> I have no love for the Black Agony, but feel insulted as to my intelligence at the majority of the press reports, which give Johnson little credit as a fighting expert, but simply state that he was 'too big and too strong' for Burns. The fact is, he was in a still greater degree too good a boxer for his adversary. From the world 'go' the ink-bottle spilled himself all over Burns and put his fire out. The spectacle was comparable to that of a gorilla toying with a light meal. … If Lang or Squires is allowed to have a go at the present champion there'll as likely as not be an elegy-writing job for some white poet shortly after.[518]

---

[515] *Referee*, December 30, 1908. *Melbourne Age*, December 29, 1908.
[516] *Melbourne Age*, December 29, 1908.
[517] *Daily Telegraph*, *Melbourne Age*, December 29, 30, 1908.
[518] *Sydney Bulletin*, January 7, 1909.

Jack Johnson's mother Tiny Johnson said Jack helped his family, often sending money to her and his sisters. He had purchased a home in Galveston for his mother. Before the championship fight, he had told his family that he could not lose to Burns, and advised them to sell the furniture and bet it all on him.[519]

[519] *Los Angeles Times*, December 27, 28, 1908.

CHAPTER 26

Racial Implications: The White Hope Era Begins

In the wake of the Burns-Johnson fight, in Australia the sport of boxing endured a great deal of criticism, which also brought out its defenders. Much of the ill-will was the result of the fact that a black man had defeated a white man for the world heavyweight title, though for some it might have been subconscious. The fact that there was such a great outpouring of anti-boxing sentiment following this particular fight, when other fights had not brought forth such strong feelings, lends credence to the position. The local Sydney newspapers printed several editorial letters, which revealed a great deal of the country's underlying racism and race issues.

Some lamented the influence that such a spectacle would have upon the general tone of the community, stimulating and glorifying brutish fighting instincts that were anti-social. Several, including clergymen, said the fight and boxing had a degrading, demoralizing, and dehumanizing influence. A reverend said, "A huge crowd of men would evidently have seen a fellow-creature pretty well battered to death if it had not been for the interference of the police. ... The only satisfaction I have in the whole business is that the despised black man proved to be the superior animal."

The *Sunday Observer*, a British newspaper, characterized the fight as a degrading spectacle. Some called for the law to prevent fights.

One countered, "The men were not forced to fight, and the public were not forced to watch them. It was done at their own free will. In my opinion the people who watched the fight last Saturday saw no more brutality than they would in a game of football."

Several writers noted the inconsistency of those who extolled football and rugby yet condemned boxing, despite the fact that there were many more injuries in the former. "The list of injured at Rugby football reads like a battle, while as for the good feeling in the game, I cannot remember of any instance where a pugilist knocked down and kicked an adversary." Football matches contained so much more brutality than boxing that "if anyone attempted to do what is often done on the football ground in the public street he would be charged with attempted murder."

One writer echoed that there was much more "inhumanity" going on affecting more people on a daily basis than was the case with boxing, yet all the church leaders were silent regarding those more serious concerns while they preached about the evils of boxing. For example, schoolchildren were being "shockingly sweated on dairy farms," "young girls were working in city factories for a shilling and even nothing a week," and "doing heavy manual labour for long hours – practically men's work."

Another agreed that the fight was not brutal if Burns, within 24 hours, was attending church and spending the day picnicking at National Park with his wife. His jaw was not broken as rumored, for he had given a vigorous speech at the Stadium. He made a great deal of money from the contest and was a well-trained athlete. The crowd was orderly and civilized. "The point which most people seem somehow to evade is that many worse things are in our midst daily than boxing contests for money of which but little notice is taken." Examples included cigarette-smoking. In this instance, the police had the power to stop the fight, which they did when they believed that Burns had no chance of winning and only would get punished more. The crowd was satisfied that the correct thing was done.

Some argued that boxing was good for the Anglo Saxon race in general, for it kept it tough and able to defend itself.

> These boxing contests, in the normal man, appeal to that bulldog nature – that desire to be on top, that in our forbears has placed the Anglo-Saxon race in the pre-eminent position it occupies today. To keep this position in the struggle for existence these instincts must be fostered. Real war is a merciless game, and to the strong in mind and body is given the victory.

Another argued, "Once the science of self-defence is made punishable by Act of Parliament, then good-bye to the good old adage of Britons never shall be slaves." Yet another wrote, "Boxing is for manly men (may we have more of them), not for ladies, nor for effeminate degenerates."

So why all the criticism? One writer acknowledged that race motivated the anti-boxing sentiment:

> They are hurt because a black man has won, and they howl, "Stop the game, the colour line should have been drawn." They are not sportsmen in any sense of the term.

> And there are others whose feelings are lacerated because they know that the downfall of the white man before the coloured will be told, sung, and cinematographed everywhere where there is a black skin; because they know that the victory of black over white will be preached among every coloured race; because they know that the story of the fight will help to promote unrest and sedition; and because they see in the triumph at the Stadium on Saturday last a grinning savage with his foot on the neck of White Australia and exclaiming, "What did I tell yah?"

Hence, the fight's result could have worldwide racial and political implications. Many whites of all nationalities were concerned about the larger symbolic impact, particularly given that most white nations had conquered and colonized most non-white nations, and had instituted racial caste systems. Whites did not want non-whites to get any ideas that they could be victorious over whites, or that white dominance might not be the result of the natural and automatic order of things.

Another writer agreed that race motivated the anti-boxing sentiment:

> If Burns had won there would have been none of this outcry. ... They listened readily to every bit of idle tittle-tattle about Johnson. ... They speak of Mister Johnson 'spitting venom' when they know well the insults he himself had to submit to. Did Burns not taunt the despised black man? ... Read Burns's book, and you will find the advice there to 'make your opponent wild.' What has Mr. Simpson to say about the gross insult by Burns that Johnson was a cur with a yellow streak? That sounds to me somewhat venomous, but I am old-fashioned. ... I was at the fight, prepared to cheer the best man, irrespective of colour or creed, and when I observed the masterful demeanour of that magnificent black man, dominating the whole of that hostile, one-eyed crowd, I was lost in admiration. ... As soon as the boomed American gets a drubbing, fairly and squarely, then the cry is raised that Australia is in danger from the aggressive coloured races. Not a word of this before the fight.
>
> Is it not the very limit of hypocrisy? All this new and well simulated abhorrence of prize-fighting is entirely due to the fact that the Burnsites are smarting over the defeat of the courageous man whom they were gulled to believe was supernatural.

Ex-champion Jim Corbett had been known as a mouthy fighter, taunting his foes, yet he still was perceived as a "gentleman."

A clergyman told his congregation that the Christmas season had been marred by a brutal prizefight. His statements also demonstrated the cognizance of the significance of race, even in Australia:

> A ray of sunshine was in the hope that the triumph of the colored man over the white would lead here to a truer conception as to the power of the non-European peoples. Believers in a White Australia – and he was one – should recognize the danger and sin in pushing that doctrine to the extreme. The asiastic neighbor as well as the negro had some marvelous capacities when trained, and Johnson was an illustration in one line of action.

Another Australian Methodist clergyman denounced the fight and boxing as a carnival of savagery which had undesirable racial and political implications, stimulating fear and concern:

> After all the boasting, bragging, and betting, those 20,000 raving white Australians beheld their white champion beaten by the despised black man. Racial hatred had been set on fire. There would be racial reprisals and recriminations. They have by this deed put back the clock of history. There was not one redeeming feature in the savagery and brutality. God grant that the defeat of Saturday may not be the sullen and solemn prophecy that Australia is to be outclassed and

finally vanquished by these dark skinned people who everywhere are beginning to realise their immense possibilities.

One writer soothed readers by saying that Burns' performance had been a credit to the white race:

> We read daily of these 'croakers' of the supposed brutality of this great contest, which proved the grit, determination, and bravery of our white race, in the person of Tommy Burns, and which was an object lesson to all those present to follow Burns's example of pluck and endurance against great odds. ... If he should meet Johnson again I am sure he would make a better show, and use other tactics to regain his title; and I hope, should this ever take place, that he will have the satisfaction of erasing that 'dirty smile' off a 'champion' full of his own conceit and self-importance. Away from Johnson's personality, he is a wonderful boxer, and any man that goes down to him has nothing to be ashamed of.

Noted was the fact that most of the anti-boxing outrage arose *after* the fight, not so much before it, chiefly owing to the result's racial implications. "This fight should be a lesson to all, for it has exhibited the superiority of the despised black over the white, and brings into satirical relief the law appropriating this large continent to one race only." Another said, "The signal victory for one of the black races may 'give us pause' amid our dithyrambics about a 'White Australia.'"

Yet another writer said, "I should very much like to have seen Burns win, because he is a white man; at the same time I have no antipathy to the dark man. Black people have taken high positions in various walks in life."

Further highlighting the racial aspects of the analysis, one noted,

> There is one phase of this brutal struggle to which I would desire to call attention. Now may we not see why there is such a spirit of hostility to the colored race (the negro race) of the States? All Americans have a true and genuine respect for men like Frederick Douglas or Booker Washington. Allowances must be made for a people so recently recovered from the barbarism of darkest Africa. As we count history our black brothers are only infants in the progress of civilization. The wonder is that so much has been accomplished. ... On the other hand, I have met large numbers of a very different style of man. Johnson is not simply unpopular at the present time, he is the subject of a race hatred much more intense than the Judenhetze of the Germans.[520] Perhaps our white people are to blame for it, for there is, apart from any idea of race superiority, a wisdom in drawing the color line. ... And so have we appealed to savage brute force as a test of superiority, we must be content with the consequences. The black man won in the war of brute force, and

---

[520] Judenhetze was the systematic persecution, incitement to hatred, and malicious propaganda towards Jews.

the cheer which followed, though restrained, was his due. And yet how humiliating!

Even the Australian Cabinet would discuss whether to make pugilistic encounters illegal.

Hence, Johnson's victory had social, political, and racial meaning and relevance even in Australia, because that country, which was part of the British Empire, had its own racial issues and concerns, particularly with Aborigines and Asian immigrants. Johnson's victory made Australians' true feelings regarding race more noticeable.[521]

The *Freeman* reported that there were schemes afoot in the U.S. to boycott the new champion. It asked, "Why should the Americans be prejudiced against Jack? Is he not an American? And did he not represent America in his fight? Tommy is a Canadian. But still home was and is against Johnson as master of the fighting game."[522] Clearly, race trumped nationality.

The *New York Age*, another black-owned newspaper, quoted Bat Masterson as saying, "Jack Johnson, like most of the Negroes in this country, is genuinely American, and if we have no white native capable of holding and defending the championship title it is far more in line with American patriotism to have it defended by a black native than an imported American whose skin happens to be white." However, for the most part, Masterson's feelings were not shared:

> Such should be the opinion of every American with reference to the result of the Burns-Johnson bout; but race prejudice is an affliction that renders the patient totally unconscious to merit, justice and fair play. As it is, we have but few white Americans to express through the press such sentiment as 'Bat' Masterson recently made in the *New York Telegraph*. There is Tad, of the *New York Journal*, who is one of the fairest writers that ever pushed a pencil and who has always evinced an inclination to judge a fighter on his merits – be he white or black – but after the two above-mentioned scribes you will find them writing, as does Edgren, of the *New York Evening World*, with a pen that has been dipped in gall and wormwood whenever a Negro fighter is the subject for discussion.

New York Telegraph writer Charles Meegan expressed the sentiment of the majority of white Americans when he said,

> Sportsmen generally did not approve of Burns risking the loss of a title to a Negro when the match was made, and the defeated champion will get little sympathy. While censuring Burns, sportsmen do not extend open arms to the new champion by any means. Johnson never will be a popular champion, although his title to the

---

[521] *Sydney Morning Herald*, *Daily Telegraph*, December 30, 1908. *Sydney Daily Telegraph*, *Sydney Morning Herald*, *Melbourne Age*, all December 28, 1908; *Sydney Referee*, December 30, 1908; *Sydney Bulletin*, December 31, 1908.
[522] *Freeman*, January 9, 1909.

honor is clear and clean. He won it in a fair, hard battle, proving that he is the better man, but the sporting world is not enthusiastic at the spectacle of a Negro occupying the position of its former idols – Sullivan, Corbett and Fitzsimmons.

The *Age* went on to say,

> It is perfectly true that the white sporting world does not relish the spectacle of a Negro being the champion fighter of the world. Every Negro, from the lad large enough to sell papers to the old man who is able to read the paper (if he can read) is happy today, but it is not natural that the white man should be. How many Negroes were happy July 4, when the news, sad to us, came from the West that Joe Gans had been beaten by 'Battling' Nelson? The writer doubts that there was one in America. Then we should not expect to see the white Americans enthuse over a Negro becoming champion of the world. However, we do expect all white Americans to show a spirit of fair play.

The *Age* noted that as a result of race prejudice, the majority of white writers had claimed that Johnson had a yellow streak, regardless of whether they truly thought it. Johnson was disproving that theory.

> This same 'yellow streak' is generally attributed to all colored fighters until they prove otherwise in decisive fashion. Johnson has stopped all talk about having a 'yellow streak' by giving Burns such a beating it took all the police in Australia who could be hastily summoned to the ringside to pull him off his white adversary before a tragedy was committed.

> Now the white writers are staying up late at nights trying to figure who can wrest the championship from Johnson. The best they can do is to resurrect a bunch of 'has beens.' They talk of Jim Jeffries, but he drew the color line several years ago after he saw Johnson send his brother to the 'Land of Dreams.' He would be the champion's most troublesome white contender. ...

> But Edgren speaks truthfully when he declares Johnson will be champion for some time. In the opinion of the writer, Johnson's strongest rival is a Negro – Sam Langford – and the champion has defeated him.

Earlier in the year, at Madison Square Garden, the Negro Elks had introduced Johnson as the next champion. In a speech, he told members that he was going abroad to chase Burns until he secured a match with him, and when he returned he would occupy a position in the pugilistic world that would make every Negro proud.

> He has not only kept his word but has also shown to the world that the theory of a Negro possessing a 'yellow streak' is only a piece of imagination on the part of many white writers, who have

> unfortunately had too high a regard of the white fighters' ability of ring generalship and too low an opinion of the Negro's. ...
>
> Every time Johnson knocked down Burns a bunch of prejudice fell, and at the same time the white man's respect for the Negro race went up a notch.
>
> Christmas in America was truly a great day for the sable contingent of our great population, and it is natural that we should assume an a la peacock pose whenever we think that for the first time in the world's history a Negro is champion over land and sea.[523]

Clearly, Johnson's victory uplifted the black spirit and served to refute many racial myths and stereotypes.

Johnson claimed that he could beat Burns in any kind of contest, whether it be motor racing, cycling, running, swimming, tennis, baseball, golf, bowling, sculling, billiards, piano, guitar, fiddle, banjo, or even the concertina. "I feel so sick of hearing the opinions of Sydney people about Burns's merits that I want to show that I can beat him at anything."

Johnson would remain in Sydney for weeks before visiting Melbourne and Adelaide. When he wasn't exhibiting, "I spend most of my spare time in the art galleries and the museums. My principal hobby is archaeology. ... I'm real interested in aeronautics. I have an idea of a new kind of flying machine, which will turn out, I think, a fine success."

Four days after the championship fight, on December 30, 1908 in Australia, New South Wales Chief Secretary William H. Wood said the government would not allow a Johnson-Burns rematch, and if they did try to fight, the police would interfere and the principals would be arrested and prosecuted. He said the contest was more brutal than scientific.

The government had shown no concern when it came to less prominent fights that were much more brutal, nor when it was a white fighter pounding on a black one. Amongst the spectators in attendance at the Burns-Johnson fight were the Australian Attorney General, the state government premier, and the chief secretary. They had no problem with boxing's brutality *before* the white man was beaten.[524]

It cannot be underestimated how significant an occurrence it was for a black fighter even to be allowed the opportunity to attain the status of heavyweight champion, let alone win it. Many believed that blacks had no right to challenge for the heavyweight championship, regardless of ability. It offended notions that blacks and whites should occupy separate existences and never intermingle in a competitive way. In the U.S., Burns drew harsh criticism for violating the norm, which affected his legacy.

Boxing champions had been revered as symbols of skill, intelligence, and courage, as well as racial and national superiority. For a black man to represent the ultimate symbol of those values was a threat to the existing social order. Either the representative would have to be changed, or the

---

[523] *New York Age*, December 31, 1908.
[524] *Sydney Morning Herald*, *Sydney Daily Telegraph*, December 31, 1908.

image of the champion boxer would have to be altered in order to satisfy the dominant ideology.

Immediately the call for a white man to regain the title and remove Johnson's golden smile began. The "golden smile" in the face of white defeat was a sign of black pride; something blacks were not supposed to show. Thus began the era of the search for the "White Hope," which Johnson noted began "with ill-concealed bitterness."[525]

Some even attempted to inoculate themselves from Johnson's victory by claiming that since Jeffries never had been defeated in the ring, he still was the champion, not a black man. Johnson laughed at the idea.

Joe Woodman, Sam Langford's manager, said he would put Langford in with Johnson for a 12-round bout, but not 20 rounds, because in a 20-round fight, Johnson's superior weight and strength eventually would tell.[526]

Previously, world middleweight champion Stanley Ketchel had drawn the color line. He thought a white man lowered himself in the respect of his associates when he fought a colored man. However, Ketchel had changed his mind, and said he would cross the color line in order to regain the heavyweight title for the white race.[527] Ketchel stated,

> I had made up my mind before the Burns-Johnson fight never to fight a colored man, but now that the great bulk of the American sporting public seems to be incensed over the fact that Johnson is the recognized champion, I am thoroughly willing to fight him, but all other negroes I will bar. ... The fact that I am willing to fight Johnson is proof positive that the talk of my being afraid of Langford is all bosh.[528]

Ketchel also said, "I was against fighting colored men, but since there is a public demand to dethrone Johnson, I am ready to comply with the demand of the people."

Baltimore's *Afro-American Ledger* noted that even Jim Corbett was discussing potentially fighting Johnson. Of course, he was 42 years old and had not fought since 1903, so he was delusional. Corbett said, "I simply feel badly to see a colored man champion." Although retired for many years, his prejudice had him considering re-entering the ring.

Yet, despite his age and inactivity, blinded by prejudice, several respected experts said Corbett would have a shot to win if he had six months to train.

> They cannot abide a Negro being the heavyweight champion of the world.
>
> Ever since the days of Peter Jackson, the white heavyweights have absolutely refused to fight with a colored man. Johnson ran Burns almost all around the world to get a crack at him. ...

---

[525] Johnson, *In the Ring and Out*, at 58-59.
[526] *San Francisco Examiner*, December 30, 1908.
[527] *San Francisco Chronicle*, December 31, 1908.
[528] *Tacoma Times*, January 6, 1909.

> The secret of the whole matter is that these fellows think there will be big money in a chance at Johnson, and it is more that than anything else.[529]

The *Freeman* noted there was a tendency to view boxing battles between white and black fighters from a racial standpoint. Hence, stirred-up whites wanted the black Johnson dethroned.

> By Jack being master of the heavyweights means that a Negro is at the lead of his class. There seems to be a sentiment predominating whenever a colored man meets a white man in the ring that it is a question of race superiority. ... The fact that it is a question of the best man winning, regardless of color, is lost sight of.

Regardless of the white desire to see him dethroned, the *Freeman's* expert believed Johnson would be champion for a long time. He had chased Burns for two years, but the "fourflushing" champion insulted him instead, calling him "quitter" and "yellow dog." Now that Jack had proven otherwise, the hunt was on to find a white fighter who could beat him:

> Since Johnson has become champion, the sporting circles have been busy looking over the list of the 'ex's' and fighters of the day...to find a man who can dethrone the black man. So ambitious are some of the old men of the fistic game to bring the laurels back to the white race that there have been a number of replies of willingness to re-enter the ring on Johnson's return home and defeat the colored wonder.[530]

Most whites wanted Jim Jeffries, believing he was the only man who could return the title to the white race. In January 1909, Jeffries started some light training under the auspices of vaudeville exhibitions. Jeffries started saying things that gave the impression that he at least was considering a comeback:

> It's awful to think that a big negro can lord it over all the white men. Maybe I'll see my way clear to make him go yet. I'll never fight again unless I am sure that I can get right. ... I must be in condition to fight if I ever return to the ring. I'd look nice taking a beating from a big coon after fighting my way right to the top. ... I never considered Burns a heavyweight champion. He always looked like a big, well developed middleweight to me.[531]

John L. Sullivan declared that Johnson never would have the prestige of a white champion. Sullivan said it was foolish for anyone to think Corbett had any chance to defeat Johnson. However, "As for Jeffries, if he can get into shape he has a good chance."

---

[529] *Afro-American Ledger*, January 9, 1909. *Salt Lake Herald, Los Angeles Herald*, January 4, 1909; *San Francisco Call*, January 10, 1909.
[530] *Freeman*, January 16, 23, 1909.
[531] *San Francisco Call*, January 17, 1909.

Unlike whites, the colored population was wild with enthusiasm and "dippy with delight" over Johnson's victory. "Negroes are proud of Johnson. ... He is the best fighter the black race has ever produced, and I think even the white followers of the ring are disposed to give him credit."

White prejudice against blacks doing well in life was nothing new. At that time, Senator Ben Tillman was giving speeches saying that he was opposed to the higher education of negroes, for it might do away with the white man's supremacy. When addressing teachers at Columbia, South Carolina, Tillman insisted that negroes should not be allowed to have higher education because it meant the final undoing of white people.

The *Afro-American Ledger* noted that there had been 101 lynchings in 1908, the most since 1903. 98 of them were in Southern States. The Night Riders had lynched and burned both colored people as well as whites. All were made to feel its power. Even some women had not escaped.

"BLACK MAN'S BURDENS."
Washington Bee, January 2, 1909

Since the 1905 race riots in which most blacks were driven from the town, the remnants of the Harrison, Arkansas black community lived a tenuous existence. In late January 1909, Harrison's transformation into an all-white town was completed by yet another violent riot, brought on in the wake of the January 18, 1909 arrest of a black man on the charge of raping a white woman. The continuing mob activity resulted in another mass exodus of black citizens from Harrison. Unprotected, most left on the night of January 28, 1909, and their property quickly was declared forfeit and seized by the town's whites.[532]

The *Sydney Bulletin* said Jack Johnson was the first "colored bruiser" to hold the heavyweight championship, and "already they are talking of his wiping out." Al Kaufman, who recently scored a KO39 over Jim Barry, was

---

[532] *Afro-American Ledger,* January 9, 1909; *Freeman,* January 23, 1909.

looked upon as the most likely man to do the job. He was bigger, heavier, and taller than Johnson, "and when the eminent black Methodist meets that white giant we shall see what sort of a losing fight he can put up."[533]

The *Freeman* lamented, "Sullivan has been continually poisoning the minds of the sporting world with the dope that a Negro has no right to hold the championship over white men."

The *Freeman* noted that racial prejudice had caused many to predict Johnson's defeat to Burns as a result of his so-called yellow streak. Now that he had proven them wrong, as a result of racial envy, whites were taking a strong interest in the heavyweight division, as predicted. Many whites engaged in all kinds of slander and schemes to deny Jack's ability and right to hold the title.

> So strong has the desire to dethrone the Negro champion become that James J. Jeffries, the only man who is thought to have an equal chance with Johnson – the retired champion who has said "Let it be understood that I will never fight again"; - has been brought back into the limelight as being the last hope for white supremacy. There is now no doubt of Jeffries' intention to re-enter the ring. He is getting into shape while on a theatrical tour. Believing it to be a certainty that the big Californian will step back into the roped square, although he strenuously denies the charge, the fans have already begun to wager on the prospective bout.

Johnson's victory was making Jeffries big money, for it brought him before the public more strongly than ever before. He could earn good money giving stage exhibitions, owing to the fact that he was a potential prospective opponent for Johnson; one who had a chance to win back the title for the white race. That made folks want to see Jeff more than ever.[534]

The *Sydney Bulletin* noted the inconsistency of Americans, particularly its reporters. One minute they were hard on Burns for not fighting Johnson, and the next they were hard on him for having fought him. It was a matter of better watch for what you ask.

> The Americans are marvelous people. Three months ago, they were yelping at Tommy Burns with one united yelp to drop his nonsense about the color line, and face Brother Johnson like a man. Jim Jeffries yelped in this regard as loudly and as persistently as any of them. When the U.S. heard that Thomas was really going to meet the Black Agony they were pleased. They started forecasting the result of the event, and many of their forecasts favored the white champion. Jim Jeffries, for example, went into details on the subject, and gave Burns the decision six weeks before the fight on his superior footwork, his infighting ability, and his gameness. Now the fickle James says this, which is what 90 per cent of the other fight fans in Hamland say: -

---

[533] *Sydney Bulletin*, January 28, 1909.
[534] *Freeman*, January 30, 1909.

> "Tommy Burns' mistake, the one great mistake of his career, was in allowing Johnson the opportunity to fight for the title. I refused time and again to meet Johnson while I was holding the title, even though I knew I could beat him. I would never allow a negro a chance to fight for the world's championship, and I advise all other champions to follow the same course. Tommy Burns has been vastly overrated as a fighter. This has always been my belief."

Of a verity, N. Brusso spoke sooth when he remarked after the Johnson chastisement, that "Americans have no use for a beaten man." They are the world's worst sportsmen.[535]

In early February, Roscoe Johnson, one of Jack's brothers, who lived in New York and was about 19 years old, died of pneumonia.[536]

On February 12, 1909 in New York City, W. E. B. Du Bois founded the National Association for the Advancement of Colored People (NAACP), which was dedicated to promoting equality of rights for colored people and eradicating caste or race prejudice.

Jim Corbett thought that Jim Jeffries would need at least one to two years of work to be prepared properly to defeat Johnson:

> There is too much at stake – a Negro has the championship and it must be won back by a white man, to whose race it belongs. Jeffries must be right in every sense of the word before he takes the chance, and he can not hope to be right until he undergoes a long course of training. The American public and the fight promoters are making a big mistake by endeavoring to force Jeff into a match.[537]

Jeffries had signed a contract to appear on the vaudeville stage for 20 weeks at $2,500 a week, which was very big money. He would do some light sparring with Sam Berger, have time to do a little training, and think over a potential fight with Johnson. Jeffries wanted to be sure that he could get into top shape again before agreeing to fight Johnson. Jeff said,

> Who said that interest in the boxing game was on the wane? After my experience of the last week I am led to believe that the gloves are more popular with the public than ever before. It may, of course, be possible that the fact that Jack Johnson, a Negro, holds the heavyweight championship of the world is responsible for the Queensberry revival. ...
>
> Everybody and his neighbor appears to believe that it is their honorable duty to ask me if I am going to fight again. ...
>
> W. W. Naughton and other experts have been kind enough to place themselves on record as saying that I have nothing to fear from Jack

---

[535] *Sydney Bulletin*, February 4, 1909.
[536] *New York World*, February 4, 1909.
[537] *Freeman*, February 6, 1909.

> Johnson. That just about expresses my sentiments. I don't fear the Negro or any other being who walks on two feet. ...
>
> Followers of pugilism are an inconsistent lot. When I was in this city last summer...everybody was criticizing Tommy Burns because the Canuck would not fight Jack Johnson. ... Now these fellows are howling out of the other side of their mouths, and they are howling longer and louder than ever. "This man Burns is a disgrace to the ring," they say. "He should never have crossed the color line. Had he refused to meet Johnson, the white people would never have been disgraced by having a Negro as the heavyweight champion."
>
> I am wondering day by day what my fate would be were I to meet Jack Johnson and be defeated. The sporting world is crying at me now to go in and fight the Negro. In some instances the criticism hurled at me is not of the kindest nature. I get letters calling me a coward and all that sort of rubbish. I pay no attention to them. I have Burns' example in front of me.[538]

Jack Kipper, a partner with Jeffries in a Los Angeles saloon business, thought that Jeff would fight again if he could condition himself:

> And, believe me, that negro will be the worst whipped coon that ever crawled from the ring when Jeffries gets after him. If it took the black man, with all his vaunted cleverness and tremendous hitting power, 14 rounds to stop Tommy Burns, a man by no means as large as he is, what will Jeff do to him?[539]

That was a question the public, both fight fans and otherwise, wanted answered. A potential Jeffries comeback was a running theme which newspapers and the public obsessed about for some time to come. The amount of ink devoted to both Johnson and Jeffries was tremendous, omnipresent, and continuous.

In picking Jeffries to win a potential contest with Johnson, the *Sydney Bulletin* wrote,

> The general opinion among pugs of all sorts is if Jeff can get back to condition Massa Johnson will climb between the ropes before 10 rounds are through. The *Bulletin* doesn't think so. Johnson may not be a heroic fighter, but he knows enough to keep the ex-boilermaker at bay for 10 rounds. It is after the 10th that he will probably begin to go to pieces.[540]

---

[538] *Freeman*, February 6, 1909.
[539] *Tacoma Times*, February 10, 1909.
[540] *Sydney Bulletin*, February 25, 1909.

CHAPTER 27

The Return

Once Jack Johnson became world heavyweight champion, a position of great symbolic relevance, the white press began scrutinizing his every move, and increasingly focused on his personal life, which previously had been given little mention in the newspapers. The shift became quite palpable as the years progressed.

While black newspapers often printed opinions of those who thought Jim Jeffries would lose to Johnson, white newspapers were more inclined to print the opinions of those who believed that Jeffries would restore the honor of the white race. As time progressed, it practically was considered sacrilege and disloyal to the white race to give an opinion otherwise. Although there were those who wondered whether Jeffries could come back, most wanted him to try, feeling that he could defeat Johnson if he got back into shape.

Unlike whites, most blacks rejoiced at the fact that a black man occupied the esteemed position of world heavyweight champion. It had a psychologically uplifting effect. This was important, given that blacks were held back by Jim Crow laws and told that they were inferior to whites. Of course, this also explains why many white folks felt the need to tear down Johnson personally and hope to see him defeated.[541]

The *Sydney Bulletin* explained why blacks were so successful in the ring:

> The Yankee is becoming perturbed over the success of the negro in the square 'ring.' There are 72 millions of white men, and only eight millions of blacks, in the U.S.A., and yet the number of clever colored boxers is out of all proportion to their population basis. Why? ... The general impression seems to be that the white bruiser gets a swelled head before the colored one. In fact, he gets it before he has learned his business thoroughly, whereas it is only when he has become 'a scientist,' like Jack Johnson and other great men, that the negro begins to inquire for 9 ½ inch hats. ... But, all the same, writer's opinion is quite different. The black man is still the child of Nature, closer to the earth. He is handier to the period when man had to rely for his defence upon his own physical powers. The white man has

---

[541] *Washington Times,* January 14, 1909; *Nashville Globe,* July 9, 1909.

passed that stage. He slays his enemies with projectiles. ... Boxing is, after all, a barbaric business, inasmuch as it is the art of pounding an opponent into submission by brute force. Brute force, scientifically applied, if you like; but, nevertheless, brute force. And in the white man's blood the idea is to apply not physical force, but mechanical power. Therein lies the difference between the two races, and naturally the race that is closest to the stage in which man fought for his life with his hands, feet, and teeth, will produce the larger proportion of boxers.[542]

On February 15, 1909, Jack Johnson left Sydney, Australia on the steamer *Makura*, heading towards Vancouver, Ontario, Canada.[543]

Jim Jeffries consistently maintained that before deciding whether or not he would fight Johnson, he needed time to get into condition and see whether he felt that he could get back to his old form again. He would not announce a Johnson fight unless and until he was certain that he could get right again. Regardless, if someone else beat Johnson, he would not re-enter the ring. "I may not need to meet this nigger."

Everywhere he went, Jeffries was given a great reception and constantly hounded with questions of whether and when he would return the title to the white race. Nevertheless, on his tour, he was advertised as the undefeated heavyweight champion.

When Jeffries arrived in New York, the throng of humanity that came to see him far exceeded that which came to greet the President-elect of the United States, William H. Taft.

Jeffries was a big hit on the New York vaudeville stage. Large crowds watched him train and spar 4 shortened rounds with big Sam Berger. "Jeffries now is the repository of

Jim Jeffries as of March 1909

a yearning of a race which longs to assert its supremacy. So it is that he is the magnet of the hour, drawing an enormous salary for an extraordinary period for spending about ten minutes a night on the stage."[544]

Jack Johnson was traveling with a white woman who purportedly was his wife. There was some mystery surrounding how, when, or where he had met her, when or if he had married her, and who she was. Various newspapers said that apparently he had married her without divorcing his first wife (who had sued him for nonsupport). The reporters were not sure.[545]

---

[542] *Sydney Bulletin*, February 25, 1909.
[543] *Sydney Bulletin*, February 18, 1909.
[544] *New York World*, March 2 - 4, 9, 1909.
[545] *San Francisco Call*, January 24, 1909. When Johnson had been in Australia, an Australian paper printed a story about his intended marriage with a white Oakland woman named Lola Toy. She entered a libel suit against the newspaper and secured a verdict for $7,500.

Jack Johnson with "Hattie McLay," a.k.a. Hattie Watson

Allegedly, her name either was Nellie O'Brien, Hattie Smith, Hattie McLay, Anna McClay, or Hattie Watson. She was with him in Sydney. At various times, Johnson called her by multiple different names, and said she was a New York Irish gal whom he had met before his trip to Europe to chase after Burns. It later would be revealed that Johnson had a habit of often calling a current girlfriend his "wife."

While on board the ship on his return journey, the champ participated in a couple of concerts, playing the bass violin. Mrs. Johnson played the piano and accompanied Jack, and they were well received.

Johnson decided to part ways with his manager, Australian Sam Fitzpatrick. Jack had a reputation for jilting managers. He had many in his time, and sporting men said Fitzpatrick was lucky to hold on to him for so long. Johnson said he had no trouble with Fitzpatrick or any ill will. It just was a matter of economics. "His contract was up, and it was not renewed."

Fitzpatrick shrugged his shoulders and said it was impossible for any man to handle Johnson after he won the title, for Jack had a "bad case of a swelled head." "Johnson was a different man before the fight. He would feed out of the hand then, but he is a hard man to handle now. We decided to split up soon after the Makura left. Anyhow, he don't want a manager now. He has got Mrs. Johnson as his manager." Another newspaper said they had split "owing to the woman in the case."

Johnson noted that Australians criticized him for his playful taunts directed at Burns, but failed to note how Burns had insulted him. Jack did not feel he had received the treatment that was his due as champion in Australia, though the better class treated him very well.[546]

Jack was surprised that even after the fight, Australians fawned over Burns. "But, on the square, they seemed to think more of Tommy Burns after I had licked him – giving him such a licking as anybody ever had – than they did of me, and me the champion." To him, this defied logic. "Australia has no reason to complain about me though. I paid my income tax all the time and I raised a good deal of money for various charities while in Sydney." Johnson said he liked to read Shakespeare for comfort.

---

[546] *Daily Province, Ogden Standard, San Francisco Call, New York World,* March 10, 1909.

The champ also noted that while in Australia, the churches there drew the color line on him, for "they did not seem to have much use for a colored man in the Methodist churches of that white Australia."

When Johnson was informed that Galveston, where he grew up, was arranging a parade for him, his eyes sparkled, he showed his gold-tipped teeth with a grin, and said, "Tell them I'll be there."

Johnson said he was a bad sailor, and often felt sick to his stomach at sea. However, he was quite popular on the ship. A score of ladies clustered around him to say good-bye when he left.

On March 9, 1909, after three weeks at sea, Johnson arrived in Victoria, Canada. A big crowd congregated at the dock to give him a great reception. Everyone wanted to shake his hand. The reception tickled the smiling Johnson. Before traveling to Vancouver, Johnson said,

> It amuses me to hear this talk of Jeffries claiming the championship. Why when a mayor leaves office he's an ex-mayor, isn't he? When a champion leaves the ring he's an ex-champion. Well that's Jeff. If he wants to try to get the championship back I'm willing to take him on. ... In all the notices I have seen, it's all what Jeffries will take. What's the matter with what Johnson will take. I'm the champion, ain't I? I want a winner and loser's end; I don't care what it is, 60 and 40, or 75 and 25, but there's got to be a winner and loser's end.[547]

Some said Jeffries wanted a small ring if they were to fight. Johnson said that kind of talk did not scare him. "I will fight him in a 16, 12, or even a 10-foot ring if he wants to have it that way."

A delegation of colored sports met Johnson in Vancouver and gave him a mighty cheer. Beautifully attired in white pants, red necktie, and lavender shirt, Johnson received the adulation of scores of "dusky skinned admirers" who had flocked to Vancouver from the U.S. He attracted more attention than "an Indian potentate."

George Paris, the Vancouver Athletic Club's boxing instructor, tried to help Johnson secure lodging at a Vancouver hotel. However, despite application at a half dozen downtown hotels, all of them essentially drew the color line. They did not do so explicitly, all saying that there was no room and they were filled, but it was obvious what they were doing. A frustrated Mr. Paris had Johnson and his white wife stay at his home.[548]

Johnson said he would not be defending his title against Sam Langford in May in London, as had been reported (and as he had agreed to do prior to the Burns fight). Negotiations had fallen through. The National Sporting Club had offered a total purse of only 1,000 pounds ($5,000) for a 20-round contest, a paltry amount for a title fight, particularly one against a well-regarded contender. Johnson said, "I wouldn't fight for that." Now that he was champion, Jack fully realized his newfound economic power. The days of being paid a fraction of his true value were over.

---

[547] *Daily Province* (Vancouver, British Columbia, Canada), March 9, 1909.
[548] *Daily Province, Tacoma Times*, March 10, 1909.

Johnson felt that it was time for him to reap the financial rewards that other champions had. "I think I should be given a chance to cut the melon. I went to Australia and gave Burns everything he asked in the way of money just to get at him, and now that I am the champion I think I should be allowed to reap the profits." He would make easy money with theatrical engagements. "Johnson got all the glory and very little of the money in the Burns battle, and it is apparent from his demeanor that he intends to get the money as well as the glory next time."[549]

The *San Francisco Call* printed a poem entitled "The Color Question."

> Says Mistah Johnsing to Mistah Jeffries:
>
> Come, now tell us, Mistah Jeffries, is yo' re'lly gwinter fight,
> Is yo' gwinter take your chance wif de culled man's delight,
> Is yo' game to face de moosic when de coon begins to play.
> Or does de whisper frum yo' hea't say, "Honey, keep away"?
> Yah! Yo' mahty gran' an' haughty as yo' walk upon de stage,
> An' puff yo' chest an' show yo' ahms an' jes' be all de rage;
> But dere's de white man's burden – which de white men couldn't pack –
> Now, is y' gwinter pick it up, or is yo' turnin' back?
> Is yo' gwinter quit yo' bluffin', is yo' comin' to de scratch,
> Is yo' gwinter quit yo' talk, is yo' gwinter to make a match,
> Is yo' hank'ring fer to step in where de udders have not dared,
> Come, tell us, Mistah Jeffries, will yo' fight – or are yo' scared?[550]

Victor McLaglen and Jack Johnson before their 6-round exhibition bout

---

[549] *Daily Province, Tacoma Times,* March 10, 1909.
[550] *San Francisco Call,* March 10, 1909.

On March 10, 1909 at the Vancouver Athletic Club in Vancouver, British Columbia, Canada, the day after his arrival in Canada, world heavyweight champion Jack Johnson boxed a 6-round exhibition against Tacoma-based 25-year-old Victor McLaglen (also spelled McLaglan).[551]

Before the bout began, it was announced that the 6'3" McLaglen weighed 198 pounds, while Johnson weighed 211 pounds.

McLaglen looked well-built and strong. However, in the clinches, Johnson was far stronger, handling Mac "as though he were a child. He threw McLaglan around at will, and made the Tacoma man look foolish most of the time." Victor tried hard to land something, but could not.

The bout almost terminated in the first minute of the 1st round. Johnson had McLaglen's arms locked, when Jack suddenly drew his left back from the clinch and shot it hard into the body. In a delayed reaction, McLaglen backed away slowly, sank to his knees, and then doubled up on the floor.

After rising, McLaglen was very weak and all-in for about 30 seconds. However, Johnson did not try to finish him.

McLaglen was too slow for the "shifty black," and "made but a sorry showing thereafter. Johnson had to take the best of care not to do any damage, and it must be admitted he succeeded admirably." The champ carried the hopelessly outclassed McLaglen, toying with him for 6 rounds. Still, Jack demonstrated his marvelous speed and skill.

Between rounds, Johnson did not even bother to sit on his stool. He stood up against the ropes and carried on an animated conversation with George Paris about the latest fashions in diamonds in London.

In 1935, the film industry's Academy Awards would bestow upon Victor McLaglen the Best Actor Oscar for his role in the film *The Informer*.

Later that same evening, a number of his colored admirers hosted a banquet for Johnson at the Bismark café. Johnson gave a speech, saying that he was glad to see the two races sitting together. He also gave Burns credit for fighting him, despite Tommy's verbal attacks. "My gracious, there is surely one mean man! He used language to me I wouldn't repeat."

> Let me say of Mr. Burns, a Canadian and one of yourselves, that he has done what no one else ever done; he gave a black man a chance for the championship. He was beaten, but he was game. Of course, he got the money for doing it, but just the same he did what nobody else has ever done.

The next day, before Johnson left on the Canadian Pacific Railroad, heading east for Chicago, at the depot was a big delegation of both colored citizens and a great many white folk as well, all wanting to see him.[552]

The *Sydney Bulletin* wrote, "Just at present half the white man's world has one eye fixed on a big, bull-necked man in New York, wondering what he will do. Will Jeffries challenge Johnson? That is the question." New Yorkers

---

[551] *Daily Province, Tacoma Times*, March 10, 1909. McLaglen's record included: 1908 KO2 Fred Russell and LKOby3 Denver Ed Martin.
[552] *Daily Province*, March 11, 1909.

"demanded what he was doing in the matter of that nigger. Was he going to wipe him out!" Sam Berger said Jeffries was "as formidable as ever."553

Jeffries said if he came back, it would be for one fight, solely to reacquire the championship for the white race, not because he wanted to be a fighter in general. "If I ever fight again it will be with the negro and then only to win back the championship to the white race." His motivation was racial. "If Johnson had been a white man, I never would have thought of fighting again; I would have stayed in retirement for the rest of my life."554

In Chicago, Johnson said,

> I am a champion who fought his way to the top by taking the small end of purses in order to get matches, and have little to show for all my trouble. Now that I am at the top, I intend to go out hard after the coin. Langford is a good fighter, and would give me an interesting contest, but would have no chance to win. I beat him once, really knocked him out two or three times, the kindness of the referee only permitting him to stay the limit.
>
> Right now I want to brand as a lie the story that credited me with saying that I would insist on a colored referee in the event that I met Jeffries. ... There is one referee, a white man, whom I believe capable and honest enough to referee any ring contest. ... The man is Jack Welch of San Francisco. ... I have been outrageously treated by referees times without number, but do not think I would be taking chances of unfair usage with Welch as judge of the bout.555

Hugh McIntosh arrived in New York on March 12 with 15,000 feet of Johnson-Burns fight films. He said, "Johnson should not be underestimated. He is one of the greatest fighters that ever put on a glove. He is the coolest proposition in the ring I've ever seen. He has no yellow streak. In fact he is a man of much bravery, big, strong, fast, and a phenomenal boxer, particularly on the defense."

McIntosh wanted to promote a Johnson-Jeffries contest, in part as a result of "a worthy ambition to recover the championship of the world for the white race, as I was perhaps, one of the humble instruments in the white race losing it."556

Despite wanting to visit his family and enjoy a parade in his hometown, it appeared that Johnson and his wife would have to abandon their planned trip to Galveston, Texas. That state had a statute forbidding intermarriage between whites and blacks. The law did not allow mixed-race couples to live together inside the state even if they were married in another state which permitted such a union. Texas did not give full faith and credit to mixed-race marriages. The U.S. Supreme Court had upheld anti-miscegenation laws as constitutional. Texas authorities said they would prosecute Johnson

---

553 *Sydney Bulletin*, March 11, 1908.
554 *Tacoma Times*, March 11, 1909; *Daily Province*, March 12, 1909.
555 *Freeman*, March 27, 1909; *Honolulu Evening Bulletin*, April 2, 1909.
556 *New York Sun*, March 13, 1909; *New York World*, March 13, 15, 1909.

if he brought his white wife there. Hence, he could face imprisonment for co-habiting with her in his own home state of Texas.

Adding to the trouble, Johnson's first wife, Mary Austin, a colored woman, declared that Johnson was a bigamist and still was married to her. She was seeking money.[557]

Johnson denied that his wife was white, claiming, "Mrs. Johnson is three-quarters colored blooded, and I did not marry her in Australia. Her maiden name was Hattie Smith, and we were married in Mississippi about two and a half years ago. She went to Australia from London with me." Others believed she actually was white, but that Jack was claiming she was black in order to avoid prejudice and appease whites who would be offended by an interracial relationship.

Johnson offered to bet $1,000 that his wife was not white. However, Mrs. Johnson decided that they would not go to Texas, for she feared that she would be forced to permit the "white Christian gentlemen" to examine her body carefully in every way to determine whether she really was white or a "nigger," and then after they had settled themselves on that point, they might rape her. She refused to submit to such indignities.[558]

Johnson's admirers in Chicago's "darktown" followed him around. Jack said he could lick Jeffries. "I am going to New York to make him fight or shut up. ... I know I can outbox Jeffries; I think I can hit as hard as he can, and I believe I am just as strong."[559]

The *Sydney Bulletin* did not believe that Jeffries was a coward for having refused to defend the title against Johnson owing to the color line, which it understood. However, now that Johnson was champion, folks wanted and expected Jeff to recover the title for the white race:

> When Jeffries fought niggers he wasn't champion of the world. When he became champion he declined to allow any nigger to have a chance of winning the fighting supremacy from the white race. And in the light of the strong racial feeling in the States this is quite understandable without any suggestion of fear to account for it. That the pressure which is being brought to bear to induce Jeffries to come out and fight Johnson is tremendous is evident enough even in this corner of the globe. From all over the world handsome purses – record swags of cash are being offered for the fight.

Jeffries was being badgered by the press and public on a daily basis.[560]

The black-owned *New York Age* said Jeffries was lucky that Johnson had defeated Burns, because as a result, Jeff was able to make several thousands of dollars weekly in variety houses posing as the undefeated champion, for folks would pay to see him with the hope that he would fight and defeat Johnson. "As it is, he is looked upon by our white fellow citizens as the

---

[557] *New York World*, March 13, 1909; *Freeman*, March 20, 1909.
[558] *Chicago Broad Ax*, March 20, 1909. *Freeman*, March 27, 1909.
[559] *Honolulu Evening Bulletin*, April 2, 1909.
[560] *Sydney Bulletin*, March 18, 1909.

Moses who will lead the race out of the embarrassing position Tommy Burns allowed Johnson to put it in."[561]

Johnson and world middleweight champion Stanley Ketchel tentatively agreed to fight, the date and location to be determined. If Ketchel were to win, it "would release Jeffries from the White Man's Burden."[562]

Although one black-owned newspaper in Tennessee cautioned that the negro press should not boast too exultantly over Johnson's success, the *Freeman* disagreed, saying the negro should be proud of Johnson and the fact that a member of the race was atop the ladder of pugilistic fame. "Our white papers all laud James J. Jeffries. Why should not we say a few words about Mr. Johnson? Shall we keep mum? Should we not feel honored to have the world recognize us as having the best, even though it be in athletic or boxing circles?" This newspaper took racial pride in Johnson and appreciated his skilled science. It noted that even white papers had said the negro should be proud of him. "Not only should we be proud, but openly express the pride we have in him."[563]

Stanley Ketchel

On March 26, 1909 in New York, Stanley Ketchel won a 10-round no-decision bout against former middleweight and light-heavyweight champion Philadelphia Jack O'Brien (D20 and L20 Tommy Burns). O'Brien boxed very well early, outpointing Ketchel through the first 6 rounds, just as he had done with virtually all of his opponents. However, Ketchel came on, wore him down, and badly hurt O'Brien late. O'Brien was knocked out cold at the end of the 10th round, but technically was saved by the bell. The bout further boosted Ketchel's stock. The feeling was that if he could catch up with a fleet-footed master like O'Brien, then Ketchel could do so with Johnson as well, and Stan hit hard enough to hurt and stop anyone.

Ketchel drew the color line on Sam Langford, refusing to give a black man a chance at the middleweight title. But when it came to recovering the heavyweight crown for the white race, Ketchel was willing to cross the line. If he lost to Johnson, he still would be middleweight champion. However, if he lost the middleweight title to Langford, it "would be too much for our neighbors," meaning whites.[564]

Johnson most wanted to fight Jeffries. "I don't bar anybody, but of course, there would be more money and more glory in defeating Jeffries than anybody else, and that's why I'm so anxious to meet him."[565]

---

[561] *New York Age*, March 18, 1909.
[562] *New York World*, March 19, 1909.
[563] *Freeman*, March 20, 1909. The weekly *Freeman* only cost $1 for a year's subscription.
[564] *Freeman*, March 27, 1909.
[565] *New York World*, March 29, 1909. In Johnson's party were his wife ("she is white O.K.") and George Little (who either was or would become Johnson's manager).

When Johnson arrived in New York on March 29, 1909, a large black crowd greeted him at the Grand Central Depot. One writer said, "Looking along 42nd Street west there was a streak of black ... Darktown was everywhere. And why shouldn't the colored brother laud the champion heavyweight of the world?"

The champ was taken to black Barron Wilkins' hotel and compelled to make a speech. That week, large crowds would congregate around the hotel, hoping to see the new champion. Whenever Jack visited a colored club, they always asked him to make a speech.

Johnson exhibited twice a day at Hammerstein's Victoria Theater on 42nd Street, and would do so for 2 weeks at $2,000 a week. When introduced to the mixed-race crowd, he was both cheered and hissed.

Johnson sparred 3 rounds with 247-pound 5'7" Kid Cutler, a previous 1st round knockout victim of his. Jack just played with him, jabbing whenever he pleased, not trying to hurt Cutler. However, blinded by prejudice, *New York* reporter William McLoughlin said,

> I saw Johnson work yesterday afternoon. He is not and never can be a genuine heavyweight champion. He lacks the punch. He hasn't any ring sense. How such a man got away with poor but plucky little Tommy Burns is a mystery to me. He showed nothing yesterday, and I don't believe he ever had anything to show.

McLoughlin said the fans agreed with him that "Johnson won't do as the heavyweight champion of the world. ... I know that Jeffries has his heart set on getting back that heavyweight title for the white men."

> And atop of all this, the law is after Johnson. It seems that last year, about this time, he was circulating in the Tenderloin and lost some jewelry. He caused the arrest of two women. They, in turn, caused his arrest on a charge of indecent conduct. Johnson has been out on $1,000 bail since his arrest.

The black-owned *New York Age* noted the white press' hypocrisy. Jeffries was sparring tame rounds, making easy money posing as the only man who could give Johnson an interesting argument. Johnson was entitled to earn easy money with tame exhibitions as well.

Johnson said, "Ah doesn't mind what the papers say about myself, Ah'm a prizefighter. But I do object to them going into my private affairs and talking about the color of – well I will stand for anything that is said about me."[566]

On April 1, 1909 in New York, Johnson appeared in court to answer the long-standing charge against him made by Aimee Douglas, a 17-year-old light-skinned negress. Most said the charge was attempted statutory assault, which had been pending since March 1908.

---

[566] *New York World*, March 30, 1909; *New York Age*, April 1, 1909.

Interestingly, prior to Johnson's appearance, Joseph Netherland, a negro porter, was arrested and charged with attempting to bribe Miss Douglas with $75 to not show up to court, which is called witness tampering.

At the hearing, Johnson entered no defense, was convicted, and the court imposed a $200 fine, which Jack immediately paid in cash. As he left the courtroom, Douglas and her friend who had been a witness taunted him and asked, "Now will you be good?" As his car started, Jack called back, "I certainly got off cheap. Why, girls, dat was just cigarette money." His car whirled away amid jeers and hoots from the crowd.

Douglas later intimated that Johnson's offense might have gone unnoticed had he not had them arrested two days after the incident and charged with having stolen two of his rings. His case was dropped for lack of corroborative evidence, but Douglas then filed a counter charge.[567]

Regarding a potential Johnson-Jeffries contest, the *Freeman's* writer prognosticated:

> It won't be Jack Johnson, but one James J. Jeffries, groveling on the canvas in defeat, and the advocates of white supremacy will be in deep mourning. Jack Johnson will be recorded in pugilistic history not one of the greatest, but the greatest of all heavyweight champions, modern or ancient, that ever graced the squared circle. Watch the calendar and see if I'm right.[568]

Jack said he could have earned $20,000 to fight McVey in Paris. "I offered him eight thousand for his losin' end, but he said he was too strong over there to risk it."[569]

On April 15, Jim Coffroth officially announced that Jack Johnson and Stanley Ketchel had been matched to fight 20 rounds for the heavyweight championship at Colma, California on October 12. The fighters would receive 60% of the gate receipts, divided 65% to the winner and 35% to the loser, with an additional $5,000 side bet.

"Michigan Lion" Ketchel had such a huge army of loyal followers that he would draw a much bigger gate attendance than any other active contender. Hence, his selection was a matter of economics.

Ketchel said, "I'll beat him, sure. I know he can't hurt me, and furthermore he can't keep away from me like O'Brien. All I want is to get home a few smashes in the body, and I will bring Johnson down so I can knock his head off."[570]

On April 17, 1909 in Paris, France, Joe Jeannette and Sam McVey engaged in an epic 3-hour battle, won by Jeannette at the start of the 49th round, when McVey, unable to continue, retired in the corner. Jeannette had been dropped and badly hurt several times throughout the bout, but

---

[567] *Tacoma Times*, April 1, 1909; *Alexandria Gazette*, April 1, 1909; *New York Sun*, April 2, 1909; *Billings Gazette*, April 2, 1909.
[568] *Freeman*, April 3, 1909.
[569] *Freeman*, April 10, 1909.
[570] *Tacoma Times*, April 15, 1909; *Freeman*, April 24, 1909.

proved his toughness, resilience, condition, and determination, eventually winning despite having suffered a bad beating.[571]

Johnson would be on the stage for about 15 weeks in various cities throughout the country, sparring with Yank Kenny and others.

On April 19 at the Gaiety Theater in Pittsburg, when Johnson announced to the audience that Jeffries was afraid of him, the crowd practically hooted Jack from the stage.[572]

Jim Jeffries kept calling himself the undefeated heavyweight champion of the world. Semi-hysterical audiences kept asking Jeff whether and when he would fight Johnson.

On April 20, for the first time, Jim Jeffries announced that he would fight Johnson. However, he needed at least ten months of additional work before signing articles of agreement.[573]

The *Los Angeles Herald* said, "The white world is waiting for Jeffries to come back into the ring." The general feeling was that Johnson would have little chance with Jeffries, who would weigh more, have an equal reach, a far harder punch, and superior gameness. This writer claimed that Johnson previously had faked fights so he could get matches.

Johnson said, "Never until I beat Jeffries will I be able to demonstrate to the American people that I am in his class, I suppose."

Jack was going to box a 6-round no-decision bout with Philadelphia Jack O'Brien in Philadelphia, "because that is easy money that I can't afford to overlook."[574]

Arthur F. Bettinson of London, England's National Sporting Club said that after Johnson won the title, he wanted more money to fight Langford than he had agreed to before he left England for Australia. Hence, Bettinson called Johnson "a nigger, and a very bad type of one."[575]

---

[571] Two months prior in Paris, McVey had won a 20-round decision over 185-pound Jeannette. *Times Dispatch*, April 18, 1909; *Tacoma Times*, April 27, 1909; *Freeman*, May 1, 1909.
[572] *Washington Times*, April 19, 1909; *Richmond Planet*, May 1, 1909. During April 1909, in Pittsburg, Johnson boxed in a 4-round exhibition against Frank Moran, whom he would meet in an official title defense several years later.
[573] *Tacoma Times*, April 20, 1909; *Los Angeles Herald*, April 21, 1909; *Honolulu Evening Bulletin*, May 1, 1909.
[574] *Goodwin's Weekly*, May 8, 1909; *Salt Lake Herald*, May 9, 1909; *Los Angeles Herald*, April 21, May 2, *Boston Post*, April 27, 1909; *Freeman*, May 1, 1909.
[575] *New York World*, May 3, 1909. On April 27, 1909 in Boston, Sam Langford and Sandy Ferguson fought to a 12-round draw.

CHAPTER 28

A Trick or a Treat?

Philadelphia National Athletic Club manager Harry D. Edwards had secured the Philadelphia Jack O'Brien versus Jack Johson 6-round no-decision bout by guaranteeing Johnson $5,000, which was very good money for a mere 6 rounds. If the bout went the distance, he would earn $277.77 per minute. "Financially, it pays to be a world's champion pugilist." That was the same amount of money the English had offered Johnson to fight Sam Langford for 20 rounds.

O'Brien cut a deal for 30% of the gate receipts, feeling that the contest would draw very well. Hence, if he was correct, he stood to make more than Johnson, or less if he was wrong.[576]

Johnson started formal training for O'Brien on May 3, just a couple weeks before the bout.[577]

The *Philadelphia Public Ledger* believed, "O'Brien will be the first really clever man Johnson has ever met in public." O'Brien had the reputation for having the fastest hands and feet of any man in the ring. Johnson was slightly taller, at 6' ¼" vs. 5'10 ½", and was much heavier than the 170-pound O'Brien. Both were 31 years old.

Philadelphia Jack O'Brien

O'Brien actually had the superior ring experience. "O'Brien is 31 years old and has been in the prize ring since 1896, taking part in more than 160 battles." The former world light-heavyweight champion held 6-round victories over Burns and Choynski, and knockouts over Kaufman (KO17) and Fitzsimmons (KO13). Many recalled that O'Brien had outpointed Ketchel clearly in the first 6 rounds of their contest, and noted that the upcoming bout was only 6 rounds, so it was possible that O'Brien could outpoint Johnson. Many said if the champion's heart was not in the right place, "he is in for a lacing." "O'Brien is without doubt the cleverest big white man in the ring today."[578]

---

[576] *Philadelphia Public Ledger*, May 3, 1909.
[577] *Ogden Standard*, May 3, 1909; *Philadelphia Public Ledger*, May 4, 1909.
[578] *Philadelphia Public Ledger*, May 4, 19, 1909; *New York Sun*, May 19, 1909; *New York Journal*, May 12, 17, 1909; *Deseret Evening News*, May 14, 1909; Boxrec.com.

The fight would give the public an opportunity to get a line on the Johnson-Ketchel fight. If O'Brien did well, it would encourage Ketchel's admirers to believe he had a good chance with Johnson in their upcoming title bout. "If O'Brien outpoints Johnson, ring experts say that there will be increased interest in the Johnson-Ketchel fight at Colma, in October."[579]

The *Los Angeles Herald* lamented that "faker" O'Brien was in the limelight again. It remembered how he would not fight Burns in a rematch unless Tommy agreed to throw the fight. O'Brien's history caused some to wonder whether the upcoming bout would be on the level. Most reporters believed Johnson had agreed to carry previous foes, so they felt that he was not beyond agreeing to do so with O'Brien for an easy payday.[580]

While in Chicago on his exhibition tour, Jim Jeffries spoke of Johnson, who was in the same town, saying,

> If that fellow comes to see me he will get a cleaning for which he might get a lot of money later on. I don't want to see him. ... Tell his friends to keep him out of my sight, for I'll knock his block off the first time I see him. ... I could whip him on one second's notice. ...
>
> Jack Johnson won an easy victory over Tommy Burns. ... Just such an easy victory will I have over the negro fighter, who says he is champion of the world, but he will be a more marked fighter than Burns was. I will batter him beyond recognition. I have harbored ill-feeling for a number of the men I met in battle, but never so bitter have I been against any other living soul. I'll batter him into such a state of helplessness that he will never fight again. I'll show no mercy.
>
> It would not surprise me if I knocked him out in a jiffy – that is, if he'll stand up and fight.[581]

The *Bisbee Daily Review* said Johnson's wife, Hattie Smith, born near Biloxi, Mississippi 26 years ago, had attracted more attention than any other boxer's wife. Married for 2 ½ years, they had lived in comparative obscurity. However, once her husband had won the title, a great deal of attention was paid. Although several reports said she was white, making her an international figure at once, others said she actually was black, but reporters were misled by her light color. She easily could pass for a white woman, "but admits a strain of colored blood."[582]

On May 15, before Johnson exhibited at the National Club in Philadelphia, when he was introduced, the hisses, hoots, and groans from the mostly white crowd were so loud that Jack could not be heard when he tried to give a speech. Nevertheless, Jack smiled and bowed. People paid to see him, whether or or not they liked him or disliked him.[583]

---

[579] *Washington Herald*, May 4, 1909; *Deseret Evening News*, May 14, 1909.
[580] *Los Angeles Herald*, May 12, 1909.
[581] *New York World*, May 11, 1909.
[582] *Bisbee Daily Review* (Arizona), May 4, 1909.
[583] *New York Sun*, May 17, 1909; *New York World*, May 18, 1909.

That day, police officers in two separate states stopped "Champeen Jack Johnsing." On his drive from Merchantville, New Jersey to Pennsylvania, a motorcycle officer saw that the license displayed on his vehicle was out of Illinois, not Pennsylvania, so he stopped him. Then, when Johnson returned to New Jersey, an officer detained him there for the same reason.[584]

JOHNSON AND O'BRIEN READY FOR BATTLE

It would become a running theme for Johnson to be stopped and ticketed for various minor traffic offenses, most often speeding. He probably was the first black man to be stopped incessantly for "driving while black," as they say; police officers using whatever excuse they could to detain and charge him whenever they could.

JOHNSON AT WORK AT MERCHANTVILLE

Reporters noted that O'Brien was training hard, whereas the overconfident and overweight Johnson did not appear to be taking the bout seriously, taking a lot of chances with his lack of training. He obviously had "inordinate confidence and conceit in his own ability." For the past few months, he had done little work, mostly eating at banquets, doing a little theatrical work, and joy-riding with a bunch of ladies in his automobile.

O'Brien certainly was the more popular local favorite with the fans. "The majority of spectators will favor O'Brien, for the white man always has the house with him when he fights a negro..."

---

[584] At that time, each state required a license be obtained to drive in that individual state. They did not honor the U.S. Constitution's full faith and credit clause.

260

Philadelphia Record, May 16, 1909

In Chicago on May 18, 1909, Jim Jeffries took the scales in public for the first time and allegedly tipped the beam at 243 pounds.

Also on May 18, 1909, in Pittsburg, Stanley Ketchel won a 6-round no-decision bout against Hugh McCann (a.k.a. Kid Hubert), decking him several times. In 1908, Hubert had fought Marvin Hart to a 12-round draw. 10,000 spectators attended, confirming that Ketchel was a big gate draw.[585]

Unlike the black Johnson, whose defensive, cautious style often was criticized and alluded to as demonstrating a yellow streak, Jack O'Brien's defensiveness and cleverness were lauded as brilliant and intelligent.

Some thought Johnson might be trying to increase interest in the fight by appearing fat and less than prepared, or to make Jeffries become more willing to fight him if he did not perform too well against O'Brien, or to stimulate interest in the upcoming Ketchel contest, for if he struggled with O'Brien, then folks might think Ketchel could beat him. "Johnson may have his faults, but he has also some of the caginess peculiar to his race." Johnson would get paid either way, and still would be champion even with a poor performance, for it was a no-decision bout. Folks did not think Johnson was above engaging in such tactics, for they believed he had done so earlier in his career.[586]

On May 19, 1909 at Philadelphia's National Athletic Club, Jack Johnson and Philadelphia Jack O'Brien fought their 6-round no-decision bout.[587]

At 2 p.m., Johnson and manager George Little arrived at the National Athletic Club and insisted on being paid the $5,000 guarantee at that time, which was unusual. Club manager Harry Edwards later said, "I learned that

---

[585] *New York Sun*, May 19, 1909.
[586] *New York World, New York Journal, Philadelphia Inquirer, Press, Record*, May 19, 1909.
[587] The following account is an amalgamation of the *Philadelphia Public Ledger, Philadelphia Press, Philadelphia Inquirer, Philadelphia Record, Philadelphia Evening Bulletin*, and the *New York World* and *New York Journal*, May 20, 1909, all of which had reporters on scene.

Johnson had taken this step to foil an army of creditors." Jack wanted to be paid before his creditors could get at the money and attach the purse. Jack said, "When I get it in my jeans they can whistle their attachments."

The bout proved boxing's popularity. The cheapest ticket price was $2 for the furthest gallery seat, which normally sold for 50 cents at regular boxing shows. The $3 seats normally sold for 75 cents, and the $5 and $10 seats normally sold for $1.

Yet, scalpers still flourished, getting double and triple the face value of the tickets. They were selling $2 tickets for $4 and demanded $10 and $15 for the $5 tickets. An estimated 4,000 people paid from $2 up to $50 to watch the bout, filling every seat and choking the narrow aisles. The crowd was so large that an extra police detail was needed to preserve order.

The *New York World*'s William P. McLoughlin said Philadelphia was a strange place. "They still employ coon policemen." Regarding the venue: "The building is in the heart of a negro district. It looked as if every 'cullud pusson' in town turned out to get a peek at Johnson and to wait for the result of the fight. The street was like a mass of black soot studded with straw hats." Black residents had saved up their money for a chance to see their champion in action. "For, although he is champion of the world, he is principally their champion and the colored population was more than well represented." Still, the majority of paying fight fans were white, and they were there to see and root for the local man, O'Brien.

The estimated and reported gate receipts included $18,300, $20,564, $22,000, $23,000, and $25,000. The receipts either were the largest or the second largest on record for Philadelphia, with Terry McGovern vs. Battling Nelson having drawn about $23,000.

Some said O'Brien earned 30% of the gate receipts. However, others reported that O'Brien had struck a new deal, wherein he purchased the right to 75% of the gate receipts, but guaranteed to pay Johnson's purse out of his end. Reports of what O'Brien earned included $6,169.20, $6,600, $8,875, $11,000, or $12,000. The club made $9,294.80. Regardless of the exact amounts, it was very good money for a mere 6 rounds. "Big bouts pay."

There was a curious absence of betting. There were all sorts of rumors floating around. Hence, the general impression was that it was a good fight to keep away from wagering hard-earned money.

At 10:20 p.m., Johnson was first to appear and enter the ring. He received many moans and hisses from the whites, with the "boohs" drowning out the cheers and mild applause he received from the several hundred black persons present. The champion wore his usual smile of assured confidence, undisturbed by the cool reception.

One minute later, "Jawn" O'Brien hopped through the ropes. He was cheered to the echo, rousingly and tremendously for several minutes. Wearing a tasteful white silk kimono, he smiled and bowed in acknowledgement. "Oh dear, but it was just too cute." The reception O'Brien received was in marked contrast to that accorded to Johnson.

Johnson walked over and shook O'Brien's hand.

A little boy entered the ring, walked to O'Brien's corner and tied an American flag on Jawn's waist. O'Brien kissed the child, who then exited.

Boxing celebrities present were introduced to the cosmopolitan crowd. Stanley Ketchel entered the ring and received a tremendous welcome.

The overall pattern of the bout would be that Johnson occasionally would rush in firing some hard blows to the body and head, knocking O'Brien about the ring and even down, hurting him, even partially closing his left eye, but then O'Brien would move and clinch, Johnson would back off, stand still, play defense, and wait for a while, while O'Brien would work, firing the far greater number of blows, mostly jabs, which were relatively light and had no effect on the smiling champ, who mostly blocked and eluded until he decided to spurt with some offense again. Johnson often grinned and laughed while allowing O'Brien to work. In the clinches, he wrestled O'Brien around with ease, smiling. The crowd hooted Johnson's efforts, while they cheered everything that O'Brien did. The local man's admirers shouted, "Knock the gold out of his teeth." They cheered O'Brien's superior activity and work rate, even though his blows appeared to have little power or effect. Conversely, Johnson's body blows "sounded as though a drum was soaked with a potato."

O'Brien went down several times, in the 1st (twice), 4th (and suffered swelling to his eye – between rounds, his second made a small incision in the swelling on his left cheek bone to reduce the puffiness), and 5th rounds (a right to the swelling eye which sent a stream of blood flowing from his badly cut cheek). In the final round, O'Brien's mouth was bleeding as well.

Several times throughout the bout O'Brien slipped and went down, and occasionally it seemed that he went down voluntarily as a defensive tactic to keep from getting hit. "Strangest thing the way that fellow tumbles." Others believed Johnson wrestled him down, and hissed him as a result. After O'Brien slipped down in the final round, one reporter said, "Honest Jawn tumbled again. He was the original fall guy."

At the bout's conclusion, the crowd gave O'Brien a vociferous ovation, standing up and cheering thunderously. He was compelled to shake hands with dozens of his admirers. When Johnson left, the crowd hissed him.

The local *Inquirer*, *Record*, *World*, and *Journal* all said Johnson had won, but the local *Ledger*, *Press*, and *Bulletin* called it a draw.

The *Philadelphia Public Ledger*, *Press*, and *Evening Bulletin* agreed that O'Brien earned a draw by using his craftiness, forcing the fight and doing a majority of the leading, mostly with his left, though they admitted that his blows lacked strength. Both fighters often sought to land counters, but their guarding was so near perfection that the bout was even.

These local writers called Johnson a disappointment, saying he lost prestige. He had worked more like a "has-been" than a current champ. "Had O'Brien followed Johnson's example there would have been a poor bout. The Philadelphian jeopardized his chances in doing all the leading, but it helped him to get a draw." "The consensus of opinion was that

Johnson...was a lucky man to hold the championship." O'Brien was the fan favorite because he was the local man, white, smaller, and had shown heart.

However, the local *Philadelphia Inquirer* said that Johnson had bested O'Brien with his harder, more effective punches. The local man did most of the leading, and landed more often, but Johnson's punches hurt when they connected. O'Brien's jabs did not appear to affect the smiling Johnson at all, for he sometimes intentionally took them in order to land a hard one to the body or jaw. The *Inquirer* scored it 4 rounds Johnson, 2 even. Regardless, "Johnson's showing did not impress those about the ringside as being that of a real champion. On the form he showed last night he would not have been common amusement for Sullivan, Fitzsimmons or Jeffries."

The *Philadelphia Record* agreed that Johnson was too big and strong for O'Brien. The local man was game, active, and aggressive, gaining credit for his showing, for the champion "seemed for the greater part of the time disposed to loaf along and make the contest as easy as possible." Johnson intermittently rushed and pounded away, giving O'Brien something to remember, but then he seemed content to wait for the smaller man to come to him, which O'Brien eventually would do. Nevertheless, O'Brien "got some very hard bumps and was pretty badly hurt at times, and there is no doubt that the negro had the better of the contest." Ultimately, this writer knew that Johnson was the better fighter. "He is a tremendously big, powerful man, and much too good for all such fighters as O'Brien."

> But in giving O'Brien full credit for the fight he put up, it must not be forgotten that he did not hit Johnson one damaging blow, and that the lefts which he finally got home to the big man's face were little more than touches. It was a fast, clever boxer against a big, clever fighter, and while the little man did remarkably well, he never had any chance of winning.

The *New York World*'s on-scene reporter William P. McLoughlin said although O'Brien showed extreme cleverness, gamely did most of the leading, and landed some good stiff jabs, he was no match. "When Johnson did send over a sweep it counted, and Jack showed the effects of the big fellow's wallops." The *World* scored it 4 rounds Johnson, 1 O'Brien, 1 even.

The *New York Journal's* famous sportswriter Tad Dorgan said Johnson was "just a bit too big and strong for Jack O'Brien." However, he also was out of shape, as "round as a baby doll," and stalled throughout:

O'Brien did practically all of the leading, but there wasn't one good solid punch throughout. He stabbed and grabbed all the way. He was afraid of Johnson and when he did lead he followed it up with a hug, fearing a mix or a return from the black fellow, who was vicious with his uppercuts and quite generous.

Quite often O'Brien flopped to the floor. "He didn't seem able to hold his feet at all." The feeling was that either Johnson knocked him off balance or O'Brien went down intentionally in order to avoid punishment. Tad scored it 4 rounds Johnson, 2 O'Brien.

Another writer said Ketchel might have beaten Johnson had he been in the ring with him. Johnson had been leading an easy life, "and unless he gets down to business and works faithfully for future battles he will not remain champion very long. He was never so big and fat before."

Johnson said O'Brien's punches did no damage, whereas he had O'Brien going on several occasions, and Jawn grabbed and held on in order to survive. O'Brien would be knocked out in a longer bout.

> Instead of fighting the Quaker spent all his time hanging on and thus saved himself. He is clever, but cannot hit with any force. ... O'Brien hung on for dear life. Ketchel is not a hugger, and in the fight with him I will show what punching means.

Still, Johnson admitted O'Brien was clever, fast, and a good ring general.

Jack O'Brien said, "I beat Johnson, and the job wasn't hard." "Fighting as he did last night he would be a cinch for Ketchel. With Jeffries he would be a joke. Johnson is a better fighter than he showed, however." "He can hit, though, as that wallop that almost closed my left eye proves."

An unimpressed Stanley Ketchel hoped that no one else would get to Johnson before he beat him. "I will prove...that I am a far better man and more entitled to the heavyweight championship than Johnson. He looks to me like a man who will not stand up under much punishment, and once I connect good and hard on him there will be nothing to it."

Upon learning of the result, James J. Jeffries said, "In my opinion the fight was a defeat for Johnson. ... A real champion of the world – mind you I never have said that Johnson was such – who is able to knock down an opponent forty pounds lighter than himself should be able to stop him." Jeff said Johnson failed to finish O'Brien because he lacked class. "I thought little of Johnson's claims to the championship before this fight and I think less of them now." "Nothing Jack Johnson can do in or out of the ring makes the slightest difference to me. ... I do not think he wants to meet me in the ring."

For several days, newsmen kept debating whether Johnson won or whether O'Brien had secured a draw. Another theme was whether Johnson had faked and carried O'Brien intentionally. There was a mix of opinion.

The *Philadelphia Record* said if mere touches counted as points, possibly O'Brien could have obtained a draw, but it was not that type of contest. There would be no demand for a rematch.

> Philadelphia would hardly stand for another meeting, for the reason that the local fight followers now know that Johnson is entirely too big for O'Brien and that he in condition and so disposed, should beat O'Brien in short order. This is not to intimate that Johnson faked on Wednesday night, for there was no indication that such was the case, but he surely did not try his best in every round. Just why he loafed Johnson knows better than any one else.[588]

The *Philadelphia Public Ledger* criticized Johnson for fighting only in spurts, for if it had not been for O'Brien's activity and aggressive tactics, "the bout would likely have developed into a disgusting exhibition."[589]

The *New York World*'s writer believed Johnson had carried O'Brien, at least to some degree. Johnson's punches seemed to lack knockout force, but whenever he did throw in a hard one for the "sake of appearances" it sent O'Brien to the floor. O'Brien was great at the tap-tap-tap and run game, but did no damage. Whenever O'Brien landed, Johnson responded with a great mouthful of gold-filled teeth and laughed aloud, "He-yi, he-e-e!" But occasionally Johnson would "forget himself so far as to swat O'Brien on the jaw. Sometimes hot and sometimes cold. Twice he did it real hard and O'Brien went down each time." O'Brien's left eye was banged up so badly that it had a cornice of deep black, and by the 5th round his eye was closed completely. "Ruling on the idea of foot racing and shadow boxing, O'Brien had it on Johnson. But when it came to sending in a smash – tee hee - why that there Jack Johnsing he just banged O'Brien to the floor when he felt he had to do it to keep up appearances."

This writer believed Johnson could have knocked out O'Brien if he had wanted or chosen to do so. "Could Johnson knock O'Brien out? Yes-s-s-s-! With one right or left punch." The author argued that Johnson was not about to knock out the man who was paying him. O'Brien engineered the making of the bout, and therefore was helping Johnson earn good money. The inference was that the smaller man had gotten the larger one to work with him somewhat so they could make money, and Johnson obliged him for the payday in which there was no danger of him losing his title.

Stanley Ketchel said, "I knocked the life out of O'Brien. I wonder what I could do to that nigger?" The *World* writer responded, "So do I."[590]

Tad Dorgan wondered whether Johnson had played possum. Some were saying, "He could have knocked the Quaker out had he tried real hard, but

---

[588] *Philadelphia Record*, May 21, 1909.
[589] *Philadelphia Public Ledger*, May 21, 1909.
[590] *New York World*, May 21, 1909.

he took it easy." Ketchel saw the fight and said he wished that he had been inside the ropes instead of O'Brien. "Maybe that's what the champ wanted. ... Some one will tell Jeff now that Johnson is a terrible joke and he may jump at an offer." The implication was that Johnson could induce others to fight him, and generate excitement surrounding other bouts if he did not look too good. Still, Johnson "was the better fighter, we could all see that." The thrill was that O'Brien did better than expected.[591]

The *Philadelphia Record* suspected a frame-up because Johnson tried only in flashes, but then failed to follow-up advantages, and instead loafed along and played defense for long spells. As a result, some spectators, carried away by prejudice or sympathy for the smaller local white man, erroneously thought O'Brien deserved credit. "It will be hard to make those who witnessed the contest believe that Johnson could not have done better work had he been so inclined." "Johnson's cautious tactics seemed quite ridiculous under the circumstances, for O'Brien is not a knocker out." Also odd was the fact that "O'Brien displayed unnatural confidence in carrying the fight to an opponent so much his superior in physical power, as well as a reckless abandon foreign to his usual crafty style of fighting." There was "no good explanation for the manner in which he met O'Brien's attack. If he knows no better then he certainly is a very poor champion, and if he did not try then the bout must have been a 'frame-up.' If it was time will solve the riddle." Johnson received his money in advance, so he was set up well financially regardless of the result. Since it was a no-decision, he might not have cared what happened.[592]

O'Brien's past record also caused suspicion. Some thought Johnson might have posted a forfeit agreeing not to knock him out, or been offered a bonus if he didn't score a knockout. O'Brien had used such methods of doing business in the past.

The *Washington Times* noted that O'Brien was a "self-confessed faker" known to take part in fixed fights. Many folks thought it bad for the sport to allow a man with a shady history to be involved in a high-profile bout. After the revelations concerning O'Brien's attempt to fix the Burns bout, O'Brien "was branded in terms that would have made a right-thinking man want to commit suicide." He was supposed to be obliterated forever under a weight of shame. However, time had passed and O'Brien was forgiven. Yet, many wondered whether Johnson had carried him intentionally pursuant to some sort of side-deal. Johnson himself had a record that "has never appealed to sportsmen."

> [C]ompetent critics at the ringside are at a complete loss to understand the tactics of Johnson on any other basis than that he was not trying his best. That he had several rallies and showed flashes in which, with his boxing ability and superior weight and reach he made O'Brien look weak is admitted, but that he absolutely failed to use his

---

[591] *New York Journal*, May 21, 1909.
[592] *Philadelphia Record*, May 23, 1909.

natural advantages and fought most of the time as if tied to a post is also admitted. Although not well trained, it is claimed he did not attempt to exert himself as much as his remaining strength would have permitted, and was content to let the white man dance in and out and take desperate chances which would not have been predicted by any critic familiar with O'Brien's style.

The presumption hinted at by some of those who have considered the queer angles of the bout is that Johnson was under a heavy forfeit not to put out O'Brien, and was too much afraid of losing the money to get too gallus in the way of heavy punches. It will be remembered that O'Brien once had Tommy Ryan sewed up in just such a manner, and that there was almost exactly the same agreement when he first met Tommy Burns. ... Jack McGuigan, the referee and guiding spirit of the National Athletic Club, which pulled off the affair, accompanied by Jack O'Brien, went to Pittsburg to see Johnson to arrange for the match, which does not sound well to start with.

Others said Johnson simply was not that good, was overrated, lucky to be champion, and just an ordinary "negro prizefighter" whose head had been "inordinately swelled by a sudden rise to prominence."[593]

Most newspapers throughout the nation were quicker to use the "draw" result version than the several versions that said Johnson had won.

Philadelphia Press, May 22, 1909

---

[593] *Washington Times,* May 23, 1909.

Many questioned just how long Johnson would be able to reign as champion. William Rocap said, "Jack Johnson's future in the ring will not be all roses. American promoters are bound to get him beaten. He must meet Stanley Ketchel on October 12, or else confess that he is afraid of the Montana cowboy." The perpetual theme of underestimating Johnson appeared to be continuing, or to have been revitalized, though some thought that was what Johnson wanted.

O'Brien said Ketchel would vanquish Johnson and "win back the world's heavyweight championship for the white race." "Johnson isn't in Ketchel's class when it comes to hitting and gameness, two qualities that make real champions invincible. I think that if the negro ever gets into a slugging bee with Ketchel at close quarters he will be the first to go down, for he cannot stand up under the smashes that Ketchel will hand out." Many New Yorkers respected O'Brien's opinion, for he had fought both. This led to many wagering on Ketchel in the upcoming Johnson fight.[594]

A *Record* writer said Johnson's true boxing ability should not be judged by his showing against O'Brien. "O'Brien could not do anything with the big black fellow, and Johnson was so lazy and indifferent that he did nothing much with O'Brien."

> Granting that O'Brien landed the most blows, which would be hard to prove, as there was no means of recording them, the difference in the effectiveness of the blows would make the contest in favor of Johnson. The best friends of O'Brien would, no doubt, be willing to admit that he was knocked down and battered around, and that he received many hard blows on the head and body. The friends of O'Brien would be hard pressed to tell when the blows of O'Brien did any damage to the black champion.

Even conservative observers believed O'Brien had been lucky to last, for Johnson evidently was not trying his best, despite the fact that he was larger and just as clever and fast. With Johnson in top shape and trying his best, no one would back O'Brien with real money to stay more than 3 rounds.

This writer said that visual perspective, based on a spectator's angle, impacted the opinion as to whether or not the punches landed. Blows that appeared to land on Johnson in fact did not, for he slipped the punches with a movement of his head.

> In fact, it appeared as if Johnson could make O'Brien miss whenever he wanted to. ... Even in the poor physical condition in which Johnson appeared...he was able to evade O'Brien's attack when he felt like it, and he carried the fight to the Philadelphian when he felt so disposed. Just why he did not train and get in shape for the bout, and just why he did not extend himself more while he was in the ring are best known to himself; but that he could have done better was evident to those close to the ring.

---

[594] *Washington Herald*, May 22, 1909.

Some said that as a black fighter, Johnson was used to taking it easy on his opponents in order to obtain matches, and old habits die hard. "It is only a short time ago since Johnson was forced, or thought he was forced to agree to go lightly with his opponents in order to get matches. But that time has passed."[595]

Clara Kerr and Johnson in happier days past

On May 21, Johnson allegedly paid $3,000 for a special speed roadster, and $1,800 for a big diamond. However, after the purchase, the auto was seized at the request of Johnson's former black girlfriend/wife Clara S. Kerr of Philadelphia, who served Jack with an attachment on the auto to recover $405.95 on an alleged board bill for Johnson's blind brother Charles.

Johnson claimed the car was not his, but belonged to his manager George Little, who confirmed the statement. However, the police insisted the auto had to go to Camden for an authority there to decide the matter. They went before a district court judge, and Little produced a bill of sale showing that he had purchased the auto. The judge asked Johnson why he didn't simply go ahead and pay the bill. Jack defiantly replied, "Before I'll pay that bill I'll go to jail for ten years. It is a very unjust bill and I will never pay it. I'll fight it to the limit."[596]

On June 2, 1909 in New York, Stanley Ketchel scored a KO4 over Tony Caponi, who back in 1904 had fought two 6-round bouts with Tommy Burns, one a draw and another a decision loss.

Jim Jeffries, who had taken off at least 40 pounds, was looking very good. Jeff said, "I don't know when it will be, but I will lick that big smoke if it's the last thing I ever do in this life."[597]

On June 9, 1909 in Philadelphia, just three weeks after O'Brien-Johnson, Stanley Ketchel fought Jack O'Brien for the second time. From the start, the extremely aggressive Ketchel rushed and tore into him like a human tornado, viciously ripping, smashing, and hammering away with fearful sledgehammer punches that broke through O'Brien's defense, decking him twice in the 2nd round, and in the 3rd round, pounding on him so badly that the referee had to step in to save the helpless O'Brien from unnecessary punishment. Stanley Ketchel had shattered and knocked out in 3 rounds the shifty man whom Jack Johnson had not stopped in 6 rounds. Ketchel's stock further skyrocketed.

---

[595] *Philadelphia Record*, May 23, 1909.
[596] *New York World*, May 22, 1909; *Los Angeles Herald*, May 23, 1909.
[597] *Pittsburg Press*, June 7, 1909.

The fans loved watching Ketchel fight, which made him a marketable attraction. "He is the sort of fighter who stands the audience on their heads with excitement. He makes them yell. He makes them jump. He is tearing in viciously all the time." The victory further heightened the demand to see Ketchel fight Johnson. "He wanted to show the fight-loving public that he was a fit opponent for Champion Jack Johnson, and he certainly did."

Ketchel said, "I am more confident than ever that I can whip Johnson. The negro's poor showing against O'Brien convinced me of this."

O'Brien said, "Ketchel is a great fighter. The best in the world today. He can beat Johnson or anybody else. He surprised me with his speed, while nobody could have stood up under his terrible punches." "Ketchel will beat Johnson to a pulp. ... He is the hardest hitter I ever met."

The result made the Johnson-Ketchel fight even more intriguing. Stan was the reigning sensation. Many saw him as the fighter who could "bring back the heavy weight crown to the white man."[598]

The *Philadelphia Record* said, "Stanley Ketchel...now enjoys greater popularity than any other fighter who is before the public." "Everyone who saw Ketchel curl O'Brien up with body blows feels confident that a few such punches would take all the fight out of the big black." Ketchel even became the odds favorite over Johnson in Philadelphia.

However, many critics said Johnson did not show his best form against O'Brien, and "the colored man now admits that he did not try."[599]

Rumors were afloat that Johnson had received an additional $3,000 for not knocking out O'Brien. "Johnson showed very plainly that he could have stopped O'Brien in one round had he tried."

One writer said Johnson was no fool, and a very shrewd businessman. It would not make sense for him to take only $5,000 for a fight that likely would generate over $20,000. Hence, it stood to reason that he had an extra $3,000 guarantee coming to him if he did not stop O'Brien.

This rumor was circulating amongst blacks who lost money betting on Johnson to stop O'Brien. Hence, they were angry at the champion. "There is the most bitter prejudice against Johnson that has ever been expressed against any man who has held a boxing or fighting championship in the history of the ring, and, strange to say, the prejudice against Johnson seems to be as bitter among the men of his own race as it is among white men."

> One of the men who is telling around that Johnson got $3,000 for not knocking out O'Brien states that Johnson told the story himself and gave that as his reason for not extending himself when the men met recently in this city. Those who saw the Johnson-O'Brien contest could see that the black champion was not extending himself ... The fact that Johnson was in poor condition, hog fat and twenty pounds at least over weight caused some to think that it was this lack of condition which tied Johnson up, but there was abundant evidence

---

[598] *Boston Herald, Pittsburg Press,* June 10, 1909; *San Francisco Call,* June 13, 1909.
[599] *Philadelphia Record,* June 13, 1909; *Ogden Standard,* June 12, 1909.

that even as he was, he was not trying to go his best pace, for the work he did was nothing like that which he could and did do on other occasions in this city.[600]

The *Ogden Standard* explained and excused Johnson's recent performance against O'Brien as being not only the result of poor condition, but because the crowd threatened him.

> When properly trained Johnson can dispose of the Quaker in a few rounds. Another cause for his poor showing was that he was threatened with personal injury if he disposed of O'Brien by the knockout route. Several times during the contest, when the colored man became the aggressor or acted on the offensive, he was hooted, jeered, and threatening remarks were heard from several sides. This unsportsmanlike method of several rowdies caused Johnson to fear for his life.[601]

Years later, Johnson said he dropped O'Brien in the 1st, 4th, and 5th rounds. The crowd did not approve of the way he was hitting their esteemed fellow citizen, and threatened him with harm if he didn't change tactics. Philadelphia was where he once got hit on the head with a bottle after scoring a knockout over a local fighter. Hence, for the most part, he and O'Brien played a gentle game. Since there would be no points decision, the result meant nothing to him.[602]

---

[600] *Philadelphia Record*, June 13, 1909.
[601] *Ogden Standard*, June 12, 1909.
[602] *My Life and Battles* at 81-82.

CHAPTER 29

Big Talk

In June 1909, Jack Johnson said Jim Jeffries most likely was bluffing about meeting him, using the excitement of a potential match with him as a way of making easy money giving exhibitions with Sam Berger (who was Jeff's sparring partner and manager), but ultimately would decline to fight.

> I am ready to box every week in the year if I am given my price for my services. I bar no man who has any right to challenge. I am ready to box Jeffries, Ketchel, Kaufman, Hart, or any one else who wants to meet me. ... I regard a match with Jeffries as the surest way of proving that I am in truth the world's champion.[603]

When shown a dispatch claiming that Johnson would attend the 6-round Jeffries-Berger exhibition in Pittsburg on June 15, an upset Johnson said it was a false story which emanated from Jeff's press agent, who wanted to draw a crowd. "I will go there if Jeff will box me instead of Berger, and I will be willing to let the box office receipts go to charity."[604]

Upon his arrival in Pittsburg, a massive crowd of 20,000 greeted James J. Jeffries. He said,

> I see Mr. Johnson is talking a lot. ... I want to meet that black fellow more than I ever wanted to fight any living man. I have always been afraid of my own strength in a ring for fear I would kill a man, but I will have no such fear when I get into the ring with this fellow. For the first time in my life I will then hit a man with all the force that is in me. I want to see how far I can knock him. ...
>
> Do I hope Young Ketchel beats this black? Yes, I hope for far more than that. I hope when Ketchel meets Johnson he kills him. I repeat, I hope he kills him!

Upon hearing of Jeff's statement, Johnson challenged Jeffries to fight or hold his tongue. "I believe he is a four-flusher in the backbone. ... I will not stand for his abuse and slurs any longer. If he means to fight me, why don't he come out like a man and set the time and place?"[605]

New York writer Charles Meegan believed if Johnson followed his usual line of battle against Ketchel, standing still, playing defense and jabbing, there would be a new champion:

> His yellow streak will beat him if nothing else will in that sort of a fight. Two or three of Ketchel's terrific smashes would open the

---

[603] *Boston Globe*, June 13, 1909.
[604] *Boston Post, Pittsburg Press*, June 14, 1909.
[605] *Boston Herald, Boston Globe, Boston Post*, June 15, 1909.

floodgates of the big negro's courage tank and he would drown himself. ... I repeat, if Johnson fights Ketchel in the same manner he has fought most of his battles he's a 'gone coon' for sure.[606]

Johnson was set to appear in Cambridge, sparring at a benefit concert given by the colored Methodist church. It was said to be the first instance of a fighter participating in a church charity entertainment.

Every day, newsmen were printing the statements of Johnson and Jeffries. "Jeffries declares that Johnson is not a real champion and Johnson hurls back the defiant cry that Jeffries is only stalling and is afraid to meet him." Jeff's popularity had soared when he announced that he would meet Johnson to redeem the title. All the talk helped build up interest in the fight to an unprecedented level.[607]

On June 16, when he arrived in Philadelphia, Jeffries said of Johnson,

> So, he calls me a four-flusher. Well, I'll make him look worse than that when I get ready to talk business. ... His great mistake was in thinking that I had no intention of re-entering the ring, but I will fool him. You can say for me that I shall be my old self when I go into the ring and I shall take a savage delight in repaying him for the many things he has said since he beat Burns. I was correctly quoted in saying that I hoped Ketchel knocks his head off, and if Stanley does not do it I will turn the trick myself. I have surprised myself with my speed and condition and in Pittsburgh last night I was as fast as ever in my life. My wind, too, is good and my friends need not worry in the slightest when I fight Johnson – that is, if he will fight me. ... My personal opinion is that the colored man is four-flushing and will refuse to sign to meet me.[608]

The *Philadelphia Record* said everyone white had been "hoping and praying" that Jeff would "knock Jack Johnson not only out, but clean out of the ring with the first good punch he could land on the Texas negro." Jeff's supporters consistently said Johnson would be a plaything in his hands, for he had a yellow streak which would reveal itself when Jeffries hit him.[609]

On June 19, a Boston court issued a warrant for Johnson's arrest for failing to appear on charges of speeding, operating without a license, and failing to register his vehicle in Massachusetts.[610]

---

[606] *Ogden Standard*, June 17-19, 1909.
[607] *Boston Post, Boston Herald, Pittsburg Press*, June 16, 1909; *Philadelphia Record*, June 20, 1909.
[608] *Philadelphia Evening Bulletin*, June 16, 1909.
[609] *Philadelphia Record, Philadelphia Evening Bulletin, Boston Post*, June 17, 1909; *Philadelphia Record*, June 20, 1909; *Washington Herald*, June 22, 1909.
[610] *New York Sun*, June 20, 1909.

CHAPTER 30

Scouting the Champ

On June 20, 1909, the *Pittsburg Press* announced that big Italian Tony Ross would fight Jack Johnson 6 rounds at the local Duqesne Gardens for the National Athletic Club on June 30, ten days away. In April 1909, Ross had fought 10 furious competitive rounds with Al Kaufman, losing a decision, but proving his durability against a big, hard-punching heavyweight. Bill Delaney said the Italian was such a tough customer that he was willing to wager $10,000 that Johnson could not stop Ross in 6 rounds. He also said Kaufman, who recently had withdrawn the color line, would withdraw his challenge for the championship if Johnson stopped Ross.

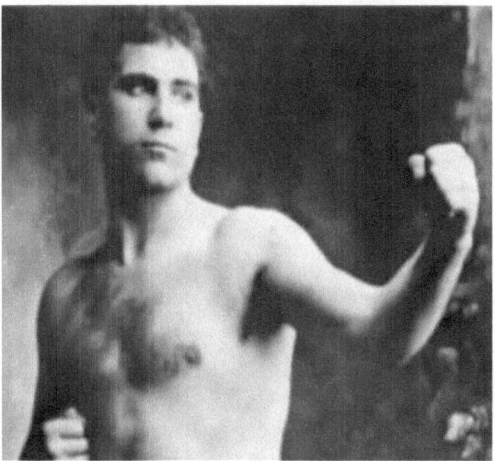

Tony Ross

Native Italian 24-year-old Tony Ross was born as Antonio Rossilano. Ross held knockout victories in 1908 over Mike Schreck (KO10) (who had beaten Hart) and George Gardner (KO7). In 1909, Ross was beating Marvin Hart, but lost via 13th round disqualification when after decking Hart he hit him while he was down. Hence, in essentially beating a big, tough, hard-hitting fighter in Hart, Ross showed that he was made of good stuff.[611]

Johnson said, "I know that I am going against a far more dangerous man than Jack O'Brien. ... Would Jeffries take any chances on a man like Ross? No, you can bet he wouldn't."[612]

Johnson declared that ever since he won the championship, his enemies had formed a conspiracy to ruin him in the public eye.[613]

There were rumors that there was a plot to get Johnson whipped as soon as possible. The Ross bout was the first step in a scheme by white managers. Ross was tough enough to test Johnson and make him fight hard, and that was what managers wanted to see, so they could scout him, note his strengths and weaknesses, and use the information in the future.

---

[611] *Pittsburg Press*, June 20, 21, 1909.
[612] *Pittsburg Press*, June 22, 1909.
[613] *Pittsburgh Post*, June 25, 1909.

I can state to you positively that Kaufman, Ketchel and several other fighters and managers will have representatives at the ringside taking careful note of everything the negro does. They will not come themselves, as they tried that in the O'Brien case, and Johnson held back purposely. He could afford to hold back with O'Brien and not risk the chance of being put out, but with a man who can hit like Ross, Johnson can take no chances. ... Ross can hit hard enough to put him away and there is a possibility of this, and then Johnson will have to show his best hand.[614]

Reporters said the bout could show how good Johnson was against a man near his own size. Ross weighed at least 190 pounds and stood 5'9". Of course, Johnson had fought and defeated several bigger men, like Fred Russell, Sam McVey, and Sandy Ferguson (who recently defeated Joe Jeannette), but many writers conveniently forgot or overlooked such facts.

The confident hard-punching Ross said that he knew the big smoke's weakness – his body - and would play for that spot for all he was worth.[615]

Whites were pulling for Ross, and "it seems to be the unanimous wish that he punch holes in every portion of the big negro's anatomy." Jimmy Dime, who was hosting the fight and training Ross, said, "Ross has got a punch that will knock anybody in the world cold, I care not who he is, and if Johnson is not in better shape than he was against O'Brien, watch out."[616]

When Jack Johnson failed to appear in Atlantic City on two charges of driving without a license, his two $25 bonds were forfeited. Jack had headed to Pennsylvania for the Ross fight.

The day before the fight, on the morning of June 29, when Johnson arrived at Union station in Pittsburg, blacks gave him a royal welcome. They, along with the Knights of Pythias Band, formed a parade which escorted Jack from the station through the streets to his hotel. Hundreds followed and clung to him, "proving that he is the idol of the negro race."[617]

That evening, "his fellow countrymen" (meaning blacks) gave Johnson a parade in the Hill district, which was a black neighborhood.[618]

---

[614] *Pittsburg Press*, June 26, 1909.
[615] *Pittsburg Dispatch, Pittsburgh Post, Pittsburg Press*, June 27, 1909.
[616] *Pittsburgh Post, Pittsburg Press*, June 28, 1909.
[617] *New York Journal, Pittsburg Press*, June 30, 1909.
[618] *Pittsburg Dispatch, Pittsburgh Post*, June 30, 1909. The Hill district later became a famous black cultural center in the area.

Some said Johnson was guaranteed at least $2,000 to fight Ross, though others were not sure what the economic terms were.[619]

On June 30, 1909 in Pittsburg, Jack Johnson fought Tony Ross in a 6-round no-decision contest. Despite the sweltering heat, a packed house of 4,000 was on hand.

When he entered the ring, the audience gave Johnson a cool reception. On the other hand, when Ross appeared, the spectators rose and cheered vociferously for more than a minute. The *Pittsburg Press* wrote, "Johnson did not get the greeting from the crowd last night that might have been accorded a champion. There were cheers, but faint ones. When Ross entered...he was received warmly and the uninitiated ones might have thought he was the champion approaching."

TONY ROSS

WHO MEETS JACK JOHNSON AT DUQUESNE GARDEN TONIGHT.

The bout nearly ended in the 1st round. In the last ten seconds of the round, Johnson dropped Ross with a series of hard rights and lefts to the head. The referee was in the process of counting him out, but the ringing of the bell saved him. Ross was lying on the floor out cold, with his face bloodied.

From the 2nd round on, Ross covered up at every opportunity, not wanting to open up and expose himself to dangerous blows. Johnson smiled continually from ear to ear. Throughout, he used his left jab, hitting the nose, lip, or eye on nearly every occasion.

In the 3rd round, Johnson again decked Ross for a five-count. Before the round was over, Tony was cut to ribbons.

Ross rarely laid a glove on Johnson, and none of his blows had any effect. Mostly he was cautious, but still took a beating over the course of the 6 rounds.

The *Pittsburg Post* said Ross was cautious after the 1st round, when he learned that Johnson could hurt and deck him. "Johnson's defensive tactics were the best ever displayed by a fighter here, and the few blows that Ross did uncork were nearly always neatly turned away by the negro."

Although for the most part Johnson toyed with Tony, nevertheless Ross "took one of the worst beatings that a fighter ever received in a local ring." "Ross was only a plaything in his hands and it is a question whether he could not have put him away any time during the six rounds." The *Pittsburg Press* agreed, saying, "That Johnson is a great fighter there is no doubt."

---

[619] *Pittsburg Dispatch, Pittsburg Post,* June 30, 1909; *Philadelphia Press,* July 1, 1909.

The local *Pittsburg Dispatch* had a completely different take, with more of the anti-Johnson stance that smacked of the typical white prejudice and bias which attempted to minimize his success and denigrate his performances. Its writer said, "Not one good, square, resounding lick was struck by either of the fighters, though a glance shot on the nose of Ross brought the claret." Opinion was that Johnson's championship reign would be short-lived and the first good challenger would put him out, for Johnson had "absolutely no good fine boxing qualities." The general cry was, "Oh, for one round of Jeffries!"

Many believed that this was another occasion of Johnson's "pulling" strategies to delude the public in view of coming matches. The feeling was that Johnson wanted to make the public think future opponents had a chance with him so as to make the bouts more lucrative. Hence he carried Ross when he could have stopped him.

The black-owned *Boston Guardian* noted that the crowd's show of color prejudice did not worry the black world's champion, who simply grinned.[620]

Speaking of press bias, the *New York Age* said it often was difficult for a white man to be fair on any question wherein members of both races were concerned, including most white sportswriters. However, Bat Masterson of the *New York Morning Telegraph* and Tad Dorgan of the *New York Journal* were the fairest of the white reporters. In a recent issue of the *Telegraph*, Masterson accused fellow white writers of clubbing Johnson over the head because he was colored. Johnson had made many a sacrifice to win the title, and now was in a position to dictate terms. He had grown tougher in negotiations. This upset many whites. The *Age* quoted Masterson, who said,

> But in all fairness, Jack Johnson has had more bricks thrown at him than he deserves. ... Johnson is the champion; newspaper denunciation and abuse are not going to take the title from him, that is certain. ... As he has truthfully said, he won the championship by conceding about everything there was in the game to his opponent. ... Johnson has the same right to demand concessions from a prospective opponent for the title that he was forced to concede to Tommy Burns.

Masterson believed most writers were not actually expressing public sentiment, but voicing their own personal views and prejudices. And if in fact they were expressing public sentiment, "Johnson could not well be blamed for refusing to fight at all. He certainly could not expect to get a square deal in this country." Masterson went on to say,

> Clubbing Johnson over the head, through the newspapers, because he is a Negro, will hardly work in this country. No doubt Johnson has left himself open to criticism on account of the way he has acted with reference to some of his contracts; but no one who has taken the

---

[620] *Pittsburgh Post, Pittsburg Press, Pittsburg Dispatch, Philadelphia Record, Philadelphia Press, Philadelphia Inquirer, Philadelphia Evening Bulletin, New York World, New York Journal, San Francisco Call, Salt Lake Herald, Arizona Republican,* all July 1, 1909; *Boston Guardian,* July 3, 1909.

trouble to go over his record since he has been champion can help but realize that a good deal of the roasting he has been receiving through the papers was chiefly due to the fact that his skin was black. Johnson's conduct since he became heavyweight champion compares favorably with that of some of his white predecessors. ...

It is all well enough to roast a man through the newspapers for the sake of filling up space, but quite another thing when it comes to putting up money to back what you say. ... Pounding Johnson chiefly because he happens to be a Negro will not get the money in this country.

The *Age* writer said Johnson's championship victory, combined with race prejudice, helped Jeffries earn more easy money in vaudeville exhibitions than ever before in his life. Jeffries was appealing to the white man's racial sensibilities, knowing that whites would herald him as a Moses-like figure. "The former champion is making money by working on the racial sympathies of the white brother, who is not wise enough to know it."

The *Age* wanted Johnson to ignore Jeffries, for Jack was giving Jeff free advertising, which led to Jeffries capitalizing even more on race prejudice, making him more money than Johnson, the current champion.[621]

On July 5, 1909 in Colma, California, "Michigan Assassin" Stanley Ketchel successfully defended his world middleweight championship with a 20-round decision victory over Billy Papke, the third time that Stan had beaten him. Ketchel later said he was weight drained in making the middleweight limit, and would be stronger as a heavyweight. Most agreed.[622]

In July 1909, Jim Jeffries claimed that he had not given his title to Marvin Hart, and therefore he still was champion. Jeff said, "Jack Johnson is not, and will not be, the champion until he whips me, and he never will do that." Still, Jeff confirmed that he would fight Johnson.

Johnson replied that Jeffries was bluffing about fighting him. "I think I am in condition now to clean up on Jeffries within fifteen rounds."[623]

On July 29 in Detroit, a motorcycle policeman arrested Johnson on a speeding charge. Jack was taken to the police station, where he was required to deposit $25 to guarantee his court appearance. Johnson produced a $1,000 bill, but they did not have change for such a large amount, so they took him to a local auto factory to obtain change.

On August 5, 1909, Jim Jeffries set sail for Carlsbad, Bohemia, near Germany (modern-day Czech Republic), to train there for six weeks.

Sam Fitzpatrick, Johnson's former manager, predicted that Jeffries would knock out Johnson. "There was never a champion so thoroughly hated as Johnson, and it is going to be a sweet menu for the fans when Jeffries hands this fellow a whaling, and he will do it sure." Johnson would be surprised by Jeff's tremendous strength and power, and his courage

---

[621] *New York Age*, July 1, 15, 1909.
[622] Ketchel was very aggressive, digging in short body shots and uppercuts, but also showed that he could box and move. In 1912, Papke would score a KO18 over Georges Carpentier.
[623] *Philadelphia Evening Bulletin*, July 13-15, 1909.

would diminish once he was hit. "I always told Johnson to be modest and keep away from Jeffries; but he knew it all and sneered at Jeffries."[624]

On August 16, despite previously having booked rooms at a hotel in Salt Lake City, Utah, when he arrived, the hotels there drew the color line on the champ. He could not secure lodging for himself and his wife.[625]

Johnson arrived in the San Francisco area to start training for his October fight with Ketchel.

Johnson did not believe Jeffries really wanted to fight him, and thought that ultimately he would not do so. "He will come back to this country with bands playing and he'll work the theatrical game for all it is worth. He may sign articles and appoint a date for the fight, but mark my words, when the time draws near there will be an accident or a doctor's certificate, setting forth that Jeffries' health will not allow him to fight." "I am going to start training for Ketchel, and if they dig up another opponent for me in the meantime I will take him on also. I am in this game to get the money."

Were they to fight, Johnson said he would not fight Jeffries in the South. "I will not fight at Oklahoma, or south of the Mason and Dixon line, or at any outside place. I am not crazy. I want to fight in or near a big city, where I will have all the protection the law affords and every chance to show that I am a better man than Jeffries."[626]

Sam Berger said Jim Jeffries was not only a "fighter in a million," but a "man among men." He was special, and could overcome years of inactivity and indulgence. "I feel sure that when Johnson and Jeffries meet, the white race will be in no danger of losing the heavyweight championship of the world."[627]

---

[624] *Philadelphia Evening Bulletin*, July 27, 28, 30, 1909, August 5, 6, 1909.
[625] *Philadelphia Evening Bulletin*, August 13, 17, 1909.
[626] *San Francisco Call*, August 22-24, 1909; *San Francisco Call, San Francisco Chronicle, San Francisco Examiner*, September 1, 1909; *San Francisco Bulletin*, September 8, 1909.
[627] *San Francisco Evening Post, San Francisco Chronicle*, September 1, 1909.

CHAPTER 31

Better Than We Thought

In mid-July 1909, Jack Johnson had accepted promoter Jim Coffroth's offer of $10,000 guaranteed to fight Al Kaufman 20 rounds in late August in San Francisco. However, Bill Delaney said Kaufman would take his time and not be rushed into a fight. He did not think Al would be ready.[628]

However, on August 24, Jim Coffroth made the Johnson-Kaufman fight. It was set to be held sixteen days later, on the afternoon of September 9 at the Mission street arena. The catch was that they would box only 10 rounds in a no-decision bout, something the Kaufman side wanted.[629]

Up to that point, 216-pound 23-year-old Al Kaufman's known record was 19-1 with 16 KOs. Many of his bouts were fights to the finish, and therefore he obtained more quality experience in one lengthy bout than most fighters do today in several years of boxing. His only loss came in his fifth pro bout - LKOby17 to Jack O'Brien, when he was just a novice and never before had fought more than 3 rounds. Since then, Kaufman had been 15-0 with 12 KOs. His very impressive resume was amongst the best of all heavyweight contenders. He had victories over Jack Sullivan, Sam Berger, George Gardner, Mike Schreck (who twice stopped Hart), Jim Flynn, Jim Barry, and Tony Ross, amongst others.[630] Based on results, Kaufman was more deserving of a title shot than any other white contender. He was known for his toughness, condition, and heavy punch.

Al Kaufman

The *San Francisco Call* said the fact that Johnson was black detracted somewhat from his reception, although he still was receiving the notoriety and recognition that came with being champion.[631]

---

[628] *Philadelphia Evening Bulletin*, July 13-15, 1909.
[629] *San Francisco Call*, August 25, 26, 28, 1909; *Philadelphia Evening Bulletin*, August 27, 1909.
[630] Al Kaufman victories included: 1906 KO14 Dave Barry, KO1 Jack Sullivan, KO10 Sam Berger, and KO14 George Gardner; 1907 KO7 Mike Schreck, KO3 Dave Barry, and W25 Jack Sullivan; 1908 W6 Joe Grim, KO9 Jim Flynn, KO14 Terry Mustain, and KO39 Jim Barry; and 1909 WND10 Tony Ross.
[631] *San Francisco Call*, August 29-31, 1909.

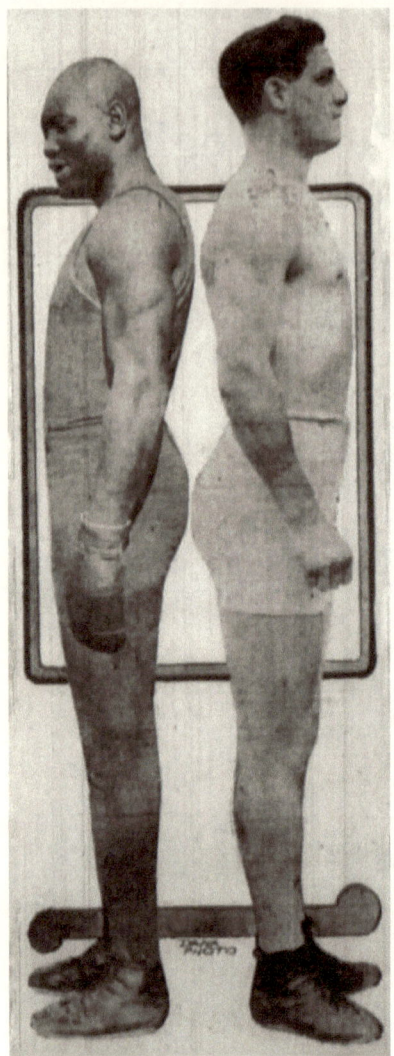

Johnson failed to appear in court for his speeding trial in Oakland, so his $25 bail was forfeited. His manager George Little said Jack was too busy getting into shape to allow ordinary Police Court business to interest him.

On September 1, after his training concluded, Johnson weighed 213 pounds. However, when asked his weight, Jack humorously told spectators, "230 pounds."

Al Kaufman said of Johnson, "Oh, he's a great fighter, all right. He can be hit, though, the same as anyone else. And if I can land on him just once I think I'll bring him down."

Johnson said he could go 10 rounds with Kaufman even if blindfolded.

Jeffries-Johnson remained the biggest fight on sportswriters' minds. "For the past year these big bruisers have taken up more space in the newspapers than anybody else in the country."[632]

Al Kaufman had been a blacksmith. Swinging a 20-pound sledge for three years had made his muscles as strong as steel. W. W. Naughton said Kaufman was extremely strong and powerful, and his winning record possibly as good as any heavyweight ever. He hit hard enough to deck a bull.[633]

Some speculated that Johnson would not try to stop Kaufman, and might even carry him so they could fight again and make more money.

The *San Francisco Evening Post* expected the "lazy negro champion" to give a tame exhibition of cleverness. Although many doubted Johnson's courage, his cleverness was undisputed. "The big negro knows every trick and artifice of the game."

Referee Eddie Smith said, "The best man will win, regardless of color or prejudice." Although it was a no decision bout, he would offer his opinion of the winner, regardless.[634]

---

[632] *San Francisco Call*, *San Francisco Evening Post*, *San Francisco Chronicle*, *San Francisco Examiner*, *Philadelphia Evening Bulletin*, September 2, 1909.
[633] *San Francisco Chronicle*, *San Francisco Examiner*, September 5, 7, 1909.
[634] *San Francisco Call*, *San Francisco Evening Post*, September 8, 1909.

The *Call* said if Kaufman landed any one of his wicked body blows, "Johnson will indeed be a fortunate man to still retain the heavyweight crown." Kaufman appeared to be in better shape than the champion. "Johnson, on the other hand, spent more of his time scorching in that big red automobile of his than performing in the gymnasium."

Local fans did not like Johnson or his style. However, he was a gate draw because he was the champion. "It is only Johnson's fame as heavyweight champion that has made him the great card he is today."[635]

On September 9, 1909 at the Mission-street arena in Colma, California, the Jack Johnson vs. Al Kaufman 10-round no-decision bout took place. The main event was set to start at around 3 p.m. A crowd of between 6,000 and 8,000 taxed the capacity of Coffroth's fight pavilion.[636]

Upon his entrance, Kaufman was given a great reception. "There was a genuine ovation for the white man." He smiled and nodded to his friends.

In contrast with Kaufman's reception, as Johnson approached and entered the ring, the crowd hooted, hissed, groaned, and booed him. The *Chronicle* said the fans were markedly unfair to Johnson. His lack of popularity was well known, "but black or white, he was entitled to fair consideration. ... As a fighter, Johnson has been uniformly fair in his actions in the ring. There are few men quicker to obey the referee or none who will fight a more fair battle than this same Johnson." Regardless of the cold reception, Johnson simply smiled, walked over to Kaufman, and shook hands.

Billy Jordan announced Kaufman as "the Native Son of the Golden West." The crowd again cheered him to the echo. Then Jordan said, "The heavyweight champion of the world, Jack Johnson," to more hoots, hisses, and boos.

They stripped and posed for photographs. Kaufman was taller and seemed to have the longer reach. Johnson wore blue fighting breeches. Kaufman wore white. Each man wore a red, white, and blue Stars and Stripes American flag belt.

---

[635] *San Francisco Call, San Francisco Chronicle*, September 9, 1909.
[636] The following account is an amalgamation of the local day-of and next-day reports from the *San Francisco Evening Post*, September 9, 10, 1909; *San Francisco Chronicle, San Francisco Examiner, San Francisco Call*, and *San Francisco Bulletin*, September 10, 1909.

The ring was cleared, and at 3:04 p.m., Uncle Billy Jordan made his familiar cry of "Let 'er go!" and the bell rang to start the fight.

Throughout the bout, the ever-smiling Johnson beat a tattoo on Kaufman's head and body, landing every punch in the book - jabs, hooks, uppercuts, and body blows, without receiving returns. Johnson clearly was superior and much too fast for Kaufman, eluding or blocking all of his attempts. "It was an illustration of the mastery of the colored man." It was one-sided, and the crowd mostly was silent, though it cheered and applauded even when Kaufman landed lightly. Johnson simply flashed his golden smile and laughed at Al's efforts. He even cracked jokes and carried on a rapid-fire repartee with the spectators, who tried to encourage Kaufman. Johnson waved his hands at various friends in the audience, or smiled at his wife, who was seated in a ringside box. She never failed to smile back. Throughout, Johnson administered a beating, occasionally rocking Kaufrman's head back and forth, lifting it high in the air with uppercuts, and backing him up to the ropes. He even showed his strength on the inside, which was supposed to be Kaufman's forte.

By the middle of the 1st round, Johnson's famous right uppercut drew blood from Kaufman's nose and lip. In the 3rd round, Johnson bashed Kaufman all over. One of his right uppercuts badly cut Kaufman's lip and broke his teeth, causing blood to spurt and spray from his mouth in profuse torrents. The *Call* said, "It was apparent that Johnson was clearly Kaufman's master and could finish him at such times as he was ready to cut loose." In the 4th round, Johnson's fierce swings carried Kaufman to the ropes, and Al bent back so far across the top rope that it looked as though he would topple over onto the ringsiders. Johnson then stood, laughed, and backed off, giving the impression that he was carrying him, despite the continued pounding. The *Chronicle* said Johnson was playing with him. The *Call* said Johnson deliberately slowed up.

There was a veritable stream of blood running down Kaufman's face, and there even were smears of his blood on Johnson's shoulders and back as the result of their coming together in clinches.

Johnson alternately would play defense, standing still and picking off blows, smiling and laughing, and then he would attack ferociously.

Throughout, the crowd hooted, hissed, and taunted the grinning Johnson. Jack would talk with all-comers. One fan in the bleachers yelled, "You ain't game! You've got an awful yellow streak, Jack." Johnson retorted, "Mebbe, but they can't find it." Several laughed at the comeback. Jack added, "Nobody has found it yet." Another yelled, "You're a big dub." Johnson chuckled and cleverly responded with, "That may be so, but I'll help spend some of yoah money tonight." To another he said, "I got your $3." Yet another said, "Wait till you meet Jeffries." Jack replied, "Then I'll get some money." Jack was "as playful as a black kitten."

At one point in the 5th round, after Al broke from a clinch and stepped back, Johnson deliberately remained standing with his back to the corner, with his hands stretched down at his sides, and laughingly dared Kaufman to keep up the attack, in taunting fashion saying, "Come on Al! Walk right into them! Youah tough big man." Al accepted the invitation and went after him, swinging several blows, but Johnson parried, blocked with his arms and elbows, grinned, and then nailed Al with an uppercut. The fans expressed their disapproval. "Why don't you fight, you big zobs?" "Oh, if Jeffries was only in that ring we'd see a fight." "Where do you think you are at; in some picnic grounds?" "We paid to see a fight, not a minstrel show." Johnson nailed Kaufman with four snappy right uppercuts, each one lifting Kaufman's head a foot in the air. "Johnson was quickness and nimbleness personified."

In the 6th round, a spectator yelled, "Look out, here comes Jeff!" Jack laughed, but suddenly attacked and landed a fusillade of blows, beating Kaufman across the ring to the ropes. Johnson followed with some hard stomach blows that sent Kaufman halfway through the ropes and almost into the press stand. Jack liked to vary defensive tactics with "spiteful spurts of fighting in which he cuffed Kaufman until the blood fell from Al's face like rain." Jack waved his hand at someone in the audience. In a clinch, he leaned his chin on Kaufman's shoulder and chuckled and laughed.

In the 7th round, Johnson blocked and grinned, but then suddenly attacked again; hooking and uppercutting Kaufman across the ring, rocking his head. "It was apparent to all that Johnson was holding himself in reserve and only opened up when the fancy took him."

The 8th through 10th rounds were similar in pattern. Johnson scored three to one. Kaufman landed a few hard rights to the body, but they had no effect. During the one-minute rests between rounds, Johnson kept up an incessant verbal exchange with the crowd. There was a scattered cheer for Kaufman at the end, because he had lasted the distance, a betting point.

All of the local reporters unanimously agreed that Johnson had won every round with ease. Kaufman was no match, and left the arena with a bloody mouth and nose. Johnson was unmarked.

What observers were not sure about was whether Johnson had carried Kaufman, or just was not able to knock him out, either because Kaufman was too tough to be stopped in a mere 10 rounds, or because Johnson didn't hit that hard, or wasn't a fast finisher owing to his cautious methodical style. Some thought Johnson was in a good mood and just chose to play around in a no-decision bout for which he would be paid regardless of result, particularly given that he was winning handily, so there was no need to try to knock out Kaufman. Others thought Johnson either wanted to leave open the possibility of a rematch, to stimulate interest in other upcoming matches, or encourage others to fight him.

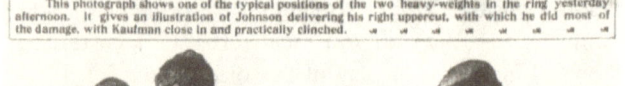

This photograph shows one of the typical positions of the two heavy-weights in the ring yesterday afternoon. It gives an illustration of Johnson delivering his right uppercut, with which he did most of the damage, with Kaufman close in and practically clinched.

The *San Francisco Evening Post* said the way the clever Johnson loafed and joked with the newspaper men made it seem more like a minstrel show than a fight, which disgusted the fans. "The big black man danced before Kaufman's glazed eyes like some giant shadow, which Al tried as vainly to capture as did the little boy who chased the rainbow." "Johnson simply toyed and played with Kaufman, and there was a general suspicion around the ringside that the giant negro was not trying very hard to put Kaufman away." "On more than one occasion Kaufman's eye took on the glassy stare of a man in deep distress, but on these occasions Johnson would step back and allow Al time for recuperation." "The big negro exchanged pleasantries with the newspaper men and spectators, and was as unconcerned about coming to grief at the hands of Kaufman as though Kaufman were in the next county." Regardless, the feeling was that Johnson was a big clever defensive fighter "without much heart and with no very damaging punch." This writer said nearly everyone at ringside agreed that Johnson would be easy pickings for Jeffries.

The *San Francisco Chronicle* said the champion handled Kaufman with such ease, deliberately playing with him, such that there was a feeling that he could have sent him down and out at any time. "The fight showed that Johnson is wonderfully clever, that he has the strength and the cunning of an ape." "In any kind of a contest the alert black man animal is his master." Kaufman was "spilling great gushes of blood from his mouth and the white of his eyes showed ghastly and staring." The contemptuous Johnson's "wicked grin" never left, which upset Al's legion of white followers. Kaufman could not strike under or above Johnson's "squirming, twisting baboon arms." Al was puzzled. "It was ape strength and ape cunning against blind stolid courage and endurance." "His gorilla arms coiled and recoiled and struck at the mealy white body before him with the speed of a rattlesnake striking." Kaufman could scarcely place a glove on the "alert man-animal before him. The black landed on him at will, making the white man look like a big, befuddled thing, a lumbering automaton. Race prejudice, which is strong in the crowds that see fights, was much in evidence."

The *San Francisco Examiner* said the fight "proved that the negro is a marvel at defensive work" and a lot stronger than folks realized.

The *San Francisco Call* gave Kaufman some credit for lasting the distance, "but none of us know whether or not the same Jack willed it this way."

> The black man gave an exhibition of boxing and clean hitting that fairly opened the eyes of every spectator. No cat ever played more skillfully or more successfully with a tiny mouse than did he with Kaufman. He never lost his famous golden smile. ... Apparently he never breathed heavily.

Respect for Johnson skyrocketed. "The fight goes to show that Jeffries is the only man who has any license to make a legitimate showing against Johnson." The only other possible exception was Sam Langford, but he was black, and the white population did not want to see the title go from one black man to another. "The San Francisco fans should raise the Jeffries cry louder than ever now, that is if they want to see a man in the ring who is capable of making the black champion extend himself."

The *San Francisco Bulletin* said, "It was child's play for the smoke and Kaufman can thank his lucky stars that Johnson was in a good humor and fought under wraps." Although Kaufman was bleeding badly from the terrific pummeling, "the big dinge did not open up and show his true speed more than twice or thrice in the contest." Most of the time he stood still, daring Kaufman to come hit him, and laughing derisively at the latter's attempts to land a blow. Despite landing lightning-like punches from every angle, "Even then he did not seem to be half trying, and the writer firmly believes that he could have knocked Kaufman out if he had cared to."

Johnson was criticized for smiling and laughing at his foe. "This grinning and grimacing, by the way, will gain Johnson little save public opprobrium and is certainly an undignified exhibition for a champion. The sooner he cuts it out the better it will be for himself and the game." He was not supposed to taunt the man who for years had drawn the color-line.

Regardless, Johnson's impressive fighting abilities were recognized:

To be sure, the white race still has another lion up its sleeve and is by no means ready to admit that the tawny one from Texas can whip him. But after yesterday's exhibition the consensus of opinion is that Jeffries, if he ever does decide to fight, will have one of the toughest arguments of his career before he puts Jack Johnson to the mat. ... Johnson demonstrated, beyond all question of doubt, that he is the greatest heavyweight exponent of the fisticuffs now before the public, and that it will take a wonderful fighter to beat him down.

The *Bulletin* argued that just because Johnson beat Kaufman did not mean that Al was not a very good fighter. "Any man who thinks he has a chance with Al because of his showing against Johnson would do well to encase himself in armor-plate before entering the ring. Otherwise he may be carried out on a stretcher a few minutes later."

Referee Eddie Smith told the newsmen that Johnson had outboxed and punished Kaufman in every round, and only Kaufman's wonderful assimilating powers had saved him from a knockout.

Johnson complimented Kaufman, saying,

> Kaufman is a big, strong fellow and can take a world of punishment. I hit him many hard blows, but he took them and showed that he is game. Why, he can whip nearly all those big fellows. Why, he can beat Tommy Burns any time. Kaufman is a tough fellow and it will take a great fighter to beat him. He is game and can hit hard. They said I would back up. Well, did any one see me back up? I forced the fighting throughout. If the fight was longer I think I could have finished him.[637]

Kaufman said, "Johnson is so clever, a man can not make an impression against him in a battle of short duration. He covers up so well and is so fast that a man can not begin to slow him down in 10 rounds."

Promoter Tom McCarey, who had scheduled a Johnson vs. Jim Barry bout for September 20 in Los Angeles, called it off. He said Barry's health would not permit him to appear on that date.

The news that the Jim Barry fight was off came within hours of Johnson's decisive victory over Kaufman. Many noted the interesting timing of the cancellation, which led sports to believe the real truth was that McCarey had decided Barry would be led to slaughter should he fight Johnson, so he canceled the fight. Some reported that before the Kaufman fight, McCarey had told friends that if after seeing Johnson in action, he saw that Barry would have little chance, he would cancel the contest.

The *Bulletin* comically said Barry and McCarey had developed a case of "tonsillitis Africanus."

> It is strange how general is this 'tonsillitis Africanus' in the fistic world. Johnson, Langford, Young Peter Jackson and a few other chocolate and coal-colored bruisers seem to be human generators of

---

[637] *San Francisco Chronicle*, September 11, 1909.

throat trouble. Let one of them get a match with a white slugger and immediately the latter feels a tickling in his throat. ... Sometimes this condition is even transmitted to the promoter.

McCarey considered Johnson "to be one of the greatest - if not the greatest – heavyweights that ever donned a glove." He further said, "Johnson is the ideal of a defensive boxer and I have yet to see him opposed to a man whom he could not beat under double wraps."

McCarey also said that if he could obtain Johnson's word of honor that he would extend himself against Ketchel, he would wager that Jack would knock him out within 5 rounds. However, Johnson rarely extended himself, and usually won however he saw fit.

In an interview from New York, Stanley Ketchel said, "There is no doubt that I will be the champion pugilist in a short time and that Jeffries will be spared the ignominy which he dreads so much in meeting a negro." Ketchel also said,

> Johnson is a good-natured sort of a big coon. I always liked him pretty well. You can't blame him for the things he has done. For years he was the under dog, and had to take the worst of everything. He fought his way up in spite of everybody, and now he's champion it would be strange if he didn't take his revenge. Of course, he does a lot of crazy things, but what should you expect? He's just a great big uneducated coon come into a lot of money and a sort of popularity, and he's lost his head a little.[638]

Neither O'Brien, nor Ross, nor Kaufman had impressed newspaper reporters or the public sufficiently to garner any momentum for lengthier title challenges.

A few days after the fight, W. W. Naughton said folks were "now freely admitting that the champion is the marvel of the age in the boxing line even if he does fool away much valuable time when he is in action." The erratic Johnson fought how he liked. "He slows or quickens as the whim seizes him and he defends his tactics by saying that he usually brings the decision away with him."

Johnson explained his cautious style, arguing,

> I came out of the Kaufman go without a scratch or a bruise and I left the other man pretty badly punched up, didn't I? What more do they expect? I don't advertise to kill a man every time I enter the ring. I have lots of fights to look forward to and I have to keep my hands in good shape and protect the title I have gained in the face of greater difficulties than any man deserving of the championship ever encountered. Those who blamed me for using my cleverness to my own advantage would be the first to howl with joy if I blundered and was knocked over by some lumbering opponent. I win my fights and I intend to win them my own way. There is no complaint when a

---

[638] *San Francisco Bulletin*, September 11, 1909.

favorite in a horserace comes home eased up half a length ahead of the next best, is there? Those who handle him know there will be other races on other days and the nag isn't asked to burst a blood vessel when there is no occasion for it. And on top of all this I'll tell you something. Knocking Kaufman out isn't as easy as it may look.

Naughton agreed that despite his faults of omission, "Johnson is now regarded by the sporting public as a real champion. It is felt that no one in the lists at present can conquer him, and our thoughts turn to Jeffries more than ever. The alfalfa baron is our only dependence."

Jim Jeffries' father did not want him to fight a black man. The Reverend Alexis Jeffries said, "If my son should ever fight Jack Johnson, I would be tempted to disown him."[639]

The black-owned *New York Age* said Johnson was a wise ring general who could whip any man in the ring, including Jeffries. "One thing about him is that he has made up his mind to fight according to his own ideas and not in the manner ofttimes desired by the white writers and the public." Johnson had Kaufman at his mercy, and took no chances of injuring his hands or exposing himself and getting caught with something big. It was not his job to win by knockout, but not to lose the title, for if he did lose his crown, whites never would give him the chance to win it back.[640]

---

[639] *San Francisco Examiner*, September 12, 1909.
[640] *New York Age*, September 16, 1909.

CHAPTER 32

Fighting For the Films

Jack Johnson's next scheduled championship bout was set to be held in mid-October 1909 against world middleweight champion Stanley Ketchel.

Known as the Michigan Assassin, the 23-year-old Ketchel was from Grand Rapids, Michigan. Of Polish descent, his birth name was Stanislaus Kiecal. A pro since 1903, he had nearly 50 career victories to his credit.[641]

Ketchel had scheduled an interim September 17 bout in New York against Sam Langford. However, New York Governor Charles Hughes (who defeated newspaper magnate William Randolph Hearst in the 1906 election) wanted the mixed-race bout canceled. Governor Hughes wired the police commissioner, district attorney, and sheriff, informing them that it was their duty to see to it that the law was upheld, whatever that meant. Acting on the district attorney's advice, the police commissioner declared that the Ketchel-Langford bout could not be held. In 1910, Governor Hughes would become a U.S. Supreme Court justice.[642]

Ketchel was upset. "I wanted to give [Langford] a good beating before I whipped Johnson, so that with Johnson, I would have cleaned up the entire circuit of negro fighters."

From Carlsbad, Jim Jeffries said, "I am more confident than ever that I will be able to beat the big tar baby."

Sam Berger said Jeffries would fight "the big tallow smoke" Johnson "more to uphold the precedence of the Caucasian, and wipe out some personal insults that the negro has heaped upon him, than for the money that will be in the fight." He never wanted to beat someone so badly in his life. Berger also said, "To compare Jeffries with Johnson on a mental, moral or physical basis is all rot. Jeff is his superior every way."[643]

Hugh McIntosh offered $50,000 for a Johnson-Jeffries match, saying,

> Johnson is willing and ready; he has been all along; he has never changed. Oh, yes, I think he is looking after himself all right; you see he cannot afford to lose his title. ... And it will be a bitter contest. That between Burns and Johnson was bitter enough, but this will be more so. There is the color prejudice, and – and Johnson's talk. ...
>
> Americans will not hear of [Jeffries] being defeated. Listen to the list of things they call Johnson: Nervy Nubian, Big Chocolate, Giant

---

[641] Ketchel's contests included: 1907 D20, KO32, and W20 Joe Thomas; 1908 KO1 Mike "Twin" Sullivan, KO20 Jack "Twin" Sullivan, W10 Billy Papke, KO3 Hugo Kelly, KO2 Joe Thomas, LKOby12 and KO11 Billy Papke; 1909 WND10 Jack O'Brien, WND6 Kid Hubert, KO4 Tony Caponi, KO3 Jack O'Brien, and W20 Billy Papke.
[642] *San Francisco Evening Post*, September 14, 16, 1909; *San Francisco Examiner*, September 14, 16, 17, 1909.
[643] *San Francisco Evening Post*, September 14-17, 1909.

Ethiopian, Scientific Senegambian, Ebony-Hued, Husky, Heaved, Lil Artha, Tantalizing Texan, Galveston Cyclone, Big Smoke, and Cloudy Clouter.[644]

On September 23, Ketchel, known as the "Michigan lion," the "assassin," and the "sensation of the prize ring," arrived in San Francisco. Stan's talkative manager Willis Britt said Ketchel would defeat "that big shine," for "Ketchel…is Johnson's master."

The *San Francisco Bulletin* said, "If any one can develop the 'yellow streak' which Johnson is said to possess Ketchel is the man to do it. … If there is one thing in the world the sporting world wants him to do that one thing is to beat Johnson." The *Bulletin* called Johnson the "Galveston Gorilla."[645]

Willis Britt was great at promoting the fight, making statements on a daily basis. With his usual big talk, he said,

> Why, if Ketchel lands on that big smoke they'll have to get a smoke consumer to dig up Johnson's remains from the debris. The Lion is going to roar loud in this fight, and I am certainly confident that he will beat Johnson and beat him so thoroughly that Jack will never be heard of again.

The *Evening Post* said Ketchel was vastly more courageous than Johnson, with a daring, slashing style, loving the bombardment of fists:

> As well compare a wharf rat to a Bengal tiger in courage. Yet, what Johnson lacks in courage, he makes up in cunning. Like some ghoulish coyote, Johnson will hang to the flank of a harassed foe until he drops from sheer weariness and then will beat him.

> There is nothing, barring finesse and finish, in the boxing of Johnson that can appeal to any one. There is more of the weasel than the lion in the negro.

However, "even Johnson's worst enemies must admit that the Galveston tar baby is a very good big man."

> Lacking heart, Johnson has all the other qualifications of a good fighter. He is without cavil or doubt the most scientific heavyweight now before the public. Johnson is a master of defense. The big dinge does not carry a leaden blow, but he is a ripping puncher, and when he finishes with his opponents he usually has them looking as though they had just completed a six-weeks' course with a sausage grinder.[646]

The *San Francisco Bulletin* said the "Galveston Shine" inherited ancestral traits which made it hard to fight him and even harder to make him fight. In ancient times, there were battles for supremacy between white nations and the darker ones, but the whites eventually won out. "Nevertheless, they

---

[644] *San Francisco Evening Post*, September 18, 1909.
[645] *San Francisco Bulletin*, September 20, 1909; *San Francisco Evening Post*, September 22, 24, 1909; *San Francisco Examiner*, September 21, 24, 1909.
[646] *San Francisco Evening Post*, September 25, 1909.

gave us a strenuous tussle for a couple of thousand years, and did not give up until a few adventurous spirits, of the Ketchel and Jeffries order, rolled them over a barrel and packed them off to Africa, where they have resided in more or less quietude ever since." The "dinge" Johnson was said to be an ancestor of the ancient black warriors who gave whites a tough time of it.

> [He] has shown the ancestral trait of avoiding punishment. On the other hand, however, he has seemed somewhat loathe to administer it, and up to the present time it is safe to say that Jack has never extended himself, being content to stall along under wraps and take a decision where he might have had a knockout just as well. ...
>
> Critics say he could have knocked out Tawmy Burns in ten rounds and Al Kaufman in five – if he had wanted to.[647]

On September 29, just before Johnson was about to start his sparring exhibition at the Seal Rock hotel, policemen appeared and informed him that until he secured a license, which happened to cost $1,200, he could give no further boxing exhibitions when an admission fee was charged. Johnson immediately jumped into his automobile and drove to Chief Cook's office, complaining that he was being discriminated against, for others, including Ketchel, had been allowed to charge money for specators to watch his training. The chief informed Jack that he would have to secure a license if he charged admission.[648]

Johnson said Jeffries was afraid of him, and had been for years. "I think he fears me more than any man living. ... I have been chasing Jeffries for six years trying to get a fight with him, and I am still on his trail. ... He was afraid of me then, and he's more afraid of me now. ... I am not yet convinced that he wants a fight with me."

Johnson predicted, "Ketchel is a pretty tough boy, but I feel sure that I will knock him out in less than fifteen rounds."

The inflammatory Willis Britt said,

> Ketchel will knock the golden smile from the countenance of that big hippopotamus. Say, on the level, if Johnson was in Africa right now, where he belongs, he would be in a cocoanut throwing competition for the championship of the world with the other baboons of the Jungle Athletic club. That smoke has got a tail a yard long sure, and Ketch will show it to the public. Johnson's got a streak of yellow in him richer and broader than the Chinese war flag.

Britt said manager George Little was just Johnson's messenger and was not even drawing a messenger boy's pay. Speaking of Johnson,

> That dinge couldn't get booked in a nickelodeon after Ketchel gets through with him.

---

[647] *San Francisco Bulletin, San Francisco Evening Post*, September 27, 1909.
[648] *San Francisco Evening Post, San Francisco Examiner*, September 30, 1909.

Stan is going to be in great shape for this match, and he's going to flatten Johnson sure. Why, there's not a chance in a million for Johnson beating Ketch inside of twenty rounds. It ain't in the dinge to do it.

Britt further said, "It's funny to me to hear this big dinge talking about what he is going to do with Ketchel. Steve and myself laughed ourselves sick over the interview in which Johnson declared he would win by a knockout. Why, who has he ever knocked out? ... Johnson is scared."[649]

Johnson drew criticism for his penchant for automobiling. The champ said, "They think I'm not training. ... Just let them come and see me box Ketchel, and then they'll know whether I am trained or not."

Some noted that Ketchel had knocked out O'Brien twice, whereas Johnson had not. "According to popular belief, Johnson is always afflicted with faintness of heart when under fire, and instead of fighting back he was wont to run for cover in the old days. According to these theories and deductions, it is up to Ketchel to bring out this so called yellow streak."[650]

George Little said,

> In reply to Britt's statement I will say that I might be a messenger boy for Jack Johnson and I might not be drawing a messenger boy's salary, but I will have the satisfaction of jingling part of that paltry $5,000 side bet.
>
> When a boy, my grandfather used to take me on his knees and talk like this: "George, when you grow up to be a man never buy any hair restorer from a bald headed barber, and never take a broken man's advice."
>
> As for Johnson being in Africa throwing cocoanuts for the championship of the world, when he gets in the ring on October 12 he will land a few on Ketchel's cocoanut that were never there before.[651]

On October 4, Johnson consented to postpone the fight date by four days, from the 12th to the 16th, pursuant to the request of the promoter and Willis Britt. They also decided to take moving pictures of the fight, and a contract was signed with the Miles Brothers to film it.[652]

---

[649] *San Francisco Evening Post, Call, Chronicle, Bulletin*, October 2, 1909.
[650] *San Francisco Examiner, San Francisco Call, San Francisco Chronicle*, October 3, 1909.
[651] *San Francisco Call, San Francisco Evening Post*, October 4, 1909; *San Francisco Bulletin*, October 5, 1909.
[652] *San Francisco Chronicle*, October 5, 1909.

Johnson did not mind Jeff's statement that he was his physical superior, but Jeff's claim that he had it on Johnson in terms of intellect had hurt the feelings of the "heavyweight from Zamboanga," for he took pride in his intelligence. The *Evening Post* quoted Johnson as responding, allegedly,

> What? Jeffries mah superior in intellect? Dat ain't so. Ah'm a smart niggah, Ah am. Ah know litterchure. Ah know joggafy. Ah knows where New York and Chicago is, and Ah knows 'rithmatic, too. Ah Figure 1can beat Jeffries in a spellin' match or any form of culture he cares to meet me in. Ah'm a smart niggah.[653]

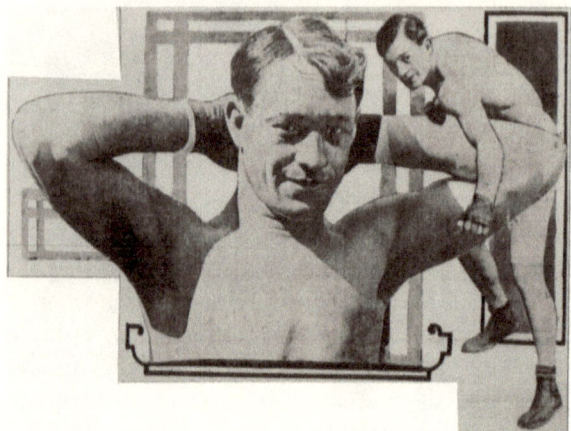

Stanley Ketchel

Johnson, Ketchel, and Coffroth agreed to pay outright the entire cost of filming the fight, which meant they would reap all of the profits. Johnson secured the greatest share at 40%, while Ketchel and Coffroth each would earn 30%. "If Johnson should win in a round or two, the pictures will be worth little, but if it is a sensational match, or by any hook or crook Ketchel would be returned the winner, there would be barrels of money for the men concerned." Hence, the more interesting the bout, the more valuable the films would be to the investors, including Johnson, who stood to earn the most money.[654]

On October 7, Britt was smoking a cigar in promoter Jim Coffroth's office, telling his friends that Ketchel would be a sure winner. Johnson walked in, wearing his automobile uniform. Smiling, Jack said, "Evenin', Mistah Britt." Willis replied, "Well look who's here....if it isn't Jack Johnson himself. Well, Jack, I'm glad you dropped in. I was just telling Mitchel that Ketchel was going to give you a fine larruping, and telling him how Ketch is going to do it." Britt continued, "I hear you're going to box with Armstrong. Well I wish we had Armstrong at our camp. I guess the reason you haven't been working with him before is because he is too tough."

Johnson replied, "You come out and box with me just once, and you can have Armstrong at your camp. I'll tell you what I will do. If you will come out I'll let you have Armstrong and give you $100 to boot." Britt replied, "Nothing doing. You might crack my jaw and I want to be behind Ketchel when that fight starts."

---

[653] *San Francisco Evening Post*, October 5, 1909.
[654] *San Francisco Chronicle, San Francisco Evening Post, San Francisco Call, San Francisco Bulletin*, October 7, 1909.

After further conversation, Johnson said, "I ain't goin' to fool too much with Ketchel. I'm going to beat that boy up some." Britt told Johnson, "You are one who holds caution almost to the point of hysteria. You never fought an aggressive battle in your life. ... But Ketchel is of a different mold. Lion or tiger like, he loves to fight, and there is not a bit of yellow in the Ketchel make-up. You know, Jack, that if yellow pigment ever became extinct all the artists would have to do would be to trepan you and they could get enough yellow to paint the North Pole."

Johnson responded, "Lawdy, how that man do talk." Britt told Johnson, "This time, you aren't going up against a Tommy Burns." Jack replied, "No, but I will have a softer one." Britt said, "You have been beating a lot of suckers who come at you just the way you want, so you can jab and counterpunch. Ketchel has something else ready for you." Jack said, "Well, let him come at me any way he wants. I am used to the tough fellows and the clever ones and the fast ones and the slow ones. I can get them all." As he was leaving, Johnson told Britt that Ketchel was in for a beating. "I'm saving up for him."

Britt noted that Ketchel had knocked out Jack Sullivan and Hugo Kelly, whom even Tommy Burns could not stop. Continuing, Britt said,

> The trouble with Johnson is that he has never been opposed to a real, live, sure-enough top-notcher, and he's trying to cover up his fear of the experiment by a lot of big talk. ... Jack's record is about the saddest excuse for a championship title-holder anyone ever looked at. It's filled with Denver Ed Martins and Sam McVeys and Joe Jeannettes, Black ills and so forth – men who have nothing but bulk as an excuse for being in the prize-ring – but there aren't many like Corbett, Ruhlin, Sharkey and those fellows. ... Ketchel, on the contrary, has been meeting the best in his class all the time.[655]

In an interview with a *Bulletin* lady reporter who visited both camps, Britt said of Ketchel, "Oh yes, he's heavy enough, 180 pounds, and a nigger is easy to beat, for a nigger is never as game as a white man."

The lady reporter noted that Jack Johnson used to be a sparring partner at a salary of $1.50 per week. However, winning the championship had brought him fame, fortune, and a newly acquired ego.

George Little said Johnson loved to eat, and always had an appetite. "He'll eat twenty-five or thirty pancakes at night and go to bed and sleep."

The reporter said current opinion was that Johnson periodically got himself arrested by the automobile police for advertising purposes. Little maintained it was because the police liked to boast of arresting a champion. Johnson said, "It's a curious thing, I always get arrested when I'm going slow." The reporter asked him whether perhaps it was because of his reputation for speeding. Johnson exclaimed, "Ah! That is not right. The law reads that a man cannot be arrested without showing cause." The reporter

---

[655] *San Francisco Chronicle, San Francisco Evening Post, San Francisco Call, San Francisco Bulletin,* October 8, 1909.

asked, "But suppose when you're speeding, something should go wrong with the car; the danger from accidents is so much greater?" Johnson again replied,

> Ah! 'If' and 'suppose'! Two small words, but nobody has ever been able to explain them. ... I would just as soon go seventy-five miles an hour as five. One man falls out of bed and is killed. Another falls from a fifty-foot scaffold and lives. One man gets shot in the leg and is killed. Another gets a bullet in the brain and lives.

Johnson spoke of crashing his car into a tree in New Jersey on a slippery night, which cost him $1,800, but he was not hurt. "I always take a chance on my pleasures. We gets in this world what we're going to get." Johnson indeed had the courage (or foolishness) characteristic of a fighter.[656]

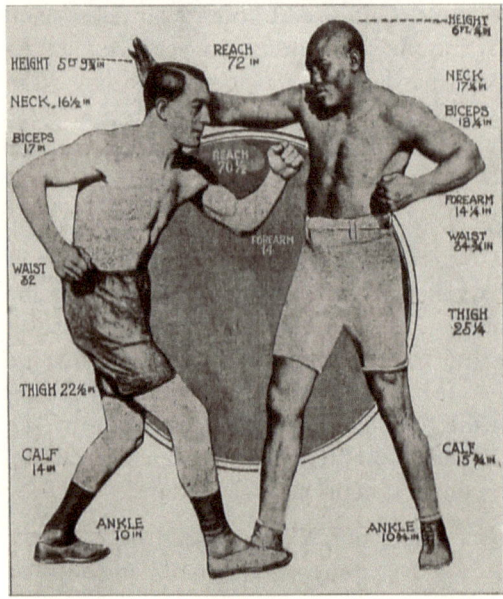

England's Hugo Corri argued that although Johnson had won the title relatively late in life, he "is one of those negroes who have the trick of aging slowly, more slowly, that is, than the average white man."

Bob Fitzsimmons said, "Jeff will beat Johnson to death. ... Johnson will never be able to hurt him enough to win, and the coon will never be able to stand big Jem's punches. Yes, I am pretty confident that Jeffries will beat the nigger if ever they come together."[657]

The *Call* wondered who would be Johnson's best foe if Jeffries did not face him next. "A careful survey of the field reveals only one man, Sam Langford. As Langford is of the same color as Johnson, a meeting between this pair would not stir up enough interest to warrant any promoter coming forth with the guarantee that these men undoubtedly would demand for a championship battle."[658]

The *San Francisco Chronicle* said, "There are many who cannot get away from the belief that Johnson has a streak of yellow, and that if hard pressed and hit he will quit." Stanley Ketchel had the punch to make him quit.

Responding to critics, Johnson said,

---

[656] *San Francisco Call, San Francisco Chronicle, San Francisco Evening Post, San Francisco Bulletin,* October 9, 1909.
[657] *Boxing,* October 9, 1909. A British magazine.
[658] *San Francisco Chronicle, San Francisco Examiner, San Francisco Call,* October 10, 1909.

I'm not a slugger, but a boxer and a scientific hitter. You all know what a great racehorse Sysonby was. Well, he never broke a record in his life, but he never ran second, either. That's me. I'm not for tearing in and knocking 'em out, just to get the name of being a hurricane. I would rather size my man up in the right way, beat him down carefully, if slowly, and then win without taking a chance of allowing him to put over any wild haymakers on me. This has always been my style and I am not going to change it now, simply because I am champion of the world.

On October 10, Johnson's auto suffered a flat tire. Ketchel happened along as Johnson was repairing the tire, and offered to help him, but Jack declined. Nevertheless, Ketchel talked with the champ good-naturedly. "Say, Jack, you ain't so big, are you? Why, from the way they talked about you I thought you were as big as one of the twin peaks. Why, you ain't got much on me, Jack, I'm nearly as big as you are." Johnson responded, "I may not be so big as they say, but I think I'll be big enough to beat you up some, Mr. Ketchel." "Well, that's where we differ, Jack. You know that little song, Jack. You know how the chorus runs, 'And he rambled till the butcher cut him down.' Well, Jack, I think I'm going to cut you down next Saturday. I like them big like you because you'll fall harder than a small fellow and it won't be so easy for them to pick you up, either." Ketchel then left while Johnson smiled and continued fixing his flat.

According to the *San Francisco Evening Post*, on October 10, 1909 at the Seal Rock house, in the 4th round of his sparring exhibition with Jack Johnson, navy seaman Gunboat Smith, who previously had been a Ketchel sparring partner, allegedly knocked down the heavyweight champion with a looping overhand right chop to the jaw coming out of a clinch. When Johnson got up, his manager called time, cutting the round short by a minute. The 500 fans present cheered vociferously.

The former amateur armed forces champion Smith had just turned professional, and was no bigger than Ketchel. Many said if a game amateur could drop Johnson, then Ketchel could do the same and more.

However, Johnson still sparred three others, 2 rounds apiece, for a total of 10 rounds that day.

> Johnson did not care to discuss the punch much. He seemed inclined to take the incident lightly and pass the matter off as a slip rather than a knockdown, but there was not one fan who saw the trick turned who could be convinced that Smith's blow was any less hefty than a real knockdown punch.

However, not every local paper reported a knockdown. The *San Francisco Call* said, "Johnson and Smith went four rounds and the exhibition proved a good one." Nothing about a knockdown was even hinted. The *San Francisco Examiner* did not mention anything about a knockdown either.[659]

The story's promotional value was that it could serve to stimulate even more interest in the upcoming championship fight, because it made Johnson seem vulnerable.

George Little denied the knockdown claim. "The thing is a cheap attempt to gain a reputation at Johnson's expense." The question was whether the *Evening Post* was engaging in yellow journalism, potentially being paid by Smith's backers to circulate the story.

The *San Francisco Call* reported, "There are a number of contradictory stories about the knockdown which Gunboat Smith is said to have scored on Johnson." Little said it was a slip, although it was a slip after Smith had landed a blow. "Johnson's foot slipped and he partially fell. That's all there was to the story." Others insisted that Johnson was dropped.

The *San Francisco Chronicle* said, "The story that Gunboat Smith knocked Johnson down in a sparring exhibition Sunday afternoon was a bit stretched. Johnson slipped on the canvas and the balance of the yarn was easy to concoct."

The *San Francisco Evening Post*, which had generated the story, insisted it was a knockdown.

> Lyttle denied the knockdown and tried to say that Johnson slipped, and some of the unwise swallowed Lyttle's statement complete. ... Johnson's canvas dive was no slip, but the result of a well-timed whack on the chin.[660]

On October 12, Johnson boxed 11 rounds, including 4 with Gunboat Smith, who could not land effectively.

Scouting the bout, an *Evening Post* writer said,

> Coming right down to taw, and without any aspersions being cast and with all respect due the colored race, I tell you from personal knowledge that I never yet have seen a negro that didn't quit under fire. ... Ever since the dawn of day the white man has been in the supremacy. It will carry in the present issue. ... Now you might think from this talk that I'm prejudiced against the colored race. Never in a thousand years. I know some of the most brilliant fellows in the world who are colored men and I am proud of their company and associations.[661]

Many were speculating that on account of the moving pictures, Johnson would allow Ketchel to last a while. George Little said that regardless, "I am

---

[659] *San Francisco Evening Post, San Francisco Call, San Francisco Examiner*, October 11, 1909.
[660] *New York Times, San Francisco Examiner, San Francisco Call, San Francisco Chronicle, San Francisco Evening Post*, October 12, 1909.
[661] *San Francisco Chronicle, Call, Examiner, Evening Post*, October 13, 1909.

certain that he will win inside of fifteen rounds and I am going to bet my money that way, and I intend to bet a good chunk, too."

The *San Francisco Bulletin* said if Ketchel knocked out Johnson, the motion pictures would be worth half a million dollars. If the battle went 20 brisk rounds, the films would be worth $250,000, and "even if Ketchel should lose to the champion in twelve or fifteen rounds, but succeed in knocking him down or punishing him badly at any stage, they would easily be worth $150,000 to $200,000." That type of money could be an incentive for Johnson to carry Ketchel for a while, and perhaps do more.[662]

The *Evening Post* said, "The public is with Ketchel almost to a fan." If he happened to win, he would be "the greatest ring hero of modern times."

This writer said Johnson lacked a champion's aggressiveness, possibly as a result of being "lazy." "Johnson has seldom shown many very open signs of courage, and there is a public belief, well founded or not, that Johnson is not a game man."

Johnson said he and Little were betting at even odds that he would stop Ketchel within 15 rounds. When asked if it would be safe for his friends to bet that he would win inside of 10 rounds, Johnson replied, "No-o. But they can go as far as they like on the fifteen round proposition. Tell 'em to bet that I stop Ketch before the end of the fifteenth round." Hence, Johnson was prognosticating the bout's termination during rounds 11 through 15. "Maybe he thinks I am not a very wicked puncher, but I think he will change his mind before I am through with him tomorrow afternoon." George Little said, "In my opinion it is all over with the exception of paying over the money."

The day of the fight, the *Bulletin* said, "[I]f the darky has a streak of yellow anywhere in his makeup the Michigander is the one who will bring it out. ... Besides, almost every lover of the boxing game who has seen Johnson in the ring wants to see him get a licking."[663]

On October 16, 1909 at Jim Coffroth's outdoor arena in Colma, California, in the San Francisco area, Jack Johnson defended his world heavyweight championship against Stanley Ketchel.[664]

Promoter Coffroth announced that every seat had been sold. "With the standing room customers that will be squeezed in within the next half hour I figure to have $40,000 when I count up tonight." No bigger crowd could have been packed into the arena. Even the aisles were crowded. Thousands were turned away at the door. "Many negroes were scattered through the crowd, but were outnumbered forty to one by the white followers."

---

[662] *San Francisco Call, Chronicle, Evening Post, Bulletin,* October 14, 1909.
[663] *San Francisco Chronicle, Call, Examiner, Evening Post, Bulletin,* October 15, 16, 1909.
[664] The following account is an amalgamation of the local next-day accounts from the *San Francisco Chronicle, Examiner,* and *Call,* October 17, 1909.

San Francisco Chronicle, **October 16, 1909**

Police officers were stationed around the corners of the ring, and many special officers were distributed throughout the crowd, which was something new.

Announcer "Uncle" Billy Jordan climbed between the ropes carrying new gloves. They were dark red, and had light-blue ribbon strings.

At 3 p.m., when Johnson entered the ring, the spectators gave him a poor reception, which included hoots, hisses, groans, and catcalls. Jack merely smiled in response. One fan told Johnson that Ketchel was going to beat him, and the champ responded by saying that he was going to give Ketchel the beating of his life.

When the popular Ketchel entered the ring, he received a huge ovation; akin to a royal welcome. The bashful Ketchel smiled in appreciation, but as he went to and sat in his corner, it appeared that his eyes were filled with tears, and he wiped them away. He either was consumed with nervous tension or touched by the warm reception. Stan told the newsmen that his mother had sent him a message wishing him success.

Johnson went over to Ketchel's corner and they shook hands. He examined Ketchel's hands and gloves, but when he tried to remain in Stan's corner so he could observe the gloves being put on, wanting to make sure no horseshoes were inserted, Willis Britt objected forcibly, argued with him, and shouldered him away. Britt said, "We've got his goat already, Steve."

Johnson returned to his corner. As the gloves were tied to his wrists, he looked over the sea of hostile faces with a half-grin.

When Billy Jordan introduced Ketchel as the middleweight and light heavyweight champion of the world, he received a powerful ovation. When Johnson was introduced as the world heavyweight champion, his reception was modest. Referee Jack Welch also was introduced.

The men stripped to their fighting costumes and posed for the newspaper photographers. Jack wore knee-length blue trunks with an American flag belt. Stan wore pinkish red trunks with no belt.

Ketchel's weight was given out as 174 pounds, and Johnson's as 196 pounds. Neither man took the scales, so no one knew for sure.

Referee Welch ordered the ring cleared. Billy Jordan announced the start of the fight by saying, "Let 'er go." The bell rang at exactly 3:09 p.m.

The fight's pattern from the start was that both were cautious, waiting, sparring, feinting often. Johnson often landed whipping left jabs to the face with lightning-like rapidity. He then would step back or to the side, circling about, capitalizing on his obvious height and reach advantages. Jack's movement was quick but efficient, moving no more than necessary. In the clinches, Johnson easily handled Ketchel. Stan usually attempted body blows, particularly his left hook, but was stifled by Johnson's ability to block, clinch, suppress, smother, or twist away. What punches Stan did land, Johnson took well. Sometimes Jack would lean back away from Ketchel's powerful swinging blows. Jack's gold teeth glistened as he smiled in the clinches or after he made Stan miss.

In the 2nd round, in a fast mix, the champion landed a right uppercut and then straight right to the jaw that sent Ketchel backwards, and in the follow-up near the corner, as Ketchel tried to stop and fire a right; Johnson landed a shorter, faster clean right to the jaw that dropped Ketchel to the floor with considerable force.

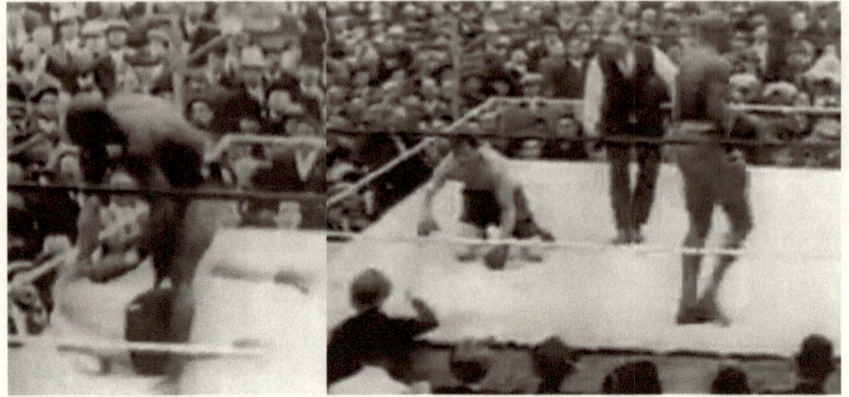

Ketchel grabbed the lower rope and rose from the knockdown at the count of six. He rushed in, and Johnson clinched, then broke and sparred, not trying to follow-up his advantage. Instead, he jabbed, defended, and grinned, merely toying with Ketchel.

For the remainder of the contest, mostly Johnson was content to stick jabs, maintain his range, feint, tie up, and only occasionally launch combinations. He either quickly attacked and then grabbed, occasionally sneaking in short inside blows, or he would wait for Ketchel to attack so he could counter and suppress Stan's arms. Both fighters were cautious, and the pace relatively slow, neither moving very much, each carefully selecting their moments of attack. Johnson was in total control, calmly outboxing Ketchel.

At one point in the 4th round, after Stan clinched, Johnson literally lifted him up off his feet like a baby and carried him to ring center, five feet from the spot where the clinch started.

Throughout the 5th round, Johnson's long left continually visited Ketchel's reddened nose and bloody lips.

In the 6th round, Johnson sent Ketchel reeling with a left on the jaw, and dropped him to his haunches with a straight left on the chin. Stan rose immediately, and received more left jabs that drew blood from his nose.

In the 7th round, on the inside, Johnson began pumping in right uppercuts for the first time, reaching the face and body. Ketchel used Johnson's shoulder as a mat to wipe the blood flowing from his nostrils.

Suddenly, Ketchel swung his left with terrific force and it caught Johnson solidly on the jaw, raising a lump there that immediately was perceptible to the spectators. The immense crowd rose to its feet yelling and cheering gleefully. However, the *Examiner* disagreed, saying the punch caught Johnson on the glove and made a noise. "It landed on his raised glove." Johnson merely laughed.

In the 8th and 9th rounds, Johnson continuously landed head-tilting left jabs, adding more force to the blows. Stan's nose was pouring blood. He kept attempting powerful swings, to no avail. Jack eluded and grinned.

By the 10th round, Ketchel was spitting blood and seemed tired. During a clinch, as they scuffled and wrestled, Johnson landed some short left hooks to the ear and jaw, and Ketchel stumbled and almost went down to the floor, but Johnson held, lifted, and swung Stan up to a standing position again, actually  preventing Ketchel from going down. The *Examiner* said, "Up to this point Johnson seemed to be under a wrap," holding back and carrying Ketchel. In fact, he literally lifted him up.

In the 11th round, Stan sent the crowd into convulsions by landing a hard right to the face, though he could not penetrate Jack's clever defense any further. Suddenly Johnson loosened up and was all over him, whipping in hard punches with both hands from every angle.

In the 12th round, after some sparring, Ketchel fired right swing. His glove seemed to curve around Johnson's neck as he was ducking, though it possibly came down on the jaw. It was too fast to be seen well. Johnson sank clumsily to the floor, his left left foot apparently starting to come off the ground before the blow even landed, with his left glove catching himself on the ground. The champion was down! The crowd was shocked, and cheered uproariously.

Johnson flipped around on the ground, ever so slightly shaking his head. Some claimed there was a slight grin on Johnson's face.

As soon as Jack rose, Ketchel rushed in to finish him, but Jack met the advance by lashing out with a series of blazing-fast rights and lefts thrown in combination, decking

Ketchel. The first right that Johnson threw landed as Stan was throwing his own right, doubling its force as he moved and turned right into it, and appears to have been the decisive blow.

Johnson threw his vicious combination with so much ferocity and abandon that he flung himself over the top of the prostrate Ketchel and went tumbling down to the canvas in his own corner. Ketchel fell on his back with his arms outstretched, as if he had been shot dead. Johnson turned around, rose, and then swiped some of Stan's teeth out of his glove.

Ketchel was out cold, the blood streaming from his mouth as referee Jack Welch counted off the ten seconds.

It was a wild and spectacular ending, given that the champion had been on the canvas, and just seconds later it was Ketchel who was down and out.

Overall, the fight had been a dominant Johnson performance, having administered a gradual beating. Johnson dropped Ketchel in the 2nd and 6th rounds, picked him up and prevented Stan from going down in the 10th, until finishing him off in the 12th round.

Debate about this fight continues to this day. Most of it centers on two issues. The first was whether Johnson was carrying Ketchel and could have knocked him out at any time, or simply was administering his usual cautious gradual beating. The second issue was whether Johnson intentionally took a dive before finishing Ketchel in order to make the motion pictures more valuable, and to bait Ketchel into a trap. Another theory was that Johnson wanted to seem vulnerable, so as to induce Jeffries to fight him. Others thought Ketchel simply was a very hard puncher who caught Johnson well, and that Jack, though slightly stunned momentarily, struck out in an attempt to get payback, as he always did when hit hard. Fans, writers, and experts engaged in the same debate then as today. Most believed the worst.

Immediately after the fight, Johnson said that although he won with ease, Ketchel was a good, tough, game man, with a very hard punch. He admitted that he had been knocked down with a fierce right behind the ear. "His punch hit me back of the ear. Of course it hurt me. Why shouldn't I admit it? I was stunned, I can assure you." Another quoted Johnson as saying he was struck on the jaw. After Jack rose, Ketchel came at him wildly, and Johnson beat him to the punch. "Jeffries can have his chance any time. I guess I showed the fans that I have a good punch."

Because the films are old and do not have a sufficient number of frames for a good slow-motion view, and the angle is not perfect, it is not entirely clear where Johnson was hit, or if he was hit at all. Many even then believed the punch missed entirely and that Johnson took a dive.

The concussed Ketchel did not remember much afterwards:

> How did he hit me? I don't know. I only realized that when I came to. ... Just where I hit him I can not say. ... He never hurt me till he landed the punch that knocked me out. Here are three of my teeth which fell out after that last punch.

Referee Jack Welch believed that Ketchel scored a legitimate clean knockdown – a vicious right swing that landed behind the ear. "Johnson was inclined to fool around too much, and I think Ketchel sneaked one over on him." The blow only served to arouse Johnson's ire, and he immediately rose and made short work of him, lashing out with a brutal right to the jaw that sent Stan down like a log. "Just look at the glove on Johnson's right hand and you will see where Ketchel caught that final right. His teeth tore holes in the leather of the glove big and ragged, as though it had been hacked with a saw."

The *San Francisco Chronicle* said it was a most spectacular, sensational ending to a fight that up until then had been thoroughly one-sided "in favor of the black." In the middle of the 12th round, Ketchel swung a hard right that appeared to glance around the back of Johnson's head. It did not appear to have much force, and there was genuine surprise when Johnson dropped down and spun around on his knees with a smile on his face.

As soon as Johnson rose, he was not so dazed as to be prevented from immediately firing more viciously than he had at any previous stage of the match, and had so much force behind his right that the glove showed where Ketchel's front teeth pierced through the leather and were knocked out. The timing of Johnson's sudden increase of speed and power seemed interesting, particularly given that he had never thrown like that at any time earlier in the fight. The suggestion was that he had been carrying Ketchel.

Although the *Chronicle* conceded that the knockdown of Johnson might have been legitimate, "the writer did not see a punch that would have such an effect, and it must also be remembered that such an ending would be of fast assistance to the handling of the moving pictures." The strong suspicion was that Johnson intentionally went down to increase the market value of the films so he could make even more money. Another *Chronicle* writer said that even while Johnson was down, it was obvious that he was planning his opponent's downfall, like a cat ready to spring.

The *San Francisco Call* said Johnson won after reeling from a "mysterious punch" that fans failed to see. It suspected he took the "ungraceful stumble" to swell the motion picture gate receipts, and had stalled up to that point for the same reason.

The sudden ending electrified and mystified nearly everyone. Veterans shook their heads and said, "It was a good show, but the last act was rotten. They should have had a stage manager to give them a few practical rehearsals." Most thought Johnson fell to help swell the moving picture revenues. The referee said it was genuine. "But even the champion himself can not explain how he came back with the speed and fury with which he responded." Fans found it mysterious for Johnson to be dropped, but within a few seconds thereafter be able to pulverize his opponent into total unconsciousness. "Nobody ever saw anything quite like it before. It was a new one in ring tricks."

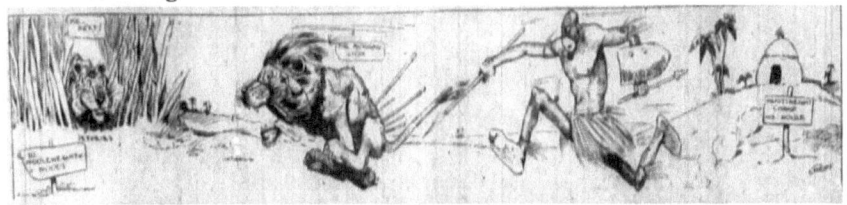

San Francisco Call, October 17, 1909

The *Examiner's* W. W. Naughton said, "Johnson has the habit of infusing buffoonery into his fights at times, especially when he has matters well in hand." He said Johnson fell like a clown. Naughton thought that if he was hit harder, it might have looked more genuine. When Ketchel went down, it was like a soldier whose heart had been cleft by a sword-thrust.

After Johnson rose, he lashed out with all of his strength, "fighting for the first time during the afternoon." Johnson so far outclassed Ketchel that he could have knocked him out in any round he wanted, including the 1st round, had he cared to extend himself.

Naughton agreed the bogus knockdown would add value to pictures, for folks would pay to see whether Johnson had sprawled in earnest.

Johnson toyed with Ketchel. He kept his dangerous right uppercut in reserve until the 7th round, and he did not use it as often as usual. In fact, he hardly used it at all, perhaps another indication that he was carrying Ketchel. He also allowed numerous openings to pass unnoticed. Jack chuckled at Stan's inability to land. In the clinches, "Ketchel was as helpless as an eel held in a vise." Even when Ketch did land, it almost seemed as if Johnson allowed him to do so. Jack even picked him up on occasion.

Johnson showed how easy it all was, undisturbed by the crowd's taunts, jibes, and guffaws. "Whatever else may be said about him, he is a cool-headed customer and ringside reviling does not rattle him for an instant."

The *Chronicle* said it was apparent that Johnson could have finished the fight much sooner had he desired, proven by the fact that "he was merely saving Ketchel even to the extent of holding him up in the earlier rounds, when the white man was almost falling."

Even before the fight started it was rumored amongst the press that Johnson would fight for the moving pictures for 12 rounds and then cut loose. George Little was credited with having told several friends that Johnson would win in the 12th round. In the 10th round, when several people remarked that Ketchel might last the limit, Little offered to bet any amount of money that Johnson would knock him out before 15 rounds had passed. Little even said to those near the corner, "What round do you want Johnson to knock him out? He can do it now. Just say the word." No one thought Ketchel was in on it, but "there is reasonable suspicion that Johnson, for the sake of the pictures preferred to allow his opponent to last a reasonable length of time."

Some believed Ketchel could have done better had he adopted his usual nonstop rushing tactics, but the *Chronicle* disagreed, feeling that if he had done so that Johnson would have stopped him even sooner. As it was, Johnson dropped him as early as the 2nd round, and again in the 6th, and had to back off, handling Stan like "a child," swinging him clear off his feet in the clinches, and making his blows miss by a foot or more. Johnson made him look foolish, and "often during the bout spared him, displaying rare good-nature until the moment when it suited his purpose to end the fight."

Another *Chronicle* writer said Ketchel was the crowd's idol, but had he been anyone else, or been of a different color, the fans would have jeered and hooted him. Instead, they heartily cheered at the slightest excuse. Even when he swung and missed, he was cheered for his courage. If he waited and made Johnson carry the fight to him, he was applauded for his wisdom, and if he landed even a light blow, the crowd burst into a howl of delight. Stan was cheered even as he left the ring. However, "It was Johnson all the way, even during the spasm of renewed hope which brought the crowd to its feet in the twelfth round."

Ketchel was the idol not only because of his skin color. "Added to the natural support of a white man by the white race, was the added hatred of Johnson for his offensive ways, which have made him the most unpopular fighter in the ring."

Unlike Ketchel, Johnson was jeered and booed. The champ simply grinned and showed his gold teeth, further increasing the fans' dislike for him and strengthening their hope that he would be defeated. Johnson's white wife was in the stands, smiling confidently, which didn't help matters.

Johnson received no applause, not even when he generously picked up Ketchel from the different corners of the ring and whirled him around to a safe space in the center, after which Jack stepped back momentarily and allowed Ketchel to get his bearings. The crowd simply hated him. "The crowd groaned and exchanged estimates as to how close Ketchel had been to the heavy-weight crown, but in the opinion of the writer, and I would have been pleased to see him win, the middle-weight champion had no more chance than the much talked of rabbit."

Angered by the result, the crowd began discussing how Jeffries would make pulp out of Johnson.

The *Call* said, "Ketchel never figured for a single second." The fight "resembled a setto between a hawk and a sparrow." Ketchel was sincere, but Johnson played. "Johnson never seemed to be in earnest. He spent as much of his time watching the crowd as he did watching Ketchel. He would answer his critics and then come on and cuff Ketchel with a right or a left, whichever suited his purpose." Ketchel was outclassed in every aspect of the trade, with the possible exception of gameness, "but what is the use of gameness for a man like Johnson, who seldom, if ever, is compelled to show this quality? There was no necessity for his taking any punches."

Johnson stalled and smiled and took his time. When he threw, his punches landed. When Stan missed, Jack smiled and winked at the crowd. Time and again he informed everyone at ringside that the battle would end before the 15th round.

The champ kept jabbing and smiling, though it did not appear as if he was hitting as hard as he might have had he felt so disposed. Still, he brought blood running from the nose and mouth and blackened Stan's eyes.

Several hundred black fans were present, but they were afraid to cut loose vocally amongst the mostly white crowd. "If Johnson did any damage the crowd would hold its breath, but if Ketchel landed one everybody seemed to jump to its feet at once and tear loose with a volley of cheers."

Johnson did not seem to mind the white fans' jeering at all. He worked his smile all the time, and the further the fight went, the broader his smile became. He remarked many times to the crowd that he intended to give Ketchel the worst beating of his life, and he did.

Afterwards, Jim Coffroth estimated the receipts at $32,300, though before the fight began, he said he expected the gate to yield about $40,000. The fighters received 60%, from which Johnson's winner's share was 65%, or about $12,597. Plus he won an alleged $5,000 side bet. He would earn a great deal more from the film revenues, of which he had a 40% interest.

One newspaper reported that there were 8,401 paid admissions at the fight, the second largest crowd that ever attended a fistic contest there. 8,704 had attended Corbett-Jeffries II.

In subsequent days, the newspapers and fight-goers continued talking about the 12th round knockdown that Ketchel scored on Johnson. Many asserted that Ketchel did not land hard enough to budge a lightweight, or that he missed, and that Johnson took a dive.

The *Evening Post* believed the knockdown was legitimate, though it only momentarily jarred Johnson. "The blow was one of those sudden and spectacular ones for which Ketchel has been noted." As a result, for the first time in the fight, Johnson showed fire in his eyes, indicating that he wanted revenge. "His face took on a demoniac look, half human, half the expression of some wild thing goaded to desperation. Johnson's...gorilla-like arms began to beat a very hailstorm of blows on Ketchel." Before that, Jack wore a "dreamy, languid expression."

The *Chronicle* said Ketchel's face was bruised, nose swollen, and there was a gap in his mouth where Johnson had knocked out several teeth. Hence, there was no foundation for the belief that the two were working together.

However, there was "plenty of reason for argument that Johnson delayed the knockout until the twelfth in order to give the moving pictures a chance. The suspicion also continues that Johnson did the spectacular in falling to the floor of the ring when he was hit, if hit at all, by a glancing blow," which did not have the force of the punch that Stan landed in the 7th round, when "Ketchel failed to stagger the black." Several parties were advised against betting that Stan would last 15 rounds.

The *Call* said nine out of ten were sure there was some sort of a job framed up, but none were sure exactly what it was. Everyone was talking about the mysterious punch which allegedly floored Johnson. "If the punch was landed it certainly was the fastest and most deceptive in history."

The *Examiner* said the only blot on Johnson's performance was his "flop to the floor, which was voted amateurish." Johnson boxed 10 rounds for the benefit of the moving pictures, and then, having fulfilled the obligation, whipped Ketchel in less than two rounds of actual fighting. Nine out of ten failed to see Ketchel's knockdown blow land.

The *Bulletin* said the big crowd reviled the black man for faking his own knockdown to enhance the value of the films. "If Johnson can recuperate from a swat like that in three seconds and then come back strong enough to knock his opponent cold a second later he is supernatural and must be ranked in the same class as...the Wizard of Oz."

The *Bulletin* called Johnson's flip-flop "grotesque." Many believed he was a "manipulator of the worst type."

This writer condemned Johnson for carrying Ketchel. Noted was the fact that when Johnson's friends asked him if it was advisable to bet on him to win in less than 10 rounds, he cautioned them not to do so, but said they could bet that he would win within 15 rounds. "How does it sound to you, gentle reader? At that, he had a hard time to keep faith with his friends. ... In the second round, and again in the tenth, Johnson almost knocked his opponent out, only saving the day by holding the latter in his arms until he had recovered his senses." "In most instances Johnson simply grinned and allowed the Michigan Lion to recover his equilibrium – probably fearing he would finish the battle if he followed Ketchel up."

Despite its racially denigrating language, the *Evening Post* said the boos and catcalls which accompanied Johnson into the ring were uncalled for:

> Black or white or brown or red, when a man enters the ring he deserves fair treatment, and this was more than the local fight fans accorded Johnson. No matter what may be said against Johnson's antics out of the ring, once he finds himself between the ropes with an opponent in front of him, he is the fairest and cleanest of fighters, and a good sportsman. He never takes unfair advantages.

Memphis, Tennessee reported that the fight bulletins had tied up traffic on the Mississippi river. There was a shortage of labor, for black deckhands remained ashore in order to hear returns from the fight as it was taking place. After the victory, they remained ashore to celebrate, which caused the big steamboats to remain docked. It was called a "Big Negro Jubilee."

Eastern followers were surprised by the ease which Johnson defeated Ketchel. "Sporting authorities now agree that Johnson has been underrated, rather than that Ketchel was overestimated, and that Jeffries has a much more difficult problem with which to contend than was known before the Ketchel fight."

Given how easily Johnson had handled light-heavyweight-sized fighters like Burns and Ketchel, there wasn't going to be much interest in a fight with Sam Langford, who was the same size and no taller. Johnson simply was too big and clever for smaller foes. Plus, Johnson already had defeated Langford clearly once before. The *Call* provided an additional reason the Langford fight would not be made, because "two colored fighters would not draw much money."

Everywhere he went, the champ was the center of attraction, and his victory brought money and joy to all those of his color who had bet on him.

Jack said he was in the business to make money, and fighting made him money. A Jeffries fight could make him the most money. He would fight anyone if there was enough money in it.[665]

---

[665] *San Francisco Evening Post, Chronicle, Call, Examiner, Bulletin,* October 18, 1909.

In his 1920s autobiography, Johnson claimed he carried Ketchel in order to "make the pictures snappy and worth seeing." He did it to help boost the film revenues, of which he was to receive a sizable percentage.

Johnson claimed to have gone down intentionally, saying,

> On the day of the fight…I was busily thinking how I could make the fight picturesque, and a plan occurred to me. This plan I did not divulge to any of my party though I told Bob Armstrong…that if he should see me down in a certain round he need not get excited. … [Ketchel] sent over a punch which landed on my jaw. It did not hurt nor disconcert me. My brain had been working rapidly – so rapidly that I recognized this to be a clean cut blow with apparently much force back of it. I said to myself, 'Now's your time! Now's your time! Here's your chance,' and so I hit the canvas. … I pretended to be groggy, but in reality I was ready to deliver the knockout.[666]

Some later claimed that Johnson was angry with Ketchel, the man he had been carrying pursuant a gentleman's agreement, for having double-crossed him and nailing him with a good one. However, this claim is not supported by the evidence. Both men had struck each other with hard blows throughout the contest.

The fact that Johnson made no attempt to finish after decking Ketchel early on, and literally held him up on occasion, combined with the odd look of the knockdown, and Johnson's instant recovery, certainly led to a strong belief that Johnson was playing a game, which he much later admitted.

Another thing to consider is whether Johnson's going down against middleweight Gunboat Smith in sparring from an overhand right, the same punch that Ketchel used to drop Johnson, actually was somewhat of a rehearsal, to see whether he could pull it off and fool folks, and was another ruse to generate interest and ticket sales, of which Johnson would earn a percentage. There was debate about that knockdown as well.

Johnson later said his only regret was hitting Stan so hard. "But that last round made those motion pictures sell like hot cakes. I made a small fortune out of them."[667]

A few days after the fight, the *San Francisco Bulletin* said the popular impression was that Johnson deliberately allowed Ketchel to last long enough to make a good moving-picture film, and then intentionally took a dive before finishing him, thus assuring himself thousands of dollars.

The *Bulletin* said this theory was strengthened by the statements of several of Johnson's seconds and camp members, who claimed the champion told them not to worry if he were to fall or be knocked down. Also, Johnson had wagered several hundreds of dollars that Ketchel would not last 13 rounds, but advised friends not to wager on a knockout before the 10th round.

---

[666] Johnson, *In the Ring and Out*, 194-196.
[667] *Saskatoon Star-Phoenix*, Apr 26, 1929.

The *Bulletin* said the pictures would show how unconcerned Jack's cornermen all were when Johnson dropped to the mat. "He practiced it daily in his training quarters." This lends credence to the theory that when he went down with Gunboat Smith that Johnson was seeing if he could fool the public. The unnamed Johnson camp sources claimed Ketchel actually missed his right swing.

The *Bulletin* writer believed Johnson could have knocked out Ketchel in 2 rounds if he had tried. He almost stopped him in the 2nd, and again in 10th round, but he helped him.

The *Examiner* said the majority thought the knockdown was bogus. Ketchel's supporters said it was legitimate, and that saying otherwise was to rob him of a little credit "where his credits were lamentably few."

W. W. Naughton said Johnson's fall was unreal and stagey. At first he thought Johnson was throwing the fight and was going to stay down and take the count. Ultimately, most gamblers did not care what Johnson did in the way of asides, as long as he protected their money and won.

It looked as though the debate over the knockdown indeed would prove the best possible advertisement for the motion pictures. Everyone would want to see them and decide for themselves.

A man wrote a letter condemning the *Bulletin* for race prejudice, saying that "it is contemptible the way you and other sporting writers abuse and revile Jack Johnson because he is black!" The *Bulletin* replied,

> In the first place, neither the writer nor any other reputable sport critic would think for a moment of condemning Johnson because of his color or race. Sam Langford, Young Peter Jackson, Joe Gans, and even Johnson himself have always received fair play at the hands of American sporting writers until they did something for which they deserved opprobrium. Then, and then only, they got what was coming to them. In the second place, the public or San Francisco goes to see two men doing their best, not one great hulking piece of fighting machinery playing for twelve rounds with a smaller – though gamer – opponent for the benefit of the cinematograph. And, in the third place, Johnson has made such evident attempts to belittle every one of his white opponents that he has made himself universally unpopular throughout the entire country.

Of course, this perspective overlooked the fact that writers, fans, managers, and opponents often used racially derogatory terms towards Johnson, verbally abused and belittled him as a fighter, and had drawn the color line on him and others for years. It also overlooked the fact that men like Corbett had laughed at and taunted his opponents, had hippodromed, and had a cautious style, and yet the press had treated him quite well.

The *Call* said Johnson's ways only served to intensify the desire to see Jeffries meet and beat him. "Johnson started upon a career of local unpopularity when he sneered and laughed at Al Kaufman. ... He rounded it out when he pitilessly and unnecessarily punished Stanley Ketchel." San

Franciscans would go en-masse to see Jeffries against Johnson, no matter what the ticket prices.

Jack Johnson, the Heavyweight Champion of the World, and George Little, His Manager, Who Continue to Claim That Jim Jeffries Is Afraid to Meet Johnson in the Ring.

W. W. Naughton said everyone wanted a Jeffries fight. "The negro so far outclasses all the other heavyweights...that it must be hard work for him to hold himself back sufficiently to make the exhibitions interesting." Jack Johnson had come full circle, having gone from being criticized for not being good enough, to being too good for his own good.

Sam Berger confirmed that Jeffries would fight the "so-called champion."[668]

Fight-goers were "disgusted" with Johnson and his tactics. "He has taken on airs that are insufferable." The hope was that Jeffries would "everlastingly wallop the pretensions out of this black fighting man."[669]

The *Bulletin* said the Ketchel contest only intensified the sporting world's desire to see Jeffries come back and "give the black champion a drubbing that will drive him from the prize-ring forever." Johnson had prolonged Ketchel's agony 10 rounds longer than necessary, had made a plaything of him, leering and laughing when Stan tried to hit him, calling out to the crowd to watch his antics, "and generally behaving like the denizens of the forests from which his ancestors came. Even the fight-followers who are hardened to the sight of a negro opposing a white man in the ring do not relish the idea of a sneering, grinning gorilla slowly annihilating one of their own race." They were praying for Jeffries to lick the "Galveston coon."

Coffroth was wise to place two uniformed policemen and a dozen plain-clothes officers in Johnson's corner. Coffroth said, "I don't want him to come to any harm at the hands of the crowd."[670]

It was looking almost positive that Jeffries would re-enter the ring "in the hope of regaining the heavyweight championship of the world for the white race." He had gone too far in his public statements to back out.[671]

The black-owned *New York Age* said Johnson had established a record for nerve. It was easy to do one's best when the crowd supported and cheered for you. "What a difference when you find yourself confronted by a crowd of 10,000 excited spectators who clearly make known to you that you are not their favorite contender by hoots and groans and loudly cheer the other fellow." Jack's nerve under such circumstances further served to dispel racial stereotypes and myths.

---

[668] *San Francisco Evening Post, San Francisco Examiner, San Francisco Bulletin,* October 19, 1909; *San Francisco Call, San Francisco Examiner,* October 20, 1909.
[669] *San Francisco Bulletin,* October 20, 1909.
[670] *San Francisco Evening Post, Chronicle, Call, Examiner, Bulletin,* October 18, 1909.
[671] *San Francisco Bulletin,* October 21, 1909.

> Colored fighters have been charged with possessing a yellow streak, which after all means an exhibition showing lack of nerve at a critical period. Possibly there have been such cases, the fighters having been discouraged by the hoots and groans of the crowd; but not so with Champion Jack Johnson. He is evidently one of those who at all times considers the source, and instead of becoming awed or nervous at the unfriendliness of the big crowd, showed that he was master of the situation by looking around cynically and then handing out one of his famous golden smiles.

Not many could face a huge audience that was against them and still keep their nerve. The *Age* saw Johnson's smile as a way to combat the ill-feeling against him. Still, the *Age* understood the racial sympathies.

> The writer does not bewail the fact that Ketchel, a white man, was the more popular. It was natural that such a situation should exist. How many colored men could you find in the United States who were pulling for Ketchel? A white man was arrayed against a colored man, and consequently there was a crossing of racial sympathies, generally speaking.

Still, the *Age* noted white newsmen's biases:

> Speaking of some of the white writers, the class that has not yet become reconciled to the fact that the champion heavyweight of the world is a Negro, they have been made monkeys of by Johnson for some time. A few of them reside in New York City, and they are certainly a bunch of sore-heads. Johnson has made them welch, dispute themselves and appear ridiculous in the eyes of their readers. One of them told in bold face type Saturday just how Ketchel was going to put Johnson, a fourflusher [bluffer], out. Sunday morning he begged that he be awarded the first prize in the guessing contest, declaring that he had predicted before the fight that the champion would knock out Ketchel. ...

The *Age* writer said the prejudiced white writers were turning to Jeffries to "lead them out of the wilderness of embarrassment and humiliation," but Jeff would not be successful, for Johnson had yet to show his best. "It looks very gloomy for the Caucasian; for all the fighters who are to be taken seriously as contenders for the heavyweight title are of ebony hue – truly a most unique state of affairs."[672]

The *Freeman* said the Johnson-Ketchel fight settled the "question of the physical prowess of the Negro." The bout was a sad spectacle. Yet, "it requires so much to convince the white man that the Negro is his physical equal." Jack Johnson had something that the white man wanted:

> Prize-fighting has always been a conspicuous factor in the world's sensations, but never before has a championship title been worth so

---

[672] *New York Age*, October 21, 1909.

much to the white man as now. And the humane societies should prevent the many inhuman sacrifices that the white man will undergo in his frantic desire to wrest the title from the giant Negro. And whatever may be said of Johnson, good, bad or indifferent, you are cheating yourself if you say he is not a fighter, even though his fight with Ketchel had many shady appearances. And the writer takes the liberty here to say that if this Johnson-Ketchel fight wasn't a prearranged affair, there was some awful clear catering to the moving picture machine.

This writer believed that not in a thousand years could Ketchel legitimately drop Johnson. "Ketchel was out in the second round with an unintentional punch." But Johnson made no attempt to finish then, because that was not the plan.[673]

---
[673] *Freeman*, September 23, 1911.

CHAPTER 33

The Future Welfare of His People

On October 22, 1909, James J. Jeffries returned from his European trip, arriving in New York on the steamer *Lusitania*. He was greeted by hundreds of fans "eager for a glimpse of the man who is expected to regain individual physical supremacy for the white race."

Jeffries said he weighed 228 pounds and was ready to fight Johnson. "That negro has made more noise and done less than any man I know." "The sooner the articles are signed the better."[674]

The day before, on October 21 in San Francisco, Jack Johnson was arrested for speeding, this time on Market street. When booked in at the City Prison, when asked his occupation, Johnson replied, "Lawyer." When the bond and warrant clerk commented on the number of times that Johnson had been arrested for his speed mania, Jack replied, "If I want to speed on Market street I intend to do so. There is a good road there, the best in the city. I never killed any one. If it suits me to speed that is my business." The *Examiner* noted the humorous irony that although Johnson kept himself in reserve when in the ring, he liked to extend his auto to the last notch when driving. It cost him $100 bail to be released.[675]

Boxing, a weekly magazine based out of England, said Jeffries was the great white hero "whom we can look to wrest the title for the dominant race." It claimed that it was not just a matter of racial pride, but one of existence, which caused the urgent desire to see Jeff triumph. The colored races outnumbered whites, but hitherto had been kept in subjection by recognition on their part of physical and mental inferiority. Great changes had taken place of late. The Russo-Japanese War proved that a colored nation could defeat a white nation. Ever since then, there had been signs of unrest amongst the colonized dark nations.

There was powerful symbolism in the fact that the dominant race was compelled to recognize that a black descendant of a slave was the sport's

---

[674] *San Francisco Evening Post*, October 22, 1909; *New York Times*, October 23, 1909.
[675] *San Francisco Examiner*, October 22, 1909.

master. Johnson's success had political, racial, and sociological implications. Such success inspired colored people with hope. A Jeffries victory was needed to help quell that hope. "While, if after all, Johnson should smash Jeffries – But the thought is too awful to contemplate." Ultimately, this writer said, "We can't see Jeffries losing, and that's a fact. Even if they made it a fight to a finish, Jeff ought to outlast the negro."

Jeffries said Johnson was not very popular even among his own people. "He hasn't had any too good a time in the States as it is; even the niggers are getting tired of him. They support him, of course, because he is their colour, but they are a bit sick of him, all the same."[676]

On October 22, Johnson left San Francisco via railroad for Chicago. He forfeited the $100 bail on the speeding charge. "For a few months, at least, the last has been seen of Jack Johnson and his gilded giggle."[677]

Fight fans were given quite a jar when John L. Sullivan allegedly said Johnson would whip Jeffries:

> I am a great admirer of Jeff and would be one of the first to bewail the fact that a negro claims the championship, but I fear that Jeff is not the man he was five years ago and that he will be unable to cope with this wily Zulu. I don't like negroes any better than I did twenty years ago, but in this case I think credit must be given to the better man, and I look upon Johnson as being the fighter of the day.[678]

On October 28, Johnson arrived in New York from Chicago to sign articles of agreement for a fight with Jeffries. A crowd of about 5,000 black folk were on hand to greet him at the train station. A grinning Johnson said,

> We will now see who is the 'four-flusher,' the black or the white man. If Jeffries signs up and behaves himself properly I will doff my hat to him and at the same time promise him the greatest thrashing of his life. ...
>
> This is the opportunity of my life and I propose to show the world that I am the best man that ever donned a mitt if I succeed in getting Jeff into the ring with me. It has always been the ambition of my life to get this man in the ring. ...
>
> It frequently has been said that somewhere in my anatomy runs a yellow streak. Does it not strike you funny that no one has ever been able to find it? And just take it from me, Mr. Jeffries will not be able to locate it, presuming that I have one somewhere. ...

---

[676] *Boxing*, October 23, 1909.
[677] *San Francisco Examiner*, October 23, 1909.
[678] *San Francisco Examiner*, October 28, 1909.

Let me give you this little tip: When Jeff and I get in the ring, don't let anybody's prejudice against the negro prevent you from getting a good-sized bet down on the black man. Of course, if you can afford to lose, why, bet on Jeffries.[679]

When Johnson arrived at his hotel on the corner of 35th street and 8th avenue, a hotel reserved for blacks, he was the hero of an admiring throng of "his own people," who crowded the streets for more than a block in every direction. Jack smiled and shook hands with hundreds of admirers.

Jeffries said, "I'll kill that fellow. It will be a short fight. In less than fifteen minutes the big negro will get all that's coming to him. I saw the pictures of his fight with Ketchel last night. He's a good defensive fighter, that's all. He couldn't hurt me with an ax. But wait till I hit him. Good night."

The *San Francisco Bulletin* said the result of the Jeffries-Johnson fistic argument would bear "almost as much weight upon the Anglo-African question as did the Civil War."[680]

On October 29, 1909 at New York's Hotel Albany, James J. Jeffries and Jack Johnson signed articles of agreement to fight 45 rounds, the fight to be held no later than July 5, 1910 before the club that offered the largest

---

[679] *San Francisco Bulletin, San Francisco Evening Post,* October 28, 1909.
[680] *San Francisco Chronicle, San Francisco Bulletin,* October 29, 1909.

financial inducements. The winner would take 75% of the purse, and the loser 25%. Jeffries, Berger, Johnson, and Little had met and agreed. Johnson wanted his name listed first, and to be called the present champion. Jeffries assented. They would fight straight Queensberry rules with 5-ounce gloves. They posed for photographers, and champagne was served.[681]

The *Chronicle* said that as a spectacle, nothing could surpass the Johnson-Jeffries bout, "combining as it does the world's title with the supremacy of the white over the black race."

On October 30, 1909, after a week-long illness, Stanley Ketchel's manager Willis Britt died from a hemorrhage flowing from a lung disease. Some said he had died of a broken heart.

Jack Johnson's home at 3344 Wabash Avenue, Chicago

Race would factor into the Jeffries-Johnson betting. "There is no question but that the national prejudice against the black race will install Jeffries a 10 to 7 or 10 to 8 favorite over Johnson."[682]

Johnson had been sending money monthly to his mother in Galveston. He built a large $11,000 12-room home on Wabash Avenue so that his mother and two sisters could come live in Chicago with him. Jack said he never would live in Texas again. Mrs. Tiny Johnson said,

My boy has always been good to me and his sisters. He promised to build me a fine home, and I am going to Chicago to be near him. He wrote three weeks before the Ketchel match that it would not last 15 rounds, and told me I could mortgage the old home and bet the money he would win. He sends me money regularly, about $200 a month.[683]

The English magazine *Boxing* said Americans were opposed to Johnson not only because of his "personal failings" but because of his color.

It is repulsive to the American nature that a black man should hold a world's fighting title over a white man. If there was another Caucasian in sight of his prowess 'we' could look to as having a chance to wrest the championship from Johnson, he would be as much favoured and lauded as Jeffries is.[684]

---

[681] *San Francisco Call, Chronicle, Evening Post, Examiner, Bulletin*, October 30, 1909.
[682] *San Francisco Chronicle, San Francisco Call*, October 31, 1909.
[683] *San Francisco Call*, November 2, 1909; *Freeman*, November 20, 1909.
[684] *Boxing*, November 6, 1909.

Boxing trainer Tim McGrath said Jeffries seemed to be suffering from what many other analysts had suffered from – underestimation of Johnson. Everyone was telling Jeffries that Johnson was scared, and he "can beat that coon in a few rounds." McGrath cautioned, "Johnson isn't afraid of him, so get that out of your head." Jeffries needed to be in top condition. "If he lacks the proper stamina it will be good night to the white race and the heavyweight title."[685]

The *San Francisco Call* said talk of a Johnson-Langford match was not taken seriously. "Johnson and Langford would not draw a large house. No two negro fighters ever did, and no two will. It is not at all probable that any promoter would be willing to give up as much money as Johnson and Langford will surely demand." Tim McGrath said Johnson could ignore Langford owing to the fact that he had defeated him clearly already, Sam was black and the public wanted to see a white man regain the championship, and because Langford was no bigger than Ketchel and Burns, whom Johnson had dominated. The *Freeman* agreed that "the physical advantages of the champion over Langford are so great that the public would hardly concede the latter a chance."[686]

When Johnson was appearing at a New York vaudeville house, from the stage he made a speech saying that he was willing to fight Langford or anyone else. The police arrested Jack and charged him with attempting to violate the prize-fighting statute. At his arraignment, the local magistrate discharged him. "There is no violation here, and the police were wrong."[687]

Although Johnson was known for speeding, wearing nice clothes, and taunting opponents while inside the ring, the *Freeman* said that when in the presence of white men outside the ring, he conducted himself in an unassuming, gentlemanly manner, such that no one could take exception.[688]

On December 1, 1909 in New York, bidders for the Jeffries-Johnson fight included Hugh McIntosh, Tom McCarey, Ed Graney, John Gleason, Tex Rickard, and others. The bids were astronomical and unprecedented. George Lewis "Tex" Rickard of Ely, Nevada, who had promoted Gans-Nelson, and was allied with John Gleason, offered $20,000 up front as a guarantee, for a total cash purse of $101,000, plus the fighters would receive 66 2/3% of the motion picture rights. It was believed that the motion pictures would be worth a fortune, for the Britt-Nelson fight pictures earned a quarter of a million dollars.

Soon thereafter, Rickard claimed that he and Gleason had won the bid, though no official announcement would be made for a day, owing to New York's anti-prize-fight laws.[689]

On December 3, 1909 in Hoboken, New Jersey, articles of agreement were signed by Jeffries, Berger, Johnson, Little, Rickard, and Gleason, for a July 4, 1910 fight. The $101,000 purse allegedly would be split 75% to the

---

[685] *San Francisco Call*, November 14, 1909; *New York Sun*, December 5, 1909.
[686] *San Francisco Call*, November 28, 1909; *Freeman*, January 29, 1910.
[687] *Los Angeles Herald*, December 1, 1909.
[688] *Freeman*, November 27, 1909.
[689] *New York Sun, San Francisco Call, Los Angeles Herald*, December 2, 3, 1909.

winner ($75,750) and 25% to the loser ($25,250). The fighters each would have a 1/3 share of the film profits (2/3 total).⁶⁹⁰

Jeffries assured the public, stating,

> I came out of retirement because the public demanded it, and because, under the circumstances, I felt it my duty to regain the title. ... I will beat Johnson, and do it in much less time than any of the followers of the ring expect me to. You can rest assured that when the sun sets on July 4, 1910, a white man will be the champion pugilist of the world.⁶⁹¹

At year end, the *Freeman* said, "We should feel proud of our race from a sporting standpoint, because we have reached the top round in every line of sport that we have been permitted to take part in." "This should be a happy Christmas day for us, recollecting that we have been so much deeper down in the mire than other races on the globe, and now we are on the top round in the world of sport." Such successes had symbolic importance to the oppressed.

Jack Johnson had not seen his mother, Mrs. Tiny Johnson, for seven years, but they spent Christmas together in Chicago in the home that he had purchased for her to live, at 3344 Wabash avenue. Speaking of the upcoming fight, Jack's mother said, "Win that fight? Why, he'll knock that white man's head off." Also present were Johnson's "wife" Hattie, his sister and her children, brother, a few other relatives, and his manager. Jack gave his wife a set of diamond earrings.

The local colored aristocracy paid their respects to the champion, coming and going all day. "And those who don't believe that it is a fine thing to be a world's champion heavyweight ought to see the way that Jack Johnson is idolized by the colored population."⁶⁹²

Christmas was not a happy time for everyone. According to the *Chicago Defender*, in 1909, 325 black men and women had been lynched, shot, and burned at the stake for fun. 28,000 colored females had been victimized by mobs or rapists. Southern state governments had failed to protect blacks.⁶⁹³

---

⁶⁹⁰ *New York Tribune*, December 3, 1909; *New York Sun*, December 4, 1909. On December 11, 1909 in Paris, France, Joe Jeannette and Sam McVey fought to a 30-round draw in a rematch of their epic battle.
⁶⁹¹ *Richmond Planet*, December 18, 1909.
⁶⁹² *Freeman*, December 25, 1909, January 8, 1910.
⁶⁹³ *Chicago Defender*, January 1, 1910.

THE NEW YEAR DINNER

"Someone Overlooked – As Usual"
Chicago Defender, January 1, 1910

Chicago Defender, January 22, 1910

Jim Jeffries said, "I am certainly not coming back after four years of farm work to be beaten by a nigger, even if that nigger did beat Burns. You can bet your life on that."[694]

De Witt Van Court said the consensus of opinion was that Jeffries would defeat Johnson with ease. "In my opinion, Jeff will win inside of six rounds."[695]

Joe Gans said,

It is almost a positive fact that all the folks who refuse to give Johnson a chance with Jeffries simply figure through prejudice against the colored fighter. He can't hit, he always backs up, he hasn't got the punch and he is always stalling, are a few things that they charge to Johnson. Now, in my estimation, and you know that I have seen them all, I think that Johnson is one of the greatest fighters of the past twenty years.[696]

Johnson had a $1,500 a week theatrical engagement, which would continue until mid-April.

On January 20, 1910 in New York, Jack Johnson was arrested on a charge of assaulting a fellow black man named Norman Pinder. The event took place between 1 and 3 a.m. at Barron Wilkins' saloon at 253 West 35th street. Allegedly, Pinder offered him a drink, and Johnson said he wanted wine. Pinder said he could buy him one, but could not afford more. Johnson said he never drank anything else. Pinder replied, "You used to drink beer. I've seen you drink it – and out of a bucket too, with your face in the bucket like a horse." Johnson then struck him several times. When asked at police headquarters why he had done it, Johnson said, "Honest to God, Cap'n, I'm sorry I didn't hit him harder. He has been casting aspersions and insults on me for a long time and I just had to hit him." Apparently there was history between the two. George Little obtained a bail

---

[694] *Albany Advertiser*, January 8, 1910.
[695] *Los Angeles Herald*, January 16, 1910.
[696] *Freeman*, January 15, 1910.

bondsman. The champ said his real name was John Jackson, age 31, and he was a boxing instructor by occupation.[697]

Boxing noted that Jeffries' supporters liked to claim that Johnson had a yellow streak. "The man who could face with a calm, broad smile such hostile receptions as those which greeted him when he entered the ring to meet Burns and Ketchel, to say nothing of others, cannot be much of a coward."[698]

There were rumors that if Jeffries was on the verge of being beaten that his adherents either would throw in the sponge or do something to get him disqualified, rather than allow Johnson to score a clean knockout.

Jeffries insisted that Johnson would have to knock him out cold to win. "But that nigger never can win from me. I'll give him the worst pounding that a man ever received. ... I will demonstrate again the superiority of the white race." Jeff claimed he often held back in fights, afraid of maiming his opponents, but he would not do so with Johnson.

The Future Welfare of His People Forms a Part of the Stake.

Chicago Defender, February 5, 1910

Sam Langford's manager Joe Woodman said Langford could defeat any heavyweight in the world except Jeffries. He said Jeff would defeat Johnson, and did not even need to be half as good as he once was to do it.[699]

---

[697] *New York Sun, Washington Herald*, January 21, 1910.
[698] *Boxing, Freeman, Chicago Defender*, January 22, 1910.
[699] *Los Angeles Herald*, January 25, 29, 1910; *Seattle Star*, February 1, 1910.

World champion wrestler Frank Gotch had wrestled with Jeff, and was certain that Jeffries would defeat Johnson with ease. Jim Corbett agreed.[700]

An impressed observer who saw Jeffries exhibit on February 3 said,

> James J. Jeffries is going to give back the heavyweight championship to the white race. I am as confident of this, barring accidents of an unforeseen nature, as I am that the sun will rise tomorrow morning. I must confess that I am slightly prejudiced, racially, but with that in mind, I can see no one but Jeffries in the coming struggle for the pugilistic supremacy of the world.[701]

John L. Sullivan allegedly said Jeffries could not win unless Johnson laid down. "I don't care what Corbett says, his talk to me has the same weight as the ashes on a cigar. He couldn't punch a hole in a pound of butter."

Some speculated that the fight would be fixed for the white man to win, because if he did, the pictures would be worth a million dollars. If the black man won, whites might refuse to see the films. Hence, the feeling was that Johnson would be bribed to take a dive.[702]

The French were backing Jeffries to win. The English thought Johnson was the best bet. Americans liked Jeff.[703]

On February 8, 1910 in Los Angeles, Jim Flynn clearly won a 10-round no-decision bout against Sam Langford.[704]

In a letter to the editor of the *Freeman*, one man criticized Langford for challenging Johnson and talking about his ability to beat him, even though Langford knew he had no chance to win. "Every time one Negro gets a little prominence, along comes another, and instead of emulating his example, tries to assist the white man in tearing him down."

The *Freeman* warned Johnson that if he was not more careful about comporting himself with the law, he would wind up in prison. Jack also failed to realize his political importance, which could have an adverse impact on the black race, as well as himself. No one ever heard of Peter Jackson creating any scenes in a barroom. He lived decently and was a gentleman. Yet, when he fell off the map, "the white man silently rejoiced."

> Johnson is undoubtedly the recognized heavyweight champion of the world, and for that one reason the colored people have something to be proud of; aside from this, there's nothing to stand on your head about.
>
> The heavyweight championship of the world carries with it a great deal more than the mere title, especially if you take into consideration the amount of good or bad that can be done the race to which such a fighter belongs. The world generally knows every 'hook or crook' made by a champion, and for that reason the colored race is up

---

[700] *Seattle Star*, February 1, 1910.
[701] *Spokane Press*, February 4, 1910.
[702] *Richmond Planet*, February 5, 1910, *Freeman*, February 12, 1910.
[703] *Salt Lake Herald-Republican*, February 6, 1910.
[704] *Los Angeles Herald, San Francisco Call*, February 9, 1910.

against two great obstacles; First, the adverse feeling such a condition will naturally arouse; and second, the inability to control to any sensible degree the conduct and general deportment of such a 'crazy' champion. The white man has no real love for Mr. Johnson. ... Then why not stick with and try and be an honor and a credit to his own race. As a matter of fact, Johnson has shown no particular liking for the colored race since he has been heavyweight champion of the world, and this is shown conclusively in his recent mix-up with Norman Pinder, a little consumptive colored man of about ninety pounds, who had about as much chance in a battle with Johnson as a bedbug would have trying to kiss him during his favorite dream. ... The cold hand of the law is reaching out for Mr. Johnson in no uncertain terms, and it looks to take the leading role in his future conduct. Why shouldn't it, when the lives, liberty and happiness of over nine million Negroes are being antagonized and jeopardized by his folly? If you don't believe it, holler 'hurray for Jack Johnson' in the hearing of any group of white men, and see how much trouble you will have. Then when you get close enough to say 'howdy-do' to Mr. Johnson, let me know if he answers. ... That Jackson Johnson is a big, strong, burly, rough darkey, I'll admit, and being champion of the world he may feel that he has a perfect right to run over, beat up, ignore and otherwise make life miserable for others, but he should not forget the fact that Samson ruled the world with his strength, but his love for a woman got him killed. ... So, when you look back into Mr. Johnson's police record, you will agree with me that unless he puts a quietus to his wild methods, the strong hand of the law is apt to chain him down.

Johnson's assault case was before a New York grand jury:

That Mr. Johnson looks upon these conditions as a very huge joke is demonstrative of another phase of his ignorance. The grand jury is in duty bound to indict him, then he is up against a No. 1 district attorney, with twelve white men in the jury box. ... It's a 'pipe' that a colored man won't have any more chance of getting on that jury than Johnson will have beating it. And with twelve white men on a jury trying Johnson, all betting that Jeffries will lick him, while down deep within their hearts they are praying that Jeffries will kill him. Can you beat it?[705]

The grand jury indeed indicted Johnson with a charge of second degree assault on Norman Pinder. His bail was set at $2,500. Conviction carried a maximum sentence of 5 years, or a fine, or both.

This writer listed several legal issues which Johnson had become entangled with since his arrival back to America as champion:

---

[705] *Freeman*, February 12, 1910.

> On landing in New York City from Australia, after he had defeated Tommy Burns for the heavyweight championship of the world, he was arrested and charged with committing rape on a colored girl; was fined $250.
> May 21, 1909—Johnson's automobile seized by sheriff in Philadelphia on a writ of attachment in suit for board bill.
> May 22, 1909—Forced to settle a bill of $406 for nursing his brother.
> May 30, 1909—Arrested, charged with violating speed laws of Boston; was fined.
> June 2, 1909—Johnson pleaded guilty to violating speed regulations; was fined $5.
> June 9, 1909—Arrested in Boston in suit to collect old debt of $41; later smashed his auto in wild ride through city.
> July 16, 1909—While at Crown Point, Ind., had road race with auto; machine skidded; opponent's axle was broken; young white woman seriously hurt.
> August 5, 1909—Arrested in London, Ont., on telegram from chief of police of Woodstock, charged with exceeding speed limit; in wild ride ran down another auto and smashed it; was fined.
> October 21, 1909—In a parade in San Francisco, drove auto recklessly through the streets; arrested. On leaving San Francisco after his fight with Ketchel, his auto was attached for a debt of $180. The Overland Limited was held twenty minutes while Johnson was sought for debts he owed; refusing to pay, his auto was held.
> January 2, 1910—Jumped contract with Terre Haute theater; manager attached trunks; was arrested by police.
> January 4, 1910—Held up by constables and made to pay costs for jumping contract to show at Duquesne Garden, Pittsburg.
> January 14, 1910—Arrested in Boston, charged with assaulting taxi driver and breaking window in cab.
> January 20, 1910—Arrested in New York, charged with assault on another Negro (Norman Pinder), in Barron Wilkin's Cafe; held in $1,000 bail for grand jury.

Freeman, February 12, 1910

Several newspapers observed that in less than one year, Johnson had been arrested thirteen times. He alleged self-defense against Pinder. The thirteenth arrest came in Detroit, when Johnson's bull pup chewed the coat of a pedestrian and Jack was hailed into court. One newspaper said he had been sued for $20,000 in damages and had paid $800 in fines.[706]

Jim Jeffries opened as a 10 to 7 betting favorite over Johnson.[707]

C. E. Van Loan said Johnson loved to spend money. Jack was making up for all of the long, lean, hungry years. "Johnson never used a manager for anything, except to draw money from hm."[708]

The English publication, *Boxing*, discussed the uneasy feeling about the Jeffries fight, which disturbed the "complacent American mind." They feared the consequences if Jeffries lost.

> Well, then, as every American realized, things would be in a very parlous condition indeed. It was bad enough to have a negro strutting about as cock of the walk as it was, although he was only enabled to strut by virtue of his triumph over a little fellow – a game and clever fighter, but nevertheless a smallish man – in Tommy Burns.

---

[706] *Salt Lake Tribune*, February 20, 1910; *Salt Lake Herald-Republican*, March 5, 1910.
[707] *Call*, February 13, 1910.
[708] *Freeman*, February 19, 1910.

> But a victory over Jeffries, the chosen champion of the white race, has become a contingency almost too awful to contemplate. Should Johnson win, not only he, but all the coloured inhabitants of the United States would commence strutting at once. And this would be a serious state of affairs from every point of view.

Boxing admitted that from a racial viewpoint, it wanted to see the white man win. If Johnson lost, it accurately prophesized what would happen thereafter – the color line would be drawn more firmly than ever.

> Of one thing, however, we may rest assured. Should Johnson lose his title...the black man will have enjoyed his last tenure of the world's championship. He will never be given another chance.
>
> The first step which any future white holder will take will be to draw a most portentous and well-defined colour line. In fact, it would not be a very wild prophecy that this will be insisted upon by fight promoters, press, and white public alike.
>
> It may not show commendable pluck on the part of the white race, but there are numerous reasons for their adopting such a course.[709]

A *Freeman* writer said it was foolish to expect Johnson to be a Booker T. Washington or a paragon of culture and refinement. Regardless, the press had overblown Johnson's actions. "While he is in the limelight, his every act is noticed, purposely misconstrued and exaggerated. Jack is a really good fellow, never a bully, and his errors of deportment are more the caprices of an overgrown schoolboy than a hardened sinner."[710]

On March 17, 1910 in the Los Angeles area, Sam Langford avenged his loss to Jim Flynn, knocking him out in the 8th round.[711]

On March 18, Johnson was in yet another auto accident, a single car collision. Many wondered how long he could continue driving the way he did without being seriously injured or killed.

Former Jeffries trainer Tommy Ryan announced that he would assist Johnson with his training. He would give Jack tips about Jeff.[712]

A *Freeman* writer did not believe Johnson would throw the Jeffries fight. It meant too much to him personally, as well as to the black race. "We are with you, Jack, old boy. ... He has proven to the race that he is worthy of their race pride. ... The white race says that Jeff must win and that the whites must be supreme. But we say that the black man must win."[713]

On March 23, 1910, Johnson was in New York to stand trial for his assault charge upon Norman Pinder. None of the witnesses showed up, including Pinder. Nevertheless, showing his bias, the judge increased Johnson's bail to $5,000, which he could not pay, so he had to spend time in jail for half a day, locked up while bail money could be secured. The

---

[709] *Boxing*, February 19, 1910.
[710] *Freeman*, March 12, 1910.
[711] *Los Angeles Herald*, March 18, 1910.
[712] *Salt Lake Herald-Republican*, March 19, 1910.
[713] *Freeman*, March 19, 1910.

judge continued the case to the next day, with warrants for the arrest of the witnesses. However, it appeared that the charge would have to be dropped, which eventually it was.[714]

No fan of the black man, the *Los Angeles Herald* said the champ was disgracing himself. "Johnson seems to disregard all common decency by almost insisting upon open defiance of law and order everywhere he goes, and he constantly is getting into trouble with officers of the law." He loved to joy ride at high speeds. Right after being released from jail on the assault charge, he was served with a breach of contract suit in Chicago. Allegedly, he was losing supporters even amongst his own race.[715]

On March 31, 1910, Jack Johnson celebrated his 32nd birthday.

Los Angeles Herald, March 26, 1910

---

[714] *Salt Lake Herald-Republican*, March 24, 1910.
[715] *Los Angeles Herald*, March 26, 1910.

CHAPTER 34

A National Obsession

The press and public were so intrigued by the Jeffries-Johnson championship fight, dubbed "the fight of the century," such that for the next three months, from April to July 1910, the press issued daily reports on the two fighters' activities and training, as well as the thoughts, predictions, analysis, and expert opinions of those involved with the fight and the sport of boxing. The public eagerly read it all. No fight or sporting event ever had received such a huge amount of daily coverage, or for so many months in advance of the event. It further built an already hugely significant fight to epic proportions. Naturally, the racial relevance of the contest was omnipresent.

On April 5, 1910, Jim Jeffries arrived at his training camp at Rowardennan, Ben Lomond, California, in the Santa Cruz mountains. He would train there for the next few months.

Jeffries received a letter from a Brooklyn man who "deeply deplores the fact that the colored youths of the Church City have corralled the goats of all the white boys there. Mr. Harmon implores Mr. Jeffries to give Mr. Johnson a proper beating, in order that the youngsters of his neighborhood may enjoy peace and, incidentally, get the upper hand in the future." Jeff received daily letters of that nature from folks across the country, urging him to restore the championship to the white race.

Chicago Defender, **April 2, 1910**

Tommy Ryan backed out of his agreement to train Johnson, fearing that training the black man would make him very unpopular.

In Boston, Jack Johnson won his breach of contract suit with Alec McLean. The court held that the contract made four years ago was illegal, for a fight agreement was a felony and therefore could not be enforced.

Johnson had demanded a jury trial on his latest speeding charge in Chicago, and the jury acquitted him.[716]

Emeryville, just outside of Oakland, California, had been selected as the Jeffries-Johnson fight site.

The *Freeman* wrote of Johnson's racial significance:

> There is not a patriotic Negro in America today, no matter what his views may be in regard to the prize ring and its principals, who is not proud of the fact from the depths of his heart that one of his race reigns supreme in his vocation. ... Supremacy in one vocation begets supremacy in another. ... We hope that when the smoke of battle clears away, so to speak, that the question of supremacy between Caucasia and Ethiopia will have been settled from a gladiatorial standpoint on its merits, and the victory achieved on Ethiopia's side.[717]

On April 15, Jeffries celebrated his 35th birthday, but put in a full course of hard training and sparring nevertheless. Jeffries would spar with men such as Billy Papke, Jack Jeffries, Joe Choynski, Bob Armstrong, Sam Berger, and eventually former champion James J. Corbett.

Jim Corbett cast the usual aspersions on Johnson, saying he was flatfooted and had a yellow streak. He also said Johnson was just the colored champ, not the world champion. "Jeff is the champ, and he will be until he dies." Corbett said Jeff would knock out Johnson within 6 rounds.

Corbett was going to spar with and train Jeffries in part because "I don't want to hear the people say, 'We have a colored champion.'"[718]

On April 21, 8,000 people gathered at the train station to see Johnson leave Chicago, heading west to give exhibitions in various cities. The *Chicago Defender's* entire staff was on hand to bid farewell to their hero.[719]

Johnson said Tommy Burns had said many unkind things about him, and when he got him in the ring he remembered them all. "Every time I forced him to his corner I would ask him if he remembered when he had made some certain statement and I followed it up with one of my best blows." Johnson said Jeffries had said many harsh things too, and on the day of their battle, he would make him atone as well.[720]

On April 27, 1910 in Philadelphia, Sam Langford and Stanley Ketchel fought to a 6-round no-decision. A poll of newsmen on scene had it 7 for Langford, 4 for Ketchel, and 2 votes for a draw. Even those who said Langford won said he only had a slight advantage and a draw would have been a fair decision as well. Some said if that was the best Langford could do, then "he is a vastly overrated fighter."[721]

---

[716] *San Francisco Call, Spokane Press*, April 6, 1910; *Richmond Planet*, April 9, 1910.
[717] *Freeman*, April 9, 1910.
[718] *Reno Evening Gazette, Los Angeles Herald*, April 17, 1910.
[719] *Chicago Defender*, April 23, 1910.
[720] *Los Angeles Herald*, April 24, 1910.
[721] *Reno Evening Gazette*, April 28, 1910; *Washington Times*, April 28, 1910.

When Johnson arrived at the Los Angeles train station on April 28, five-hundred cheering blacks greeted him.[722]

The parties argued about the choice of referee. Johnson said he had to protect himself because of his color. Berger accused Johnson of using his race as a stall tactic to get the best of it. Berger did not want Johnson's selections of Jack Welsh or Eddie Graney, though few could understand why. Both had good reputations, were white, and were known for honesty and integrity. Johnson said he could name fifty men who would be suitable to himself. Berger said perhaps one of them would be agreeable. Jack replied: "I know that none of them will suit you." Berger: "Well, why not?" Johnson: "Because they are all smokes."[723]

The *Freeman* wrote, "Jack, please show this haughty world that color don't make the man."[724]

Boxing did not believe rumors that the fight might be fixed. Even if it was fixed, neither could trust the other, and the fight meant too much to both. "There is far too much at stake and there are far too many prejudices concerned for any 'frame-up' to come within the bounds of possibility."[725]

Sig Hart, Jack Johnson, George Little, Sam Berger, Tex Rickard, Jack Gleason

The parties met again on May 16 to address the referee issue. Johnson wanted a fair man, saying, "There is not a man that lives that would dare to give Jeff the worst end of the contest. The white people would hang him to a tree. It would be very easy for any one to give me the worst end of this contest on account of my color." Johnson blamed the Marvin Hart loss on the referee. Berger called Johnson a racial slur, and Johnson called him an "educated dog." Eventually, after they settled down, Berger asked promoter

---

[722] *Spokane Press*, April 28, 1910.
[723] *San Francisco Call, Reno Evening Gazette*, May 5, 1910.
[724] *Freeman*, May 14, 1910.
[725] *Boxing*, May 14, 1910.

Tex Rickard if he would referee. Rickard said, "Yes." Berger said that suited him. Johnson said, "All right," and the debate was over. As was the case with Johnson-Burns, the promoter would referee the fight.[726]

Joe Choynski, Sam Berger, James Jeffries, Farmer Burns

Jeffries was the betting favorite in part because of race prejudice. Whites simply could not believe that the vaunted representative of their superiority could be defeated by a black man. Many whites believed Johnson would reveal the stereotypical black trait of cowardice when opposed to a man like Jeffries. Many overlooked the top black opposition that Johnson had met; only seeing white.[727]

A good percentage of observers of Johnson's training at his Seal Rock, California camp on May 18 were women, including white women.

While he was in Chicago, California Governor James Gillett said he did not foresee any reason why the big fight could not be held in California. "The law authorizes the contest to take place and there is nobody to prevent it. I haven't the slightest doubt the club can get a permit in San Francisco without any trouble." He also said,

> The fight seems to be of the biggest national interest ... It will bring hundreds of persons to the coast and leave thousands of dollars in San Francisco. ... To the people of the United States, at least, it is a bigger thing than the passage or defeat of important legislation, Roosevelt's triumphal tour, or even the approach of the comet.[728]

After Rickard's discussion with local San Francisco politicians, the local supervisors and police commission approved the bout. However, the religious community was applying political pressure to stop the fight.[729]

A *Freeman* poet wrote of Jack Johnson's symbolic value and ability to uplift black folks' spirits, saying, "Dear people, take it from me: I'm no fighter and don't want to be; if both were white I wouldn't care a minute. But since our race is represented, we all would like very much to shout: 'Hooray! Jack has knocked Jeffries out!'" The *Chicago Defender* said, "While pugilism does not compare favorably with the intellectual forces of mankind, yet, the same pluck, patience, perseverance and stick-to-itiveness characterized by the colored champion is essential to success in all vocations in life." Hence, "we do hope as a loyal race" that Johnson would

---

[726] *San Francisco Evening Post*, May 16, 1910; *San Francisco Call*, May 17, 1910.
[727] *San Francisco Call*, May 15, 1910.
[728] *San Francisco Call*, May 19, 1910.
[729] *Reno Evening Gazette*, May 19, 20, 1910.

win. The *Defender* said that never before in pugilism's history had the public been aroused to such a pitch of excitement.[730]

In his well-attended exhibitions, the "hope of the white race" was introduced as "A Native Son," "the California Wonder," and "the undefeated champion of the world, James Jeffries." He was received with wild enthusiasm. Jeffries was popular in part because Johnson's claim to the title was "savagely resented by the Caucasians who follow the fighting game." Impressed and excited fans were certain that Jeff would slaughter Johnson.[731]

The *Chicago Defender* found all of the white Christian clergy and religious organizations' fight-opposition to be amusing and hypocritical. They had set "a new Christ-like mark in their color line," working overtime in an endeavor to prohibit the match. These religious folks even were taking up the matter with the U.S. President. The real "national disgrace," as these organizations liked to call the fight, was the fact that "supposed Christians faint at the sight of prize fights, but laud the raping of colored girls and lynchings. ... If this is Christ, excuse me."

> Why, sure these gentlemen object to the national disgrace of a white and black man struggling for physical supremacy as man to man, etc. I wonder if these same men have stopped to consider how hypocritical their present efforts seem to the fair-minded public, who cannot help but wonder if these gentlemen are really sincere from a Christian standpoint ... [W]ith all of the lynchings and mob violence that is prevalent in this land of supposed freedom, you have never heard or read of a Christian body of white ministers even raising their voices in their annual conferences, much less appealing to the authorities to put a stop to it. But possibly they reason this way: That lynchings are perpetrated by a mob against one man, and as the motto of our beloved country is 'In Union There is Strength,' it is no national disgrace. But in the case of Messrs. Johnson-Jeffries, it is man against man, and as a Negro has an equal chance, that in itself, in their opinion, is enough to constitute a national disgrace. Now I may be wrong, but it seems to me that if this same 'Christian' body would direct their combined efforts to abolish Jim Crow cars and advocate the enforcement of the fourteenth and fifteenth amendments, along with the abolishment of mob violence, they would be following a

---

[730] *Freeman, Chicago Defender*, May 21, 1910.
[731] *San Francisco Call, San Francisco Evening Post*, May 28, 1910.

course more in keeping with the Christian consistency that we all expect to see in one who wears the cloth. But for them to ignore these vital questions that affect the moral and Christian welfare of seventy-five millions of people, and concentrate their influence upon an incident that only affects a few, is, in my opinion, the very zenith of that most despicable of curses known as hypocrisy. Wake up, my white brethren, and show to us that your hearts are right. ... [A]s this is the first time that a black man and a white man have met as the pick of their respective races in a contest of this kind, on behalf of the Negroes of this and other countries may Jack succeed in knocking Jim's block off, just to make it a good national disgrace.[732]

True to the traditions of his races Jack Johnson holding a prize chicken about to be transformed into pie for the champion's dinner

When Johnson was doing some preliminary calisthenics and exercises, an impatient spectator of his training shouted, "Oh, put on the gloves. Quit your kidding." Johnson grinned and won the house when he invited him to come up and do a little boxing with him. There was no further disturbance. Jack eventually sparred 8 rounds, and afterwards said, "Well, I just hope that Jeffries is as good as they say he is. I want to beat him at his best. ... I want credit should I beat him." Jack said he would have Jeff down on the canvas for the first time in his career within 15 rounds.[733]

Jim Corbett's comment that Johnson had a "yellow streak" roused Jack's ire. He said no one had been able to find it, if he had one. Jack noted that against Tom Sharkey, Corbett hollered to the police to help him. When they fought again, after taking a good licking, his second jumped into the ring "by a prearranged plan to again save this coward, Corbett." Johnson said Corbett was the one with a yellow streak.[734]

The *Call* claimed the "big smoke" was "lazy" and lacked ginger in his work. Many believed he was not training hard or often enough.[735]

While in Chicago, California Governor James Gillett shockingly said the Jeffries-Johnson fight was a "frame-up" for Jeffries to win. He further said, "All fights are fakes" to fool fools, and this fight was just a scheme to make a lot of money:

> Anybody with the least bit of sense knows that the whites are not going to allow Johnson or any other negro to win the world's championship. ... Johnson is no fool. He knows he would have to whip every white man at the ringside in order to win. ...

---

[732] *Chicago Defender*, May 28, 1910.
[733] *Reno Evening Gazette, San Francisco Call, San Francisco Evening Post*, May 30, 1910.
[734] *San Francisco Call*, June 1, 1910.
[735] *Los Angeles Herald*, May 22, 1910; *Call, Chronicle, Bulletin*, June 2, 1910.

There was no chance to get Jeffries back into the ring until he had been assured that he would win. ...

I would like to interfere if I could, but the only thing that would justify my interference is a riot. I do not think that will occur.

When Jeffries wins, every white man in the country will be told that a white man has demonstrated his physical superiority over a negro and everyone who has no sense will rejoice in the victory.

Gillett also said he would stop the fight if he could, but "all sorts of frauds are allowed that nobody has the power to stop."[736]

Gillett's interview caused a storm of comment, and increased suspicions about the fight's genuineness. The next day, Governor Gillett denied making such statements. Others reported that Gillett admitted to making the statements, but said he merely was expressing his own private personal views, and did not intend his words to be used for publcation.

Most commentators believed the fight would be genuine, for Johnson had too much pride to take a dive. They thought the governor did not know what he was talking about, and either was seeking publicity or "talking through his hat." His comments were given little weight, particularly since previously he had said that he knew nothing about the fight game.

An insulted Jeffries said he never had been involved in a fake in his life.

Johnson squares off with George Cotton; with George Little at center

On June 3, when Johnson exhibited at the Dreamland rink, some spectators hissed and verbally abused the champion. A smiling Johnson said, "I got their money, anyhow, so let 'em holler."

In a speech, Johnson said that when the crowd congregated at the fight, he hoped that "they will see," and then someone in the gallery immediately hollered "a nigger funeral," and then laughter followed, "two well trained men, both in the very best physical condition, and that the battle will be between man and man and may the best man win." Applause followed.

---

[736] *San Francisco Bulletin*, June 2, 1910.

The *Evening Post* said no matter what private thoughts one had about Johnson, it was unsportsmanlike and reflected ill-breeding to treat him unfairly and indecently with jeers, hisses, and interruptions.

Bill Delaney, who once had been a trainer/manager for both Corbett and Jeffries, agreed to work with Johnson. New Yorkers who wanted to see Jeff win offered Delaney $10,000 to train Jeffries instead. Delaney replied that under no circumstances would he work with him. "I quit Jeffries for welching on a gambling debt and running out on the Squires match. … From a white man's standpoint I admire the stand you take – but I could not conscientiously have any more dealings with James J. Jeffries."[737]

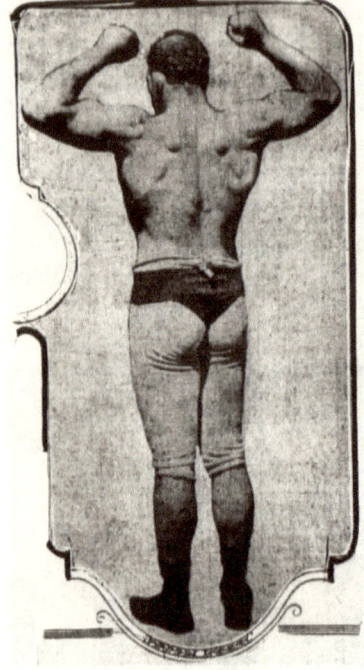

The *Call* said the retired champion certainly was a wonder. Watching him work provided ample evidence that he still was a great fighter.[738]

Governor Gillett declared that he would not interfere with the fight, no matter how many petitions he received. He said the remark he made the other day was a casual one, not meant to be taken seriously.

News out of the Johnson camp was that Jack had fired George Little as his manager. However, Little had a contract to earn 25% of the champ's profits, which he intended to enforce. He also said he helped pay Johnson's bills, and was owed money.[739]

In Chicago, a $10,000 bet was made on Jeffries, with the "hope of the white race" the odds favorite at 6 to 10.[740]

The majority of New Yorkers were picking Jeffries to win with ease. Tom O'Rourke's opinion was common: "If Jeff is half way right he ought to beat the nigger good and proper."[741]

The *New York Age* said,

> There is going to be thousands of dollars placed on the Johnson-Jeffries fight on purely sentimental grounds, and the money will not be bet and lost by Negroes, either. Really, when you look at the pugilistic situation void of racial prejudice and only from a true sportsman's standpoint, it looks as if Jack Johnson is the one best bet.

---

[737] *San Francisco Call, Reno Evening Gazette, Chronicle, San Francisco Bulletin, San Francisco Evening Post*, June 4, 1910. Jeffries had failed to pay a gambling debt accrued in Reno when he was there to referee the Hart-Root fight back in 1905. Delaney claimed that Jeff had agreed to fight Squires back in 1907, but Jeff said he never agreed to terms, for the financial inducements were insufficient.

[738] *San Francisco Call, San Francisco Chronicle*, June 5, 1910.

[739] *San Francisco Bulletin, San Francisco Examiner, San Francisco Call*, June 6, 1910.

[740] *San Francisco Call*, June 8, 1910; *Reno Evening Gazette*, June 8, 1910.

[741] *San Francisco Chronicle*, June 9, 1910.

However, whites were not only betting on Jeffries, they were so confident in him and betting so heavily that they were giving odds, making him the betting favorite. Hence, blacks could make a lot of money by betting on Johnson, the underdog, if he won.[742]

Jim Corbett said white folk could put their minds at ease:

> The call of the white race has brought Jeffries out of retirement and believe me, if the white population of the United States knows what a game, determined effort this man Jeffries has made to get back into condition to make good and what a terrific grind he has put himself through to attain his present splendid shape, he'd be a popular hero on the strength of that alone.[743]

Johnson was sparring with Al Kaufman, Kid Cotton, and Dave Mills.

After sparring with Jeffries on June 10, Jim Corbett said, "The big fellow has got the old punch and everything else. Honestly, he is a marvel." The *Examiner's* C. E. Van Loan said, "The hope of the white race worked impressively today, and there was not a spectator in the audience who did not think he was fit."

Jeffries said he never felt better, and the black fellow would jump with fright. "I do not think it will last ten rounds. The minute I get one good chance at that fellow I am going to pop him and he will go down for the count." If defeated, he would offer no excuses; and furthermore, would be satisfied that Johnson could have beaten him at any time during his career.

One writer favoring Jeffries said blacks were followers more than leaders, and whites had better brains. Others questioned Jack's courage.[744]

Al Kaufman said, "Johnson is a wonderful fighter. ... I look to see him beat Jeffries, and I don't think that the retired champion will be able to lay a

---

[742] *New York Age*, June 9, 1910.
[743] *San Francisco Bulletin*, June 10, 1910.
[744] *San Francisco Call, Examiner, Bulletin, Evening Post, Freeman*, June 11, 1910.

glove on the negro." Eddie Graney said of Johnson, "Don't let anybody talk you into thinking that he is loafing on the job."[745]

Stanley Ketchel said Johnson was one of the greatest fighters ever. Even if Jeff was able to come back, he still could not beat Johnson.[746]

Many gamblers believed Johnson would show a yellow streak after he realized that Jeff was too strong, powerful, determined, and impervious to being hurt. Sam Berger bet $1,000 on Jeff, the favorite, at 7 to 10 odds.[747]

William T. Rock, Vitagraph company president and representative for several other film companies, offered $150,000 total to Johnson, Jeffries, Rickard, and Gleason to purchase the moving picture rights. Johnson sold his rights for $50,000. Jack received his money and was satisfied, saying, "Some of my friends tell me that I can make more by taking a chance, but I am satisfied to get this money outright. Then there will be no chance to mix me up in any suits. The ready cash looks good." It did not matter whether the fight lasted 1 round or 45, because the picture men were taking all of the risks. "They can't say now that I am fighting for the films, because I have sold my interest in them." Rock said that within a week after the fight, up to 8,000 theatres would show the films in the U.S., Canada, and Europe.[748]

Despite previous promises, in mid-June, California Governor James Gillett buckled under to the religious community's anti-fight political pressure. He declared that boxing was illegal, and sent a letter to the attorney general instructing him to take steps to prevent all boxing contests.

Upon hearing about the governor's decision, Jeffries responded, "I can't believe it. I did not think that the governor would do that after he has repeatedly said he would not interfere." A politician failing to be a man of his word? Never heard of such a thing.

Tex Rickard was quite upset, and criticized the governor's "11th hour" pronouncement, saying, "I have already expended $25,000. ... Why Governor Gillett should wait until this late day in declaring that he would stop the fight, particularly in view of his accredited statements in the past that under no circumstances would he interfere, is inconceivable."

Rickard had spent a great deal of money in reliance upon the governor's prior representations, having constructed a special arena for the fight. San Francisco businessmen, particularly hotel owners, were not happy about the governor's new position either. Big fights boosted the local economy.[749]

---

[745] *San Francisco Call, Chronicle, Examiner*, June 12, 1910.
[746] *Reno Evening Gazette, San Francisco Call, Bulletin, Evening Post*, June 13, 1910.
[747] *San Francisco Call, Chronicle, Examiner, Bulletin*, June 14, 1910.
[748] *San Francisco Call, Reno Evening Gazette*, June 15, 1910.
[749] *Reno Evening Gazette*, June 15, 1910.

Governor Gillett said boxing was illegal, corrupted morals, was offensive to the citizenry, and should be abated as a nuisance. His decision applied equally to the upcoming Langford-Kaufman fight. The governor said they would be arrested if they fought. Cynics might say it was no surprise that the governor was preventing two high-profile mixed-race bouts.

San Francisco's mayor criticized Gillett's timing, saying if he had informed everyone a couple months ago that he would prevent the fight, they would have avoided a great expenditure of money.[750]

Governor Gillett sent two companies of the California state militia to San Francisco to ensure that the scheduled Langford-Kaufman fight did not take place. He said California had been disgraced long enough and the intolerable outrage would not be allowed. Any man who attempted to stage a boxing bout would have to fight the State of California first. So the governor was willing to use violence to prevent a violent sport.[751]

The black-owned *New York Age* noted, "An unsportsmanlike attempt of some writers to inject racial prejudice in the coming championship contest…has been severely criticized by a number of fighters who well know that the question of color should not figure in the big fight." Some newspapers, particularly black-owned, were critical of this aspect of the reporting. The *Cincinnati Commercial Tribune* wrote,

> A number of the daily newspapers both in the North and the South are working themselves into a terrible state of excitement over the possible consequences of the defeat of Jeffries by Johnson…. They refer to it as a struggle between the champions of the Negro and Caucasian races.
>
> Now this is in no wise a struggle for supremacy between representative champions of the two races. It is utterly foolish to attempt to surround the fight with any sentimental halo of race supremacy. …
>
> The only danger of any racial difficulty arising from this battle comes from the ill advised and unthinking people and papers who try to make a struggle between two bruisers…assume the guise of a battle for race supremacy. Such characterization of the fight will make the ignorant members of both races have an exaggerated idea of the importance of its result.

Likewise, the *New York American* was concerned by the pervasive racial overtones and hype surrounding the fight, and feared violence.

> In many quarters there has been an evident desire to stir up a racial prejudice in the coming battle. … Some have even gone so far as to claim that the Negroes throughout the country would become unbearable in the event of Johnson winning and race riots would surely result. …

---

[750] *San Francisco Call, Chronicle, Reno Evening Gazette,* June 16, 17, 1910; *Freeman,* June 25, 1910.
[751] *San Francisco Bulletin,* June 17, 1910.

This writer noted that several black men had won championships and defeated white fighters, and no race riots had resulted. "The big affair is a contest between men, not race of men." However, not everyone agreed. For many, this fight was about race.[752]

The *Freeman* said "the object is to have the white man win if there's any way to do it. It is squarely a case of Negro versus white man in the matter of brawn and nothing will be undone to make for the supremacy of the white man." It believed the odds were designed to boost Jeffries and reduce Johnson's courage and his friends' faith.[753]

On June 21, Tex Rickard confirmed the fight would be held in Reno, Nevada, which had promised to construct a special arena, furnish the site, and pay the $1,000 state license fee. Nevada was a sparsely settled region, and the fight would be good for the economy. Boxing definitely was legal in Nevada, so it was anticipated that Nevada Governor Denver S. Dickerson would not do anything to prevent the fight. Locals were excited.[754]

However, Johnson ran up against the color line even in Reno. The owner of the Laughton Springs resort said he would not allow him to train there. "The color line has always been drawn tight in Reno. Old-timers relate that a black face was never seen here in the early days and up to four years ago a colored hotel porter was the only negro in the city."

Johnson's new manager Tom Flanagan struggled to find a place that would accept the world champion. He finally secured a roadhouse three to four miles southwest of Reno, known as Rick's resort. "Certain persons interested in it were against letting it out to a colored man."[755]

On June 21, John L. Sullivan watched Johnson train, and was impressed. Sullivan and Johnson met and shook hands. Sullivan said he still was uncertain about his choice in the fight, and previously published reports of his opinions were false.

Battling Nelson said that when scouting a bout, one had to cast aside sentiment, race prejudice, and personal feelings. Johnson was a real fighter, and "Jeffries never did care much about boxing him at any time, and I doubt if it was altogether because of his color." Even at his best, Jeffries "would have the time of his life to defeat the negro."

---

[752] *New York Age*, June 16, 1910.
[753] *Freeman*, June 18, 1910.
[754] *Reno Evening Gazette, Nevada State Journal*, June 21, 1910.
[755] *Bulletin*, June 20, 21, 1910; *Call*, June 21, 1910.

Terry McGovern said Jeffries would defeat Johnson decisively. "Jeffries has an awful wallop. If he lands it in true style he'll cave in Jack's ribs."[756]

Bill Delaney said,

> I know Jeffries well and know that he is now and always has been afraid of Johnson. The mention of Johnson's name sends cold shivers up and down Mr. Jeffries' spine. He never wanted any of Johnson's game. When I was with Jeffries merely mentioning the black man's name was like casting a pail of cold water in Jeffries' face. ... I believe honestly that Johnson, as good as he is today, could lick Jeffries the best day he ever saw. Make no mistake about it, this Johnson is one great fighter. He is one of the cleverest big men the ring has ever seen.[757]

On June 22, when Jeffries arrived in Reno, the city's entire population greeted him at the train station, giving him the greatest welcome ever afforded to anyone who ever visited, including U.S. presidents. Jeffries was the "wonder of the age, the most important man who had ever found his way into the Sagebrush state." Tex Rickard and the mayor greeted him.

PHOTOGRAPH OF IMMENSE CROWD THAT GREETED JEFFRIES AT RENO STATION. TAKEN BY 'EXAMINER' STAFF PHOTOGRAPHER—ARROW INDICATES JEFFRIES AND TEX RICKARD

On June 22 in San Francisco, once again Jack Johnson was arrested for speeding. The officer claimed he saw Johnson speeding at about 45-miles per hour and ordered him to stop, but he did not. He went to Jack's hotel and attempted to place him under arrest. Initially, Johnson refused to be arrested. The officer then went and got a couple other officers. Jack locked the door of his room. When they returned, the police broke the door in and seized Johnson, who resisted their efforts until Delaney advised him to allow the law to take its course. Jack unsuccessfully attempted to convince them to let him go, given that he was leaving town the next day. When the police chief greeted him, he said, "Arrested again?" Johnson replied, "Yep, but it took three of them."

Johnson paid $10 bail and was released. "Being arrested has become such a common thing with Johnson that his admirers are not alarmed when they hear that their idol has been taken before a magistrate. He seems to thrive on this kind of recreation." Some thought Johnson would love Nevada, given that there were no speed laws.

---

[756] *San Francisco Examiner*, June 22, 23, 1910.
[757] *New York Age*, June 23, 1910.

The *Call* said Johnson was a 10 to 6 underdog in part because of the "common feeling that the powers in control – human and otherwise – will not allow the black man to win over the pride of the white race."

Johnson said, "Many sports seem to think that I can not take a punch. They say I am not game. ... I am glad I am meeting a big, strong man like Jeffries, because it will give me a chance to show the public what I can do."

Johnson settled with George Little for $16,000.

In Reno, nearly everyone faithfully supported Jeffries. "It's Jim all the time. This goes for them all. They would fire Governor Dickerson tomorrow and give the job to Jim if he only put it up to them."

Nevada Governor Denver Dickerson promised that he would not stop the bout, for boxing was legal, and he believed the fight was legitimate.[758]

Jeff trained in Reno for the first time on June 23. "They were all unanimous in their belief that the white man's only hope will bring back the championship."

When John L. Sullivan showed up at Jeff's training camp, Jim Corbett barred him and had the gate closed, saying that Sullivan had knocked Jeff and the fight. Sullivan denied it.

When Johnson did not show up in court to answer the recent speeding charge, the judge declared his $10 bail forfeited and asked the policeman if he wanted a bench warrant to be issued for Johnson's arrest. The officer replied, "No, I do not think that will be necessary. I think that will be enough." The judge agreed. Johnson had taken a train to Reno.

Already local Reno hotels were packed. Gambling joints and restaurants were thriving.[759]

Johnson told *Boxing*:

> I have been doing quite a lot of thinking about this fight. I could see it away off as soon as I had beaten Tommy Burns out in Sydney, just because I left dead certain that you white men wouldn't like to see me riding around as champion; and there wasn't any other man you could possibly pick but Jeffries with anything like a chance of knocking me out of the championship.[760]

Johnson told the *Afro American Ledger*:

> Now…fighting is a simple matter of business with me. I'm in the game for what I can make out of it. … Of course I'm proud of being the first Negro that has held the world's heavyweight championship. It's only human nature that I should be. … Where do some of these dopesters get the hunch from that I'm a chicken compared to him?[761]

In Reno, Jeff was the favorite at 10 to 6 odds. One writer said Johnson was up against the sentiment of the whole white race.

---

[758] *San Francisco Call, Chronicle, Nevada State Journal, San Francisco Examiner*, June 23, 1910.
[759] *San Francisco Call, Nevada State Journal*, June 24, 1910.
[760] *Boxing*, June 25, 1910.
[761] *Afro American Ledger*, June 25, 1910.

UNCLE TOM'S CABIN — AS IT WILL HAVE TO BE PLAYED IF JOHNSON WINS.

UNCLE TOM (to Simon Legree).—DID AH HEAH YO' SAY, WHITE MAN, DAT YO' DONE OWN ME, BODY AN' SOUL? HUH?

Puck, June 22, 1910

JEFF AND CORBETT TALKING IN RENO RING—JEFF PUNCHING THE BAG BEFORE BIG CROWD

Rickard and Jeffries sold their motion picture rights to William Rock for $100,000 total. Jeff would receive 2/3 ($66,666.66) and Rickard 1/3 ($33,333.33).

On June 24 in Reno, 5,000 folks greeted Jack Johnson when his train arrived.[762]

One observer of both Jeffries and Johnson's training said,

> Jeff is tremendous. ... The white race have got the best man they could get to represent them in the battle. As for Johnson, he is the finest specimen of his race I ever saw. ... The colored race has in this man a real representative, a man that will be very hard to lick, for he knows if he can win this fight he will do more to make the white man respect his color than a thousand Booker Washingtons.

William Muldoon spoke about the great pressure that Jeff was under:

> No man ever stepped into a prize ring with greater responsibilities, in the fact that he will represent the white against the black race. He fully appreciates the importance of his undertaking ... He knows the entire world has their eyes upon him, expecting him as the white man, to make good. It is an awful responsibility for any one man.

Jack London said Johnson and Jeffries were vastly different types. Johnson was "happy-go-lucky in temperament, as light and carefree as a child. He is easily amused. He lives more in the moment, and joy and sorrow are swift passing moods with him." Jeffries was "more primitive, more ferocious, more terror inspiring." He was like a warrior from thousands of years ago; a perfect type of physical manhood. London felt that the fight did not mean to Johnson what it meant to Jeffries.

> If Johnson loses the fight, he won't be worried much. If Jeff loses, it will almost break his heart. Under that dark and rather somber seriousness that characterizes him, there is a race pride of which he is intensely self-conscious. Then, too, there is the pride in himself as a man and as a subduer of men. ... Of one thing I am certain the loss of any half dozen of his other fights would be less of a blow to Jeff than the loss of this coming fight with Johnson.[763]

---

[762] *San Francisco Call, Examiner, Bulletin, Nevada State Journal,* June 25, 1910.
[763] *Reno Evening Gazette, San Francisco Evening Post, San Francisco Chronicle,* June 25, 1910.

On June 25, the Sullivan-Corbett feud came to an end. At Jeff's request, Sullivan visited the camp again, and when John L. met Corbett, they shook hands and engaged in cordial conversation. Jeff told Sullivan that he was willing to take his word that John L. had not knocked him or the contest.[764]

The *Call* said the majority of sports were picking Jeffries to win. One man predicting a Jeffries victory said, "I'll be there to assist at the autopsy." A real estate man who rented to blacks said, "If Johnson wins I will have to raise my rents to get even." The confident Tom Corbett said, "Jeffries will win. ... I look for him to bring the heavy weight championship back to the white race. I am going to bet everything I have on him." Another man said, "I can see nothing to it, only a badly frightened negro, fighting on the defensive, trying to withstand the rushes of the greatest heavyweight punisher that ever climbed into a ring. I can not see anything to it but a white celebration." Sam Langford said, "I think that I can beat Johnson and I know that I can't beat Jeffries, so that's my answer. Johnson is not there with the heart to trim that great, big white man." Joe Jeannette predicted a Jeffries victory within 10 rounds. James J. Corbett said, "I look to see a big, clever, defensive coon trying to keep out of the way of the greatest fighting machine that ever stepped into a 24 foot ring."

Most of those who had been skeptical about Jeffries' ability to come back had been convinced otherwise. Others said he did not need to come all the way back to lick Johnson, he was so good. Yet, one color-line advocate said, "Any white man who fights a negro ought to lose."[765]

The majority of those who saw Johnson train on June 26 said he looked inert, sluggish, tired, disinterested, and lacking vim and ginger. They said he was a careless worker. Others said Johnson picked off blows with such ease that he appeared to be loafing, and he fought the same way. T. P. Magilligan said Johnson's apparent carelessness and indifference actually was studied defense. "His simplicity is more complex than the most complex system." Jack Root said Johnson's work was done so easily and with such little effort that it appeared slow and slovenly. "Johnson's work is deceptive." He described Jack as a "big, good-natured darkey out for a frolic." He always wore a smile, and had a light-hearted demeanor.

Battling Nelson said the general public did not give Johnson due credit. They liked to say he was a big black faker, quitter, no good, not game, and would lie down. It was true that Jack had pulled and stalled in several fights, but never had he quit or laid down. Many liked to cite the Hart fight, but Nelson, who was at the fight, said Johnson was robbed.

---

[764] *San Francisco Chronicle, Call, Nevada State Journal,* June 26, 1910.
[765] *Call,* June 26, 1910.

Nelson said the claims about colored fighters - that they lacked gameness, would not take punishment and fight back, would run away and quit - were false. He said just as many white fighters were quitters as black fighters. The public and so-called experts previously had claimed incorrectly that Johnson would quit against Burns. "The general public at large seems to think that we should not have any negro champions in their respective classes because this is a white man's country – and I agree with them." However, that was not clouding Nelson's judgment when scouting the bout.

Nelson did not think it made sense for Jeffries to take the fight. If he lost, "a white man would stand a fat chance of walking down Market street, or any other one, without being humiliated, or otherwise roughly treated, if he passed by any of Johnson's race."[766]

Reno police planned to have plenty of law enforcement present, both plain clothes and uniformed, to maintain order. Local police captain Cox declared that the first fellow to shout "Kill the Nigger" would be hurled out of the arena. No alcohol would be allowed. Quite frankly, the ticket prices were high enough such that the rough element would be minimized.[767]

Johnson said he was confident that the spectators would give him a square deal, regardless of his color, and just see them as two boxers.

After training, for relaxation, Jack played bass violin, cello, and piano.

In terms of personality, Muldoon said Jeffries was a silent, serious, introverted iron man who avoided attention and found his huge popularity and adulation annoying. He preferred private training. He trained how and when he liked, rarely letting anyone know when he would work, and at times he would vary his schedule based on how he felt, which upset fans and reporters who wanted to see him. Jeff said he was training for a fight, not running a three-ring circus. He did nothing for show, and wanted to be left alone. He had a brusque way of speaking. Jeffries was "merely himself, with the strength of character to be himself." He felt no impulse to be pals with everyone he met, "and he is honest enough not to simulate a feeling he does not possess. All the same, it is darned hard on the public."

With Johnson it was just the opposite. Jack liked training before crowds. He was care-free, happy, personable, and reveled in and craved attention. He was jealous of the fact that the fans and reporters were more interested in seeing Jeff than him, and was upset when they did not come out to his camp. He enjoyed talking with and entertaining reporters, and liked performing for them. This actually caused many reporters to take a liking to him, for Jack was affable, congenial, and accommodating.

> Nobody was ever more gregarious than he, ever happier to greet old friends and make new ones. He likes crowds, thrives upon them, and in turn does his best to give them a good time. Let him decide on a certain day that he is not going to spar, and then inform him that 200 persons have journeyed all the way out to his camp to see him work,

---

[766] *San Francisco Evening Post,* June 27, 1910.
[767] *San Francisco Call,* June 27, 1910.

depend upon it, Johnson simply couldn't let them go away disappointed.

Conversely, if Jeff had decided not to spar or work, then he would not do so even if a massive crowd was on hand to see him.[768]

Famous authors and boxers from all over the country and world had flocked into Reno, which was seeing a celebrity a minute. Never before in boxing's history had such a galaxy of boxing stars and famous men been congregated for a fistic show. Over 150 writers were in town.

Lou Houseman offered to bet $10,000 that Johnson would not last 7 rounds.

Jack London said boxing was developed by and belonged to whites, and inherently was part of the white race, suggesting that was why Jeffries was the favorite:

> This contest of men with padded gloves on their hands is a sport that belongs uniquely to the English-speaking race and that has taken centuries for the race to develop. It is no superficial thing, a fad of a moment or a generation. No genius or philosopher devised it and persuaded the race to adopt it as their racial sport of sports. It is as deep as our consciousness and is woven into the fibers of our being. … We like fighting. It is our nature.[769]

On June 28, the 209-pound Johnson boxed 12 rounds in front of a large crowd that included Nevada Governor Denver Dickerson. After George Cotton drew some blood from the champ's lip, Johnson knocked him out cold with a left hook to the jaw. Tales that Jack was slow and lazy were proven to be unfounded, though some reporters kept calling him lazy.[770]

---

[768] *San Francisco Chronicle*, June 30, 1910.
[769] *San Francisco Bulletin, San Francisco Chronicle*, June 29, 1910.
[770] *Chronicle, Examiner, Nevada State Journal*, June 29, 1910; *Reno Evening Gazette*, June 28, 29, 1910.

Members of the Australian party which arrived on the steamship *Wilhelmina*, l to r: Bill Lang, W. F. Corbett of the *Sydney Referee*, Hugh McIntosh, and Tommy Burns.

Hugh McIntosh picked Johnson to win. He had a $500 wager with Tommy Burns, who bet on Jeffries. Although McIntosh "would prefer to see it rest with the white race," nevertheless, he said, "I am putting my money in the dark column."

On the 28th, Jeffries did not box, saying that he had a stomach ache after eating. Jeff suffered from some dysentery, though it soon abated.[771]

The consensus of opinion was that Jeffries would be the best conditioned man, better than Johnson, too strong, and would wear down the colored man, no matter how long it took.[772]

Pistols were banned from the arena. Anyone who tried to bring one in would be barred from taking their seat. Taking no chances on his security, Johnson had hired an army of gun fighters to ensure that no one tried to make trouble for him. Both he and his friends kept guns with them.

Much of the black population was afraid to bet on Johnson, in part because white sporting men were so confident and eager to wager large sums of money on Jeffries, even offering 2 to 1 odds. Nevertheless, Johnson sent his mother a telegram saying, "Don't believe what you see in the newspapers. I am in condition. Will win sure."[773]

The *New York Age* said the "Battle of the Century" had aroused more widespread interest than any other match in prize-ring history. It was the all-absorbing topic of discussion everywhere. It would be a long time before there was another fight of this magnitude.[774]

Jim Corbett said that when Johnson realized he could not hurt the impervious Jeffries, his heart would evaporate. Corbett also said it was a contest between men not only of different races, but of different traditions as a result of race, which would impact the fight:

> Jeffries is the embodiment of all that is powerful and brutish in the white man. He has always lived close to nature. ... Had Jeff lived thousands of years ago, when strength and courage made kings, he would have reigned supreme among his fellow men. It must have been the same with Johnson, say you, and you are right. But don't you remember reading the tales of how the blacks bowed down to, worshipped, and feared – there's the word – feared the white man.
>
> Psychologists say that in times of great stress, in great moments, we go back to original principles, the inborn characteristics that, while they may be buried deep by disuse, invariably spring to the surface when a great crisis arrives...Will Johnson be able to check and master the overwhelming fear of the powerful white man...? I doubt it.
>
> No one realizes better than I do the fact that I am prejudiced in favor of Jim Jeffries. I am. ... I know that Jeffries is the pugilistic marvel of the age. Why, then, shouldn't I be prejudiced in his favor? Undoubtedly there is a racial prejudice there, too. In sizing up this fight I have made allowance for that prejudice and have not allowed it to influence my judgment. I have carefully weighed Jeffries' fighting

---

[771] *Call*, June 29, 1910; *Examiner*, June 30, 1910; *Nevada State Journal*, June 28, 1910.
[772] *San Francisco Chronicle*, June 29, 1910.
[773] *Reno Evening Gazette*, June 29, 1910; *Nevada State Journal, San Francisco Call, Bulletin*, June 30, 1910.
[774] *New York Age*, June 30, 1910.

abilities and compared them one by one with Johnson's. And Johnson has suffered by the comparison.[775]

On the 30th, Jim Jeffries said, "I am ready to go into the ring to win the championship back for the white race." Jeff said he would keep in mind all those who had bet on him. He had worked for more than a year preparing for the fight. "It has been a long, hard pull, but I believe I have brought myself into the greatest physical condition of my life."[776]

The *Chronicle* said nine out of ten men in Reno were picking Jeffries to win. De Witt Van Court said Jeffries was better than ever. "Those stomach punches of the big fellow will fix Johnson."[777]

Jeffries refused to step on the scales. His trainers thought he was about 218, though others estimated anywhere from 220 to 230.

Tommy Burns, James J. Corbett, Jams J. Jeffries, John L. Sullivan

Sam Langford said Johnson had better look over his insurance policy. Jeffries looked "big enough to eat up de whole black race. Ah'll fight Johnson any morning before breakfast, but Ah'd rather step in de 'lectric chair than stand up before dis terrible being." "I hope Jeff breaks Johnson's jaw in the first punch."

From Louisville, Marvin Hart said he hoped Jeffries would win, but in his heart, he thought Johnson would have it on him. Abe Attell said, "I think there is nothing to it but Jeff."

Johnson laughed at predictions favoring Jeffries. "Many a time when I was training for my early fights I didn't have any attention at all, and sometimes I didn't have any too much to eat, but I pulled through."[778]

---

[775] *San Francisco Bulletin*, July 1, 1910.
[776] *San Francisco Call, Chronicle, Examiner, Nevada State Journal*, July 1, 1910.
[777] *San Francisco Examiner*, July 1, 1910. *San Francisco Chronicle*, July 1, 2, 1910.
[778] *Reno Evening Gazette*, July 1, 1910; *San Francisco Call, Nevada State Journal, San Francisco Examiner*, July 2, 1910.

The *Freeman* said, "Jeffries has the white man's burden. ... Will it help Jeffries, this terrible responsibility?" He was under an immense amount of pressure. "Jeffries knows that he is the Atlas of the white race in fistic matters. The white man's terrible responsibility is on him and he is leaving nothing undone to give a satisfactory report of himself."

Johnson's camp was like a picnic. Jack enjoyed kidding with his sparring partners. For recreation, he would shoot craps and play roulette.

Governor Dickerson assured Johnson that if he was good enough to whip Jeffries that no race prejudice or outside influence would be permitted to wrest the decision from him. Johnson said, "I'll go to sleep on that, Mr. Governor. I'll trust to the square men of Nevada and the others around the ring to see that I won't get none of the worst of it from anybody but the man I'm fighting, and I'll attend to that part of it myself."

Jack Johnson at the roulette table. Jack has been playing them pretty high up in the sagebrush State, and has been having about an even break with Dame Fortune.

The *Freeman* said the entire civilized world was interested in the outcome, owing to the fact that it was promoted as a race supremacy battle, a fight on the nation's birthday between mankind's two best specimens, for the biggest prize in sport. Fearing harm to blacks, it cautioned,

> This is by no means a race supremacy battle. It is a battle for thousands of dollars. The race question was raised by sporting editors throughout the world on Jeffries as the bull fighters would raise the red flag to enrage the bull. And it had its effect on Jeffries. It is well that the colored man does not take this race question too seriously. ... This race question will get many a man in trouble on the Fourth of July if he carries it too far.

No living man had gone through what Johnson had gone through to get to the highest point. "He has been accused of everything – yellow streak, quitter, four-flusher, trickster and all kinds of denouncements." He had to whip all of the top colored fighters before top whites would face him. Even after doing so, many still drew the color line on him, or he had to suffer a raw decision against Hart. "All this went to make him what he is today. His record will show that he has defeated more men than any heavyweight champion has ever defeated; traveled the world over to do it."

Johnson's method was compared with "Isaac Murphy, the race horse rider, who made all of his finishes close. The same with Jack Johnson. ... He has never been classed a slugger; for if he had been so classed he would not have got the chance he has today."

The crowd would encourage Jeffries, but they could not fight for him. "Johnson won't care how much noise they make; he is used to that – in fact, all colored fighters are. ... All this talk about Jeffries putting Johnson away with one punch is silly talk and bad noise."

Johnson advised his admirers not to bet on the fight's duration. "Don't bother about the number of rounds, just get your money down that I will bring home the bacon and then sit back and wait until the time comes to cash in."

Viewing the fight grounds, Jeff said, "It was on this very spot that I gave away my title exactly five years ago, and now I have come to get it back."[779]

The *Chicago Defender* wrote, "Think, in 1776 the colored man fought the British to give the American his freedom and today (1910), which should be a nation's fight, the colored man is forced to fight Jim Crow delegations, race prejudice and American public insane sentiment. If he wins in the face of all this, he is truly entitled to a Carnegie Hero Medal." This writer estimated that $2.5 million dollars had been wagered on the fight.

The *Defender* believed that Johnson had obtained his shot at the championship by carrying fighters and not knocking them out. Champions did not want to fight tough propositions. Johnson showed rare business tact by not giving it his all.

> Had he shown his true form the laurels of champion would never have rested on his sable brow. ... Knowing that his color would be a barrier to him in reaching the coveted goal of his ambition, if he performed too brilliantly, hence he fought his battles systematically.
>
> Johnson, being a past master of feints and guards, his exceptional cleverness, great speed and almost impenetrable defense, enabled him to wage battle the full limit of scheduled rounds, winning by a narrow margin, whereas a quick victory over his opponents would have put his future interests in jeopardy. Hence the public was misled as to his real form.

His long quest for the championship showed unparalleled pluck, patience, and perseverance, for no one had to work harder or longer to obtain a title shot. "When the smoke of the battle clears away, so to speak, and when the din of mingled cheers and groans have died away in the atmosphere, there will be deep mourning throughout the domains of Uncle Sam over Jeffries' inability to return the pugilistic scepter to the Caucasian race."[780]

---

[779] *Freeman*, July 2, 1910.
[780] *Chicago Defender*, July 2, 1910.

An *Examiner* writer said, "When I watched Johnson box, I couldn't see how any man could hit him. When I watched Jeffries box, I couldn't see how any man who stood in front of him could keep from being hit."

Famous sportswriter Tad Dorgan said the Jeffries men outnumbered the Johnson men three to one.[781]

Jack London said the equals of Johnson and Jeffries would not meet again in a generation. There never had been anything like this fight in the history of the ring. It truly was the fight of the century. "It is the fight of fights, the crowning fight of the whole ring, and perhaps the last great fight that will ever be held."[782]

Several *Bulletin* writers predicted a Jeffries victory. He was stronger, had the better punch, an underrated defense, "and as for courage, he lays over the darkey like wool over a sheep. These little advantages, combined with race psychic reasons, give him an edge that makes the 10 to 6 price figure about right."

Bob Fitzsimmons, Joe Choynski, Jack Munroe, and Bob Armstrong, who had boxed with or fought both combatants, all favored Jeffries.[783]

Bill Delaney never thought Jeffries would fight Johnson:

> When Jeffries was fighting and at his best Johnson used to follow him about the country and hurl challenges at him. Jeffries refused to meet him on the ground that he was black. The fact that he had already fought colored men like Bob Armstrong, Peter Jackson and Hank Griffin cut no ice: Jeffries turned Johnson down cold. Why? Because he was afraid of him.

Of course, Jeff argued that he did not want to give a black man a chance to win the championship. Back then, Delaney was as insistent or more so that Jeff would not cross the color line as champ; that he would not allow it. Bill had changed his tune. Delaney said of Johnson and the upcoming fight,

> [T]he sporting world does not know how good a fighter he really is. In my mind he has been fighting under wraps. ...

> It has been stated in the press, and I have heard experts who have seen Johnson perform, say that Johnson was a coward. In reply to this attack upon his courage, please name me a fighter, white or black, that he has ever refused to fight. As I have already mentioned, when Jeffries was in his prime Johnson was dogging his footsteps with challenges. Cowards never taunted Jeffries. ... Another point they attempt to make against Johnson is that he can't punch – can't deliver a knockout. ... Jim Jeffries will find that Jack Johnson can hit before he is through with him. ... In my long connection with the ring I have seen few fighters who knew more about fighting than Johnson. He has lots of brains. ...

---

[781] *San Francisco Examiner*, July 2, 1910.
[782] *San Francisco Chronicle*, July 2, 1910.
[783] *San Francisco Bulletin*, July 2, 1910.

> The betting odds do not startle me. I looked for Jeffries to be the favorite. There are four or five reasons for it. Johnson's undeserved reputation of being a coward, also his reputation of being a weak hitter, and Jeffries a hard one, his color and the suspicion that if there is anything doing in the crooked way Jack would be the one to lay down, all these have contributed to make Jeffries a red-hot favorite. But that does not fease me. ... In regard to the fight being 'shady,' there is no reason to have any fear. If I even suspected a crooked angle I would never have consented to go behind Johnson.[784]

Johnson said the talk of his having a yellow streak made him laugh:

> I am glad that all of the critics pronounce him to be in the best shape of his entire career, for then I'll get the full credit for licking him. ....
>
> That talk of 'yellow streak' in my make-up is a joke. Nobody ever saw me show it, did they? ... It's only a question of how long Jeff can stand the gaff.

T. P. Magilligan said Johnson never had been given full credit because he often had his hands tied by stipulation. "No one knows exactly how good Johnson is. ... He beat all his men of late years with such apparent ease that even the veriest novice might see he was holding back."[785]

William Slattery said many picked against Johnson because of race and personal prejudice. "He is not a popular fighter, even with those of his own blood. Many of them bet against him because of their hatred for him." However, when picking a fight, one had to use cool, calculating judgment and overlook "caste hatred."

Many Southern white citizens had dire apprehensions, greatly fearing the social result of a Johnson victory:

> The negro population of the south is intensely interested in the outcome of the great battle, believing that the fight will determine the social position of the black man in the society of the nation.
>
> It is the contention in the south that if Johnson wins at Reno white ladies will be crowded off the sidewalks and insulted generally.
>
> Southern congressmen...see many dire evils in the defeat of the white man by the black.
>
> "Dangerous exultation" is the term used by those who deplore the effect of the fight.
>
> Negro government clerks are said to be nervous and excited as they expect their race to be greatly exalted in a social way by the fight.[786]

---

[784] *San Francisco Bulletin,* July 2, 1910.
[785] *San Francisco Evening Post,* July 2, 4, 1910.
[786] *Nevada State Journal,* July 3, 1910.

Black churches would be praying for a Johnson victory. About a thousand "dusky sports" were expected to be on hand at the fight, and most of them were betting their money on Johnson.

Public interest in the fight was so tremendous, one writer called it ravenous. Newspapers throughout the nation were devoting an enormous amount of space to the fight on a daily basis.[787]

One writer who gave Johnson the edge said Jack was underrated in part because of prejudice against the colored race.

Joe Woodman said Johnson was a dog, and Jeff would bring it out within 15 rounds. Denver Ed Martin said, "There will be one 'white' colored man in the ring next Monday afternoon." He liked Jeff.

Johnson would face a hostile audience. It was safe to predict that fully 90% of the spectators would be rooting for a Jeffries victory, regardless of whom they had wagered upon. However, Johnson was used to derision.

When John L. Sullivan asked Johnson how he felt, the champ responded, "Captain John, I never felt better in my life. If I felt any better I would be afraid of myself."

Johnson was not bothered by the odds. Since most who wagered on the battle were white, "it is only natural that they should select Jeffries to carry their money. It makes it nice for my friends because they are getting good odds for their money."

All of Johnson's trainers said he would win, for he was the finest boxer ever, the hardest hitter, as well as the hardest to hit, with the heart, stamina, and confidence. Dave Mills said, "I think the fifteenth round will see the finish." Tom Flanagan said Jack had no fear and was game, despite what folks imagined.

On July 2, Jeff said, "I am going to keep faith with the public that has kept faith with me." "I guess that Johnson and myself can claim the record of bringing together more celebrities of the sporting world than any two boxers ever drew before."

Jeffries claimed he once told Johnson that they could go down into a cellar together and the man that came back up would be champion. Johnson replied, "I ain't no cellar fighter." Jeff took it as a sign of fear.

Speaking of why he had come back, Jeff said the whole world was begging and pleading with him to defend the white race's supremacy, feeling that he was the only man on earth who could beat Johnson. Eventually, "the pressure became too great." Sam Berger said, "He wants to bring the championship back to the white race and he is going to do it beyond the question of the slightest doubt."

Jeffries had a lot of support. Jack Jeffries said Jeff would make Johnson jump over the ropes before the fight had gone long. Jim Corbett said Johnson "lacks the heart and the courage and Jeffries will surely beat him down." Tommy Burns said, "Take it from me, Jeff will rush that big 'coon' off his feet." He said if Jeff's left hook hit the body, Johnson would be down squirming on the mat. Tom Sharkey said, "Johnson trained me for a

---

[787] *San Francisco Chronicle*, July 3, 1910.

couple of fights. He is a classy boxer, but he hasn't the steam." Jack London said, "A trifle of prophecy, if the fight goes any decent distance, bent and dented ribs for Johnson, if not broken ones." Fight announcer Billy Jordan, famous for his call of "Let 'er go," anticipated that Jeffries would win in about 15 rounds. "He is going out to bring the championship back to the white race, where it belongs."

A *Call* writer said the 10 to 6 odds were ridiculous, "and they have been made ridiculous because of the prejudice against Johnson on account of his color. He is not a popular fighter, even with those of his own blood."

The *Call* reported that the $101,000 purse actually was going to be divided evenly, 50/50, and not based on winner and loser. Such was decided in a secret meeting in Hoboken. It said the real truth had leaked out. Others said the $101,000 purse would be divided 75% to the winner and 25% to the loser, plus a $20,000 bonus to each fighter.[788]

Bill Delaney said that after Johnson beat Jeff's brother, he pleaded for a fight, saying that he had licked Jack Jeffries, and could lick Jim too. Jeffries would not fight Johnson no matter what the financial inducements. Delaney had to take all of the blame and act as a bumper.

U.S. President William Taft said he would receive reports of the fight through a local newspaper wire. His son Charley was betting all of his money on "the pride of the white race."

In response to boxing's critics, Jack London said there were many things a lot worse than prize-fighting, a sport which had rigid rules that gave its participants more fair play than the outside world offered. In the real world, food was adulterated, legislators were bribed, children worked in factories, and merchants compelled women to labor long hours on a semi-starvation wage. By comparison, boxing seemed lucrative, safe, and fair. "If some of the fairness of the prize-ring were carried into business life it would be a much more beneficial world in which to live."

A southerner told Jeff that the South was with him, and emphasized the fight's larger implications. "For God's sake, Jeff, beat the negro. We are all with you; do your best. It is more than the fight to us."[789]

Writer Rex Beach believed Jeff would win in part because "he possesses a mentality lacking in his antagonist, and mind after all is stronger than matter. ... The man of education will outlast the man of ignorance in any test of endurance be they evenly matched in strength."[790]

Battling Nelson said, "Racial prejudice seems to influence almost everyone here."

A *Call* writer said the battle would "decide whether the white or black race shall rule supreme over the pugilistic world."

Another *Call* writer said those who insisted that Johnson was a dog with a yellow streak had no basis for such claims. True, he had loafed a good deal during his career, but never had he quit cold. "And they say Johnson

---

[788] *San Francisco Chronicle, Examiner, Call,* July 3, 1910; *Los Angeles Times,* July 4, 1910.
[789] *San Francisco Chronicle,,* July 4, 1910.
[790] *Reno Evening Gazette,* July 4, 1910.

must be a dog because he's colored." However, other colored champions like Dixon and Gans never had dogged it. "No man should be branded with the failings of his race until he has exhibited these failings himself. There is no trait that is absolutely universal in any one race."

When Stanley Ketchel came to visit Jeff at his training camp on the 3rd, he was ousted. Obviously, Jeff was upset that Stan had picked Johnson.[791]

On July 3, the day before the fight, Jeff wrote that he was glad, hungry, and anxious for the contest, like a boy waiting for Christmas day:

> When the gloves are knotted on my hands tomorrow afternoon and I stand ready to defend what is really my title, it will be at the request of the public, who forced me out of retirement. I realize full well just what depends on me, and I am not going to disappoint the public. ... That portion of the white race that has been looking to me to defend its athletic supremacy may feel assured that I am fit to do my very best.

Jeffries also said that some had discussed what harm might come to Johnson should he win. "They have pictured the negro as being shot, hanged or mobbed in case he won." Showing his true sportsmanship and humanity, Jeffries said,

> I would consider any move to intimidate Johnson as cowardly and a disgrace to the American spirit of fair play. It is my honest belief that should Johnson be fortunate enough to win from me that the negro would not only be allowed to walk unmolested from the ring, but that he would be accorded all the honors due to the victor. I want it understood that I want no friend of mine to make a hostile movement towards Johnson. . ... If Johnson should by any chance win...he must not be harmed. I demand this.

An *Examiner* writer said Johnson had toiled for years, fighting anyone who would fight him, battling against the color line. He had heard the hisses of race feeling in the shouts and yells at countless ringsides. The color line had prevented a Jeffries fight. But he knew that if one day he held the championship, public clamor would force Jeff out of retirement, which it had. "And had the championship remained in the keeping of a white man, he never would have fought again. So, after all, it is Johnson's black skin that has won him his chance to fight Jeffries." The irony was that his skin had kept him from a fight with Jeff, but now that he was champion, his black skin is what got him the fight.[792]

On the morning of the championship contest, Jim Corbett said they were fighting "for glory, money, title, and to prove the physical superiority of the white race." Jim cited Jeff's prodigious strength, wonderful hitting power, and gameness under punishment as "the things that will bring the pugilistic supremacy to the white man."

---

[791] *San Francisco Call*, July 4, 1910.
[792] *San Francisco Examiner*, July 4, 1910; *New York Times*, July 4, 1910.

Ashleigh Simpson said if the colored man were white, the odds would be considerably different from what they were.

Many suggested several potential negative effects if Johnson won. "If Johnson wins there will be a riot in the south. If Johnson wins the game of pugilism will suffer."

Johnson too was cognizant of his and the fight's importance. He thought that he was a greater deliverer of his own race than Frederick Douglass or Booker T. Washington.[793]

Thousands of newspaper pages had been devoted to the fight, analyzing and discussing it exhaustively on a daily basis for months, more than any single upcoming sporting event in history. In fact, no sporting event ever again would parallel the level of discourse which surrounded this single event. The wait was almost over.

---

[793] *San Francisco Bulletin, San Francisco Evening Post, Nevada State Journal,* July 4, 1910.

CHAPTER 35

Battle of the Races

On Independence Day, July 4, 1910 in Reno, Nevada, reigning world heavyweight champion Jack Johnson fought undefeated ex-champion James J. Jeffries in the most racially charged fight of all time, hyped as a battle for racial supremacy. For whites, it was supposed to be white Independence Day, for Jeffries was supposed to liberate whites from a black champion who never was supposed to be in such a position, and to put blacks in their place. Conversely, blacks were rooting for Johnson to prove to whites that if and when given a fair and equal opportunity, they could prove themselves to be just as good as whites, and sometimes even better, that race did not and should not necessarily determine the outcome of anything in life.

Jim Jeffries was 19-0-2 with 16 KOs, several of which were 20- and 25-round bouts. He had become world champion in June 1899 and fought until August 1904, before retiring in 1905. Since early 1909, immediately after Johnson had won the title, Jeffries had been in training to come back for the specifically stated purpose to reclaim the crown for the white race.[794]

Reno was packed with people. The town was so overflowing with humanity that several restaurants ran out of food.

The night before the fight, Johnson said he was thinking of the hard road that he had traveled since he left home when he was 12 years old. "I ran away as a kid and stowed away on a cotton steamer and landed in New York. I didn't have a nickel." Since then, he had traveled most of the world, had his ups and downs, but his ambition had been realized. He had taken his mother out of the Galveston shanty where he was raised, and put her in a big house in Chicago. "She's got everything she wants, and I'm happy."

Most elaborate preparations were made for Jeff's corner. In addition to the regular paraphernalia, his corner would be equipped with a sunshade, an electric fan, "and drugs enough to start an apothecary shop."

Doctor William Porter visited Jeff and administered some medicine to him for the prevention of nose bleed.

At 10:45 a.m., Johnson was in the yard posing for news photographers. He was laughing and joking as though he had not a care in the world.

Rex Beach was one of those who harped on the bout's racial significance. "Out from the jungle shadows of Ethiopia had stalked an Afric-giant to measure his strength against the white man's champion. It was again a battle of the races." As a result, people paid enormous amounts

---

[794] The following account and discussion of the fight is from an amalgamation of sources which had reporters on the scene, including: *Nevada State Journal, San Francisco Chronicle, San Francisco Call, San Francisco Evening Post, San Francisco Bulletin, San Francisco Examiner, New York Times,* July 5, 1910; *Reno Evening Gazette,* July 4, 5, 1910; *Freeman,* July 9, 1910.

to witness the fight. Tickets sold for $10, $15, $20, $25, $30, $40, and $50. It was like the Roman Coliseum. Even women were there.

Ticket scalpers flourished, more than doubling their investments. The cheapest seats had been marked up to $25, and still there was more demand than supply. Rickard admitted that his friends had been correct in advising him to ensure that a large arena was built.

It was a very hot clear day, with dry air, and not a cloud in sight. The intense heat was tempered faintly by a slight cool breeze.

At 11 a.m., ringside telegraph instruments began humming. A force of 100 expert telegraph operators were present. Both the Western Union and Postal Telegraph companies said at least 750,000 words of press matter at an average cost of two cents a word were sent out over the wires that day.

Above each of the four arena entrances was an American flag, dropped on its staff. At 12 p.m., the arena gates were opened, and thousands entered. The fight was scheduled to start at around 3 p.m.

So as to prevent rowdiness or violence, alcohol and weapons were forbidden. Before entering, men were frisked. Only the police were armed. There was no drunkenness. Hence, the police did not have to do much.

Inside, the arena's bare pine boards generated a terrific amount of heat from the scorching sun, which beat down fiercely.

A long booth of boxes specifically built for women atop the enclosure's outer walls, at the crater's rim, were filled with 75 to 100 women who wore striking gowns and gaudy hats. Never before had so many women attended a fight. Every section was dotted with them, from the cheapest seats to the $50 ringside section.

The Reno military band entered the 22-foot ring and played various American airs to celebrate the nation's birthday. At 12:50 p.m., they played "The Red, White, and Blue." An enthusiastic fan jumped into the ring, waving a silk American flag, and the vast crowd cheered. The band next played "Dixie" (the de facto anthem of the Confederacy) to another tremendous cheer.

At 1 p.m., the heat was intense, as the midday sun poured its rays into the crater-like structure. Green visors were sold by the hundreds for eye shields against the glaring sun. They cast reflections across the ring.

When the band played "America," the crowd made a feeble attempt to sing, but soon went back to their fans and handkerchiefs. The brass band also played "Just Before the Battle, Mother," "Star-Spangled Banner" (which was not yet the national anthem), and other tunes appropriate on the nation's birthday.

Contrary to popular belief, it merely was rumored that the brass band would play "All Coons Look Alike to Me," but it did not do so, for racial feeling was too high. The authorities had barred anything that might cause a disturbance. However, some subsequently claimed that it was played.

There was an undertone of fairness and good fellowship amongst it all. There was little bad language, and no disputes or disturbances in the crowd. Lemonade was the only beverage served.

Tex Rickard announced that they were fighting for $121,000. The purse was $101,000, which Rickard said the fighters were splitting 60% to the winner and 40% to the loser. However, Rickard also awarded a $10,000 bonus to each fighter, regardless of result.

Ringside betting favored Jeffries at 10 to 6 odds, and remained so, with plenty of money in sight to be wagered on the white man.

Estimates of the crowd size varied. Every seat was occupied. Rickard said the seating capacity was a little over 19,000. One or two thousand more were crowded like sardines into the bowl-shaped yellow pine arena in the standing room sections, and a six-foot platform that extended all the way around the upper edge was covered with a human fringe of standing spectators as well. It was the biggest crowd that ever saw a prize fight to that point, and the receipts were so far ahead of any similar event that the record was shattered.

Reports regarding the gate receipts also varied. The most specific number offered was $270,778.50. Some said $380,000 was generated.

Rickard estimated that the San Francisco losses, including the expenses of the unused arena, cost him about $21,000 to $30,000.

After deducting both major and incidental expenses, Rickard estimated that they would make a profit of about $120,000 to $128,000, which he and Jack Gleason would split. Gleason estimated the profits at $150,000. Plus the promoters also would profit from their interests in the motion picture proceeds. Rickard sold his 1/6 interest for $33,333, but Gleason still held a 1/6 interest, which he refused to sell. It certainly was the battle of the century from a financial perspective; by far the most lucrative fight ever up to that point.

One reporter claimed that someone brought a thermometer to ringside and it registered 102 degrees in the sun. The *Nevada State Journal* later said the temperature got up to a high of 86 degrees. Either way, it was hot.

It was a wonderful crowd in that it was most orderly and well behaved, even under the broiling sun. Perhaps the sun had something to do with it. It was so hot, no one wanted to perspire any more than necessary. The tickets were not cheap, so no one wanted to be thrown out, and only the respectable class could afford the seats. Further, the deputy sheriffs' strong presence and lack of alcohol ensured civility.

William Muldoon entered the ring and gave a speech complimenting the state of Nevada and Governor Denver Dickerson for having the courage to stand by the laws. The entire vast assemblage rose and gave three rousing salvos for Governor Dickerson, who was in attendance.

Billy Jordan introduced Tex Rickard as the "gamest sport of the world. All the credit you can give belongs to this great sport, Tex Rickard. I call for three cheers for Our Tex." The crowd responded with a will.

Never in history were so many pugilistic celebrities at a fight. All of the old-timers were there. Billy Jordan continually introduced the vast throng of celebrities. "I introduce to you the great and only champion, big hearted John L. Sullivan." The ex-champ climbed through the ropes, which set the spectators wild. Bob Fitzsimmons was introduced as "the greatest warrior of them all." Tom Sharkey was next. "Gentlemen, the great Roman gladiator, Frank Gotch." Others introduced included Hugh McIntosh, Tommy Burns, Stanley Ketchel, Jack O'Brien, Los Angeles promoter Tom McCarey, moving picture man William Rock, Bill Lang, Jim Coffroth, Joe Choynski, Abe Attell, Battling Nelson, Jack McAuliffe, and Sam Langford, all of whom were photographed in the ring.

McIntosh, Burns, Sullivan, Coffroth, Gotch, Jordan, McCarey, Lang, Fitzsimmons, Sharkey, Harting, Ketchel

At 2:28 p.m., Jack Johnson came down the aisle and entered the ring to a relatively chilly reception. He did receive a few scattered friendly cheers, and the jeers were not very noticeable, though a few did stand up and hiss.

Wearing a mocha or black and gray silk dressing gown/bathrobe with thin white and black stripes running through it vertically, Jack smiled, waved his hand, and bowed to the crowd, which included a small sprinkling of folks of his own race. He greeted friends and acquaintances. He was not nervous, but seemed happy, calm, and only semi-serious.

Ed Cahill said Johnson entered wearing an elaborate gorgeous robe. "Don't get away with the idea that his high sense of his own importance is offensive. Not at all; he is just the simple-minded, elemental savage, basking in the sunlight of popular admiration. There is no pose. He can not help it."

Johnson's then girlfriend, the white Etta Duryea, whom he called wife, was sitting in a $40 seat. Jack waved to her, and she responded in kind.

A few minutes later, at 2:31 p.m., Jim Jeffries' approach was like the coming of an emperor. With Jim Corbett leading the way, Jeff's entry was the signal for a tremendous outburst of enthusiasm and cheers. "The crowd was there to yell, and to yell for the white man."

Bob Armstrong acted as a palm-bearer, holding a great fan or sunshade which could be used to cool the fighter between rounds and shelter Jeff from the sun.

As had been his custom in prior fights, Jeff was chewing a big chunk of gum nonchalantly. One said he looked primordial as ever, with an expressionless face. Another said he was dark, somber, ominous, grim, serious, and savage. Most thought he seemed calm.

Corbett requested a toss for corners, but Delaney said Johnson would allow Jeffries to take either corner. Jeffries took the corner with his back to the sun.

At 2:35 p.m. Johnson was led to ring center and presented by Billy Jordan: "Gentlemen, the heavyweight champion of the world, Jack Johnson." He was given a weak reception. Richard Barry said, "When Johnson was introduced he got about nine handclaps and there were upwards of twenty thousand people within sight." Jack smiled and waved his hand at his white girlfriend Etta Duryea. His hands were bandaged with black adhesive tape.

Johnson was stripped and ready, wearing blue trunks with a silk American flag as a belt entwined around his waist.

Abe Attell wound cotton or white muslin bandages around Jeff's hands, as well as some tape. Jeff wore purple trunks (slightly of a blue hue) and the American flag for a belt. The multitude stared at him in awe. He looked good, like a gnarly

rugged oak, huge, stolid, stoical, and well-tanned.

Jeff came to ring center and was introduced: "The great and only undefeated heavyweight champion of the world, James J. Jeffries." The adoring crowd roundly cheered, howled, clapped, tossed hats in the air, and punched each other with joy, excitement, and anticipation. Johnson smiled and clapped as well. Coffroth thought Jack was pretending to applaud. Jeff folded his arms behind him and gazed over the vast assemblage which cheered him again and again.

The men donned their gloves, and Jordan cleared the ring. Johnson's golden smile was much in evidence.

Johnson was willing to shake hands, but Jeffries refused, saying there would be no handshake, so Johnson assented with one of his many smiles.

Billy Jordan said, "Gentlemen, this will be a forty-five round contest, honest and on the square. They will break by the order of the referee. May the best man win. Let 'er go!"

George Harting rang the bell to start the fight at 2:46 p.m.

In the 1st round, Johnson smiled at Jeff, who calmly chewed gum and smiled back. Jack said, "Now, come on, Jeff; do your best." After cautious sparring, Johnson led and landed the first blow, a light stabbing left to the nose or mouth. In a clinch, Jack pushed Jeff's left arm backwards and showed his strength. Jeff tried to crowd Jack and bear his weight upon him. There was a great deal of clinching.

Corbett said, "Wonder how long that black man is going to do the brother act? Will he never let go? Break 'em, Tex." However, John L. Sullivan said it was Jeffries who was doing all of the clinching. Both men seemed willing to rough it at close quarters.

On a break, Jeff landed two short-arm lefts to the face and the crowd cheered. Corbett shouted, "Why don't you laugh?" Johnson winked and smiled back.

Jeff landed a left to the body. Corbett said, "That's it, Jeff, right there, that's where it hurts." Jack landed a left on Jeff's cheek and told him, "Be very careful, for you have got one too many eyes to look out of."

At the gong, Johnson grinned and playfully tapped Jeffries on the back of his shoulder. Jeff returned to his corner smiling as well, and he winked at his cornermen.

Summarizing, observers said it was a tame, uneventful round with considerable hugging and clinching. No telling blows landed, though Jeff received cheers for anything he did. Most said the round was about even.

Between rounds, Corbett entered the ring and stood in the vicinity of Johnson's corner, near the neutral corner. From there, he taunted Jack with cutting remarks, trying to rattle him. At first, Jack was surprised, but soon became accustomed to it and had a ready and witty response every time that Corbett flung a remark his way, winking and smiling at Corbett.

In the 2nd round, Johnson came up chatting and smiling, while Jeff advanced with his famous crouch and smiled in return. Corbett cried out to Johnson, "He's going to fight a little bit now." Jack replied, "All right,

Mistah Corbett, I feel like fightin' a little bit myself." Corbett said to Jeff, "He wants to fight a little bit, Jim." Jack retorted, "You bet I do, Mistah Corbett."

Jeffries generally tried to crowd and put his weight on Johnson in the clinches. With his golden smile, Johnson said, "Don't love me so much, Jim, don't love me so." Jack followed his comment with a short stinging right uppercut to the jaw that tilted Jeff's head.

Johnson also landed a right on Jeff's eye, which caused it to flush.

Johnson attempted to break out of clinches and punch. Corbett hollered, "That left hand hook is a joke. Jim, he can't reach you with it. It's a little slow yet." However, Jack then landed some short left hooks.

Johnson's lip showed some blood, either from a punch or a head butt. A cut on his lip that George Cotton had caused in training had been re-opened. The crowd drew inspiration from the blood.

Nevertheless, in the clinches, Johnson landed uppercuts and pushed Jeff's left arm back. Jack was as jovial as ever, laughing gleefully.

Jack London said a repetition of what happened in Australia when Burns fought Johnson took place. Each time someone said something harsh to Johnson in the hope of making him lose his temper, Jack responded by giving the white man a lacing. Jeff did not talk as Burns did, but Corbett spoke, and each time Jim cried out, Johnson promptly landed a blow.

Summarizing, the *Bulletin* said Jeff's punches missed most of the time. Johnson's aim was by far the more accurate. Every blow he landed meant business, especially a left hook that hit the right eye. The *Evening Post* said Johnson put a little more steam into his left jabs, which disconcerted Jeff. The *Nevada State Journal* said they kidded and talked to each other continually. The *Reno Evening Gazette* said, "It was a case of strength against cleverness, with the Nubian having the better of it." Several noted that Jeff was not making the whirlwind fight generally forecasted. Richard Barry said that in the middle of the round, they scrapped for the first time in earnest. Everyone said, "Now wait till the coon feels that bear strength." However, instead, Johnson matched Jeffries' strength, which stunned everyone.

Between rounds, Johnson and Corbett kidded each other incessantly.

In the 3rd round, the confident Johnson smiled at and talked to Jeff, deriding him as he feinted. "Come in Jim." When Johnson landed some blows, Corbett yelled, "You've got a fat chance of hurting him, Jack. Everybody is laughing at you. He's making you look like a fool. How do you like that stinger to the stomach, eh? It hurts, don't it? Wait till that yellow streak begins to show. Go on, Jim, you'll knock his block off." Johnson replied, "That's what they ALL say, Mistah Co'butt." JC: "Jim will make you show your yellow streak after awhile." JJ: "Then we'll be in the same class, Corbett. He certainly made you show plenty of yellow once." "If he makes me quit I'll come out and get you. That will make us even." Johnson kept up a constant cross-fire of conversation with both Corbett and Jeffries. They were smiling and kidding one another. They would punch and clinch, and punch in the clinches.

Jeff swung a hard right to the body and they clinched again. Corbett said, "Dat's funny; I know that feeling myself." Johnson winked over Jeff's shoulder at Corbett and said, "Come in and help him." Corbett then became very vulgar, and everyone around Jeff's corner was susceptible to his remarks. "Show the yellow streak in the nigger." However, some of the crowd did not appreciate Corbett's mouth and fired back at him to keep quiet.

Johnson blocked the punches with his arms, shoulders, and gloves. The *Chronicle* said, "The white man finds it hard to break through the clever defense of Johnson." When the round ended, Jack again patted his antagonist on the shoulder. He waved his hands to friends in the audience and chuckled as he went to his corner.

Most observers, including John L. Sullivan, agreed that Johnson had the better judgment of distance, and had done most of the hitting and landing thus far. Jeff only landed a few harmless punches, for Johnson was blocking cleverly. In the clinches, Johnson was able to seize Jeff's left, his best arm, and prevent its use. Johnson's big smile showed his confidence. Jeff's defense was of no use. He took the punches - right uppercuts, chopping lefts, and short snappy jabs.

In the 4th round, the confident Johnson said to Corbett, "They all say I can't hit – here is one of them," and he fired a right uppercut which knocked Jeff's head as far back as it could go. Jack was all smiles. Jeff hit the body with his left, but Johnson landed two stiff left uppercuts and smiled some more. Jeff also smiled to show that he could stand the gaff.

Johnson kept joshing and taunting Jeff all the time. Rickard admonished him that it was a fight and not a talkfest. Jeff rushed, crowded, and struck with more vim than before. In response to Jeff's rush, Johnson said, "Don't rush me, Jim. You hear what I'm telling you?" Jack backed his statement with a right uppercut to Jeff's jaw. Despite attacking more frequently, Jeffries found it difficult to land.

When Johnson landed a left, Jeff said, "This is a tough old head to crack." Johnson responded, "I'm a sure enough nut cracker." After Johnson struck him, Jeff asked, "Did you hurt your hand?" Jack replied, "No," and hit him again.

Jeffries landed a couple lefts to the body, one into the pit of the stomach. Cries of glee came from Jeff's corner. Corbett hollered, "You've got him winded, Jim." Jeff landed a good hard right to the mouth which started the blood flowing more noticeably from Johnson's lips again. Some in the crowd cried, "First blood for Jeff."

Corbett was trying to disconcert Johnson, but as Jeffries advanced and ducked, Jack timed him on the way in and landed a short right on the jaw.

Johnson dared Jeff to bring forth those demon punches for which he was so famous. However, it was Johnson who landed a hard left on the jaw.

Most said the round was even, while some thought Jeffries had the edge, for it was his best round thus far. He was the more active. Still, most of Jeff's blows were blocked or smothered. Some said Jeffries planted a few choice raps on the body, but apparently he could not land with any force or effect, for Johnson only smiled, though his mouth was bleeding.

In the corner between rounds, Johnson looked down at Sullivan at ringside and said, "He can't hit hard."

In the 5th round, Johnson chuckled, "I am all open if you can find the place and land it." They wrestled for a spell. Corbett said, "Johnson is trying to goad Jeffries into losing his head, but it doesn't work. He might as well talk to a stone wall." Corbett called out, "Why don't you go in and mix it, Jack? Go on, Jeffries, he's only stalling." Johnson replied, "Great stall it is, too." They feinted into a clinch. Jeff said, "Break free," and then leaned his weight on Johnson.

As Jeffries crouched, Johnson kidded and said, "I will straighten him up in a minute." Someone in the crowd heard him and said, "He will straighten you up, nigger." Johnson led and landed his left on the stomach. In the clinch, Jack looked over Jeff's shoulder and grinned. Jeff smiled and remarked, "Gee, I love you, Jack."

Jeffries shot two rights to the body, but Jack responded with a left uppercut that cut Jeff's lip, though Sullivan said it was a short right that cut the upper lip. Eventually, Jeff's lip bled more profusely than Johnson's. Some noticed that Jeff's nose was bleeding as well, from the right nostril.

Suddenly, from the down-low crouching position, Jeffries sprung up to his toes with a straight left to the mouth that sent Johnson's head back a foot. It was a clean punch and the crowd cheered. Corbett said, "Jeff jolts his left to Johnson's head and the coon's head wabbles back. Don't cry, Johnson, the worst is yet to come." However, Johnson was not jarred, for he clinched and laughed loudly.

Still, Corbett was trying to get his goat. It was so quiet at ringside that his comments could be heard from far away. Corbett said, "My, oh my! That's an awful bad left! Worst left I ever saw! Jim, I thought this fellow could box. He can't box a lick on earth." Johnson looked over and grinned.

Corbett's running fire of words only served to make Johnson smile even more merrily and to wink at him over Jeff's shoulder in the clinches. Johnson was not flustered in the least by any of Jeff's punches, talking to him in a manner that exuded confidence and relaxation. Jeffries could not land effectively. Conversely, Johnson was ripping in rights and lefts that had a wearing effect. A steady stream of blood had started to flow from Jeff's lip and right nostril.

Before the 6th round began, Jeffries remarked to his seconds, "I'm going to mix with him now." He continued chewing gum. Jeff attacked, but did not land with any effect. Corbett yelled, "Go it, Jeff, slam 'em in. Make him back up." Jack grabbed Jeff around the shoulders and said, "That's right, Jim, do just as your seconds tell you." Jeff ducked a left and shot a right to the body. A fan asked Johnson if he would like a drink. Jack responded, "Too much on hand now." He then said, "Now we'll mix it a bit. Come right on, Jeff, let's mix it." Jeff replied, "All right."

Johnson showed his class in a flash of real fighting. With startling quickness, Johnson fired a hard left to the body and three stinging left hooks on the sore mouth and face, driving Jeffries to the ropes. They were the most effective blows of the fight thus far, and Jack's first real fierce aggressive rush. It took only a second or two, but at its conclusion, Jeffries clinched, and it could be seen that blood was seeping from a cut high on his cheek bone, and his right eye was closing. Jack laughed, "Ha ha."

Corbett said, "Yes, I guess Johnson did have the better of that. I'd like to see Jeff cut loose a little. Gee, he's got Jim's right eye on the blink. Be careful, Jim, take it easy, you'll get him."

Jeffries kept trying to rush, but his blows lacked accuracy. Johnson fired the quicker blows, and more of them. A hard left caught Jeff's eye. Sullivan said Johnson's blows were harder than they seemed.

Jeff waded in, but on the inside, Johnson freed his arm and met Jeff with a nasty left uppercut that further puffed up and closed his right eye. Johnson also landed his right uppercut. After the bell rang, Jeffries rubbed his swollen eye as he walked to his corner.

Jeffries was bleeding from his nose, lip, and cheek, and his right eye was puffy, affecting his vision. His face was all marked up. Jeff had been aggressive, rushing and hitting the body, but ineffectively. Johnson was fighting and smiling strong. He jerked himself loose from clinches and fought savagely, peppering and hooking Jeffries, who seemed bewildered.

During the intermission, his seconds worked hard on Jeff's damaged optics, but only irritated him, and he told them to leave him alone.

In the 7th round, Johnson stepped in with left hooks. As they clinched, Johnson said, "Come on you, Jeff." When Jeff tried a right at close quarters, Johnson laughed sarcastically. Jeff rammed his left into the body. Jack said, "Try it again; once again, Jeff," and then drew Jeffries nearer to him. Jeff landed a left to the face and Johnson again laughed. Johnson was fighting cleverly and stopping leads, or at least smothering them.

Locked in an embrace, Johnson freed his left, jolted Jeff three times over the damaged right eye, and followed with a right uppercut to the jaw. Johnson also landed a left on the nose, bringing more blood.

Jeffries certainly was getting the worst of it. His nose kept bleeding. In the clinches, Jack kept freeing his left and jolting Jeff's head. After landing, he flippantly said to Jeff, "Well, old man, it's all over but the shouting."

Jeffries was showing the effects of the punishment. His right eye was swollen, his upper lip puffed, nose bloody, and cheek bone cut with gore dripping from it. He showed signs of weariness as well. The hot sun beat down on the fighters, and they perspired freely. The *Bulletin* said Jeff's blows were missing, and he was taking a beating.

Between rounds, Johnson kidded Corbett, "Too late now to do anything, Jim; your man's all in."

In the 8th round, after landing two hard left jabs, Johnson said to Corbett, "Hello, Jimmy. Did you see that one? How do you like the way things look?" Even Delaney said, "Why don't you smile, Corbett?" Jim replied, "He who laughs last laughs best."

Johnson kept landing. Jeff bore in with a show of anger, but Johnson clinched. Through his blood-bespattered face, Jeff shouted, "Break away, Johnson." But the champ did not break for a while. Jack drew away from a vicious left swing to make it miss, and then laughed.

Bill Naughton was dictating blow-by-blow to a telegraph operator. He said, "Jeff took a left hook to the jaw." Johnson heard him and replied, "Is that all he takes, Mr. Naughton?" Jack then landed twice with fast, short jolting hooks that brought blood.

In another clinch, Jack grinned over Jeff's shoulder, and, winking to the newspaper men, kept his left hand busy, generally landing. Jack said, "I've got your measure, Mistah Jeffries, and I am going to put you out any time I want to." To encourage Jeffries, Corbett said, "It only takes one or two, Jim." Then Johnson, as if to answer, landed a stinging left uppercut to the battered eye and said, "That's all it takes, Mister Jeffries." After a pause, Jack landed another, and said, "See that?" They hugged all around the ring.

Jeffries showed perceptible signs of tiring and slowing down, rushing and crowding less often. Conversely, Johnson was maintaining or increasing the pace, and was as quick as a flash. Yet, many still believed that eventually Jeffries would land a big one and turn the tide, as he always had done in the past.

When the 9th round began, Corbett said to Jeffries, "Go in and make that big stiff fight, Jim." Johnson replied, "That's right; that's what they all say." Jeff grinned and said, "Come along." Johnson replied, "Come on, I'll mix with you." Jeff led and landed a left on the body. Corbett hollered, "That's it, put that left in there again." While they were clinched, Johnson continued to fire and hurl terse statements at Corbett.

On the outside, Jack jabbed away at Jeff, stopping his forward progress. Corbett said, "Look out, look out. Keep away from those lefts, put up your guard. Don't let him keep putting them over."

Jeff shot in a couple of rights to the ribs and stomach. Corbett said, "Stick it into his stomach there, he can't take them."

In one clinch, Jeff leaned his chin on Johnson's right shoulder, where he was safe from the uppercuts. Johnson was smiling, and seemed brighter and happier than when he entered the ring.

From the outside, Jeffries stepped in, ducked a left and drove a solid right into the pit of the stomach that sounded like the beat of a bass drum. Jeff's men exclaimed, "That's the stuff. A few more like that, and he'll stop!" However, Johnson again smiled and invited Jeff to punch his body as hard and as often as he pleased. "Hit me again. You haven't found that weak spot in my stomach. Now, hit me in the belly, won't you?"

Newsmen agreed that Jeffries was looking very bad. The *Bulletin* said Johnson had opened a gash on Jeff's forehead, and he staggered him with successive left uppercuts. Jeffries planted an occasional body punch, but his efforts only brought smiles from the confident Johnson.

The 10th round saw Johnson continue landing, methodically poking, prodding, and pounding on him. As usual, Jeffries could not land cleanly.

When Jeff landed on the ribs, Corbett said, "Ha ha, he's getting tired now, Jim." However, Johnson effectively landed short lefts and rights to the face. Corbett said, "Look out for that right swing. I guess that one must have stung." Jeff landed a left on the face and drove a good left into the body. A spectator said, "Why don't you smile Jack." Over Jeff's shoulder, Johnson grinned at the crowd.

Jeffries blocked and eluded some blows. Corbett said, "That's it, Jim, block 'em; show him up. You've got it on him. He can't hurt you." Farmer Burns said, "Jeff, you're getting better."

However, Johnson always was on the alert to land or block. Jeff's head kept bobbing up from the whipping blows. Corbett lamented, "Jeff always lets them uppercuts go through." Jeff received a good hard left hook on the liver that put a sickening expression on his face. Mrs. Johnson, in the sixth row, shouted, "Keep it up, Jack."

Jeff's face presented a sorry spectacle. He was growing slower and more tired. His few rushes had been futile. Conversely, Johnson was fresh, aggressive, and smiling with confidence. His blocking was marvelous.

In the 11th round, Corbett said, "Short, snappy one, Jim." Jack replied, "Huh. Easy to say, but hard to do." Johnson feinted his left and landed the right sharply across the jaw as they clinched. Jeff shook his head as though stung. They wrestled for a while, but Jack landed several left hooks.

Jeffries was getting the worst of it, but kept trying to fight back like a tiger. However, he didn't seem to worry Johnson one bit. Jeff was spitting blood, breathing laboriously, and holding on a great deal as well.

Johnson was very good at yanking or working his arms free from the clinches and smashing in his famous short punches like piston rods, particularly uppercuts. Corbett said, "There's that right to the jaw. That coon certainly is outboxing Jim. Go on, I've handed him the same thing, Jack, and he just eats 'em up. He don't even feel 'em."

Jeffries kept trying to hit Jack's body with both hands. What punches he did land had no effect. However, Corbett said to Johnson, "You're getting tired, ain't you? That's it; now Jim, bore in. That's what he should have done at the start and he'd have taken the heart out of that coon."

Johnson smashed Jeffries time and again. The blood spouted freely from Jeff's mouth and nose in a stream. Jeffries was doing most of the clinching. A straight right on the chin caught Jeff and he wobbled.

However, suddenly Jeff electrified the crowd by making a rally, landing his right to the jaw and hard left to the body. This brought the crowd to its feet. Yet, in response, in a flash, Johnson bombarded him and banged a left on the bloody mouth, which left Jeffries unsteady at the bell.

No one was betting against Johnson anymore. Jeffries had freshened up on occasion, but none of his blows had any effect, and often Jeff was laying against Johnson for support. Jack was smiling and confident all the time, apparently toying with him.

At the start of the 12th round, Johnson looked at Corbett, laughed and said, "I thought you said you were going to have me wild." Whenever Johnson saw a friend at ringside, he smiled, nodded, or winked. He'd say, "Howdy, Joe," and then sent a left to Jeff's eye. "Hello, Tom," followed by a right uppercut. Corbett said, "Look at that coon nodding and bowing to the crowd. He's grinning now, but will he keep it up?"

Corbett lamented that Jeffries was not doing enough and was too slow, while Johnson was hitting him whenever he pleased, "making a sucker out of him." Still, he remained hopeful. "Jim will get one of those lefts over yet, and then it'll be good night. Johnson is landing left and right almost at will. Jim's bleeding pretty freely from the mouth."

At the bell, Johnson went to his corner smiling. In his corner, the tired Jeffries was spitting blood.

The majority of observers said Jeffries was in a pitiable condition, his energy sapped by the vicious grinding mauling. Johnson kept smiling and making sarcastic, cutting comments at Jeff's efforts. Still, the spectators hoped that Jeff had one big rally left. Richard Barry said, "If the white race must go down, we wanted it to go down in a blaze of glory."

The 13th round opened with Johnson saying to Corbett, "Hello, Jimmie; isn't it wonderful?" Johnson continually yanked his arms loose from clinches and landed hooks and uppercuts, pretty much as he pleased.

Jack cleverly evaded Jeff's blows, and just laughed at the ones which landed. In the clinches, when Jeff threw lefts to the stomach, Johnson looked over his shoulder, smiled, and did not attempt to resist the punches. A Johnson right uppercut almost lifted Jeff from the floor. Corbett was noticeably silent.

Johnson drove Jeff back against the ropes and smashed him full in the face with right-left-right. Jeff tumbled forward into a clinch, the blood pouring from his nose and mouth.

The round ended with Corbett advising Jeff to cover up and stay away.

At the bell, Jeff stared rather blankly into the middle of the ring. He appeared very tired, and slowly returned to his corner bleeding profusely. His face was all cut up, bloody, and swollen. He sat down, huddled over with his chin on his breast, appearing thoroughly discouraged.

All of the writers agreed that things looked very dismal for Jeffries. Johnson had chaffed Jeff's corner-men, defeated Corbett in the mouth fighting, and battered Jeffries in every way, inside and out.

In the 14th round, Johnson kept landing. Jeff swung a left on the cheek, but Jack just bowed to the audience and smiled. Jeffries landed a left jab, but it only brought a laugh from Johnson. They drew close and Johnson said, "Ain't that a nice belly Jim, why don't you hit it?" Johnson again dared Jeffries, "Hit me. Let's see how hard you can do it." Jeff put all his weight into a body blow.

There was a long clinch, with Johnson consistently ramming away at the face with both hands, bringing the blood. Corbett said, "Gee, but Jim's right cheek is battered up. That coon must be hitting hard. There goes that left again. It doesn't help Jim's face any. He tells me that he can't see out of the right eye." Members of the audience called out, "Talk to him, Corbett." A crestfallen Corbett had said little from the 7th round on.

Yet, Johnson took one of his characteristic loafing spells, laying back and playing with the big man. He was as cool as a cucumber, smiling as broadly as ever, confident, yet also careful, taking no chances, for he had matters well in hand, gradually punishing and breaking down his foe.

Corbett said, "Jeff lands a left high on the head. I wish Jim would lead oftener. He seems satisfied to just wade in and take them."

Three times Jeffries hit the body with his left. Johnson simply laughed and said, "My belly's gone to pieces – eh?" After breaking, Jack came back with a left jab on the face and left hook on the chin before they clinched. Corbett observed, "Johnson rests and then suddenly shoots over those punches and Jeffries looks as if he expects them, but he doesn't block 'em."

Johnson grinned and said to Jeffries, "Right on the hip; hit me heah, hit me heah." Jeff managed to land a left on the hip. Johnson said, "They say my belly is awful weak, Jeff. Awful weak." "Find that yellow streak you said I possessed." Taking body shots with a smile was Johnson's response to all those, including Jeffries, who claimed that Johnson and other black fighters could not take it and would show yellow as soon as they absorbed body punishment. Corbett then said to Johnson, "Why don't you do something? You're doing a lot of talking, why not fight?" Johnson replied, "Too clever, too clever, like you."

The *Call* said Jeff was just about done. The *Chronicle* and *Nevada State Journal* said Jeffries kept coming forward and springing in with blows, but the clever Johnson was able to block leads with the greatest ease, while frequently landing his own blows.

In the 15th round, Corbett shrieked advice. Johnson chuckled, "Do as they told you, Jim," and then landed a left to Jeff's stomach that hurt.

Johnson freed his right arm from the clinch and fired a vicious right uppercut to the point of the chin that jolted Jeffries' head back. Then Johnson fired three consecutive left hooks to the jaw, each one knocking Jeffries backwards towards the ropes, where he turned around and went down, grabbing the lower rope with his right hand. It was the first knockdown of his career.

The inexperienced Tex Rickard failed to count. Johnson hovered close to Jeffries, a few feet away. Corbett hollered, "Get up, Jim. For God's sake get up. Throw some water there, you fellows, are you turned to stone?" Of course, he was suggesting illegal assistance. Sam Berger yelled to Jeff's brother, "For God's sakes, Jack, throw in the towel and stop this fight."

Jeffries rose in about nine seconds; though some said it had been more.

As soon as Jeffries rose, Johnson quickly took one step in and nailed him with a powerful left hook to the jaw, and Jeff tumbled backwards through the ropes. His rear end and right arm were on the canvas outside the ropes, but his legs were draped over the ropes, hanging there, with his left hand grabbing the lower rope. Essentially, Jeff was in a sitting posture outside the ring with his legs caught on the ropes. Hundreds of his friends and admirers yelled for the bout to be stopped. "Don't let the old man get knocked out; stop it." "Don't let the negro knock him out." "Stop it, Tex! Stop it!" Corbett asked, "Why don't the bell ring?!"

Once again, Rickard failed to count. Jeff's cornermen mounted the apron. One walked on the apron over to Jeffries, outside the ropes. Two others entered the ring, including Corbett. Berger remained in the corner, standing on the apron. Another person who was not a second, whom Sullivan said was a newspaper man, mounted the ring from the other side of the ring and ran to Jeff, and he, along with one of Jeff's cornermen, lifted and picked up Jeffries from the canvas and helped him get back inside the ring again. A photographer also had entered the ring and moved over to the far side. Johnson coolly watched. Was the fight over? Referee Rickard did nothing to indicate that the contest was at an end.

Once Jeffries was back up and inside the ring again, Johnson quickly advanced and attacked. The cornermen exited the ring as the fight resumed. Johnson fired a left hook, and then momentarily paused with his left outstretched in stiff-arm fashion and his right help up high, as if he was uncertain whether he should continue. Jeff moved backwards and then across the side of the ring as Johnson gave chase, firing two more left hooks, a right, and another left hook as Jeff staggered on the retreat and slightly turned away and went down again on his hands and knees on the opposite side of the ring from where the first two knockdowns had taken place. Some in the crowd yelled, "Save him from a knock out; throw the sponge into the ring."

Once again, Rickard seemed confused, failing to count, while Johnson hovered about, calmly walking around his foe. Timekeeper Harting was counting the seconds. Once again, several of Jeff's cornermen entered the ring. The huge Sam Berger seemed intent upon stopping the fight this time, and approached Johnson, apparently hollering something, raising and pointing out his arm as he spoke, acknowledging defeat. In the meantime, Jeff rose, unassisted. Johnson pointed towards Berger and stepped away, to the side. Bill Delaney demanded the fight for his man. Tex said he already had awarded the fight to Johnson.

Berger led Jeff back to his corner, while Johnson's cornermen entered the ring and started celebrating Jack's victory, surrounding him on his side of the ring, while Jeff's seconds surrounded him over on his side of the ring. Others who were sitting at ringside entered the ring as well. The fight was over. John L. Sullivan congratulated Johnson.

The *Chronicle* said a hushed silence fell over the audience, like a funeral.

Johnson showed his sportsmanship by going over to Jeff's corner to shake hands, but either Corbett waved him away, or Jeff refused, depending on the verison. "He has never shaken Johnson's hand. He probably never will."

Jeff remained on his chair in his corner for several minutes, bleeding profusely from the mouth. He was in a stupor, with his head bowed down.

In his corner, Johnson was besieged by a mob of excited fans. The crowd inside the ring was so dense that the police had to keep people back. Jack seemed a bit concerned about potential violence to his person. His trainers and seconds formed somewhat of a circle around him. Johnson told Delaney, "No, I don't want to go through that crowd. They might mob me." Delaney replied, "Oh, come on, they are all your friends." Eventually, Johnson walked out, but he had his seconds around him as bodyguards.

Spectators tore the ring to pieces as souvenirs. In five minutes, the ropes, canvas, and other material had vanished.

The press, fighters, trainers, and managers all virtually were unanimous in their analysis of the fight. They agreed that Jeffries was not even a shadow of his former self, but was just a shell, while at the same time they granted that Johnson was a magnificent boxer who could not be beaten by anyone. Jeffries gradually faded as Johnson methodically broke him down. Jeff could not land effectively against Johnson's magnificent defense. He was dead game, smiling through the blood, always trying, but always failing. Conversely, Jack could land almost at will, chopping away, particularly on the inside, slowly beating Jeffries down.

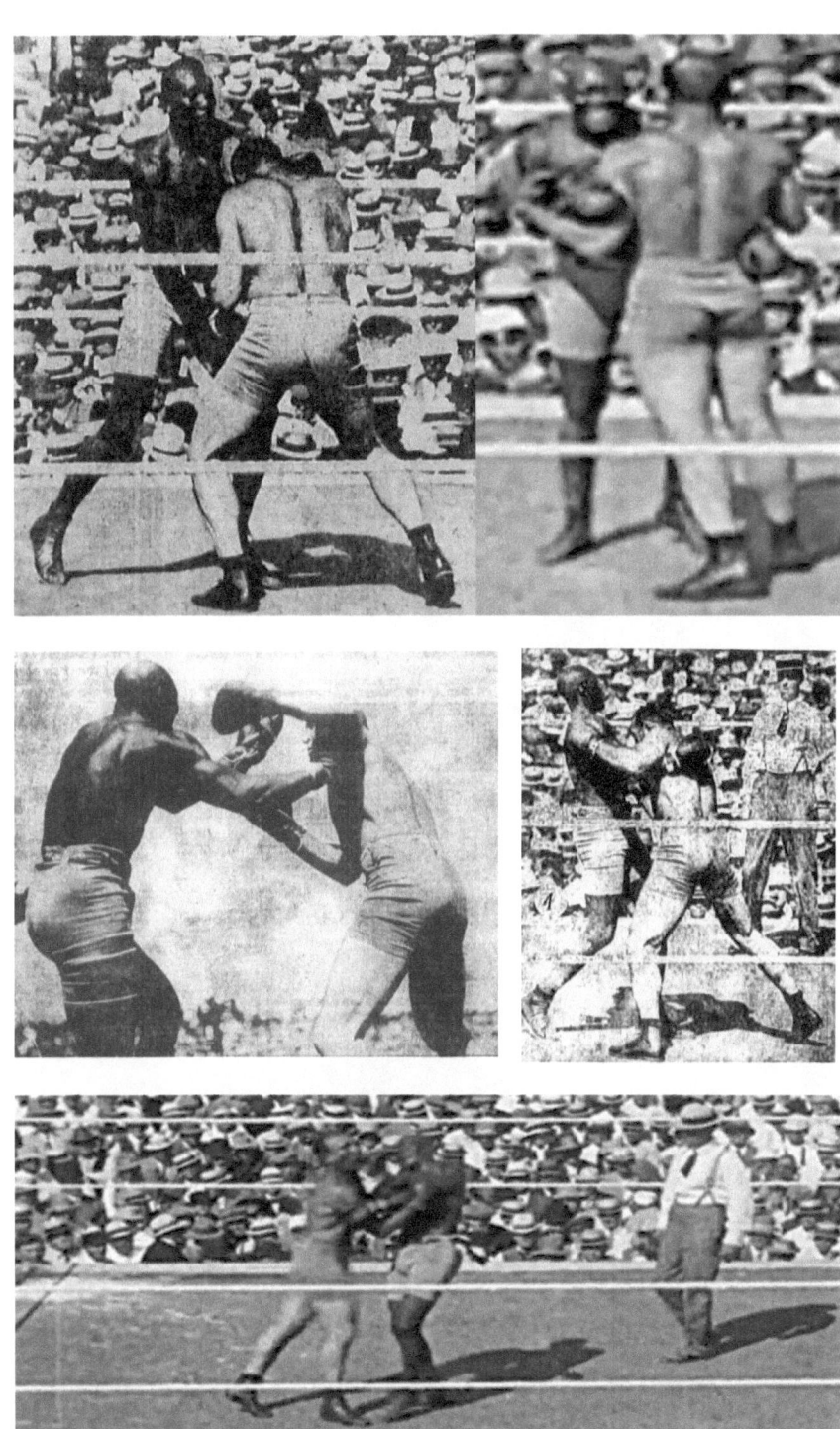

Observers agreed that the confident Johnson had played with Jeffries. He had been good-natured, light-hearted, smiling, laughing, joking, and nodding in the clinches. His golden smile was the most prominent feature in the ring. Jeffries jested with him as well, but not as often. At the conclusion of several rounds, Johnson gave Jeff a patronizing slap on the shoulder. When he wasn't making flippant remarks to Jeff he was amusing himself by chaffing Corbett or the audience.

Even a novice could tell that it was Johnson's fight from the start. However, no one dared express such a belief amongst the thousands of Jeffries admirers. He remained the favorite with the vast throng which cheered whenever he threw, regardless of whether the blow landed, carried any force, or had any damaging effect. "The mere fact that Jeffries had reached the negro with a blow was considered sufficient for loud applause." Even mere attempts found cheers. Whenever the crowd voiced its approval of what appeared to be a well-placed body shot by Jeffries, Johnson giggled and then peppered Jeff's face with several left hooks.

Seldom was there a positive word for the dark man, who was slamming away at Jeff's face, bringing the red blood flowing. During the bout, Pauline Jacobson said of Johnson, "Oh, he is giving it to him; he is giving it to him!" A spectator told her, "Oh, shut up! We've got to hope for the best. All the more credit to Jeffries if he wins." However, in the next breath, that same spectator said, "Oh, where are his famous stomach punches?" Later Jacobson said, "There's one thing, by God, they can't say now this was a frame-up. Johnson got him outclassed in every way; he's got him outboxed." A spectator responded, "Ah, cheer up. Jeffries is liable to get Johnson yet when Johnson is looking at the grandstand. He's too fond of that." But Jeff continued growing groggier. "God, it is awful." Many called the fight a "pitiful tragedy."

Between rounds, Corbett liked to stalk nearby to annoy Johnson, but Jack was cheery and buoyant. After the 13th round, Jim ventured forth no more.

When the fight was over, Johnson said to Frank Hall,

> I was only having some fun when the finish came. Not one blow hurt me. It is Jeffries that can't hit. He will never forget two punches I landed on him, and he will never order John L. out of his camp again for giving his opinion of a fighter. He won't be so grouchy now.

When Hall asked for Johnson's gloves, in declining, Jack replied, "I will give one to Corbett and one to Jeff."

The *Chronicle* believed Jeffries should have been counted out the first time he went down. It said he was down for twelve seconds. Even Jim Corbett said, "He was on the floor many seconds more than ten, but it seemed a year to me."

After the second knockdown, Jeff laid there until several of his handlers picked him up and tossed him back into the ring. William Slattery said, "It is a question as to whether Jeff ever would have risen but for the assistance of his brother, but, anyhow, [his brother] Jack [Jeffries] committed a rash foul, and had Referee Tex Rickard acted in accordance to the rules, he should have disqualified Jeffries then and there and awarded the battle to Johnson." Richard Barry agreed. "Technically, the fight should have been stopped right there, but Tex Rickard, the referee, who had not said a word nor lifted a hand until that moment, paid no attention to the irregularities."

The *Bulletin* said the illegal act of lifting Jeff up and back into the ring "brought a roar from the Johnson supporters," but Johnson did not complain or appeal to the referee. He had his man safe, and wanted no technical victory, but to end it cleanly. There were enough of Jeff's advisers in the ring to have disqualified Jeff had the referee so chosen.

The *Bulletin* said that as soon as Jeffries was lifted to his feet illegally, Johnson attacked, slugged, and mauled the "tottering hope of the white race" across the ring, and Jeff went down for the third time. Jeffries was not counted out, but rose at eight. "Whether or not, it probably will be counted as a knockout." Berger entered the ring to stop the fight. "We lose, Tex." Jim Coffroth said, "He would have gone down for a fourth time had not Berger made himself understood to Rickard that defeat was acknowledged by the Jeffries corner." Berger humanely stopped the fight. Jeff was like a man in a trance. Rickard raised Johnson's glove as a signal that he had won.

The *Call's* William Slattery said Tex Rickard did not initially give a formal technical decision as to how the bout ended. All folks knew was that Jeff went down three times and obviously had enough, Berger entered the ring to ensure that the fight was stopped, and Rickard declared Johnson the winner. The question was whether Jeffries was disqualified or knocked out.

Jack London said the end was pitiful. "Never mind the technical decision. Jeff was knocked out. That is all there is to it."

W. W. Naughton said, "Johnson will receive the credit of a knockout. It is the law of the ring that if anyone intervenes when a knockout is imminent, a knockout is recorded."

Another wrote, "Rickard finds it difficult to make an official ruling on the technical points involved, but is disposed to rule that the interference of Jeffries' seconds in helping him to get up after the second knockdown constitutes a disqualification." Rickard said Jeffries was disqualified.[795]

Rickard also said, "I thought the seconds were going to carry Jeff to his corner, Instead, they shoved him into the ring again to be beaten further, while I was doing all I could during the confusion to stop the fight." Yet, another quoted Rickard as saying, "I stopped the fight only when I saw that Jeff could not keep on his feet. It would have been brutal to have let Johnson hit him again."

Rickard's statements were not at all consistent with Rickard's actions in the ring, and do not match what the films show. Even though he could have disqualified Jeff for the assistance given to him in rising after the second knockdown, in truth that is not what he did. He allowed the bout to continue after Jeff was assisted up, and does not appear to make any attempts to stop the contest at that point. He also appeared willing to allow it to continue even after Jeff went down a third time, until Berger entered and made it clear that he wanted it stopped. Regardless, everyone knew that the real reason it was over was because Jeff had enough.

The *Chronicle* said, "It was pitiful in a way, this vanquishing of the hope of the white race, the effort of a man to drag himself back into athletic condition in order to wrest back to his own race the title that he had relinquished." Regardless, "The best man did win. No one of us can gainsay that, black man though he is."

Jack Johnson was given a great deal of credit. Newsmen agreed there was nothing that he could not do. He was a marvel of accuracy, a whirlwind for speed, a giant for strength, a masterful boxer and game fighter, with superb cleverness and ring generalship, like a panther, beautiful in alertness and defensive tactics, the "most wonderful big man that the prize-ring has ever seen." He presented an "almost impregnable defense," and was a "cracking good hitter."

W. W. Naughton said Jeffries was mastered, whipped, and cut to pieces by a grinning, jeering negro's merciless attacks. "It was a one-sided fight. ... Johnson proved more clever than many expected."

Jack Densham said Johnson smiled and took body blows with nonchalance, to the surprise of those who expected him to be hurt. He even intentionally allowed Jeff to land some body punches, causing wonder to sweep throughout the crowd.

---

[795] *San Francisco Bulletin,* July 6, 1910.

Ed Cahill said Johnson sat on the sunny side of the ring, and unlike Jeffries, required no sunshade protection, for his black skin protected him. "No naked lizard on a rock was more immune from heat stroke than he. Is the Caucasian fighting man played out?" Jeff kept boring for the body, and landed many times, but Johnson just grinned and patted Jeff on the back in a patronizing way. Jeff simply could not affect Jack's good nature. Cahill called Johnson a "grinning savage."

Frank Herman called Johnson a "shifty coon."

The *Nevada State Journal* and the *Chronicle* believed Johnson could have finished off Jeffries earlier had he wished. Some said he wanted to punish Jeff for the things he had said, and for drawing the color line on him for years. Others said he employed his usual cautious methodical style to wear down his man gradually.

The *Afro-American Ledger* said Johnson was "today without fear of contradiction the undisputed champion heavyweight of the world."[796]

The *Freeman* said Johnson was "as cool as an iceberg." Having longed for this fight for well over six years, he wanted Jeff to have everything in the way of terms so there could be no excuses afterwards. When Berger asked him to toss for corners, Johnson said, "Help yourself. Take that one over there so that Jim can have his back to the sun. I'll sit in the other corner. I don't mind a bit." Jeffries would not shake hands or pose together with Johnson for photos before the fight, a clear indication he thought Johnson was beneath him. Afterwards, the spectators looked like they were returning from a funeral. "Johnson is invincible and will remain so for years." "Long live Johnson!"[797]

Nearly every reporter and expert agreed the fight had disproved the theory that Johnson had a yellow streak, "the thing that has been written and talked about ever since he came into ring prominence." Jack London said Johnson went up against a bigger man with a huge reputation, but was not intimidated or scared at all. "And he played and fought a white man, in a white man's country, before a white man's crowd."

Frank Hall said Johnson's coolness "was the most remarkable exhibition of nerve I have ever had the good fortune to witness." Corbett kept up a streak of fire at Johnson, telling him that he was yellow and it would appear shortly, but Jack responded by smiling, unaffected.

Pauline Jacobson said everything was against Johnson, because the audience was white and the referee was white. She asked how Jeff would feel if he was fighting in front of a colored audience with a colored referee.

The *Bulletin* said Johnson was the coolest and most unconcerned man in the arena. His golden smile never deserted him. He showed "gameness in facing unruffled a man whom experts had pronounced invincible."

> Nor can credit be denied Johnson for winning under conditions absolutely unfavorable. There are many States in the Union where

---

[796] *Afro American Ledger*, July 9, 1910.
[797] *Freeman*, July 9, 1910.

black men enjoy a greater vogue than in the sagebrush commonwealth. The talk of possibly gun play in event of the negro's winning, taken in connection with the fact that practically every cent of Nevada money was bet on Jeff, was not idle twaddle. In the arena not one person in twenty was an admirer or backer of the negro, and not one person in forty was of his own blood. But the champion never worried and never laid aside his good-natured grin, not even when jeers and even insults were hurled at him by those about the arena.

Johnson "proved to the satisfaction of the writer, at least, that the 'yellow streak' so commonly reported to be one of natural inheritance of the negro was 'left at home' in his case, and that he could take, as well as administer, a glove punching at the hands of the foeman of equal girth and measurement."

Even Tommy Burns said, "Let no man now say Johnson has a yellow streak. He demonstrated beyond any manner of doubt that he is game to the core." He was shocked to see Jeffries at his mercy. "I heard hundreds of people applauding Jeffries for scoring body blows when from my seat I could plainly see that they had been cleverly blocked by the other fellow."

Jim Coffroth said,

> Let us now call Jack Johnson the champion of the world and not tell about all his poor fights and the little men he has whipped. He was asked today to meet in the ring the greatest fighting animal we have known. He met him in an arena where but few of his race were about him. ... He was fighting on a soil that has been referred to by the effete east as the 'wild and wooly west,' where gun plays are thought to be as common as the click of the ball on the roulette table. ... We will no longer hear of the 'yellow streak.' That's good.

Timekeeper George Harting said, "Johnson proved to the world that he is not yellow. On the contrary, he is game and aggressive."

The ongoing war of words and wits between Corbett and Johnson always resulted in a Johnson victory. Several times when Jack whispered to Jeff to break or he would uppercut, he did exactly as he threatened. Jack laughed and joked with the crowd, winked at Corbett, "who had been boisterously noisy during the opening stages," and time and again challenged Jeff to try to land a body punch. Johnson was the master of the situation so completely such that after the 10th round, Corbett's face turned grey and sullen, and he was silenced. The *Reno Evening Gazette* said the "white man with a grouch has been defeated by a colored man with a continual smile, one that won't wipe off, and the battle of all battles has been finished."

Stanley Ketchel said Johnson could have knocked Jeffries out whenever he wanted. "I never said a harsh word about Jeffries in my life; yet he ordered me out of his training quarters just because I picked Johnson to win this battle."

John L. Sullivan said:

> I was in such a peculiar position. I all along refused to announce my choice as to the winner. I refused on Jeff's account, because he was sensitive, and I wanted to be with him some time during his training. I refused on Johnson's account, because of my well-known antipathy to his race, and I didn't want him to think that I was favoring him from any other motive than a purely sporting one. He might have got this impression, although since I know him better in these few weeks I am rather inclined to believe that he has not many of the petty meannesses of human character.
>
> You will deduce from the foregoing that I really had picked Johnson as the winner. My personal friends all knew it, and even Jeffries accused me of it one day, but I denied it in this way. I said, "Jeffries, I have picked a winner, but haven't done it publicly."

Bob Fitzsimmons said the way Johnson patted Jeff on the shoulder after the rounds was as if to say, "Poor old fellow, I am sorry for you, but I have to do it." Fitz said Johnson was big, strong, powerful, clever, and cool. "He made me change my opinion of him as a fighter. I don't think there is a man in the ring today who would have a chance against Johnson."

Jack O'Brien also admitted that he was wrong in his estimation of Johnson: "I feel that he would defeat me in a long contest."[798]

Tex Rickard said, "Jack Johnson is the most wonderful fighter that ever pulled on a glove. ... Jeffries couldn't hit Johnson, and Johnson could hit Jeffries whenever he pleased." "It was the same old story. No two men can whip Johnson today. He fooled the whole world. All his previous fights have apparently been phony."

Afterwards, in his dressing room, Johnson said, "I never had any doubts about licking him, as I had seen him fight Corbett, Sharkey, Munroe, Ruhlin, and several other men and knew that I was his master." "He was only half the trouble that Tommy Burns was." "I outclassed him in every department of the fighting game."

> It was a game and courageous man whom I defeated. ... He simply could not hit me. I have always known this and he just found it out. ... I gave Jeffries a beating he will never forget. As I thought, I was too fast for him. ... I might have won sooner, but why take chances when so much was at stake. ... It may have looked easy, but Jeffries was certainly a tough one to put away.

Jack said his victory entitled him "to wear the championship crown without any 'ifs' or 'buts' to it."

Johnson believed the fight debunked several myths about him, including his alleged inability to absorb stomach punishment. What landed had no effect, though quite often, when the crowd cheered, thinking Jeff had landed, "my glove was between Jeffries' blow and my body."

---

[798] *Boxing,* January 14, 1911.

> Those clinch blows to my stomach did not bother me in the least. I have been saying it for years, and I say it again, although nobody seems to want to believe me, my stomach is the least vulnerable part of me. I am not bothered by blows there. I can stand up and let Jeffries do what he did to me in the clinches all day long and never bat an eyelid. ... It's a funny thing that every pugilist who fights me thinks he can hurt me by playing for my stomach.

Amused by those who liked to claim that he had a yellow streak, Johnson asked, "Did I back up? Did I run away? Who did the most of the leading? Who made the first lead?"

> One of the many things that are said by the people who cannot bring themselves to acknowledge that I am any good as a fighter is that I have no punch. Well, I think today's exhibition of punching should send that story to the waste basket along with the 'yellow streak' fable.

Regarding his interactions and talk with Jeffries inside the ring:

> Jeffries was quite good-natured in the ring. The only words we spoke to each other were joshes. There was no bitter feeling on my part, and I do not think there was any on the part of the big fellow. There was no personal satisfaction in knocking Jeff out, only the mechanical pleasure of winning a big fight.

Regarding Corbett:

> I had a lot of fun with Jim Corbett while today's fight was going on. Corbett is one of the men who thinks he can outbox me, and also that I am lacking in courage. ...
>
> Corbett was a failure as a second. He tried to rattle me by his talk, but what a chance! ... I'm just as good a jollier as I am a boxer.

Johnson complimented the crowd, for "instead of getting shot or hit on the head with pop bottles as some of the people expected" he was treated fairly. "I have a warm spot in my heart for Reno and the thousands of spectators that were in the arena."

Bill Delaney said if Johnson were white, he'd be Vice-President of the United States in a few years, given how affable and bright he was.

Speaking of his career, Johnson said, "It was not my fights themselves, but my fight to get those fights that proved the hardest part of the struggle." For years he had wanted to fight Jeffries.

> It was my color. They told me to get a 'rep,' but how was I to get a 'rep' without meeting fighters of class? But I made them fight me. I just kept plugging along, snapping up what chances to fight I could grab, until by and by the topnotchers saw that sooner or later they'd have to take me on. As soon as I had shown what I could do, the fight public – most of the fans, anyway – took sides with me, and that helped a whole lot.

It was the general belief that Johnson held back in his fights, lest he make potential opponents too afraid to fight him. He preferred to toy with his foes. He had a good temperament, never rattled, and usually smiled during his fights, even in the face of "coarse and insulting jibes that frequently greet him from fight spectators." He never lost his poise.

Johnson displayed a check for $60,600 for his share.

Regarding potential future fights, Johnson said, "I don't care who I fight next. Anybody who can draw a gate will be acceptable to me, but now that I have been in a battle in which $101,000 was the purse I'm liable to become an expensive luxury for the promoters, and it isn't likely that I would be attracted by anything but a big purse." If they wanted Johnson to take the time to train and fight and risk his valuable title, they would have to pay him very well. He knew his value.

Johnson's white "wife"/girlfriend Etta said, "I had a good seat, facing Jack, and at the end of every round, I waved my hand at him and smiled my encouragement. ... I hope the public will give Jack due credit for what he has done."

From Chicago, Johnson's mother was upset and insulted by the fact that Jeff had declined to shake Jack's hand before the bout. Her son promised her that he would win, and he always kept his promises.

After the fight, Jeffries had tears in his eyes. As he sat in his chair, Jeff said, "If it was only four or five years ago. I felt I was gone after the third round. It's no use; my stomach went back on me. Oh, this is awful." Once in his dressing room, Jeff sobbed, broken-hearted. "Just think, he knocked me out; yes, knocked me out. Oh, this is awful."

Jeff's wife said the loss would break his heart. He had worried and worked so hard, for such a long time.

One of Jeff's friends said, "He was forced into the match, and now I guess the people who lost on him will roast him. This is the saddest day I have ever known."

Later, various newspapers quoted Jeffries as saying:

San Francisco Chronicle:

> This hurts me worse than anything I have ever experienced in my life. I do not hold anything against the negro. He fought fairly, and beat me fairly, and I am not going to make excuses. ... I trained hard and thought I was there and my friends lost, that's what gets me. It's all over now. ... I guess it is Old Jeffries now, and people will knock.

San Francisco Examiner:

> I would have remained the retired and undefeated heavyweight champion of the world but for the fact that the American public demanded of me that I try to take away the championship from a black man.
>
> I don't regret the fact of my defeat so much as I do that it was a negro who beat me, thereby establishing himself as the best man in

the world. I would rather have been beaten three times over by a man of my own race than to have been the means of placing a negro in this position. It was to tear Johnson away from this honor that I consented to fight. I shot at the mark but missed it. There is nothing left to do but congratulate the winner. The color line should be drawn outside the ring. It cannot be done inside the ropes. When two men face each other for battle one of them must not be discriminated against because his skin is black. Keep him down entirely or give him fair place. ...

I went down trying with every ounce of energy in my body to bring back the world's heavyweight championship to the white race. ... I did everything that mortal man could do to bring myself back into fighting form. I actually believed that I had accomplished this. I felt that I was myself again ... I was mistaken. ... Had I met Johnson when I was in my prime the result would have been different. I would have beaten him. ...

I slaved to obey the will of the public. Had I neglected one single item in my long battle for condition I would feel that any criticism directed toward me was deserved. As it is I believe that I deserve consideration from my people; what is more, I feel that I will get it.

San Francisco Call: "Johnson is a great fighter and the people cannot imagine how clever he is."

Freeman:

> I was getting along nicely and living peacefully on my alfalfa farm, but when they started calling for me and mentioning me as the white man's hope, I guess my pride got the better of my good judgment. ...
>
> Six years ago the result would have been different, but now – well, I guess the public will let me alone after this.

That evening, Jeffries was quoted as saying, "What will mother say when she hears that I have ben licked by a nigger!" His mother was a Southern woman.

Jim Corbett said,

> We hailed Jeffries as the hope of the white race. Now we must hail him as the 'goat of the white race,' for it was the clamor and the howl of the white people who dragged Jim Jeffries out of retirement, who hounded him and fired him, by this hounding, to go into the ring against his will, and this was the result. The blame is upon our shoulders.

The fact that Jeff was beaten by a black man is what hurt Corbett the most. "If it had been a white man that beat him I would not feel it so keenly. But it gets to me pretty hard to think that Jeff was never knocked down in his life and after fighting half of the greatest fighters the world has produced, until he lifted the color line and fought a black man."

A *Reno Evening Gazette* writer said that before contest, people believed Jeffries had come back, or made themselves believe it. Frank Hall said the public had fooled itself into thinking that Jeff could come back. "We fool ourselves every day more than other people fool us."

Edward Hamilton said fans clung to their idolatry for Jeff throughout. "The race feeling was strong within even the men who had taken the benefit of the odds."

The chairman of the Board of Police Commissioners said, "Most people thought the negro would win, but they didn't like to say they thought the black would whip a white man."

San Francisco's mayor, P. H. McCarthy, noted that California Governor Gillette had claimed the fight was fixed for Jeffries, but the result spoke for itself, and showed how little he knew.

Sam Davis said,

> The odds in favor of the white man were purely fictitious and arose from the ridiculous touting of his condition and endurance from the pens of the so-called sporting writers of the San Francisco papers. These men have little judgment in such matters, but are influenced almost solely by their sentiments. ... This fight demonstrates that you cannot add an ounce to a fighter's blows or endurance by newspaper touting and the backing of the betting ring. Johnson could have licked Jeffries and all his training camp in the same ring this afternoon.

Frank Hall said,

> It seems a terrible thing for a white man to go down to defeat at the hands of a black. There was too much sentiment in this battle. People seemed to forget that it was a question of which was the best fighter, and there is no question of a doubt in my mind that that was the cause of the odds.

The *Bulletin* also said the glowing tributes of his trainers, Corbett, Berger, and Choynski, and newspaper scribes who were all more than friendly towards Jeff, deceived the general public and installed Jeffries as the betting favorite at a false price. Also affecting the odds were the constant qualifying phrases used in conjunction with Johnson's chances: "If he did not show his yellow streak." "If his disposition did not make him weak." "If he had not been bought off." Such statements fooled the public into the belief that Johnson was going into the ring to lose, and caused many to bet on Jeffries. "The popularity of Jeff with the fight-loving public of the world caused them to be easily swayed to bet on him against their better judgment."

Bob Fitzsimmons admitted that he had allowed his sentiments to carry him away. Deep down he thought Johnson might win, but he pushed that thought from his mind and only could think of Jeff's former greatness.

Gamblers on Jeffries lost a great deal of money. The estimated amount bet on the fight in the U.S. was over $3 million. The Johnson bet proved to be the greatest short-end wager ever. Many gamblers were angry at Jeffries, his trainers, and newsmen for deceiving them.

In another interesting twist, the *Evening Post* took a jab at the *Bulletin*, which prematurely claimed that Jeffries had won. The *Bulletin's* effort to be first, to have an inside scoop before anyone else, led to the early release of an incorrect special edition. It got carried away with the belief that he would win. A member of the *Evening Post* secured a copy of the first fight extra, which it teasingly called the *Bulletin's* only scoop in the past two years. When one man saw the paper announcing Jeffries' victory posted in the *Post's* window, done to embarrass the *Bulletin*, he growled, "Get out! The coon won all the way. I saw it. What does this mean?" Someone explained and he laughed. Even today, some news agencies rush to publish before having all of the facts. Fake news always has existed.

Naturally, everyone liked to speculate about what the result of a fight between Jeffries and Johnson would have been had they fought years ago, with some arguing that Jeff would have won, while others admitting the result would have been the same. Arguments amongst the general public could become quite heated and violent, particularly when they were between blacks and whites.

Jack London said, "Jeff was not the old Jeff at all. Even so, it is to be doubted if the old Jeff could have put away this amazing negro from Texas, this black man with the unfailing smile, this king of fighters and monologists."

Frank Herman said,

> In my opinion Jack Johnson is the most wonderful heavyweight that ever donned a glove. If his color was white instead of black he would be the most popular boxer in the world. His cleverness, combined with his coolness and great hitting powers, as well as his good-nature, would make him as big an idol as John L. Sullivan was in his prime.
>
> I believe Johnson would have defeated Jeff when Jeff was in his prime. I think that the coon-hued swatologist is the most marvelous piece of fighting machinery that the prize ring has ever known. He has every requisite that goes to make a champion.
>
> His enemies have always pointed to his past battles as flukes, and they have never failed to refer to the 'yellow streak' that he has never

shown in any of his contests. Yesterday he proved that he was game when he refused to run away and back up against a man who was supposed to be the strongest and most powerful heavyweight in the country. ...

Of course, many will try to console themselves by saying that Jeff wasn't in condition and that he would have wiped up the earth with Johnson when he was in his prime. However, the most expert trainers in the country pronounced the big giant to be in perfect trim, and they backed up their opinions with real money.

Bill Delaney said he always knew that Johnson would win.

Jeffries was always afraid of Johnson. When I was with him he repeatedly refused to sign with Jack. ...

Jeffries promised me faithfully he would fight Squires. I made a match at his request and he ran out on it. Had he met Squires, as he promised to do, he would have defeated Squires and Burns, the man who lost the championship to Johnson. Johnson would never have become champion, and, therefore, Jeffries is directly responsible for Johnson being champion of the world today.

Ed Hamilton said, "The gorilla is greater than the bear."

Helen Dare said, "I have shared with zest and felt the thrill of what has always been regarded as exclusively a man's game, a man's holiday. Shocking? Is it?"

The *Bulletin* said the crowd was more sportsmanlike than expected. There was no anti-negro demonstration.

Notwithstanding the fact that every white man wanted to see Jeffries win, as a matter of principle, Johnson received a generous ovation when he entered the ring and another when he left it. This is perhaps due to the fact that Johnson had been friendly with the people, while Jeffries and some of his trainers – notably Farmer Burns – had been exactly the opposite.

Another *Bulletin* writer said Johnson's victory was not popular. He was given less applause upon leaving the ring than his vanquished opponent received.

One *Chronicle* writer said the crowd response was muted. "It was like the passing of a funeral. Hardly a white man cheered, and few blacks." The end was taken with solemn silence. Helen Dare said Johnson's victory was unpopular, unanticipated, and undesired.

Sullivan said the fans pitied Jeffries. Although no friendship was exhibited towards Johnson, and little cheering, he was treated fairly. "The negro had few friends, but there was no real demonstration against him."

Ed Cahill said the crowd scarcely said a word about race, and when someone did say something offensive, there was a strong outcry of crowd disapproval; "Cut that out!"

Battling Nelson said the applause Johnson received for annexing the undisputed title was anything but flattering.

Bill Delaney noted that whites were upset with him for working with Johnson. "I received all sorts of threatening and insulting letters."

Tom Flynn noted the advances in racial tolerance.

> Thirty or forty years ago if Johnson had commenced to whip his white antagonist, the ropes would have been cut, the ring invaded by ruffians and he might have been lucky to escape with his life. He got few cheers today at Reno, but nevertheless, his treatment as compared with that of the old fighters was courteous.

W. W. Naughton said the crowd reaction at the end differed from most fights. There was one yelp when Jeff went down the first time. "Then those who yelled seemed to suddenly remember that a negro was beating down a white man. In the other knockdowns Jeffries fell in silence." After it was over, there was more silence as the big throng left the arena.

Former San Francisco Mayor E. E. Schmitz said, "I'm sorry to see a white man go down that way." He "spoke what was in everybody's mind."

Throughout the country, huge crowds stood in front of newspaper bulletin boards, reading news dispatches. Some newspapers hired look-a-like boxers to demonstrate the punches from inside a makeshift ring.

Baltimore's *Afro-American Ledger* noted that amongst the crowd standing near the news office where the fight returns were megaphoned out to the multitude, a white man exclaimed, "I hope Jeffries will kill the damn nigger." The black writer replied to him, "Johnson is right there in the ring with him." The white man said, "If Jeffries can get at him he will knock his damn head off." The writer replied, "There is nobody in between Johnson and Jeffries and Jeffries has every chance in the world to get him." When the fight ended, there was no applause from the crowd.

Helen Dare said that for over a year the entire civilized world had been interested in this fight to an extraordinary degree, and for the past two months had talked about little else. Millions of dollars had been wagered. An arena had been built just for one day. Men from all over the world had made special journeys. An army of writers had been engaged. Governors of two states and opposing and supportive moral factions had been mightily exercised. Jeffries had been training for more than a year. Yet, the actual event which meant so much to so many only lasted sixty minutes.

Rex Beach said the victory would help the black race:

> [Johnson] demonstrated further that his race has acquired full stature as men; whether they will ever breed brains to match his muscles is yet to be proved. But his heart, his yellow streak of which so much had been said, it was not there. He fought carefully, fearlessly, intelligently. He outpointed, he outfought, he outlasted his opponent. There remains no living man to dispute his title as the world's champion.

Clearly the fight could serve to dispel many racial myths about the inferiority of blacks, which could uplift the spirits of black folks.

One man who was ashamed said,

> I'm ruined. Think of it! A big black man beating Jeffries. Why, I would have bet old Bearcatcher against a truck horse that Jeffries could whip all the black men fighting at the same time in the same ring. ... This is a big blow to a man from down where we think a white man can whip a whole passel of men of Johnson's color. I can hardly believe it. It is a shadow on the white race. It's awful. I tell you I hate to look my friends in the face.

A captain of detectives said,

> Johnson did the trick, but he had to do it to convince the people that he was made out of championship material. ... There was more interest taken in the fight than in any similar contest, and the fact that a negro won it is not a fact that the average white man takes to kindly. Race prejudice should not interfere with judgment in boxing contests, and in this case the stronger, cleverer man won the fight.

A *Bulletin* writer said it was doubtful if ever there was a less popular champion than Johnson. "There are several reasons contributing to this, but probably no one factor was more potent than the sight of the beautiful and apparently educated and refined white woman whom Johnson calls wife standing up in the arena between rounds and throwing kisses and waving salutes to the black man." Whites were disturbed by Johnson's association with a white woman.

The *Call* called Johnson, the son of a former slave, the "new champion." The fact that some did not give Johnson full recognition as the true champion until he defeated Jeffries

Johnson with then girlfriend Etta Duryea, whom he called "wife."

explains why the bout was so important to Johnson and black folk, aside from economics. He needed the victory to obtain universal status as champion. Even John L. Sullivan noted that even though Johnson technically became champion with his victory over Burns, the rank and file of sporting people never gave him the full measure of his title until he defeated Jeffries.

Jack London lamented, "Once again has Johnson sent down to defeat the chosen representative of the white race, and this time the greatest of them all. And, as of old, it was play for Johnson."

A local Reno writer called it the greatest tragedy in ring history. As the "pride of the white race," Jeffries had been the idol of countless thousands throughout the world, all of whom were disappointed.

Pauline Jacobson said some had wondered whether blacks throughout the country would become demoralized and refuse to work if the white man won. Instead, the opposite had occurred. Whites were crushed. Allegedly, when a black woman who was boarding a train took off her hat, someone asked why she removed the hat, and she said, "Cause ah wants everybody to know that ah's a niggah, das why, an' ah'm prahd of it."

Years later, Johnson said he had wanted to punish Jeffries, as he had done with Burns, for all the rumors Jeffries had spread attacking his courage. Jeff had told a false story that he had offered Johnson the opportunity to fight him in a cellar, alone, claiming that Johnson had said, "I ain't no cellar fighter. I want to fight in public, with a referee." Jeff replied, "Oh, you aren't even a four-flush. You're a three-flush." Johnson said it was Jeff who had been afraid to fight him. Jeffries had "indulged in many hateful and venomous remarks" towards him. Even James J. Corbett, who was in Jeffries' corner, called Johnson names in an effort to upset him. In retaliation, during the fight, Johnson laughed at and taunted Jeffries and spoke to Corbett and ringsiders to reflect his confident control over matters. He wanted revenge, and he got it.[799]

Johnson made $70,600 from the fight purse and bonus. Jeffries received $50,400. Johnson sold his motion picture interests for $50,000, while Jeff sold his for $66,666. Including the bonuses, Johnson earned a total of $122,600. Jeffries earned about $117,066. Others noted that Jeff also had made another $75,000 in theatrical engagements. Johnson made aplenty on the stage as well. "Yet some people say fighting is a bad business." Jim Coffroth asked, "How would you like to be a 'white hope'?"

---

[799] *My Life and Battles* at 90-91. Johnson, *In the Ring and Out*, at 171.

CHAPTER 36

A Nation's (and the World's) True Colors Revealed

There was much more on the line in the Jeffries-Johnson fight, psychologically, than a mere battle between two men. The fight often was promoted in the press as a battle of racial supremacy between the white and black races. During this era, many politicians, scientists, and social theorists believed that blacks were inferior to whites in every way, physically, mentally, and socially. They believed and fostered the idea that whites were in superior power positions as the result of the natural order. Because world heavyweight champions had been viewed as symbols of national and racial superiority, Jack Johnson's victories challenged such theories.

Racial myths led the public to believe that Johnson lacked the physical and mental abilities needed to defeat Jeffries; that the best black never could beat the best white. For example, Johnson's relaxation and pacing in the ring, something actually beneficial to speed and condition, was considered black laziness, lack of focus, and lack of training. Jack's intelligent defense and cautiousness was called black lack of gameness. Much of the public and press had so built up Jeffries as invincible and so believed racial myths of black inferiority that it helped make Johnson the betting underdog.

The fight's racial contrast and strong racial feelings and issues made it a pervasive hot topic of discussion, leading to financial success, but also caused its racial symbolism to have serious political consequences and repercussions, both in the immediate aftermath and for a very long time thereafter. Not only was race pride at stake, but there was fear that a black victory could be used to upset the social and legal caste system that placed blacks at the bottom. Whites feared that a Johnson victory meant that blacks would demand more rights.

Jack Johnson realized that the magnitude of the event went beyond mere boxing. "It wasn't just the championship that was at stake - it was my own honor, and in a degree the honor of my race."[800]

Ironically, although the spectators inside the arena and in Reno had been well-behaved, it is an understatement to say that such was not the case elsewhere. The fight's racial implications and result set off an immediate wave of racial violence and riots across the nation, "between whites, angry and sore because James J. Jeffries had lost the fight at Reno, and negroes jubilant that Johnson had won."

---

[800] Johnson, *In the Ring and Out*, at 183.

When the national fight bulletins came in on July 4, 1910 announcing Johnson as the victor, many whites did not appreciate blacks' joyous, unbridled, and sometimes raucous celebration of their de facto representative's victory over the whites' representative in the battle for supremacy. The psychological impact and toll was tremendous, and it brought out the worst in many whites who did not want the fight's result to threaten the status quo or for blacks to think it was an argument for equal opportunity or rights. Therefore, they felt the need to lash out at blacks, particularly those who celebrated the victory. It was sheer anger meeting unmitigated joy; which in the racial climate of the time, proved to be a powder keg that ignited into violence throughout the nation. However, the violence was not limited merely to white on black; but included black on white, black on black, and white on white. Many blacks, uplifted and encouraged by the victory, which refuted racial myths, sought to exact revenge against a white society that had kept them subjugated. Any excuse could be used by either side to engage in violence in the wake of the fight.

Thousands were injured in the national riots, and there were many deaths. Not until the assassination of Martin Luther King, Jr. in the late 1960s would one event cause such widespread national rioting. Incidents in various cities included, but were not limited to:

Atlanta, GA – Whites chased many blacks, one of whom the police saved from being killed.

Baltimore, MD – As a result of arguments about the fight, several blacks were stabbed and injured in a race riot with whites. One was cut badly, and two others injured severely. 70 blacks were arrested for disorderly celebrations.

Charleston, MO – Unrelated to the fight result, two blacks were lynched for allegedly committing a murder. One black man who allegedly used rough language when addressing a white woman was about to be lynched, but eventually he was set free. The sheriff and his deputies claimed they were powerless against the crowd which attacked the county jail. An exodus of the black population was reported to be in progress.

Chicago, IL – Until daylight the next day, the streets were filled with blacks celebrating Johnson's victory. Whites were made the butts of boisterous wit. 36 blacks were arrested for disorderly conduct and for blocking traffic. Women were as wild as men in the excitement, and even some children accompanied them.

Many fights and riots were reported in the negro section, called the "black belt." Scores were injured. A negress was shot by a negro. One black man was stabbed and seriously injured.

Cincinnati, OH – Intermittent rioting followed the announcement of the fight result. Whites took blacks from their homes and beat then. A mob of hundreds of whites chased a black man who allegedly made offensive remarks.

Clarksburg, W. VA – Angered by black celebrations of Johnson's victory, a posse of 1,000 white men drove blacks off the streets. One black man was being led with a rope around his neck when the police interfered.

Covington, KY – Several whites stabbed a black man, who barely was saved from lynching.

Enoka, LA – Wild with enthusiasm, blacks paraded the streets cheering for the champion and taunting whites. Infuriated whites beat and shot to death a black man and his father, as well as a negress who shouted for Johnson.

Fort Worth, TX – Several white-black fights and race disturbances. Two negresses badly beat a white woman with beer bottles.

Houston, TX – When a negro on a street car vociferously announced the fight's outcome, a white man slashed his throat from ear to ear, and he later died. Another version of this incident claimed that a white man, who was stabbed by a negro, killed his negro assailant.

White men attacked and badly beat three blacks. Reports of a few persons shot. Police were called to quell several disturbances.

Hutchinson, KS – More than a thousand blacks that had gathered specifically for the purpose of praying for Johnson's victory were jubilant upon hearing of his victory. No riots.

Kansas City, MO – Street rioting.

Keystone, W. VA – In most instances, whites could not stand blacks cheering for their hero, so they attacked. Blacks fought back and eventually took possession of the town. A negress stabbed a negro to death.

Lake Providence, LA – A white man killed two negroes, and a negress was struck by a stray bullet.

Little Rock, AR – Several fights on trains. White men killed two blacks. A white conductor was killed.

Los Angeles, CA – Several white-black clashes occurred throughout the night. The *Call* wrote, "Flushed with small cash winnings, several negroes sallied forth, filled themselves with liquor and looked for trouble." A dozen were arrested on charges of drunkenness. When a white man spoke disparagingly about the champion, a black man severely cut him with a razor. Another white received two rib fractures in a fight with a black man who declared that he could lick any white man in California. Yet another white took a bad beating when he disagreed with an "arrogant negro" on Spring Street. Members of both races were treated at hospitals after interracial fights.

The next morning, the courthouse was packed with more than 200 cases of disorderly conduct and battery charges from the riots the previous day. Blood-stained bandages covered wounds made by clubs and knives. Fines of $5 to $10 were the rule. One white man, defending his actions in fighting, said a colored man was using some awful language in the presence of women and children, including that white people did not have any business on the street, given the fight's result.

Louisville, KY – Crowds of blacks attacked white newsboys selling extras telling of race riots and the fight.

Macon, GA – Authorities doubled the police force to prevent a race clash. Blacks were boisterous in celebrating the victory. Several were beaten. "The negroes have angered the whites by insolent remarks about Jeffries."

Mounds, IL – Four blacks killed a black constable who was attempting to arrest them for shooting up the town in celebration of Johnson's victory. One white man was killed and another mortally wounded.

New Orleans, LA – There was rioting near newspaper bulletin boards issuing fight result reports. Two whites shot and seriously wounded two blacks. The whites approached and said, "Johnson won, but we will get even with all negroes." Then they started shooting. One was hit in the head and the other in the arm and side. A negro who shouted, "Hurrah for Johnson!" was seized and beaten severely until the police rescued him. Several other relatively minor outbreaks of violence occurred as well.

Newport, RI – Between the announcement of the fight result and 1 a.m., there were 24 white-black conflicts.

New York, NY – Race rioting broke out in the seven different points of the city, affecting all of the boroughs. "The irritation caused by the defeat of Jeffries at the hands of the negro caused scores of street fights, negro hunts through the streets and outbreaks all through the night." There was rioting from the time the result was announced until long after midnight. Police reserves were out in all negro sections, called upon to quell mobs.

A negro waiter was killed in an altercation with a white man over the question of what Jeff in his prime could have done to Johnson. The white man ended the argument by striking the black man over the head with a blunt instrument. He later died in the hospital. His assailant escaped.

Whites pulled blacks from street cars and beat them. Some were found in the streets unconscious. One negro was dragged from a street-car and badly beaten before being rescued. Some white men were beaten in the negro sections of the city.

One black man almost was lynched for yelling to a crowd of white men in the San Juan section, "We blacks put one over on you whites and we're going to do more to you." After his revolver missed fire, the crowd was upon him. He was being hauled to a lamppost when the police rescued him.

A gang of white men set fire to a negro tenement on the West Side, but it quickly was put out.

One report said that sailors from the various battleships in the port were the leaders in nearly all of the attacks on blacks. About 50 badly injured blacks were in hospitals recovering from injuries.

The next day, the police were patrolling the "black belt" to try to check any further race trouble engendered by the bout's outcome.

Norfolk, VA – Fifty blacks and several whites were taken to hospitals for injuries received in riots. They had broken faces and stab wounds. Many blacks were in severe condition. There were riots in all parts of the city. Much of the trouble was caused by enlisted men from the various battleships who attacked blacks wherever they met them. Nearly a score of white U.S. sailors were fined from $5 to $20 for their assaults.

Omaha, NE – One negro killed and several injured.

Philadelphia, PA – Fights with fists, bricks, and missiles broke out nearly everywhere in the city where the two races intermingled. Police freely used clubs to quell the disturbances. Over 100 whites and blacks were arrested.

The next day, the arrested rioters, some with heads bandaged, went before a police magistrate. Most received a fine, but those more seriously involved were held with bail or sent to prison for short terms.

Phoenix, AZ – A mob seriously injured a negro.

Pittsburg, PA – In the negro district, street cars were held up, and insulting epithets were hurled at white passengers until police used their clubs to beat back the crowds to permit the passage of cars.

Scores hurt in race riots in which a thousand blacks attacked white men. 100 rioters were arrested.

Pueblo, CO – Two white men were stabbed and 25 hurt in a white-black race riot in Besemer City Park.

Roanoke, VA - There were street scuffles all over. Mostly, there were broken heads and black eyes. However, some knives were used and a few scattering shots were fired. Six blacks were beaten and badly injured. One was wounded fatally. Six white men were locked up.

One negro, upon hearing the fight result, said, "Now I guess the white folks will let the negroes alone." A white man replied, "No," and they clashed. The police jailed the negro, but allowed the white man to go free. However, another black man shot that white man in the head. The bullet went through his skull.

St. Joseph, MO – A mob of whites attacked a fellow white man who came to the defense and aid of a black man who was being struck and beaten by another white man. A policeman finally rescued him.

St. Louis, MO – Blacks blocked traffic and made threats. Eventually, a score of police clubbed the blacks into submission and dispersed them.

Blacks had planned a celebration to be held the day after the fight, but the authorities interfered and forced the plans to be canceled. Blacks were cautioned against assembling in the streets.

Shreveport, LA – Three blacks killed, one white fatally injured, and scores of both races hurt in the post-fight riot.

Uvalda, GA – Riots led to the deaths of three blacks; and many injured.

Washington, D.C. – At over 100,000, the largest black population in the U.S., blacks were in a frenzy of delight over Johnson's victory. The police were ready for trouble and quickly stopped many fights. The *Call* reported, "The negro saloons were crowded with coons filled with gin." Hundreds of drunken blacks proceeded through the streets.

Blacks were wild with enthusiasm, and their boisterousness increased as the evening progressed. Police tried to quiet them but there was invariable conflict, and several persons were injured seriously.

One report said 7,000 blacks and whites rioted throughout the night.

Three white men chased a negro who had been shouting, "Hurrah for Johnson, champion of the world!" Fight after fight followed in quick succession. Police arrested members of both races for rioting.

Some blacks attacked whites. Three negresses dragged white women into the streets and beat them and tore their clothing away. An enlisted U.S. marine had his throat cut and was at a hospital in serious condition. Another white man was found unconscious after a free-for-all fight on Pennsylvania avenue. He was taken to a hospital, where it was determined that he had a concussion. A negro stabbed a white man, which required hospitalization.

Every policeman was on duty. There was a question as to whether federal troops should be ordered into the nation's capital to restore order. The fighting was continuous along Pennsylvania avenue between the Capitol and the White House. Rioting continued all night.

At least 200 blacks were arrested and more than 30 whites. Others said there were 246 arrests. Two hospitals were crowded with the injured. Heavy police detachments patrolled negro settlements. Daylight brought little cessation to the celebration. One or two shooting affairs occurred during the evening. Many were severely injured, but none fatally.

Washington, PA – Blacks shot two persons in cold blood.

Wilmington, DE – Whites attempt wholesale lynchings. Scores were injured in the resultant riots. Police clubbed whites and blacks who were fighting. Police threatened to shoot into a crowd of 5,000 whites that were throwing stones at an arrested negro.

There were race riots in nearly every sizable city in the U.S. Thousands of blacks were beaten and many were dead or dying. The mob spirit seemed to rise up wherever a negro cheered for Johnson or permitted his exultation over the victory to grow to an extent that made it offensive to whites. Blacks were chased through the streets. Many fought back, injuring and killing several whites.

The *Bulletin* said scores of cities saw fighting that raged all night. Most victims were black. Up to noon on July 5, 19 blacks and 5 whites had been killed, hundreds of both races were badly injured, and hundreds were in jails and prisons. Hospitals were filled as well.

The *Chronicle* reported that most of the trouble was in the South, but large cities in the North were not immune.

Ironically, there were almost no troubles in Reno, where the fight had taken place. The week of the fight, at least 300 known criminals were arrested. Over half were drunks. Many were taken into custody on suspicion of theft. The police were on guard to arrest anyone who even hinted at making trouble. Hence, most known troublemakers were incarcerated on the day of the fight. The City of Reno was determined that there should be no issues, and it had been successful.

Some blamed whites for the riots, some blamed blacks, and some said it was a mixed bag, varying from situation and locale. The *Call* said the blacks celebrating Johnson's victory precipitated trouble with whites. The *Evening Post* said the irritation caused by the defeat of Jeffries at the hands of a negro caused scores of fights and negro hunts.

Mrs. Tiny Johnson, the champion's mother, deplored the riots, and said it all was due to white unwillingness to allow blacks to express themselves. "The white ones do not like for a black man to be on top, but Jack's there, and his victory will help the entire negro race."[801]

Blacks rejoiced at the victory in the greatest celebration since the issuance of the Emancipation Proclamation. To them, it proved what they could do if allowed to compete on an equal footing, and was an extremely significant psychologically uplifting and liberating event. Furthermore, Johnson and his victory was the symbolic representation of black revenge upon historic and ongoing white indignities.

The powers-that-be were aghast. The fight result and the riots had a ripple effect. Some wanted to ban boxing; some wanted to ban the fight films; while others attempted to disavow the very racial meaning that much of the press and public had conferred on the bout before it had occurred.

In Los Angeles, it was said that the city council would pass a law to prohibit all boxing exhibitions.

The *Los Angeles Times* was concerned that as a result of Johnson's victory, blacks might become too uppity, confident, and demanding of more civil rights. It sought to disabuse blacks of such notions, and to diminish the fight's significance. It told whites that the fight meant nothing, and to take the loss in a more honorable fashion:

> It was a fight between a white man and a black man, but it is well at the outset not to pin too much racial importance on the fact. The conflict was a personal one, not race with race. ... Even if it were a matter of great racial import, the whites can afford the reflection that it is at best only a triumph of brawn over brain, not of brain over brawn. ...
>
> The white man's mental supremacy is fully established, and for the present cannot be taken from him. ... His superiority does not rest on any huge bulk of muscle, but on brain development. ...

---

[801] *Nevada State Journal, Reno Evening Gazette*, July 6, 1910; *San Francisco Evening Post, San Francisco Call*, July 5, 1910.

The members of the white race who are not a disgrace to it will bear no resentment toward the black race because of this single victory in the prize ring. That would be to manifest lamentable weakness, not strength; stupid foolishness, not wisdom; a cowardly disposition, not manliness.

Let the white man who is worthy of the great inheritance won from him by his race and handed down to him by his ancestors "take his medicine" like a man. If he put his hope and the hope of his race in the white man who went into the ring, let him recognize his foolishness, and in his disappointed hope let him take up this new "white man's burden" and bear it like a man, not collapse under it like a weakling.

And now a Word to the Black Man.

Do not point your nose too high. Do not swell your chest too much. Do not boast too loudly. Do not be puffed up. ... Remember you have done nothing at all. You are just the same member of society today you were last week. Your place in the world is just what it was. You are on no higher plane, deserve no new consideration, and will get none. ... No man will think a bit higher of you because your complexion is the same as that of the victor at Reno.

The *Times* further said the fight did not mean the black man was on top. "You are no nearer that mark than you were before the fight took place." But it also said, "White men who are men worthy of the name will not join in any fresh crusade against your race, already too long and too cruelly persecuted."[802] The fact that whites spent so much time trying to diffuse the Johnson victory was an implicit acknowledgment of what a powerful occurrence it really was. Whites also were trying to quell further violence.

Ministers throughout the country started a movement to get the fight films banned. Christian societies believed the films were as bad as the fight itself. They lobbied politicians, saying the film exhibitions would be demoralizing, the cause of more violence, and harmful to the morals of women and children. Most police chiefs supported the ban, fearing that public exhibitions would encourage race riots and crime.

Given the national violence which had occurred merely in the wake of verbal and written fight reports, many politicians throughout the country feared that the film exhibitions might cause further violence. As a result, most cities and several states banned the Jeffries-Johnson fight films.

Some cities said they would allow the films, some banned them outright, while other cities said the film exhibitions would be permitted provided that no disturbances were created, taking a wait-and-see approach. Usually the films were barred by executive order of the mayor, or sometimes by emergency legislative action. Some police departments simply banned them on their own. Most jurisdictions which outright banned the fight pictures

---

[802] *Los Angeles Times*, July 6, 1910.

argued that the films would cause race hatred and riots, or they called the films detrimental to public morals, brutal, and degrading.

Major cities which outright banned the exhibition of the Jeffries-Johnson films included: Baltimore, MD, Berkeley, CA, Boston, MA, Buffalo, NY, Cincinnati, OH, Fort Worth, TX, Houston, TX, Indianapolis, IN, Little Rock, AR, Los Angeles, CA, Louisville, KY, Milwaukee, WI, Minneapolis, MN, Mobile, AL, Norfolk, VA, Oakland, CA, Portland, ME, Providence, RI, Richmond, VA, St. Louis, MO, San Francisco, CA, Savannah, GA, Springfield, IL, Springfield, MA, and Washington, D.C.

A local Baltimore Cardinal said children had to be protected from the films. The picture shows would have a bad effect upon the community, and would "tend to induce attacks upon the blacks," as well as cause riots. "The black people could not profit by seeing the pictures and I am sure the whites would not." The Los Angeles city prosecutor said he would enforce the city ordinance prohibiting the exhibition of motion pictures that were subversive of morals or harmful to the young, which to him included fight films. St. Louis police officials "believe that negroes...eager to show their admiration for Johnson and the belief that the black can whip any white man living will become riotous after viewing the pictures." San Francisco's Board of Motion Picture Censorship banned the films. One member of the board of censors said prize-fight pictures had a demoralizing effect on the young, while another said suppression was necessary to prevent race war. The Topeka, Kansas mayor said the police would stop any show and arrest the managers of any theater who showed the films.

In Atlanta, a bill prohibiting the display of moving pictures of any prize-fight was introduced in the general assembly. "The pictures would inflame the anti-negro sentiment and the result would be disastrous."

Some places, like Kansas City, Missouri, said the pictures would be allowed unless they provoked race rioting. In New Orleans, initially the mayor issued an order to the chief of police to arrest the proprietor of any theatre attempting to show the moving pictures. Later, New Orleans decided to allow them to be shown, but only when blacks and whites saw the films at different times. Segregated exhibitions would reduce the possibility for violence. Pittsburg police said the pictures would be allowed unless when shown they proved to be the cause of race trouble.

Some welcomed, or at least refused to ban the films. The mayor of East Liverpool, Ohio said there was no more harm in showing the fight films than in allowing the presentation of Wild West shows. "This agitation over the country is simply advertising the pictures. If people remained quiet the public soon would forget the fight."

In New York City, the International Association of Police Chiefs said boxing film exhibitions were illegal because prize-fighting was illegal in New York, and therefore the film exhibitions would be the reproduction of an illegal act. However, New York City mayor William Gaynor had a tolerant attitude towards the films. He said, "New York hasn't a large negro population, and I am sure the pictures will not engender any race feeling here." The mayor said he had no more right to stop the films than to stop publication of the stories of the fight. He would not use arbitrary power to suppress the exhibitions. In a letter to a reverend who represented an international reform bureau, the mayor said,

> Ours is a government of laws and not of men. ... I shall not take the law into my own hands. You say that you are glad to see that the mayors of many cities have 'ordered' that these pictures shall not be exhibited. Indeed? Who set them up as autocrats? ... The growing exercise of arbitrary power in this country by those put in office would be far more dangerous and is far more to be dreaded than certain other vices which we all wish to minimize.

Portland, Oregon's mayor said, "I cannot see that the displaying of the pictures is any worse than the printing of the minute details of the fight in the newspapers."

In San Jose, California, the mayor refused to be swayed by the ministerial hysteria, and allowed the showing of the films. He said,

> I do not see any reason why the Jeffries-Johnson pictures should not be shown in San Jose. Under the English common law every idiot, insane person and incompetent, as well as every minor, was provided with a guardian to care for him, but anyone else might do as he pleased. So it is here and it seems to me that the proper way to deal with the situation is to prohibit those from seeing the exhibition who are incompetent. There is nothing about the pictures of the fight which can be very injurious to persons of sound mind and faculties.

Seattle, Washington's mayor, confident that the police could do their duty and handle any problems, said there would be no interference with the fight pictures. "Whenever I am convinced that the city is unable to handle any riot that may result from the exhibition of fight pictures in Seattle, I will immediately tender my resignation."

Many state governors were supportive of a ban, including the governors of Alabama, Arkansas, California, Colorado, Illinois, Indiana, Iowa, Maine, Maryland, Michigan, North Dakota, South Carolina, South Dakota, Texas, and Virginia. California's governor said, "The interest in the fight was exaggerated into hysteria. Now comes the natural reaction, following the collapse of that hysteria." The *Bulletin* noted, "The Governor intimated that the prejudice against the pictures might not have been so general and so pronounced had the white man defeated the negro." Missouri's governor said if the fight pictures started race riots or produced public disturbances in the state, he would prohibit their display as a public nuisance. Several governors left it up to individual towns to decide, but encouraged them to ban the films.

Even foreign cities and countries considered whether or not to allow the Jeffries-Johnson fight film exhibitions. Most who banned them feared incitement of racial animosity. One must keep in mind the political and racial context. Much of the world contained nations whose darker-skinned majorities had been conquered and colonized by white minorities. From the conquerors' perspective, the films could send a dangerous message to those who were oppressed – that their lot in life was not inevitable. Such a message could foment agitation, demand for more civil rights, and ultimately rebellion. The films' potentially powerful symbolic message led to their banishment by many towns and countries throughout the world:

British Columbia, Canada – Films barred by executive order.

Calcutta, India – The demand to prohibit the pictures was spreading. The newspapers there suggested that the American authorities destroy the films and compensate the owners.

Cape Town, South Africa – There was widespread demand to prohibit the films, "owing to their effect on the natives. Signs already are evident among them of excitement on account of the victory of the negro." South Africans were refusing to order the films at all, fearing racial unrest.

Havana, Cuba – The government prohibited exhibition of the fight pictures.

Johannesburg, South Africa – All of the newspapers demanded the suppression of the moving pictures. It was believed that the town council intended to forbid the exhibitions as detrimental to the public peace.

London, England – A movement in favor of government action to suppress the fight pictures was extending to a considerable section of the House of Commons. Some morning papers advocated for suppression. Sir Howell Davies said he would ask the Home Secretary in the House of Commons to prohibit the fight films in the interest of public decency. The London City Council voted to deprecate the showing of the films. Although there was no law preventing the halls from showing them, it was thought that theaters would be hesitant to do so, given that the Council granted discretionary licenses every year, and the halls would not want to incur their ire.

Manila, Philippines – Fearing the effect that the bout might have on the Filipinos, the municipal board of Manila resolved to prohibit the picture exhibitions.

Melbourne, Australia – The clergy sent a petition to the Australian premier asking him to prevent the pictures. A similar movement was afoot in New Zealand.

Mexico City, Mexico – The pictures would be welcomed. The Governor of the district said, "Happily, we have no negroes here."

Ontario, Canada – Barred by executive order.

Pretoria, South Africa – The government sent instructions to the police to prohibit film exhibitions of the fight.

The majority in the U.S. held that the fight films were injurious to the morals of the young and provocative of race war. The feeling was very strong in the South, where the black population equaled or exceeded the white population. Many reverends said the pictures would have a demoralizing effect, that children would be influenced by them, and the films "would inspire them with false ideals," whatever those were.

San Francisco Evening Post, July 8, 1910

Those of us who understand our 1st amendment constitutional rights to be something time-honored and sacrosanct might be asking how the government could censor and ban fight films. Well, the U.S. Supreme Court did not hold that the 1st amendment was applicable to the states in any way until 1925, in *Gitlow v. New York*, 268 U.S. 652 (1925). Hence, until then, the 1st amendment only applied to the federal government. At that time, cities and states could do whatever they wanted when it came to censorship, unless deemed unlawful by the state constitution.

Various noted clubwomen joined the hysterical war on the fight pictures, demanding the protection of children from the degrading spectacle. The District President of the San Francisco Federation of Women's Clubs said, "Any sort of prizefight is debasing, but the one at Reno was particularly degrading. It aroused primitive passions. The white race is not depending for supremacy on brute force, and no man of the caliber of a prizefighter fosters the ideals of our civilization." The lady Vice-President of the California Club wrote,

> The fact that this man Johnson is the champion fighter of this country deludes the colored race into believing that they have made great progress. It gives them a false security, sets up a degrading ideal for them, and immeasurably retards their growth in real intelligence.
>
> One reads about these race riots everywhere. The pictures prolong the degrading event that happened in Reno on the Fourth by emphasizing it in the minds of children and of persons of immature

intelligence. The negroes are to some extent a child-like race, needing guidance, schooling and encouragement. We deny them this by encouraging them to believe that they have gained anything by having one of their race as champion fighter. Race riots are inevitable when we, a superior people, allow these people to be deluded and degraded by such false ideals.

Let alone the injury that will be done our children by allowing them access to such a spectacle as these fight pictures, we also owe something to these negroes. As a superior people we are under responsibility show them a better way than this.

Naturally all of this was a big concern for the companies and men who had invested a great deal of money into the films, such as the American Vitagraph Company. Financial interests were at stake.

The motion picture syndicate said they would not show the pictures in any city where adverse legislation existed. They did not intend to buck the law. "We do not think these pictures are any different from those which have been displayed of the Johnson-Burns and Johnson-Ketchel fights, but if we find that popular sentiment is against them we will lay them on the shelf and not show them at all." However, they reputedly had invested $200,000, so they were going to need to show the films in the locations that would allow them, or via underground private clubs, exhibitions, and stag parties. Subsequently, the Vitagraph Company said they only would display the films privately, not publicly, in order to ensure that the younger generation would not be allowed to see them.

Apparently, the motion picture men made the announcement that the films would not be shown at public exhibitions because they felt that putting up a fight to show the films would have resulted in the passage of additional laws making the exhibition of fight pictures a crime. By gracefully withdrawing, without opposition to public clamor, the pictures still would have the option of making money via private displays, which could give them a chance to earn some money, although not as much as would have been the case with public exhibitions. Plus, perhaps after all of the hysteria and ill-will died down, eventually the films could be displayed publicly.

Black folk wanted to see the films. Unlike most white ministers, the Negro Ministers Conference refused to endorse a resolution favoring suppression of the fight films. One Methodist bishop admitted that he had prayed for a Johnson victory. "[He] wanted to see the black man win, especially as the whites had made a race issue of the encounter. He urged that no appeals be made by colored men to suppress the pictures and declared that men advocating such suppression were doing so only because the black man had won." Most blacks believed the main reason why the films were being suppressed was because Johnson had won.[803]

---

[803] *San Francisco Chronicle*, July 5-7, 1910; *Reno Evening Gazette*, July 5-7, 12, 13, 1910; *San Francisco Bulletin*, July 6-8, 1910; *San Francisco Call*, July 5-8, 12, 1910; *Nevada State Journal*, July 6, 8, 1910; *San Francisco Evening Post*, July 6, 11, 12, 1910; *San Francisco Examiner*, July 9, 10, 1910.

San Francisco Examiner, July 9, 1910

San Francisco Bulletin, July 16, 1910

Sympathizing with American whites, many newspapers in London, England were excusing the white violence that followed in the wake of the fight result, feeling that it was understandable, and perhaps even necessary. A *Freeman* correspondent said the queer thing about the reaction was that the English, who usually took delight in anything that reflected adversely upon Americans, suddenly reverted to support for black suppression. Race appeared to trump nationality, particularly since the British had colonial considerations. "The *London Afternoon Star* is practically the only afternoon paper that has criticized the outbreak of anti-Negro violence." The London *Globe*, which usually was anti-American, was not so in this instance. It said,

> Our sympathy runs more to the man with the rope than to the blatant blacks. It is against human nature to expect white men to accept the negroes' insolent assertion that Johnson's victory established the superiority of the black without instant protest. The Reno contest was the most injudicious one ever permitted and the racial effects will continue for years.
>
> The Americans are the trustees of the predominance of whites over blacks and we believe they will prove true to their trust.

Writing in support of white-upon-black violence, the London *Daily Telegraph* said,

> It is useless to hold up the hand of reprobation here. These things are brutal and vile, but behind them lies the absolute necessity to keep the negro race a little in check, for if it once gets out of hand there will be worse scenes under the stars and stripes than have yet been witnessed there.

The *London Times* said the fight proved nothing, for a thousand American whites probably would beat a thousand negroes in any conflict or form of physical endurance. It commented on the fact that Americans disliked seeing a white man beaten by a Negro, and remarked,

> The American feeling must frankly be recognized. The feeling, we think, is not confined to America. It is very easy for us in England, where we have no color problem, to talk with indignation and abhorrence of the lynchings and the outrages which occur so frequently in the Southern States of America. We have yet to see how the English would act if confronted with entirely similar conditions. There is much reason to fear that our attitude would be no more tolerant.

The *San Francisco Evening Post* wrote, "The *Times* thinks that the pivot of the whole question is the world-wide instinctive feeling against color intermarriages." It didn't help matters that Johnson's girlfriend was white.

Many newspapers deplored the fact that a white man had consented to meet a black, and some reiterated condemnation of former champion Tommy Burns for ever having consented to fight Johnson just so he could earn money. They blamed Burns for having given a black man a chance at the title, which ultimately forced Jeffries out of retirement.[804]

Several writers said pugilism's death seemed imminent. John L. Sullivan replied that talk of boxing's future being gloomy was ridiculous. "Now this Jeffries-Johnson fight marks the end of the sport. BOSH. When they change human nature, and put a mollycoddle's heart in every good, red

---

[804] *Reno Evening Gazette, San Francisco Evening Post*, July 7, 1910; *Freeman*, August 6, 1910.

blooded American citizen then the game might die," but until then, there was scant danger of pugilism ceasing.[805]

Thomas Bannerman, president of the San Francisco Board of Education, said the fight's result was a "proper rebuke to the Caucasian race." He was glad that the black man had won.[806]

The *Bulletin* said the fight game was dying by inches, for politicians used the sport to serve their own personal and political ends. It looked as if California officials had their minds set upon boxing's complete abolition.

Tex Rickard said the country was being run by crooked politicians. He called the anti-fight-film movement hypocritical. He noted how San Francisco Mayor McCarthy had been a friend, had brought the fight there, fully supported it, and a permit was paid for and granted, but now the mayor was jumping on the bandwagon, saying that the fight films were illegal and corrupted morals. "I suppose it is a case of politics." The *Bulletin* also called the mayor a hypocrite.

Rickard argued that if the fight really was such a brutal affair, the best way to convince people for all time that such was the case would be to let them go and see the pictures in question and judge for themselves.

> Every day in the week all over the country the youth of the big and small cities are shown on the canvas the commission of murder, robbery and trickery of all kinds, and these shows go on without censure. Why this sudden disposition against the pictures on moral grounds is hard to understand.

He said there was more brutality in amateur bouts with raw and inexperienced youngsters than in a pro bout with trained and experienced fighters.

Tex said the attempts to ban the pictures would make the investors more money in the end, for it was the best advertising in the world.

Rickard said it was impossible to promote fights unless one first got himself "right" with politicians, "and I guess you all know what that means." He said Governor Gillett misled him willfully, told him in person that he would not interfere with the fight, but then when the time was right, turned on him by panning the fight and getting it barred, making a play of political pyrotechnics. "I don't know what politics is behind this, but you can gamble it's crooked politics." It showed that the whole game of government was "rotten to the core." "If Gillett had told me that he would not allow the fight to be pulled off in this state I would never have thought of coming here. But Gillett lied and lied repeatedly." Tex said stopping a fight or the fight game never was done to serve any alleged high moral purpose, but to secure further political power.

Rickard said Governor Gillett had been drinking a few too many highballs on the day he gave the purported interview in Chicago alleging that the then-upcoming fight was fixed for Jeffries.

---

[805] *San Francisco Bulletin*, July 11, 1910.
[806] *San Francisco Examiner*, July 5, 6, 1910.

Tex said the fight game would go on. In a year or two there would be even more of it. Some states would legislate against it, while others would be more liberal. He would stage any bout which he thought would draw a crowd and make money. To him, it was just like mining or oil-drilling. If he saw a chance to earn money, he would take it.[807]

The next day, Rickard said his alleged interview printed in the *Bulletin* the night before, criticizing the mayor, was a fake. He denied having said anything. Regardless, the point was made.[808]

Professor W. L. Hamilton of the University of California, in a lecture to a sociology class, declared that the Jeffries-Johnson fight proved that the negro no longer belonged to an inferior race. Johnson's success demonstrated the improvement of the entire race, and was an instance of the black race's remarkable advances in in all areas. "He is rapidly approaching equality with the white so far as civilization is concerned and I should not be surprised, were I alive to watch his progress, 300 years hence to see the negro and the white intermarry and meet everywhere on common ground." Of course, many were concerned about that.

A black reverend in Washington, D.C. said,

> I believe that because Johnson won, prize fighting will be stopped forever. The white people are unjust to Johnson, but this does not change the principle that fighting is wrong. The newspapers are most to blame for the interest in prize fighting. If negroes attach undue importance to this fight, the whites are no more rational.[809]

The *New York Age* said even presidential elections never had aroused the strong interest manifested in the fight by millions of Americans of all races. Blacks were joyous, many richer in the pocket, while whites were somber.

> And the result of the fight has had a peculiar effect on the populace. … Seldom was a white brother seen to smile and appear as if pleased. The only people whose faces were bright and who went about in a light-hearted manner were the colored citizens. …

> For the Negro citizens to enthuse over Johnson's victory and try to buy up all the newspapers is perfectly natural. I have never seen so many colored people reading newspapers as since the fight. I saw one enthusiastic citizen of color with every New York daily paper of July 5, including a German and a Hebrew paper. He told me that he wanted to cut the pictures of the fighters out of two papers he could not read. Then, again, never have I seen such few white people read the papers as within the past two days. …

> That the Negro race should feel highly elated over the fact that a member of their race is champion of champions is to be expected. There would be something wrong with us if we felt otherwise. All

---

[807] *San Francisco Bulletin*, July 7, 8, 1910; *San Francisco Call*, July 8, 1910.
[808] *San Francisco Evening Post*, July 8, 9, 1910.
[809] *San Francisco Bulletin*, July 7, 1910.; *Afro American Ledger*, July 23, 1910.

other races feel proud of their members who achieve name and fame; then why not we?

> There is one regrettable feature about the Johnson-Jeffries fight that I deem it opportune to comment upon at this time and that is the attempts of many white writers and Caucasians to provoke a race issue. The fight between Johnson and Jeffries was not to decide whether the colored race was the superior of the white race as fighters. It was to settle the question of who was the superior…Jeffries, who happened to be a white man, or John Arthur Johnson, a Negro.

The *Age* noted that many white writers unnecessarily attacked Johnson simply because he was a colored man. Whites liked to contend that a black fighter always would show the yellow streak when he faced a white man, and that black fighters lacked heart. Even Jack London, who admitted that Johnson did not show a yellow streak in the fight, despite so many predictions that he would, still did not grant that the question was settled for all time. "How nonsensical! How can some of the 'doubting Thomasas' be convinced that Negro fighters do not possess yellow streaks?"

Some black folk had not wanted the fight to happen, feeling that whatever the result, the contest would do more harm to colored citizens than good. However, this writer disagreed.

> I have always wanted to see Jeffries and Johnson meet, in the first place believing that Johnson would win, and secondly, feeling that the victory of the Negro over the white man would cause the white brother to hold us in higher esteem.

> Despite the fact that we are acquiring education as well as wealth, we are not only as a race, but as individuals considered the inferior of the Caucasian. Almost any white man, no matter how ignorant or illiterate, thinks he is the superior of every black man, and while any Negro would be foolish for a moment to compare his race with that of the dominant race, yet we are willing to make comparisons as to superiority when it comes to individuals.

> The case of Jack Johnson shows the superiority of individuals, irrespective of color, and by defeating Jeffries we are bound to be more highly respected. From now on the white man will not generally underestimate us as he has been guilty of doing heretofore.

> Some of the yellow journals are endeavoring to work up race riots throughout the country, now that Johnson has won.[810]

Lithographs of Johnson appeared in the windows of practically every black apartment in New York. Most blacks lived in the negro districts of San Juan Hill and Harlem. Folks across the country even purchased statues of Johnson.

---

[810] *New York Age*, July 7, 1910.

JACK JOHNSON
Champion of the World

His Statute 18 in. high finished in bronze

An Ornament for every Negro home as he is the first Negro admitted to be the best man in the world, sent upon receipt of price $2.50. Agents wanted in every locality. Send $2.50 for outfit and liberal terms.

The Champion Statuary Co
1535-41 Melrose St., Chicago, Ill.

The Irish district of "Hell's Kitchen," which was next door to San Juan Hill, was agitated, and a number of bitter clashes between whites and blacks took place on July 7, three days after the fight. "Serious trouble seems inevitable and the 'cockeyness' of the colored population seems to have increased a hundredfold since July 4."

The police reported that shops had sold more revolvers in the four days since the fight than at any similar time in recent years. Most of the purchasers were white.[811]

The *Afro American Ledger* criticized white newsmen and others for hyping the racial aspects of the fight, which in part caused the riots and all the trouble regarding the fight films:

> [The] world stood spellbound, with eager anxiousness never occasioned before by any event in the sporting world. The prime reason for this anxiety was the unwise accentuation of the racial features of the fight. The world was made to feel that it was the white man against the black man, and that in order to show the superiority of the Saxon brain and brawn over the Negro brain and brawn, Jeffries must win. He was published up as the hope of the white race, and as their representative must show his superiority over the Negro. ... This emphasizing of the racial element in the contest, prepared the way for the trouble which has arisen throughout the country, as we had expected, and the newspapers, these public educators, are responsible for it.[812]

The black-owned *Broad Ax*, published in Chicago, Illinois and Salt Lake City, Utah, said the entire civilized world stood against the cool, steady nerve and boldness of Johnson, whose well-directed, scientific, sledgehammer blows could defeat any heavyweight on the face of the earth.

Many erroneously believed the rank speculation of Governor Gillett, who said the fight was a frame up, that Johnson had a weak back and like any common Negro would lie down or be bought off. The governor's wild talk, combined with racial prejudice and stereotypes, caused many white sporting men to be guided by false sentiment, and therefore they went bust by placing their money on their white idol. On the other hand, colored folks raked in lots of money by betting on Johnson at long odds.

To the great astonishment of those who knew nothing about Johnson's fighting qualities, he did not display the yellow streak so much talked about

---

[811] *San Francisco Bulletin*, July 8, 1910.
[812] *Afro American Ledger*, July 9, 1910.

by the California governor, fight fans, white newspaper writers, and the public in general, aside from black folk, for the former falsely labored under the impression that Jeff would lay Johnson out cold with one or two body blows, and that "no Negro could look him or any other white man in the eye and live thereafter." The entire civilized world was in shock.

The fans and Jeff's cornermen were so hell-bent upon making sure that Jeffries was not knocked out by a black man that they urged the fight to be stopped, and the cornermen rushed into the ring to save him.

Still, the fans who attended the bout "displayed more tolerance than the preachers and so-called Christians who hated to see the black Samson win, and who think it is a burning shame and an everlasting disgrace for a Negro prize fighter to knock out a white prize fighter."

Because of the great rejoicing by the colored population throughout the country, some "pinheaded" city and state officials would not permit the moving pictures to be exhibited. "Many members of the so-called superior race have vented their spite and bitterness against the Colored people because they were on the losing side." The fight's outcome settled none of the serious problems which confronted Americans.

This writer said it was wonderful that a black man held first place in at least one thing in the world. It proved that if given the chance, blacks were capable of producing folks who were tops in other fields as well.[813]

George Knox, publisher of the *Freeman*, also commented on the racial hype, analysis, and impact of the fight:

> It has been well said that the white people are responsible for the turn of affairs in pugilism, especially as it concerns the Johnson-Jeffries fight, and which, by the way, will have much influence in the future in affairs of the kind. The impression was made that the aim of the fight was to win back the laurels from the Negro, a contention never denied at any time up until the day of the fight. The championship, according to men, means that the one who wears the title of champion is the best man physically in his particular class.

Being a champion of the human race was an honor and a symbol of great manhood. However,

> [Johnson] is a Negro, and the Anglo-Saxons are not quite prepared to see Negroes shattering their traditions. ... The many expressions in the newspapers at all times and in Jeffries' favor always were inflammatory to a race like the colored people, who feel to be getting the nasty end of things always. ...

> The result of the fight will be far reaching in its consequences; the end is not promised. But whatever the end, the white people should think as to who knocked the chip off of the shoulder. Already conditions are assuming an ugly shape. The fight pictures are being prohibited in localities and mostly because of who Johnson was. The

---

[813] *Chicago Broad Ax*, July 9, 1910.

colored people did many silly things; to be honest, they aggravated the white people, but simply through a spirit of victory, and one must confess of race rather than of individual. It should have been the other way; it would be far now for the general peace if the fight had been considered merely a contest for the supremacy of man, physical man, rather than a contest for race superiority which counts nothing for more than the moment, excepting prejudice.

The *Freeman* recognized that the fight "meant nothing by the way of securing supremacy for the race." Johnson himself had avoided talking about the fight in racial terms. And yet, "The *Freeman* feels as though the race should be grateful and thankful for having an opportunity to display its athletic ability, which has been denied by Sullivan, Corbett and others."[814]

Fight fans dreamt that Johnson had a yellow streak that Jeff would bring out, but it only was a dream, and they finally were awakening to reality.

Race analysts believed that the Negro's body was his vulnerable part. "And that you may beat him over the head all you care to and that he will not even be dazed. This is carrying a joke too far." Johnson had disproved the myth by allowing Jeff to hit his body. The fact was that fighters of both races had been knocked out by punches to both the body and head.[815]

A New York theater on Broadway claimed to be showing the Reno fight films, but when the spectators realized the films were fakes and the theater owners swindlers, they rioted and tore up the theater.

A writer for the black-owned *New York Age* said the question in the wake of the fight was whether its result would intensify race feeling. Being an optimist, this writer felt that more good would result than bad:

> Those of the white race who have heretofore held the Negro cheap at all times will commence to regard the race to which Champion Johnson belongs in its proper light – a child race, while true, but having members who are capable of competing with other races in most every walk of life, providing an opportunity is given. There is no doubt that the Negro will be accorded more respectful consideration.

True, the fight caused several disturbances in which white toughs attacked blacks, and several people died.

> Yet, if one does not size up the post-fight situation in the role of an alarmist he will find that at a general election more murders are committed and more brawls take place between whites of opposite political parties than occurred between the two races after July 4.

> Of course, the sensational newspapers will seek to attribute every clash between whites and blacks for the next year to Johnson's victory over Jeffries, but the people of this country are beginning to learn that the yellow journals incite more race antipathy than do the most radical elements of both races.

---

[814] *Freeman*, July 9, 1910.
[815] *Freeman*, July 9, 1910; *New York Times*, July 5, 1910.

All Negroes and all well-thinking white citizens regret that a number of colored persons were killed because Jack Johnson won the fight. But had Jeffries come out winner I venture to make the statement that the list of Negroes killed by white toughs would be three times as large as it is today. Irrespective of the termination of the fight, conflicts between the races would have been inevitable, but in view of the far-reaching effect the fight at Reno is bound to have on this body politic I think the casualty list has been small. There is one thing the Negro must learn, and that is that races, as with individuals, must sacrifice in order to succeed. Many races have lost thousands of people to gain a point.

There was an issue involved in the fight on July 4, one which the Negro did not make but which was brought on by many of the white newspapers and Caucasians. A week or so before the fight even a colored minister, clothed in his ecclesiastical garb, could not talk for long before he was called Jack Johnson in derision. No one can deny that by reason of color the Negro has been greatly underestimated. To be other than white usually means inferiority to the majority of white citizens, and when Johnson whipped Burns it was then that Jeffries was called upon to regain the championship title and relieve the white race of what was considered an embarrassing situation.

So, before the fight at Reno when the betting should have been even money the odds strongly favored Jeffries to win, and not because conditions should have been rightfully such, but because one fighter was white and the other colored, and the white bettors could not for the world see why in such a great contest for physical supremacy a Negro should come out first best.

Therefore, the blindness, due to color prejudice, cost many a white man a neat sum of money, and any time you touch a white American's pocketbook it is then he sits up and takes notice. In an endeavor to correctly size up the Johnson-Jeffries contest the white bettors will very likely conclude that after all color is no bar to success and does not necessarily mean inferiority.

But the movement against the exhibition of the fight pictures is about the most childish and idiotic crusade that has been inaugurated for some time. Had Jeffries won there would have been no opposition to showing the pictures, but as Johnson came out victorious the cry "Don't show the fight pictures" was set up which now extends as far as India. In fact, even abroad various authorities do not favor the pictures being shown to the darker races in which a black man is pictured as soundly thrashing a white man. …

What is particularly pleasing is that both races are taking the result of the fight in a becoming and praise-worthy manner. True, a number of white toughs have seen fit to vent their spleen by attacking Negroes, but they are the dregs of society, and their actions must be attributed to ignorance. And the colored brother has exhibited unusual reserve during these moments of unbounded enthusiasm for him and has not been arrogant or insulting as many whites presumed he would be. So, despite the fact that a Negro is the undisputed champion of the world, the sun continues to rise and set and there are no evidences that the affairs of this great country are to be chaotic and unsettled because Johnson won.[816]

Some blamed white newspapers and Jeffries himself for causing the riots, for they made too much of the race issue. The *Washington Times* noted that Jeff was advertised as the "champion of the white race," and announced that his only purpose in re-entering the ring was to re-establish Caucasian supremacy. He forced the race issue, which resulted in riots, largely precipitated by white men and boys who attacked blacks. He stirred up needless animosity, and was aided and abetted by the news-writers who incessantly demanded that he leave his farm and "uphold the supremacy of the white race."

The *New York Sun* said some thought Jeff would win because of his race, some simply wanted the white man to win, so they picked him, and others thought Jeffries would win because business interests would make it worth Johnson's while to lie down, because they could make more money long-term if the more popular man won. Johnson's victory saved boxing by showing that it was not always or necessarily the most popular man that won. "As for the talk about the bad effect of Johnson's victory, it seems to be largely nonsense. If a white man is willing to go into the ring with a Negro, he and his friends ought to be willing to take the consequences."

The *Indianapolis News* said, "Fairness to the Negroes compels the statement that all the talk about the fight Monday as a struggle for race supremacy came from the white man. As far as we know no colored man made this silly assertion. Johnson himself said that it was simply a battle between two men, which, of course, is all it was." The race issue was "nonsense," but Jeff and many newspapers had supported and fostered the idea. "What wonder is it that some of them [black people] came to accept the white view, and to celebrate the triumph of Johnson as victory for their race?" The whites were to blame for the black exuberance, for whites were the ones who advanced the "idiotic theory" that there was a race question at issue. It believed that Jeff's true motivation was to earn a big chunk of money. Of course, some argued that white newspapers were trying to diminish and minimize the race aspect only once Johnson won.

Psychologically, some whites overcame their disappointment by viewing Johnson's victory as a victory for the South. The *Richmond Times-Dispatch* noted that Jack was Southern born and raised, which made him fit for a fight with a Northern Yankee.

---

[816] *New York Age*, July 14, 1910.

This newspaper further noted that most post-fight racial disturbances had taken place in the North, or in cities of the new South, like Atlanta. "In the old South, of which Richmond is the soul, there has been no trouble." Blacks knew their place in the old South.[817]

A white minister in Cleveland said the attitude and movement against the fight films was unworthy of the white race:

> While I deprecate the prize fight, and the display of the brutal in these moving pictures, I believe there is in this matter an issue more serious than the fight itself. It is the race prejudice that it reveals.
>
> The prize fight has always tended to arouse the brute in man, but why should the matter be treated differently when a Negro participates? Race prejudice is a contemptible passion, and is only aggravated by the present discussion.
>
> Reports show that white men have been the great offenders in the post-fight disturbances – men who are not sportsmanlike enough to wish to see the better boxer win. If the white man had won, the white man would have exulted, the Negro would have borne defeat, and the pictures would have been shown. The disgrace is to the white man whose mean intolerance belies his boasted superiority....
>
> It is a pity to degenerate into lovers of the prize fight; but it is a greater pity to become self-confessed slaves of an intolerance that is bigoted and fanatical. Let every white man prove his worth by bearing defeat as a 'white' man should.[818]

The black-owned *Chicago Broad Ax* said religious organizations, preachers, and the press throughout the country were crying out against the fight pictures because a black prize fighter had put to sleep a white fighter.

Their hypocrisy was duly noted. Neither religious organizations, preachers, nor the press ever attempted to suppress the *Clansman*, which depicted a black man raping a white woman. On the contrary, they "glorified it from their pulpits as the noblest work of their hand made God." Nor did they cry out against bloodthirsty anarchists such as Benjamin Tillman, James Vardaman, Reverend Thomas Dixon, Jr., and their brood of rank enemies to society and law and order, whose sole object was to stir up race hatred and prejudice and to uphold mob and lynch law so that the "highly civilized Christians" could to their hearts content murder innocent and law-abiding colored men, women, and children in cold blood, upon some pretext or other.

Hypocritical newspapers were bitterly opposed to the moving pictures, even though those same newspapers for months had contained extensive daily coverage of the training, and the fight itself, including photos, which had entered into millions of homes where children resided. Those same

---

[817] *New York Age*, July 14, 1910, quoting the *Washington Times*, *New York Sun*, and the *New York World* in quoting the *Richmond Times-Dispatch*.
[818] *New York Age*, July 14, 1910, quoting *Cleveland Plain Dealer*.

papers crying out against the pictures had set forth gleefully every detail of thousands of fights, as well as the most revolting crimes committed by mankind, in particular when it came to illustrating black crimes.

The *Broad Ax* noted that those who were fearful that Jeffries might not defeat Johnson, mainly the "so called Christians," were the ones who cried out against permitting the fight. They were afraid of the message that a potential Jeffries loss would send. Other Christians felt that Jeffries' likely victory over Johnson could be used to instruct the colored folks never in the future to attempt to fight anyone with a white face. Millions of Christians prayed to their white God to ensure a Jeffries victory. Ultimately, they all were upset that a black had defeated a white.[819]

Chicago Defender, **July 30, 1910**

The Baltimore-based *Afro American Ledger* printed more views of the black press about the fight:

Lodge Journal and Guide, **Norfolk, Virginia:**

> Prize fighting is becoming a menace to the peace and happiness of the races and ought to be abolished. In a great fight like that between Johnson and Jeffries race feeling will creep out and race pride will be injured. ... For the sake of peace let us have no more prize ring comparisons of the physical prowess of the Negro and the white man.

West Virginia's *Advocate:* "Racial superiority is not decided by tests of physical endurance."

Atlanta Independent: "It is quite natural that the blacks should sympathize with Jack Johnson and the whites with Jim Jeffries."

Nashville Globe:

---

[819] *Chicago Broad Ax*, July 16, 1910. James K. Vardaman was Mississippi's Democrat governor from 1904-1908, and later served in the U.S. Senate from 1913-1919. Known as "The Great White Chief," he advocated for slavery's return. He further said, "If it is necessary, every Negro in the state will be lynched; it will be done to maintain white supremacy."

> If the daily papers would stop publishing the groundless rumors about riots and near-riots the matter would soon be forgotten.

> The latest agitation about the moving pictures is another mistake the daily press is making. ... The whole affair shows inconsistency of the rankest nature. When the "Clansman" was staged a few years ago the doors of every theatre in the country were thrown open. Billboards were covered with pictures that were of a nature, of a truth, to create a hatred toward a helpless people, but no city forbad the show being exhibited, but when a Negro prize fighter defeats a white prize fighter, a great howl is set up about race riots, race domination and the like. If the perpetuity of this government is now threatened by one Negro prize fighter the predictions of the statesmen of the old world that our form of government would not stand the test of time has virtually come true.

Philadelphia Tribune:

> The white Philistines throughout the country bet on their Goliath and when he was done up they got sore in the head as they were in the pocket and began to maltreat black people. He is a poor sport who howls like a dog when he is whipped and tried to take revenge of those of him who whipped him. ... There may be no more legalized prize fighting in this country. In that case the championship of physical prowess will remain with the black Samson and his people. Very good.

A black reverend from Philadelphia's Mount Olive African Methodist church said Johnson's decisive victory would have a tendency to increase the spirit of independence in the Negro race.

An *Afro American Ledger* writer said the effect of Johnson's victory upon the country had been phenomenal, disastrous, and far-reaching. Regrettably, it had rekindled race prejudice in people and sections where it barely existed or was dormant. The blame was laid at the door of those who were dissatisfied with the result and gave vent to their feelings by mercilessly attacking the innocent.

> The rough element of both Negroes and whites has brought disgrace upon themselves and the community by their thoughtless acts of violence. As to the legal suppression of the moving pictures...it is absurd and looks more like child's play than the work of grownups in a civilized country like this, the boasted land of the free and home of the brave.

Allowing whites to brutalize blacks in mob violence fostered general lawlessness, which would have a greater social impact.

> There is a class of persons to be found in almost every community which seems to have lost all respect for the law. The reason for such misguided judgment may be traceable to the fact that the law winks at crime and disorder when it ought to apply its legal authority.

However, we are thankful that greater civil war did not follow Jack Johnson's victory.[820]

Even the white-owned *Brooklyn Daily Eagle* said:

> The effect of the Negro's victory on the ruffians or animals of his race and on the animals and ruffians of the white race has been what was expected. ... A strain has been put on law and on the police as the enforcers of law. Had the result been reversed there would still have been a strain, but it would have been less, and law and civilization would not have been so severely wrenched.[821]

The black-owned *Washington Bee* also quoted what the Negro Press throughout the nation said about the fight's implications:

Dallas Express:

> The fight, however, is not without its helpful lesson to us all. We have had placed before us a striking example of the fact that excellence along no line of human endeavor lies in race or color. Superior training is the thing. Preparation is what counts. ... Johnson has taught his own race a lesson from which they should take courage – not courage to fight, perhaps, but courage to try.

Afro American Ledger:

> It was a race question from the start to the finish, for which the negro was not and is not responsible. The results, riots, deaths, and injuries lie at the door of the white man and his prejudices, and the negro is not and should not be held responsible.

Kentucky Reporter: "What Johnson has done in his line of work is only a demonstration of what the negro can do in any chosen profession, if given a fair chance."

Muskogee Cimeter, Oklahoma:

> If the Ministers' Alliance and other organizations which are fighting the exhibitions of the Johnson-Jeffries fight pictures would put forth as much energy in suppressing such plays as *The Clansman* and suppressing the lynching and burning of negroes, then the general public could well commend their efforts.

Advocate Verdict, Harrisburg, Pennsylvania:

> "To win back the championship for the white race" was the keynote of the entire affair. The race issue was raised by the white men alone. Besides, some of them were so sure that Jeffries would win back the championship that they bet large sums of money on him. Naturally, a man would feel a little sore after losing a big sum, or his last dollar,

---

[820] *Afro American Ledger*, July 16, 1910.
[821] *Afro American Ledger*, quoting *Brooklyn Daily Eagle*, July 16, 1910.

but he would be a better sport if he shouldn't try to take his revenge on an innocent person.

Atlanta Independent: "Our white neighbors ought to be liberal enough to allow the blacks to exult a little enthusiasm over the victory of Johnson, and the negroes ought to have sense enough not to tantalize our white neighbors over the defeat of Jeffries."

Amsterdam News, New York: "The negro race rejoices over the victory, and why not? The white people would have done the same if the results had been the opposite. We needed a Booker T. Washington, a Kelly Miller, a Paul Lawrence Dunbar, and certainly a Jack Johnson."

Chicago Defender: "This fight has taught the white man that boasting has caused him to lose heart as well as his money, and that the other fellow, though black, can fight like hell."[822]

The *Freeman* said there would have been no trouble had Jeffries won. Whites should have been better sports and taken their medicine like men instead of being poor losers and getting ugly over their champion's defeat.

Some tried to minimize the fight by saying Johnson only proved that he was the biggest brute. Notwithstanding this, most sporting experts could not help but give Johnson credit for being the most scientific boxer the world had ever seen, one whose brains helped quite as much as his muscles.

White preachers and newspapers deplored the resulting disorder, and vociferated loud and long about prize-fighting's brutality. Colored ministers, while not sanctioning prize fighting as such, could not conceal the satisfaction they felt, owing to the practical demonstration Johnson had given to the world that blacks were not inherently inferior to whites.

The *Freeman* said most thinking people recognized that the opposition to boxing and the films was all due to race prejudice. There would have been no hue and cry raised had Jeffries won.

The only reason whites put forth for barring the films was that they might infuriate the mob. However, this writer asked why society should concede so much latitude to the mob such that the course of events must be disturbed to appease its angry passions. The correct position that officers of the law should take is that people should be able to enjoy their natural rights, and if mobs do not approve of obedience to the law and constitution and insist upon getting ugly, the right thing to do is for the police to suppress the mob, not the films. "The Negroes of Washington [D.C.] are particularly sensitive on this score, for the policy of yielding to every objection of the mob to the civil equality of the races here on federal soil, has gradually forced us out of every place of public enjoyment, of intellectual profit and of ordinary public accommodation."

There was no more reason to suppress the films than there was to keep the pictures and articles out of the daily papers, which reached everyone. Newspapers had done more to stir up the excitement than any other

---

[822] *Washington Bee*, July 16, 1910.

agency. "Why cry down the pictures, which reach a limited number, and allow the newspaper undisputed sway?"

Another *Freeman* writer said if the pictures were opposed merely on the score of brutality and immorality, then all should join in. However, that hardly was the case. The truth was that such arguments were a front and façade for the real reason - that there was a "darkey in the woodpile." The omitted argument was well understood by everyone. The opposition was an example of hypocrisy and a growth of the race feeling.

One poet wrote,

> They called big Jack a smoke, out at Reno;
> Said his boxing was a joke, out at Reno;
> But despite his yellow streak,
> And his heart so very weak,
> He put big Jeff to sleep, out at Reno.[823]

England's *Boxing* said the big fight was over, "and now we are being told that the racial war is going to commence. Was there ever a more lamentable confession of panic?" The "prophets of evil" were inciting "the more truculent white men in America to ensure that bloodshed shall follow the defeat of Jeffries."

> That some bloodshed was bound to follow, everybody who knew anything about the racial trouble in the States was aware. The black man is, and will be for many generations, very like a child. ... But the negroes could no more help strutting round and gloating over their champion's triumph than they could help breathing. Their boastings may not have been in the best possible taste perhaps, but one might have expected that the whites would have been sufficiently strong-minded to recognize that the blacks were only children showing off in somewhat noisy fashion. If the white men hadn't been so sore about the matter!

> Because there is no use in disguising the fact that the whole white race is feeling a bit sore over this Reno battle.

> Everybody has been telling everybody all about the yellow streak which every Negro conceals in his make-up, and which Johnson was certain to reveal in the ring. Well, every negro may conceal a yellow streak somewhere, as quite a number of white men do (although we never acknowledge the fact); but its existence has still to be discovered in Jack Johnson's composition.

> Had Jeffries emerged victorious from the struggle should we not have heard of bonfires, feastings, and general jubilation? Here and there a negro would probably have been killed, but these murders would only have been isolated cases, for the simple reason that the negroes would have accepted their hero's defeat with more equanimity than

---

[823] *Freeman*, July 16, 1910.

the whites have done; while, on the other hand, the white men's jubilation would have been more restrained and less personally offensive. The white's superiority to all the races, which is his cardinal faith, would merely have been confirmed, and he would consequently have been far less excited.

As matters turned out, however, the black's growing hopes of equality, as well as his peculiar vanity, the vanity of a subject race, were all appealed to, and no power on earth could have prevented him manifesting his joy over the event.

The attacks on boxing as a sport, and its meaning, were related to race. A year prior, generally boxing was recognized as the finest form of physical exercise and hailed as the "Noble Art." Now, it was "brutal," "degrading," "a relic of the barbaric ages," and "a blot on our civilization."

And all this just because a white man – who was coaxed, badgered, and bullied out of a well-earned retirement – found it impossible to recover his old prowess...and consequently went down to defeat before a despised negro.

The Americans built the fight to a racial conflict of the highest order.

They lifted, of their own free will, this championship contest out of the realms of pugilism and converted it into a racial trial of strength. The negroes would probably have still regarded it as such, without any assistance from the white men; but it was because the white men insisted that Jeffries "would show the nigger what a contemptible thing he was when he came up against a real good white man" that the coloured people were so dead-set on the issue. ...

It was the whites, and the whites mainly who converted the Reno contest into a test of racial superiority. They insisted on this fact from every standpoint. Brain, brawn, speed, agility, stamina, wit, and courage were the points to be tested. ... Can it be wondered at that the black men were jubilant?

The fight was not just about boxing superiority alone, as it should have been, "but moral, mental, and physical superiority, as one race insisted and the other accepted, with the under dog's champion coming out on top."

So now the white men wanted to stop the fight pictures:

Why? He may say that they are indecent. Some of the influential whites are built that way, but they have only just discovered that boxing pictures are indecent; they never found it out before.

Then they say that their exhibition will conduce to race riots. Well, the rioting so far has been mainly on the white side, though we will readily admit that the blacks probably went about asking to be ill-treated. What do the mayors, town councilors, and other guardians of law and order say of the pictures?

That the blacks will ask for more ill-treatment and will be accommodated, or is it that they are anxious to avoid all reference to their champion's downfall.

Really it looks as though the latter were the sole reason which appeals to them. We can rest assured that, had Johnson been beaten, there would have been a tremendous run on these pictures. Everybody knew this beforehand, and it was openly asserted that such would be the case.

Jeffries was given credit for ensuring that the local fight crowd was sportsmanlike, for he had issued a statement prior to the fight demanding such, and they acceded to his appeal.[824]

Some said the present wave of agitation against boxing would pass and the game would resume its normal condition. Others thought the recent happenings had injured the sport rather seriously.

The *San Francisco Bulletin* blamed many in the press for instigating riots by continually harping on the bout's racial aspects. Those who were amenable to the powers of suggestion eagerly devoured such talk. It said that in truth, Johnson beating Jeffries was not such a big deal. Johnson was not the first black man to beat a white man. Other blacks, like Gans and Walcott, beat whites, and no racial difficulty took place. However, for Jeffries-Johnson, the press and some participants "went Hades bent on telling open-mouthed fools that it was to be an ethnological test, a test of the physical superiority of the races. Merest balderdash, but it was bad seed and grew a bitter harvest." This writer said no sensible white man would believe that racial superiority depended on a Jeffries victory any more than would any black man believe that Johnson's victory meant the superiority of his race. The hysteria had hurt pugilism, potentially beyond recovery.

Also noted was the fact that Johnson's victory did not lead to one scrap at ringside. The paying boxing fans behaved themselves. It was the general public that did not.

Georgia passed a bill barring exhibition of any fight pictures of fights between whites and blacks, although films of whites against whites or blacks against blacks could be exhibited. The majority of the legislators felt that black vs. white fight pictures would be degrading and lead to riots.[825]

Some white writers said Johnson's victory had been a serious set-back to black boxers in all classes. "There will be quite a number of cities, not only in the South, but in the North as well, that will bar the black fellows." City officials in Memphis told promoters not to match any colored men.[826]

Mayor Brand Whitlock of Toledo, Ohio noted that the press, after discussing the details of the anticipated brutality for months, now was against the fight pictures, and even against boxing. Their hypocrisy was "simply sickening." He also scored his fellow politicians:

---

[824] *Boxing*, July 16, 1910.
[825] *San Francisco Chronicle*, July 19, 1910.
[826] *San Francisco Evening Post*, July 21, 1910.

For months newspapers, periodicals and magazines have been filled with intimate personal accounts of both fighters, giving as if it were of the last importance to humanity, the thoughts and opinions of defeated former pugilists. ... And now, after reveling for two months as a nation in all this, we experience a recrudescence of Anglo-Saxon morality and suddenly wake up to the fact that all this is brutal and likely to corrupt somebody. This is declared in resolutions, and interviews and hundreds are greedily seizing the opportunity to obtain a reputation for morality by opposing prize fighting. Meanwhile in the tenements and slums of New York, yearly, children are dying; half of all the children in these districts die before they reach the age of six years. Furthermore, last year by the industrial machines of the country, half a million men were killed or maimed. Most of these lives might have been saved by the improvement of working conditions, by the enactment and observance of safety appliance acts. They or their families might have been recompensed in a measure by the passage of employers' liability acts or by the repeal of many ancient provisions of the law such as the fellow servant rule. No resolutions now, no appeals, or threats. Why? Because to oppose this kind of brutality is dangerous – economically dangerous.

Because to oppose this kind of brutality involves an economic risk – it might hurt business, it might cost men their soft positions.

Since the fight ended it has suddenly been discovered that some questions of race superiority was involved in it.

That question is not involved and it can't be settled that way anyway. For instance, I have no doubt that Jeffries, even in his battered and bruised condition, could whip Booker T. Washington, or that Johnson could whip Tolstoy whenever he wanted. Perhaps he could whip Colonel Roosevelt and many other of the leading representatives of our race. But even if he could and did, nobody would say that demonstrated the superiority of one race over the other.[827]

A writer for the *Chicago Broad Ax* said the U.S. constitution would be violated if the fight-film exhibitions were stopped. Article V of the Constitution said the government could not take private property for public use without just compensation. The films were of no value if they could not be exhibited, and therefore were as worthless as if destroyed. The public could not ex post facto pass laws against what was legal at the time of the fight, which was to film it and exhibit the pictures.

This author noted that subsequent to the fight, white writers had been encouraging the idea that not too much importance should be placed on the fact that Johnson won. "All that froth talk before the fight about the white

---

[827] *New York Age*, July 21, 1910.

man being so superior to the black man has quit. It was confidently said that the presence of Jeffries in the ring would scare Johnson out of it." The sudden change in discourse, now that Johnson had won, was noted. The reasons were obvious. However, the writer agreed that blacks could not improve the race's standing just by hurrahing for their prize fighters. Much more would be necessary.[828]

The *Freeman* further quoted expressions from the nation's black press:

"Yet Jeffries was the most perfect specimen of the white man's superior physical manhood." - *Exchange*.

"Both Johnson's 'yellow streak' and Jeffries' 'superior stamina' received some severe jolts." – *Detroit Informer*.

"The *Atlanta Constitution* published for the first time in its history a Negro on the first page when it placed Jack Johnson on there. Great Scot!" – *Chicago Defender*.

"Why suppress moving pictures of the Jeffries-Johnson fight and allow Dixon's lying, vulgar book to be sold and theaters to play the disgusting dramatization, 'The Clansman'?" - *East Tennessee News*, Knoxville.

"Well, the white press and white sports, and as for that matter the whites generally, made the Johnson-Jeffries fight a race issue. Then why get mad? If the whites had been victorious they would have been yelling yet. Let us have a little fun out of the victory." – *Georgia Broad-Axe*.

"We knew that the white man is drunk with power and pride, but we contended that since he had so many monuments to his achievements to point to that he could stand a 'little thing' like a Negro whipping a white man in an exhibition of brute force without any display of feeling." - *World*, Indianapolis.

"Pride of race made the white man's friends beg the black champion to desist, that the 'hope of the white race' be saved the humiliation of a knockout at the hands of the greatest fighter the world has ever known – a Negro." - *New Century*, Norfolk, Virginia.

"If the Negroes are boasting and rejoicing elsewhere in the United States as they are in and around Muskogee over the victory of Johnson over Jeffries, their actions are going to damage the race in many sections." – *Baptist Informer*, Muskogee, Oklahoma.

"Johnson is undoubtedly the most skilled fighter that ever donned a glove. Thus we plainly see that when individual members of our race are given half a chance in America they prove the equal of the best of the Anglo-Saxon and often their superior." - *Iowa State Register*.

"It was a clear case of science and endurance triumphing over bigotry and egotism." - *Columbian*, Louisville, Kentucky.

---

[828] *Chicago Broad Ax*, July 23, 1910.

"In this hour of Johnson's victory the Negroes of the country should exercise considerable self-control, good judgment and discretion and should refrain from indulging in demonstrations." - *Southern Reporter*, Charleston, South Carolina.

"The success of Jack Johnson on the Fourth of July should be an inspiration to the Negro of this country. He has shown in unmistakable manner what can be done by thorough preparation for anything he undertakes." - *Star*, Newport News, Virginia.

"The Johnson-Jeffries fight may have injured us in some sections and increased race prejudice in some others but on the whole it has proved a God-sent blessing in showing that certain traits and characteristics are inherent in us and when fairly and fully developed make us one of the most powerful races of people on the face of the globe." – *Richmond Planet*, Virginia.

"The exhibition of race and color hatred was the most marked feature of the whole affair. There was enough of it before the fight, but the amount since the battle clearly shows how far away we are from the sentiment which has made the Star-Spangled Banner one of our famous National airs." - *Dallas Express*.

"[T]he daily press tried for months to make [the fight] a racial contest for supremacy.... Now that same daily press is trying to recede from the position it has been holding and is offering such editorials as sane, fearless organs should have offered long ago." - *New Age*, Los Angeles.

"Before the battle was waged the public press, with all energies that it was capable of, declared that this would prove the assertion that the darker-skinned race could not achieve the physical condition; could not undergo the stamina that the Caucasian race, with its thousands of years of development behind it, has achieved. They claimed it absolutely impossible; the developments of this fight have emphatically refuted this argument and have proven that such is not the case." – *Advocate*, Portland, Oregon.

"The most intense race prejudice was the occasion of the Johnson-Jeffries prize fight. This city was a scene of the most bitter race feeling. The police could not handle the mob. Hundreds of fights were allowed to go on, and dozens of colored citizens were assaulted almost under the eyes of the police without being molested. Of course, the defeat of Jeffries was a bitter pill for a prejudiced class to swallow." - *Bee*, Washington, D.C.[829]

>Commenting on race analysis in boxing, the *San Francisco Bulletin* said,
>
>>As for the superexcellence of the white race, it is almost doubtful if negroes have not been their equals in the ring game at all stages of the sport's history. ... At the present time negroes rule the prize ring with Johnson, Langford and Jeannette at the helm.

---

[829] *Freeman*, July 23, 1910.

> Boxing is undoubtedly a good sport, but the writers always maintained that certain "authors" placed too much stress on the racial aspect of the Reno battle. ... The head, not the fists, make for a superior race. ... Barring the difference in the color of their skins, Johnson was a far more civilized and better mannered man than Jim Jeffries, with a better intelligence, a keener sympathy for the amenities of life, and as he has subsequently proven, possessed of a better fighting brain, better fighting hands and a better fighting heart.[830]

The *Chicago Broad Ax* noted that Chicago's mayor and chief of police, while originally not objecting to the fight films, did an about-face and said they would not permit exhibitions of the Johnson-Jeffries fight. There would have been no storm of protest against the films had Jeffries won the championship, but it was "galling to many so-called Christians to think that a Negro carried off that honor."

Initially, the mayor had said that in the past, white fighters had been knocked out by colored ones, there was nothing to get excited about unless acts of lawlessness were committed during the exhibitions, there was not as much race prejudice in Chicago as in the South, and no harm would come from the exhibitions, for pictures of the fight already had been scattered to all parts of the world through the daily papers.

However, the mayor had changed his mind. The *Broad Ax* believed,

> [I]f Jeffries would have won in his contest with Johnson; he would have been hailed by the so-called Christians throughout this country as divine evidence of the superiority in every respect of the white race over the black race.
>
> But as it turned out the other way, it is very galling indeed to hypocritical Christians, who roll up their eyes Heavenward in holy horror at the very idea of permitting the exhibition of the moving pictures. But if a lynching bee was on tap, of a Negro, charged with raping some low white woman, who wanted to be raped, thousands and thousands of this same class of Christians who are bellowing out against the moving pictures, would attend the lynching bee with their sweet innocent little children to witness the Negro being burned at the stake and gladly pay out their money for slices of his quivering flesh, and the preachers would have exclaimed from their pulpits that such demoralizing scenes have been productive of much wholesome and moral influence.
>
> And yet they are bitterly opposed to one class of moving pictures, the Johnson and Jeffries, and we are again reminded that there is more hypocrisy to the square inch among the Christians in America than any other country in the world.[831]

---

[830] *San Francisco Bulletin*, July 27, 1910.
[831] *Chicago Broad Ax*, July 30, 1910.

William Pickens, a Talladega College professor, gave his analysis of the fight and the race issues it revealed:

> The average Negro wished to look at the fight as only a pugilistic contest between individuals, while certain clamorous newspapers of the white race, north and south, insisted and kept insisting that it was to be "a great race battle." ...
>
> If Jeffries had won the fight, it would have aroused no resentment in the Negro race against the white race.

However, blacks knew if Jeffries won, whites and their newspapers were ready to preach lies about black inferiority. Many editors already had composed such editorials before the fight. Therefore, blacks could not conceal their satisfaction at Johnson's fists figuratively knocking such homilies into the waste basket. "In this he did missionary work."

Contrary to what they said before the fight, whites ex post facto tried to spin the fight as being about brute force only, but really it was about more:

> We are not sorry that Johnson showed other points of superiority besides mere physical superiority. Most of us had already conceded the latter. But during all the months of preparation and clear through the battle he has carried the sunshine and good-nature of his race. His good-nature was impregnable against insult and unshaken by the battle itself. ...
>
> Even the insulting words of Corbett, the "bully," could not shake him. The jeers of the audience fell on him like rain upon the testudinate back of a turtle. ... The black man was merry all through the game. ...
>
> And not only in physical and temperamental qualities, but in magnanimity the black man was superior. His race has noted with pride that he has never tried to bully his enemies or to detract from the worth of his opponent. ... [H]e gave them choice of corners without "tossing." ...
>
> White editors who so nobly fought Jeffries' battles before the fight, have found one consoling reflection since the fight, viz; that the victory of the black man "will do the Negro race harm." How, I ask, in the name of heaven can it harm a race to show itself excellent? ... These results have simply impressed the Negro with an undue sense of its importance. It was poor tact again on the part of white people.
>
> But, sincerely now, it was a good deal better for Johnson to win and a few Negroes be killed in body for it, than for Johnson to have lost and all Negroes to have been killed in spirit by the preachments of inferiority from the combined white press. It is better for us to succeed, though some die, than for us to fall, though all live. The fact of this fight will outdo a mountain peak of theory about the Negro as a physical man – and as a man of self-control and courage. ...

It will do Johnson's race good and no one knows this better than the white men who are responsible for the overestimation of the event – before the event. After the event, however, it is called a pure contest of brutality, and Johnson is represented as simply the "best brute."[832]

A *Freeman* poet wrote:

> The Fourth will be remembered, as long as we are a race;
> For a noble black man, who wore our flag about his waist.
> Jeff, he was a good man, as ever struck a brace.
> But when he walked up to Jack, Jack struck him in the face.
> Hurrah for the champion of the world! For he is of our race;
> Hurrah for Jack Johnson! Sound it in every place.
> The flag has floated from the mast, it has floated from every place.
> Henceforth it will always be worn, around the Negro's waist.
> I hope he long may live, and bear his distinction with grace.
> Jealously maintaining your honor, for you are one of the race.

The *Freeman* said Johnson's victory revealed a great deal about society:

> Johnson, by defeating Jeffries, has brought about the true color of the average American white man. ... This fight has drawn them out from Governor on down. Their actions after Johnson had won proves beyond the slightest doubt the brain and blood of this fair country, which is advertised the world over "the land of the free and liberty." Ministers laid down their Bibles, lawmakers set aside their duties to meddle with the much-called low, degraded pastime of prize-fighting. All these choice picked public servants, whom the public has selected from among the thousands of men to help lead the nation to peace and prosperity, turned and advocated race riots on the whole-sale order. ...
>
> Their reason for objecting to the pictures being shown is that it would ruin the morals of the young American. Because Jack Johnson, black-born American, defeated James J. Jeffries, white-born American, the child must not see this horror; yet they have seen "The Clansman," heard the great Tillman lecture, read for years what Vardaman had to say and know the art of burning Negroes at the stake by heart. All this they claim as pastime, but a picture that would show them what a Negro can do if he is given a fair chance would ruin their little pure hearts. ... If Jeffries had won...these same persons would have advocated that these pictures be shown in the public schools every Friday in order to show the little tender buds of morals the superiority of the white man over the black man. ... They would claim that the pictures and books would give them courage. ...
>
> [A]ny Representative from the South can shoot a defenseless Negro while lying helpless on the ground and should be awarded a Carnegie

---

[832] *Chicago Defender*, July 30, 1910.

brave medal. Yet it is a state's prison offense to show a picture where a Negro defeated a white fair and square.

The hypocritical daily papers showed photos of the fight and provided descriptions of the bout in order to sell newspapers, while at the same time knocking the pictures, in which they had no financial interest. Hence, if prize-fighting was a disgrace, then so too were the newspapers that described it in every detail and created and promoted race hatred and riots.

> The battle was a white man's own affair. Had it been left to the colored race to finance and promote the fight Mr. Johnson and Mr. Jeffries would have received about a two-thousand-dollar guarantee and it would have been a hard matter to collect…if they had depended on the Negro for their support.

In truth, the fight was not about race supremacy. Blacks had been winning championship battles for the past 15 years. Jeff's fall was the same as his predecessors. They all eventually lose if they keep at it long enough.

> There will be prize fighting as long as the world stands. It is a lot of folly to hear the comment that the last heavyweight fight has been fought in this world. There will be another fight here in this country just as soon as a man shows up who can beat Johnson. The same crowd that has been doing all the hollering will demand it. Don't be worried – Johnson will never retire. The sporting writer will not allow him to. As money is a factor, he has his price, the same as James J. Jeffries, who returned to the ring to get that pile of money regardless of whom he was to fight. [833]

Some wondered if the protests about the big fight would cause the sport's obliteration. Many states already either outlawed boxing or had restrictive laws.[834]

On July 29, 1910 in Slocum, near Palestine, Texas, white racial hatred ignited again. White mobs took up rifles and shotguns and hunted down and slaughtered an estimated 18 to 25 blacks. Most of the known victims were unarmed and shot in the back. Investigation of the "race war" revealed that it was a "'nigger killin' pure and simple. Hundreds of white men, armed to the teeth, forayed through the district and shot the scurrying blacks wherever they overtook them."[835]

An English observer reporting on the American race riots said, "I see that white hoodlums in various American cities have been manifesting their sportsmanship by shooting down the Negroes for no other offense than that they made merry over the victory of their black champion."

---

[833] *Freeman*, July 30, 1910.
[834] *San Francisco Chronicle*, July 31, 1910.
[835] *Reno Evening Gazette*, August 2, 1910; *Washington Post*, July 31, 1910; *New York Times*, July 31, August 1, 1910; *Fort Worth Star-Telegram*, February 27, 2011.

A black correspondent for the *Freeman* in Glasgow, Scotland said Jack Johnson had "established world-wide fame for himself and the downtrodden race."

> The American whites are now showing up their ignorance, unjustness and brutality to the world in a way that will make them less popular than ever in sporting circles at any rate. There is no doubt but that the whole population of the white world would rather have seen "the white man's hope" at the top of the pole. ... If the civilized world knew more of what the American Negroes were doing, it would go a great way in obtaining world-wide respect for the race and more denunciation of the treatment dealt out to them by the unjust white Americans, who wish so much to be at the top of the pole in all things.

This Scottish correspondent believed there would be a world-wide move to prevent the picture exhibitions, because their symbolism was a threat.

> Why? Because the black man was the victor. Our victories must not be kept before the youth of a white man's country; it's too humiliating. Here in religious Glasgow the town council has been petitioned not to allow them to be shown. ... Had Jeffries won would this be so? No, they would have been used to cower these poor, simple, good-hearted natives, to make them fear the power of the white man and make them feel their own insignificance before him. The world must know only of the white man's superiority and only of the inferiority of the Negro and all dark races, robed in its shadiest garb. ...
>
> The press, as you all know, is the greatest educator today. ... Bear in mind that there are many here, and elsewhere, as bitter toward the black man as can be found in America. Why drink in all the poison of the one-sided press against the colored man, who is stigmatized as being possessed of all the vices America contains and not a single virtue. ... My eyes are open to all that is going on through the press, commercially, socially and otherwise. One thing is certain: The black man must make his own way; no white man will do it for him, nor yet help him to do it. Why not? Because the united white press, the united white Christian civilization, and the united white state rulers are at one in all things where a Negro's interest is at stake. In America they are bold with it – out and out – in other countries they are sneaking.
>
> They would rather not offend the American cousin. He is generally wealthy. Why should he not be rich, I often ask, after obtaining for nearly 250 years the unpaid labor of from three to ten millions of slaves. ... Jack, the slayer of the white man's hope, which I hope may be forever, has opened many new avenues for the Negro if he will take the opportunity to work upon them. Take new courage now.

> Three cheers for Jack the Giant Killer and the same for the colored journalists and the Afro-American press, the black man's hope.

The *Freeman* noted that even the *Chicago Tribune* had called "attention to the ludicrous inconsistency of the newspaper protests against the display of the Johnson-Jeffries fight pictures." Correspondents were "appalled by the journalistic hypocrisy which can devote a year to giving publicity to the preparations for the fight, surrender pages to a detailed account of it, supplement this by printing photographs of its most agonizing moments, and then complacently demand the suppression of the moving pictures."[836]

Some saw the Johnson-Jeffries fight films. The motion pictures ran 2 ¼ hours long, including both pre- and post-fight scenes, and the entire 15 rounds. They were the clearest and best fight films ever taken.[837]

An editorial in the *Evening Times* of Glasgow, Scotland noted the fight's fair play, despite the strong racism in the United States:

> Emphasizing still further the point regarding fair play is the fact that into the contest entered the very strong racial feeling of black and white. It is difficult for the citizens of this country to thoroughly appreciate the depth and the vehemence of these feelings in America. The animosity which unfortunately exists between the white man of the Southern States especially and the Negroes can not be exaggerated. It explains the vast difficulty surrounding that bugbear of the American statesman, the color problem. [The] exhibition of a white man getting publicly pummelled into partial unconsciousness by a representative of the hated and despised Negro race, must inevitably tend to fan the flame of racial hatred. Perhaps the best feature about the business is the fact that despite the existence of these feelings, Johnson was permitted to defeat Jeffries. That is at least a further evidence of fair play.

The fight pictures were big in Ireland. Despite denunciations by Archbishop Walsh, threats by the police, and protests, the pictures were drawing tremendous houses in places like Dublin. At the end of the day, the "Celt is a dead game sport," and folks wanted to see the fight.[838]

The *Chicago Defender* reported that in order to justify, explain, and minimize the racial impact of Johnson's victory, a desperate Kentucky colonel named Jack Collins was telling his black workers that Johnson actually was white. Collins said,

> The negroes, seh, have shown signs of becomin' unendurable. It was a matter for diplomacy, seh. We did not like to use force upon the negroes, foh they are mere children, seh. Also, we need 'em to work the crops. So I delivered 'em a lecture.

---

[836] *Freeman*, August 13, 1910.
[837] *Boxing*, August 6, 1910; *San Francisco Evening Post*, August 15, 1910.
[838] *Freeman*, September 3, 1910.

> "This heah Jack Johnson," I says to them, "is the finest example of a Numidian athlete that ever lived. The Numidians are a white race, but owing to their having lived in a southern latitude for many generations, they looked somewhat dark on the outside. But they most fiercely resent being called negroes." ...
>
> "Col. Collins," says my old Jack darky, "we folks always been told this heah Misteh Johnson is a cullud man." "Don't you believe it, Jack," says I. "Johnson is a Numidian. No coon could ever lick a white prizefighter." .... "All right, cunnel," says mah old Jack, "But them Numidians mus' be mighty dahk w'ite folks, cunnel."[839]

Hugh McIntosh said this was not the first time that issues related to Johnson fight films had arisen. He discussed the impact of the Johnson-Burns films, as well as the effect of Johnson's victories on non-whites:

> The coloured superiority in the sport of boxing – the greatest of all athletic sports, wherein the actual domination and complete mastery of an opponent is the strongest and, we might say, the most striking feature – is exciting the minds of thinkers as to the possible influence for evil this will have upon the coloured races.

McIntosh said the Earth's colored people took a keen and eager interest in Johnson. The Burns-Johnson film exhibitions caused thousands of Kaffirs in South Africa to surround a poster of Johnson. They were so excited that the police asked the management to refrain from exhibiting posters or photos of Johnson, or "from publishing in their advertisements anything that might excite the Kaffir mind. Each exhibition of the pictures was attended by Kaffirs, who were highly delighted each time their coloured champion landed a decisive blow."

Concern about Johnson's impact was so great that the South African Parliament discussed whether to bar the Johnson-Burns fight film exhibitions. McIntosh did not want to annoy the white race's feelings. Hence, he voluntarily terminated the film tour there, and decided that no pictures with a colored contestant would be shown in South Africa.

In India, there was a similar state of affairs. The "Hindoos" and "Cingalese" on the island of Ceylon flocked to see the Johnson-Burns pictures. There was fear and concern that the films would inspire the natives to rebel, emboldened by seeing a member of a darker race beating up a white man. There was unrest and discontent prevailing amongst a section of the natives, given that they had been colonized by the British. Hence, there was clear recognition of the fact that Johnson's victories and the fight film exhibitions of those victories had political, racial, and social influence and implications. The white colonizers' concerns were intensified further when it came to the Jeffries-Johnson fight films.[840]

---

[839] *Chicago Defender*, September 3, 1910.
[840] *Boxing*, September 24, 1910.

CHAPTER 37

Revisionism

A *San Francisco Evening Post* writer said that because he picked Johnson before the fight, some accused him of having some grudge against Jeffries. It was common to score severely anyone who picked Johnson. It seemed as if folks felt it was the press' duty to boost Jeff and show race loyalty, rather than write what they honestly felt. Anyone who picked Johnson to win was banned from Jeff's training camp. The public had been "led badly astray." Most authors had praised Jeff's condition and other qualities. Jeff's admirers had been saying that even if he was half as good as he once was that he'd make Johnson jump over the ropes. They were hysterical in their belief in him and in their denigration of Johnson, whom they treated with contempt.

Jeff's flatterers were his worst enemies all along. They filled his head with his invincibility and told him that Johnson was not well trained, that he was yellow, a quitter, and could not fight.

Although on the day of the fight Jeffries said that in years past the result would have been different, the day after the fight, allegedly Jeffries said in very humble fashion, "I never could have hit that fellow in my prime. He is the devil. I never could have reached him in a thousand years."[841]

San Francisco Examiner, July 7, 1910

Jeffries had lost friends in a degree never before experienced by a former champion. Typically, an ex-champion found sympathy, praise, and applause. Not with Jeffries. The public was fickle. Jeff was goaded into a fight by a public which convinced him that he had to do it, and that Johnson would be easy prey. Jeff's "flatterers led him into molasses, and when big Jim began to sink they deserted him."

Many said Jeff was overcome with fear, which shattered his nervous system. "But the public remembers that these 'wise ones' did not stir the air with any warning note of Jeff's disinclination, his unfitness to fight, that they dropped no ink to warn them of such conditions."[842]

Many were angry with Jeffries, accusing him of hiding the true facts from them. Some blamed Corbett and the other trainers for constantly boosting Jeffries in the press; accusing them of deliberately misrepresenting his condition.[843]

---

[841] *San Francisco Evening Post,* July 6, 1910.
[842] *San Francisco Evening Post,* July 7, 1910.
[843] *Nevada State Journal, San Francisco Bulletin,* July 6, 1910.

Jeff drew little sympathy from the *Bulletin* and other reporters, owing to the fact that during training, he was morose and uncivil, "and nowhere nearly as highly civilized a person as the black boxer who opposed him."

Unlike Jeffries, who was surly and gruff towards the reporters who had helped make him a fortune, Johnson made friends and was a gentleman. He proved that "he is a likeable negro." He was smiling and friendly, and his quick wit gained him "as many friends as any black man could expect to gain." Jack was pleasant and very obliging. He had open training and gave the press full access, unlike Jeffries, who trained when and how he pleased. If the crowd wanted to see Johnson box, he boxed. If the photographers wanted pictures, he posed. If correspondents wanted inside information, he gave it to them. True or not, he gave them good copy. He shook hands with the people and gave speeches. He was everything that Jeffries was not. "It is little wonder, therefore, that we of the fourth estate have kindly feelings toward him for his unfailing courtesy." The only excuse made for Jeffries was that it was his nature, and he had been just as discourteous to others, including the governor, as he was to the newsmen.[844]

Jim Corbett said, "All this talk about his being the hope of the white race had got on his nerves." Jeffries worried a great deal because so much was expected and depended on his showing.

Before the fight, Corbett said, "Jeff, you have got that nigger scared to death. If you wade into him you can lick him in one round." However, "Jeffries acted like a man who didn't hear what was being said to him. ... [H]e acted as if he was in a stupor."

Joe Choynski said Jeffries had a "thousand and one worries that no one but his trainers will ever know. I tell you he had his mind loaded to overflowing." For weeks on end Jeff received hundreds of letters daily from admirers imploring him to whip Johnson, telling him that he was the hope of the white race. "That preyed upon his mind" and "unnerved him."[845]

Jeff's friend and business partner, A. F. Jack Kipper also said worry ruined Jeff's chances. He received hundreds of telegrams from men who pleaded with him to win, saying he had to win, and that they had bet all of their money on him. That sort of psychological pressure got to him.[846]

Ben Benjamin said it was the same old story of when a once-great man starts downhill everyone who was not great who envied his prior success gave him a kick. Men had glorified him and made capital out of his reputation and friendship, but now were doing all they could to blacken his character. Regardless, if Jeff had been a bit friendlier and more obliging to the press and public, he would have received more sympathy.[847]

The *Bulletin's* W. J. Jacobs said Jeffries was being maligned by the same men who egged him on to come out of retirement and return the title to the

---

[844] *San Francisco Bulletin, San Francisco Examiner,* July 5, 6, 1910.
[845] *San Francisco Chronicle, Bulletin,* July 7, 8, 1910; *San Francisco Evening Post, Nevada State Journal, Reno Evening Gazette, San Francisco Bulletin,* July 12, 1910; *San Francisco Call,* July 12, 13, 1910; *San Francisco Evening Post, Bulletin,* July 19, 1910; *Freeman,* August 20, 1910; *Boxing,* August 13, 1910.
[846] *Reno Evening Gazette, Call,* July 9, 1910.
[847] *San Francisco Bulletin,* July 7, 1910; *San Francisco Chronicle, San Francisco Call,* July 8, 1910.

white race. His failure to win was "such a grievous and unpardonable sin that his honor has been assailed, his courage doubted, even his disposition held up as a horrible example. And all this because he lost a fight."

Jeff also was roasted because he had been less than genial. However, he never had been a social mixer. He always had kept close within his own small circle of friends and avoided "glad-handing every Tom, Dick and Harry." He just was being himself. There was no hot air or bull-con stuff in his make-up. "In an ordinary human being, open-facedness of this sort would be a trait to be generally admired, but because it happens to be in the loser of a championship battle it's downright surliness."

The public had enticed and begged him to fight. Jeff had trained long, hard, and faithfully, and was in great shape. Many a condition expert looked him over and all agreed he was physically perfect. It seemed that the critics were kicking a man when he was down.[848]

Boxing wondered whether all of the quotes attributed to Jeffries, both before and after the fight, were genuine at all, or fabricated by news reporters, press agents, trainers, or managers on Jeff's behalf. Jeff was not a talker. He was not a bragger, nor was he the kind to say that he could not whip Johnson at his best. Most likely, he would not say anything at all.[849]

Since the fight, Jeff's café, which usually had been jammed packed, was as silent as a cave.

Bulletin writer T. P. Magilligan still questioned Johnson's toughness, and still wondered whether he had a yellow streak in him.[850]

England's *Boxing* believed that ironically, prejudice actually had benefitted Johnson's career. "Had he been a white man it is certain that he would have been snapped up by some enterprising manager quite early in his career, billed as coming world-beater," and then thrown into fights with the elite prematurely, before he had acquired sufficient ring experience or knowledge. For a long time, early in his career, Johnson often went hungry and rarely had enough money. He lived from contest to contest. The long hard gradual road to success had made him a better fighter.[851]

Charlie White, who had been the back-up referee for the championship fight, said of Johnson, "If he were a white man the public would accord to him the title of the greatest heavyweight that ever donned a boxing glove."

Jeffries had known that he was going to be in a tough fight. When he started training for the big fight, he told one writer, "This - - nigger is going to give me the toughest fight I ever had."[852]

White writers and fans previously had contended that Johnson's punching powers were mediocre. However, he proved them wrong. During the fight, Jeff said in his corner, "Gee, but that coon can hit some. I feel as though my jaw was cracked." Stanley Ketchel had told everyone that

---

[848] *San Francisco Bulletin*, July 9, 1910.
[849] *Boxing*, July 16, 1910.
[850] *San Francisco Bulletin*, July 22, 1910.
[851] *Boxing*, July 23, 1910.
[852] *San Francisco Evening Post*, July 27, 1910.

Johnson could punch. "I say he is the hardest hitter in the world. Look here, if a fellow couldn't hit, how could he dislodge three teeth?"[853]

In late July, Jeffries claimed that he had been doped. He said, "There was something the matter with me. They sure did something to me and it will all come out in time." He did not specifically use the word "drugs," but essentially he was alluding to it. Yet, he never fought again or ever sought a rematch.[854]

Few believed the dope claim (Fitzsimmons claimed the same after his loss to Jeffries), and just thought Jeff needed an excuse for the loss and his performance.

However, before the fight, Jeffries was administered a drug to prevent nose bleed, which one could speculate might potentially have affected him. If one really wants to engage in speculation, one might also wonder whether Abe Attell, who worked Jeff's corner, might have slipped him something. Years later, Attell was involved in the fixing of the 1919 World Series, likely in conjunction with Arnold Rothstein. There was a lot of money to be made with a wager on the underdog Johnson. In 1912, Attell lost his world featherweight title to Johnny Kilbane via 20-round decision. Kilbane claimed that Attell's gloves were laced illegally with chloroform in order to blind him. Attell previously had admitted to fixing a 1904 Chicago fight with John Reed to end in a draw.

Jack Gleason criticized Tex Rickard's refereeing, for Tex improperly allowed Corbett between rounds to look in on and taunt Johnson, and failed to stop the fight when Jeff's seconds illegally boosted him back into the ring.[855]

Australian promoter Hugh McIntosh claimed that one of Jeff's admirers insisted on the band playing "All Coons Look Alike to Me," which was received with great enthusiasm. This assertion contradicted the news reports that this tune was not played, having been barred by the authorities.

As for the future, McIntosh said, "The search for a white man to wrest the championship from the black holder has commenced, and the white sporting public of the world will not be content until they have proved the white superiority in the sport of boxing."[856]

At this point, most writers and experts believed that Jack Johnson was invincible, no heavyweight had any chance with him, and only Father Time would defeat him. Jack London asked, "And where now is the champion who will make Johnson extend himself, who will glaze those bright eyes, remove that smile and silence that golden repartee?" Jim Coffroth said promoters would have to find another white hope. H. M. Walker said,

> Nowhere in the world of pugilism is there a man who has one chance in a thousand of wresting the title from the shambling, smiling, good-

---

[853] *Chronicle*, July 27, 1910.
[854] *San Francisco Bulletin*, July 25, 1910; *San Francisco Evening Post*, July 27, August 2, 1910, citing the *New York Telegraph*.
[855] *San Francisco Evening Post*, August 8, 1910.
[856] *Boxing*, August 13, 1910.

natured black. He whipped the grizzled Jeffries in each and every one of the fifteen rounds, and what is more, Jack accomplished this feat with such ridiculous ease that his continual tantalizing smiles and nods wore a deep canker into the souls of the friends and supporters of the white champion.

Johnson's superb defensive skill would discourage anyone. "He punishes in a cruel, rasping, deliberate manner that suggests the snake prolonging the torture of a helpless victim. His sting is poisonous. ... Jack Johnson's skin is black, but he is a real heavyweight champion of the world."

The *San Francisco Bulletin* said that for the first time, a negro was the undisputed heavyweight champion (finally giving him credit as the true champion), and no white man could change that. Therefore, without a big fight on the horizon, Johnson probably would not fight for a long while. "Here he is loaded down with money, a fine theatrical engagement, and nobody to fight. Nothing to do but pose, show those gold teeth, and strut about the world." Sam Langford was too small, had lost clearly to Johnson once before, and besides, "a fight between two colored men is not especially attractive from a box-office standpoint."[857]

Tex Rickard did not support a Langford-Johnson bout either, saying, "Langford could not make a showing against Johnson. He's too small. Then, two black men fighting would not draw a crowd. Johnson told me he would be willing to meet Langford, but he knew that a fight between blacks would not make any money." The paying public was white, and they wanted to see a white man regain the title. The *Chronicle* and *Evening Post* agreed that "two negroes never make an ideal card."[858]

The *Call* said Johnson reveled in wine, women, and song. He enjoyed being in the limelight. "If Johnson cares to he can act just like the other champions. He can lay off for the next year and reap the golden harvest which the theatrical field offers. Notwithstanding his color he is a great attraction before the public."[859]

San Francisco Evening Post, July 13, 1910

---

[857] *San Francisco Bulletin*, July 5, 6, 16, 1910.
[858] *San Francisco Bulletin*, July 7, 20, 1910; *San Francisco Chronicle*, July 24, 1910; *San Francisco Bulletin, San Francisco Evening Post*, July 21, 1910.
[859] *San Francisco Call*, July 10, 1910.

CHAPTER 38

Reverberations of the Big Fight

When Jack Johnson's train from Reno arrived in Ogden, Utah, heading to Chicago, Johnson said, "I'm just the same old fellow that I was before I had the pleasure of Mr. Jeffries' company for a short time." "He made a mistake to fight me, but the people forced him to do it. Therefore he should not be roasted too strong. If you will believe me he did the best he could all the way through." "We were kidding each other continually. ... When I landed on him he usually asked me if I did not think he had a hard old head, and I would retort by asking him if he did not think I was a pretty clever fellow."

Between rounds, Corbett came over to his corner. "That only amused me. I don't think he had a right to step over that way as it is a time-honored custom for the seconds to keep their own corners. But I did not mind in the least. I kept talking to him and kidding him all the time and don't consider that I had the worst of the verbal exchanges."

Before Johnson left Utah, three burly young white toughs walked up to the train's open window and used a vile epithet to Johnson in the presence of his white girlfriend/wife and dared him to come to the platform. One of Johnson's trainers exited, spat a mouthful of tobacco juice onto one of them, and then kicked him. Officers rushed up and forced the crowd back.

As a result of the incident, railroad officials placed two detectives on the train to accompany the champion.[860]

When Johnson arrived in Chicago on July 7 at 2 p.m., "the black king of the fistic ring" was accorded a warmer welcome than anyone ever before had received upon entering the city. About 5,000 blacks and a big sprinkling of whites were at the railway station to greet him. The crowd yelled, "Jack, Jack, Jack." Miles of sidewalks were lined with a living wall of humanity seeking to catch a glimpse of him as he passed. Men, women, and children cheered and waved banners. Some pinned the extra papers with Johnson's picture across their breasts. It was estimated that blacks in Chicago had won at least $600,000 wagering on Johnson. Some said he was so popular that if Johnson ran for alderman in Chicago's Third Ward, he would win in a walkover.

Johnson drove to his home at 3344 Wabash Avenue, where his mother Tiny Johnson and members of his family awaited. A huge crowd was outside their home as well. Amidst roars and drums, Jack entered the house and embraced his mom. Mrs. Johnson served him chicken and watermelon.

---

[860] *Call,* July 5, 1910; *Nevada State Journal,* July 6, 1910; *Examiner,* July 6, 1910.

Johnson said, "I am going to New York Sunday afternoon to begin a thirty weeks' vaudeville tour. ... If it looks like a good thing I may accept offers to go to Europe." Johnson was quite wealthy, could make even more easy money on the stage, and did not need to fight any time soon. Joking, he said, "I have enough money to last me till next week."[861]

Johnson said Jeffries fought gamely to the end, and those who said otherwise were sore about losing their bets. "He could hit, too. ... [H]e landed several punches that let me know that I had been hit." "Some people say that I might have finished things quicker, and perhaps I might. But it wasn't safe to take chances with a man like Mr. Jeffries."

> Yes, I was a bit sore when they introduced Mr. Jeffries as the champion of the world, because you see I fancied that that title belonged to me all right. Well, it does now, you know, so I am not kicking about it at all any more.[862]

Explaining why he had broken away from former manager George Little, Johnson alleged that Little had attempted to get him to throw the Jeffries fight, asking him how much it would take. "I asked him what he meant by asking me to throw away the title which I had worked hard for eight years to win." Little said someone was offering big money for him to lie down. "Now if I ever called a man in my life I certainly told Little a few things then and wound up by telling him I was through with him."

Little told Jack that he could not dismiss him, because he owed him a lot of money, and threatened to let the world know a few things about him. "By this he meant that I was not training, that I was not leading a decent life, and a lot of other things which he knew were not true." Johnson called upon the authorities for protection, and after they heard his story, they compelled Little to keep away from his camp. Johnson wanted the public to know, "I am an honest fighter."

> I could have dragged down $350,000...had I agreed to throw the fight, but no amount of coin is ever going to induce me to figure in a shady deal as long as I am in the ring. I intend to retire and nobody will ever accuse me of pulling off a crooked fight.

Johnson subsequently said that in trying to induce hin to throw the fight, Little reasoned, "Don't you see, Jack, the pictures will be worth $1,000,000 more if Jeffries wins? Get wise." Jack laughed. No amount of money could get him to throw the fight he always wanted, for he truly believed that he could whip Jeffries at his best, and furthermore, too many of his friends had wagered their money on him.

In response, Little denied Johnson's allegations, and instead alleged that Johnson had agreed to carry Kaufman the distance or forfeit a certain amount of money, and to carry both Ketchel and Jeffries a certain number of rounds for the motion pictures.

---

[861] *Nevada State Journal, San Francisco Call*, July 8, 1910. *Freeman*, July 9, 1910; *San Francisco Evening Post*, July 7, 1910.
[862] *San Francisco Evening Post*, July 13, 1910; *Boxing*, July 16, 1910.

Johnson was winning numerous admirers by "carefully avoiding the 'racial' issue."

The champion also was praised for remembering those from his past. He sent gifts ranging from $250 up to $750 to eight men in Galveston who helped him early on in his career. Jack sent $750 to Ed Harrison, who taught Johnson to fight when he was a young boy working on the docks. Receiving $500 was Cafferty Williams, who saved him from drowning in the bay at the docks when Jack was sucked under a vessel.

Jack financially supported his brother and his mother. He also had three sisters living, all of whom were married.

Four days after the fight, on July 8, a St. Louis machinist armed with a rifle was arrested after he attempted to force his way into Johnson's Chicago home. Neighbors thought he intended to kill Johnson, so they called the police. The man admitted that he had lost $25 on the fight, but denied that he intended to harm Johnson. Why then was he attempting to break into his home with a rifle in hand?[863]

On July 11, 16,000 black citizens of the San Juan Hill area of New York, also known as the "Black Belt," swarmed the train depot to see Johnson arrive from Chicago. They were there even though the train was several hours late. The police, fearing trouble, refused to permit a parade.

Baron Wilkins, reputedly the city's wealthiest black man, wanted to make a welcome speech from his saloon's balcony. However, fearing that hundreds of idle whites might start a riot, the police told him not to give the speech, and he complied.

Jack would make his first appearance that night at Hammerstein's roof garden, and would collect $3,000 per week. There were no riots.[864]

Johnson said, "Jeffries was forced to fight me. He did not want to, but the newspapers and magazines haunted and hounded him until there was no other course left him but to come out of retirement and take up the white man's burden."

The champ hoped that black folk would not be like the French were with Napoleon. The people were with Napoleon when he was winning, but turned against him when he lost. Jack said he never would be broke.[865]

In New York, after he was arrested for reckless driving, an upset Johnson said the police were dogging him and trying to get him however and whenever they could. He had followed the instructions of a police inspector who told him after he left the theater to get away as quickly as he could from the crowds. Jack told the judge that it was a matter of necessity. "I had to drive hard to dodge the hoodlums, who call me names and throw stones at me. The officers told me to go fast and get away as soon as I could. I have never run down or injured anyone, but I don't want to be struck by stones." The judge told Johnson that he would wind up running down someone yet, and noted that he had been arrested in almost every city

---

[863] *Reno Evening Gazette, Call,* July 9, 1910; *San Francisco Chronicle,* July 10, 1910; *Freeman,* July 16, 1910.
[864] *San Francisco Evening Post, Chronicle,* July 11, 1910.
[865] *Freeman,* July 16, 1910.

he had visited. The champ said the arrests were made for advertising purposes. The judge found him guilty and fined him $15.[866]

The *Bulletin* noted, "There is very little disposition on the part of promoters to match whites and negroes since the Johnson-Jeffries affair."[867]

Hattie McLay, who lived in Philadelphia, claimed that Johnson was her husband, and she was about to sue him for divorce and $50,000 in damages. However, she could not produce a marriage certificate. She claimed the champ had carried it off. McLay said she first met Johnson in August 1907 in Marshall's café, went with him to Atlantic City, and then Boston, where she was married to him on September 28, 1907 by a magistrate. She lived with Johnson until December 30, 1909. She had witnessed his fights during that time, including the one with Burns. She said Johnson had deserted her, and for the last six months, George Little had supported her.

Johnson denied that she was his wife, and accused Little of influencing Hattie to make trouble for him.

The *Broad Ax* was amused that a white lady was willing to acknowledge to the world that "she has been seeking social equality with Colored people; and that she is willing to call Johnson her black darling in order to grab on to some of his money."[868]

Governor Gillett said, "It makes me laugh when I read that Johnson has demonstrated that a Negro can be honest. He's a fine example of an honest Negro. He'd double-cross his best friend." Some alleged that Gillett had kicked the fight out of California after he learned that it was fixed for Jeffries but Johnson was going to double-cross him and fight to win.[869]

On July 25 in New York, Jack Johnson was arrested, not for speeding, but for standing still. He was accused of obstructing traffic by stopping his car seven feet from the curb. He also was charged with having a wrong number on his car. He gave $100 cash bail for his court appearance.

The next day, Johnson was found not guilty of obstructing a highway. Jack said, "Most generally, they get me for speeding and always fine me, too. This time I was caught for standing still, but they let me off."[870]

Paul West composed a poem about the police harassment that Johnson endured:

> Jack Johnson on a summer's day
> Motored up Broadway, blithe and gay!
> He wanted to get from Thirty-fourth
> Maybe a dozen blocks up north.
> But the moment he showed his visage bright
> A million policemen hove in sight,
> And each individual copper grim
> Fell on the Smoke and arrested him.

---

[866] *Bulletin*, July 20, 1910; *Chronicle*, July 21, 1910.
[867] *San Francisco Bulletin*, July 21, 1910.
[868] *Chicago Broad Ax*, July 23, 1910.
[869] *Freeman*, July 23, 1910.
[870] *Bulletin*, July 26, 1910; *Chronicle*, July 27, 1910.

They hailed him to court without a word,
And these were the charges that Johnson heard:
Disturbing the cop upon his beat,
Casting a shadow across the street,
Tooting his horn till it lost its breath,
Making men cheer themselves to death,
Wearing the pavement asphalt down,
Making a Jeffries bettor frown,
Waking a copper from his rest,
Scaring a sparrow from its nest,
Stopping the trade in five saloons,
Distracting attention from three balloons,
Scattering fourteen swarms of flies,
Straining a hundred thousand eyes,
Crossing a street without a permit,
Stretching the neck of a Harlem hermit,
Neglecting to check his hat and coat,
Getting Jim Corbett's peevish goat,
Doing as other people do,
And smiling without a license, too,
Battery, arson, theft and treason,
Blinking his eye with no good reason,
Mayhem, piracy, breach of trust,
Beating the customs, spreading dust –
Every crime and felony,
From truancy up to bigamy –
And he paid his fines and he went away,
To travel again that great Broadway,
And to be arrested from time to time
And charged with every heinous crime
Because – the reason is easily found;
He knocked out Jeff in the fifteenth round![871]

Johnson wanted to engage in automobile races on the track, to prove himself a champion race-car driver as well. However, the Indianapolis Motor Speedway turned down his request and refused to allow Johnson to race there. White citizens applauded the decision, while blacks resented it.

Johnson instead asked to be allowed to engage in an exhibition race, but the directors also refused that request. "Johnson has been opposed on account of his color, barred from entering certain automobile races, including one in Indianapolis."[872]

Reports were that the white woman whom Johnson currently called wife (Etta Duryea) never was married to him. The alleged Hattie McLay, a.k.a. the real Mrs. Jack Johnson, was upset. "He can't run out on me. I've got the

---

[871] *Freeman*, August 27, 1910.
[872] *Bulletin*, July 27, 1910; *Evening Post*, July 28, 1910; *Freeman*, August 20, 1910.

deeds to his house in Chicago in a safe deposit vault and I've got the key to the vault." She also had love letters from Johnson. Johnson had left McLay in late 1909 and had been with Etta Duryea ever since.[873]

The white-owned *New York Telegraph* thought Johnson should stop motoring around the streets with the new white woman, for such an exhibition was subversive to the city's morals, conducive to race hatred, and should be a matter for police regulation. Johnson's real wife, though very light, had a trace of negro blood. The newspaper believed that the moving pictures of the Jeffries fight were much less vitiating, upsetting, perverse, and debasing than the spectacle of Johnson in real life parading around with his white paramour through the streets in his automobile.[874]

Regarding a possible Johnson-Langford fight, the *Evening Post* said, "In this country, no matter how evenly matched or how clever the scrappers may be, the promoters have found it to be a risky undertaking to bring two colored boxers together."[875]

Johnson noted that legislators were attempting to kill boxing. "I have practically given up all hope of defending my title in this country. … I don't care where they hold them as long as they offer purses which are worth training and fighting for."[876]

Boxing said Johnson had been a first-class show-business headliner, attracting large crowds. Many thought that no whites would pay to see a black man, but they did. "This proves for sure one of two things, either that the real American values the satisfaction of his curiosity above his race prejudice, or that he deems the successful man the god in the car to be run after, whether he be black or white in colour."[877]

Johnson allegedly told a *Boxing* writer,

> I need not tell you that in America the racial question is very rampant just now. Our country taken from us is ruled by whites, and any sign of superiority on our part is regarded as a crime. They regard people of my colour as little better than dogs. Education does not count, and neither does refinement nor high breeding. Colour with them is everything. … Here am I, a cultured man, fit to converse on any subject – from astronomy right down to ancient classics – tabooed by white individuals whom I regard, both as regards race and education, as my inferiors.
>
> These people – these Christians – attend church, pray regularly, and yet pick out of the New and Old Testaments only those things which are agreeable to themselves. Worse than this, the very clergymen recognize that unless they pander to the popular taste they might as

---

[873] *Bulletin*, July 28, 1910.
[874] *San Francisco Evening Post*, August 2, 1910, citing the *New York Telegraph*.
[875] *San Francisco Evening Post*, August 8, 1910. On August 10, 1910, Joe Gans, the old master, passed away as a result of tuberculosis.
[876] *Freeman*, August 13, 20, 1910.
[877] *Boxing*, August 13, 1910.

well shut up shop. My blood boils as I think of these things, and only deep and solemn prayer calms me.[878]

At her brother's home, Lucy Johnson, the champion's sister, got married to Otto Bowlden, a professional ball player for the Oklahoma City club. As a gift, Johnson gave his sister a check for $3,000.

The English kept talking about white Bombardier Billy Wells, whom they thought had a chance to defeat Johnson. The 6'3" 21-year-old had many impressive fights and knockouts in India while in the army. Eugene Corri said, "I am quite confident that he is the coming man – the man to whom we can look to wrest the championship from Johnson."

A Paris promoter offered Johnson $20,000 to fight Joe Jeannette to a finish in Paris. Johnson did not think the offer was large enough for such a fight, particularly since he was earning easy money with his theatrical tour.[879]

On October 15, 1910 in Conway, Missouri, Stanley Ketchel was murdered by Walter A. Dipley, who shot him in the back, took Stan's money, and then fled with his girlfriend/wife Goldie Smith. Both Dipley and Smith were captured, tried, and convicted of murder in the 1st degree. Smith's conviction was overturned after she spent 17 months in prison. Dipley's life sentence was confirmed.

On October 25, 1910 at the Brighton Beach track in New York, Barney Oldfield defeated Jack Johnson in two consecutive 5-mile heats of auto racing in a best two out of three competition. Afterwards, Oldfield said,

> I raced Jack Johnson for neither money nor glory, but to eliminate from my profession an intruder who would have had to be reckoned with sooner or later. If Jeffries had fought Johnson five years ago, the white man would have won. ... I am glad if my victory over Johnson today will have any effect on the 'white man's hope' situation.[880]

The American Automobile Association later blacklisted Oldfield for racing Johnson without obtaining its sanction.[881]

The *Freeman* called Johnson a racial asset who showed the world what a black person could do if given the opportunity. "It helps the Negro to tell the world that opportunity is its greatest need in any avenue of life."[882]

On November 2 in Chicago, Johnson unintentionally got caught up in a labor dispute. Thousands of taxicab workers were striking. Johnson got into a non-union taxicab that drove past a crowd of striking union drivers, one of whom threw a brick through the window. It hit Johnson in the forehead, cutting him badly and stunning him for a few minutes.[883]

---

[878] *Boxing*, September 3, 1910.
[879] *Freeman*, September 17, 24, October 1, 1910. On September 6, 1910 in Boston, 170-pound Sam Langford won a clear 15-round decision over 190-200-pound Joe Jeannette in a fierce contest.
[880] *Salt Lake Herald-Republican*, October 26, 1910; *Freeman*, November 5, 1910.
[881] *Freeman*, December 24, 1910.
[882] *Freeman*, October 29, 1910.
[883] *San Francisco Call*, November 3, 1910.

Abe Attell claimed that in order to get Jeffries to fight, Johnson had agreed to throw the contest, but gave Jeff the double cross. Jeffries branded Attell's story a lie, but claimed that he had been doped.[884]

In November 1910, while in Lawrence, Massachusetts, Jack Johnson was suffering from memory loss and depression. He told his girlfriend Etta to take his revolver, for something told him that he might do harm with it. On November 17, a Lowell doctor told Jack to stop stage work for a while and rest, for he was suffering from nervous prostration. Jack said, "I attribute my condition to overwork. I haven't had a rest since my fight with Jeffries. ... I'm going to take a long rest."

The champ might have been suffering from a bad concussion, given that recently he was hit in the head with a brick. In his vaudeville performances, he was sparring 3 rounds with Walter Monahan, so perhaps he was not allowing his brain to heal.[885]

From New York, the National Negro Committee, speaking about the black race's condition in the U.S., said,

> Our people were emancipated in a whirl of passion, and then left naked to the mercies of their enraged and impoverished ex-masters. As our sole means of defense we were given the ballot. ... No sooner, however, had we rid ourselves of nearly two-thirds of our illiteracy...than this ballot...was taken from us by force and fraud. ...
>
> This attempt to put the personal and property rights of the best of the Blacks at the absolute political mercy of the worst of the Whites is spreading each day.
>
> Along with this has gone a systematic attempt to curtail the education of the Black race. Under a widely advertised system of 'universal' education, not one Black boy in three today has in the United States a chance to learn to read and write. The proportion of school funds due to Black children are often spent on Whites ...
>
> In every walk of life we meet discrimination, based solely on race and color...
>
> We are, for instance, usually forced to live in the worst quarters. ... When we seek to buy property in better quarters we are sometimes in danger of mob violence, or, as now in Baltimore, of actual legislation to prevent.
>
> We are forced to take lower wages for equal work, and our standard of living is then criticized. Fully half the labor unions refuse us. ...
>
> A persistent caste proscription seeks to force us and confine us to menial occupations where the conditions of work are worst. ...
>
> A widespread system of deliberate public insult is customary, which makes it difficult, if not impossible, to secure decent accommodation

---

[884] *Freeman*, November 19, 1910, January 28, 1911.
[885] *Chicago Broad Ax*, *New York Times*, November 19, 1910.

> in hotels, railway trains, restaurants and theaters, and even in the Christian church we are in most cases given to understand that we are unwelcome unless segregated.
>
> Worse than all this is the willful miscarriage of justice in the courts. Not only have 3,500 Black men been lynched publicly by mobs in the last twenty-five years, without semblance or pretense of trial, but regularly every day throughout the South the machinery of the courts is used, not to prevent crime and correct the wayward among Negroes, but to wreak public dislike and vengeance and to raise public funds. This dealing in crime as a means of public revenue is a system well-nigh universal in the South.[886]

On November 25, 1910 in New York, Jack Johnson was arrested for assault and disorderly conduct. Allegedly, one month prior, he had made an indecent proposition to Annette Cooper, a show girl, and grabbed her wrists when she repulsed him.

When Cooper failed to appear in court the next day as required, claiming she was ill and requesting a two-week continuance, the magistrate refused, and discharged Johnson.[887]

Johnson was investing in Chicago real estate. He had a cash balance in a local savings bank of nearly $165,000. Jack said, "I will show you one prize fighter who never will end up broke."[888]

The highest offer Johnson received from either French, British, or Australian promoters to fight either Sam Langford or Joe Jeannette was $20,000. However, Johnson believed he was worth a lot more, for he had just earned nearly six times that amount from the Jeffries fight.

John L. Sullivan said the fight game was not dead, but in critical condition. The one chance for its recovery was to find a young white talent who could beat Johnson.[889]

On December 21, 1910 in a Pittsburg bar, Brooks Buffington, a white Southerner, shot and killed Robert Mitchell, a black man, after the two engaged in a racial debate. One report said Buffington actually had sought to kill Johnson, but the intoxicated man was not allowed to enter the arena where Johnson was acting as a cornerman for a white boxer, so, perhaps frustrated, he killed a Johnson admirer instead.[890]

At year-end 1910, the *Chicago Defender's* editor lamented,

> When in the last days of departing year we look backward and see the bodies of 200 heroes lynched and 5,000 innocent girls rushed into motherhood by our Southern white friends, we mourn and hide our faces in shame at a government, the greatest the world has ever seen,

---

[886] *Chicago Broad Ax*, November 19, 1910.
[887] *Salt Lake Herald-Republican*, November 27, 1910.
[888] *Chicago Broad Ax*, December 3, 1910, quoting *Chicago Tribune*, December 3, 1910.
[889] *Freeman*, December 10, 17, 1910. Carl Morris of Oklahoma was an emerging white hope. He was a huge 6'4", 235-245-pound heavyweight. On December 20, 1910 in Sapulpa, Oklahoma, Morris stopped former champion Marvin Hart in 3 rounds.
[890] *Washington Times*, December 21, 1910; *New York Times*, December 22, 1910.

which would permit such crimes to be instituted in her domain. We look with shame upon our churches for not raising a dissenting voice; and we look with shame on American priests who at no time during a lynching have they tried to stop the mob or offer a prayer for the lynched. While others of the race rejoice and gloat over their success, we humbly beg God's mercy on the American government and its citizens.[891]

On January 1, 1911, after spending the holidays there, Jack Johnson left his mother's home in Chicago. Allegedly, he had a disagreement with his mother over his white girlfriend Etta Duryea, whom for the past year Johnson had been calling wife. Earlier in 1910, Duryea had been divorced from her white husband Charles Duryea. Mrs. Tiny Johnson allegedly barred Etta from entering the home again. Johnson's devotion to Etta caused him to leave his mother and sisters, or so the story was told. Others said he simply was retuning to his vaudeville tour.

On January 18, 1911 in Pittsburg, Jack Johnson actually and legally married Etta Duryea, whom he had been calling wife for some time.[892]

W. W. Naughton said the overwhelming desire to locate a "paleface" capable of defeating Johnson caused many to overlook the fact that some of the best fighters in the world were black.[893]

Most American promoters and the fans wanted to see a white man recover the crown for the white race. If Johnson lost to a black fighter, it made no difference to whites, for the crown still would remain in black hands, a situation they wanted to correct.

Johnson said he was willing to fight Langford, or any other man, but insisted on at least a $30,000 guarantee. "I am not in need of money...so if I fight it will be on my own terms."[894]

On March 25, 1911 in San Francisco, Jack Johnson pled guilty to a speeding charge. However, in a huge surprise, the judge sentenced him to 25 days in jail. Johnson admitted that he had been traveling at 62 miles per hour. An auto dealer, who was trying to sell a car to a white man, was about to be passed by Johnson. The dealer's prospective client said, "I'm a southerner, and if you let that fellow pass you, I'll not buy your car." So the dealer raced Johnson. That got them both pinched.

Justifying the lengthy jail sentence, the judge cited Johnson's long record of speeding infractions. Jack started his jail term on March 28. Subsequently, the judge agreed to reduce his sentence slightly and release him on Easter morning, Sunday April 16, but then, for whatever reason, the

---

[891] *Chicago Defender*, December 31, 1910.

[892] *Freeman*, January 14, 21, 1911. On January 10, 1911 in Boston, Sam Langford won a 12-round decision over Joe Jeannette, dropping Joe in the 1st round with a left uppercut to the jaw and clearly beating him thereafter.

[893] *Freeman*, February 18, 1911, quoting W. W. Naughton in the *Cincinnati Enquirer*.

[894] *Freeman*, March 4, 11, 18, 25, 1911. On February 21, 1911 in London, England, Sam Langford defeated Bill Lang via 6th round disqualification, having dropped the larger Lang in the 2nd, 3rd, and 5th (twice) rounds, though when Langford went down in the 6th round (either from a slip or a knockdown), Lang hit him while down, leading to his disqualification.

judge had a change of heart and made Johnson spend the full 25 days in jail. This was the second time that Johnson had spent nearly a month of his life in jail; the first being when he was arrested for fighting Joe Choynski.[895]

The black-owned *Chicago Broad Ax* hoped the jail term would do Johnson some good, "to learn that he must have at least some respect for the laws of this country and not to feel just because he has plenty of money that he can just for the pleasure of the thing run his automobile at full speed at all times."[896]

However, others said the sentence was extremely excessive and ridiculous, for Johnson had victimized no one, the sentence was disproportionate to the crime, and simply was one way the white man was attacking and punishing Johnson for beating Jeffries.[897]

Johnson said the judge had treated him unfairly.

> I think I was stung just because Judge Tredwell wanted to get a little notoriety out of me. They have never put any one else in jail for speeding. ... [The judge] told me that if I would plead guilty he would fine me. ... He promised to release me on Easter Sunday. When Saturday came, although I had a parole paper signed by the district attorney and the sheriff, the judge refused to sign it.

When leaving San Francisco, heading home to Chicago, Johnson was asked, "Are you going to be good now, Jack?" He replied, "I think I will drive as fast as ever. I have never hurt any one." However, Jack was not interested in returning to California, for boxing or any other reason.[898]

An apocryphal story has been told of Johnson, in which a police officer stopped him for speeding through a town, and when informed how much the fine was, he gave the officer double the money and told him to keep the change, for he would be returning the same way going the same speed.

Staunch slavery advocate Senator Ben Tillman allegedly was suffering from brain trouble, and his mind was decaying. The *Chicago Defender* said, "Tillman was the monster who once incited mobs which caused maddened, sweating men to abuse the golden rule as imps do in the lowest depths of hell with all its iniquity." Yet, "After all his rage and after all his vilification of the race and all that, great credit is given him for being a man to fight out in the open and not like the Northern assassin." He was forthright about his racism, unlike those in the North who concealed or denied it.[899]

On May 15, 1911 in New York, Jack Johnson was cited for driving his auto too slowly, at 5 miles per hour, and for having Chicago plates. Johnson noted that they pinched him both for going too fast and for going too slow. "Next thing somebody'll arrest me fur bein' a brunette in a blonde town. Ef

---

[895] *Freeman*, April 1, 8, 1911.
[896] *Chicago Broad Ax*, April 1, 1911.
[897] *San Francisco Call*, April 23, 1911, quoting the *Wisconsin Weekly Defender*, a black newspaper.
[898] *Freeman*, April 8, May 6, 1911. On March 28, 1911 in Sapulpa, Oklahoma, Carl Morris knocked out Mike Schreck in the 6th round. On April 1, 1911 in Paris, France, for a $10,000 purse, Sam Langford and Sam McVey battled to a 20-round draw.
[899] *Chicago Defender*, April 22, 1911.

I goes fast they arrests me, and now it seems like ef I go slow they does the same. White men, whut's the trouble now?" However, the magistrate dismissed the charges.[900]

Set to exhibit in England, Johnson said he would fight British heavyweight champion Bombardier Billy Wells while there if guaranteed $30,000. He wanted the same amount for Langford or Jeannette. He hoped that when he returned to America that a white hope would have been developed who could garner a large purse offer.[901]

---

[900] *New York Evening World*, May 15, 17, 1911; *New York Times*, May 16, 1911.
[901] *Evening World*, June 5, 1911. On April 24, 1911 in London, Bombardier Billy Wells knocked out Iron Hague in the 6th round to win the National Sporting Club's British heavyweight title. On May 5, 1911 in Kansas City, Missouri, Jim Flynn knocked out Al Kaufman in the 10th round. This was a huge upset victory for Flynn, for many, including Johnson, had considered Kaufman to be the best of the white hopes. This victory once again put Flynn on the map as a contender.

CHAPTER 39

The British Empire's Color Line

On June 6, 1911, Jack Johnson, accompanied by his wife Etta Johnson, as well as his chauffeur, trainer, and sparring partners, sailed from New York for England. The trip's main objective was to make money in theatrical engagements. However, Johnson said if offered $30,000, he would fight too.[902]

Johnson landed at Plymouth, England on June 12, 1911.

When he arrived in London at Paddington station, the cheering crowd was so large, dense, and frantic; it required the police to assist Johnson and his wife through.

Having been invited to see King George's coronation, Jack said, "I'm going to see King George try on his new hat."

Johnson's jovial good nature and his flow of stories quickly made a decided hit with all those whom he met. This would serve him well during his music hall tour.[903]

The *Defender* said, "Perhaps the reason why Theodore Roosevelt condemned prize fighting in America is best described from the lionization of Mr. J. Arthur Johnson in England. ... When the black world laughs the white world cries. ... But sport has done its holy work..."[904]

On June 22, 1911, Johnson attended the coronation of King George V and Queen Mary. He saw them try on their new hats, so to speak.[905]

The English magazine, *Boxing*, said the friendly Johnson was totally unlike the average man's idea of a pugilist, or a black man:

---

[902] *Evening World,* June 6, 1911; *Freeman,* June 17, 1911.
[903] *Manchester Guardian,* June 13, 1911; *Freeman,* July 1, 1911.
[904] *Chicago Defender,* June 17, 1911.
[905] *Manchester Guardian,* June 23, 1911.

He is a man well worth meeting – and studying, too, at that, for the simple reason that even a brief acquaintance with him at once disabuses your mind of numerous prejudices which you first imbibed with your mother's milk, and have since sedulously cultivated by the study of much expert opinion from ethnological and education authorities so called.

In the first place, Johnson belongs to a race which is frequently asserted to be only partially developed from our animal ancestors. All the apologists for the ill-treatment of coloured men and women by white lords of creation have always insisted that the black man was, and is, a brute, and must be treated as such.

In the second, Johnson is a man of comparatively humble origin, who went through a long series of hardships in his youth, and who at many times during his career has known what hunger, thirst, and the lack of a roof to cover him mean in reality. ...

For Jack Johnson in the flesh is really a merry, unaffected, shrewd, and likeable man. He will deliver himself of his views on life in a carefully-reasoned, philosophic fashion which affords instant proof that there is not only plenty of brain inside that shaven skull of his, but that brain has also undergone careful cultivation.

He is a consummately cool man, indifferent to danger, and yet in many ways as simple almost as a child; kind-hearted to a degree, sentimental of course – like most coloured folk – wonderfully humorous, especially in a dry vein, and positively a really charming host.

Musical taste is almost universally allowed to be convincing evidence of a refined disposition, and Johnson is not only a great lover of classical music, but also a really good executant himself on his favourite instrument, the bass viol. He might even earn a decent living as a musician were he not able to collect a much better one with the gloves.

Jack preferred talking about most anything but fighting, but would talk about boxing if pressed. He delighted in motor-driving, horse-racing, swimming, athletics, and books. Johnson's wife was an excellent pianist.[906]

The champ said if a challenger sufficiently proved himself worthy, there would be great demand for a fight, which meant a promoter would be able to offer the money that he wanted. It was up to the challengers to garner sufficient public demand, just as he did.

> Now to settle this tiresome controversy, let me say that if any responsible promoter in America, England or France hangs up a suitable bunch of coin and there is no interference I will fight Langford under any conditions Woodman may name. ... But I'd

---

[906] *Boxing*, June 24, 1911.

rather box with a white man because that's where the interest is, and also the money.[907]

The *Freeman* noted the irony of the fact that Jeffries had begun his career by stopping a black man, but ended it by being stopped by one. Regardless of the impact the latter fight had on his legacy, the fact was that he got paid mighty well for the beating he received. Similarly, no one could fault Johnson for wanting to get paid handsomely for taking risks as well.

In July, it was announced that Johnson was going to fight England's champion, 190-pound Bombardier Billy Wells in London in September for a guaranteed purse of $30,000, win, lose, or draw. Johnson's demands were met, so he took the fight.[908]

In late July and early August, Johnson gave nightly exhibitions inside a large dance hall at Magic City amusement park in Paris, just east of the Eiffel Tower. He even sparred with then welterweight Georges Carpentier.[909]

On August 13, 1911, in Coatesville, Pennsylvania, a black man named Zachariah Walker was lynched by a white mob which set him on fire and burned him alive. The day before, as a prank, a drunken Walker had shot over the heads of two Polish steel workers. Edgar Rice, a police officer who worked security for the steel mill, informed Walker that he would have to come with him. Walker refused, a tussle ensued, Rice was shot, and he died a few hours later. Walker attempted suicide by shooting himself, but only managed to shoot from his ear to his jaw. Walker was taken to jail, and claimed that he had been acting in self-defense. Reports circulated that he was proud of what he had done. Eventually Walker was taken to a hospital.

A angry crowd of 2,000 gathered outside, entered the hospital, beat, grabbed, and took Walker away, bringing him to a field. Walker again insisted that he killed Rice in self-defense. Nevertheless, the mob created a bonfire and threw him in. A charred Walker, with seared flesh, escaped, but he was beaten with rails from a fence, then thrown back into the fire, which was increased by the addition of fuel. Yet, Walker escaped a second time. He was beaten again, the foul smell and sight of his burnt flesh hanging off his body quite evident. A rope was placed around his neck, and he was pitched in one last time. His screams of agony were heard a half-mile away. Mob members collected pieces of his burnt flesh as souvenirs.

News of a black man's lynching was nothing out of the ordinary. In fact, the same day, another black man was hung in Durant, Oklahoma. What made the Walker lynching unusual and national news was that it took place in the supposedly enlightened North.

Fifteen people eventually were indicted for their role in the lynching, but all were acquitted by a jury of their peers. Walker had become the eighth

---

[907] *Freeman*, July 1, 1911.
[908] *San Francisco Call*, July 16, 1911; *Freeman*, July 29, 1911.
[909] *New York Sun*, August 2, 1911. On August 1, 1911 in New York, which on July 26 had legalized boxing with the passage and signing of the Frawley Act, 190-pound Joe Jeannette fought 200-pound Tony Ross to an unofficial 10-round newspaper draw.

person lynched in Pennsylvania. Black leader W. E. B. Du Bois lamented that sadly, "the best traditions of Anglo-Saxon civilization are safe." John Jay Chapman said the jury had acquitted "because the whole community, and in a sense our whole people, are really involved in the guilt. ... A nation cannot practice a course of inhuman crime for three hundred years and then suddenly throw off the effects of it."[910]

Further demonstrating that race relations were not improving in the U.S., Georgia Governor Hoke Smith (who was President Grover Cleveland's former Secretary of the Interior, Georgia's future U.S. Senator, and former publisher of the *Atlanta Journal*, which fostered racial animosity that led to riots) spouted off inflammatory racial rhetoric and encouraged and signed into law bills designed to disfranchise blacks, so as to give the white man the ability to control the government under all circumstances. He did not believe that blacks were citizens, but rather simply a "debauching influence" that reaches "the man who uses the ballot." Governor Smith said, "The true policy in the United States should be the development of the white race, with no mixture in matters of government by the yellow, the brown or the black races." He believed that white men must rule even where blacks outnumbered them, as was the case in Georgia. "[W]e made it lawful to keep 200,000 Negroes from registering and voting, and only permitted 10,000 to register. ... The Negro has been permanently eliminated from politics in Georgia."

The *Chicago Defender* bemoaned the fact that blacks had to pay taxes to support white men who spent the money to benefit only white men. The spirit of white rule had sunken so deep into the hearts of white Southern citizens such that "some of them count it a privilege to insult a Negro anywhere and in any place." It argued, "The blood of the soldiers that was spilt in the Civil War ought not to be spilt in vain. The Negro cannot protect himself unless he is given a fair chance. He must have the ballot."[911]

The English were treating Jack Johnson so well, he even said he would consider making England his home. "Johnson seems to be very popular in England – much more so than in the United States." Jack did not like how he was treated in America on account of his race. "What has America done for me? Has it ever given me a square deal? Did it give me a shout when I won? Not on your life." He even was quoted as saying, allegedly, that he never would take up a musket for the United States.

The question was whether Johnson just was playing to his hosts, or genuinely meant what he said, if he said it. Another question was whether the good treatment he was receiving simply was the honeymoon phase for a world famous athlete who just was visiting. The *Freeman* cautioned that the race struggle knew no national boundaries; something Johnson soon would learn.

---

[910] https://timeline.com/the-forgotten-lynching-of-zachariah-walker-was-one-of-our-most-shameful-and-it-was-in-the-north-678871b13f2d
[911] *Chicago Defender*, September 2, 1911.

Americans were upset with Johnson for making what they called unpatriotic remarks. Subsequently, Tom Flanagan, Johnson's manager, denied the reported interview in which Johnson was "alleged to have declared against America and for England." He said it was a fake.[912]

In August, Johnson signed a one-year contract with Hugh McIntosh to begin October 31, for a guaranteed $125,000, which would include fights in Australia against whomever McIntosh selected.[913]

There were reports that Johnson's white wife was being treated for nervous prostration in Paris. Etta had mental issues.[914]

For the upcoming title fight, Johnson would earn $30,000 and Wells $10,000, regardless of the fight's result. The picture rights had been sold to the Barker Motion Picture Company for $100,000.

Johnson was a diplomat. While in England, he praised everything English, and while in Paris, he praised everything French. He told the Parisians that after he disposed of Wells in England, and McVey and Langford in Australia, he would finish his theatrical engagements, retire, live in Paris, and open a gymnasium.[915]

The *London Times* confirmed that Johnson was well-liked in England. "He is popular, and has so far deserved his popularity."

The local *Times* claimed that Billy Wells was the speediest and most skillful of the "white man's hopes." The fight had been moved to October 2, to be held in the Empress Hall, Earl's Court, London. The match was attracting a lively amount of interest, including from those who did not want the fight to take place.[916]

Despite claims that race prejudice was not as great in England as in the U.S.; a *Freeman* writer feared that such was not true entirely. "If Johnson wins, I am very much afraid that prejudice will come up a bit in England. Even that fairly fair country does not care to have a black-a-moor putting it over Englishmen, the very lords of the fighting business in all respects. I may be mistaken in this, but we shall see what we shall see. Kindly watch the prediction." It turned out that this writer had some valid insights.[917]

With the Johnson vs. Wells fight looming large; race, religion, and politics coalesced and garnered momentum to prevent the bout. Regent Park Chapel Reverend F. B. Meyer, a Baptist secretary of the National Free Church Council, a coalition of churches in England, in the name of race and religion began a crusade against the scheduled Johnson-Wells contest, as well as its reproduction and exhibition via cinematograph films, saying it

---

[912] *Freeman*, August 5, 12, September 2, 1911.
[913] *Freeman*, September 2, 1911; *Rock Island Argus*, August 16, 1911; *Hawaiian Star*, August 25, 1911.
[914] *Freeman*, September 9, 1911. Some estimated Johnson was weighing 245-250 pounds.
    On September 5, 1911 in New York, Sam Langford (who in August had stopped Jack O'Brien and Tony Ross in the 5th and 6th rounds respectively) narrowly won a 10-round newspaper decision against Joe Jeannette. Still, Joe put up a game and clever fight, some calling the fight a draw, for on scientific points, Jeannette won, landing three to one, but Langford landed the harder blows, hurting and dropping Jeannette a few times. As a result, some said Langford would be no match for Johnson. *Freeman*, September 16, 30, 1911.
[915] *Freeman*, September 16, 1911.
[916] *London Times*, September 12, 1911.
[917] *Freeman*, September 16, 1911.

would be a bloody and degrading white vs. black fight. Meyer urged Winston Churchill, the Home Secretary, to prevent the fight.

On September 13, London City Council chairman Edward White sent a letter to W. H. Bond, the Earl's Court Exhibition, Ltd.'s licensee, strongly urging that the Johnson-Wells contest scheduled to be held there had to be prevented, and threatening that if the show was not stopped that the location's license might be endangered when it came up for renewal. The council had received a resolution passed unanimously at the Wesleyan Methodist Church's Second London District Synod's meeting, emphatically protesting against the fight. The City Council already was on record with its opinion that public exhibitions of the Jeffries-Johnson motion pictures were undesirable. "Bearing in mind the very widespread feeling of disgust which the Johnson and Jeffries contest in America caused in this country, I feel bound to add my personal view that if the proposed contest takes place at the Earl's Court Exhibition it may very seriously imperil the renewal of the licence by the Council in November next."

The Earl's Court directors responded that they had nothing to do with the contest other than leasing the Empress Hall to the promoters. Legally, it was impossible for them to take steps to stop the contest, for if they did, the promoters then would be within their legal rights to sue the Earl's Court for damages for breach of the lease.

James White, one of the promoters, noted, "Boxing contests take place in London every week during the winter, and no efforts are made to stop them, so why should this one stop? The law will not be infringed in the slightest degree, and absolute order will be maintained throughout the building. The police authorities will be invited to be present."[918]

Reverend Meyer protested that the fight "would embitter the feeling of the white people against the Negroes in America, South Africa and India." Home Secretary Winston Churchill was looking into the fight's legality. The promoters said they would not be deterred by ignorance, prejudice, and misconception.[919]

Reverend Meyer and the National Free Church Council said they were not attacking the art of self-defense in general, but argued that this particular fight would be a brutal match and not self-defense. Meyer claimed the Reno fight had attracted a horde of profligate people, there was much gambling, and noted that the pictures had been banned.

The Earl's Court Press Manager questioned the London City Council's jurisdiction over the matter, saying,

> The only distinction between the Johnson-Wells contest and others was that this one might conceivably be complicated by the colour question. It might be urged that Imperial considerations rendered it undesirable that such a contest should take place at all. If that were

---

[918] *London Times, London Daily Mail*, September 14, 15, 1911.
[919] *Freeman*, October 7, 1911.

so, the matter was for the Home Secretary and not the London City Council.[920]

The National Free Church Council was urging ministers in England to speak out against the fight from their pulpits in order to arouse the national conscience against the spectacle. The Johnson-Wells fight was denounced in countless sermons in London.[921]

The London weekly *Observer* supported the bout's prohibition, saying, "We think that there are objections which may be legitimately taken to the exhibition, and its subsequent display at the music halls, and should not be sorry to see it prohibited." Its objection had nothing to do with boxing's purported brutality, for it did not believe that boxing was brutal. Quite the contrary, it believed boxing to be fine physical and moral exercise. "We do, however, think that the great publicity given to the heroes of these events has a tendency to cause the youth of the realm to follow after false gods. Estimable a darkey as Mr. Jack Johnson may be – and, we believe, is – we do not want him as a popular hero."[922]

Members of Parliament, metropolitan mayors, members of city and county councils, and the clergy overwhelmingly opposed the fight, owing to racial considerations. Alderman A. Shirley Benn, a member of parliament and the London County Council, said,

> I am strongly in favour of the London County Council doing everything in its power to prevent boxing contests between white men and negroes. My objection is based not on any dislike to boxing pure and simple, but on the effect on the minds of negroes of contests such as the one to which you refer.

Southwark's mayor said, "I think boxing is good sport, but such contests as suggested between Johnson and Wells do not meet with my approval."

Reverend Meyer said, "At this time we ought to bring the races of the world together rather than increase the bitterness of the antagonism between white and black."

One reverend who opposed the opposition said, "Why all this fuss? There are so many real evils to be got rid of that it seems a pity to waste energy on matters of this sort." A Lord who supported the bout said those who did not approve of the fight were under no obligation to witness it.

James White, the contest's promoter, said of Reverend Meyer,

> I make him the following sporting offer: If he can prove there will be more brutality in this contest than in any of the contests being staged nightly at all the boxing halls throughout London and the provinces, including England's premier club, I will cancel this contest, though it would mean serious financial loss to me.

---

[920] *London Times*, September 16, 1911.
[921] *London Daily Mail*, September 16, 1911. *Freeman*, October 7, 1911.
[922] *Observer*, September 17, 1911.

He also said that he would cancel the contest if Meyer would agree to indemnify him from loss.[923]

White said the contest would take place, so far as he was concerned. Every seat had been booked. White "ridiculed the idea of a match between Johnson and Wells being calculated to create racial prejudice, as had been put forward in argument by certain persons, including a member of the London County Council."[924]

The *London Daily Mail* called it a "Black & White Fight." Many focused on the brutality of boxing in general. However, they could not overcome the argument that they opposed this specific bout but not others. Lord Harris said, "I think it inconsistent to oppose one and not others." One London Council member admitted why there was a difference. "I am most emphatically against the proposed contest between a white man and a negro, as it is bound to create racial antagonism in certain quarters, whatever the result may be."

A London Council member who was not opposed to the fight said, "My own personal view is that the colour or racial question is not of very serious importance in this country." Hence, he did not see any reason for objection. Fulham's mayor said people should be able to spend their money however they wanted, including witnessing the contest.

Jack Johnson could not understand the objections to the fight, for black men already had fought white men in London without trouble. He said his championship title gave him the right to defend against England's best man. "I see that they are trying to raise a storm of protest against the match. I don't see why, as it will not be different in any way from scores of others which take place nightly in London."[925]

There was some degree of hypocrisy to the opposition. However, the real difference was that this fight had greater symbolic value, because it was a black world heavyweight champion going up against the white British heavyweight champion, so it was not just an ordinary contest. The opposition was not about boxing itself, but the potential powerful symbolic racial and political message that the world would receive, particularly British colonial subjects, should a black champion pummel a white British champion. It was all about race and power.

Several public school headmasters went on record against the match. Even the Archbishop of Canterbury wrote a letter to the Home Secretary opposing the fight. They feared the contest's influence on British youth.

A sportsman who was not opposed to the fight, Sir C. Champion-De-Crespigny, said, "I most certainly do not agree with the London County Council in trying to stop the contest. My only objection is that if the 'nigger' is fit and fine it will prove a burlesque and probably not last a full round."

Some argued that Reverend Meyer was not in a position to criticize the Johnson-Jeffries fight, for Meyer admitted that he had not even seen the

---

[923] *London Daily Mail*, September 18, 1911.
[924] *London Times*, September 18, 1911.
[925] *London Daily Mail*, September 19, 1911; *Boxing*, September 23, 1911.

fight films. Regardless, Meyer thought the Home Secretary would support his viewpoint.

The *South African News* was leading an agitation against the fight as well. It appealed to the Union Government to prohibit the importation of the bioscope films into South Africa should the contest take place. "The paper further expresses fears as to the effects which the fight may have upon the South African natives, and protests that the country cannot afford to invite any expansion of the black peril."[926]

In his relentless crusade against the fight, Reverend Meyer said,

> The eyes of millions of the black and subject peoples are watching the issue of the contest (so widely advertised by the fact of it being held in the heart of London) as being in their judgment a decisive test in the matter of racial superiority, and, however you may guard it, you cannot alter its essential effect.
>
> Whatever safeguard you may adopt in the matter of referees, you must admit that the present contest is not wholly one of skill, because on the one side is added the instinctive passion of the negro race, which is so differently constituted to our own, and in the present instance will be aroused to do the utmost that immense animal development can do to retain the Championship, together with all the great financial gain that would follow.

South Africa's Cape Town correspondent said many prominent men, including the Moderator of the Dutch Reformed Church, wanted a prohibition in that country of any illustrations or newspaper descriptions of the Johnson-Wells fight.[927]

The *Freeman* reported, "There is no doubt that the feeling against the match is of the strongest sort and that it is growing stronger."

> [T]he color question has been introduced, and never before has the color question been so discussed in England. It is not based upon conditions in England, but upon conditions in parts of the British Empire where the question looms large.
>
> The *Outlook* asks the pertinent question: "If we were convinced that Wells could outclass the victorious black should we be so serious to deny him the triumph?"[928]

The feeling was that the black world champion would crush their white champion. That would send the wrong message to those darker races who had been colonized by the British throughout the world. It could give them hope and foster rebellion.[929]

A large number of prominent people, including the the Bishop of London, and even Lord Lonsdale, who was a lover of boxing, supported

---

[926] *London Daily Mail, London Times*, September 20, 1911.
[927] *London Times*, September 22, 1911.
[928] *Freeman*, October 7, 1911.
[929] *London Daily Mail*, September 22, 1911.

Reverend Meyer's proposed ban. Several London newspapers supported the prohibition as well, including the *Times* and the *Daily Telegraph*. Major General Sir Alfred Turner said, "The Home Office should prevent the exhibition, which my lead to lamentable racial disturbances."

The *Times* and the *Daily Telegraph* argued that race relations in Africa were such that Great Britain could not afford an encounter likely to cause the racial ill-will that was provoked in the U.S. after the Reno affair.

The *Freeman* noted and predicted, "Never in the history of public sport has so much government influence been directed against the holding of a glove contest; and there will be no fight."

From Paris, Johnson said, "It's just this, you don't want me to win, and that's the truth, but I am going to win. ... Lonsdale is sore at me because I would not fight for $5,000."[930]

Petitions to the Home Secretary said the fight should be stopped in the interests of public order and national well-being. A South African man said,

> I state unhesitatingly, and I write with inner knowledge, when I say that such a contest, with all its concomitants, must necessarily have a most harmful effect throughout South Africa, where white and black are seeking amid great difficulties to establish permanent and equitable relationships based on justice to both.
>
> We have hitherto in South Africa attempted, with success or with partial success, to maintain the supremacy of the ruling caste – viz., the European element. ... Surrounded, as we are, by natives in all stages of civilization, from the sea to the Zambesi, we seek to establish our supremacy ...
>
> How can we look them in the face when such a fight is permitted to take place in the heart of the Empire? It will have a bad effect on the native races within the Empire and it will inflame race feeling throughout South Africa. ...
>
> Why pit black against white at all, and why do so with all the odds in favour of the black man? ... The baneful effects will be felt far beyond the spectators who witness the fight. It will make the position of the white man more difficult still in distant parts of the Empire.[931]

Hence, the truth was that when push came to shove, the British Empire had a vested interest in maintaining white supremacy and suppressing anything which symbolically threatened it.

South Africa had prohibited the exhibition of the Jeffries-Johnson fight films. Blacks could not be allowed to see or even hear about a black man beating up the best Englishman either.

A writer named Stanhope said that even a few weeks after Johnson beat Tommy Burns, when the writer arrived at Suva, in the Fiji Islands, a policeman told him that he had more trouble with the colored people since

---

[930] *Freeman*, October 7, 14, 1911; *London Daily Mail*, September 23, 1911.
[931] *London Daily Mail*, September 23, 1911.

that fight than at any other time previously. A colored man said to him, "White man he no use; black man he knock him down every time." The policeman promptly proved to him that not every colored man was a Johnson. "The fact remains, however, that physical force had to be used, and once that is the case the safety of a white population, many times outnumbered by a coloured, becomes seriously menaced." After all, white minorities were ruling black majority populations. Even press reports of the Burns contest were sufficient to cause trouble. Although boxing in general produced more good than harm, once the color question became injected, the analysis changed entirely. Blacks were taught that it was a heinous offence to attack a white. A mixed-race bout shattered that doctrine. Therefore, a mixed-race championship fight would have "effects which both we and those who live under the British flag in distant lands may live bitterly to regret."[932]

South Africa's Bishop of Grahamstown said, "I am Bishop of a colonial and missionary diocese where there are nearly as many Kaffir adherents of our Church as there are Europeans, and I believe a fight between a black and a white man cannot fail to do infinite harm and cause bitter racial feelings."

A Nigerian correspondent argued that the Johnson-Wells fight would weaken the British Administration's supreme authority.

> There can be no doubt that in this part of British West Africa, and in such places as Sierra Leone and Cape Coast, the news flashed over the wires that a physical struggle between a white man and a black man, attended by thousands of spectators, has been waged in the capital of the Empire, would have a thoroughly mischievous effect – especially if the black man won.

Because Johnson was so well respected, it was presumed that he most likely would win, even if the talented Wells gave him a tough time of it. This writer said that "one can imagine few things more calculated to do us (and them) harm…than the…astounding incident of masses of Englishmen assisting at the public thrashing – if it so turned out – of an Englishman by a negro."[933]

The *Freeman* was not surprised; and said Johnson should not be surprised either. "He should have had the feeling that white men are white the globe around and that black men are black men in the meanwhile. They can't doff their feelings like they can their shoes, and furthermore they don't want to." It believed the Wells bout would be canceled.

This was a time in which conquered darker races were trying to assert themselves, and whites were resisting, in all ways. South Africa, England's Cape colony, was a reflex of the United States. In fact, the British Empire's racial conditions in many ways were even more problematic than in the

---

[932] *London Times*, September 23, 1911.
[933] *London Times*, September 26, 1911.

U.S., given that fewer whites ruled over a far greater number of darker people, and in many more countries.

> Other countries yet in South Africa are beginning to take notice, and England hopes to avoid a peril from its black belt stretched around the globe. So it does the very wise thing – from its viewpoint – self-preservation, keeping down all unnecessary possible causes of race comparison and friction. ... Great Britain has a race problem of her own. Such a notable defeat of a white British champion by a Negro would have its effect, it is thought, upon British South Africa, where there are one million whites dominating five million blacks, and in India, where only 150,000 whites are ruling over 300,000,000 nonwhites. And so in Jamaica and other parts of the empire.
>
> The Briton who has been spending his time analyzing our colored problem and writing gloomy predictions suddenly awakens to the realization that our colored question is nothing compared with his, for in the British Empire there are only sixty million whites, as compared with almost 350,000,000 nonwhites.

The Brits feared the fight's psychological effect. The Russo-Japanese war had shown the effect of a defeat of a white country by a nonwhite one. It was the germ of unrest in India. Time after time in the white-ruled world, "it has been shown that it is unwise to let the nonwhite races physically humiliate one of the 'ruling race.'"[934]

A Johannesburg correspondent lamented the fact that South Africa's white population was not keeping pace with the colored population, and feared the implications. At such a pace, eventually the darker peoples would outnumber the whites even more than they did already. "And what will become of the system of self-government under such conditions? Bearing in mind the progress of the backward races, is it certain that half a century hence twelve millions of coloured men will be content to be ruled without representation in the Legislature chosen by a few hundred thousand white men?" Black and brown races already constituted over 78 percent of South Africa's population, but they had no say in the government whatsoever.[935]

Ultimately, regardless of the fact that boxing bouts took place all the time in Great Britain, Home Secretary Winston Churchill, on behalf of the Home Office, concluded that the Johnson-Wells bout would be illegal, and issued an edict that unless the promoters abandoned the contest voluntarily, steps would be taken to prevent it by issuing a summons against promoter James White in the Police Court for a prospective breach of the peace.

However, James White did not want to give up on the promotion. He said the bout's rules would be no different than others held in England. If there was no breach of the peace for all of those contests, there should not be one this time either. White felt that he had the right to be treated the same as any other boxing promoter.

---

[934] *Freeman*, October 7, 1911.
[935] *London Daily Mail*, October 9, 1911.

Reverend Meyer was pleased. He had received letters from reverends and bishops throughout the British Empire, including Uganda, Australia, and New Zealand, all saying that a black vs. white fight would cause bitter racial feelings and disturbances throughout the Empire.[936]

Reverend Meyer believed that all black vs. white contests should be prohibited, saying,

> So far as battles between coloured men and whites are concerned, I am absolutely opposed to them. ... When white opposes black it is not a game of skill, for the black nature has more fire in the blood than the white, and has more passion. The reason men like to see blacks fighting whites is because the black men fight so passionately; it introduces the element of animalism which you do not see in the case of two white boxers. ...
>
> As I have lived in one country – South Africa – where the racial problem enters into these matters, I emphatically endorse the 'Stop-the-Fight' campaign now being engineered in that country, where it is believed by many that the contest will have a grave and harmful influence on the natives, who place altogether exaggerated importance upon the fact of a black successfully pommelling a white man.

Yet, Meyer admitted that he had never seen a professional boxing contest in his life. In response to this admission, *Boxing* said, "Comment is needless."[937]

On September 26, a local magistrate issued summonses to John A. Johnson, Billy Wells, James White, and others to answer for the contemplation of a breach of the peace.

Johnson said, "If they stop this fight it means that every other boxing contest, no matter where held, must be stopped too. If they stop this fight, England can never claim again that she is a nation that allows fair play."[938]

Supporters of boxing said what was taking place was an absolute farce. People who knew nothing whatsoever about boxing were dictating what was or was not brutal. There had been many black vs. white fights without problem. Boxing fans feared that the upcoming legal proceeding could deal a death-blow to the sport.[939]

The Metropolitan District Railway Company, which owned the property where the bout was to take place, filed a suit to obtain an injunction against the fight being held on its premises. The company feared that if the fight was allowed, its license to operate would not be renewed. Specifically cited was the letter from the London Council threatening such.

---

[936] *London Times, Manchester Guardian*, September 26, 1911.
[937] *Boxing*, September 30, 1911.
[938] *London Daily Mail*, September 27, 1911.
[939] *London Times*, September 26, 1911.

The Defendants cited fights such as Slavin-Jackson, Johnson-Burns, and Langford-Lang, all of which were black vs. white fights which had taken place in the British Empire without incident.

Nevertheless, Justice Lush granted the temporary injunction against the fight, given that the bout had a strong probability of endangering the owners' license. The judge passed no judgment on the contest's legality, but simply agreed that because there was a reasonable likelihood that the license was imperiled, the injunction could be granted.

On September 27 at the courthouse on Bow-Street, there was a separate case and hearing brought by the Crown at the instance of the Home Office, regarding the alleged contemplated breach of the peace. The court was packed. Well-known sporting men were present, showing support for the fight. Reverend F. B. Meyer had a seat upon a back bench. Outside the courthouse, a crowd of about 2,000 people was dense enough to hold up traffic. Wells arrived in a taxicab. Great cheers greeted him. The police had to help him get through the crowd.

John A. Johnson entered the courtroom with his shining golden smile. Even Magistrate Marsham was amused. When the Solicitor-General said, "Mr. Johnson will defend himself," Johnson replied, "Absolutely." His voice's emphatic strength left no doubt about his confidence in his ability to plead his own case. The champ stood beside Wells, as well as their respective managers, promoter James White, and the lawyers.

When permission was given for the men to be seated, Johnson chose to remain standing. During the Solicitor-General's opening statement, Johnson leaned easily against the rails, looking about and smiling. When Johnson had occasion to speak, his words were clear, and his sentences as straight to the point as one of his left leads. He addressed the Magistrate as "His Worship," and referred to opposing counsel as "the honorable solicitors."

The government argued that the fight would constitute a breach of the peace and was illegal, as opposed to a legal sparring match. The Solicitor-General said the last time a championship contest was decided, it took place at Reno, and the title was maintained successfully by "Jackson." Johnson interrupted, "Johnson, if you please." The Solicitor-General bowed his head in acknowledgement of the correction. Continuing, counsel argued that a sparring match was legal, but intent to injure or do harm was illegal.

The Solicitor-General said Johnson had taken part in three championship contests. With a broad smile, Johnson interrupted, "A few more than that, if you look into the records." The Solicitor-General replied, "Well, three or more." Burns, Ketchel, and Jeffries all had been stopped before their scheduled limits. He argued that was proof of intent to injure.

Police Superintendent McIntyre was called as a witness. The defense lawyers objected to questions of the witness regarding published records of the results of previous championship contests and newspaper descriptions of them contained in the *London Sporting Life*.

The magistrate asked Johnson whether he had objections he wanted raised. Johnson replied,

Yes, I object, for the witness is refreshing his memory of something he probably knows nothing about. I object because these papers printed in England are no authority upon contests in America. ... From these records the witness is simply refreshing his mind. Reading a paper refreshes his memory of things he has perhaps never known.

Nevertheless, the magistrate overruled the objections, admitted the newspaper into evidence, and the fight descriptions contained therein were read into the record. When asked whether, after hearing the descriptions, the witness apprehended that the upcoming contest would lead to a breach of the peace, the Superintendent replied, "I do."

The lawyers reserved cross-examination for a later time, but Johnson wanted to cross-examine him at that point. "I want to cross-examine him now." The magistrate suggested that it might be better for him to leave it until the legal gentlemen had undertaken theirs. Johnson persisted, however. "Are you familiar with the Queensberry rules?" "No, I am not." "Why did you say I knocked Tommy Burns out in the fourteenth round?" The superintendent started to look at the records. Johnson: "Don't look at the book. I object to you looking at that book every time I ask you a question. You are simply refreshing your memory." The superintendent said he meant the contest ended in 14 rounds. "I said at first that you knocked him out, but I find that the police interfered." Magistrate: "He admits he made a mistake." Johnson said, "The witness does not know what he is talking about. If he only goes by the book his evidence is very thin." Continuing, Johnson asked: "Why do you say that when Jack Johnson and Mr. Wells box on October 2 there will be a breach of the peace?" "I said I feared there might be." "Did Sam Langford and Bill Lang cause a breach of the peace?" "I do not know." "Did you see that fight?" "No." "Have you ever seen a boxing contest?" "No." "Then you have no idea of what they are like?" "No." With a scornful wave of his arm, Johnson turned to the magistrate and said, "The witness may go now. I am through."

Johnson's cross examination of the police officer was a "very sharp, swift attack, very skillful for one not experienced in courts." Of course, what they did not realize was that Johnson had been in court many times in the U.S. The case was adjourned until the following day.

As they left the courthouse, huge crowds loudly cheered and hailed the Defendants. It took a while for Johnson's taxicab to drive away slowly, given that a crowd of men clung to it as it went down Bow-street. Wells literally ran down the street to escape the cheering crowd.[940]

The next day, on September 28, 1911, matters came to a sudden conclusion. The bout was declared off "voluntarily." Pursuant to the agreement of the parties, the Justice of the Police Court granted an injunction against the fight. It appeared that promoter White had agreed to abandon the bout, fearing the potential repercussions of an adverse decision

---

[940] *London Times, London Daily Mail*, September 28, 1911.

against boxing in general. Such would hurt potential future contests as well. So instead of risking a decision that might implicate boxing's legality in general, they agreed to abandon the contest. Another reason given was that in light of the injunction issued by Judge Lush, it was impossible to hold the contest at Earl's Court, and as no other premises would allow the fight in London, it would be impossible for it to take place as advertised.

Unfortunately, the Johnson-Wells fight could not be held anywhere in the British Isles, where it would be the most attractive and financially lucrative, given that Wells was the British champion. However, the injunction would not affect Johnson's lucrative friendly sparring exhibitions at music halls, which continued.

The *London Times* was happy that the fight had been called off. It said the pressure of public opinion had achieved the desired result:

> We have assumed throughout the Empire great and unparalleled responsibilities, and it is impossible to ignore the widespread effect which this contest must undoubtedly have had in those countries where "colour feeling" unhappily exists. We have opposed the fight in the belief that it was contrary to the best interests of the Empire for this country to allow it to be held. The fine and manly English sport of boxing has been neither assailed nor displaced by its prevention, nor has the opposition been based upon any personal feelings towards either Johnson or Wells. Indeed, it is only fair to recognize that both men have adopted an attitude of most commendable restraint ever since public opinion began to range itself against their meeting. In his cross-examination of Superintendent McIntyre in the proceedings at Bow-street on Wednesday, moreover, Johnson showed a power of advocacy which proves he is possessed of an acute brain as well as formidable fists. Neither the men nor boxing as a sport have been arraigned and the justification for the opposition to the holding of the contest at Earl's Court is founded, as we have declared from the first, upon the public interest of the Empire.[941]

The *Freeman* noted that although the Earl's Court lease had been secured for 21 years, the London County Council had full powers over the granting or revoking of licenses, and without its consent, it was impossible to run the place. Hence, long-term economic concerns forced the promoter to acquiesce to those in power who sought to stop the fight.[942]

A frustrated Jack Johnson announced his retirement:

> I am now through with boxing. I will finish my contracts in England, but I will never put on the gloves again in public after those contracts are through. I shall retire as the heavyweight champion of the world.
> ...

---

[941] *London Times*, September 29, 1911.
[942] *Freeman*, September 30, 1911.

> I had only one other fight fixed up, and that was in Australia. But as Australia is governed by England, I do not want to run the risk of making that journey and then find the fight declared illegal. So that fight is off.

That evening, Johnson said,

> I had originally intended to fight three more fights, but as Australia is governed by British law, and they don't seem to want me any more in this country, I don't want to force myself on the public. I have made enough money to retire on, and the last chance the British public will have of seeing me with the gloves on will be at exhibitions which I am about to give in the music-halls through the British Isles.[943]

Some hoped that a 10-round Johnson-Langford bout could be arranged in New York. However, New York Governor John Dix, who recently had championed boxing, had changed his mind, and was discussing with Senator Frawley the advisability of repealing the enacted law that legalized the sport. "The English opposition to the Johnson-Wells match commands much sympathy here, even in sporting circles."[944]

A month after the bout was prevented, in the House of Commons, Mr. Thorne commented, "Does the right honorable gentleman think that if there was any possible chance of Wells beating Johnson we should have heard anything about it?" Laughter followed, and no answer was given. The obvious point was that if they thought Wells had a real chance to beat Johnson, most likely those whites in power would have allowed the bout.[945]

In the end, Great Britain and the British Empire was no better than the U.S. in its racial attitudes about white-black competition on a heavyweight championship level, despite what it often professed about itself. Ultimately, in a world where whites sought to maintain domination over darker races, concerns about racial conflict came to the forefront, and a Johnson-Wells fight was viewed from a racial and political perspective. The English had colonies throughout the globe, dominating darker folk. Fear about the bout's symbolic effect, particularly if Johnson won, derailed the bout. Johnson was a symbol of subversion to the racial status quo. These concerns were particularly sharp in South Africa, where in the Second Boer War (1899-1902), the Brits had sustained massive casualties in obtaining Afrikaner lands. Nationalist movements threatened British rule in places like India and Egypt as well. In all of these locales, non-white subjects outnumbered the whites. A black man defeating a white British champion would send a message the Empire did not want and did not think it could afford, for such would foster ideas it did not want encouraged. A European nation which maintained colonies throughout the world could not afford to be any more tolerant than Americans; and in fact was even less tolerant.

---

[943] *Manchester Guardian, London Daily Mail, London Times*, September 29, 1911; *Freeman*, October 7, 1911.
[944] *Freeman*, September 30, 1911; *London Times*, September 29, 1911.
[945] *Manchester Guardian*, November 2, 1911.

Like it or not, Jack Johnson was a political and racial symbol throughout the world.

The *New York Morning Telegraph* lamented that the world's best heavyweights were black, asking, "Where is the white man who will take the conceit out of the big Negro, Jack Johnson? It seems as if this gross dark throwback stood invincible in the prize ring and defied the world to find a white man who can whip him."[946]

It was reported that Johnson had many quarrels with his white wife, the last occurring in a Paris café, where she declared that Jack did not pay enough attention to her, and allegedly he slapped her face.

There also were rumors that Johnson was low on cash and had to pawn his car, having spent most of his money. Others countered that Johnson had over $150,000 in various forms of securities, and had plenty of money. One never knew which rumors were true, or which were designed to cast aspersions on a famous black man.

Johnson said, "I possess more than $100,000 cash, four automobiles, three here and one in America, and all fine ones, a bag full of diamonds and a lot of other property." He recently had a car made according to his own ideas and specifications, which cost more than $7,500. His wife wore jewelry worth between $60,000 and $70,000. "Tell them that Jack Johnson is still a long way from the bread line."

Johnson blamed the ministers for the fight game's decline. "It is all the preacher's fault. ... This is supposed to be a free country, and it would be but for the preachers. They look sharply after everybody's morals except their own. ... I am a sober man. I am told the great majority of preachers in England are boozers. ... Great fighting is dead from an overdose of sanctimoniousness." Jack was going to Paris, the warmest town on earth.[947]

One *Freeman* writer said Johnson's declaration of retirement was met with little comment, owing to the fact that ever since defeating Jeffries, "the Galveston black has made himself obnoxious to both the members of the white and black races as a result of the way he has conducted himself."

Johnson was in a difficult position. White patrons wanted to see a white man recapture the crown. They did not care as much to see another black man challenge for the title, because at the end of the day the title would remain in black hands. Hence, such a fight would not be as lucrative. However, whites did not want to see or even allow a fight in which the white fighter had little chance to win. That sent the wrong message too. They only wanted a fight in which the white fighter had a good chance to defeat Johnson.

The *Freeman* again noted the reason why Johnson was not allowed to fight was because of the potential "bad influence on the darker races, so many of whom are of the English possessions." The potential Wells fight had "quickened the public conscience."

In Newcastle, England, Johnson was fined $100 for speeding his auto.

---

[946] *New York Age*, September 21, 1911, quoting the *New York Morning Telegraph*.
[947] *Freeman*, October 7, 14, 21, 28, 1911.

W. W. Naughton said Johnson's pompous ways and the flashiness he displayed with his white wife had caused a reversal of feeling against him in England. He put himself on too high of a pedestal to suit even mild-tempered Britons. "In spite of the strong feeling against Negroes in many quarters, Johnson would never have been as unpopular in America as he is now if it were not for his actions outside of the ring since he won the championship."

The *Cleveland Gazette* said the truth was out at last:

> The plain fact was, in the case of England, that the spectacle of a Negro whipping a white man would give too much encouragement to the blacks of the English provinces, in several of which that country was and is having more or less trouble to keep them subjugated. The same thing is true in the case of the whites and our people of the South.

The *Freeman* agreed. "The truth plainly presents itself, if we conclude that racial relations are similar around the globe, a fact patent for years." In fact, many English newspapers had agreed that Johnson was likeable, before the issues surrounding the Wells fight were raised.[948]

Dr. T. Rhoudda, a Brighton, England Congregationalist preacher, called attention to religious leaders' hypocrisy by asking, "Will the forces that came together to stop the fight remain together to stop the terrible treatment which the white man is dealing out to the black?"

The *Freeman* noted that Johnson had brought attention to the worldwide color line and race politics, regardless of country. In the end, race mattered throughout the world, not just in the U.S. "Poor, innocent Jack Johnson and his Reno have brought forth this world discussion, and perhaps for the better. What has been brought out had a latent existence, and which would out at some period, sooner or later." Johnson made it obvious that the world's whites did not want racial fairness.[949]

On December 6, 1911 in Clifton, Tennessee, a group of "white caps," or white farmers who sought to eliminate competition from black farmers by using violence and intimidation, lynched a black farmer and his two daughters. They shot the father, hung his daughters, and burned them.[950]

---

[948] *Freeman*, November 4, 11, 18, 1911; quoting *Cleveland Gazette*.
[949] *Freeman*, November 25, 1911.
[950] *Freeman*, December 9, 16, 1911.

CHAPTER 40

Best White Hope

In late December 1911, Jack Johnson and his wife Etta returned to the U.S. to spend the Christmas holiday with his mother. He brought back from England 13 trunks of clothes.[951]

The *Freeman* believed that black success in sports had symbolic value which threatened the race caste and demand for white supremacy in all areas of life. "There seemed to lurk a fear that the Negro all over the land would feel his ability to meet the white man on an equal footing."

As a result of black success, "The press has taken an unusually active part in trying to push the Negro out of the limelight. ... For two years the papers have been devoting column after column to Jack Johnson and magnifying whatever little thing the champion may do into some act against the public safety." Some policemen never saw their names in print until they grasped the opportunity to secure a medal by arresting the champion. "If he is to be made the scapegoat of every little cheap newspaper reporter it is because he is black and a member of a race which most people of other races take a delight in looking down upon."

The *Freeman* said if Johnson lost to a white hope, those same kickers of the sport would want the moving pictures to be shown to all American children and "to the savages in Africa, to show how much greater the white man's powers were than the black man's."[952]

On December 26, 1911 in Sydney, Australia, 18,000 spectators saw Sam McVey win a 20-round decision over Sam Langford, decking Langford in the 3rd round, outboxing him, bloodying his mouth, and swelling up his eye. Although some thought Langford had earned a draw with his aggression, the victory boomed McVey's stock.[953]

Back in Chicago, Jack Johnson vigorously denied the "rumor" that he had retired, and said he had no intention of retiring. "With me it is purely a question of money whether I will fight again, but I have not retired and do not intend to do so for some time yet. I was sorry I did not get to fight Bombadier Wells in England. .... [A]ll those stories about me running around and drinking a lot of champagne are lies." Either he had changed his mind about retiring, or the initial reports of his retirement were false.

The champ said promoters only had to meet his $30,000 price, the same as what Burns got for fighting him, and he would fight anyone.

---

[951] *Chicago Defender*, December 23, 1911.
[952] *Freeman*, December 23, 1911.
[953] *Hawaiian Star*, January 31, 1912; *Freeman*, December 30, 1911; *New York Age*, December 28, 1911, February 15, 1912.

Rumors were that Johnson weighed nearly 300 pounds and his wife was seriously ill. Jack said he weighed 233 pounds. "If I am supposed to be down and out, why don't some of these promoters take advantage of staging a fight between me and one of these 'hopes,' whom so many persons think have a chance of beating me in a contest?" White hopes were the nation's craze. Every promoter was trying to develop a white heavyweight who could defeat Johnson.[954]

On December 30, Johnson agreed to fight Sam McVey for Hugh McIntosh in Sydney on or about Easter Monday, April 8, for a $30,000 guaranteed purse, plus $5,000 in training expenses. McVey's victory over Langford made it a lucrative bout.[955]

Unfortunately, Sydney's clergy immediately began agitating for the prohibition of the scheduled McVey-Johnson fight. Fearing a repeat of what had taken place in England, businessmen interested in the fight engaged legal counsel to test the contest's legality; to ensure that they would not be investing money in a venture that could not proceed. Once again, it appeared that another potential Johnson bout might be derailed.

While Johnson had been overseas, on September 15, 1911 in New York, 180-pound "Fireman" Jim Flynn clearly won a 10-round no-decision bout over the emerging 6'4" 230-pound heavyweight Carl Morris, who had earned knockout victories over Marvin Hart and Mike Schreck. Despite being five or six inches shorter and weighing about 50 pounds less, Flynn badly beat Morris, showing that he could handle much larger men, as he had proven in his 10th round knockout over the much larger Al Kaufman earlier that year. Those victories made Flynn the top white contender.

Negotiations for a Johnson-Flynn fight for July 1912 were ongoing with Promoter Jack Curley, and it appeared that they were close to a deal.[956]

Ultimately, as a result of all the opposition to a Johnson fight being held in Sydney, the champ received notice that the McVey match could not be held in Australia, at least not on the scheduled date, and it might need to be moved to another country like France and held in the summer. Things were looking uncertain, and the fight promotion appeared to be on the ropes.[957]

Chicago's *Day Book* said, "Flynn looks like the best 'white hope' in sight at present. He is a rough and ready, tearing, clashing fighter, who does not know the meaning of fear."[958]

Promoter Jim Coffroth said he too would give Johnson his $30,000 price to fight Flynn.

On January 6, 1912, Jack Johnson and Jim Flynn signed articles of agreement to fight in July 1912. Johnson would be paid a guaranteed $30,000, $1,100 for expenses, and also earn 1/3 of the moving picture

---

[954] *New York Age*, December 28, 1911. *Freeman*, December 30, 1911; January 6, 1912.
[955] *San Francisco Call*, December 30, 1911. *Observer*, December 31, 1911.
[956] *Manchester Guardian*, January 3, 1912; *Salt Lake Tribune*, January 4, 1912.
[957] *Call*, January 4, 1912.
[958] *Day Book*, January 6, 1912.

rights. Flynn's undisclosed share would be paid by his manager, Jack Curley, who represented the unnamed promoters.[959]

H. C. B. Fry, publisher of the new *Fry's Magazine* in London, England, said the Negro constitutionally was a better scrapper than the Caucasian, for he was quicker and had superior ability to absorb punishment. Fry claimed that England did not have anti-color feeling, yet admitted that "we do not much like not having a man who is either champion of the world or thereabouts, one of our own blood, I mean – a white man."[960]

There had been talk of Johnson boxing in an interim 10-round bout in New York, to be held prior to the Flynn fight, against Joe Jeannette.

However, on January 11, 1912, New York Boxing Commissioner Frank O'Neill announced that he would not allow Johnson to box in that state. "I have come to the conclusion it is against public policy and expediency to have Johnson box here. This is final."

After reading that he had been barred from boxing in New York, Johnson objected, saying the commissioner could not ban him without just cause.

> Do you know why they try to bar me in New York and London? Well, it is because they know no white man alive can whip me. They believe in their hearts that Jack Johnson is the greatest fighter that ever lived and just because he is colored they don't want to give him a chance.
>
> Why, if they had a big white fellow in New York that they thought could trim me, there wouldn't be the slightest objection in the world to the match. They would let me fight Jeannette, too, because he also is colored. But just because I have it on the white fellows, they say, 'Let's bar him.' That's not justice and I will leave it to any fair-minded person if it is.[961]

---

[959] *New York Times, Washington Herald,* January 7, 1912; *El Paso Herald,* January 6, 1912; *Freeman,* July 20, 1912; Boxrec.com. Copy of the signed articles of agreement.
[960] *New York Age,* January 11, 1912.
[961] *Salt Lake Tribune,* January 12, 1912; *Tacoma Times,* January 11, 1912. On January 17, 1912 in Toronto, Jim Flynn knocked out 200-pound Canadian champion Al Williams in the 2nd round.

On January 29 in Cincinnati, the Methodist Ministers Association adopted a resolution protesting against the Johnson-Flynn fight, and even sent its protest to the U.S. Congress.

Black newspapers often liked to call attention to the clergy's hypocrisy, for religious folk condemned boxing while engaging in total blindness regarding lynchings and the barbarism of mob rule. The *Chicago Defender* said Christianity was a "peculiar kind of religion. Can these worthy (?) men of God explain?"

> It is a peculiar coincidence that the barbarism of prize fighting is never uppermost in the minds of the more sanctimonious (?) of the white race until the name of Johnson is mentioned. ... Can these worthy (?) men of God explain why the battles between the white exponents of the art fail to arouse their antagonism? Truly the ugly sprit of prejudice is a most opposing force and Christianity is powerless to obliterate it. For the protestation against prize fighting is no more than another exhibition of the white man's pet hobby – prejudice, and only a true insight into a Christian life and a casting of the sham religion will uncover the eyes of the divines to the things that warrant protesting against. Daily, yes, hourly are members of the other race scheming to degrade and perpetrating the crime of lynching on their fellow-man and if the religion of the white man was a thing of the heart and not of the head their bills to Congress would be filled with prayers and entreaties of the suppression of such diabolical crimes against humanity.[962]

Jim Flynn, the Best White Bet In Sight; Johnson's Next Opponent

In February, Las Vegas, New Mexico was chosen as the Johnson-Flynn fight site. New Mexico recently had been admitted to the Union as a state on January 6, 1912, and had no laws against prizefighting. Local businessmen welcomed the publicity and revenue which they thought would flow from a big fight.

However, anti-boxing folks came out in force and protested the bout. New Mexico Governor William McDonald said he would stop it if he could, for he did not want to permit a white vs. black fight. He appealed to the legislature to pass a law against prize fighting. As usual, church groups called the bout a detrimental disgrace.[963]

In early February in Chicago, Johnson was appearing on stage, singing and playing the bass violin in a show called "Down in Melody Lane."[964]

---

[962] *Chicago Defender*, February 3, 1912.
[963] *New York Times*, February 9, 1912.
[964] *Chicago Defender*, February 10, 1912. On February 24, 1912 in Milwaukee, Jim Flynn knocked out Leopold McLaglan in the 3rd round.

The U.S. government was pursuing Johnson, intending to prosecute him for smuggling, alleging that he failed to declare and pay taxes on a $6,000 diamond necklace when he returned from abroad. The government claimed he owed $9,600 in duty taxes on the necklace, including the penalties. The secret service raided his home in Chicago and departed with the necklace.[965]

On April 8, 1912 in Sydney, Sam Langford avenged his defeat by winning a 20-round decision over Sam McVey.

On April 15, 1912, in its maiden voyage, the *RMS Titanic*, the largest passenger ship ever built to that point, struck an iceberg and sunk. As a result of the ship having an insufficient number of lifeboats, 1,502 people died. There were no safety regulations requiring more lifeboats. In an ironic twist of fate, owing to the color line, there were no black Americans allowed on board, although there was one Haitian family.

On April 24, 1912 in Pittsburgh, Jack Johnson and his brother Henry Johnson were passengers in the back seat of the champ's car, which was driven by valet Randall Wright. When the car came to a stop, a heavy truck rear-ended it, crushing the car like an egg-shell. The impact strained the tendons and muscles in the champ's back and spine. Johnson had been set to start active training for the scheduled July 4 Flynn fight, but on the doctor's advice, he would rest for a while instead.[966]

On May 23 in Albuquerque, New Mexico, before giving a sparring exhibition, Jim Flynn told the the crowd, "I will bring back the championship to the white race, where it belongs." He was cheered loudly.

On May 25, 232-pound Johnson, his wife, four sparring partners, and chief trainer Professor William Burns left Chicago, heading to Las Vegas, New Mexico, the fight site.[967]

Many believed that Flynn's ferocious style and powerful explosive blows were well-adapted for Johnson. The 215-pound Flynn was 32 years old and had been fighting for almost 12 years.[968]

---

[965] *Chicago Defender*, April 6, 1912.
[966] *Chicago Defender*, April 27, 1912. *New York Times*, April 25, 1912. From 1891 to 1911, the official spelling of the city's name was changed to "Pittsburg," but from July 19, 1911 on it was known by the original spelling, "Pittsburgh."
[967] *Albuquerque Evening Herald*, May 24, 25, 1912.
[968] *Albuquerque Evening Herald, Albuquerque Morning Journal*, May 30, 1912.

Johnson said, "Mistah Flynn will touch me but twice in our coming battle. The first time will be when he shakes hands at the beginning of the fight, and the other will be when he tries to hold on to keep from being knocked out, when I put over the anaesthetic punch."

Jack Curley insisted that the fight would occur. The legislature would adjourn on June 8, and most of them favored the fight.[969]

The game, hard-hitting Flynn daily lambasted his sparring partners. "It was a case of slug, slug, slug and butt, butt, butt from the time each setto starts until it ends." Flynn said, "I'll only win by fighting the big smoke. He would make me look like a huge sucker if I tried to box with him."

All of his sparring partners said Flynn was the strongest man in the game and dealt the hardest blow of them all. Flynn had been active throughout his 50-fight career, and had gone 10-0 with 9 KOs over the course of 1911 and 1912 alone.

Conversely, Johnson was coming off a two-year layoff, during which time he had engaged in a great deal of high living, and therefore many thought he would not be as good as he once was. Plus, he was 34 years old.

The very confident Flynn said,

> I'll knock the big smoke stiff. ... I'll win and win sure. Why shouldn't I win? Doesn't every good white person around the country want me to trim Johnson? Then, won't the best people at the contest in Las Vegas July 4th be white people? I know I won't disappoint, and inside of a month's time the whole world will know what I know now.

Johnson too was sure of victory. "While I figure Jim Flynn a tough ringster, the best of the white crop, I am confident I will defeat him July 4th inside 15 rounds."[970]

Johnson had planned to exhibit in nearby Albuquerque, but declined to do so when no assurances could be given to him that he and his wife would be permitted to stay at a first-class hotel. He was told that there were a "lack of accommodations," but in truth the color line was at work. Johnson said, "I don't want to be humiliated by being refused first class hotel accommodations."[971]

Flynn's trainer Tommy Ryan said Flynn was in great shape: "Don't say that I am claiming that the title is going to be returned to the keeping of the white race, but if Johnson doesn't cop Flynn while he is fresh I think my entry will just about score."[972]

On June 14, Johnson was given a list of fifteen names of potential referees, but he objected to eleven of them as unfit as a result of pronounced antipathy against his race. The *Chicago Defender*, which had a special correspondent with the Johnson party, wrote, "They tried to fake him, but he wouldn't stand for it. ... At least a half dozen of those crossed

---

[969] *Albuquerque Morning Journal*, May 31 - June 3, 1912.
[970] *Albuquerque Evening Herald, Albuquerque Morning Journal*, June 5-6, 1912.
[971] *Albuquerque Morning Journal, Albuquerque Evening Herald*, June 11, 1912.
[972] *Kansas City Star*, June 13, 1912.

off were men known as Negro haters. One of them openly declared that 'the Negro had no business at the head of anything.'"

Ed W. Smith, the *Chicago Examiner*'s sporting editor, eventually was chosen to referee, for he got along with both Johnson and Curley.[973]

On June 17, Tommy Ryan abruptly quit and left the Flynn camp. Most believed the reason was financial. Others reported that Flynn practiced foul tactics on his sparring partners, so much so that a disgusted Ryan quit. He predicted that Flynn would lose on a foul.[974]

Much to promoter Curley's chagrin, Governor McDonald had declined to put himself on record regarding whether he would try to stop the fight. Curley feared that might lower attendance, for folks would not want to pay to travel to a fight that might be prevented. Las Vegas men of prominence allegedly had spent from $65,000 to $75,000 on the enterprise.

Curley insisted that the fight would happen, for there was no law to prevent it in New Mexico. The bout likely would be better than the Jeffries fight, for Flynn was younger, more consistently active, and in great shape.

On June 18, those who watched "the hope of the white race" in training agreed that he had "more than an even chance to carry off the heavyweight title." New chief trainer Abdul 'the Turk' Malgan said, "Flynn deserves to bring the heavyweight title back to the white race."[975]

On June 21, 1912, federal officials indicted Johnson and his wife for smuggling, alleging they had failed to report and pay import duties on a $6,000 diamond necklace that Jack had purchased for her in England.[976]

One reporter in Las Vegas said the Mexicans, who outnumbered the American citizens in the area four to one, were strong for Johnson:

> Every afternoon at the ink's camp the insurrectos congregate and applaud his efforts. John Arthur can spell a fair line of Spanish, while a smattering of English and profane is Jim Flynn's line. The negro appeals to the 'Mex' because he is good natured and looks lazy. They don't like anything here in the animated line.[977]

Ten days before the fight, on June 24, New Mexico Governor William C. McDonald said the contest would not be prohibited. All he could do was enforce existing laws, and the legislature had passed no law against boxing. Las Vegas was jubilant. Seats were selling for $10, $20, and $25.[978]

Hugh McIntosh was offering Johnson $30,000 to come to Australia to fight next, presumably against Sam Langford. Johnson would require assurances that the British Empire/Australian authorities would allow him to fight there before he would travel such a long way and spend time and money training, forgoing other opportunities.

---

[973] *Chicago Defender*, June 15, 1912; *Albuquerque Morning Journal*, June 16, 1912.
[974] *Albuquerque Evening Herald, San Francisco Examiner, Call*, June 18, 1912; *New York Times*, June 22, 1912.
[975] *Albuquerque Evening Herald, Kansas City Star*, June 19, 1912.
[976] *New York Times*, June 22, 1912.
[977] *Albuquerque Morning Journal, Albuquerque Evening Herald, Kansas City Star*, June 22, 1912.
[978] *Albuquerque Evening Herald, Albuquerque Morning Journal*, June 25, 1912.

Tom Flanagan noted that fans and writers loved to criticize the champ, regardless of whether or not he fought, or whom he fought. Most folks failed to consider what it cost to train for a fight, both physically and financially. However, when Johnson got his fair price, he was willing to fight anyone.[979]

Intrigued by the contest, W. W. Naughton arrived in East Las Vegas. He said Flynn had proven himself to be the best of the white hopes.[980]

John Perkins, Marty Cutler, George DeBray, Jack Johnson, Professor Watson Burns, Calvin Rastus Respress, Kid Skelly, William Brown

There were the typical rumors and speculation that Johnson might throw the fight. Harry Smith responded, "Johnson thinks too much of his title and the glamour with which it surrounds him to give it up for what Flynn and his backers could afford to hand over." Curley was promoting the bout on the chance of Johnson not being in the best shape owing to his long inactivity, not because of a fix. "Naturally such gossip is to be expected."

The *Chicago Defender* did not think Johnson would sell out and throw the fight, for he had too much at stake. "Such report seems absurd when one views the obstacles that the champion had to overcome to reach the coveted goal of his ambition. ... The champion would struggle to stem the tide of defeat as long as an ounce of strength would respond to his dominating spirit." Although Flynn was the pugilistic "Titanic of the Caucasian race," the *Defender* did not believe the title would be transferred "to the brow of the Anglo-Saxon."[981]

The champ was confident that he would win soon after the 10th round. "This talk of high life and wine dinners for Johnson seems to be a joke."

The *Star* reported that the 5'6" black Calvin Respress, who was built like Joe Walcott, was the only man left in Johnson's camp who was able to assimilate the "smoke's" jolts. "Johnson appears to take keen delight in

---

[979] *Albuquerque Evening Herald*, June 25, 1912; *New York Times*, June 26, 1912.
[980] *Albuquerque Evening Herald*, June 26, 1912.
[981] *Albuquerque Morning Journal*, June 27, 1912; *Chicago Defender*, June 29, 1912.

slaughtering this gorilla-like ink spot. ... [Respress]] was so cute [that Johnson] brought him along with the other animals."[982]

New York's Garden City Athletic Club wired Johnson an offer to fight on Labor Day against Al Palzer, who recently knocked out Bombardier Billy Wells in the 3rd round. "How Johnson is to fight in New York unless the boxing commission relents hasn't been explained. Six months ago the commission announced that the champion ink was barred."[983]

A local straw ballot of 24 votes had 17 favoring Flynn as the victor. The majority believed he would be able to wear down the "Big Smoke."[984]

Johnson was willing to bet $2,500 that Flynn would not survive the 15th round. The champ said the claim that he had been idle and taking life easily for the past two years was false and misleading. He had trained for Wells, and had been exhibiting constantly on theatrical circuits. "Flynn will find me an opponent who has been working union hours right along and has had mighty few holidays." Johnson told his detractors,

> Stick to your opinion, but don't back it with your money. Then when it's all over you'll know better and you won't be poorer in pocket. ... One of the wagers I would like to make is a few hundreds at even money that Flynn will not hit me ten clean blows during the fight. ... And here's a hunch for you. The last man I licked was named Jim. I have been beating Jims all my life and I don't think Flynn ever got the better of a man named Jack.[985]

Tommy Ryan predicted, "I would not be surprised to hear of Flynn losing the fight by a foul. When he sees that he can not hit Johnson he will do anything he can... [N]owadays the butthead fighter is a thing of the past."[986]

The *Albuquerque Evening Herald*'s W. H. Lanigan said,

> [Flynn's] present form is marvelous. He will go into the ring a three to one better man physically than Johnson. He can go a route; Johnson can't. Flynn never puffs after his hour's work in the gym and the Fireman's work is WORK compared to what Johnson pulls. Johnson always puffs, to an extent, after completing his toll. A colored man does not belong in this high altitude. It's in the swamps where they thrive. Johnson is one sterling, high-class, likeable, appreciative fellow. The ring would have owned its most popular champion were he a white man. He is confident. ... But give me a ticket on Flynn Thursday. Jim will win sure, and I think he will cop inside of 11 rounds.[987]

---

[982] *Kansas City Star*, June 27, 1912; *Albuquerque Evening Herald*, June 28, 1912.
[983] *Kansas City Star*, June 30, 1912. On June 28, 1912 in New York, 228 ¼-pound Al Palzer knocked out 188 ½-pound Bombardier Billy Wells in the 3rd round. Although Wells had decked Palzer in the opening round, Palzer came back and dropped Wells once in the 2nd and twice in the 3rd round. *Albuquerque Morning Journal*, June 29, 1912.
[984] *Kansas City Star*, June 29, 1912.
[985] *San Francisco Examiner*, July 1, 2, 1912.
[986] *Albuquerque Morning Journal*, July 1, 1912.
[987] *Albuquerque Evening Herald*, July 1, 1912.

If Johnson won, it was "highly probable" that his next fight would be in Australia. McIntosh had offered him $30,000 to fight either Langford or McVea, promising to place a $10,000 guarantee in the hands of a reputable sporting man before Jack sailed. Johnson said, "That looks good to me. I will cable McIntosh today, asking for further particulars. If everything is satisfactory I will sail for Australia in September."[988]

Meanwhile, in Washington D.C., in the U.S. Congress, a Senate bill had been proposed which would prohibit the interstate shipment of prize-fight films. Representative Thetus Sims of Tennessee, a Democrat, had proposed the bill, and sought to pass the measure immediately, explaining that the Johnson-Flynn fight was scheduled for July 4, and he hoped that the films might be barred from leaving New Mexico. However, a quorum was not present in the house, so the bill was delayed temporarily, despite Mr. Sims' vehement protests. Still, the bill was pending. And it was proposed specifically with the intent to limit the spread of Jack Johnson fight films.[989]

Special trains from Denver, Pueblo, Kansas City, El Paso, Trinidad, and other places arrived in Las Vegas, New Mexico. The genial Johnson met all of the trains and gave folks an opportunity to meet him.

Someone recalled that Flynn had showered verbal abuse on Johnson during their prior 1907 contest, calling him a nigger. Johnson agreed: "He surely did, but you bet he suffered for it. He called me vile names in the sixth round and after that I gave him the punching of his life."

If he won, Flynn said he would draw the color line and never defend the title against any black fighter. "It is his idea that the white and black races should have separate champions and he argues that there would be less prejudice against boxing if the promoters of the future would set their faces against 'magpie matches.'" He would refuse to give Johnson the same opportunity that Johnson was giving him. Hence, one can understand why it was so important for Johnson not to take too many risks inside the ring, for if he lost, he would not be given another chance at the crown.[990]

Flynn would not receive any pay until Johnson received his $31,000 and the other expenses were deducted. Then Curley and Flynn would divide the remainder, if any. Jim said, "It may be a bloomer and I may get a beating, but I have risked all that in an attempt to restore the title to the pale-faced race. If I win I wouldn't care if the receipts were only three dollars, for I feel that I will get mine after that."

On July 4, 1912 in Las Vegas, New Mexico, Jack Johnson defended his world heavyweight championship crown against Fireman Jim Flynn.[991]

As usual, the exact weights were not recorded officially, but it was estimated that Johnson was 212-214 pounds, though some said he was

---

[988] *San Francisco Examiner*, July 2, 1912.
[989] *Albuquerque Morning Journal*, July 2-3, 1912.
[990] *San Francisco Examiner*, July 4, 1912.
[991] The following account is an amalgamation of the same-day and next-day July 4 and 5, 1912 reports from the *Las Vegas Optic*, *Albuquerque Evening Herald*, *Albuquerque Morning Journal*, *Santa Fe New Mexican*, *Denver Post*, Claude Johnson of the *Kansas City Star*, W. W. Naughton of the *New York American* and *San Francisco Examiner*, and Sandy Griswold of the *Omaha World Herald*, all of whom were at the fight or had reporters present at the fight.

closer to 219. The morning of the fight, Flynn allegedly weighed 192 pounds at his quarters. Johnson was 34 years old to Flynn's 32 years of age. Their Queensberry rules fight was scheduled for 45 rounds.[992]

The weather was nice and warm, but not too hot. The arena walls were built of pine lumber and canvas.

Sandy Griswold said the fight attracted all kinds of people. Rich ranchers, stockmen, miners, men of the commercial world, summerishly-gowned women, Americans, Mexicans, Indians, Negroes, and Chinese all constituted a jumbled mass.

Unfortunately, the crowd was small, far less than expected. Only about 3,000 men and 500 women paid admission. About 4,000 total were present.

Promoter Curley said the total gate receipts did not amount to over $29,000, and were below Johnson's $30,000 guarantee. Some said Governor McDonald's action in delaying his statement that he would not interfere with the fight cut down on attendance. Still, Curley could earn very good money with the films, which would generate enough revenue that the gate receipts were less of a concern. Plus he was banking on Flynn's winning, which would earn them a great deal of money in the future as a result.

Shortly before noon, Jack Curley handed the champ a certified check for $31,100, which represented his purse and expense guarantee.

Mrs. Etta Johnson was present, wearing expensive jewelry. She looked happy, as if the battle was over already. Mrs. Johnson and the wives of the champ's trainers occupied a box near the ring.

Soda pop was retailing for 15 cents a bottle. Soft cushions were selling for 25 cents. Souvenirs included Mexican gold-work and official programs.

The arena, inside and out, was patrolled by 75 armed members of the state police, under the leadership of Captain Fred Fornoff. "They look like moving picture bandits and carry more artillery than a first class cruiser. That they maintain the peace at all hazards, the betting is 1 to 10."

When Flynn arrived at the arena shortly after 2 p.m., he received a tremendous ovation as he walked to his quarters. The Mexican band greeted him with the popular song, "All Coons Look Alike To Me."

Announcer Tommy Cannon called attention to the "several hundred ladies who have graced this occasion by their attendance." He asked the spectators to remember the ladies' presence when it came to shouting comments.

At 2:27 p.m., Johnson entered the ring. The champ wore the same striped bathrobe that he had used in Reno.

At 2:38 p.m., Flynn received wild applause as he approached and entered the ring. Jim was in exceptionally good humor, and spent much of the time sauntering about the ring greeting friends. Upon seeing Mrs. Johnson, Flynn shouted, "Ain't you pulling for me, Mrs. Johnson?" The champ's wife smiled but said nothing. At Johnson's request, Mrs. Johnson was transferred to another box, closer to his corner.

---

[992] *Freeman*, July 20, 1912.

Flynn was introduced as the "Fighting Fireman of Pueblo." His earlier warm reception of cheers was duplicated. When announced as the champion heavyweight of the world, Johnson's reception was lukewarm.

In the 1st round, Flynn asked, "Will you shake hands, Jack?" but then proceeded to rush in. Johnson clinched and replied, "Gee."

Throughout the bout, Flynn quickly and constantly advanced and bulled his way in with his head lowered and leaning forward or slightly crouched to the side, with his hands up or arms crossed in front of him. From the inside, Flynn tried to work short overhand left hooks and rights to the head, as well as body shots.

Johnson smiled constantly. He looked into the crowd as he played defense, blocking and clinching. He fought with great care, sending in light jabs, often clinching between punches. Johnson was very good at either holding or just placing his hands on Flynn's arms, shoulders, or elbows, applying some force to smother and suppress so that Flynn either could not punch or had the force of his blows greatly diminished. Sometimes Jack would push Flynn off to move him back to the outside. Occasionally Johnson would hit him with a jab or give him a stiff arm, or try to time him on the way in with a hook or uppercut. The champ would slide back or around off to the side to maintain range. But Flynn was relentless, quickly moving in close, where Johnson clinched. Jack would play defense for a while and allow Jim to work. The champ also would let go, fire a short inside blow, and then suppress Flynn's arms again. This would be the fight's pattern.

During the 1st round, the calm and smiling Johnson nailed Flynn with a right uppercut that cut a deep bloody gash under his left eye.

In the 2nd round, Johnson landed several left jabs and head-tilting right uppercuts. He grabbed around the shoulders, all the while "grinning like an ape," laughing at Flynn's attempts, and exchanging his usual repartee with the spectators. Flynn's mouth was bleeding as he went to his corner.

In the 3rd round, the smiling champion looked into the crowd as Flynn tried to dislodge himself from clinches and fire away. After Flynn butted, the champ cut loose with several short right uppercuts to the jaw, tilting Flynn's head. Flynn's mouth, eye, and nose all bled profusely.

In the 4th round, Johnson jabbed and grabbed, and snuck in uppercuts, laughing out loud as Flynn tried to hit him. Jack constantly invited Jim to blaze away at his stomach. "Go ahead, Flynn. Hit it hard. Go ahead, man."

In the 5th round, while Flynn banged away at his body, Johnson nonchalantly turned his head towards the spectators, hardly noticing him, smiling and intentionally taking the blows. Mrs. Johnson waved at her husband. Jack kept jabbing, grabbing, and uppercutting.

The champ aroused the crowd to merriment by smiling, releasing his hold on Flynn and clapping his own gloves together "like a happy school girl" behind Jim's head as Flynn was leaning forward on the inside.

In another clinch, Johnson rebuked Flynn for butting. Flynn loudly protested to the referee, "Make him let go. I can't fight while he's holding me." The round ended with Johnson carrying on a running conversation with his wife and seconds.

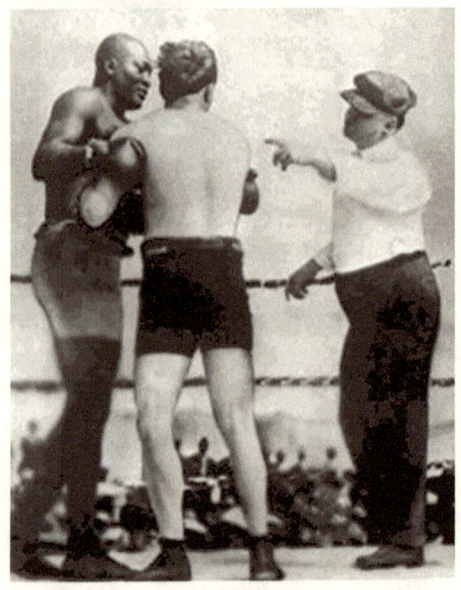

In the 6th round, Flynn allowed his frustrations to get the better of him. While being held, Flynn jumped up into Johnson's face with his head. Shortly thereafter, Jim tried a left hook that was blocked, and then he intentionally jumped up with his head into Jack's face again, butting him. Referee Smith cautioned Jim. Flynn complained about Jack's holding.

Leaning forward on the inside, Flynn jumped up with his head into Jack's face yet again. This drew another stern warning from the referee. Flynn complained that Johnson's holding justified his actions. Jack's seconds were in an uproar.

After Johnson landed jabs, a right, and a right uppercut before grabbing, Flynn flagrantly and brutally launched himself into the air and landed the top of his head into Johnson's face again. The referee broke them and administered another warning. Flynn reached out with his right to touch gloves, and Jack reached back, but they did not touch, for Flynn pulled his hand back just as Jack's glove came close.

Johnson jabbed and grabbed again, and Flynn leapt up into the air with his head, striking Jack's face. The referee broke them, administering yet another warning. Flynn complained, "He's holding me."

After resuming, Johnson fired off a combination of jabs and right uppercuts before grabbing again. Flynn gave him a more subtle butt and Jack turned and looked at the referee. Flynn also looked at the referee and complained about the holding. The referee chided him and they broke.

Flynn had head-butted flagrantly and intentionally six times in the round. Between rounds, Flynn's own seconds warned him to stop butting.

In the 7th round, as usual, Flynn worked the body, while Johnson jabbed, grabbed, and uppercut. As he was suppressing Jim's arms with his palms, Jack looked into the crowd and smiled.

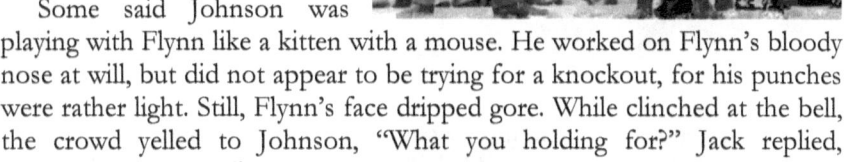

Flynn complained that Johnson was holding, but Referee Smith replied, "Fight. I'm referee of this battle."

Some said Johnson was playing with Flynn like a kitten with a mouse. He worked on Flynn's bloody nose at will, but did not appear to be trying for a knockout, for his punches were rather light. Still, Flynn's face dripped gore. While clinched at the bell, the crowd yelled to Johnson, "What you holding for?" Jack replied, "Because I'm strong."

In the 8th round, Johnson would punch, clinch, punch, and clinch. Sometimes he pushed Flynn off and then hit him with jabs as Jim forced his way inside. He also landed left and right uppercuts to the badly battered nose, bringing the blood afresh. While being held, Flynn unsuccessfully tried to land short body shots, looping hooks, and overhand rights.

As the referee stepped in close to break them, Flynn flagrantly jumped up, butting Johnson in the face. Jack then strongly grabbed both arms and spun around. Flynn followed with two more leaping head butts in a row.

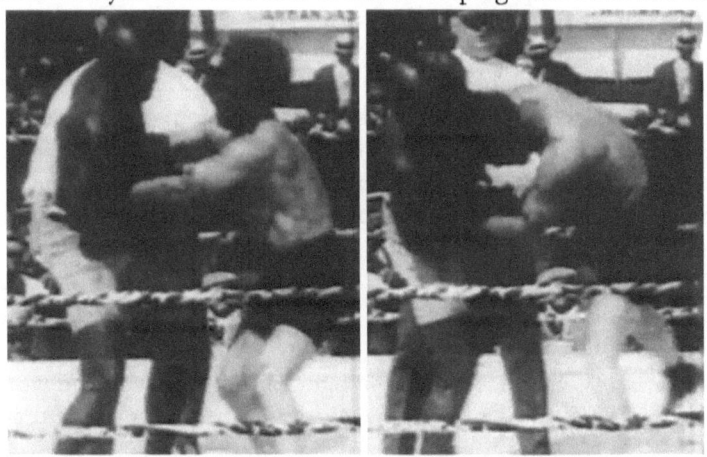

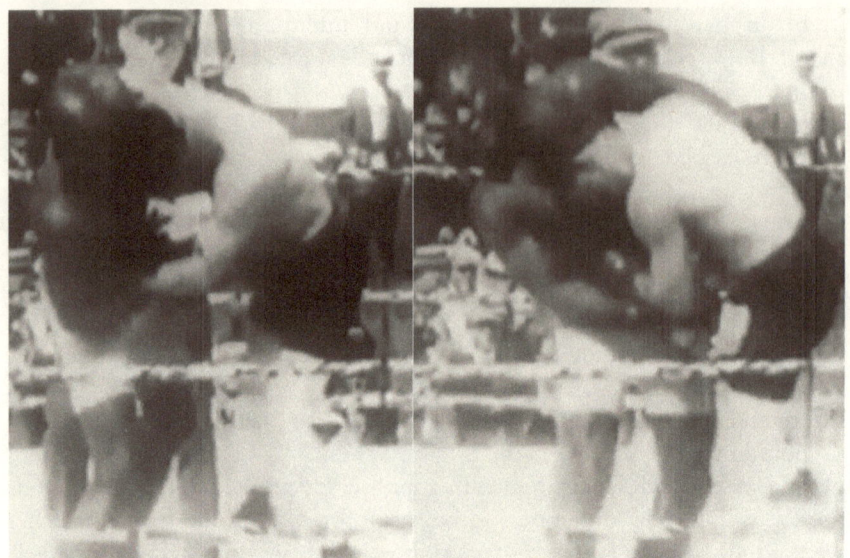

The referee broke them and sternly warned Flynn. Soon thereafter, on the inside, Flynn leaned in with his head again. The referee broke them and lectured Flynn, threatening to stop the fight. "Once more and I'll disqualify you." Flynn said, "He's holding." They resumed and it was more of the same – Flynn getting in and trying to punch while being held. Jack would jab from the outside and uppercut on the inside, though he mostly held and smothered. Flynn had been warned for butting at least three times in the round; the tenth time in the fight.

In the 9th round, Johnson timed Flynn on the way in with a right uppercut. He pushed off, struck Flynn with a left hook and then held again.

Flynn threw a hook to the body and then leapt up with his head, butting. The referee simply broke them. Jack kept landing jabs and uppercuts.

Johnson landed an upward jab and then grabbed. The leaning-in Flynn launched himself up into Jack's face, flagrantly butting again with the top of his head. Flynn followed with some body shots as the referee broke them and issued yet another warning.

Flynn put his hands on his sides and argued with the referee, complaining about Johnson's holding, motioning with his hand in an upset fashion. Flynn then grabbed the referee as if to demonstrate Johnson's holding. The referee pushed him back and waved them on to continue.

However, at that point, Captain of the Mounted Police, Fred Fornoff, realizing that the referee was loath to terminate the fight on a foul, entered the ring and declared, "The fight is over. We will have no more fighting of this kind." He had his men with him, and they carried revolvers. Flynn briefly protested, grabbing hold of the policeman, but was pushed back gently. Johnson's cornermen entered the ring, followed by many more folks. The fight obviously was over.

Referee Ed W. Smith awarded the fight to Johnson, who had won every round on points. The champion was given a terrific cheer, while the crowd vented its wrath on Flynn with jeers and boos. They had wanted to see the fight come to its natural conclusion, but were sore at Flynn for his clearly intentional fouls which forced the stoppage.

After Flynn is warned for intentionally butting yet again, state Police Captain Fred Fornoff enters the ring to stop the fight.

The sportswriters put forth two extreme views about this fight. Some argued that Johnson was dominating every round, toying with Flynn, could have put him out at any time, and was breaking him down gradually. A frustrated and bloody Flynn foresaw a bad ending for himself, so he intentionally fouled with head butts to get himself disqualified.

Another view was that although Johnson was outpointing him, he was tiring from Flynn's relentless attack, throwing less punches, and holding more as the fight progressed. Had the bout continued and Flynn not lost his head, or used it intelligently instead of in foul fashion, he had a chance to wear down Johnson eventually, for Jack was not in the best condition, while Flynn was strong and active throughout, and in excellent, superior shape.

The truth probably lies between the press' two extremes. Johnson used the style he typically used, and he used it from the start. He clinched early and often, played defense, allowed Flynn to work, and carefully chose when to punch, usually landing. He was not punching very hard or often, and though he might have been marking-up and cutting Flynn, Jim never once was hurt. Flynn was an absolutely relentless ferocious ball of energy, firing away on a consistent basis, moving in quickly, and constantly trying to work his hands free to punch. He obviously was very frustrated by Johnson's defensive tactics and holding, feeling that he could not land effective blows. He totally lost his composure and fouled flagrantly and often. It appeared that both men could have continued fighting in the same manner for many more rounds.

The local *Las Vegas Optic* reported,

Flynn displayed no ability throughout the fight. He was cut about the face until blood ran down his breast in a stream. He was utterly helpless from the first round on and by the sixth was deliberately trying to butt the champion's chin with his head. ... Smith warned him repeatedly but it did no good. ... Flynn's feet were both off the floor time and again with the energy he put into his bounds. Sometimes he seemed to jump two feet into the air in frantic lunges at the elusive black jaw above him.

Referee Smith forced Flynn back toward his corner a half dozen times. "Stop that butting," he would say, shaking his finger in Flynn's face. "Stop it or I will disqualify you." "The – nigger's holding me," Flynn roared back. "He's holding me all the time. He's holding me like this," and he offered to illustrate on the referee. Smith evaded the blood-smeared arms held toward him and waved the men together again.

Flynn continually butted despite the constant warnings and threats of disqualification. Seeing that the referee was loathe to disqualify him, the police stopped the fight in the 9th round.

The crowd accepted the police action. "Long before the end did come, ringside opinion seemed to favor the view that Flynn was eager to be disqualified. He was helpless as a child and certainly made no effort to disguise his attempt to do with his skull what his gloves could not accomplish." Flynn was roasted roundly for his unsportsmanlike tactics.

Smith could have disqualified Flynn at any time, but he hated to deprive the fans of a full fight after their long journey and the money paid.

Some thought it a strange coincidence that a police finish occurred. At a conference held a few days before the fight, both Flynn and Johnson anticipated and dealt with the potential issue of police interference. Both agreed that a decision should be given if the police stopped the contest.

The *Optic* believed the police interference saved Flynn from the humiliation of a knockout by the "inky boxer."

Claude Johnson of the *Kansas City Star*, who was on scene, noted his prediction that if Flynn lost, it probably would be through disqualification. "Flynn told the writer this morning that he would never take the full count and if the going got too rough he was liable to bite or kick rather than suffer humiliation at the hands of a negro." Tommy Ryan had predicted the same.

Flynn's nose was broken, eyes black, cheek cut open, and his lips and both ears were puffed. Johnson only had slightly puffed lips from the deliberate butts to the mouth.

However, offering a completely different perspective, W. W. Naughton said Johnson was used up badly from the effects of the fast pace, and broke the rules as well with his holding. Flynn had squandered his chance at victory, for if only he had kept his temper in check, he possibly could have worn Johnson down and won.

The *Denver Post's* Otto Floto, who also was present, agreed with Naughton. "Flynn lost the chance of his life. He had Johnson worried to death." Floto thought Captain Fornoff was too hasty in stopping the bout. "Flynn's foul tactics and overofficiousness on the part of Captain Fornoff spoiled what probably would have given the white man an excellent opportunity to wear the crown of supremacy in the realm of fistiana."

Floto believed that father time eventually would make the gradually slipping Johnson lose, and "there will no longer be an argument as to whether the white race or the black race owns the title."

Yet, regardless of the criticism, on a personal level, Johnson was fairly well liked. "No matter how we may criticize his fighting ability, we are forced to concede the fact that Johnson is a shrewd, clever diplomat who knows how to handle himself in all kinds of going. He is well behaved and impresses all he meets with his bearing."

The *Omaha World Herald*'s Sandy Griswold, who saw the fight, said Flynn had a split and fractured nose, his cut face was a mask of smeary gore, and his torso swathed in a scarlet sweater. Johnson had given his "bruised and busted visage an awful thumping, bringing the blood in torrents from gashes and rents in cheek and from mouth and nose and ears." Yet, Flynn's eyes were wild and fierce, with the ravages of hatred and vindictiveness. He threw away his great chance. Griswold called Johnson lucky.

Tom Flanagan said Johnson was the same peerless champion as ever.

Afterwards, Johnson was in good humor, and his golden smile in evidence. He insisted that he did not have to exert himself at any stage:

> I have many times overlooked foul tactics of other fighters, but I cannot understand why this fellow Flynn was allowed to go on so long as he did without being disqualified. I complained to the referee several times, but there was nothing doing except warnings until the police took the matter into their own hands.

Johnson further said, "His aim was to lose on a foul. He was taking punishment the spectators neither saw nor understood." Johnson said he was taking things easy and allowing Flynn to fret himself. "Now there is a prospect of my being matched with Al Palzer for ten rounds in New York. To show that I believe I am as good as ever, I will bet $10,000 of my own money that I will stop Palzer inside of ten rounds."

Flynn said it was Johnson who started the dirty work. "I could feel Johnson's punches, never hard ones at any stage, getting weaker and weaker. ... He wouldn't fight and I had to do all the fighting.... I was in to keep going and break Johnson's heart and bring out the yellow streak that I know is in him."

Still, Flynn did not blame the referee for giving the contest to Johnson, conceding he was behind on points. "I am not a bit sore excepting at myself for having lost my head the way I did. But he started the foul work first and I think I was justified in doing what I did."

Referee Ed Smith said the fight was won via a points decision, as the parties agreed would be the case if there was police interference. Both men transgressed the rules, but Flynn was the greater offender with his harm fouls. Flynn deliberately tried to lose the contest on a foul when it was plain to him that he was beaten and outclassed, for Johnson was superior from start to finish. "There is much more praise for a man who will take a punch on the jaw and die the death of a real gladiator on the floor than there is for the man who, seeing himself in for a trimming, will seek the subterfuge of a foul, the cowardly refuge of the man who is not game."

> Johnson was not holding as much as he was smoothing Flynn at all stages. He placed his thumbs in Flynn's elbows and simply held the fireman's arms helpless, completely blocked. ... It was not a foul move, because Flynn's arms were free in a way and he was able to tap Johnson's stomach and short ribs with both hands, but in a way that did not seem to do much damage.

Ultimately, "Maddened by the fact that he was being checkmated and outguessed at every stage of the contest, Flynn resorted to the most barefaced system of fouling." Smith said he was about to disqualify Flynn when the police entered the ring.

Hundreds in Chicago's "Black Belt" celebrated the news that their man still was champion. A riot call was sent to the police, and the blacks who had begun a parade through the streets were routed by a small army of bluecoats. The police were not about to allow a black celebration.

Johnson returned to Chicago. He "gave the impression he likely would accept the offers he has had to go to Australia and fight Sam Langford."[993]

Johnson said he cleared $31,000 from Curley, and won $5,000 more by betting on himself.[994]

Jack Curley said about 3,000 men and about 500 women paid admission to "witness the failure of Jim Flynn to restore the pugilistic championship to the white race." Curley said he would promote a Johnson fight with any white man who seemed to have a chance, "but I will never promote a match between Johnson and any other colored man for the title, because I am quite sure it is not what the public wants and would fail as an attraction."[995]

The *Freeman* said "Caucasia" had "long been humiliated by Ethiopia. ... I have begun to feel ashamed for the white people at the poor prospect for their fighters. Will they abandon the field, feeling it unworthy of them...?" The point was, if whites could not beat the black champion, they might simply quit trying, and instead denigrate and attack the sport itself as barbaric and try to taboo it.

> But regardless of the rhetoric; the white fighters are cutting a sorry figure. And yet as long as the game is in vogue it's right from the viewpoint of race pride to keep up the attack. ... From our viewpoint: We, the Negroes, have so little by way of triumphs to make merry over that we religiously cling to our one pugilistic hero. ... [T]he victories of old Jack Johnson are glory added unto us.

---

[993] *Omaha World Herald*, July 6, 1912.
[994] *Albuquerque Morning Journal, Albuquerque Evening Herald*, July 6, 1912; *San Francisco Examiner*, July 7, 1912.
[995] *Freeman*, August 17, 1912.

Where but little is expected a little will do very well. ... Jack Johnson won over Jim Jeffries two years ago. The victory stood for an idea. Oppression lifted a bit. Negro stock did a little bulling on the racial market.[996]

The *Freeman's* Billy Lewis noted that in a series of fights in Australia, Sam McVey was victorious in all of his bouts with white men, causing Australians to make racial conclusions:

> [The Australian papers] attempted an analysis of the races physically, concluding that white men were not meant to cope physically with black men; insisting that black men more nearly approached the brute creation. ... Whatever it may be, it can be set down, that, with equal conditions, weight, age, preparedness to fight, a white man will not whip a black man. ... The Negro boy will concede a white boy long on intellect...he will see something almost superhuman at his case in doing intellectual things....

However, in athletic endeavors, the tables were turned. "Now the pale faces hover alongside, struck with amazement at the ease with which Negro boys do physical things. ... No Negro boy thinks a white boy of equal age and size has any business monkeying around him."[997]

Many praised Johnson for maintaining his poise and composure even when Flynn acted in a rank manner. Lester Walton of the *New York Age* said the Flynn fight exploded the ancient and decrepit opinion that the Negro was the possessor of butting proclivities. Flynn with malice aforethought sought to use his head in billy-goat fashion, compelling the police (not the referee) to stop the farce. Those who argued that the Negro skull was thick and that butting was "as much of a racial trait with him as it was with the goat tribe, are now reluctantly confessing that the black man has no corner on the butting game. The admission is also made that in recent years the prize ring has shown the Caucasian to be more addicted to using his head as a human battering ram than his dusky brother." Therefore, the "American idea that the Negro is instinctively a butter has been dissipated."

Johnson maintained his poise no matter what, once again countering the white ideology that blacks could not control themselves. In this instance, is was the white boxer who could not exhibit self-control.[998]

The *Freeman* also noted the importance of the fight outside of the boxing world. "The very Negro nature cries out for the great splendid things as the desert yearns for the rain; and Johnson stands for the idea at its best. He has wrested the key from the hand of adversity."[999]

It too noted that blacks were relieved to see that it was the white man who lost his head, was overcome with emotion and rage, and could not exhibit self-control, all of which were qualities that whites argued were black

---

[996] *Freeman*, July 6, 1912.
[997] *Freeman*, July 13, 1912; *Omaha World Herald*, July 5, 1912.
[998] *New York Age*, July 18, 1912.
[999] *Freeman*, July 20, 1912.

traits. Another blow had been struck against race prejudice. "Johnson is one of the fairest and most decent men ever known in the prize ring, and his complexion is all that prevents him from being the most popular pugilist of his time. He has many charms and fine graces of manner, he is tirelessly good natured, he appreciates favors, he is generous and he is loyal to his friends."

When Flynn had been in training for the fight, he referred to Johnson "in contemptuous terms and called him by insulting names." When Johnson heard about it, he simply smiled and said, "I certainly do feel sorry for Mr. Flynn."[1000]

JACK JOHNSON FAIRLY PLAYED WITH JIM FLYNN

"DAR'S SOM'PIN MIGHTY FUNNY 'BOUT DESE WHITE-FOLKS LAWS. DEY ARRESTS A GUY AN' PUTS 'IM IN JAIL FO' FAST DRIVIN' IN A AUTO' AN' DEY ARREST 'IM AN' RAISE A AWFUL ROW WHEN HE BUYS DI'MONS IN LONDON AN' FERGITS TO PAY DE DOOTY—

'BUT, LAN'S SAKES! DEY FRAMES UP A SCHEME FO' DAT SAME GUY TO BEAT UP A PO' LIL' WHITE MAN LIKE MISTO FLYNN FO' A BIG POT OF MONEY, WHICH IS SHOLY LIKE STEALIN' CANDY FROM A BABY, AN' DEY AINT NO LAW 'BOUT DAT NOHOW — SEEMS MIGHTY FUNNY, DA'S ALL!"

Chicago Day Book, July 5, 1912

[1000] *Freeman*, August 10, 1912.

CHAPTER 41

Under Siege

On July 10, 1912 in Chicago, at 41 West 31st street, Jack Johnson officially started his night-club business, opening the Café de Champion. It was the most beautiful and elaborately furnished establishment of its kind. An orchestra played music. A crowd packed the streets, waiting to enter.

The next day in Chicago, Johnson and his wife Etta appeared in federal court for their arraignments on the diamond necklace smuggling charges. The maximum penalty was two years in prison and a $5,000 fine.

On July 12 in Chicago, Johnson was arrested and charged with striking and intimidating Charles Brown, a black chauffeur who was one of the government's principal witnesses in the smuggling case. Johnson formerly employed Brown. The allegations were that when Brown entered Johnson's café, Jack asked him what he told the Grand Jury. Brown declined to tell him, and the champion struck him in the face.

Johnson was arraigned and furnished a $5,000 bond. He denied assaulting or even touching Brown, and explained that when Brown came into his place he ordered him out. When Brown refused to leave, one of Johnson's friends pushed him out.[1001]

In late July, Johnson had Homer Kerchfield arrested for stealing an extra tire from his auto.

Billy Gibson of New York's Garden Athletic Club wanted to make a Jack Johnson vs. Joe Jeannette fight. Gibson believed the State Athletic Commission's barring of Johnson only applied to a mixed-race contest.[1002]

Johnson said it was his same old price, win, lose, or draw - $30,000. "I don't care who you name to fight me, the price will be the same for my services or I won't appear."[1003]

Johnson explained why his financial demands were firm:

> New York does not like me and I don't like New York. ... They won't let me fight a white man in that town, but expect me to box only negroes. I don't care about that, of course, as long as I get the money. The reason they won't let me on with a white man is because they know I can beat Palzer and all the rest of them in one ring on the same night.
>
> However, this fellow Jeanette will be just as easy. I can punch holes in Joe for ten rounds and don't be surprised if I stop him. I'll be

---

[1001] *San Francisco Examiner, Washington Post*, July 12, 1912; *Chicago Defender, New York American*, July 13, 1912.
[1002] *New York American*, July 8-10, 1912.
[1003] *San Francisco Examiner*, July 26, 1912.

tickled to death to show New York just how easy Jeanette is if I get my $30,000.[1004]

Johnson subsequently said, "Jeanette and myself would draw at least $60,000 in Madison Square Garden. I'm certainly worth 50 per cent of that amount. Jeanette could not draw $10,000 with anybody else."[1005]

The *Freeman* said at present, Jack's most dangerous foes were members of his own race – Langford, Jeannette, McVey, and Battling Jim Johnson, all of whom could box better than any of the big white hopes.[1006]

W. W. Naughton said a fight with white Al Palzer (who had defeated Kaufman and Wells) would "excite more interest than any the champion could be a party to."[1007]

On July 31, 1912, the United States Congress passed and President William Taft signed into law the Sims Act, which banned the transportation of prizefight films in interstate commerce, making it a federal criminal offense punishable by a year in prison and/or a $1,000 fine. So much for freedom. For the next 28 years, until 1940, when President Franklin Roosevelt signed a repeal of the law, fight films only could be shown in the state where they were taken. This seriously limited the economic value of fight films, and limited fans' ability to see filmed fights. However, bootlegging allowed some folks to see fight films in private exhibitions. Regardless, boxing had taken a very big financial hit, and it was clear that the motivation of Tennessee Congressional Representative Thetus Sims' bill had been to prevent or limit the world's ability to see Johnson's fights, and to limit the earning potential of those involved with the sport of boxing; a punishment for the sponsorship of mixed-race fights.

In Chicago, Johnson appeared in court to testify against the black youth who stole a tire from his car. Johnson said, "Your honor, I know this boy is guilty, but sending him to jail won't get me my tire back, and it may do him harm. If you are willing, I am satisfied to have the charge changed to one of disorderly conduct and a small fine imposed." The judge honored Johnson's request, and asked the champ what he thought the fine should be. Johnson said, "One dollar would suit me as well as anything else," and the judge made that the fine. Johnson showed that he could be merciful as well.[1008]

On August 13, the government dismissed the charge against Johnson of intimidating a witness for the prosecution in the smuggling case.

On August 14, 1912, Jack Johnson signed an agreement to fight Joe Jeannette in a 10-round no-decision bout at the St. Nicholas club in New York City on September 25. Brothers Jesse and Eddie McMahon, New York promoters, made the fight by guaranteeing Johnson $25,000 regardless of the gate receipts, but if the receipts totaled $60,000, Johnson would receive $30,000 plus an additional 25% of any amounts exceeding $60,000.

[1004] *San Francisco Examiner*, July 27, 1912.
[1005] *San Francisco Call*, July 29, 1912.
[1006] *Freeman*, July 27, 1912.
[1007] *San Francisco Examiner*, July 28, 1912.
[1008] *Freeman*, August 3, 17, 1912. On August 3, 1912 in Sydney, Australia, Sam Langford clearly won a 20-round decision over Sam McVey.

Johnson also would receive a one-half interest in the fight films, which could be shown in New York and overseas.

Johnson was confident that he would beat Jeannette with ease, saying,

> The only time he ever did make a showing with me, I was under wraps a bit.... You know I had a hard time getting matches in those days.
>
> But believe me when I say I'll convince the public that I'm still a great fighter by whipping the life out of that fellow. ... I expect to make more than $30,000 out of it, too.

The *Salt Lake Tribune* said Johnson's assertion that he was under wraps when he met Jeannette was the truth. "Under wraps" meant he had to agree to carry his foe in order to get his opponent to fight.[1009]

The *New York Age* theorized that some whites wanted to see Johnson fight a black man; because the feeling was that no white could defeat him, but if he was defeated by a fellow black, then that fighter might be more vulnerable to a white fighter. Some black fighters, such as Langford and his manager, used that argument as a sales pitch to white promoters.

The *Age's* Lester Walton noted Johnson's symbolic value to the race, and was glad that he was dark enough such that no one could dispute that he was a black man. "That Johnson is a Negro without any question of a doubt has always been a source of gratification to me; for had he been even of a dark brown in hue, long ago some white writers would have sought to prove that he was other than of African extraction."[1010]

Johnson said that when the Jeannette match was made, the promoters had told him that they had everything fixed with the commission, but according to recent reports, such did not appear to be the case:

> I honestly don't believe I ever will be allowed to fight in this country again. Whenever my name is mentioned in connection with a fight in any part of the country the ministers and reformers immediately get busy with the governor, with the result that there will be nothing doing for Jack Johnson.[1011]

Unfortunately, Johnson was correct. On August 22, after holding a long conference behind closed doors with the state athletic commission, the McMahon brothers called off the Johnson-Jeannette match. New York boxing commissioners O'Neill and Dixon refused to allow Johnson to box anyone in New York, and threatened to revoke the license of any club which held a bout with him involved. "Johnson had been booted out of nearly every State in the Union, and it was believed that his appearance here would bring odium to the boxing game." Senator James Frawley, who had framed the bill legalizing boxing in New York, was opposed to Johnson's boxing there, and had urged the commissioners to stop it. The commission

---

[1009] *Salt Lake Tribune*, August 15, 1912.
[1010] *New York Age*, August 22, 1912.
[1011] *The Milwaukee Journal*, August 20, 1912.

thought it best for the game of boxing to keep Johnson from appearing in New York, although they insisted that they had nothing personal against him, nor was he barred on account of his color. They wanted to keep the boxing situation "healthy." Hence, their decision was spun as being for the betterment of the sport. Edward McMahon said, "The commissioners don't want Jack Johnson to appear in a match in New York City."[1012]

Commissioner Frank O'Neill said, "The commission decided long ago that Johnson would not be permitted to fight here. We believe now, as we did then, that the presence of Johnson in a ring contest in this state would be inimical to the best interests of boxing, the status of which has greatly improved under the Frawley law."[1013]

That same day in Chicago, Johnson attempted to spar 3 rounds at a ball park to make a charitable donation to a local hospital. However, a policeman carrying orders from the chief of police said, "No boxing." Johnson replied, "Dis am foh charity, boss." The reply: "No sparring."

The *New York World's* Robert Edgren congratulated the commission for its decision, and said keeping Johnson out would benefit the sport of boxing greatly. "The trouble is that whenever Johnson appears race rancor develops."[1014]

The *New York Age's* Lester Walton criticized the commission's decision:

> They were not clear as to how the leading exponent of the manly art of self defense would cause boxing to deteriorate, and it is hardly probable that they could explain if given an opportunity to do so. Of course the action taken by the Boxing Commission was not due to Johnson's color. Such a charge most likely would be deemed unjust by them. But if the heavyweight champion was a white man how different things would have been.
>
> If the word 'inconsistency' was not in the English language there would be times when the question of color prejudice would not be raised by the dusky citizens of this country. But so often do we observe instances in which the color of one's skin (not circumstances) alters cases that we have grown to regard with suspicion this 'Malice toward none, good will and equality of opportunity for all' spirit which is supposed to pervade every nook and corner of the United States.
>
> It is difficult for colored citizens to understand why the leading fighter of the world is refused the privilege to exhibit his fistic prowess in New York when big, burly white fighters appear before the local clubs in boxing matches which are brutal in every respect and are oftimes so sickening that the police have to stop the gory and badly-battered contestants. Such contests, it will be presumed, are regarded with high favor by the Boxing Commission. In a match

---

[1012] *New York Age, New York Daily Times, New York World*, August 22, 1912.
[1013] *Freeman*, August 31, 1912.
[1014] *San Francisco Call, New York World*, August 23, 1912.

between Johnson and Jeannette, although both are big men, the absence of brutality would have been a pleasing feature, as they are boxers of great skill.

Ultimately, Walton said the "door of hope" was closed against the champion, for he was barred from appearing in bouts in the majority of cities in the U.S., as well as England. France and Australia currently were disposed to have him appear there, "but if the color prejudice germ, which is so perniciously active in this country, is transplanted to such cities as Paris and Sydney, there will not be a place where Johnson can defend the championship title, unless it be at the North or South poles."[1015]

Government authorities had prevented yet another Johnson fight.

Some white writers argued that Johnson's personality and disregard for decency and propriety were to blame for his banishment, not his race:

> He is the most unpopular Negro boxer who has ever been in the ring. ... There has been more scandal connected with Jack Johnson since he became prominent in pugilism than there was with the names of all the other Negro boxers put together.[1016]

On September 5, 1912, a white woman in Forsyth County, Georgia claimed that an unknown black man had attempted to rape her, but fled when her family member opened the bedroom door. After a black preacher remarked that the woman was caught in bed with her black lover and just claimed it was rape to save face, an angry group of white men whipped him with horse buggy whips on the street, in front of the courthouse. Close to death, the sheriff took the preacher into the courthouse and locked him in the vault after a crowd of 100-200 demanded that he be lynched. Governor Joseph Brown had to send the National Guard to restore order to the town.

Section of a Robert Edgren cartoon, *New York World,* **August 23, 1912**

Several days later, on September 9, 1912 in the same county, a young black man raped and killed a young white girl. He freely confessed.

Whites used the recent incidents as an excuse to harass, intimidate, threaten, and forcibly drive out the town's blacks, who left in fear for their lives. Within four months, 98% of the county's over 1,000 blacks were gone, and from the surrounding counties, 50% to 100% were forced to leave as well. It was the largest mass exodus of black folk based on race in U.S. history. To this day, the county remains virtually all-white.

[1015] *New York Age*, August 29, 1912.
[1016] *Freeman*, September 7, 1912.

During the early hours of September 12, 1912 in Chicago, Etta Johnson, a.k.a. Etta Terry Duryea, a.k.a. Mrs. Jack Johnson, telephoned her sister-in-law, Jack's sister, Mrs. Jennie Rhodes of 3344 Wabash avenue, and asked her to come over. Etta was in her room above her husband's new business, the Café de Champion, at 41 West 31st street.

Etta then called her two black maids to her, saying, "I want you to pray for me." They got on their knees and Mrs. Johnson joined them in prayer. She then asked them to leave her for a few minutes. As the maids were leaving, allegedly they heard her say, "God have pity on a lonely woman."

Shortly thereafter, at about 2 a.m., Etta Johnson took a revolver from a dresser and shot herself in the right temple. The bullet passed completely through her head, leaving a hole in both sides. Mrs. Johnson was lying on the floor, the blood oozing from her temple. She was not yet dead, but was unconscious.

Henry Johnson, the champion's brother, was running the café, and was told of the incident first. His sister Jennie Rhodes arrived. Henry ordered the orchestra to play loud music, and he rushed to his sister-in-law's room.

When the champ arrived, he was told that his wife had shot herself. He began wiping his eyes with a big handkerchief and cried, or as they then called it, "made audible manifestations of grief."

Etta was taken to the hospital, but there was nothing the doctors could do. At her bedside, Johnson said, "My little pal, you ain't going to take the count, are you?" At 3:25 a.m., Etta Johnson was declared dead. She was 31 years of age.

Jack Johnson's wife had been Miss Etta Terry of Brooklyn before marrying Clarence Duryea, a wealthy millionaire New York and Long Island clubman and horseman. While married to Mr. Duryea for six years, Etta associated with an exclusive upper-class society.

In the spring of 1910, Etta sued for a divorce, which she soon obtained. She and the champion had been seen everywhere together well before that.

On January 18, 1911 in Pittsburg, at Frank Sutton's hotel on Wylie avenue, Etta and Jack Johnson were married. The records showed Johnson's age as 32 and Etta's age as 29.

Immediately after her suicide, speculation abounded regarding why she had killed herself. Many believed that remorse for having left her place in exclusive high-class white society and associating with those of Johnson's race ultimately led to her suicide. She was ostracized for marrying a black man. For more than a year, she had suffered from severe nervous prostration; brought on by the realization that she was forever barred from the world she voluntarily left.

On her recent trip to Las Vegas before the Flynn fight, Mrs. Johnson was said to have remarked that everyone shunned her because she had married a Negro, and she was unhappy about it. She had been in ill health and despondent for a year.

Some said she was a depressive, and had been battling depression and suicidal thoughts for quite some time, even before she met Johnson. Her nervous ailment often caused her to become hysterical.

Johnson explained to the police that for the last two years, Etta had suffered from nervous attacks, and several months prior, while suffering an attack, she had tried to throw herself through a train window.

Two maids were employed to watch her continually. She often spoke of dying, and said she never expected to recover from the nervous prostration from which she suffered.

Others later said the champ was unfaithful, and some even suggested that he was violent towards his wife. "The champion was very much annoyed by several sensational stories in the daily newspapers harping on domestic troubles. He emphatically denies this."

Johnson wept as he denied that he ever had been brutal to his wife:

> If it had not been for Etta I would have killed myself by leaping from a window of a hotel in Portland, Maine, a year ago. ... There is no telling what I shall do now. I may kill myself. There never was a better wife. I never expect to marry a woman like Etta. All talk of family trouble is false. A few days ago I bought her a diamond ring and a sealskin coat.

Johnson said his wife's efforts to keep him from committing suicide broke down her own health. He said the nature and extent of his suffering after the Jeffries fight had been kept secret by his wife and himself.

> I am still suffering from the effects of that fight to some extent. ... I believe that I incurred brain fever or some similar derangement from the exertions of the Jeffries fight and the heat that prevailed at the time. I was not myself for a year, but the secret was closely kept between me and Mrs. Johnson. She saved me twice when I tried to choke myself to death. She seized me and struggled with me, and prevented the act.

> She had an awful time taking care of me for over a year. ...

> During the last two years she often told me she was tired of living. She tried twice before to kill herself. Once she attempted to jump out of a window in a London hotel, and before that she tried to take her life by leaping from a train out West.

> I did everything I could to make her happy and spent money on her lavishly, but most of the time she seemed despondent. Her father died four months ago, and since then she seemed more nervous and despondent than before.

> I employed two maids to watch her after she attempted to end her life the first time. ... The stories that there was much domestic trouble between my wife and my mother and sister are untrue. They both were very fond of her.

The *Freeman* asked, "Can it be possible that Jeff hurt the big Negro more than was apparent to those at the ringside?"

Etta's mother said, "My daughter was insane. She was insane when she married Johnson. She was insane when she ended her life. We did our best to prevent her marrying Johnson. But Johnson had money and we were poor, and she would listen to no one." However, if money was Etta's only concern or issue, she could have remained married to Clarence Duryea.

Funeral services were set to be held at 11 a.m. on September 14, 1912 at Johnson's 3344 Wabash Avenue mansion. Fight promoter Jack Curley was in charge of the funeral arrangements.

Without Johnson's consent, the Pekin Theater arranged to take and exhibit films of Mrs. Johnson's funeral. The champ went before a Superior Court judge and obtained a temporary injunction against the theater's owners, restraining the management of the black theater from exhibiting motion pictures of the funeral. Johnson said, "The exhibition is an injustice to me and may cause the impression that I am profiting financially from the pictures." The chief of police said he would prevent any such exhibition.

Police estimated the outside crowds surrounding the funeral at 20,000.

Right or wrong, the suicide was used as an example of the adverse results of interracial marriage; with many writers arguing that her death was the inevitable result. Even the *Freeman* said,

> In view of racial relations, past and present, she ran a great risk of her personal happiness when marrying Jack Johnson. It is not urged that she was weighted down with unpleasantness owing to her marital relations, yet the marriage was ever considered unfortunate.

Some said the bitter fruits of the interracial marriage came when her friends and family in the East socially ostracized her. Blacks regarded her as an outcast from the white race and thought she was after the money. They continually called her Johnson's "white wife." She was caught in the fire of two races, and both turned her down. "Like so many of the well-to-do of the white race, she had no way of knowing of the living death, socially, just across the line. ... She possibly knew of some racial disadvantages... She did not know of the terrible sacrifice that would be hers to make."[1017]

In the meantime, wanting to match Johnson with Sam Langford on Boxing Day, December 26 in Australia, Hugh McIntosh sent Johnson his assurances that he need not fear police or government interference.[1018]

On October 12, 1912, Jack Johnson announced that he had agreed with Hugh McIntosh to fight both Sam Langford and Sam McVea (previously known as "McVey") in Australia for $60,000 total, plus five round-trip tickets to Australia.[1019]

[1017] *Freeman*, September 7-28, October 5, 1912; *Salt Lake Tribune*, *El Paso Herald*, September 12, 1912; *Manchester Guardian*, *Chicago Day Book*, September 13, 1912; *Chicago Defender*, September 14, 21, 1912. On October 9, 1912 at Perth, Australia, Sam Langford stopped Sam McVey in the 11th round. McVey's claim of a foul was not recognized.
[1018] *Chicago Defender*, September 21, 1912; *Freeman*, October 5, 1912.
[1019] *Freeman*, October 19, 1912; *Missoulian*, October 13, 1912.

On October 14, 1912 at a political rally in Milwaukee, Wisconsin, former U.S. President Theodore Roosevelt was shot, but not killed.

On the afternoon of October 18, 1912, just over one month after his wife's suicide, Jack Johnson was arrested on a charge of abduction. He was released on $800 bail. He was accused of abducting Lucille Cameron, an alleged 19-year-old white woman who was the daughter of Mrs. Cameron-Falconet of Minneapolis, a divorced woman.

Initially, Lucille Cameron had come to Chicago with her mother's consent. She met Johnson before his wife committed suicide. Rumors were that Mrs. Johnson killed herself after discovering her husband with his arms around Cameron.

When a newsman told Mrs. Cameron-Falconet about her daughter's infatuation with the black pugilist, she immediately came to Chicago. She pleaded with her daughter to come home with her and leave Johnson, but Lucille refused, saying, "I cannot go back and I don't want to go back to Minneapolis. I expect to become the wife of Mr. Johnson shortly, though he has not proposed marriage to me. I love him and want to stay in Chicago." Her mother alleged that Lucille told her that she had "gone too far to go back." Mrs. Cameron-Falconet further said, "I was convinced at that time that the Negro had a hypnotic influence over her."

Mrs. Cameron-Falconet claimed that she called Johnson by telephone. He then came to see her in his auto. When she entered his car, she drew down the shades so as not to be seen. This nettled him. She alleged that Jack said, "Oh, some of the best white women in Chicago ride in this car." Mrs. Falconet also claimed that Jack laughed in her face and said, "Why I can get any white woman in Chicago." She begged him to give up her daughter. "He said he would not and leered in my face." Johnson allegedly told her that "he would give every dollar he has to hold her."

Therefore, Mrs. Cameron-Falconet had her own daughter arrested on a disorderly conduct charge and Johnson arrested on an abduction charge. She also swore out a warrant charging that her daughter Lucille was insane, for she had to be insane to be with Johnson. Judge Owens of the County Court issued a commitment order for Lucille's detention at the Detention Hospital pending an investigation as to her mental condition.

It was obvious that Mrs. Cameron-Falconet had her daughter and Johnson arrested in order to facilitate the breaking up of the relationship. It had nothing to do with abduction, for it was clear that Lucille Cameron was a willing participant in the relationship. But her mother was hell-bent on trying to break them up, and was willing to use whatever means she could to make it happen. Law enforcement and the courts were willing to help her, even though it involved an abuse and misuse of power and the law. It entirely was the result of the general objection to interracial relationships.

In light of the allegations, rumors were flying around that 90 of Johnson's white neighbors had met and formed a vigilance committee, sworn to drive Johnson out of the city by any means.[1020]

The next morning, Johnson was arraigned in the Chicago municipal court. When attorney Charles Erbstein, representing Mrs. F. Cameron-Falconet, demanded that Johnson's bond be increased, Johnson replied to the court, "I don't think it is necessary to increase the bond. I am a responsible citizen. I have a business worth $60,000." Erbstein fired back, "It may be worth that to you, but it's illegal and you ought to be put out of business." Johnson replied with a laugh, "All right, 'Mr. Mayor.'" Erbstein retorted, "If I were mayor of Chicago you wouldn't be in business three days." Judge Hopkins set the bond at $1,500, the usual amount in abduction cases. A professional bondsman posted a cash bond for the champ. The case was continued to October 29.

Two agents from the U.S. Department of Justice were present at the arraignment. Apparently, a few hours after Johnson's arrest, James Wilkerson, the U.S. Attorney for the Northern District of Illinois, ordered a thorough investigation, with the intention of pursuing prosecutions under the White-Slave Traffic Act, otherwise known as the Mann Act, which prohibited aiding or assisting with the transportation of women from one state to another for the purposes of prostitution, debauchery, or immoral practices. "The government is determined to go the limit in investigating Johnson's alleged relations with the Cameron girl and others. Information has come to the department of justice that the negro prize fighter has associated frequently with young white girls."

On Wilkerson's application, U.S. Commissioner Foote granted an order detaining Lucille Cameron, holding her in custody under $25,000 bonds as a witness in a federal grand jury investigation against Johnson. Department of Justice agents questioned her for two hours, but allegedly she refused to discuss her relations with Johnson.

Johnson and his attorney attempted to visit Cameron, but were denied permission.

When they heard that Johnson planned to bail her out, at the request of federal officers, Commissioner Foote authorized Cameron's removal to the county jail at Rockford, Illinois. Wilkerson then ordered her taken to the federal building, where she would be held under special guard until she appeared before the federal grand jury. She told the police that she loved Johnson and expected to become his wife.

Crowds followed Johnson wherever he went. Occasionally, loud voices would be heard saying things like, "Shoot the nigger! Lynch him!"

[1020] *Chicago Day Book*, October 18, 1912. *Freeman*, October 26, 1912. Johnson had planned to leave for Australia for the Langford fight and to take Cameron with him.

When Johnson was leaving a downtown Chicago bank, an unidentified man dropped a large ink-well from a 10th floor window, and it narrowly missed the pugilist's head, exploding when it hit the ground.

Because hysterical race prejudice was putting Johnson's life in danger, he hired Burns detectives to guard him from assassination attempts.[1021]

Even some black newspapers started to come down on Johnson. The *New York Age's* Lester Walton said that since Johnson had become champion, he had been the central figure in numerous escapades which tended to make him less and less popular with both black and white citizens. Walton called Johnson a mental weakling. Though he was shrewd and nervy, he also was so "deeply impressed with his own importance that he sincerely believes that he is a privileged character." He ignored those who implored him to avoid potentially harmful notoriety.

Many blacks viewed Johnson's involvement with white women - from the death of his wife and now a pending abduction charge - as a potential cause of prejudice and violence by whites upon blacks. Hence, he would be blamed, rather than the white perpetrators of the violence.

Johnson had mixed value as a symbol. When he defeated Jeffries, "the Negroes of this country were truly happy." It taught white citizens "a good lesson – that the color of a person's skin is not the determining factor to success. The race looked upon Johnson as a hero – one who would play an important part in breaking down prejudice."

However, Johnson also had proven to be a disappointment in some respects. "Instead of lessening prejudice he has increased it."

> It is unfortunate in this country that the entire race is subjected to criticism when one member does something discreditable. It is not so with the white race, however. It is not pleasant to contemplate just what would happen if an insane Negro attempted to kill a high Government official [as a white man recently had done in an assassination attempt on Theodore Roosevelt]. In Chicago we learn that race riots are imminent. If there are any disturbances growing out of the Johnson-Cameron incident, investigation will show that the trouble all started over enraged whites attacking innocent Negroes who are in no way connected with the affair. The Negroes throughout the United States do not think so much of Johnson that they are willing to become victims of race prejudice unnecessarily occasioned by him. In the first place we have never relished any more than the white brother the unusual attention the fighter pays to white women…
>
> True, he has a right to admire whatever type he sees fit, but the Negro has every type imaginable – the race really has a varied assortment.

[1021] *Ogden Evening Standard, Chicago Day Book,* October 19, 1912; *Bennington Evening Banner,* October 21, 1912; *Freeman,* October 26, 1912.

> There have been other colored fighters who have had white wives, for instance George Dixon. Yet Dixon was one of the most popular fighters that ever stepped into the ring. He did not crave for notoriety and was discreet. ... But Jack Johnson, due to his woeful lack of judgment and his exaggerated ego, has become a menace.[1022]

Black leader Booker T. Washington denounced Johnson, saying,

> It is unfortunate that a man with money should use it in a way to injure his own people in the eyes of those who are seeking to uplift his race and improve its conditions.... In misrepresenting the colored people of the country this man is harming himself the least. I wish to say emphatically that his actions do not meet my personal approval, and I am sure that they do not meet with the approval of the colored race.[1023]

The *Freeman* said Johnson was in bad as a result of the Cameron case, and was being condemned even by his own race. "Never before in the history of Chicago has one man had as much newspaper matter printed about him in so short a time as Jack Johnson. ... The daily newspapers have worked up an awful case on the champion." Even prominent blacks were calling meetings for the purpose of "taking action against" the champ, whatever that meant. Letters were being sent to Johnson, even by blacks, informing him that he was a menace to humanity and the black race in particular.

Hugh McIntosh called off Johnson's fights with Langford and McVey. McIntosh said Australian sporting people were disgusted by Johnson's relations with the Cameron girl. The allegations had so angered the Australian sporting public as to make Johnson a doubtful attraction, even though he was the world champion.

Several *Freeman* writers commented on why everyone was so mad at Johnson. Given his white wife's recent suicide, many thought Johnson was "obtuse" and "foolish" to be with another white woman, given the pain his previous wife had to endure. True, the woman was of age, a legal adult, and could make her own choices. "Granted. But Mr. Johnson should bear in mind that sentiment and custom are often stronger than written laws. For instance, most of the states have laws that permit Negroes to do what other men do, but when it comes to doing those things then it is something else." Hence, Johnson might have been in the right legally, but he had violated powerful unwritten social rules.

Some blacks were insulted that Johnson only sought white women. "Jack Johnson evidently thinks his own folks are not good enough for Jack Johnson." One said, "Let Mr. Jack Johnson kindly cut the female white people out of his operations and he will have plain sailing." Another said, "Some colored folks got together at Washington, D.C., and voted to repudiate Johnson as a member of the race. That's going a bit too far. ...

[1022] *New York Age,* October 24, 1912. Joe Jeannette had a white wife as well.
[1023] *Afro American Ledger,* October 26, 1912.

All of us hope that Johnson will avoid doing things that stir up race feeling."

Another wrote that Johnson had shown a weakness for white women. His past relations had been somewhat overlooked. Most thought his marriage to a white woman was a "mere chance affair and not a thing studied out by the champion in the sense of a demand" which also implied the inferiority of his own race of women.

However, "The experiences of his wife should have cured him of all desire to take on another one, who, in the nature of things, would have to undergo the same experiences. The woman needs protection against the fate that awaits her should she step foot across the racial line." After what happened with his first wife, white and black folk alike thought it cruel and inconsiderate of Johnson to associate with white women. Blacks also feared a white backlash against their race:

> We have been kindly disposed to Mr. Johnson, criticizing him some, but praising him more. We can not side with him in this matter in view of what we know. It is a humane question as well as a race question. The young woman, perhaps, thinks herself strong; thinks the strong support of affection and regard can buoy her up all her days. She is mistaken. When she finds that she must run a gauntlet of turned-up noses daily with only an occasional look of sympathy, she will find herself finally crushed between the milled edges of racial societies. ...
>
> We should only be interested in knowing that the persistent pursuing of his course will cause a wide-spread feeling of opposition to Negroes. He has no moral right to anything that promises so much mischief. He's free, and all that, as he says, but there are 'invisible' laws to which he must subscribe – the agreements of society – if he would enjoy a large measure of that freedom of which he boasts.

Johnson needed to remember that as the king of boxing, unlike other boxers, he had no private affairs. "It's a mean condition all right, but it's the penalty of greatness and exacted by a punctilious public, most rigorously." Other black boxers could have white wives and go unnoticed, but the heavyweight champion of the world had powerful symbolic meaning.

Despite the abuse of the law and courts, this *Freeman* writer said, "I hope the mother and the courts will succeed in vetoing their 'hearts legislation.' More than the two are involved, since the race is held as one. I am satisfied the white people have no sympathy in the matter. I am satisfied that the Negroes have no sympathy in the matter."[1024]

On October 21, federal authorities raided Johnson's café. Attorney Charles Erbstein, Mrs. Cameron-Falconet's attorney, was with the officers. Johnson, who was eating dinner, called the attorney "the fighting name," and ordered him out, threatening to break him in two unless he left.[1025]

[1024] *Freeman*, October 26, 1912.
[1025] *Chicago Day Book*, October 22, 1912.

Johnson emphatically denied the allegations against him. He met with 100 representative black citizens at the Appomattox Club. Jack told them,

> I want to say that I never made that statement, attributed to me, to the effect that I could get any white woman I wanted. I lay my hand upon the Bible, and swear that I never made such a statement.
>
> I want to say that I never said anything of the sort about any woman of any color. But I do want to say that I am not a slave and that I have the right to choose who my mate shall be without the dictation of any man. ... So long as I do not interfere with any other man's wife I shall claim the right to select the woman of my own choice. Nobody else can do that for me. That is where the whole trouble lies.

His lawyers declared that there were no legal grounds for his prosecution.

The Conference of Representative Chicago Colored Citizens issued a statement adopting strong resolutions asking the daily newspapers to be fair and not to condemn the entire race for the alleged misconduct of one person:

> That the tone of the daily newspaper expressions regarding this episode manifestly does the negro race an injustice by impliedly condemning the entire negro race for the alleged misconduct of one of its members.
>
> That we, as law abiding citizens in common with all good citizens of whatever race, condemn any immoral conduct or violation of the law...
>
> That we disavow any and all implied publications that the negro race as a race approve the alleged utterances of Jack Johnson or any alleged act or acts which either violate the laws of the land or are repugnant to decent society. ...
>
> That Jack Johnson at the invitation of this conference of representative negro citizens appeared in person and unqualifiedly denied that he made the statement, "He could get any white woman he wanted," or any statement reflecting upon the womanhood of any race, and being corroborated in such denial by Joseph Levy, a white man who was present at the time the statement was alleged to have been made.
>
> We therefore appeal to the sense of fairness of the public and press alike to discontinue the unfailing disposition to indict the entire negro race for any infraction of the law by an individual member of the race.

The *Chicago Broad Ax* said the minions of the law, like a pack of wolves, were hunting Johnson day and night. It concluded that the statements attributed to Johnson were a pack of lies created by newspapers for the purpose of stirring up race prejudice.

The *Broad Ax* said white men were ready to shoot dead any Negro who even winked at a white woman. That was the white man's idea of fairness and justice in America. Lucille Cameron for several months had resided at an expensive hotel, and, being unemployed, it was obvious that a man was taking very good care of her. She also demonstrated an inclination to associate with the "sporty element," meaning prostitutes. She was no angel, and needed no protection. Her relationship with Johnson was consensual. Conversely, when black women were raped, they could obtain no justice whatsoever.

This writer alleged that newspapers were not interested in Cameron's welfare, but in selling newspapers. An incident such as this was exactly what they were seeking. They could not only "hurl their fiery and race prejudice darts" at Johnson, but at the entire colored race.

The *Chicago Defender* said the daily newspapers were engaging in malicious and vicious attacks upon a man who was not guilty. They were trying to incite riot. One newspaper suggested that if Johnson were living in the South he would be lynched, for they lynched folks for offenses much less severe than the one for which he was accused.

The Chicago City Council was attempting to close Johnson's café. On October 23 they adopted a resolution instructing the mayor to make an investigation of the café's conduct, and if any infractions could be found, to revoke his license promptly. They condemned his alleged boasts and said he was a disgrace to his race. Initially, Mayor Carter Harrison resisted, saying, "The council will pass resolutions on most anything so long as it is popular."

Cameron's mother was said to be hysterical, upon the verge of insanity, and under the care of physicians over the whole ordeal.

One man wrote the *Defender*, saying of Johnson, "His manner of living as regards his conduct and habits are to me revolting in the extreme. However, he is an American citizen and as such is clothed with all the rights and privileges of any other citizen of this city. If however, he has violated the laws…I am frank to say he should receive the full penalty of the law."

A black reverend said,

> Every man, colored or white, who acts in a way or conducts his business in a manner as to injure public morals, and who persists in doing so after having been warned to desist, should be tried by the courts, and, if found guilty, punished; and whether he is convicted or not, he should be ostracized by all who believe in common decency and good morals.

Another local black citizen criticized the criticism of Johnson, saying,

> The Johnson-Falconet case from the beginning, was plainly shown to be an out-burst of race prejudice. Hence, Mrs. Falconet's statement: "I would rather see my daughter spend the rest of her life in an insane asylum than see her the plaything of a nigger." Other

statements show that it is merely Johnson's race and color that Mrs. Falconet objects to.

Now, any act or statement by anyone of his, Johnson's race, tending to favor the Falconet side of the case is treason, and this particular one is a traitor to his race. There is only one way to oppose race prejudice and that is by exercising race loyalty. ...

The charge of abduction, under which Mr. Johnson is held, and the many statements of Miss Cameron (who has passed the age limit of womanhood), of her determination, volition and love for Mr. Johnson, reveals the weakness of the law in this strange case of the color of skin. Our white brethren, whose minds are enslaved by prejudice, and whose daily papers, with their brimstone and bloodthirsty articles of condensed suggestions, seem to be laboring very energetically to provoke violence against this Negro whom the world has failed to conquer by fair play. The Negro as a man, as a race, and as a unit, should stand as a solid phalanx against and encroachment of his rights (no matter how insignificant), or any attempt that tends to limit the rights of a deserving and liberty-loving people.

Unrelated to the Johnson case, but insightful regarding the general perspective of the South regarding black rights, Hoke Smith, the U.S. Senator from Georgia, who was seeking re-election, said,

> The uneducated Negro is a good Negro; he is contented to occupy the natural status of his race, the position of inferiority. The educated and intelligent Negro, who wants to vote, is a disturbing and threatening influence. We don't want him down here; let him go North. I favor, and if elected will urge with all my power, the elimination of the Negro from politics.[1026]

Mrs. David Terry, mother of Etta Johnson, said of her daughter,

> I believe she killed herself, not in a fit of madness, but in a fit of sudden clear-seeing and understanding. I believe the mental fog lifted from her for a moment, and revealed her position in all its hideousness.
>
> No one will ever know how cruel Johnson was to Etta. She was mortally afraid of him.
>
> He beat her so she had to go to the hospital for treatment. ... I have seen Etta with her eyes black, and great bruises all over her face.[1027]

There were some allegations that Johnson recently had been shot in the leg by a married black woman, Mrs. Ada Banks-Davis, who may or may not have been his lover. The allegation was that she had shot him in a jealous rage over his attentions to the Cameron gal. Banks-Davis, who was a singer

---

[1026] *Chicago Broad Ax*, *Chicago Defender*, October 26, 1912. *Freeman*, November 2, 1912. *Mahoning Dispatch*, October 25, 1912.
[1027] *Chicago Day Book*, October 24, 1912.

in Johnson's café, was called to testify before the grand jury, which was seeking something tangible against Johnson to substantiate the many horrible stories published in the daily newspapers. Banks-Davis said, "I never shot Jack Johnson. This story is ridiculous. I never handled a revolver in my life. ... I have tried to get the reporters to publish the facts, but you know that they are only looking for a new sensation." She said that while she was employed by Johnson, he was a considerate employer.

However, Banks-Davis' husband filed a lawsuit against Johnson for $25,000, accusing him of alienating his wife's affections.[1028]

U.S. government officials insisted that the singer had shot Johnson in his café. Some said Johnson had been walking with a limp. Others said he was seen at the bank the next day and seemed fine. Johnson strenuously denied that he had been attacked.

The grand jury also wanted to ask Banks about Johnson's alleged connection with the importation of Cameron into the city from Minneapolis, so as to obtain facts to substantiate a Mann Act charge.

Lucille Cameron was confined to the Oxford, Illinois jail. Johnson tried to get her released on a writ of habeas corpus.

A subpoena was issued for a West Side manufacturer, who federal officers said had introduced Cameron to Johnson.

Johnson deeded his property at 3344 South Wabash avenue to his mother, Mrs. Tiny Johnson.

The champ briefly went into seclusion, fearing for his life. A mob had besieged him in the First National Bank and forced him to flee through a side entrance. He received many threats and warnings of assassination by letter, telephone, and personal messengers. Concerned authorities declared and warned that widespread race war would follow if the threatened assassination took place.

> It is an unconcealed fact that plans are being discussed in various quarters as to some method whereby he can be killed, and his friends are urging him to forfeit his $1,500 bond to the government and get out of the country.
>
> It is realized by the authorities that his assassination or attempted assassination would precipitate an ugly race war, not alone in this city, but in other localities. Whites and Negroes in many cities would choose the occasion to even up old scores, dating back to the Reno battle.

In an about-face, changing his prior position, Mayor Harrison said he was seeking some legal excuse whereby he could close up Johnson's café and drive him from the city. "The feeling against him and other Negroes is growing in intensity all the time, and trouble is being expected on the street cars and other places where the races meet. The killing of Johnson would start something that the authorities might have difficulty in handling."

[1028] *Chicago Defender*, November 2, 1912. *Democratic Banner*, October 25, 1912.

During all of the tumult, Johnson had his brother Charles Johnson arrested for theft or embezzlement.

Figuring correctly that Charles Johnson would not be happy with his brother for having him arrested, the government subpoenaed him to testify before the grand jury, which he did for nearly two hours, allegedly giving them a fair amount of information about Johnson's trips from state to state with white women. He furnished names and addresses. Charles said Jack expected trouble, and as a result, deeded about $200,000 to their mother.

On October 31, the City Collector refused to renew Johnson's saloon license. Another reported that the license under which he was operating was owned by a brewery. His contract to use it expired on November 1, and they refused to renew it. Hence, Johnson was forced to retire from the saloon business.[1029]

Explaining why so many were against Johnson, the *Freeman* wrote,

> Johnson bucked the unwritten laws of this country. These forbade racial amalgamation as it concerns Negroes and white people. Others may do so, may marry as they choose. ... With us poor sons of Ham, who live mainly by sufferance, this program of diversity is denied. And I may say right here that the Negroes have no desire, no general desire to change sentiment. ... He was aware of the sentiment against interracial marriages, and which is almost as strongly opposed by our own race as by the white people.[1030]

West Liberty, Kentucky's *Licking Valley Courier* said if the Johnson case had been south of the Ohio river, Johnson would have been "put over," for "The Southerner knows how to handle such cases." Meaning that they would have lynched him. It said Johnson had "tried the stunt that every nigger who is given the opportunity tries – to equalize himself with white people." Johnson's money and the "glad hand" of "white negrophiles of the north" made him as good as white people, such that he married a white woman. "But the horrors of the situation was such that even she could not endure it and did the sanest act of her life in committing suicide." When he seduced another white woman, Chicago finally became shocked by his conduct, for Cameron's humiliated mother "managed to stir up enough of the dormant manhood in that Sodom."

> The Southerners know the nigger; know his nature, his capabilities, his limitations; hence know how to handle the problem that is becoming a grave national menace. But the Northerner's chickens are coming home to roost. The nigger himself is demonstrating to them the pitiful fallacy of their clamor to educate their black 'brother' and make a good citizen of him. The white man of the South long ago realized that Omnipotent Omniscience had made that impossible. The leopard can not change its spots. Neither can 'education and

---

[1029] *New York World*, October 23, 1912; *Freeman*, November 2, 1912. *San Francisco Call*, November 1, 1912.
[1030] *Freeman*, November 2, 1912.

culture' make a good citizen out of the nigger. There's no moral foundation in his nature to build upon.[1031]

On November 7, 1912, Jack Johnson was arrested on four indictments returned by the federal grand jury for violations of the Mann Act. His bond was fixed at a whopping $30,000, and Judge Kenesaw Mountain Landis refused to reduce it. Born in 1866, Judge Landis was named for a mountain peak where his father had been wounded in the Civil War.

The Mann Act, a federal law officially known as the "White-slave traffic Act," was drafted by Republican U.S. Congressman James Mann of Illinois. The Act made it unlawful to aid or assist the transportation of women (specifically including the aiding or assisting in the procurement of any tickets or form of transportation) across state lines for the purposes of prostitution, debauchery, or other immorality. Although intended to eliminate forced prostitution, the language of the act was so vague and overbroad that prosecutors could persecute even sexual encounters between unmarried consenting adults that didn't involve prostitution. It was a morality crime. Hence, anyone providing finances to a woman not his wife who traveled across state lines, if the intent was to have sexual relations, technically could be found guilty of a federal criminal felony. The law was approved by the U.S. Congress on June 25, 1910, signed by U.S. President William Taft, and went into effect on July 1, 1910.

Contrary to popular belief, Jack Johnson was not the first person prosecuted under this Act. In fact, in the Northern District of Illinois alone, there were forty Mann Act prosecutions even before the Johnson case.

Initially, the U.S. Department of Justice alleged that over two years ago, on August 10, 1910, one month after the Jeffries fight, and one month after the law went into effect, Jack Johnson had brought a then 24-year-old Belle Schreiber of Pittsburg, a white woman, to Chicago for an unlawful purpose. Johnson had set her up in business as a part owner of a resort (another way of saying brothel) on the south side. A government lawyer said the case would not be open to dispute. "There could not be a plainer case of white slavery in violation of the Mann act."

Although briefly released, when there were issues surrounding the validity of the bond posted on his behalf by a friend, on November 8, Johnson was taken back into custody.

On his way in to the jail, Johnson struck a newspaper photographer with a cane that he was carrying in his free hand; not happy about the attempt to photograph him.

Johnson was forced to remove all of his clothing and wear prison garb. He was assigned to a cell in an upper tier. He asked for a dozen candles, a box of cigars, and a case of champagne. He was told that he could not have those items. Johnson replied, "You're not as accommodating as they were in San Francisco. I got everything I wanted there." Johnson requested a bottle of milk, and that was given to him.

[1031] *Licking Valley Courier*, November 7, 1912.

Responding to the allegations, Johnson said, "I was in New York playing at Hammerstein's on August 10, 1910, the day they say I brought this Schreiber girl into this state. After that I played in Brooklyn for a week. I never transported her anywhere."

U.S. District Attorney James Wilkerson opposed the acceptance of payment of Johnson's bond in cash. He understood that Johnson intended to leave the country on November 30 if he obtained his release. The offense with which Johnson was charged was not subject to extradition. Wilkerson wanted two men of good character with unencumbered real estate to post the bond. U.S. District Court Judge Kenesaw Mountain Landis agreed, and refused to accept the $30,000 in cash. Hence, they kept Johnson in jail despite the fact that he had the money necessary to post the bail set.

Belle Schreiber was the white daughter of a Milwaukee policeman. She had preceded Etta Duryea in Johnson's affections. The start of their relationship pre-dated the passage of the Mann Act. The champ continued to associate with her after his marriage to Duryea, for she was his vaudeville combination after the Reno fight. She finally was abandoned by him, and at that time threatened to get even with him. She was a willing witness, though government detectives kept her in seclusion.[1032]

Meanwhile, Lucille Cameron had been held in jail on a $15,000 bond, but when a bondsman offered to pay it, Judge Landis refused to accept it. The government continued to hold her against her will – ironic given the allegations that Johnson had abducted her, which he had not. In fact, it was the government which had abducted Lucille Cameron.[1033]

The black-owned *Seattle Republican* opined,

> If Jack Johnson has broken the law he deserves the punishment of the law and we hope he gets it, but it looks to us as if all this publicity is given to it because Jack is a Negro and the women are Caucasians. Had Johnson mistreated girls of his own race in a similar manner the federal authorities would have considered it beneath their dignity to give it a moment's consideration. ...
>
> He was evidently untrue to the white woman he called his wife, which drove her to commit suicide, and he had no sooner returned from her tomb than he began to lionize a bunch of others, and became defiant when the parents of one of the girls protested. In good plain English, he was a damphool and deserves no mercy.[1034]

Many colored editors of various newspapers across the country were opposed to Johnson's affinity towards white women, for they considered it a slap at his own race, and believed it engendered further race prejudice:

St. Louis Advance, quoting Major John Lynch: "Some of his race have been proud of him as a prizefighter, but never as anything else."

[1032] *Freeman*, November 23, 1912. *New York Tribune*, November 9, 1912.
[1033] *Daily Ardmoreite, El Paso Herald, Chicago Day Book*, November 8, 1912.
[1034] *Seattle Republican*, November 8, 1912.

Star of Zion, Charlotte, North Carolina: "This time he is arrested from trafficking in white slaves. A great injury is done the race when any of its members are exploited whose lives cannot be emulated by the youth of the race. We do not subscribe to the doctrine that the champion pugilist is a racial asset."

The Star, Newport News, Virginia: "No Negro, who has any spark of manhood and who prayed and hoped that Jack Johnson would win his battle with Jim Jeffries...now feels that he did himself the slightest tinge of honor. What a pity it is that Johnson ever was successful in obtaining the great amount of money which came to him if it is to be put to no better use than being spent in a desire to parade a white woman as his wife."

Exchange, Birmingham, Alabama: "As to the physiological ability of Jack Johnson, we believe we voice the sentiment of every intelligent Negro, when we say that we glory in him. ... [but] we say that we most indefatigably denounce his debase allegiance with the other race's woman, and only express our feelings mildly when we say that we hope that he will get everything that is coming to him as far as the law is concerned."

Detroit Informer: "The camel's back is broken with too much Johnson. That he is a menace to the race is conceded by all. Johnson should not nor does he deserve the touch of pity or defense from any source."

Pittsburgh Courier: "Negroes have had quite enough of Jack Johnson and his 'high life.' ... We think Jack Johnson a failure as a representative of the race; and experience no hesitancy in saying that we have had too much Johnson."

Illinois Idea: "Mr. Johnson may be the most scientific boxer in the world, but he is not the best diplomat...and he or no other man has ever suppressed public sentiment or public morals, and the moment that he attempts to do it he will be destroyed of his popularity and business opportunity as have all other men who defied public sentiment."

New York Amsterdam News: "It has been too often the case...that colored men who have achieved prominence have apparently sought to forsake their race by taking as the companion of their bosom either a cast-off or mediocre woman from the Caucasian race....an evidence of the black man's lack of race pride."

Texas Freeman: "Jack Johnson's temporary prosperity, his dense ignorance and misuse of power is doing more to crystalize sentiment against our race."[1035]

However, Johnson had his defenders, too. The editor of the *X-Rays Democrat* of Topeka, Kansas said,

> Jack Johnson, the Colored champion pugilist of the world, is in the lime light once more. They claim he has disgraced Chicago. What a pity to disgrace so pure a city. Better see to the thousands of poor

---

[1035] *Freeman*, November 9, 1912.

white girls who are living in the underworld of Chicago and give Jack Johnson and the 19 year old White gal a rest as she may not be worth the space she is receiving in the press.

The *Chicago Broad Ax* agreed, saying the people of Chicago and the rest of the country were deceitful and hypocritical, and would hang their heads in shame when it fully dawned upon their race-prejudice-befuddled minds that they permitted themselves to go crazy not on behalf of a pure and innocent young lady, but an experienced prostitute who took money from both races. Cameron had been in his employment for a year.

The *Broad Ax* criticized that the law and law enforcement only sought to protect white women, but never black women. After all, the law itself was named the White Slave Traffic Act.[1036]

Lester Walton of the *New York Age* wrote,

> There is a difference between prosecution and persecution. If John has violated the White Slave Act then let the Chicago officials give him a fair trial and not seek to keep him in jail before he has been adjudged guilty. The actions of the Chicago authorities are more disgraceful than the notorious conduct of the champion.
>
> Evidently with a view to playing to the gallery and winning popular favor, the authorities are determined to make as much political capital out of the Johnson incident as possible. They are demanding all kinds of bonds and Tuesday refused a $40,000 cash bond, preferring to keep the fighter in jail. Investigation might show that the white women mixed up in the case are too low in morals to warrant the fixing of Johnson's bond even at $100.
>
> Johnson has been severely criticized in these columns for his lack of judgment, but we are unalterably opposed to seeing him railroaded to jail because of his color.[1037]

The *Freeman* agreed that "it seems to us that they are pushing Jack Johnson too hard in the matter of his bond." A $40,000 bond was extremely high, and the court would not accept cash, but wanted it secured by property, which was an odd and unusual request. Clearly, they wanted to keep him in jail. They were "pursuing the champion in a way not warranted by the custom of the courts." Although it did not support his relations with white women, the *Freeman* also opposed unfair treatment by the courts:

> We can not see that it is up to the law or court to see that Jack Johnson does not get Lucile Cameron, as much as we are opposed to it. We oppose it not as a thing of right and wrong, but as a matter of sentiment, knowing the general opposition to mixed relations and the possible bad effect on society as it is now constituted.

[1036] *Chicago Broad Ax*, November 9, 1912.
[1037] *New York Age*, November 14, 1912.

The concern was that the court was being "too readily influenced by sentiment growing out of racial feelings," for it appeared as if judges had become prosecutors and persecutors, rather than neutral arbiters.

The *Freeman* noted that Johnson had assaulted the unwritten law of non-amalgamation. Although the country was filled with mixed marriages, including other fighters, they were "not advertised by men in high places." Johnson was the heavyweight champion, the man on top. Hence, his relationships had greater symbolic value and were advertised more widely. "Johnson laid on the last straw when he took on the Cameron girl. He broke the camel's back. Rage that had smothered and smoldered long – the old fires that had died down…revived, and are now fanned by the gust of passions that promise to cease when he has drained his cup of bitterness."

The government was coming at Jack hard. He could furnish a sufficient bond, which already was ridiculously huge, and yet they still kept him in jail.

> Johnson's case is getting dangerously near to persecution if it is not there already. … Johnson is being maltreated right in the courts. … If the court means to punish him under the white slave law act, it acts extraordinary when it scours heaven and earth to find evidence, going into ancient history, so to speak. … The courts are to protect those whom others would devour, they are not to go into the devouring business themselves.[1038]

The *Chicago Defender* lamented that it appeared to be the U.S. government's policy of "All white people up, all black people down." The fundamental principle of the land of the free and home of the brave was justice to all. However, that principal seemed to have been trampled in the mud in the Johnson case. The world wanted to know why he was held in custody with three times the amount of bail required in his case than any other, and the amount was guaranteed but still not accepted, which was unfair. "Has colorphobia such a stronghold in Chicago?" Johnson was being "persecuted beyond endurance."

Johnson's unsuccessful attempts to be released on bail had caused some of the public sentiment to switch in his favor, particularly by his own race.

Johnson's lawyers, Edward Morris and Benjamin Bachrach, went to Washington D.C. to argue the case before the U.S. Supreme Court. The case was heard on November 11, 1912. They argued that the bail was excessive, cash should have been accepted, and the Mann Act was unconstitutional. "The Mann Act is particularly to prevent the traffic in women and is aimed at their debauchery. It cannot however interfere with the personal liberties of citizens and be constitutional." Johnson's attorneys argued that under the 10th amendment, the regulation of morality was a matter for the states, not the federal government. They further argued that Congress lacked constitutional authority to make something not commercial

---

[1038] *Freeman*, November 16, 1912.

a matter of interstate commerce under the commerce clause. The case was continued so the government could respond.[1039]

The federal grand jury returned four more Mann Act indictments against Johnson. Eventually, it would indict him on eleven counts. The penalty for each offense was maximum imprisonment of up to 5 years, or a fine of up to $5,000, or both.[1040]

From jail, the champ declared his innocence. Hundreds daily visited him, white and black, including his mother, brother, and sisters. Johnson had both white and black lawyers working on his case.

Solicitor General Bulitt filed a brief with the U.S. Supreme Court, opposing the motion to admit the pugilist to more reasonable bail terms, arguing that Johnson might escape prosecution by fleeing the country.

U.S. federal Judge George A. Carpenter also refused a $40,000 cash bail payment on Johnson's behalf, and refused to reduce the bail.

The *Chicago Broad Ax* noted that even the white-owned *New York World* thought matters were being taken too far, quoting it as saying:

> The prosecution of Jack Johnson is becoming interesting in more ways than one. It is no longer a mere record of incidents in the life of a dissolute pugilist, it is an issue of equal rights in the courts.
>
> There is a growing suspicion that no matter how bad a man Johnson may be, and he is bad, undoubtedly popular clamor and race prejudice are making him blacker than he is. Whatever he may be, he is entitled to his rights under the laws impartially administered.
>
> The amount of bail required for him is larger than has ever been asked in similar cases. It is probable that no such sum would be demanded of any other man in America upon a like charge. ... No man should have to go to the Supreme Court at Washington to get reasonable bail in a criminal case not capital.[1041]

On November 15, 1912, after eight days of incarceration in the Cook county jail, Jack Johnson was liberated. Friends and family furnished the $30,000 bond, guaranteed by $70,000 in property, including that of Mrs. Tiny Johnson and Matthew Baldwin, a real estate dealer. Johnson's mother put up the property at 3344 Wabash avenue, valued at $32,000.

Johnson walked out of court in company with his black attorneys Anderson and Wright, and his mother and sister. The crowd outside gave him three cheers.[1042]

As Johnson was leaving the federal building, two local police detectives re-arrested him on a warrant sworn out by a newspaper photographer charging assault and battery, alleging that Johnson struck the photographer with a cane at the county jail entrance on November 8. The pugilist was

---

[1039] *Chicago Day Book*, November 11, 1912; *Daily Missoulian*, December 13, 1912.
[1040] *Washington Herald*, November 12, 1912.
[1041] *Chicago Broad Ax*, November 30, 1912.
[1042] *Washington Times*, November 13, 1912; *Chicago Defender*, November 16, 23, 1912.

taken to a police station, and a cash bond of $400 was accepted. The photographer also filed a civil suit asking for $10,000 in damages.

The *Freeman* said Johnson's primary offense was "failing to get himself born white." "The spectacle of two great American cities lashing themselves into the fury of a Georgia lynching mob" over the allegations against Johnson was "contemptible beyond expression, and as much worse than Johnson's alleged offense as the Armenian massacres or Russian atrocities surpass in degree a barroom row down in Bath House John's bailiwick."[1043]

The Reverend Judson Thomas, pastor for the First Baptist Church of Austin, Texas declared, "If Jack Johnson was swung up from a lamp post and his body riddled with bullets it would be light punishment for his sins."

Several Midland, Texas citizens sent letters to Charles Erbstein, the attorney for Lucille Cameron's mother, offering him $100,000 for his defense if he would kill Johnson.[1044]

A black attorney said the Chicago press was exploiting the Johnson situation in a mischievous manner, which was a disgrace to the profession of journalism and a sin against the peace of the community. "It has the effect to inflame the feeling of the masses of the white race against the Negro, who is having a hard enough time as it is."

This writer also criticized the black press and black religious community:

> Many colored papers, preachers and other Negroes continue to harp on one line, that Johnson owes the Negro race something. I disagree utterly with that assumption. The Negro race has done nothing for Johnson, has given him nothing, aided him in no way to attain any prominence and is entitled to nothing, considered as a race. When Jack Johnson needed money to go to Australia to fight Burns, did the Negro race come forward with help...? This idea Negroes have of criticizing is too common; just as soon as a Negro, great or small falls afoul of the white man's one-sided law all the Negroes like rats deserting a sinking ship begin to outdo the white in denouncing him. Cowardly conduct I call it. ... The fact that he likes white women is no reflection on the race; you make too much of that point. Most men like fair women, if you don't believe it just go into the best Negro homes...and you will find a yellow or almost white woman occupying the leading place of wife. ... If he gets in 'bad with the law' let him take his medicine, if he can't get out of it like other people have to do, but this eternal question of mixing up the race with everything he does is foolish and playing right into the white man's hands. Exactly what he wants us to do is to acknowledge that we are not good enough to marry his old bold, brazen women, while he takes great delight in running every black girl he can get his dirty paws upon. ... Don't let white folks bluff us all the time on this old mixed marriage question. ... and never admit for an instant that black men

---

[1043] *Freeman*, November 23, 30, 1912; *New York Tribune*, November 9, 1912. *Evening Standard*, November 15, 1912.
[1044] *Chicago Broad Ax*, November 16, 1912; *Chicago Day Book*, November 15, 1912.

and black women are not good enough to mate with white men and women, for that is the whole thing in a nutshell and you know it. As long as we admit inferiority we are inferior.[1045]

A white writer for the *Cincinnati Enquirer* said Johnson was the greatest fighter who ever lived, and a lot of ill feeling against him, both personal and professional, had been caused by the fact that he was colored. This writer lamented the unfair treatment that Johnson was receiving, saying,

> It is an unfair way to try to get the championship away from the Negro. I want it back to the white man and I want it bad, but I want him to win it like he lost it. ... Now, to all men who want to be fair, let's give the Negro a fair deal and win back on the level.
>
> If we could kill or put the ban on all men who get mixed up with the opposite race we should have about one-half of our own people out of business. I want to see the championship won as it was lost – in the ring. ... not the courts.[1046]

On November 19, 1912, the groundless abduction charge against Jack Johnson was dismissed quietly. Municipal Judge Jacob Hopkins dismissed it; owing to the fact that the prosecution could not prove Johnson had abducted Cameron. The sensational story started by the daily newspapers and Cameron's mother had no basis in fact whatsoever. Of course, everyone had known this all along, yet they had put Johnson through the ringer anyhow, because of the fact that he was dating a white woman. Using the prevarication was an abuse of the justice system, it was unethical for the prosecution to pursue a case that had no factual or legal basis, and unethical for the judiciary to support the charge and the high bail amounts.[1047]

Johnson compared himself to Napoleon, saying, "All great men have been persecuted."[1048]

On November 21, Johnson pled not guilty to the charge of smuggling a diamond necklace into the country.

Jack dropped the case against his brother Charles, whom he alleged had stolen $150 in furs.[1049]

On November 22, at his arraignment, Johnson pled not guilty to the charges of having transported Belle Schreiber from Pittsburgh to Chicago, Milwaukee, and Detroit for immoral purposes.

Ida B. Wells-Barnett, a former slave, suffragist, journalist, and civil rights leader who documented how lynchings often were used as a way to control or punish blacks who competed with whites, often under the guise of false rape charges (when in fact most liaisons were consensual), called a meeting of 2,000 citizens. They passed a resolution declaring that the sensational exploitation of charges against Jack Johnson had done great injury to the

---

[1045] *Freeman*, November 23, 1912.
[1046] *Freeman*, November 23, 1912.
[1047] *Harlowton News*, November 22, 1912; *Chicago Broad Ax*, November 23, 1912.
[1048] *Mathews Journal*, November 21, 1912.
[1049] *Chicago Day Book*, November 21, 1912.

civic, industrial, and business relations between colored and white citizens. They appealed to the public for the presumption of innocence to which every man was due, to the press for respite from harmful sensationalism, and to government officials to subordinate prejudice to principle.

The *Chicago Defender* said the Cameron case was a lesson for all races. Her mother had resorted to the hysterics of the stage in her spectacular newspaper attempt to reclaim her adult child. In fact, "Cameron knew the turns and twists of State street before she knew the outs and ins of Café de Champion." Regardless, the entire black race was nailed to the cross. The lesson was that black folk should "move carefully in the future when they are called on to condemn one of their own upon the testimony of harlotry."

Tom Flanagan, writing for the *Evening Telegraph*, said Johnson never had been forgiven for defeating Jeffries. On that day, Jack made thousands of enemies. He could have laid down and retired rich, but he did not because he was a better sportsman than the white gamesters who had hoped to clean up on the trusting public. Johnson was on the square, and could be depended upon to do his best in training and fight to win.

Flanagan said Johnson may have sinned against morality, but those who were hounding him probably were not any cleaner. "Jack Johnson is black and they are white. There seems to be a separate code of morality for whites and blacks in the United States and Johnson is the goat." Jack was no saint. He simply gave in to temptation. "Some people may be surprised to know that the famous pugilist has actually been hounded by women in nearly every city he has visited – white women, supposedly respectable."

Flanagan found Johnson to be a fair and honest man. "He is black, and naturally can never hope for much justice across the line."[1050]

The black-owned *New Amsterdam News* said there was no doubt about the attempt to put it over on Johnson. The government was run by white men, and they were only human, affected by race shame the same as anyone else. They did not like Johnson at the top of the ladder, nor did they like his dating of white women. The Cameron "abduction" case was utterly groundless. Lucille was willing to testify all along that she was seeing Johnson of her own volition, and everyone knew it. "It is openly reported in Chicago that white men not related to the Cameron girl were behind the prosecution." Had the case come to trial and Johnson been given a fair hearing, the entire fabric of race persecution would have been exposed.

Noted was the inconsistency of Mann Act prosecutions, which were based solely on race. White men lusted after colored women in every city, in both the North and South:

> Yet in all this the government has never yet invoked the white slave law. The stench of the unjust and unholy race persecution in which the entire country is joining hands in railroading Jack Johnson cries to heaven for redress. … The persecution of Johnson will not hurt only

---

[1050] *Chicago Defender*, November 23, 30, 1912.

Johnson, but disturb for a long time to come the peaceful relations of the white and colored people of the nation.

It was obvious to this writer that the government was prosecuting Johnson because he was black, he slept with white women, and he was the world heavyweight champion, plain and simple.[1051]

On December 3, 1912, Jack Johnson married Lucille Cameron at the family home at 3344 South Wabash avenue. Johnson placed a $2,500 diamond ring on her finger. Cameron was 18 years of age, as revealed by the marriage certificate, for her birthdate was February 22, 1894.[1052]

The new Mrs. Johnson said,

I am a free woman and have a perfect right to marry whom I please. Why don't the United States government stop southern and northern white men as well from living and raising children by colored women out of wedlock; look in the south and see the advantage taken of the colored people. Look at that case where the white men in Georgia fought and killed each other for the love of a colored woman. There are no gleaming headlines in the nice big papers. Well, let them holler who will; … I want my fellow citizens to know that I am still living in the 'land of the free and the home of the brave.'[1053]

A motion picture concern offered Johnson $5,000 for pictures of the wedding, which he accepted. However, in most places, the films of Johnson's wedding were barred from being exhibited. The Indiana Motion Picture Exhibitors' League decided to deny patrons the privilege of witnessing the mixed-race wedding.

Picture-show owners in Paducah, Kentucky also placed a ban on any films showing the Johnson-Cameron marriage. They passed a resolution that the pictures were greatly deplored by all respectable people, were an insult to common decency, and would not be allowed to be displayed. Of the four local theaters, colored patrons were admitted only to one.

[1051] *Freeman*, November 30, 1912.
[1052] *Chicago Day Book*, December 4, 1912; *Tacoma Times*, December 3, 1912; *Chicago Defender*, *Chicago Broad Ax*, December 7, 1912.
[1053] *Chicago Defender*, December 14, 1912.

> Another blot has been given the Negroes by Jack Johnson's craze for white women, which he exhibited in marrying Lucille Cameron....
>
> It is said the citizens of Texarkana telegraphed Mayor Carter Harrison of Chicago saying that if Chicago wanted to get rid of Johnson to just send him to Texarkana for three minutes. It now begins to appear that Jack Johnson is determined to commit suicide.[1054]

At a governors conference, South Carolina Governor Coleman Blease said those who lynched black men accused of assailing white women would not be punished:

> I will never order out the militia to shoot down its neighbors and protect a brute who commits the nameless crime against a white woman. Therefore, in South Carolina, let it be understood that when a Negro assaults a white woman all that is needed is that they get the right man, and they who get him will neither need nor receive a trial.

Never mind due process, the right to counsel, the presumption of innocence until guilt is proven beyond a reasonable doubt in a court of law, or a unanimous verdict by an impartial jury of one's peers. According to the state's own governor, mob justice was perfectly acceptable.[1055]

The *Freeman* said black folk had become "more reconciled to Jack, since they saw plainly that they were trying to put something over him. At first they took the extreme attitude that white people took, insisting that the champion had committed an unpardonable sin." Noted was the difference in treatment based on race. John L. Sullivan was a drunk, who swaggered, bluffed, swore, and got into extracurricular activity not in his favor, yet he was treated as a "national pet."

After the Cameron case dismissal, Johnson said, "As soon as we can get away we will go to Paris." The *Freeman* responded, "Not a bad idea, owing to the very much perturbed racial relations in this country. Of course, Johnson can stay in this country if he chooses, but he would not get very much pleasure out of the staying." Yet, the government was determined not to allow him to leave the country until it had its way with him.

The *Freeman* reported that a New York newspaper (which it did not name) had decided to draw the color line in pugilistic matters. Black fighters' names were barred from its columns. "Never again will the besmirched 'Jack Johnson' be set up on its linotype machines as part of a boxing story, and the only way it can creep into the general news pages of the paper is as an essential integer in tales of justice meted out for criminal acts." That New York newspaper suggested that other papers should follow suit. "It meant further that Johnson is to be 'bludgeoned' out of his title in the one way that it seems possible to do it."[1056]

On December 7, officials of the French boxing federation declared that they would take steps to prevent Johnson from boxing there. They said the

---

[1054] *Freeman*, December 21, 1912, January 4, 1913.
[1055] *Freeman*, December 7, 1912.
[1056] *Freeman*, December 14, 21, 1912, January 4, 1913.

police would forbid any fight involving Johnson on the ground that it might cause trouble.[1057]

On December 10, 1912 in Vernon, California, in an elimination bout for the "white championship," 205-pound Luther McCarty administered a beating to and stopped 190-pound Fireman Jim Flynn in the 16th round (decking him thrice in the 9th and twice in the 16th).[1058]

On December 11, both of Johnson's black attorneys, Anderson and Wright, withdrew from their representation of him, saying their disapproval of his recent marriage was so strong that they no longer desired to be associated with him.[1059]

Also on December 11, U.S. Congressional Representative Seaborn Roddenberry, a Georgia Democrat, from the House floor demanded a federal constitutional amendment prohibiting the marriage of whites and blacks. He said, "We have heard much of slavery in the South, but in all the years of Southern slavery there never was such brutality, such infamy as the marriage license authorizing that black African brute, Jack Johnson, to wed a white woman and to bind her in the wedlock of black slavery." Roddenberry declared that in the South, blacks "respected the superiority of their former masters and would commit self-destruction before entertaining a thought of matrimony with a Caucasian girl." He prophesied that legal sanction of mixed marriages could bring the country to a bloody conflict.[1060]

At that time, in the 48-state Union, 29 states legally prohibited whites and blacks from marrying one another. They were: Alabama, Arizona, Arkansas, California, Colorado, Delaware, Florida, Georgia, Idaho, Indiana, Kentucky, Louisiana, Maryland, Mississippi, Missouri, Montana (as of 1909), Nebraska, Nevada, North Carolina, North Dakota (as of 1909), Oklahoma, Oregon, South Carolina, South Dakota (as of 1909), Tennessee, Texas, Utah, Virginia, and West Virginia. Illinois was one of the 19 states that allowed interracial marriage, but that did not mean it generally was supported. It simply was allowed legally. The following year, in 1913, Wyoming would become the 30th state to pass an anti-interracial marriage law, bringing the total to 62.5% of the states forbidding interracial marriage between blacks and whites.

In 1883, in *Pace v. Alabama*, 106 U.S. 583 (1883), the U.S. Supreme Court had ruled that individual states were within their rights to prohibit marriage, cohabitation, and sexual relations based on race. The Court argued it was the duty of the state to protect married couples against disturbances such as interracial relationships, because relationships between whites and blacks "must naturally cause discord, shame, disruption of family circles, and estrangement," and therefore were incompatible with the family life the state needed to protect. This interpretation of the constitution was the law

---

[1057] *San Francisco Call*, December 8, 1912; *Daily Capital Journal*, December 7, 1912.
[1058] *Freeman*, December 21, 1912.
[1059] *Omaha Daily Bee*, December 12, 1912.
[1060] *Chicago Day Book*, December 12, 1912. The *Herald and News*, December 13, 1912; *Chicago Broad Ax*, December 14, 1912. Ultimately, no amendment passed and it remained up to individual states to pass their own laws regarding the interracial marriage issue.

for the next 81-plus years, until the ruling was overturned by the Supreme Court in 1964 in *McLaughlin v. Florida*, 379 U.S. 184 (1964)(holding that laws prohibiting interracial cohabitation of unmarried persons were unconstitutional) and in 1967 in *Loving v. Virginia*, 388 U.S. 1 (1967)(holding that laws prohibiting interracial marriage were unconstitutional).

On December 12, Jack Johnson was fined $50 on the charge of assaulting a newspaper photographer with a cane.

Hugh McIntosh said Johnson was forever exiled from the Australian ring. "The whole current of popular feeling is so strong against him that no promoter would dare to bring him here." Several days later, McIntosh said,

> As far as I am concerned, Johnson will never come to Australia again. He dare not show his face in London; he is barred in New York, and now that he will have difficulty in doing anything here, the only place that is left for him, as far as I can see, is France, and I doubt if they will stand for him even there.[1061]

Johnson intended to move his wife Lucille into a mansion in the Lake Geneva area in Chicago. However, many local folks said they would try to keep him out, even if physical measures had to be taken.[1062]

On January 1, 1913 in Vernon, California, Luther McCarty stopped Al Palzer in the 18th round to win the White World Heavyweight Championship. McCarty said he was drawing the color line, and considered himself the world champion. All fair-minded sportsmen knew that Johnson could lose the title only by being defeated in the ring. Hence, McCarty simply was the white champion, and unwilling to fight Johnson.

Some said blacks were suffering on account of Johnson, losing their places and jobs as a result of his actions. Whites were taking out their wrath about Johnson upon other blacks. Others said the Johnson situation simply illuminated blacks' status in the country, and gave whites an excuse to do to blacks what they had been doing already. The *Freeman* said,

> More than Jack Johnson is at stake. The Negro is on trial before the world. What is his status in America? The champion is simply a means to an end. He, if you will notice, has abused every canon of good taste from a racial viewpoint, socially considered, yet he has done no violence to the laws. He is an object lesson on the Negro's status in this country, whether by design or accident, and from a sociological viewpoint, worth the while.

When Jack and Lucille Johnson attended the dance of the Eighth regiment, a Negro regiment of the Illinois militia, he and Lucille appeared on the dance floor, but then the blacks present hissed them and backed away. The music ceased, and Johnson and his white wife stood alone in the center of the dance floor. All eyes were upon them, and the hissing

---

[1061] *Honolulu Star-Bulletin*, December 16, 1912. *San Francisco Call*, December 21, 1912. On December 26, 1912 in Sydney, Sam Langford knocked out Sam McVey in the 13th round (having dropped McVey in the 4th round as well).
[1062] *Freeman*, January 4, 1913.

increased until the entire place joined in. An upset Johnson said, "Come, Lucille, let's leave this place."[1063]

Little known is the fact that Johnson attempted to leave the U.S. before his trial. On January 14, 1913, at the request of Charles DeWoody, superintendent of the Department of Justice in Chicago, local police in Battle Creek, Michigan stopped a Grand Trunk train and removed Jack Johnson and his wife from it. Federal officers received a tip that Johnson had left Chicago the previous night bound for Toronto, Ontario, Canada.

Johnson said he only intended to remain in Toronto a couple days, for he was on his way to see his manager Tom Flanagan regarding an offer he had received from Tom O'Rourke for a fight in Paris against Al Palzer. A telegram from O'Rourke showed that Jack had been offered $25,000 or 60% of the house. The message said, "Palzer was ill in McCarty fight. The latter refuses to box."

Superintendent DeWoody had learned that the train was due to arrive in Battle Creek at 2:48 a.m. DeWoody called the local police chief and asked him to stop the train, for Johnson was on it. At 4 a.m., DeWoody was awakened by a long distance call from Johnson, who pleaded, "You know I wouldn't leave my old mother and my country. I'd rather go to jail. I told my attorneys I was just going to Toronto to see my old trainer Tom Flanagan, and they said it was all right." DeWoody asked, "Did you have a round-trip ticket?" "No, I told them to get me one but they got it only one way. But I was going to get one." He begged to be kept out of jail.

DeWoody was not buying it, for Johnson, his wife, and valet all had one-way tickets. Another indication that Johnson did not intend to return was the fact that he shipped his automobiles to Canada as well. DeWoody tersely declared to reporters, "A great chance he was coming back!"

That morning, at Johnson's home, two hours after Jack had been arrested at Battle Creek, without having been made aware of his arrest, Johnson's mother said, "Jack is upstairs sleeping, but I can't wake him now. … His wife is here with him. My boy would never run away."

Johnson was taken back to Illinois and spent the night in the Chicago county jail to await U.S. District Court Judge George Carpenter's decision as to whether Jack's $30,000 bond should be forfeited.

On January 15, Johnson went before Judge Carpenter. Jack told the judge he had no intention of evading trial, but went to Toronto on business matters. The judge asked, "But you shipped two automobiles, didn't you?" Johnson said that was true, but he merely intended to enjoy a few days' vacation before shipping them back to Chicago. Johnson's bond was allowed to stand, for he had not failed to appear at any required court hearing. He was given time to secure a $5,000 bond on the pending jewelry smuggling charge.[1064]

The *Freeman* observed, "What is happening to him is happening to every member of the race. Jack Johnson has violated public sentiment, not the

---

[1063] *Freeman*, January 11, 1913.
[1064] *Freeman*, January 18, February 1, 1913.

laws, as far as it is known." It believed that a coterie of defeated, slanderous white reporters wanted to mob Johnson out of his title.

When Johnson went to O'Connell's gymnasium in Chicago, he was ousted. Jack had boxed 6 rounds there the previous day, but the next day, O'Connell told him he was barred. O'Connell told reporters, "Johnson's presence was hurting my business. Several of my pupils said they would quit if he came here again." The city's other big gyms likely would take the same action against him.[1065]

Meanwhile, on February 3, 1913, the 16th Amendment to the U.S. Constitution was ratified, enabling the U.S. to levy an income tax.

That same day, the U.S. Supreme Court denied Johnson's habeas corpus appeal, holding that the issue was moot, since Johnson had posted bond and had been released. It also held that Johnson could not attack the Mann Act's constitutionality with an appellate court before trial, but had to exhaust all of his legal remedies first, starting with the district court.[1066]

However, on February 24, 1913, the U.S. Supreme Court decided *Hoke v. United States*, 227 U.S. 308 (1913), holding that although Congress could not regulate prostitution per se, as that was strictly within the province of the states, Congress could regulate *interstate travel* for purposes of prostitution or "immoral purposes," finding the Mann Act to be a constitutional exercise of Congressional power.

That same day, the Supreme Court also decided *Athanasaw v. United States*, 227 U.S. 326 (1913), finding that the Mann Act was not limited strictly to prostitution, but to "debauchery" as well.

The ongoing race issues in the U.S. were not limited to the South. Legislatures in New York, New Jersey, Ohio, Michigan, and Minnesota were considering the interracial marriage question.

The *New York Age* noted that Jim Crow laws and the 'separate but equal' doctrine protected whites at every point, but left the darker races without legal protection. Whites were free to insult, order about, and even strike and murder blacks, and be justified by a white judge and white jury of their peers. "The thing now happens at some place in the country every day, and is growing worse instead of better. Separate marriage laws and the discussion of them are adding fuel to the flames."

Matters had reached the point where a black man could not even look in the direction of a white woman without arousing a policeman's suspicions, which could lead to the black man's arrest on a disorderly conduct charge; the thin excuse the police used to arrest someone. Alleged disorderly conduct, or violation of noise ordinances, or interference charges could be the overbroad catchall way for some police to arrest anyone for doing or saying anything they didn't like. The *Age* urged,

> The Negro must fight for his rights, the least and greatest, whenever they are assailed, or he will have none in the end. The Separate

---

[1065] *Freeman*, January 18, 25, 1913, February 1, 1913.
[1066] *John A. Johnson v. Luman T. Hoy*, U.S. Marshal, 227 U.S. 245 (1913).

Marriage law scheme should be fought to the bitter end. At the bottom of the whole scheme to isolate the Negro citizens in all of the public and private relations of life…in segregating them, separating them to themselves in living districts…and in branding them by law as so far inferior that they may not marry…as other races of the citizenship are free to do; in eating and drinking in places of licensed accommodation and amusement, and in accommodations in travel, by land and sea, as others are free to do – at the bottom of the whole scheme is to be found the slave-holders' doctrine, as formulated into the law of precedent by Chief Justice Robert B. Taney of the Federal Supreme Court in 1856, that "it has been so far held to be good law and precedent that a black man has no rights that a white man is bound to respect."

Blacks could not vote, which eliminated their political rights. True, technically they could vote, but their rights had been destroyed by the violence of organizations like the Ku Klux Klan, the Knights of the White Camilia, and the Red Shirts, and by legislative enactments upheld by the Supreme Court, which intentionally and functionally served to disfranchise most blacks. Only registered voters could serve on juries, so all-white juries passed judgment on blacks accused of crimes, and upon whites accused of crimes against blacks. Without political representation or protection in the courts, whites could pass whatever laws they wanted and practically do whatever they wanted.[1067]

Jack Johnson was famous the world over. Even in West Africa, the Nigerian-based *Lagos Standard* reported that Johnson was a practical prisoner in his own hotel, where he was guarded by about a dozen of Chicago's biggest roughs. He was afraid of being mobbed if he appeared on the streets.

Although initially he had drawn the color line, Luther McCarty changed his mind and said he would fight only one black man – Johnson, if a club would guarantee him $30,000 or give him 30% of the gate. His manager Billy McCarney said, "Johnson is the recognized champion, and we are after the real championship, and some money with it. Those dark skinned babies are real tough propositions, and I don't propose to give Langford a chance to earn all that Luther has worked so hard for, at least not right away."[1068]

On February 16, Johnson became very ill with a diagnosed case of typhoid-pneumonia. He was confined to bed-rest. The pneumonia was so severe that it caused a postponement of his trial.[1069]

Although there was discussion of Johnson potentially fighting Al Palzer in France, the *Freeman* noted, "The bout is planned for June, but there is little interest, as Negro pugilists just now are under the ban in France."

[1067] *New York Age*, February 6, 1913.
[1068] *Freeman*, February 8, 15, 22, 1913. New York was holding firm that it would not allow black fighters to box against white fighters. In Nashville, Tennessee, Johnson's prominence was blamed as being most responsible for the proposed bill to repeal the law allowing prize fighting.
[1069] *Chicago Defender*, February 22, 1913.

The *Freeman* observed how the white press gave top white boxer Luther McCarty different treatment than Johnson. No one gave McCarty grief for asking for a guaranteed $30,000. When Johnson asked for that much money to box Langford, he was called a hog. "Yet Johnson is a world's champion. McCarty is hardly out of the preliminary class."

The Canadian government declared that owing to moral turpitude, Johnson was designated as an undesirable and barred from admission into its country. The *Freeman* said the reason Johnson was hounded by the government and branded as an undesirable was because he was a black man who had won a white woman's heart. "Ten thousand pulpits refuse to thunder the Christ spirit as we understand it in this matter, seeing man as man."[1070]

On March 24, 1913 in Brisbane, Australia, Sam Langford and Sam McVey fought to a 20-round draw. In June, after Langford also fought a 15-round draw with Colin Bell, the *Freeman* noted that although some argued that Langford had a chance to beat Johnson, "nobody much believes it."[1071]

On March 31, Jack Johnson turned 35 years old. He celebrated at his residence at 3344 Wabash avenue.[1072]

On April 22, 1913, Jack Johnson via his attorney Ben Bachrach cut a plea deal in the jewelry smuggling case. He pled no contest, was fined $1,000, and forfeited the $2,000 diamond necklace. Judge Carpenter said there was no evidence to show that Johnson had smuggled the necklace personally (it was his now deceased wife Etta), though he attempted to conceal the fact of the purchase once he was in Chicago. Johnson initially claimed that the necklace had been brought to Chicago by a friend three weeks after he and his wife returned home.[1073]

[1070] *Freeman*, March 15, 22, 1913.
[1071] *Freeman*, June 28, 1913.
[1072] *Freeman*, September 20, 1913.
[1073] *Chicago Defender*, April 5, 12, 26, 1913.

CHAPTER 42

The United States vs. John Arthur Johnson

On May 5, 1913 in Chicago, in the United States District Court for the Northern District of Illinois, Eastern Division, in federal Judge George A. Carpenter's court, Jack Johnson's "White-slave traffic Act" trial began. Formally, it was entitled, "The United States vs. John Arthur Johnson, otherwise known as Jack Johnson." The trial would last nine days.[1074]

The White-slave traffic Act, informally known as the Mann Act, approved on June 25, 1910 and effective as of July 1, 1910, said in part,

> That any person who shall knowingly transport or cause to be transported, or aid or assist in obtaining transportation for, or in transporting, in interstate or foreign commerce...any woman or girl for the purpose of prostitution or debauchery, or for any other immoral purpose, or with the intent and purpose to induce, entice, or compel such woman or girl to become a prostitute or giver herself up to debauchery, or to engage in any other immoral practice; or who shall knowingly procure or obtain, or cause to be procured or obtained, or aid or assist in procuring or obtaining, any ticket or tickets, or any form of transportation or evidence of the right thereto, to be used by any woman or girl in interstate or foreign commerce...in going to any place for the purpose of prostitution or debauchery, or for any other immoral purpose, or with the intent or purpose on the part of such person to induce, entice, or compel her to give herself up to the practice of prostitution, or to give herself up to debauchery, or any other immoral practice, whereby any such woman or girl shall be transported in interstate or foreign commerce...shall be deemed guilty of a felony, and upon conviction thereof shall be punished by a fine not exceeding five thousand dollars, or by imprisonment of not more than five years, or by both such fine and imprisonment, in the discretion of the court.

The *Freeman* believed Johnson was on trial for daring to brave public sentiment and continuing his relations with white women. The charge against him, of white slaving, was an afterthought. White men were eager to see Johnson in prison owing to his known relations with white women, and because he was the "physical Zeus." If he had never bothered with white

---

[1074] Johnson was charged with violating 36 Stat. 825 (1910), 18 U.S.C. § 2421, by its own terms officially called the "White-slave traffic Act." (61st Congress, Sess. II, chapter 395, section 8). The bulk of the following description of the trial comes directly from the official court transcript and record.

women, he never would have been charged. The *Freeman* urged that under the circumstances, colored people, many of whom were hoping the worst for Johnson, should pray for his deliverance. If he was imprisoned, symbolically, it would be the biggest calamity to the black race since the days of freedom.

The *Chicago Defender* said, "Public sentiment is largely in favor of the champion, many persons believing that he has not received a square deal." His friends claimed the white newspapers had treated him unjustly.

Johnson complained that James J. Jeffries' admirers had hounded him since the Reno battle, and the court case was a direct outcome of his victory over Jeffries. Jack said, "All I want is a fair show." Johnson's attorney said, "If Jack goes free he will leave the United States at once."

The judge only allowed inside the courtroom the champion's immediate friends and duly accredited newsmen. Comparatively few of those in the big courtroom crowd were black.

Pursuant to attorney Benjamin Bachrach's advice, Johnson's wife Lucille did not attend the trial, for fear of inflaming the jury's passions. Bachrach said, "I am afraid it would prejudice the jury against Johnson. The jurors might think he was flaunting her in their faces."

The early part of the week was consumed with jury selection. One prospective juror who was challenged and excused admitted that the circumstances surrounding Etta Duryea's suicide might influence his voice in the jury room. An all-white all-male jury was seated. Women could not serve as jurors, and blacks rarely were included in jury pools, owing to restrictive laws which today would be considered violations of the 6th and 14th Amendments of the U.S. Constitution.

The eleven-count indictment, obtained by U.S. Attorney James Wilkerson, charged that on October 15, 1910, Johnson caused, paid for, aided and assisted the transportation of Belle Schreiber, "otherwise known as Mrs. J. Johnson," from Pittsburg to Chicago by railway for various illegal purposes, depending on the counts, which included prostitution, debauchery, unlawful immoral sexual intercourse (sex outside of marriage), and for committing the crime against nature with and upon her (anal and/or oral sex), all against the peace and dignity of the United States.[1075]

In his opening statement, U.S. government attorney Harry A. Parkin said that when traveling across the country, Johnson liked to have the company of women. Johnson had brought Belle Schreiber with him on a theatrical and fight tour for immoral purposes starting in 1909, taking her to New York, Boston, Pittsburg, Indianapolis, Toronto, Montreal, and then to Oakland at the time he had the Kaufman and Ketchel fights. Subsequently, he took her to places like Atlantic City, Boston, Pittsburg, and Chicago. During this time, he "posed and passed her as his wife."

[1075] At various times, "debauchery" has been defined as the leading of a chaste woman into unchastity, or to corrupt in morals, or to lead a lifestyle of habitual, excessive, unrestrained, or uninhibited indulgence, typically involving alcohol or drugs, which leads to sexually immoral activities.

Parkin alleged that at one point, in one city, Johnson had three different white women, Hattie [Watson, a.k.a. McClay], Etta [Duryea], and Belle Schreiber, having sexual intercourse with each of them. From 1909 to 1910, he took the three women with him to various cities at the same time, sometimes on the same train. He continued relations with these and other women even while married to Duryea, sometimes under the same roof where he lived with his wife, and said relations continued after her death.

The specific legally relevant allegations were that on or about October 15, 1910, Johnson paid Belle Schreiber's fare for a train ride to come from Pittsburgh to Chicago for immoral purposes. He sent her a telegram telling her to come to Chicago and wait at a certain place for him, and he sent her $75. Johnson had a sexual relationship with her, both before and after her arrival in Chicago. Once in Chicago, Johnson provided funds for Schreiber to use to set up a house of prostitution, and he purchased her furniture. Johnson further engaged in debauchery. Finally, "Another immoral purpose is one which is too obscene to mention, almost, to the jury trying the case, the purpose being for the defendant to compel these women to commit the crime against nature upon his body." Parkin also said,

> Now, it will appear, of course, that the defendant is a prize fighter; and in that connection it will be interesting, as the evidence develops, to see upon what victims he practiced the manly art of self defense. It will appear that these women who he carried about the country with him were, very, very many times, when he either had a fit of anger, or when the girls refused to do some of the obscene things which he demanded of them, - that he practiced the manly art of self defense upon them, blacking their eyes and sending them to hospitals, where he took care of them and paid their expenses until they recovered from the wounds which he had inflicted upon the faces and bodies of these women. Something may appear with respect to the prize fighting career of the defendant. We expect to put some evidence upon the stand which will develop the character of champion which the defendant professes to be; and also the real facts with respect to his championship, prior to the Jeffries fight.

Parkin further said that sometimes when Johnson had the three women with him, because of their differences and for other reasons, he would drop one off and put her into a "sporting house" (meaning house of prostitution) temporarily in order to relieve himself of the necessity of spending money carrying her about the country while he had the others.

In his opening statement on Johnson's behalf, defense attorney Benjamin C. Bachrach said that when Johnson came into prominence, "as is customary with a certain class of women, sporting women, they are attracted by an exhibition of physical prowess, and throw themselves in the way of a pugilist." Belle Schreiber was an "inmate," or member of the Everleigh Club in Chicago (a famous high-class sporting house/brothel), when Johnson first became acquainted with her.[1076] Johnson did not put her there. She was an ordinary regular prostitute well before she met Johnson. She worked in sporting houses across the country. Schreiber had consorted with many negro men, not just Johnson.

Bachrach said the law applicable to the case began on July 1, 1910, and hence anything done prior to that was irrelevant. The evidence would show that Johnson did not take Schreiber anywhere after the law went into effect, and did not send her a telegram asking her to meet him in Chicago, or aid her in doing so, but that Schreiber came of her own accord, and then, once in Chicago, asked Johnson for money for her residence, because she wanted her mother and pregnant sister to come live with her. Jack then paid for her furniture. This was in November 1910, before he married Etta Duryea (in January 1911). If Schreiber subsequently changed the residence into a house of prostitution, Johnson had nothing to do with it.

The government's first witness was Mervin Jacobowski (otherwise known as M. Mervin). He testified that in 1909 at Cedar Lake, Indiana, before the Ketchel fight, he saw Schreiber, who then was known as "Jack Allen," with Johnson at a party.

About a year later, on August 14, 1910 (after the Jeffries fight), Mervin came to Chicago and started working for Johnson as his chauffeur. That month, Mervin left Chicago for Cleveland with Johnson and then girlfriend Etta. Jack was on a theatrical tour. While in Cleveland, Johnson sent Mervin to a local hotel to pick up Schreiber/"Allen" and bring her to the Star theater, where Johnson was part of a twice-daily burlesque performance. After the performance, Mervin took Allen/Schreiber back to the hotel.

While in Detroit, Mervin again picked up Schreiber at Johnson's direction and brought her to the theater. An hour later, Mervin took her back to her hotel. He did this daily while in Detroit that week. He saw Schreiber on the stage; for she was a part of the vaudeville act.

He also saw Schreiber in Toronto, while Johnson and Etta Duryea were there. Belle also was in Buffalo, Montreal, and Boston while Johnson was in those towns. During Christmas 1910, in Milwaukee, Mervin saw Schreiber

---

[1076] The Everleigh Club was so famous and expensive that it was considered prestigious to be one of its clients. Moguls, actors, senators, athletes, and foreign dignitaries all used its services. The phrase "getting laid" came from this club, for patrons would say, "I'm going to get Everleighed." The mansion contained about 30 prostitutes, called "butterflies," who earned about $100 to $400 per week, much higher than the average salary of regular prostitutes, who earned about $25 - $50 per week. That said, even ordinary prostitutes earned quite well, especially given the limited economic opportunities for women. A 1916 U.S. Department of Labor study found that for the major legitimate occupations for women - department store clerking and light manufacturing - the average weekly wage was $6.67. Even skilled *male* trade union members only averaged roughly $20 per week. Hence, prostitutes earned very good money. The Everleigh Club paid about $800 a month in protection fees to law enforcement officials. Chicago was known as a place where prostitution thrived. The 1910 Chicago Vice Commission's study, whose report entitled *The Social Evil in Chicago* was issued in 1911, counted at least 1,020 brothels in the city, and 5,000 full-time prostitutes, not including streetwalkers and part-timers, and about 5 million clients. As a result, politicians and police began cracking down on prostitution, which eventually led to the closing of the Everleigh Club. Abbott, Karen, *Sin in the Second City*, Random House, 2007; "The Golden Age of Chicago Prostitution: A Q&A with Karen Abbott," by Melissa Lafsky, August 1, 2007, freakanomics.com; Russell, Thaddeus, *A Renegade History of the United States*, Free Press, 2011.

in a hotel with Johnson. No other woman was there. Johnson was ill at the time. This was all before Jack formally married Etta Duryea in January 1911.

Mervin said the only time he saw a woman named Hattie with Johnson was back in 1908 or 1909, in Chicago.

The government next called Lillian Paynter, who testified that in 1910 she ran a sporting house in Pittsburg. Belle Schreiber came to her house in March 1910 and stayed with her for about eight months. Julia Allen, a colored woman, also stayed there. Paynter was sick and hospitalized in late September or early October 1910, and when she returned home in October, Belle was gone. "My sister put her out of the house because she heard that Belle was mixed up with a colored man." Paynter said she had never seen Johnson there. "I don't know if Mr. Jack Johnson was the colored man, the name wasn't mentioned to me." She did not know where Belle went.

Estelle Paynter, Lillian's sister, testified that she ran the sporting house in 1910 with her sister. "Jack Allen," now known as Belle Schreiber, lived there for eight months, starting in March 1910. At one point, Belle briefly went to Atlantic City before returning. While Paynter's sister was in the hospital, after a man came to the house and spoke with Belle, Estelle ordered Belle out of the house, and she left the next day, somewhere around mid-October 1910. "I sent her away; I asked her to leave."

The next witness was John T. Lewis, who managed and rented apartment houses in Chicago. In 1910 he handled the Ridgewood at 28th and Wabash Avenue in Chicago. The building contained seventy apartments, from three to seven rooms each. "Jack Allen" rented a seven-room apartment, with first rent due on November 1, 1910, though she might have moved in sooner. She occupied that apartment for four months, until February 1911. She paid the rent. He did not know anything about her occupation. He stayed in apartment 425, while she was in apartment 424. Each apartment on the 4th floor was quite large, for there were only four on that floor; each containing several rooms. He could not say how many flats of prostitution were in the building at that time, or whether there were any.

Bertha Morrison testified that during 1910 she ran a sporting business in the Ridgewood Apartment building. In November 1910, she was in apartment 757. She saw Belle there from November to January. The entrance to apartment 425 is near the elevator, so that as Morrison passed up and down in the elevator, she could look right at the door. "I know that was a sporting flat. All flats in the Ridgewood Building were sporting flats, all of them to my knowledge." She had seen Johnson in the building in the elevator, and saw him entering Apartment 425 two or three times.

On cross examination, Morrison admitted that she had been inside only five of the seventy flats. She had never seen inside the Schreiber flat. She only knew (or believed) they were sporting flats through hearsay.

Chicago police officer John O'Halloran specialized in booking women into houses of prostitution for two years, and had booked women into houses of prostitution in the Ridgewood. (Yes, you read that right – a police officer was a booker of prostitutes.) He said about 20 apartments were out-

and-out houses of prostitution. The rest of the residents were "call girls" who went out on call to meet men at another location. However, he could not say for certain that every one of the residents was a prostitute. It just was the building's general reputation.

John T. Lewis was recalled, and again said he had no opinion or knowledge regarding the character of the apartments in his building.

Leopold Moss testified that he sold mattresses and furniture at Marshall Ventilated Mattress Co. at 908 Michigan Avenue in Chicago. During late October 1910, Johnson and Schreiber visited his business together. The government admitted into evidence a November 1, 1910 bill of sale, showing that the purchased goods were to be delivered to "Miss Jacque Allen" at 2730 Wabash Ave., Apartment 424, and included pillows, tables, beds, mattresses, springs, a three-piece suit, a rocker, chairs, dressers, commodes, rugs, carpet, table cloths, doilies, blankets, lace curtains, portierres, pillow cases, sheets, bed spreads, comforters, a table pad, sweeper, cuspidors, a kitchen set, socket poles, curtain poles, curtain rods, silverware, dishes, and pictures. Johnson paid $700 cash on a $1,196.53 bill, and signed a 30-day note for $500, which note was paid by Miss Schreiber sometime afterwards. The note was entered into evidence. After Schreiber complained that some of the articles were scratched badly in delivery, Moss went to the apartment one afternoon to see about it, and he saw Schreiber, her mother, sister, and Johnson there, as well as the furniture.

During the trial, Johnson had not been wearing the flashy clothes that hitherto characterized his dress. He wore a blue suit, black bowtie, and black shoes. There was an absence of his normal flash of diamonds, stickpin, or diamond rings, and the golden smile was not so apparent.

On Thursday May 8, Belle Schreiber took the stand at 11 a.m. and remained until 4 p.m. She testified that she was born in 1886 in Milwaukee and was 26 years of age. She first saw Johnson in April 1909 (when she was 22) at the Everleigh Club, a Chicago sporting house (of prostitution) where she was an inmate. The Court continually overruled throughout the trial Ben Bachrach's several objections that information prior to the passage of the Mann Act was irrelevant. Bachrach said the defense was admitting that the relations between Johnson and Schreiber were "intimate carnal relations."

Belle Schreiber, a.k.a. Jaque Allen, a.k.a. "Mrs. Jack Johnson"

Schreiber said she next met Johnson in New York City in May 1909. She received theatre tickets and several notes from him, and money via his manager George Little. "I met him frequently in New York, and had sexual intercourse with him." Johnson paid her expenses. She then went to Boston with him by motor car. A photo of Johnson and Schreiber seated in his automobile, surrounded by other persons, was admitted into evidence. Schreiber testified, "In my travels with the defendant I went under the name of Mrs. Jack Johnson, and registered at hotels under that name when I lived with him." They next went to Providence, then New York again, and then to Chicago via train. For a while, she stayed with his manager, Mr. Little, at 22nd and State Street. "I met the defendant frequently; I lived with him as his wife." She next went to Cedar Lake with Johnson and lived with him there for a few weeks. Jack started training for the Kaufman fight.

Throughout her testimony, Schreiber often would use hotel bills provided to her to refresh her recollection of the dates and locations. Interestingly, she had kept the bills for all these years.

Johnson traveled to San Francisco, and took with him a woman named Hattie, who had been with him in New York. Throughout the trial, Bachrach's objections to evidence regarding Hattie as being irrelevant and prejudicial were overruled. Johnson told Schreiber that he would send for her once he got located, which he did. "I received a telegram telling me to come to the ticket office, and to get a ticket and expense money and come out to San Francisco." She went to the ticket office and got the ticket and money that was waiting for her. She arrived in nearby Oakland in about September 1909 and stayed there, going by the name of "Mrs. Belle Leslie." Johnson met her there. At that time, Johnson was living with Hattie. However, "My intimate relations with the defendant continued during this time in Oakland."

After the September 9, 1909 Kaufman fight, Johnson took Schreiber to the Seal Rock Hotel in San Francisco. Johnson paid for her expenses. He kept introducing her as "Mrs. Jack Johnson." She lived with Jack at the Seal Rock Hotel until after the Ketchel fight in mid-October 1909. Next, she went to Chicago, traveling on the same train with Johnson, Hattie, George Little and his wife, and trainers.

When they arrived in Chicago, Schreiber lived on Indiana Avenue with a family. Johnson lived on Dearborn Street between 22nd and 23rd with Hattie. Nevertheless, Belle still saw Johnson frequently.

After Johnson went to Indianapolis in November 1909, he sent Schreiber money to follow him there. She used the name "Mrs. J. A. Gilbert." Little and Johnson both paid for her room, splitting the cost. She continued the same relations with Johnson there as at other places.

They went to Pittsburg for Thanksgiving. While there, she went by the name "Mrs. Jack Johnson." Then they traveled to New York.

Jack next went to Philadelphia, bringing Hattie with him, and subsequently sent Schreiber the money to purchase a ticket to Philadelphia. The same relations were maintained there. However, "This girl Hattie was living with him as his wife, and a girl by the name of Duryea, Etta Duryea." She claimed that Johnson introduced her to Duryea while all three were on the telephone line. Belle next left for Chicago and then home to Milwaukee.

Schreiber remained in Milwaukee until late January or early February 1910. However, at one point while she was there, she took a day trip to Chicago with her sister and saw Johnson, who told her to stay home until he sent for her.

When Parkin asked whether Johnson told her why he wanted her to stay home, Schreiber answered, "I was pregnant at the time." She told Johnson, who wanted her to have the baby. "He asked me to have this child and not to do anything to get rid of it."

Sometime during early February 1910, of her own motivation, Schreiber went to Cleveland, then Pittsburg, and then Detroit. She saw Johnson in Detroit. He bought her a ticket and sent her to Chicago, telling her to wait for him until he arrived. She went to Chicago with her sister. While Jack was in Milwaukee, he sent her money to come up there. Jack gave her money to pay the hotel bills.

Schreiber then returned to Chicago for a few weeks before going to Pittsburg and residing at the Paynter home, which was a sporting house. She was an inmate there for several months.

A month after the Jeffries fight, in early August 1910, Schreiber claimed that she received a letter from Johnson, along with money, asking her to come to Atlantic City. "I received a letter and money from the defendant before going to Atlantic City; I have not got the letter. The letter stated I was to come to Atlantic City. I destroyed the letter." For whatever reason, she had kept the bills, but not the letters (if such letters ever existed). She went to Atlantic City and stayed with him for two days at Young's Hotel. While there, she used the name Mrs. J. A. Gilbert. Her relations with Johnson were similar to those described at other places.

Before leaving Atlantic City, Schreiber alleged that Johnson told her to come to Chicago and look for an apartment; for "he said if I was sporting I might as well make the money for myself as to make it for others. He gave me the money to come to Chicago. I came." Johnson paid for her ticket from Atlantic City to Chicago. She was not able to find an apartment at that time. Johnson subsequently joined her in Chicago, and they maintained relations, just as they had at other locations.

Then Belle went to Cleveland, where she saw Johnson again. Mervin, the chauffeur, took her to the theatre. She stayed there for a week. Again they had relations.

Johnson took her to the train station, gave her money, and told her to purchase a train ticket and go to Detroit and meet him there, which she did. He arrived the next day. They were not living together at that point, but they maintained relations.

The next trip was to Buffalo. He went first, but gave her the expense money to follow him, telling her to meet him there. They had relations there every day. She did not see Etta in Cleveland, Detroit, or Buffalo.

In early September 1910, again Johnson "gave me my money, and told me to get a ticket and meet him in Toronto." She did. Etta Duryea was with him at that time. Yet, the same relations were maintained with Johnson in

Toronto. Next stop was Montreal, and again he gave her money for the train ticket, and again they maintained relations. Etta still was with him. Johnson gave Belle money for a ticket to Boston, the next stop, which still was during September 1910. She said their same relations were maintained there as well.

Johnson purchased and gave Schreiber a ticket to go to Pittsburg. She returned to the Paynter sisters' house. "Defendant knew where I was going, and what I was going to do when I got there. The Paynter house is the same house of prostitution that was testified to yesterday. I stayed there about two weeks. I was asked to leave the house." A man had come to the house and talked with Miss Paynter, and thereafter she was told to leave.

Belle went to the home of her maid, Julia Allen, and stayed nearly a week. "While there I received a telegram – I received several; I received money while I was there, $75. After I received the $75 I purchased my ticket and came on to Chicago."

At this point, Ben Bachrach made several objections, and outside the jury's presence, argued that the White Slave Traffic Act was unconstitutional, for the power to regulate vice and immorality was within the exclusive power of the state, and hence the act violated the 10th amendment of the U.S. Constitution, and that under the commerce clause, Congress could regulate interstate commerce, yet the acts forbidden by the Act were personal and not commercial, and that transporting a woman from one state to another for the purpose of having sexual intercourse with her was not within the spirit of the Act. He also made jurisdictional challenges. Judge Carpenter overruled all of the objections.

Parkin resumed his direct examination. Schreiber said, "I received the $75 from the Postal Telegraph Company in Pittsburgh, on the 17th of October, 1910, while I was still staying with Julia Allen. I left that same day for Chicago. I got my ticket with that money that I got." When she arrived in Chicago, as per Johnson's directions, she went to a private family's rooming-house on Indiana Avenue. After arriving, Johnson telephoned her there and asked her to meet him at the Vendome Hotel, which she did. "I went to a room with him." Johnson asked her, "Did you receive the $75 I sent you?" She responded, "Yes."

Johnson spoke to her about looking for an apartment. In a few days he had to go to New York. He said he would help her obtain furniture. "He said to me, to get my furniture and open a flat, and I might as well make the money as to give up half of what I was making to some one else, and for me to keep a couple of girls...and make money in that way."

The next day, she met Jack again, and he gave her between $100 and $150 and told her that it was to pay her rent and expenses. She went out and got a flat at the Ridgewood apartment building. She then went to purchase furniture, but did not recall whether Johnson was with her. She paid for it with Johnson's check. After one month, Johnson gave her more money to pay the remainder owed for the furniture. Schreiber got a sporting girl to come live with her.

Johnson came to the flat sometime after she opened up. Belle remained in the sporting house from October 1910 through February 1911. "Defendant called upon me there from time to time, between the first of November and the first of March. My relations with him were the same as I have detailed in other cities."

Schreiber also claimed that she went from Chicago to Milwaukee with Johnson for Christmas in December 1910, arriving via auto, and returning with him, traveling back and forth every day via train.

After his marriage to Etta Duryea in early 1911, Johnson told Schreiber that he would send for her.

When Parkin asked whether she ever gave Johnson any money, Schreiber replied, "I gave the defendant some money that I made once, $20, - that was in Chicago."

Admitted into evidence was a photograph of Johnson, with writing at the bottom in his handwriting saying, "To My Little Sweetheart, Bell, from Papa Jack, with best wishes." This concluded the direct examination.

Ben Bachrach cross-examined Schreiber. Belle said she lived in Milwaukee until she was 20 years old, and while there, she was a stenographer and typewriter. She then came to Chicago and became a regular sporting woman at the Everleigh Club, from December 1907 to April 1909. She first met Johnson while she was an inmate there. George Little was with him. She met up with Johnson a few days afterwards. "I received gifts from him in the way of theatre tickets and money." She saw him next in New York City, though Johnson had nothing to do with her going there on that occasion. "I practiced the profession of prostitution there." She and Johnson met up while there and became quite friendly.

Bachrach asked Belle about the photograph introduced into evidence, reading the inscription.

> Q. Were you his little sweetheart? A. I suppose I was. Q. Were you in love with him? A. I don't know. Q. What? A. I don't know. Q. Don't you know now – did you think you were then? A. I don't know what love is. Q. The favors that you extended to him, were they extended simply for money? A. I don't know. Q. What? A. I don't know. Q. You cannot say now whether you were in love with the defendant, or not? A. No. Q. At this time? A. I don't believe I ever was in love. The Court: No. the question is, did you give yourself up to the defendant out of affection or for compensation. A. Compensation mostly.

Schreiber said Johnson gave her clothes, jewelry, and diamonds, and paid for her expenses during their many trips. Each time they went to a new city, he gave her some money. "I always received money from him when I asked him for it." It paid for all of her expenses, and "gave me a little over to have in my pocket."

She had no explanation for why she had saved all of the hotel bills for so many years, and denied that her intent was to get out of him all the money she could. She usually showed Johnson the bill so he could see what expenses she incurred, and to ensure that he would believe her. Still, she did not explain why she kept the bills for years thereafter, but none of the alleged letters or telegrams. "I don't know why I saved the hotel bills and didn't save anything else."

Belle went to Pittsburg in early March 1910, to the Paynter's house of prostitution. "I had not seen the defendant at that time since January, 1910. The defendant and I were not on good terms between January and February at that time, so that my going to Pittsburgh, to go to the Paynter house, had no connection with the defendant whatever." Hence, going to the Paynter's home was her own decision and not influenced by Johnson. She went there to make money. She did not say why she was not on good terms with Johnson at that time. (Her testimony seems to contradict prior testimony that she still was seeing Johnson in January and February 1910).

About August 1, 1910, Schreiber traveled to Atlantic City, on the same train as Miss Paynter. She subsequently saw Johnson in Chicago, and then in Cleveland around August 15. She telephoned the theatre where Johnson was performing, informed them that she was in town, and gave the name of the hotel where she was. Johnson's chauffeur Mervin came and got her.

When she had been in a sporting house in Detroit back in 1909, Mr. Little saw her there, and reported to Johnson, who came and got her out. Her treatment there had not been bad; it was just as good there as at any other location. She had stayed at several houses of prostitution in several different cities, some for a short while, some longer. However, Johnson gave her money to leave and come to Chicago.

After the July 1910 Jeffries fight, she sent Johnson a telegram congratulating him. She did not hear from him until he was in Atlantic City in August 1910. "I don't remember whether I wrote to him at Atlantic City, or whether I called him up." It had been six or seven months since she and Johnson had been in contact. (So she reached out to him; not the other way around, as testified to previously. Recall also that she had testified that around February 1910, Johnson had told her not to get rid of the baby, and to remain home, but instead she returned to Pittsburg to practice prostitution, and she had testified that she and Johnson were "on the outs" around that time. Although she did not say why they were "not on good terms," one might possibly infer or speculate that it was because she had an abortion, though none of this was asked.)

Schreiber admitted that occasionally she contacted Johnson and asked for money whenever she was put out or refused admission into a house of prostitution, or was out of funds. So whenever she had financial issues, Johnson sent her money when she requested it, in order to help her. This happened about three or four times, and had nothing to do with him inducing her to travel to see him.

Schreiber was put out of the Paynter house in Pittsburg in mid-October 1910. She attempted to contact Johnson in New York. She spoke with his chauffeur, not Johnson. "I told him that I was put out of this place; that I did not know where to go and that I needed some money, and he said he would talk to the defendant and wire me the next day, which he did. ... I got a telegram the next day, asking me what my expenses would be." She later testified that the wire was signed, "Jack." She did not recall the exact amount she gave in her reply. "I received a wire saying that he was sending me $75, for me to go to Chicago and stay at Graham's and wait for him until he came back. I have not got that telegram now. I have not got any one of the other telegrams that I claim he sent me."

Schreiber had saved all of Johnson's telegrams until January 1912, when she destroyed them. So, despite the fact that she had kept all of the hotel bills, she had not kept Johnson's alleged telegram at issue in the case. When Bachrach asked whether she had destroyed the telegrams at an earlier point in time, right after she heard that Jack had married Etta, Belle denied doing so then. Bachrach was trying to show that she was jealous. Belle said,

> I don't know when he was married to her, whether in January 1911, or not. I heard of it; Johnson avoided talking to me about it. He never talked to me about it. I heard it from his mother; she told me around Christmas time of 1910, -- either that he was going to be or was married, - I don't remember.

Continuing her testimony, Schreiber said,

> The place at Graham's is that of a private family on Indiana Avenue. I had been there before. ... When I was put out of that place in Pittsburgh, I asked the defendant for money to help me get away because I didn't have any more friends. I lost all my friends, and he was the only one I could turn to. I suppose I regarded him as my friend, too. I thought it was due for him to see me through my trouble. Q. And did you love him then? A. I told you I did not know what love was.

Schreiber rated all of the hotels where she had stayed in various cities. Some were better than others, and some were the best in the city, but she was satisfied perfectly with the accommodations at all of them. She never was forced to go anywhere. She was asked, and she willingly accepted.

Again discussing the telegram sent to her while she was in Pittsburg, Schreiber claimed it said, "I am sending you $75; go to Chicago at Graham's, and wait until I get there," signed "Jack." She picked up the money from the Postal Telegraph Company, took a train to Chicago, and went to Graham's, arriving on October 18. Three or four days later, Jack called her on the telephone, and then she saw him at the Vendome Hotel.

Belle denied having asked Johnson to fit up her apartment so she could have a home for her mother and sister. Her mother always had a home in Milwaukee. However, she admitted that she mentioned to Johnson that her sister was in the family way and had to be taken care of, and wanted her sister to come live with her. She claimed to have made that statement after Jack told her that he wanted to get an apartment for her. Her mother came to visit, but did not live there. Her sister lived there while Belle was practicing prostitution there.

Schreiber testified that she had been in sporting houses in Chicago, New York, Pittsburg, Washington, and Detroit.

The first time she spoke with a government agent about Johnson was in Washington, D.C. in November 1912, at the time of the grand jury investigation. "I spoke to Mr. Horne, Chief of the Bureau of Investigation at the Department of Justice at that building in Washington." Since then, she had been earning money doing stenography work for a new reform association in connection with the Department of Justice in Baltimore. The Department of Justice was in charge of it. She was paid $15 a week, and the government paid her board at a rooming house, which was $5 a week. Government agents were watching and accompanying her everywhere.

She did not recall telling Mr. Horne about her claim that Johnson told her that she should get an apartment and he would fit it up, that as long as she was in the sporting business, she could make money for herself. "Q. Isn't it a fact that you did not tell it before the Grand Jury? A. I don't know." (The suggestion was that she had never before made such a claim, and it was a recent fabrication.)

The only ones with whom she had discussed her testimony were DeWoody and Parkin. She had gone over her testimony two or three times with them. DeWoody told her to refer to Johnson as the defendant.

After Etta Duryea died on September 14, 1912, Schreiber sent Johnson a telegram saying, "Dear Jack, - Bernice King and I sympathize with you in your recent bereavement. Sincerely, Belle Allen."

On re-direct, Schreiber testified that the jewelry and diamonds which Johnson gave her were taken away from her by him, and then the next girl, Etta Duryea, was wearing them. She testified that Hattie had worn the same jewelry before she did, before they were passed on to her. She said the money Johnson gave her was enough to pay expenses, but no more (contradicting her earlier testimony).

Schreiber claimed that she had practiced prostitution in Chicago from the time she first got the Ridgewood apartment.

On re-cross, Schreiber stated that at the time she started the Chicago flat, Johnson gave her money besides paying for the furniture, about $100 or $150. When she left with unpaid bills, Johnson later told her that he had paid them for her. She gave some furniture to her mother, sold the rest, and kept the money.

Some newspapers said it appeared that Schreiber was Johnson's girlfriend or common-law wife more than anything, and that he took care of her, starting well before the Mann Act's passage into law, but continuing thereafter as well.

Not reported in the official record, one newspaper claimed that Parkin asked her, "Did you have any discussion about coming here?" Schreiber responded, "No discussion. He beat me up so bad that..." An objection was interposed and the Court adjourned.

At that time, Judge Carpenter refused to allow the government to try to prove that Johnson beat Schreiber or other women, for such facts were irrelevant to the charge, even assuming they were true.

The next day, Julia Allen, colored, from Pittsburgh, testified that she had known Belle Schreiber since Thanksgiving 1909. Belle was known then as Mrs. Jack Johnson. That was how she was introduced. People called her Johnson's wife. Belle was in Pittsburgh with the champ. In August 1910, Belle received money via telegram and then left for Atlantic City.

In October 1910, Belle was living with Allen at Allen's house. Allen had been Belle's maid. After a telegram came, they went down to the Postal Telegraph, and Belle received $75. Allen went with Belle to Frank Sutton's hotel, had supper, and then Belle bought a ticket for Chicago and left.

Hattie Watson testified next. She first met Johnson in New York City in August 1907, after he had fought Fitzsimmons. At the time she met him, she was living in a "Call House," going out on sporting calls. The Court sustained Ben Bachrach's objections to further testimony from the witness, feeling that in light of the relations between Schreiber and Johnson and the admissions made already, it was not necessary to go into a state of affairs involving another woman. Regardless, the point was made. The woman named Hattie, whom Johnson for several years had been calling his wife, was a prostitute, like Schreiber. Both women had several aliases.

James Stillwell, the Pennsylvania Railroad company's attorney, testified that the rail company had routes between Pittsburg and Chicago during October 1910.

The government rested its case. At that point, Ben Bachrach moved for a judgment of acquittal as a matter of law. He particularly asked for a dismissal of those counts for which no evidence was introduced. At that point, the government agreed in part and asked for a withdrawal of counts 6 and 11, which charged that the purpose of Johnson's transportation of Schreiber was to commit the crime against nature. The Court granted the motion as to these counts. Bachrach again attacked the Act's constitutionality, as he had done before.

Regarding the lack of evidence in the case, Bachrach noted that no evidence had been introduced substantiating Schreiber's claim that Johnson had sent or asked someone to send on his behalf the purported telegram to Schreiber telling her to come to Chicago, or that the telegram said what she claimed it did. Furthermore, even assuming he had sent such a telegram, there was no evidence showing that his purpose at the time was for prostitution, debauchery, or some other immoral purpose. Further, even assuming that once she arrived in Chicago he told her to make money in the business of prostitution (which the defense did not grant), that was consistent with the theory that such thought and purpose occurred to Johnson *after* she arrived, not at the time the money was sent to her. The statute required the government to prove that at the time he assisted her in making interstate travels, his purpose in rendering such assistance was that she would engage in prostitution and/or immoral acts. The evidence was purely circumstantial, and the rule was that the circumstances proven must exclude the theory of innocence and not simply be consistent with guilt. Judge Carpenter denied the motion for judgment of acquittal.

The defense called witnesses on its behalf. First up was Charles Lumpkin, a Johnson chauffeur. On Christmas day, 1910, he drove Johnson, trainer Barney Furey, and Miss Schreiber to Milwaukee. Johnson became sick and urinated some blood. Owing to his illness, he did not box at the theatre that day. Schreiber was not around when he took Johnson to the train station.

Barney Furey testified that he had been Johnson's trainer for eight or nine years. Furey lived at 3344 Wabash Avenue, in Jack's mother Tina Johnson's house. The family lived there – Johnson, his wife, mother, sister, niece, nephew, Joe Levy, the maid, and himself.

In August 1910, Furey was with Johnson on all of his trips. They left Chicago on August 15 heading for Cleveland, and traveled all over the East. Furey said he had seen Schreiber in Cleveland on the stage with Johnson. He did not recall seeing Belle in Detroit. The woman who traveled with Johnson was Etta Johnson, as he called her, though technically she was not yet his wife. He did see Belle on the stage in Buffalo, speaking to one of the show girls, but that was the only time he saw her there. He either saw her in Toronto or Montreal, on the same stage where Johnson was working. He did not see Belle in Boston. Belle was not in the traveling party; Mrs. Etta Johnson was.

The Johnson party was in Scranton on October 15, 1910, and left for New York on the 16th. They were in seventeen different cities over the next month or so, some for one or two days, some for a week or more, before returning to Chicago.

Back in Chicago, at the Ridgewood, Furey had seen Schreiber, her mother, sister, and a girl named Lillian (most likely Lillian Paynter).

Furey was in the car with Johnson and "Jack Allen" when they went to Milwaukee in December 1910. On the train ride back, Allen/Schreiber was not there.

Mervin Jacobowski testified that Schreiber was not with their party in Milwaukee in December 1910, nor was she on the train ride back.

Charles Bud Redd said Schreiber came to Milwaukee during Christmas 1910 in an auto driven by Lumpkin, and she stayed at his house that week.

Testifying next was Frank Sutton, a Pittsburgh hotel proprietor. In September or October 1910, Belle Schreiber came to his hotel seeking information regarding where Johnson was. "I says I don't know where he is at, he is somewhere with his show, and I says if you telephone to Barrett Wilkins on 35th Street, New York City, probably he can let you know just where the show is at." Schreiber got the telephone number. She called but they did not know where he was. She came back the next day and telephoned again. "I heard her say something about money and she said she was in trouble and she needed a favor of him."

A few days later, she came back and had a check in the name of Jack Allen. She couldn't get it cashed under that name, so Sutton cashed it for her. It was $70 or $75. A colored lady by the name of Allen was with her, as well as Belle's sister and her sister's husband.

They had dinner, and after Belle finished eating, "she bid me good-bye, and she said her sister and her husband were going to Chicago and she was going to Washington City."

James Morrison, a theatrical man, said that during October 1910 he was in New York, and on October 17, he saw Johnson, who was there for several days. Peter M. Doyle confirmed that on October 17 he was with Morrison in New York.

John A. Johnson, popularly known as Jack Johnson, decided to waive his 5th amendment rights, and testified on his own behalf. He was 35 years old. He said that between October 1 and October 20, 1910, he was not in Chicago. "I did not receive any communication from any person about Belle Schreiber in October. The last part of September I received a telegram from her." He spoke with her via long distance telephone either on the 2nd or 3rd of October. "She asked me if I would send her $75, that she was sick and needed it, and I told her I would." A couple days later, he sent her money via telegram, but not a written message with it.

> Only a money order. Q. Only an order for money? A. That is all. Q. Did you in the month of October or September...send a telegram to Belle Schreiber in Pittsburgh instructing her to go to Chicago at Graham's and wait for you there? A. I don't think I did. The Court: What is the answer? A. I don't think I did. Q. Well, do you know? A. I am not positive. Q. Have you any doubt about it? A. Well, I might have sent her one. Q. You might have what? A. I might have sent her one telling her that, but I don't remember doing so, and my reasons for that are that other fellows attended to all my business. ... Q. What do you mean by that, you personally did not send one but somebody else might have? A. Yes, sir, that is it. Q. I am asking you, did you send one yourself? A. No, I did not. Q. Did you give any one authority to send it? A. I did not. Q. Did you instruct any person to send a telegram of that kind? A. I did not. The Court: Do you know of any one at that time sending a telegram to that effect? A. I do not, sir. ... Q. When was the first time you ever heard of such a telegram being sent, if there was one sent? A. When I was sitting in the chair. Q. And when Belle Schreiber said it on the witness stand? A. Yes, sir.

Johnson further testified,

> I did not, while in Atlantic City [in August 1910], tell Belle Schreiber that, inasmuch as she was engaged in the sporting business, it would be better for her to go into the business for herself, and that she should take an apartment and that I would furnish it for her in order that she might be in the sporting business, or words to that effect. At the time I sent that $75 to Belle Schreiber I sent it from New York,

> and at the time I sent that $75 I did not intend that Belle Schreiber should go from Pittsburgh to Chicago in order to engage in the business of prostitution. At the time I sent that $75 I did not intend that Belle Schreiber should come to Chicago for the purpose of leading a life of debauchery. At the time I sent that $75 I did not intend that Belle Schreiber should go from Pittsburgh to Chicago in order that I might have sexual intercourse with her. At the time I sent that $75 I had no intention at all as to where Belle Schreiber should go from Pittsburgh, or if she should leave Pittsburgh at all. She didn't say where she was going; she said she was sick. I had no intention on the subject. I did not directly or indirectly, -- by word of mouth or otherwise, give her any direction at the time I sent that money, or shortly before that time, to the effect that she should go to Chicago.

Johnson said the Barney Oldfield race took place about October 25, 1910, and a few days before that race he went to Chicago after Mr. Beerly telephoned him and asked him to come there, because they had a lawsuit pending with George Little regarding a diamond ring.

> I did not go there to see Belle Schreiber. After I got to Chicago I met Belle Schreiber at the Vendome, she called me up at my mother's home. When I met her at the Hotel Vendome she told me that her sister was going to be sick, that she was pregnant, and that she wanted a place for her mother and her sister, and she asked me would I furnish a flat for her. I said certainly, I will do anything to make you happy; and she says, 'All right,' and she asked me where to go and I gave her a card of introduction to a furniture man, --- and she went there and got what she wanted, and I gave her the money to pay for it. ... Besides the furniture at that time I gave her $500 to start with, to start a home and keep her mother until she got a position, -- she told me she was going to work at stenography. She had done stenography work for me, lots of it.

Hence, his version was that after he had helped her, Schreiber subsequently came to Chicago of her own accord, and that she called *him* once she arrived, not the other way around, and none of this had been done at his request. He meant to help her, and did so with no particular purpose in mind.

Johnson denied several of Schreiber's claims, including her allegation that when they met at the Vendome in Chicago that he told her that since she was sporting she might as well make money for herself with her own flat and that he would furnish it. "I never spoke any such words to her, or any one else. I never gave her any diamonds. I never loaned her any. I never permitted her to wear any. She bought some in Buffalo, but I did not pay for them."

Johnson said he paid some unpaid bills at the Ridgewood for Schreiber before he sailed to Europe on May 6, 1911. "I have not thought over the exact amount of money that I have given to Belle Schreiber since I have known her. As near as I can guess, it would be between nine and ten thousand; that includes all that I spent on her, everything – expenses and everything. She did not give me $20 at any time."

Regarding Christmas 1910, Jack said they made a trip by auto to Milwaukee. He, Lumpkin, Furey, and Belle were in the car. Jack was ill at the time. Schreiber did not return with him. She was not on the train. He later spoke with her. "In explanation, she said she was a little angry because I was coming to Chicago every day and was not paying the proper attention to her." He told her that preparations were being made for his marriage to Etta, which explained his lack of attentiveness to Belle.

Regarding Belle's claims that she was with Johnson on many trips in a drawing-room of a train car, Johnson said, "I never rode with her on a car any time in my life but once on a train, that was in 1909. Q. And since then you have never ridden with her? A. Never in my life."

Johnson said he had nothing to do with her selection of the Ridgewood apartment. He went there when she complained that the furniture had been scratched, and saw the furniture dealer there, as well as her mother and sister. "I don't know that I was there at any other time. I think I was there once."

Jack sent the $75 to her either from New York or Pennsylvania, but was not in Chicago at the time.

Of his testimony, a newspaper said that at first, Johnson spoke in a slow voice, and at times hesitatingly. Sweat stood out on his forehead and trickled down his face. After 15 minutes on the stand, his voice grew more distinct and he seemed more at ease. The direct examination lasted a little less than 30 minutes.

Harry Parkin cross-examined Johnson. Jack said he told Belle in Milwaukee that he had become engaged and could not pay any more attention to her because of his approaching marriage. Etta was in the Chicago hospital at the time. Over Bachrach's relevancy objections, Judge Carpenter allowed Parkin to ask Johnson the following questions about Etta Duryea:

> Q. What was the occasion of her being in the hospital? A. She was sick, that is all I know. Q. That is all you know about it? A. That is all I know. Q. What was the cause of her sickness? A. I don't know. Q. As a matter of fact that was a sickness caused by blows from your hands, wasn't it? ... A. No. ... Q. Well, was it caused by blow or blows from your hand? A. No, no. Q. Was it not caused by blows received by Etta Duryea in Pekin Theater here in Chicago at your hands? A. No. Q. Did you not carry her out or have her carried out and put in the automobile and taken to the Washington Park hospital after you had beaten her up? A. No, no, and I will take an oath on it, no.

Johnson said he did not know that Schreiber had been running a sporting house at the Ridgewood. He again denied ever taking money from her. He pointed out that such a claim was ridiculous, given that he was making $2,500 a week. He did not see Schreiber in Chicago until a couple of weeks after he had sent her the money. He arrived in New York on the 16th. He did not recall exactly when or where he was when he sent the money or spoke with Belle.

The champ again said he did not recall whether or not he sent Schreiber a telegram telling her to go to Graham's. He could not say he did not, nor could he say that he did. "I don't remember."

Jack denied having Belle come to Atlantic City, and said he did nothing with her while there. "I never had her come to Atlantic City." He did not give her any money while there either, or pay for her bills. He denied having sexual relations with her while there.

Jack denied knowing the character of the Ridgewood as a sporting house. "Q. And you did not know it was full of fast women? A. I didn't know anything about the fast women. I was not keeping up with them. Q. You were not keeping any of them. You kept Hattie, didn't you?" Objections were sustained.

Several times Johnson denied having as many as three women at a time in his travels. He denied having Hattie, Etta, and Belle with him at the same time. He did not have them traveling with him. The judge overruled Bachrach's relevancy objections to this line of questioning.

Johnson denied ever calling up Belle and introducing her to Etta over the telephone.

Jack said the woman who testified using the name of Hattie Watson was known by him as McClay. "She had three or four names. I called her by the name Mac – McClay. I called her Mac. Her first name is Anna, or something. I knew her by the name of Anna – Anna McClay. I never called her Hattie, never in my life that I know of."

Parkin attacked Johnson's relationship with Etta Duryea, even though said relationship had nothing to do with the charges. "How long prior to the time she got her divorce were you living with her and going around the country with her? A. I don't know, I don't remember." Judge Carpenter overruled Bachrach's relevancy objections, saying, "This is not a question of the cross-examination of an ordinary witness. The Government is entitled to go into the history of any defendant." Jack said he first met Etta in New York City in 1909, but was not certain of dates or who he was with when. "I have told you I never kept tab of those things. I am here today and gone tomorrow. I never kept any tabs. I was too busy; I had too much to think of."

Johnson said he did not have Belle and Anna "Mac" in San Francisco with him. He did not pay Anna's way out there. Lots of people came to see him. He denied having sexual intercourse with Anna "Mac" on the day of the Kaufman fight. "I did not. After a man has a fight, he is not feeling like it." Judge Carpenter continually overruled Bachrach's objections that such questions were totally irrelevant to the issues at hand, particularly since the questions pertained to acts prior to the Mann Act's passage, and with different women than Schreiber.

Johnson denied having Hattie and Belle with him while training for the Ketchel fight in 1909. They may have been in the city, but they were not with him.

Parkin even asked about the Ketchel fight:

> Q. Did you win the Ketchel fight? A. Did I win it? Q. Yes? A. It is in the book, doesn't the book say so? Q. Just answer my question. Did you win the fight? A. I suppose I did. Somebody might say I did not. Q. You knew you were going to win it before you went into it, didn't you? A. I did. The Court: Now you are going into the question of a man's self confidence. Parkin: No, no, not at all. Bachrach: No, he wants to show that the fight was crooked or something like that. Johnson: They are all crooked.

Eventually, after some debate between Parkin and Bachrach, the Court sustained objections to this line of questioning.

Johnson did admit to bringing both Belle and Mac back with him from San Francisco to Chicago. Part of the way, they were in the same drawing-room on the train. At times, they occupied the same state room as well. Of course, that was in 1909, before the Mann Act was passed.

Parkin again asked suggestive questions to Johnson about violence towards the women, and the Court overruled Bachrach's objections.

> Q. Hattie was in the hospital while you were there, was she? A. Not that I know of. Q. Did you have any difficulty with her about putting her in a hospital? A. No. Q. Did you have any similar difficulty with Belle, -- fisticuff difficulty? A. I don't understand the definition of the word. Q. You had had with Belle, hadn't you? A. What is that? Q. You had struck Belle on various occasions? A. Never in my life. Q. Do you remember using an automobile tool on her? A. Never in my life. Q. You never did that? A. Never. Q. You say you did not? A. I say no; emphatically no. Q. And bruised her side until it was black and blue?

The Court finally put an end to this line of questioning, although prior to that point Judge Carpenter had overruled all of Bachrach's objections.

Jack said Belle did not return from Milwaukee with him on the train in late December 1910. "She never made a trip with me but once in her life on the train." An upset Belle left him in Milwaukee because she said he had not paid her enough attention. He told her that he was going to get married. He did not go to see her after that, but she came to see him.

> Q. And you and she were living there together during that time? A. During what? What she? Q. You and Belle? A. What she are you talking about? You have got three shes mixed up. Which one? Q. Were there so many you couldn't tell? A. No sir. But there were three you just named. I want to know which one. Q. I am talking about the Milwaukee trip, did you have any more than one up there? A. I did not. ... Q. I say subsequent to the time that you told Belle, and

subsequent to the time that you made up your mind to marry Etta, you and Belle were living together at Milwaukee? A. Some of the time. Q. Yes. A. Yes, sure.

Jack said he married Etta Duryea on January 18, 1911 in Pittsburg.

Parkin asked Johnson whether he had any other women with him that he traveled with besides Hattie, Belle, and Etta, since July 1910. "No." Parkin kept pressing the issue, suggesting there was a girl from New Jersey who was on the train with him in Philadelphia, upon whose finger he placed a diamond ring, took to Pittsburg, then sent back, and then gave the ring to Hattie, or "Anna Mac." Johnson denied the allegations contained in each question. Bachrach's objections to each question were overruled.

On re-direct, Johnson said that prior to being charged, he did not know there was such a thing as the White Slave Traffic Act. Bachrach again asked him whether he had sent a telegram to Schreiber telling her to come to Chicago and stay at Graham's. "I never sent such a telegram in my life. Not in my life. Never in my life. I never sent it. I never have known it was sent."

The Defense rested its case.

The government called rebuttal witnesses. First up was Roy Jones, who formerly had been in the saloon business. He had a conversation on Christmas Eve 1910 with Johnson about Etta Duryea. Judge Carpenter overruled Bachrach's objections. Jones said, "Mr. Johnson asked me if I would not go out to the hospital with him to call upon his wife. ... Well, he told me that his wife was sick, that she had been in a little trouble, and they had a fight or something." Jack told him the fight was at Bob Mott's café. "I guessed there was some misunderstanding between them, and he asked me – he told me that she had always – that she had always had a lot of confidence in me and had known me for quite a little while and he tried to get me to intercede and bring them together again." ... "Q. I will ask you if he did not also state that he wanted to go there to see her so that any prosecution by her against him might be stopped? A. Yes, sir."

Jones also confirmed that he saw Johnson with Schreiber in Milwaukee during Christmas 1910.

On cross-examination, Jones admitted that he had his saloon license taken away a month ago, but recently had it restored. Bachrach implied that the government got him his license returned after agreeing to testify against Johnson.

The government rested its case.

Bachrach again made motions for acquittal, which initially were denied. However, later, in addition to dismissing the charges of crimes against nature, the Court also dismissed the counts charging that Johnson's reason for sending Schreiber money was for travel for the purposes of debauchery. No proof had been submitted sustaining those counts.

A night session was held so the attorneys could make their closing arguments to the jury. Unfortunately, those arguments were not recorded by the court reporter. However, the press reported that in his closing argument, U.S. government attorney Harry Parkin said, "If you should find this defendant not guilty, knowing as you do the evidence in the case, I do not see how any of you can go home and look squarely into the faces of those you respect and admire."

Defense attorney Ben Bachrach maintained that the jury was not to consider Johnson's general record and behavior. "If he sent her the money to come to Chicago for immoral purposes he is guilty. That is the only thing to be considered by the jury." He argued that Johnson sent her money because Schreiber asked for it, because she was in need of help, not because he wanted her to come to Chicago for immoral purposes. Bachrach also argued there was no proof that Johnson had aided or abetted in some way the transportation of one or more women from state to state for his commercial gain through their immorality.

Judge George Carpenter instructed the jury that they were to determine whether, on or about October 15, 1910, Johnson caused Schreiber to be transported from Pittsburgh to Chicago for the purpose of prostitution, or for the purpose of having unlawful sexual intercourse with her. He also said to the all-white male jury,

> Gentlemen of the jury, you must realize, and I shall charge you, that a colored man in the courts of this country has equal rights with a white man. He is entitled to the same kind of a trial and the same laws protect him, and you must return the same kind of a verdict in this case as you would render to a man of your own color were he accused as is the defendant. ...
>
> When you get into your jury room and discuss the matter here you will look at these things from a great many different standpoints, but you are entitled to take into consideration that the prosecuting witness in this case is an abandoned woman, she is an unfortunate creature. You might, so far as the evidence in this case is concerned, call her the discarded mistress of the defendant. That you are entitled to take into consideration. You are also entitled to take into consideration the fact that the defendant himself testified. He did not have to testify. The law permits him, and when he does testify his evidence must be given, if you believe it, must be given the same weight that you would give the evidence of any other competent witness; but you not only have a right to take into consideration, but you must take into consideration that the defendant himself is vitally interested in the outcome of this case, and so you must look at the evidence here from every conceivable standpoint. We have had prostitutes, we have had trainers, we have had hangers-on and we have had all kinds of unfortunate people here, but the mere fact that they are unfortunate does not bar them from testifying, it does not necessarily mean that they have not told the truth, but it is your duty, pleasant or unpleasant, to sift all this evidence through and through to see where the truth lies. ...

The law does not apply solely to innocent girls. It is quite as much an offense against the Mann Act to transport a hardened, lost prostitute as it would be to transport a young girl, a virgin. You are not concerned either with the location of the defendant when the money was sent or telegraphed, if you find from the evidence that he did send or telegraph the money. ... Now, he says that he sent it out of the goodness of his heart. She tells you an entirely different story. Now, it is for you to take all the evidence in this case and to satisfy yourselves beyond all reasonable doubt what the purpose of the defendant was in sending her the $75. The defendant himself admitted that he sent it. He claims that his purpose was good; the Government charges that his purpose was bad. Now, that purpose is one of the essential elements in this case and is something that you will have to settle to your own satisfaction beyond a reasonable doubt. ... You are not concerned with the defendant's morals save only as it may give you some light on his general character; it may give you some information as to what his intention was when he did the things, if he did the things that he is charged with here.

It is not necessary in order to constitute a violation of this law that it be charged that the defendant shall have received some profit out of the woman transported. I mean pecuniary profit. That is not an essential element at all.

But there is one thing that I neglected to state, gentlemen, that the Government has not introduced any evidence under counts 2, 4, 6, and 11 in this case, and I instruct you, therefore, when you take the indictment to your consultation room you are to disregard entirely those four counts, so that your deliberations will be based solely on counts 1, 3, 5, 7, 8, 9, and 10. ...

No evidence has been introduced on the debauchery counts, or on the counts charging the defendant with the crime against nature. The counts remaining are the counts which charge that the woman was transported from Pittsburgh to Chicago for the purpose of prostitution and the counts which charge that she was transported for the purpose of sexual intercourse.

Judge Carpenter dismissed four of the counts as a matter of law, ruling that the government had presented no evidence of debauchery or crime against nature. Of course, the question is why then did the government put forth such charges, other than to try to prejudice the jury against Johnson by mere suggestions?

The *Freeman* believed that Mr. Parkin, realizing his inability to make a case, resorted to irrelevant matter wholly immaterial to the case at bar, in an attempt to prejudice the jury. It was a character assassination, rather than a case based on evidence. Mr. Parkin unsuccessfully tried to show the jury that Johnson at times beat and slugged Schreiber and forced her to do things that otherwise she would not have done.

On May 13, 1913 at 10:45 p.m., the case was given to the jury to decide. After about an hour of deliberations, that same evening the jury returned guilty verdicts on all seven counts of violating the federal White Slave Traffic Act, otherwise known as the Mann Act. When the clerk announced the word "guilty," Johnson's smile faded. The cherished hope of his enemies had been realized. A moment after the guilty verdict was read, a force of deputy marshals surrounded Johnson.

Johnson's attorney immediately made a motion for a new trial. The judge scheduled a hearing for arguments on the motion for May 19.

Judge Carpenter overruled Parkin's motion on behalf of the government that Johnson immediately be ordered confined in the county jail. Johnson would be allowed to be free on bond until he was sentenced.

Afterwards, Johnson said, "I have nothing to say. My attorney will speak for me." Bachrach said, "I can't account for the verdict. The case was a hard one but I was confident of an acquittal." Later, Johnson said, "I have fought a good fight but I lost."[1077]

Afterwards, a gloating Assistant U.S. District Attorney Harry Parkin said,

> This verdict will go around the world. It is a forerunner of laws to be passed throughout the entire country forbidding miscegenation. Many persons believe the negro has been persecuted. Perhaps as an individual he was, but his misfortune will be a foremost example of the evil in permitting intermarriage between whites and blacks. He must bear the consequences.[1078]

The *Freeman's* Billy Lewis said that Parkin's comments proved that Johnson had been struck below the belt. It was obvious that Johnson was not being prosecuted for being good to Belle Schreiber, but persecuted for marrying his white wives.

> Perhaps this is the first time in the history of the country where a federal court officer has given it out that a prosecution was not based on the charges preferred; that a race prejudice was the underlying motive of the prosecution; that it was in the interest of the race division. All of this is appalling in view of the source from which it came. Judge Carpenter completed this iron bed of Pisistratus, when he said that the "character of the prosecuting witness must not be considered." Says he further: "The fact that the prosecuting witness is a discarded mistress, an abandoned woman, does not affect the issue in this case."

> And then this far fetched assertion: "We have had many unfortunate people here in this case – trainers, fighting camp hangerson and women of the underworld – but because of their status in life their evidence must not be disregarded."

[1077] *Chicago Defender*, May 10, 17, 1913; *Freeman*, May 10, 17, 24, June 7, 1913; *Daily Capital Journal*, May 8, 1913. *San Francisco Call*, May 9, 1913. *El Paso Herald*, May 9, 1913. *Day Book*, May 10-12, 1913.
[1078] *East Oregonian*, May 14, 1913.

Lewis was certain that if other cases were cited, in which men had been convicted and sentenced to prison,

> I am quite sure not a single one will be anything similar to the Belle Schreiber affair. Here was a woman living with a man as her husband. She was carried about the country and introduced as Johnson's wife, at least. It was so understood. He sends her money, oodles of money, more money than most Negroes have ever seen, and she is worked within the meaning of the law. I am basing my judgment on Mr. Mann's sound sense, that his law was conceived to correct a well-known abuse, that of deceiving innocent, unsuspecting women into houses of disrepute, or decoying them to assignations of which they were not aware, and not to interrupt the movements of seasoned women of the world, when moving about with a full knowledge of what they are doing.

However, the judge also had said, "It is as much an offense under the Mann act to transport a hardened woman as an innocent girl. It is not necessary that a person accused of violating the act shall receive a profit through transportation of a woman."

Johnson's attorney rightfully contended that an individual's right to travel from place to place could not be denied. Johnson said he did not invite Schreiber to Chicago. He had no particular purpose in giving her the money, other than she asked for help. Even if Johnson had asked her to come to Chicago, without stating a purpose, he clearly had that right. "He might send and invite the Queen of Sheba, and if she don't want to come, let her stay at home. Johnson beat the case to a frazzle, it is very evident to see. ... It is to be hoped that the government will not be put in the unenviable light of persecuting a race."[1079]

On May 16, the proposed Illinois state anti-interracial marriage bill was killed in committee.[1080]

As of May 18, Johnson said he was broke and needed money, and wanted to fight Luther McCarty. He asked the court to defer his sentencing for 60 days, and for permission to leave the district so he could fight. The Court denied his motion.[1081]

On May 24, 1913 at Tommy Burns' arena located just outside the city limits of Calgary, Alberta, Canada, after 2 minutes of fighting in the 1st round, 210-pound Arthur Pelkey knocked out cold 200-pound "white heavyweight champion" Luther McCarty with a clean left hook to the jaw. McCarty did not wake up, and was pronounced dead at the scene.

Some said it was a dislocated neck. A blood clot was found on McCarty's brain. His spinal cord was ruptured and there was a hemorrhage.

[1079] *Freeman*, May 24, 1913.
[1080] *Freeman*, May 10, 1913; *Chicago Defender*, May 17, 1913.
[1081] *Grey River Argus*, May 29, 1913.

The next day, Tommy Burns' arena was burned down, likely by arson. The incident would end boxing in western Canada for a while.[1082]

On June 1, 1913 in Belgium, French light heavyweight Georges Carpentier won the European heavyweight championship by knocking out Bombardier Billy Wells in the 4th round.[1083]

On Wednesday June 4, 1913 in Chicago, after his motion for a new trial was denied, Jack Johnson was sentenced. When imposing sentence, Judge George Carpenter said,

> It has been hard to determine what punishment should be meted out in this case. We have had many cases where violations of the Mann act have been punished with a fine only. We have had other cases where defendants have been sentenced to one or two years in the penitentiary. The circumstances in this case have been aggravating. The life of the defendant, by his own admissions, has not been at all a moral one. The defendant is one of the best known men of his race, and his example has been far reaching. The court is bound to take these facts into consideration in determining the sentence to be imposed. In this case the defendant shall be confined one year and one day in the Leavenworth penitentiary and that he shall pay a fine of $1,000.

Well known for being a rabid white supremacist and segregationist, U.S. Attorney General James C. McReynolds, whom U.S. President Woodrow Wilson had appointed earlier that year, had sent a telegram to James Wilkerson before the sentencing, informing him that the Leavenworth penitentiary was designated as the place of confinement specifically for Johnson. "This is special designation in this case only and does not affect generally existing designation Joliet institution for United States prisoners convicted [in] your district. Please have court order entered accordingly. McReynolds." Judge Carpenter had honored the request and ordered Johnson confined to the maximum security Leavenworth prison instead of the usual Joliet penitentiary. The following year, in 1914, McReynolds would be appointed to and confirmed as a U.S. Supreme Court Justice. He would serve until 1941, and his open racial bigotry would permeate his opinions and conduct as a justice.

Ben Bachrach and Gustav Beerly were granted time to prepare a writ of error for an appeal. Johnson was allowed to remain free upon bond, pending his appeal's disposition.

[1082] "White heavyweight champion" Luther McCarty was only 21 years old. His father was an Indian "half breed" and his mother Irish. His loss and death were shocking, for McCarty had been boxing's hottest contender, with quality victories over Carl Morris, Jim Barry, Al Kaufman, Jim Flynn, and Al Palzer. He had never before been stopped. Now he was gone. Conversely, Arthur Pelkey's record contained no prior big-name victories. Sometimes flukes happen in boxing. Some speculated that a previous injury had been aggravated.

[1083] *Freeman*, June 7, 14, 1913. Carpentier previously had been decked twice by the hard-punching Wells, taking 9-counts in the 1st and 2nd rounds, but showed his resilience by coming back to win by knockout in the 4th round by using body blows.

Many whites and those in government thought the sentence was too light. Most blacks thought the sentence was way too harsh.[1084]

The *Freeman* said the truth about the trial was that the evidence did not support the allegations. Billy Lewis said most colored folk could see nothing but color prejudice in the whole business, and with good reason. The prosecuting attorney said as much, which sounded very bad coming from a government official. "There are times when it does not pay to tell the truth. No; an individual can not doff his prejudices any more than a leopard can lose his spots, yet there is such a thing as sacrificing sentiment, prejudice in the interest of the general good."

Still, even the most liberal-minded blacks had thought all along that Johnson was a bit "too fresh" for his own good. No other champion had attracted so much attention to himself. Of course, some of that attention was owing to the fact that he was a *black* heavyweight champion.

Johnson's business had been taken away, he had been prohibited from boxing, thousands of dollars had been taken from him in bonds and defending court proceedings, and lost opportunities cost him many thousands more.

The *Freeman* felt that the iron had entered the judge's soul, for Johnson just should have been fined. Not only was the case not an aggravated one as the judge claimed, it was not a case at all. Furthermore, not a single case wherein a prison sentence was ordered paralleled Johnson's case at all. Schreiber was provided money to defray her expenses. Johnson lived with her. She was his girlfriend, and the argument that he could not pay her expenses legally was ridiculous. The act was passed and conceived with the interest of protecting innocent people and to prohibit trafficking in immoral business. "Technically, the Schreiber woman falls under the classification because the inference is that she was transported for an immoral purpose. One can see how far reaching such an interpretation would be if it were generally applied." The case was a reach in terms of what the law was intended to prohibit. She was his common law wife, or a lover engaged, and as such had a right to receive money from her husband or boyfriend.

The judge viewed Johnson as a race leader, and as such, treated him more harshly in order to send a message to blacks generally, saying, "The defendant is one of the best known men of his race, and his example has been far reaching." The judge explicitly considered race in his sentencing, something which today would be illegal, improper, and grounds for reversal. Billy Lewis further said that Johnson might have been an immoral man, but such had no relevance to a proper legal sentencing consideration.[1085]

On June 23, 1913, Benjamin C. Bachrach and Gustav Beerly filed Jack Johnson's appeal. The appeal alleged that the verdict was not supported by sufficient evidence; that District Attorney Harry A. Parkin made improper highly prejudicial remarks in his opening statement (including stating that Johnson beat women; that he kept three women at the same time, that

---

[1084] *Chicago Defender*, June 7, 1913. *San Francisco Call*, June 5, 1913.
[1085] *Freeman*, June 14, 1913.

when the three women he had with him had differences between them, he would drop one off and put her into a sporting house temporarily to relieve himself of the necessity of spending money carrying her about the country while he had the others; and alleging that Johnson committed crimes against nature even though the government had no evidence of such); that the court erred in admitting improper evidence, allowing irrelevant, immaterial questions not germane to the specific charges at hand regarding the transport of Belle Schreiber (including questions about Hattie McClay and Etta Duryea; questions about Johnson's violence towards women; and incidents that preceded the passage of the Mann Act), all designed to prejudice the jury; and that the Mann Act was unconstitutional because under the 10th Amendment, the power to regulate vice and immorality was a state function, not federal; and also that the Act was an unconstitutionally overbroad use of Congressional power under the Commerce Clause, for transportation of a woman for sexual purposes has nothing to do with commerce, because it isn't commercial; and that the court lacked jurisdiction because Johnson was not in Illinois when he sent Schreiber the money.

The *Defender* said there was a general difference of opinion as to Johnson's guilt or innocence. He was released on a $15,000 bond posted by Tiny Johnson and Matthew S. Baldwin, pending the disposition of his appeal by the U.S. Circuit Court of Appeals for the Seventh Circuit.[1086]

[1086] *Chicago Defender*, July 5, 1913.

CHAPTER 43

Escape

Twenty days after being sentenced, the day after his appeal was filed, on the evening of June 24, 1913; Jack Johnson left Chicago and escaped to Canada via train, disguised as a member of the Negro Giants baseball team. On Wednesday June 25, he and his wife Lucille reached Toronto via the Canadian Pacific railroad. They met Tom Flanagan, his manager, and then departed for Montreal. They intended to sail to France the following week. Flanagan said, "He has no intention of going back to Chicago, where he is positive he will have to serve out his sentence."

At Johnson's home, his family claimed that he was on a fishing trip at Cedar Lake, Indiana. In fact, Johnson had been selling off his belongings, and even had a couple of his automobiles shipped so he would not have to return.[1087]

On June 26, Jack and Lucille arrived in Montreal. They already were booked to sail for Havre, France on the Alian steamer *Corinthian* the following week. At that time, Jack said he did not intend to forfeit his bail bond, and would return to the U.S. after fighting abroad.

Government agents believed Johnson had left for good. Department of Justice Superintendent Charles F. DeWoody raised an outcry and strongly urged the Canadian police to arrest and deport Johnson as an undesirable, given his conviction. Still, the U.S. appellate court's decision was not yet final. DeWoody said,

> There is a paragraph in the laws...which says the police have the right to turn back into this country any person whom they may deem objectionable. If that provision can be enforced and Johnson does not leave Montreal before we get the Canadian authorities to act he will be brought back and kept under surveillance until his appeal is disposed of.

However, Johnson's deportation was unlikely, for he showed that in Chicago he had purchased a through ticket to Havre, France via Montreal. Under such conditions, under Dominion law, he could not be deported. By using this legal strategy, Johnson tied the hands of the Canadian immigration authorities, who were powerless to act further than to see to it that he left the country on the ship upon which he was booked to sail.

Johnson's sudden maneuver was no surprise to his friends. He boasted for several days that he was about to slip one over on the government.

Tom Clark, a saloon proprietor, said both Johnson and his white valet Joe Levy had discussed their plans with a crowd of blacks for more than an

---
[1087] *Rock Island Argus*, June 27, 1913.

hour before their departure. Johnson first went to a fishing resort in Wisconsin, and there donned some old clothes. He boarded a train containing members of the American Giants, a colored ball team going to Detroit, and he escaped notice. From Detroit he went to Toronto, and then Montreal; his wife and Joe Levy following. Once in Montreal, he telegraphed his friends in the U.S.

If Johnson remained abroad, the government would be enriched when it forfeited his bond. DeWoody said Johnson was in desperate straits financially. Bachrach said the bond could not be forfeited until after the court's decision on his appeal, probably the following April.

On June 29, 1913 at 3 a.m., Johnson and his wife left Canada on the Alian line steamer *Corinthian*, heading to Havre, France. They boarded in the presence of Canadian immigration officers. Johnson reiterated that he had no intention of forfeiting his bond. He took with him four automobiles.[1088]

The *Defender* believed that Johnson had been crucified and persecuted for being a Negro; one who whipped Jeffries. It was no one's business if he chose a woman of a different color for his companion, or if he married her. He had done no different than any other big sport.

The *Defender* noted how governments had prevented the moving picture exhibitions of Johnson's victory over Jeffries. The federal government then prohibited interstate transportation of fight films altogether, in order to limit severely the exhibition of Johnson's victories, for such exhibitions "would make the white children grow up with certain fear or dread of the colored boy. It is the negro boy that would have to fear the white boy." They failed to beat him in the ring, so they had to discredit him, hide his victories, and prevent him from fighting.

To marry whom he pleased was a right guaranteed by the Illinois statutes and the laws of a number of Northern states. The country for centuries had mulattoes – black children with white fathers who did not recognize their own offspring, yet it was a crime against nature for a black man to marry a white woman by her own consent. Also, Jack lived in a mansion and owned a $10,000 automobile. "They don't like that, of course."

> How many congressmen, governors, judges and clergymen of the white race have consorted with colored women? From the present day appearance of four millions of negroes in America, hosts of whom God alone can only tell whether they are white or colored, there must be left very little loyalty among white men, and less confidence among white women in them.

Still, Johnson had invited the envy of his own race as well, and "pricked the ever-growing abscess of American prejudice by spending his money like he had a plenty." The spotlight was a fearful ordeal.

[1088] *Chicago Defender*, July 5, 1913; *Freeman*, July 5, 1913. *Chicago Day Book*, June 30, 1913.

Likewise, the *Freeman* said Johnson's own people sought to repudiate him, believing that they were suffering more prejudice because of him. Hence, he left a country nearly entirely turned against him.[1089]

The *Mirror of Life and Boxing World*'s correspondent wrote,

> No one should worry over Jack's departure, as the boxing game is better off without him. Negro boxers, like the black race riders, are a thing of the past. They have been eliminated from the sport to a great extent. ...
>
> [T]here has been a revolution of feeling against the black man in America, the true cause of which is hard to find, but which has been illustrated more clearly perhaps in connection with sport than in any other line. Legally the negro may be the equal of the white man in this country, but in sport there is little room for him any more. In professional baseball the negro never figured. He was never given a chance to figure.[1090]

On July 4 in Chicago, Jack Johnson's deceased wife Etta's seized necklace was sold at public auction for $2,160.

On July 10, 1913, Johnson, his wife Lucille, nephew Gus Rhodes, and Jewish secretary Joe Levy arrived at the French port of Le Havre. Jack said, "I have done no wrong, the whole world is with me and I am over here to make some money. ... I have never had any idea of running away. My attorneys have been fully advised." However, some reported that privately, Jack was saying that he would not return.

Harry Parkin, who prosecuted Johnson, said the judge had ruled that Johnson's appearance bonds could not be forfeited until Jack failed to appear at the time designated by the Court.[1091]

The *Freeman* said, "Everyone is free in the United States except the eight million Negroes. Prejudice on every hand is manifest against them." Ultimately, what brought down Johnson was that he "was indiscreet; he flew in the face of sentiment, but in doing so he stood for manhood rights."

Johnson said Paris would be his headquarters, for that town did not take as much to the anti-Negro business. Parisians loved McVea, and he had a white wife too; a beautiful French woman. However, there was some race prejudice in France too, as was the case with the entire world. France had colonized many nonwhite nations, just as had other powerful European nations.

Johnson had trouble finding a Paris hotel that would allow him to stay there. He was refused repeatedly at several good hotels before he finally found accommodation. The *Freeman* said, "It is just about the same prejudice which exists between races the world over. Whites and blacks will

---

[1089] *Chicago Defender*, July 5, 1913; *Freeman*, August 2, 9, 1913.
[1090] *Mirror of Life and Boxing World*, July 19, August 2, 1913.
[1091] *Chicago Defender*, July 12, August 9, 1913; *Freeman*, July 19, 1913.

never be on rapport. They can get along, however, much better than they do in this country, just the same."[1092]

Happy that Jack had left, Jim Corbett said, "Johnson was a disgrace to pugilism and his continued presence was a menace to the sport."

In order to earn money, Johnson took to the stage in Paris, making his first appearance in *La Revue Chemise* at the Folies Bergeres music hall. There was some hissing, but also applause from a full house. Overall, Johnson was received favorably.

Each night, Johnson threw a medicine ball and boxed 4 exhibition rounds with various French heavyweights. After midnight, he danced the grizzly bear with Mrs. Johnson. He drew $1,200 a night for eleven nights.[1093]

Jack planned to leave on a tour through Belgium's summer resorts, then to Bordeaux, Lyons, and Marseilles, leaving France on August 20 for a three-week Russian tour, as well as vaudeville tours throughout France, Germany, and Spain. His fame as champion earned him easy money.[1094]

In New York, Sheriff Julius Harburger attended an August 13, 1913 bout between a white boxer named Paddy McCarthy and a Chinaman named Ah Chung, won by Chung via 6th round knockout. The sheriff and Bat Masterson called attention to the New York State Athletic Commission's hypocrisy, allowing this mixed-race bout between a nonwhite foreigner and a white man, but not those between black citizens and whites.

> Since the days when Abraham Lincoln issued his proclamation of freedom there was to be no distinction as to American citizenship, but how the Boxing Commission can come to the conclusion that a Chinese, who is a nonvoter and a non-citizen should have preference over a citizen is one of the mysteries that runs through the labyrinthian minds of commissioners.[1095]

As a result of the black-white bout ban, New York club managers were heard to say, "What sense would there be in matching a Negro and a white man and have the boxing commission revoke our license?"

Writing for the *Evening Telegram*, James Crowell looked at the commission's actions from a different angle. He said,

> The boxing game has enough enemies already without trying to increase the number by opening the way for a hue and cry of much more extensive proportions than that which it already has to contend with. The racial prejudice that a bout between a white and a Negro boxer incurs is detrimental to the sport.[1096]

Jack Johnson was enjoying Paris, for overall he was being treated fairly well. Jack told a French sporting paper,

---

[1092] *Freeman*, July 19, 1913.
[1093] *Freeman*, August 2, 9, 1913. *Mirror of Life and Boxing World*, August 9, 1913.
[1094] *New York Age*, August 14, 1913; *Freeman*, August 16, 1913.
[1095] *New York Age*, August 21, 1913. Recently, by a 2 to 1 vote, the New York State Athletic Commission had upheld the rule barring mixed matches between whites and blacks.
[1096] *New York Age*, September 18, 1913.

Since my return from France to America I must say that I have been the most persecuted man in the whole world. The Americans decidedly unable to stomach my victory over Jeffries…have tried to destroy and ruin me. There has not been a day on which I was not the victim of some plot, on some dubious charge, which ended only with great loss of money for me.

One day they accused me of violence to my chauffeur when in fact he menaced me and I was forced to give up heavy damages. At the same time I was in trouble for exceeding the speed limit when I had made 10 miles an hour, and on the charge that my auto smoked, which was absolutely false, and the fines were always drained from me. They accused me of trading in white female slaves when I had simply traveled with my legitimate wife from one state to another.

I was arrested and was not released until I had deposited a bail of 50,000 francs. It was always my money that they were after… One day when I was punching the bag in public a cord holding the ball broke and the bag projected 10 meters, struck a woman spectator lightly, without hurting her in the least. The woman's lawyer hailed me into court and claimed enormous damages. Do you know what she demanded? Simply $2,500 (125,000 francs). Notwithstanding the bad faith of the complaint, the court condemned me to pay $250 (12,500 francs) – a sum absolutely ridiculous under the circumstances.

In brief, with all these attacks and persecutions the American judges had already forced me to pay, in some months, more than 400,000 francs ($120,000) and as there was no reason why I would not be continually arrested until my last dollar was gone, I resolved to take to flight. … I resolved to use a ruse. I organized a baseball team composed of Negroes. I had chosen for it fifteen men as big and black as possible, all of whom resembled me marvelously. … I sent a challenge in the name of the Negro team to one of the best teams in Canada. The challenge was accepted and a date quickly fixed. Disguised in baseball outfits, it was very hard to identify me. My secretary, wife, and domestic embarked for Canada by another route. I had bought in advance tickets direct to Harve by the steamer Corinthian. When I arrived at Montréal this precaution saved me. I had arranged with a big Negro who resembled me closely and when he said he was Jack Johnson the police would have taken him back triumphantly to my house in Chicago. I promised to pay him well. Fortunately all went well in Montréal. The local authorities, unfriendly, demanded how long I would stay in Canada, and if I had not had my ticket I might not have been so fortunate. As I was only going through their country, the Canadians could say nothing. Once on board the Corinthian I was safe. … The officers and passengers of the Corinthian were truly charming to me. I count on settling permanently in [Paris] and never returning to the United States.

The *Freeman's* Billy Lewis said Johnson spoke the truth about his persecution. The government previously had the reputation of making out good, plain, unmistakable cases, but in this instance fell to the small business of pettifogging (engaging in legal trickery or arguing about unimportant details), and the prosecution was glad to get rid of the pestiferous (annoying) Johnson at any cost. It was a flimsy case, one based on race prejudice and public demand rather than justice.

The *New York Age* also noted that the American spirit of fair play had not been in evidence since Johnson defeated Jeffries. Owing to the prevalence of "Negrophobia," law enforcement had harassed and inconvenienced him all the time. Every police officer wanted publicity by arresting him for speeding. "We do not condone the champion's rank disregard for public opinion, for his indiscretions have done the members of his race much harm; but even had he not erred in judgment his color in this country would have operated against him."

The *Freeman* noted that despite black boxers' proven courage; there remained a certain class of boxing fans who claimed that every black boxer was "yellow." To the extent that some lacked self-confidence, it was because they suffered from the effects of being subjected to the white man's will. Regardless, as a class, black boxers were every bit as game as white boxers, as proven by men such as Dixon, Gans, Walcott, Jackson, Langford, and Johnson. Langford was so yellow that few whites in the world wanted to fight him. There were fifty white boxers for every black, and yet blacks had won many championships. Even the "unbiased critic will admit that the Negroes are natural-born fighters." Black soldiers also had been of great assistance to Uncle Sam, having fought well in the Civil War and the Spanish War, covering themselves with glory.[1097]

On August 25, 1913, in London, England, Johnson was scheduled to appear at the Euston Palace, a South London music hall. Two white American women comediennes told the audience that they refused to appear if Johnson did. One said, "I do not object to Johnson on account of his color, but of what the man is alleged to have done." The gallery then replied, "What's he done?" The women were booed from the stage with whistles, cat calls, and hisses. There were only a few cheers. The average Englishman on the street did not share the hostility towards Johnson. They regarded him as the victim of persecution due to color prejudice.

When Johnson appeared, the crowd roared with cheers for several minutes. Jack smiled and bowed. He appeared majestic to his supporters, and ignored with a wave of the hand those few who hissed and booed him. He made a speech, saying, "My only crime is that I beat Jeffries." Seeing that he was standing under the flag of the United States, he stopped talking, had it removed, and had the French flag hung in its place. Johnson thanked

---

[1097] *Freeman*, August 23, 30, 1913; *New York Age*, September 4, 1913.

the crowd for its reception and remarked that he was glad that English people were so fair-minded.[1098]

Johnson was a vaudeville attraction in England, receiving a $2,500 weekly salary, larger than any vaudevillian abroad.

On September 3, 1913 in New York, 194-pound Frank Moran scored a surprise 7th round knockout over 6'3" 227-pound Al Palzer. England's *Mirror of Life and Boxing World* said, "Moran is now in the forefront of the white heavyweight division." The English, who had seen Moran win five fights, thought well of him.

Dan McKetrick, who managed both Moran and Jeannette, was trying to match either one with Johnson. Many felt that Jack was putting up the color bar against men of his own color, only seeming interested in white hopes. Regardless, "The champion cannot last forever, and the general feeling is that he may fall a victim to the first good husky fellow that comes along."[1099]

Although France had colonial holdings in Africa, Asia, the Americas (including San Domingo and Haiti), and the Pacific Islands, apparently its racial concerns were not quite as great as the British Empire's. France seemed willing to allow Johnson to fight.

Eventually, an announcement was made that Johnson had agreed to fight Frank Moran. The fight likely would take place in December (later changed to January) at the Velodrome d'Hiver in Paris.

On September 4 in London, Jack Johnson was injured when a taxicab collided with his motor car. Johnson sustained some tendon sprains which required treatment. About $1,000 in damage was done to the auto. The taxicab driver was arrested. Johnson noted, "They would have me in the penitentiary by this time if this incident had occurred in the United States."

In an ironic twist, one of the grand jurors who indicted Johnson under the Mann Act was arrested for a violation of the same act in Los Angeles, after being trailed from Chicago by a woman who claimed to be his common-law wife and had him arrested. Increasingly, women were using the act as a sword rather than as a shield, blackmailing their boyfriends from leaving them, sometimes demanding marriage or money, threatening them with prosecution under the Mann Act.[1100]

Jim Corbett said Johnson had arrived at the stage of his career where money counted a great deal. Corbett thought Jack might take a dive if there was enough money in it. Was he speaking from experience?[1101]

On September 12, by a unanimous vote, the New York State Athletic Commission refused to allow Sam Langford and Gunboat Smith to box in that state, again ruling that it was against the sport's best interests to allow blacks and whites to box each other. New York State Attorney General

---

[1098] *Chicago Defender*, August 30, 1913. Jack's nephew Gus Rhodes was with him in London.
[1099] *Mirror of Life and Boxing World*, September 13, 1913.
[1100] *Chicago Defender, Freeman*, September 6, 13, 1913.
[1101] *Freeman*, September 20, 1913.

Thomas Carmody said New York was entitled legally to prevent mixed-race bouts if it believed such might prompt disorder or bitter racial feeling.[1102]

FIRST PICTURE OF CHAMPION JOHNSON PUBLISHED IN AMERICA.

This is the first picture published by any newspaper of the champion since his exit from the United States. Facing the champion, with back ha'f turned towards you, can be seen Mr. Joe Levi, private secretary. Facing the champion with straw hat is Lord Pettiford, multi-millionaire and special friend, who has always admired the champion and is about to take his yacht to the lord's private summer home about thirty miles from London. Mrs. Johnson can be seen with her usual smile. Just outside the wharf are 10,000 or more people waiting to see the world's greatest champion, who has fought and won from Jeffries to Uncle Sam, making a clean breakaway, and has never fouled either. The champion says, owing to the ill health of his twenty-second cousin, he will not return to the United States on October 4.

Chicago Defender, September 27, 1913

The *Mirror of Life and Boxing World* believed Johnson was following the example of white boxers in avoiding his toughest challengers who were black. He showed no disposition to endanger his title in matches with either Langford or Jeannette. It had been hinted that Johnson wanted to go down in history as the only colored man to become heavyweight champion, "but it might be a great deal nearer the truth to state that Johnson is in no way anxious to lose his crown, and that the possibility of defeat makes him pass up his tough coloured rivals and give preference to the more or less idolized white warriors."[1103]

Furthermore, Johnson could make as much or more money fighting whites. Few promoters were willing to put up big money for a black vs. black title fight. The general public wanted to see a white man win the title back, and far more whites than blacks paid to see fights. At the end of the day, Johnson was a shrewd businessman.

[1102] *Freeman*, October 4, 11, 1913; *Thames Star*, September 16, 1913.
[1103] *Mirror of Life and Boxing World*, September 27, 1913.

Johnson continued earning money in French and English music halls, giving performances of sparring, dancing, singing, and playing bass violin. Some greeted him warmly, while others reviled him. He could not escape global prejudice entirely.

In Paris, France, Johnson's home was the Grand Terminus Hotel. Jack had purchased property at Joiville le Pout, a Parisian suburb, and was building a bungalow there.

For two weeks, Johnson appeared at the Apollo theater in Vienna, Austria. Besides giving boxing exhibitions, he and Mrs. Johnson danced the tango, and audiences went wild.

While in Germany and surrounding countries, Jack and Lucille Johnson were received royally. He had a ten-week engagement for an alleged $5,000 per week.[1104]

Thomas Dixon Jr.'s play, *The Leopard's Spots*, was having a successful tour. In North Carolina, in a speech given before the play was performed, Dixon said that white civilization was being destroyed by educating the Negro.[1105]

[1104] *Chicago Defender*, October 4, 1913. On October 3, 1913 in New York, 195-pound Joe Jeannette outpointed 199 ½-pound Sam Langford in a fast 10-round no-decision bout, winning 7 out of 10 rounds, controlling Sam with his long left jab. Each man was staggered at times. At the finish, the overweight Langford's right eye was damaged, his nose bruised, and his lips slightly puffed. Jeannette was unmarked. Some thought Langford had gone back or was out of shape. *Freeman*, October 11, November 8, 1913; *New York Tribune, Chicago Day Book, Rock Island Argus*, October 4, 1913.
[1105] *New York Age*, October 9, 1913.

CHAPTER 44

The French Dispute

In late 1913, there was some suggestion that Parisians might be growing tired of Johnson. They thought he was funny, until he started talking about Napoleon. Jack said he possessed a library of works about Napoleon, and remarked, "Napoleon was a great man, too." They believed that Johnson suffered from a badly swelled head.

The community of Asnieres, a Parisian suburb, was shocked at the thought that Johnson was going to live among them permanently. A movement was afoot to petition the authorities to bar him. They called him an undesirable creature. "To tell the truth, Parisians are heartily ashamed of themselves and the foolish enthusiasm with which they received this man." It was one thing if he was just visiting; quite another if he was going to be living among them long term.[1106]

As of October 29, the touring Johnson was in Budapest, Austria-Hungary, playing at the Royal Orpheum theater, which was packed nightly. He was a popular attraction wherever he went. "They wished to see the colossus of the nineteenth century." Johnson planned to leave in a few days for Bucharest and then Berlin.[1107]

Johnson's European theatrical contracts would keep him busy for a year at $1,500 a week. Lucrative cozy theatrical contracts made it less likely that he would fight unless offered big money. This upset some French promoters, for it made it tougher to negotiate with him. He wasn't going to take the time to train and then risk his title, which had tremendous economic value to him, unless he was offered a great deal of money.

At a meeting of the French boxing commission, a letter was read from promoter Victor Breyer of the French Federation of Boxing Clubs in Paris, stating his belief that Johnson should no longer be considered champion, and the winner of a fight between Langford and Jeannette (which he was promoting) should be declared the new champion.[1108]

Bat Masterson, fight expert for the *Morning Telegraph*, wrote that the International Boxing Union (IBU), "whatever that is," had voted to bar Jack Johnson from boxing in France. It also proposed to declare vacant the heavyweight championship because Johnson had been sentenced to imprisonment and for other reasons too numerous to mention.[1109]

At the November 5 IBU meeting, French delegates proposed that the title should be declared vacant, and named Jeannette and Langford as best

---

[1106] *Freeman*, October 18, 1913.
[1107] *Chicago Defender*, November 15, 22, 1913; *Freeman*, December 6, 1913.
[1108] *New York Times*, October 29, 1913.
[1109] *New York Times*, October 29, 1913.

qualified to compete for the championship. Of course, it was no coincidence that the French promoters who were members and voting accordingly were promoting an upcoming Langford-Jeannette bout, and that was good marketing for the fight. The United States still held that Johnson was champion. Belgium and Switzerland expressed no opinion. As a result of the lack of a majority vote, the IBU decided to summon an emergency meeting of its delegates, set for December 24 in Paris. So, in truth, the IBU had not declared the title vacant.[1110]

However, some erroneously reported that the IBU had declared the title vacant on the grounds of Johnson's conviction in the American courts and his refusal to fight. Regardless, Americans "will hardly take the verdict of the 'I.B.U.' seriously." Still, things did not look bright for Johnson. "Barred in this country by a jail sentence and popular sentiment as well, not wanted in England or Australia, and finally given the gate in France, the 'champion' is getting his bunches."[1111]

Many black writers thought the U.S. Supreme Court would or should reverse Johnson's Mann Act conviction. Had his conviction been obtained in a fair manner, no tears would be shed for him. However, "sending him to prison on the testimony of a notorious degenerate is quite another thing." Schreiber had testified that she made money in an immoral manner and gave the proceeds to Johnson. "But the woman's testimony was so glaringly false to all who heard it that even those who utterly detest the Negro refuse to believe it."

Johnson did not deny that he had sent Schreiber money to help her out, but emphatically denied that he ever had compelled or encouraged her to prostitute herself, or that he intended to benefit financially. He also swore, and his testimony was corroborated, that instead of forcing her to engage in immoral practices, he put her up in elegant apartments, and did the same for her mother and sister. All three women lived in luxury at his expense. "If such actions mean anything, they mean that Johnson was endeavoring in his own peculiar way to rescue the woman from a life of shame and degradation, which she had been following in Pittsburgh."[1112]

On November 17, 1913 in Boston, 182-pound Gunboat Smith won a 12-round decision over Sam Langford, who appeared overweight at about 195 pounds. Smith easily landed left jabs, clearly outboxing the hard-punching Langford by using his height and reach advantages.[1113]

On November 25 in Paris, Johnson engaged in a wrestling match against a German named Urbach. After Jack secured a couple falls and had won the bout, Urbach punched him on the jaw, but Jack did not retaliate. "A small riot followed and several arrests were made." Jack occasionally engaged in wrestling bouts.[1114]

[1110] *London Daily Mail, London Times*, December 19, 1913.

[1111] *Freeman*, November 15, 1913. *Chicago Day Book*, November 6, 1913. *El Paso Herald*, November 16, 1913.

[1112] *New York Age*, November 13, 1913; *Freeman*, December 13, 1913.

[1113] *Freeman*, November 22, December 6, 13, 1913.

[1114] *Chicago Day Book*, November 26, 1913.

To give one a better sense about the serious money that top boxers were earning, the New Jersey State Bureau of Statistics of Labor said the average wage of a person employed in factories there was $557 *per year*. The industries with the lowest average yearly earnings were the manufacture of shirt waists, with an average annual pay of $386.88, and women's and children's underwear, at $289.86 per year. Fighting made sense.[1115]

In early December, millionaire Matthew S. Baldwin, who had helped post a bond for Jack Johnson, was found dead.[1116]

On December 6, it was announced that Jack Johnson would box fellow black Battling Jim Johnson 10 rounds in Paris on December 19, a mere 13 days away. Johnson also had his upcoming January bout with Frank Moran.[1117]

Chicago Defender, November 8, 1913

The French Boxing Federation's director, Paris boxing promoter Theodore Vienne, who was associated with promoters Victor Breyer and Leon See, stated that Johnson was being stripped because of his criminal conviction in the U.S. and because he was refusing to box top contenders like Langford or Jeannette, despite the promoters' efforts. Hence they declared the upcoming Langford vs. Jeannette bout would be for the vacant title.[1118]

The French Federation's Victor Breyer and Paul Rousseau sent the New York State Athletic Commission a cable stating, "French Federation proposes to International Boxing Union Jack Johnson no more world's champion. Please cable if in agreement with France."

However, the New York Commission responded that it recognized Johnson as the world champion until he retired or someone defeated him in the ring. This was somewhat ironic given that it refused to allow Johnson to box anyone in New York.[1119]

The *New York Age* said Johnson would be the world's champion regardless of what the IBU or the NYSAC decided. Any attempt to strip him via highway robbery methods would be to no avail.

> Pugilists do not forfeit their titles because of acts of indiscretion in private life. If so, many white fighters would have been bated of their

---

[1115] *New York Journal*, December 19, 1913.
[1116] *Chicago Day Book*, December 5, 1913.
[1117] *Wanganui Chronicle, Northern Star*, December 8, 1913.
[1118] *Syracuse Journal*, December 14, 1913; *Omaha Daily Bee, Salt Lake Tribune*, December 15, 1913.
[1119] *New York Herald, New York Journal*, December 17, 1913.

honors in the past. Rousseau stripped him because he refused to fight those fighters picked out for him to fight. On the theory advanced by Rosseau, the Philadelphia Athletics would be forced to forfeit its world's championship title for refusing to play the Lincoln Giants or some other strong colored baseball team.[1120]

Arthur Pelkey said he would draw the color line when it came to Langford, Jeannette, McVey, and other blacks, but would step over the line if there was a chance to fight Johnson for the title. Pelkey was in training to fight Gunboat Smith (who recently had beaten Langford) for the white championship.[1121]

Johnson wrote a letter to the *New York Herald*'s European edition, saying,

> I strongly protest against three or four so-called sportsmen who have pretended to form that which they called an international boxing union in the object of letting the public believe that I was no more the undisputed world champion.
>
> But, as you have seen, some genuine sportsmen have taken up my defence and everyone knows now that I am still the real and only title holder.
>
> Besides, I am willing to defense my title against any challenger, and those who will see me box my first opponent, 'Jim' Johnson, at Premierland, on Friday night will be convinced that I am still the man who beat Jeffries, Tommy Burns, etc., and I really deserve the name of 'invincible,' which the Americans themselves gave me.[1122]

On Friday evening December 19, 1913 inside the Premierland Francais, Elysee-Montmartre, 72 Boulevard Rochechouart, at Montmartre, in north Paris, France, Jack Johnson fought Battling Jim Johnson in a scheduled 10-round contest. Battling Jim was 26 years old to Jack's 35 years of age.

Battling Jim Johnson was a big, strong, durable fighter, typically weighing around 225 pounds. Amongst the experienced Battling Jim's 39 known bouts, he had fought a high caliber of opponents, including the big three – Jeannette, Langford, and McVey, and more than held his own. The French thought of him as a quality opponent, for they had seen him box in France against McVea (D15), Jim Maher (KO3), and McVea again (LKOby21), all in 1910, and again in 1913 against Kid Jackson (KO10). He had fought and won several times in the United Kingdom as well, so Europeans were familiar with him. The *Freeman* argued that Jim Johnson was amongst the top black fighters who were better than any white hope, for he was powerful, skillful, and could take a punch.[1123]

[1120] *New York Age*, December 18, 1913.
[1121] *New York American*, December 18, 1913.
[1122] *New York Herald*, December 19, 1913.
[1123] Battling Jim Johnson's record included: 1910 DND6 Tony Ross, LND6 Sam Langford, D15 Sam McVea, and LKOby21 McVea; 1911 KO4 Fred Drummond and KO11 Jewey Smith; 1912 L20 Fred Storbeck (despite dropping Fred three times and hurting him on several other occasions), WND6 Joe

The *London Times* said Jim Johnson held a victory over Joe Jeannette, and many regarded him as likely to provide the champ with a serious fight. When in Brussels, Belgium, the gigantic Jim had been mistaken for or passed himself off as the champion, fooling people into thinking that he was Jack Johnson.

With the champ indeed about to fight, it would make it harder for the promoters of the Langford-Jeannette contest to declare that it was for a vacant title. Some believed that the reason why Johnson was fighting again was to forestall talk about his title being vacant. Johnson said, "What? I'm no longer the champion? We'll see about that."

En haut : JIM JOHNSON — En bas : JACK JOHNSON

Probably it was no coincidence that Johnson vs. Johnson was scheduled to be held the day before Langford vs. Jeannette. The champ likely also saw it as a tune-up in preparation for the lengthier upcoming Moran title bout.

Le Temps said that despite claims, the International Boxing Union had not actually stripped Johnson, for only one member, France, voted that the title was vacant.

Some of the French press erroneously reported that Jack Johnson had not fought in two years. The Brits drew the color line on him in 1911, but he had fought Jim Flynn in 1912. Most American cities would not allow him to fight, and even the Australians did not want him. Plus, there were the legal troubles.

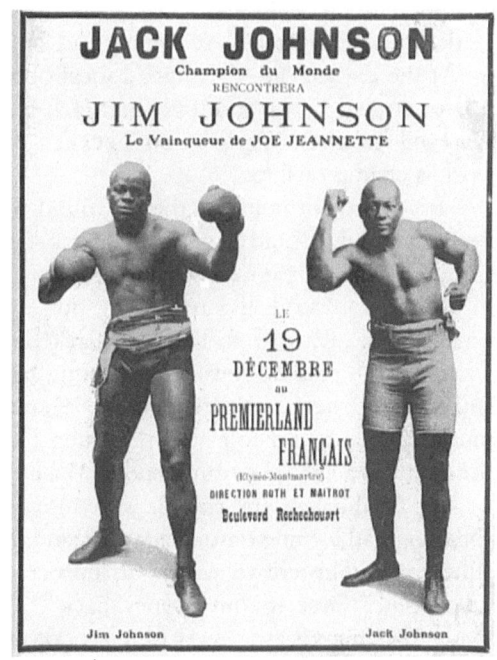

Jeannette (dropping Joe in the process), LND10 Jeannette, KO7 Black Bill, and KO2 Bill Tate; and 1913 LND10 and LDQby15 Jeannette, KO11 Con O'Kelly, KO8 Gustave Marthuin, KO10 Kid Jackson, and KO6 Bob Scanlon. *London Times, London Daily Mail, New York Herald, Le Matin, Le Petit Parisien, L'Humanite, L'Intransigeant*, December 20, 1913; *La Presse, Le Temps*, December 20, 21, 2013; *Le Matin*, December 19, 20, 1913.

L'Humanite said Jack Johnson was the world's most well-known person, and the actual incontestable champion. In the face of the threat to take away his title, he was returning to the enchanted circle against Jim Johnson, a reputedly dangerous man. Jack had to flee his own country, but his real crime was not being pardoned by the Americans for defeating and crushing their idol, James Jeffries.

La Presse said, "It's the return to the ring of the extraordinary pugilist, the best who ever existed." It anticipated an excellent contest, for Jim Johnson was respected as "the strongest fighter in the world" and "one of the most qualified to meet the world champion."

Their measurements were listed as Jack Johnson – height 1 meter 85 centimeters, weight 97 kilograms (about 214 pounds)(though he likely weighed much more), Jim Johnson – height 1 meter 79 centimeters, weight 101 kilograms (222 ½ pounds).

The hall was well-filled with a huge crowd, and many women were present. Following the preliminaries, the main event began at 11:45 p.m.

In the early rounds, Johnson displayed his assortment of punches, as well as his clever defense. It was evident that the champion was far from being past-it, as some reckoned him to be. Jack showed his gold teeth in broad smiles when Jim missed. But Jim was clever and tough as well, landing some occasional solid punches of his own, making the contest competitive. "The blows might have upset a weak white, but they only made Jack grin." Both were smiling and laughing quite often.

At the end of the 4th round, a local observer wrote, "The contest up to that point had proved not only that Jack Johnson was no back number, but that still another negro stood between the many white hopes and the world's championship."

Jack really got going in the 5th round. His fierce jabs and hooks to the head and body would have finished most fighters. Jim was very defensive, and there was a great deal of clinching.

In the 6th round, Jim rushed in, but Jack was as hard as a "café au lai wall," and retaliated well. The pace slackened, and they continually clinched.

In the 7th round, both seemed quite tired. There was very little action, and some of the crowd occasionally began shouting, "Fake." There was too much clinching and too little punching for their tastes. Jack's blows were becoming weaker. The round ended to a chorus of hoots.

The 8th through 10th rounds were more of the same, with a great deal of clinching and leaning on one another, and not much punching or landing by either man. The crowd was in an uproar, wanting more of a fight. Some called out, "Give us our money back." The house became quite rowdy, loudly shouting disapproval of the monotony.

The *London Times* said Jim appeared to be giving it a little more of an effort, while Jack seemed glad to rest in the clinches at every opportunity. Conversely, the *London Daily Mail* said that despite the fans' discontent, the men were trying hard. However, the "arrangement" idea had spread, the spectators believing the boxers were faking and working together. By the end, the malcontents were in the vast majority, and the contest was called a thoroughly unsatisfactory encounter.

Owing to the crowd noise, boos, and hisses, several minutes elapsed before the decision could be heard. One judge gave it to Jim Johnson, one judge called it a draw, while Referee M. Maitrot shared the opinion that the fight was a draw. Hence, because two out of the three officials called it a draw, the fight was ruled a draw. In today's parlance, it was a majority draw. When the decision was announced, some spectators demanded their money back, while others cheered derisively.

When the explanation was added that Jack Johnson had broken his left arm in an early round and had been unable to use it effectively, some contemptuous laughter was heard. The audience dispersed, continuing to express its disapproval of the proceedings.

Jack Johnson complained of pain in his left arm, which was swelling. Two doctors examined him and issued a statement that his arm indeed presented a fracture in the middle of the left forearm. He had fractured the third part of his left radius.

As of 1:45 a.m., a doctor confirmed the fracture of the radial bone in Jack's left forearm. Jack said his arm was broken when swinging on Jim's head in the 3rd round. *Le Matin* said the broken arm explained to a certain degree the champion's poor performance.

Summarizing, the *London Times* said it was a draw after 10 inconclusive and most unsatisfactory rounds. After the first few rounds, the constant clinching brought forth outspoken criticism from the spectators, who shouted "Fake!" They continued expressing their discontent all the way to the end, but especially so after the 7th round.

The *New York Herald* said Champion Jack was spoiled by too much tango dancing and catch-as-can wrestling. He never showed a glimmer of his old form, and before the fight was half over, he was blowing like a bull as a result of all of the bout's wrestling. Both boxers seemed to treat the matter as a huge joke, and neither one ever made a real effort to fight.

The *Herald* said the Paris press called it a huge fiasco. The *Matin* said it was more of a laughing contest than a boxing match. The *Excelsior* believed that the referee should have declared it no contest, for it was clear that neither man was trying.

Alluding to the recent dispute regarding whether Johnson should be stripped of the championship title, *Le Matin* said that perhaps France was correct in the conflict which divided the two countries.

Le Petit Parisien was not as harsh. It said the fans came in droves to see two famous colossal black fighters. However,

> To say that they returned satisfied doesn't exactly tell the truth, because a certain number expressed disappointment. Yet these two Negroes fought conscientiously. Jack placed many fabulous hooks to the jaw and not too shabby ones directly to the stomach. Already one counted on his victory, but when the fourth round was reached one remarked that he had stopped using his left arm. He continued

nevertheless, and until the end of the fight he used only his right arm and resisted Jim. The referee declared that the match was a draw, and announced to justify this unintended result that Jack Johnson had his left radius broken.

L'Humanite said the fight represented the fall of an idol.

> When I read the notes taken from the course of the match, I am astonished at the difference from the first rounds and the last ones.
>
> At the end of the 1st round, Jack had a huge advantage. ...
>
> For four rounds the champ was mastering the dance, hitting when and where he wanted. He was happy to show a golden smile when Jim would counter.
>
> The following round, it was Jim's turn to do the forcing. Jack could hardly do much to stop him. This continued until the end of the match, when it was called a draw.
>
> The public was informed that Jack broke his left arm in the course of the match.

Le Temps said although Jack Johnson was "gifted with remarkable means," and threw his punches with "astonishing virtuosity," nevertheless he was fat and out of shape, and the 10-round fight monotonous.

> The winner of tonight's battle [Langford-Jeannette] would seem to be more of a champion than the one who showed up yesterday. It is annoying to think that the invincible could consent to present himself before the eyes of the knowing public in such a state as he was in last night. This excellent athlete who is in retirement perhaps thought that we didn't know what boxing was in our country.

American newspapers, via A.P. wire, had similar reports. One was entitled "Jack Johnson Hooted As Faker."

> The spectators loudly protested throughout that the men were not fighting, and demanded their money back. ... The organizers of the fight explained the fiasco by asserting that Jack Johnson's left arm was broken in the third round. ... During the first three rounds he was obviously playing with his opponent. After that it was observed that he was using only his right hand. ... Doctors who made an examination certified to a slight fracture of the radius of the left arm. The general opinion is that his arm was injured in a wrestling match early in the week, and that a blow tonight caused the fracture of the bone.[1124]

Some erroneously reported that Jack was "battered" around the ring, barely saved from a knockout, and was "plainly groggy" when the bell ended the bout.

[1124] *Los Angeles Daily Times, Omaha World Herald, New York American,* December 20, 1913.

Others said Johnson left the ring amid a storm of jeers and hisses, for the angry crowd was disappointed by the lack of action. After being informed that Johnson broke his left arm, the crowd responded, "When does he say he broke it?" The reply was, "In the 3rd round."

> This announcement was followed by more jeering and hissing, as the spectators had failed to notice any sign of an injured arm at that stage or later. ... It was the general impression among the spectators that the injury had been sustained in the last minute of the fight, when Jim Johnson rushed Jack to the ropes and the two went to the floor with Jack's arms closed about Jim's waist. Both men jumped up quickly but Jack was plainly exhausted and he fell against the ropes as the gong sounded. Then he tottered to his corner, holding his left arm and declaring it was broken.

Some said the fight was so dull that it had cost Johnson his power as a drawing card. However, others noted that it was the general impression that if Frank Moran had been in the ring that he would have won the championship. That actually made more folks intrigued by their upcoming fight, for they thought Moran had a real chance to return the championship to the white race. However, as a result of his broken arm, the scheduled January 1914 Johnson-Moran bout had to be postponed.[1125]

The next day, on December 20, 1913 at the Wonderland Francais in Paris, in a match advertised as being for the world's championship, 185-pound Sam Langford decisively won a 20-round decision over 187-pound Joe Jeannette, decking Joe three times in the 13th round. Many in France started calling Langford the heavyweight champion, or at least felt that Johnson should defend his title against him.[1126]

On January 1, 1914 at Jim Coffroth's arena in Daly City, California, Gunboat Smith, who held a recent victory over Langford, knocked out Arthur Pelkey in the 15th round with a right to the jaw, winning the white world heavyweight championship. Coffroth confirmed that Johnson was willing to fight Smith if the money was right.

With his arm in splints, on January 8, 1914, Johnson said,

> I am ready to fight if the offer meets my terms, which are $30,000, but the fight must be subsequent to that which has been definitely fixed to take place in Paris during the first week of June against Frank Moran, the Pittsburgh heavyweight, for which William Astor Chanler...is guaranteeing me $35,000.
>
> I expect toward the end of the same month to meet Sam Langford, provided the $30,000 I demand be forthcoming.[1127]

[1125] *New York Times, New York Journal,* December 20, 1913.
[1126] *La Presse, New York Herald,* December 21, 1913; *Le Plein Air* December 25, 1913.
[1127] *New York Times,* January 9, 1914. William Astor Chanler was a former explorer, New York State Assemblyman, soldier and military leader (including the Spanish American War), Congressman (a Democrat), businessman (real estate and mining made him a millionaire), and hotel and race-horse owner. He later was known for anti-Semitic writings.

Johnson and Moran were scheduled to meet in a 20-round contest in Paris in June. A group of American millionaires financially backed the contest. They gave Johnson and Moran checks for $35,000 and $5,000 respectively, which were not payable until the day of the fight. The group, represented by Charles McCarthy, intimated that it was motivated by the desire to see a white man re-take the championship, and, impressed by his annihilation of Palzer, they liked Moran's chances.

Billy Lewis said that man's physical supremacy had been a theme of mankind. Therefore, the "best physical man is yet an object of distinction whether savage or civilized." Hence, the heavyweight championship, as the symbol of the world's top man, was important.

The *New York Age* noted that at first, white sporting writers in the U.S. were disposed to accuse Johnson of faking in his bout with Battling Jim Johnson, but the x-ray evidence of his broken arm had caused many to give him credit for refusing to quit and enduring a most painful ordeal. Johnson was called nervy and courageous.

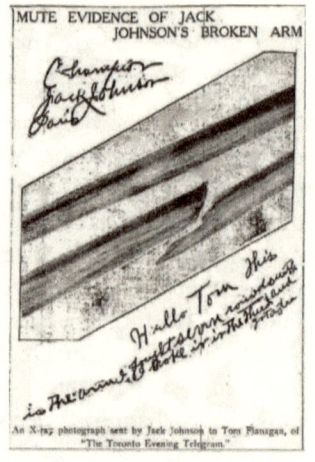

The *Evening Mail*'s sporting editor believed the real reason why the New York Boxing Commission had drawn the color line was to protect white boxers from the humiliation of defeat by a black man. Of course that was manifestly unfair to black fighters. "Fear is all that makes a boxer draw the color line. Either Jeannette, Langford or Johnson, if only half trained, could murder any white heavyweight now in the ring."[1128]

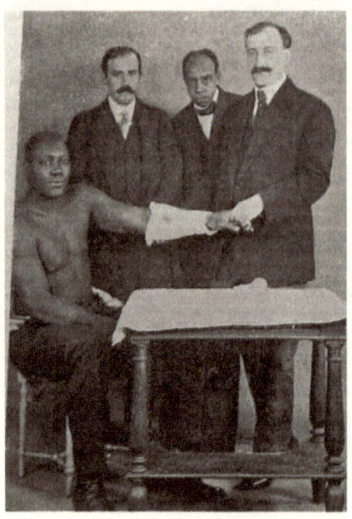

Some remained bitter over the fact that Johnson had been allowed to escape the United States. In January 1914, various stories and rumors circulated insinuating that large sums of money had changed hands in bribes to federal officials who aided Johnson in his flight from Chicago. A gloating Johnson allegedly admitted to making such payments. U.S. District Attorney James Wilkerson instituted a grand jury investigation, although ultimately no one was charged. Regardless, the reports only increased the government's ill-will towards Johnson.

The *Chicago Defender* contended that the champion was more sinned against than he had sinned. The whole case was a plot to get Johnson.[1129]

[1128] *New York Age*, January 29, 1914.
[1129] *Chicago Defender*, January 31, February 7, 1914.

Jack Johnson was persona non grata in England, even when it came to some of his exhibitions. Johnson tried to give an exhibition at Hanley, in North Staffordshire, England, but the newspapers raised such a holler that all performance venues were barred against him.

> More than once I have said England is beginning to feel what the Negro problem means. She has nearly total Africa for redemption. ... She must deal with the raw recruit from the bush. ... The leading sentiment moulder, the statesmen, the politicians, have given it out that a bad precedent is established when a black man whips a white man. They have in mind the turbulent state of Africa...where England controls.

The notion that Johnson was through and all-in as a fighter was widespread. Thus, there was growing suspicion that whoever paid Johnson to fight next was going to reimburse himself by betting on the other man. The feeling was that Moran's backers paid Johnson big money because they believed Moran would win, and they would be rich as a result of the wagers, foreign film rights, and future value of the championship.[1130]

In a letter dated February 24, 1914, Jack Johnson said he would fight anyone if his financial terms were met:

> The whole world wants to see a white man champion. I have signed to fight a white man and because I refused a ridiculously small price to meet Langford the proposed promoters and Langford's manager tried to create the impression that I would never fight again. Langford or his agent never would induce anyone with real money to back him against me. That's the reason for his soreness.
>
> I am the same John Arthur Johnson, undisputed champion of the world, and after Moran I will fight the white man who stands out, be he Gunboat Smith, Battling Levinsky, Jess Willard or Georges Carpentier.
>
> I bar no one when I get my price. Moran's backers met my terms, and all the others have the same chance as Moran. I understand that Gunboat Smith defeated Langford. Here's the gunner's chance to get a crack at my title.
>
> The public wants a white man to be my successor. I am ready to fight 'em all, and bar no one, at $30,000 apiece.[1131]

The *Chicago Defender* noted that despite suppressing films like Jeffries-Johnson, the Chicago Board of Censors failed to suppress moving pictures that bred race hatred, allowing a recent film called *Levinsky's Holiday*, which featured a frolic called "Hit the Nigger."[1132]

[1130] *Freeman*, February, 14, 1914; *Mirror of Life and Boxing World*, February 21, 1914.
[1131] *Chicago Defender*, March 14, 1914.
[1132] *Chicago Defender*, February 28, 1914. *New York Age*, March 26, 1914.

On March 21, 1914 in Paris, Joe Jeannette won a 15-round decision over Georges Carpentier, the French and European heavyweight champion.[1133]

Johnson had done much to popularize boxing, not because of love for him, but because white men wanted to see a white man on the throne. Hence there was a wide advocacy of boxing bouts almost everywhere in order to develop the man who would bring back the crown to Caucasia. Conversely, the Negro ranks were not being reinforced.

Johnson was in Stockholm, Sweden, scheduled to engage in wrestling matches. However, he was forced to leave Sweden, owing to the hostile demonstration against him.[1134]

The latest report was that Johnson's $30,000 purse would be paid to his white wife on the day of the Moran fight. "I say white wife, the words used in the dispatches, to show that that thing rankles deep yet. When Johnson went to Paris nothing was thought there of his intermarriage. It may be now that his new countrymen have gone to thinking about it. ... [S]ome go so far as to say the authorities think of sending Johnson out of the country as an undesirable citizen."

Frank Moran said if he could deliver the knockout over Johnson it would be worth a million dollars to him, "and he is right, it will be worth more; it will bring him the plaudits of the white civilization."[1135]

[1133] *New York Age*, March 26, 1914. On March 27, 1914 in New York, Sam Langford won a 10-round no-decision against Battling Jim Johnson.
[1134] *Freeman*, March 28, 1914.
[1135] *Freeman*, April 11, 1914.

CHAPTER 45

Prejudice Pervades the Record

Many folks were dissatisfied with how the Mann Act was being interpreted and enforced. A lot of blackmailers were using the act to their advantage. Men were being trapped into violating the law and then being forced to pay large sums of money to female schemers in order to avoid threatened prosecution. Many declared that "the champion pugilist is vindicated in the present dissatisfaction with the law. The department of justice will probably recommend an amendment of law, as a result of the operations of blackmailers in all parts of the county." The proposed amendment would limit its application to commercial vice. Most prosecutions had been one-sided affairs, with the man suffering, and the woman, even if she was willingly guilty, going free, which gave them the power to blackmail or get revenge on lovers who jilted them.[1136]

On April 14, 1914, Jack Johnson's appeal of his White-Slave Traffic Act criminal convictions resulted in a partial legal victory, and a partial loss. The U.S. Court of Appeals for the Seventh Circuit in Chicago upheld Johnson's convictions on two counts regarding his payment for the transport of Belle Schreiber across state lines for the immoral purpose of having sexual relations with her. It also upheld the law's constitutionality and Congress' broad grant of jurisdiction.

However, regarding the counts charging Johnson with inducing Schreiber to come to Chicago so that she might engage in prostitution, the Court of Appeals held that the evidence was insufficient as a matter of law, and his convictions on those counts were overturned. Such a holding essentially meant that no rational juror applying the beyond a reasonable doubt standard could have found him guilty of the prostitution counts, even viewing the evidence in the light most favorable to the government, because the evidence simply was not substantial enough.

The government petitioned for a rehearing, which was granted, but on June 9, the Court again reversed the convictions on the prostitution counts and upheld the convictions on the sexual intercourse charges.

The Court also held that in light of the fact that his sentence improperly took into account his erroneous convictions on the now overturned prostitution counts, Johnson should be re-sentenced.

In its ruling upholding the convictions on the sexual relations counts, the Court found that the government had proven that after Schreiber (whom it called "the girl") had told a Johnson employee of her plight; the next day she received a telegram saying, "I am sending you $75. Go to

---
[1136] *Chicago Defender*, March 28, 1914.

Chicago at Graham's and wait until I get there, Jack." She drew the money from the Postal Telegraph Company, purchased a ticket from Pittsburgh to Chicago, and traveled there on the Pennsylvania Railroad. Johnson testified that he would not or could not say that he had or had not sent the telegrams (and the telegram had not been produced at trial), but the fact that upon his arrival in Chicago he called Schreiber by telephone at Graham's (something he disputed), combined with Schreiber's testimony that Johnson asked her, "Did you receive the $75 I sent you?" warranted the jury in finding that he authored the messages. (Of course, Johnson claimed she called *him* from Graham's, not the other way around.)

Proof that Johnson's intent was to have sexual relations was bolstered by the fact that even before aiding her, "defendant habitually indulged in promiscuous sexual intercourse, that this girl was a prostitute; that defendant first met her several years before in a brothel; that throughout the period of their acquaintance they maintained sexual relations; and that frequently defendant in his journeys about the country took the girl with him, or had her travel to meet him, and always for the purpose of sexual intercourse." Johnson and Schreiber had traveled to and from Pittsburgh, Atlantic City, Chicago, Cleveland, Detroit, Buffalo, Toronto, and Montreal, and the finances were provided by Johnson, and at each place sexual relations were maintained. Hence, the Court deduced that Johnson's prior conduct and intent while he was traveling the country with Schreiber and paying her expenses to travel proved that his intent in this instance when providing her with money was to have sex with her yet again.

However, the Court also ruled that there was insufficient evidence to prove that at the time he provided Schreiber with money to travel that Johnson's intent was for her to cross state lines for the purpose of engaging in prostitution. The mere fact that he subsequently supplied her with sufficient money to enable her to open up and run a brothel was not enough, for it only raised suspicion regarding his intent at the time he provided her with the money for the train ride. There were no supplementary facts. There was no proof that Johnson had been connected with or interested in brothels or ever had aided anyone to engage in prostitution. In fact, the Court held that the prostitution evidence was "slight and dubious."

Furthermore, the Court criticized the government for its improper methods and tactics designed to inflame the jury's passions in order to prejudice them against Johnson, and for not dismissing counts it knew it could not prove. The Court said,

> In his opening statement the government's attorney said:
>
> "Another immoral purpose is one too obscene to mention, the purpose being for defendant to compel these women to commit the crime against nature upon his body. ..."
>
> We must assume that the government's attorney, when he made the statement, believed he could produce the evidence. But at some time

before he closed he knew that the picture he had drawn of the negro pugilist could not be verified. Yet not until after defendant's attorney had made a motion to that effect after the close of the government's case were the crime against nature counts withdrawn from the consideration of the jury. A desire, if not a duty, to be fair should have led the government's attorney to withdraw that heinous charge the moment he knew it could not be substantiated.

The Court opined similarly with respect to the unsupported and unproven claim in the government's opening statement that Johnson from time to time had three women with him and would drop one off and put her into a sporting house to relieve himself of the necessity of spending money carrying her about the country while he had the others. There was no proof of such allegation.

Further, the Court noted that the government improperly attempted to inflame the jury with its questioning of Johnson on cross examination:

Q. As a matter of fact that sickness (of a woman called Etta) was caused by blows from your hands, wasn't it?
A. No.
Q. Well, it was caused by blow or blows from your hands?
A. No, no.
Q. Was it not caused by blows received by Etta in Pekin Theater here in Chicago at your hands?
A. No.
Q. Did you not carry her out or have her carried out and put in the automobile and taken to the Washington Park Hospital after you had beaten her up?
A. No, no.
Q. Hattie was in the hospital while you were there, was she?
A. Not that I know of.
Q. Did you have any difficulty with her about putting her in a hospital?
A. No.
Q. Did you have any similar difficulty with Belle— fisticuff difficulty?
A. What is that?
Q. You had struck Belle on various occasions?
A. Never in my life.
Q. Do you remember using an automobile tool on her?
A. Never in my life.
Q. You never did that?
A. Never.
Q. You say you did not?
A. I say no, emphatically no.
Q. And bruised her side until it was black and blue?

The government's lawyer persistently repeated insinuating questions "with the obvious object of having his innuendoes taken in preference to the sworn answer."

A witness for the government was asked about a conversation he had on Christmas Eve, 1910 with Johnson regarding Etta. "He asked me to go to the hospital with him to call upon her. He told me he had had a fight with her at Bob Mott's Café on State street." The Court noted that Johnson's attorney duly objected to such testimony. "We find nothing in the record to justify the injection into the case of the collateral question whether defendant exercised his fighting abilities upon women." Such questions and answers had absolutely nothing to do with the charges at hand, and therefore were not relevant.

The Court held that all of these improper questions "show the atmosphere of prejudice that pervades the record." Hence, "When the situation thus improperly created is measured against the doubtfully sustainable prostitution counts, we are all convinced that defendant did not have a fair trial on that issue."

Yet, despite the government's improper inflammation of the jury's passions, creating an atmosphere of prejudice which pervaded the record, the Court did not reverse the convictions on the sexual relations counts, for "the record demonstrates that, no matter how improperly the prejudices of jurors may have been aroused, no other verdict could properly have been reached." Many folks, then and now, might strongly disagree. Johnson was entitled to have a fair trial with a decision made by an unbiased jury whose passions were not inflamed improperly against him. Such improperly inflamed passions easily could have affected the jury's judgment on all counts.[1137]

A less than pleased U.S. District Attorney James Wilkerson noted that although the evidence was held to be sufficient to sustain two counts charging improper relations, "Apparently the court holds the evidence insufficient to sustain the other counts, notwithstanding the known character of the woman and the known facts that Johnson met her in a disorderly house and subsequently furnished her money to run her flat."

Ben Bachrach was happy. "It is a great victory for us. Jack will come back now, pay a small fine and that will end it."

The *Chicago Defender* said the High Court's decision and recent efforts to amend the Mann Act showed the champ's friends that their contention that he was persecuted and not prosecuted was nearly right.[1138]

A few years later, in 1917, in three concurrently decided and reported cases (*Caminetti v. United States*, 242 U.S. 470 (1917), *Diggs v. United States*, and *Hayes v. United States*), the U.S. Supreme Court confirmed that consensual illicit fornication (sexual intercourse between unmarried persons), whether or not for the commercial purpose of prostitution, was an "immoral purpose" under the Mann Act. Caminetti and Diggs had taken their mistresses from Sacramento, California to Reno, Nevada. Their wives informed the police, and both men were arrested in Reno. They were

---

[1137] Johnson v. U.S., 215 F. 679 (7th Cir. 1914).
[1138] *Freeman, Chicago Defender*, April 18, 1914.

convicted on September 5, 1913; four months after Jack Johnson had been convicted.

In 1922, U.S. President Warren G. Harding nominated and the U.S. Senate confirmed former U.S. District Attorney James H. Wilkerson as judge for the U.S. District Court for the Northern District of Illinois, the seat vacated by Kenesaw Mountain Landis. On November 24, 1931, Wilkerson was the judge who sentenced Al Capone to 11 years in prison for tax evasion.

Judge Kennesaw Mountain Landis, who had set Johnson's bail at $30,000 and would not accept cash, and had helped Wilkerson keep Lucille Cameron in police custody, eventually became major league baseball's first commissioner in late 1920. He was known especially for banning eight Chicago White Sox players in the wake of the fixing of the 1919 World Series, causing the team to become known as the "Black Sox." Their individual involvement, or lack thereof, has been the subject of historical debate. The players had been acquitted in their criminal trials.

Former world featherweight boxing champion Abe Attell (a cornerman for Jeffries in the Johnson fight) apparently was involved in the World Series fixing fiasco, allegedly acting as an intermediary for gambler Arnold Rothstein, though charges against Attell were dismissed before the trial, for he defeated extradition from Canada. Rothstein never was charged.

As baseball commissioner, Kennesaw Mountain Landis was such a staunch color line advocate, no black player ever was allowed in major league baseball throughout his tenure as commissioner.

CHAPTER 46

Reversal of Opinion

Writing for the *Chicago Defender*, Ernest Stevens visited Paris and found the champ to be the most prosperous man of color in the city. He maintained a beautiful residence in a nice area.

Regardless, Stevens said the black race had a slim chance abroad. He had not seen many blacks, and there were very few avenues of employment open to them. Both Stevens and Johnson advised friends to remain in the U.S. France was not so great for blacks after all.

> There is only one Afro-American in Paris who can say that he is happy and that is Jack Johnson. I went to his house in Ansieres, a fashionable suburb, about ten miles ride from the city. He looks as robust and healthy as ever. He occupies a fine residence, with a large playground and poultry yard. He maintains a garage which houses several first class cars. He is prosperous and is kept busy running from one country to another doing theatrical turns. He sends greetings and like the writer, advises his friends to remain in the United States. There were also very few blacks in Holland and Hamburg. What few there are were of the unfortunate type that give the dominant race a bad impression of the whole. I may add that the German people give the race a squarer deal than the English.[1139]

On May 6, 1914, the French Boxing Federation, which previously refused to recognize him as champion, reversed course and said it now was accepting Jack Johnson's claim to the title. Lending some insight into why the French Federation had changed its mind, Theodore Vienne, a prominent member, had assumed the general management of the fight between Johnson and Moran, obtaining the right to 1/3 of the profits. He signed a contract to stage the match on June 27 as scheduled, succeeding Emile Maitrot, who "retired." The fight would be held at the Velodrome d'Hiver, which contained 26,000 seats and had standing room for 4,000 more. It was all about economics after all.[1140]

Joe Jeannette said, "Well, I tell you it's just this way; If all the stories that are going the rounds about the way Johnson has gone to pieces through drink and other kinds of dissipation are true, it ought to be easy for Moran

---

[1139] *Chicago Defender*, April 25, 1914. On May 1, 1914 in New Orleans, Louisiana, more than 5,000 fans watched 28-year-old Sam Langford and 24-year-old Harry Wills fight to a 10-round no-decision draw. Some writers thought Langford won, some said Wills won, while others argued it was a draw. The local *Times-Democrat* said the local fighter Wills had won. *Freeman*, May 30, 1914.
[1140] *New York Times*, May 7, 1914. *Freeman*, May 16, 23, 1914; *Denver Post*, June 25, 1914.

to whip him. But, on the other hand, if these stories aren't true, Frank Moran won't win." Johnson was weighing around 240 pounds.[1141]

Apparently, while in Paris, Johnson had punched Charles W. Galvin, a Johnson masseur who uttered something about salary in a fashion which Johnson thought was rude, and the Dutchman had a vague recollection of being lifted from the floor and thrown through the air, landing with a bump. Johnson settled out of court by paying Galvin 100 pounds.

The *Mirror of Life* reported that the majority of Americans were confident in Moran, and a lot of money was backing him. They believed Johnson was past-it. "Perhaps they take their wishes for realities!"[1142]

A veteran of 39 professional contests, Pittsburgh's 200-pound 27-year-old 6'1" Frank Moran was a strong, husky, tough, and durable fighter. His claim to fame was his last fight, the September 1913 KO7 over then highly touted 227-pound Al Palzer. Moran had won all five of his fights in London. He had fought once in Paris and won.

Frank Moran

Many felt that a Moran victory depended upon how far diminished Johnson was. There were many "Ifs." If Johnson had slowed up, if he had lost his punch, if dissipation had cut down his stamina, if he failed to train properly or underestimated his more youthful opponent, etc. Johnson claimed to be the same well-trained man as ever.

During sparring on June 16 with Tom Kennedy, Moran slipped and collided with his partner's head, splitting his left eyebrow. The 2.5-inch wound healed rapidly, but in order to avoid any risk of it reopening, he stopped sparring. Today, such a cut would force a postponement, but these were different times and men, particularly since they did not stop fights on cuts back then.[1143]

It was announced in England that the Home Office no longer would allow any boxing matches between whites and blacks. English promoter C. B. Cochran wanted to arrange a Sam Langford vs. Gunboat Smith bout, but, "I was advised by the Home Office that it met with their disapproval and that they would take steps to stop any further contest between black men and white."[1144]

Otto Floto said that 999 out of 1,000 fights were on the square, but the rare fake made folks become suspicious even about genuine fights.

[1141] *Freeman*, May 30, 1914. On June 9, 1914 in New Orleans, Joe Jeannette and Harry Wills fought a 10-round no-decision draw, though some thought Wills won. On June 13, 1914 in Melbourne, Australia, Sam McVey knocked out Arthur Pelkey in the 4th round.
[1142] *Mirror of Life and Boxing World*, June 13, 1914.
[1143] *Freeman*, June 20, 1914.
[1144] *New York Herald*, June 21, 1914.

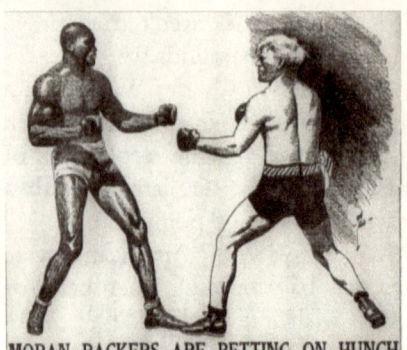

MORAN BACKERS ARE BETTING ON HUNCH

William A. Brady offered reasons why he had wagered on Moran to defeat the "big smoke." "I know that the big black is 36 years old; I know he has been drinking hard, living the fastest kind of life; going the pace that kills for five years." Such a life was bound to catch up with him eventually, especially at what was an advanced age for a boxer, particularly since he was going up against a young, strong, rugged, in-shape fighter like Moran. No champion ever had successfully defended his title at Johnson's age, and Brady did not believe Johnson would be the exception. Therefore, the "world will once more have a white man in the top division of the boxing game."[1145]

The *New York Journal*'s Tad Dorgan said no boxer alive could compare with Johnson in kidding. He was the greatest goat-getter the ring ever saw. Jack took his time, and no one could rush him, or outbox him:

> It's his style. He never yet has made a great impression in the ring, because he is not a showy fighter. He is just a big strong fellow with an eye like a hawk and a slam like a pile driver. He ignores the yelps of the mob or the abuse from rival corners, looks his man over well and then gets down to work. He has no fancy footwork. He doesn't need it. . . ... He can pick off punches that 99 out of 100 other boxers would stop with their chins. His strength is equal to that of two men. He showed that in Reno when he tossed Jeffries around like a baby.
>
> ... Johnson will be in shape, as he usually is, when a title is at stake, and just as careful.

Tad said many were wagering on Moran based on a hunch that Johnson was due to lose given his age and alleged dissipation. On a daily basis, William A. Brady, former Corbett and Jeffries manager, was writing that Moran was a cinch to win, for Johnson was too old. However, Tad said Moran was an ordinary man facing an extraordinary one.

The confident Moran claimed that he would tear into Johnson and break him after about 7 or 8 rounds, for the champion's best days had passed. "A champion worries when he goes into a fight, because he's had all the good things, and he's afraid he may lose them."[1146]

Dr. Gaston Dupau examined Johnson. He said that except for a slight trace of pneumonia, detected by a whistling sound near the top of the right lung while his breath was expelled, from which Jack had suffered back in March 1913, his condition was perfect. The doctor said there was nothing serious in those symptoms, which usually disappeared within two years.[1147]

[1145] *Denver Post*, June 24, 1914.
[1146] *New York Journal*, June 25, 1914.
[1147] *New York Journal*, June 25, 1914.

A couple days before the fight, William Brady declared that Johnson's training was a farce, for he was fat, not in shape, and had impaired wind.

Brady believed there would be a new world champion, one whose skin was white. Moran had a college education and an "abundance of native intelligence." Victory would mean half a million dollars to him, plus "the lasting gratitude of the white people of the world."

Dr. Joseph Goode of Chicago examined Moran and said, "I have seen Johnson also and I believe Moran is physically a better man."

In his training, Moran was more powerful, and never fatigued, working rapidly and effectively, with livelier footwork than Johnson, and he was more energetic. Willie Lewis said, "Moran is really the first good man Johnson has ever met. None of the others could hit as hard as Moran."[1148]

Nothing was talked about in Paris other than the big fight, from the gutter to the homes of the aristocracy.

Johnson cabled his mother in Chicago, telling her that he would win, and there was nothing to fear.[1149]

En haut, FRANK MORAN
En bas, JACK JOHNSON

James J. Corbett said, "I would give my right arm to see Moran win because it would help boxing a lot."

Although Tom Flanagan was sure that Johnson would win, he believed the battle would go the full 20 rounds.

William Muldoon said Johnson would lose. "He hasn't faced on his merits a clever or even moderately clever boxer in years. ... If Johnson defeats Moran in this bout, it will be by far the most creditable performance of his entire pugilistic career."[1150]

The *New York Herald* estimated that the receipts would reach at least $100,000. French champion George Carpentier's selection to referee likely would help attract an even larger attendance, for he was an idol amongst Parisians.[1151]

The *Denver Post*'s Otto Floto called Johnson the "Inky Kink" and the "Cinder," who was expert at tricking fighters to come after him so he could pick them apart. Still, Johnson's dissipation was proverbial, with wine, women, and song being his slogan.[1152]

The *Cincinnati Enquirer* said,

[1148] *New York American*, June 25-27, 1914; *New York Herald*, June 26, 1914; *New York Journal*, June 27, 1914.
[1149] *New York Journal*, June 27, 1914.
[1150] *New York American*, June 27, 1914.
[1151] *New York Herald*, *Omaha World Herald*, June 27, 1914.
[1152] *Denver Post*, June 27, 1914.

The trouble with Johnson is that he has had a flock of enemies to contend with and is seldom given his just dues. ... [I]t is not fair to judge a man's fighting ability by what takes place in his private life. Throw aside the prejudice and Johnson stands out as the champion in all the word implies. He is a natural-born fighter and did not get to the top by any boosting from the press agent. His color was against him, and he had a hard row to hoe.[1153]

Every seat in the big arena had been engaged, including by some members of royalty. Ringside seats were going for $75, $100, and $125.[1154]

The *New York American* said Moran was a college student, baseball player, football player, sailor, clerk, and pugilist. Moran and Johnson actually had boxed a 4-round exhibition in Pittsburgh four years ago.[1155]

The *New York American* listed Moran as 203 to Johnson's 215 pounds. *L'Humanite* said Johnson weighed about 99 kg (218 pounds).

La Presse said it would be the biggest fight in France's history.

L'Humanite said that for the past four years, Johnson essentially had abandoned the ring for exhibitions, punch bowls, and fun, dancing the bear-step in music halls. Regardless, he had trained seriously for the fight.

Le Petit Parisien said those who saw Moran in training were unanimous in the opinion that the white man was capable of victory.

L'Intransigeant said it was a nearly even fight. Johnson had lost much of his fat. Those who saw him had trouble believing that this amazing athlete could be beaten.

Le Matin said Johnson had to flee the United States essentially because the Americans were not happy with his color. The U.S. population would be very satisfied to learn about Johnson's defeat.[1156]

On the evening of June 27, 1914 in Paris, France, Jack Johnson defended his world heavyweight championship against Frank Moran.[1157]

[1153] *Freeman*, June 27, 1914.
[1154] *Chicago Defender*, June 27, 1914.
[1155] *New York American*, June 28, 1914.
[1156] *La Presse*, June 27, 28, 1914; *L'Humanite* June 27, 1914 *Le Petit Parisien*, June 27 1914; *L'Intransigeant*, June 28 1914; *Le Matin*, June 27, 1914.
[1157] The following account is an amalgamation of *Le Petit Parisien, New York Herald, New York American, London Times, Le Matin, Denver Post*, June 28, 1914; *La Presse*, June 29, 1914; *Mirror of Life and Boxing World*, July 4, 1914.

The *New York American* said the $30,000 check, made out in February, had been photographed and placed in the Credit Lyonnaise's vaults, to be handed to Mrs. Johnson at noon on the day of the fight. That was in addition to the $5,000 in training expenses already paid to Johnson.

The fight was held at the Velodrome d'Hiver, where they hosted bicycling races, near Champs de Mars. The French said it was the largest arena in the world for this type of event. The place was beautiful and represented a small fortune. There were both upper and lower galleries.[1158]

Several French reports said there were about 30,000 or 35,000 spectators. Every seat in the arena was taken. Ticket prices anywhere near the ring ranged from $40 to $60. Every ticket's price had a 10% surcharge added, the money going to charitable organizations.

The *Mirror of Life and Boxing World* said the reported gate was 12,000 pounds ($60,000). The *New York American* believed the gate would approach $100,000, and Johnson would earn nearly $50,000, greater than his guarantee, owing to the generally accepted theory that he owned an interest in the promotion. The motion picture rights were held by Johnson, Moran, and Promoter Vienne, which would generate additional revenue.

All of Paris was present, including every element of society - sportsmen, intellectuals, artists, and people of high society. The crowd included counts and countesses, princes and princesses, dukes and duchesses, famous French statesmen, boulevardiers, jockeys, American millionaires, theatrical people, and even the English and a bunch of rowdy Americans who had crossed the Atlantic just for this match. Local writers noted that a bout between a man of color and a paleface brought out a lot of passion.

The several hundred Americans present included Herman Duryea, former Senator C. W. Watson of West Virginia, Frank O'Neill, Alfred and Reggie Vanderbilt, Anthony and John Drexel, and Willie Ritchie. Several hundred women were in the audience, wearing beautiful gowns and jewels, including Baroness Henry de Rothschild, who was with Baron James de Rothschild. Spencer Eddy, former American minister to Argentina, sat near the ring, as did England's Duke of Westminster, the Earl of Sefton, and former French Premier Louis Barthou.

Johnson's wife Lucille occupied a prominent position, handsomely gowned and wearing many diamonds. During the fight, she would cheer and clap every time her husband landed a good blow.

There were some dark faces present as well, including those from Senegal, Dahomey, and the West Indies, two members of the Guadeloupe Chamber of Deputies, Prince Dauleep/Duleep Singh of India, and Omar Sultan Pasha of Egypt. It was an amazingly international crowd.

The Americans put in place a special telegraph post which allowed them to send direct trans-Atlantic cables, all at the expense of a couple thousand francs. Round-by-round reports were sent to New York.

[1158] Years later, the velodrome would be where they kept Jews before they shipped them off to concentration camps.

The 16-foot ring was roofed in with a panoply of purple silk, beneath which were rows of yard-long tubes of electric lamps, whose lights cast reflections of different colors on the spectators, making them and everything in the vicinity of the ring appear ghastly. Some had a greenish tint, while others appeared pink, etc.

The bright lights combined with the mass of humanity made the arena quite hot and uncomfortable. Men quickly removed their coats. Women in evening dress perspired. The *London Times* said it was doubtful if even the opportunity to see Georges Carpentier would have brought out so many women had they known before-hand about the lighting arrangements. However, the lights were necessary for filming the indoor fight.

The bout was scheduled to start at 10:30 p.m. in Paris, which was 5:30 p.m. in New York. The two combatants entered the ring at 10:15 p.m.

Le Petit Parisien said Johnson was smiling, looking superb and confident. His body was slightly thickened, but he gave the impression of a muscular black Hercules. He dropped his long, striped dressing gown to the floor, then bowed and nodded to the crowd with a smile.

Frank Moran, the "hope of an entire race," entered second, and he received a boisterous greeting from the delirious crowd, for they were pulling for the blonde. After all, he was a white man.

The local French press said Moran, the hope of the white race, was big and muscular. He appeared more serious than Johnson, but very confident, with a will to win.

Johnson was wearing blue trunks. Moran wore green trunks with the stars and stripes flag around his waist.

While putting on his gloves, Johnson talked to his seconds. The electric rays of light ricocheted off of his constantly smiling golden teeth.

Several writers said Johnson looked fitter than most people had expected, though there still was some fat around his midsection.

Referee Georges Carpentier entered the ring to acclamations. He wore flannels - a white shirt, white pants, and white shoes. Carpentier appeared to be the most nervous person in the ring.

Announcer Max Sergy used a long megaphone to make the introductions. At 10:33 p.m., the bell rang to start the fight.

As usual for a Johnson fight, Jack was in control, boxing carefully, pacing himself well, exhibiting his clever defense, landing jabs on the outside, and uppercuts on the inside. Moran tried to vary his tactics, occasionally attacking and fighting on the inside, and at other times, moving and circling around, trying to draw Johnson's attack and counter. Sometimes Johnson would move in and pressure Moran, while at other times he waited, stood still, and either would block and counter, or step back and counter. Hence, both took turns advancing or leading. However, nothing that Moran did worked on the clever Johnson.

For the most part, the fight was slow-paced, with both fairly cautious and defensive. When Johnson advanced, he would land a fast punch, usually a jab or straight right, and Moran would clinch. Occasionally they had a fast back-and-forth scuffle of punches up close until the inevitable clinch. There was a lot of feinting and sliding back and forth as well. Moran liked to keep his left arm out to measure Johnson. But it was Johnson who did most of the landing. Between rounds, the cornermen waived towels to cool off the men.

By the 4th round, Moran's nose was bleeding from the repeated jabs, and the crimson flowed. Johnson was dominating more and more, smiling confidently as he met Frank's attack, landing uppercuts on the inside.

As the fight progressed, the spectators complained about the lack of action, for there was too much sparring, feinting, and clinching to suit their tastes.

In the 6th round, Johnson nonchalantly said to the waiting Moran, "Come on, come on." George Considine called out to Johnson, "You don't know how to lead; never did." Johnson playfully replied, "No. ... All right, Jim Corbett."

The French press said that even if the white man could not win, at least he could resist. Johnson seemed to think exactly the same thing, treating his rival with great respect.

In the 7th round, Johnson opened wider a small cut on Moran's nose. George Considine yelled, "Moran's the first good man you ever fought." Jack simply smiled back.

Johnson would fire a jab and then a clinch would follow. He was infighting successfully, landing short rights, uppercuts, and body shots in close.

At one point in the 10th round, as Moran was pushing off to break from a clinch, Johnson landed a right uppercut that jolted Frank's head back, and Moran stepped back to complain. He walked to a corner as Carpentier warned Johnson for hitting after the break was ordered.

At this point in the fight, Johnson was doing all of the leading and landing. Moran was bleeding abundantly from the cut on his nose, which was bothering him, and also bleeding from his mouth as well. Jack sarcastically asked, "How are you feeling now, Frank?"

By the 11th round, Johnson was inflicting punishment, having a huge advantage in the fight. A tired Moran often hid his face behind his gloves. Johnson cut Moran's eyebrow and scored frequently on the jaw.

Johnson dominated the 12th as well, landing several effective uppercuts and straight lefts. Moran was breathing hard and bleeding badly. His attendants were solemn-faced.

In the 13th round, Moran rallied gamely, attacking with determination, though Johnson presented a very fine defense and also worked in his short blows.

Moran missed a right, but shifting with lightning quickness, finally landed one powerful left hook to the neck. The blow made a lot of noise. Johnson smiled, laughed, and applauded with both hands along with the cheering crowd as Moran stepped away. They both smiled as Frank extended his right arm as if to shake.

Thereafter though, Johnson was in control, landing jabs, counter right uppercuts, a lead hook, and a snappy, sneaky-fast left uppercut.

In the 14th round, Moran tried but could not land. His attempts brought smiles from Johnson.

La Presse believed that the cautious Moran's only idea was to last the distance. Johnson seemed to be amusing himself, having a good time.

In the 15th round, at least four times, Moran circled around the entire ring and avoided Johnson, who stood at ring center, pivoted in place, and watched and laughed at the moving Moran. The crowd booed, while Johnson put his hands on his hips and smiled as he watched Moran circle him.
Considine said, "You're the champion; show something." In fact, Johnson did most of the leading from the outside, firing quick jabs, and he did all of the effective work on the inside. He kept ripping in right uppercuts. When Moran attempted to lead, Jack would step back and make the blows fall short, and sometimes counter with a jab.

Le Petit Parisien said the fight had become tedious, consisting of faraway hits with little power. It was a good fight between two friends. The still-smiling Johnson kept hitting him again and again, but the white man's face showed no emotion, and he did not seem to be affected by the blows, although several noted that Moran was bleeding abundantly. A series of Johnson uppercuts had the blood spurting from Moran's left eyebrow.

By the 18th round, the crowd started shouting, dissatisfied with the lack of combat.

In the 19th round, neither landed anything significant. Referee Georges Carpentier frequently separated them from clinches.

Le Petit Parisien said that even before the 20th and final round began, the tired and upset audience started toward the exits, knowing the result already.

In the 20th round, Johnson kept sticking jabs and holding Moran safe on the inside. Moran's attempts  to land from the outside were futile, for Jack always moved just out of range of the blows. The *Herald* said Johnson landed frequently and at will. Moran hung on and tried ineffectively for the body. *La Presse* said that Johnson seemed to be at the end of his force. However, Moran faded into emptiness. Both were tired.

Le Petit Parisien said that when Referee Georges Carpentier appointed Jack Johnson as the winner, everybody recognized it. Without any possible discussion, Johnson was the winner and still "champion du monde."

All of the ringside observers agreed that Johnson clearly won, though most said he was slipping and no longer the same.

Max Hogmanay, writing for *Le Petit Parisien*, said Johnson easily beat Moran on points. He also concluded that Johnson no longer hit very hard, but granted it was possible that the white hope simply could take it very well. Either way, Johnson had the science necessary to retain his title.

Daniel Cousin for *La Presse* said Johnson beat Moran in an amicable fight. The fight seemed a bit bizarre and weird. It was not a fight, but rather a bunch of smiles and grimaces. Neither man was effective. Johnson was a shadow of what he once was, but Moran did nothing. He rarely attacked, but simply tried to finish the 20 rounds. He often ran around the ring, while Johnson stopped and waited for him.

L'Humanite said that as early as the 3rd round, one could see Johnson's superiority. He allowed his adversary to hammer his chest; at the same time smiling with his big golden teeth, as if he was having a good time. The champion was happy just to await the attacks and counter. Moran did not have the same class. Frank saw that it was impossible to hurt his opponent, and nearly impossible to hit him. His body blows had no effect. Even after landing a big hook in the 13th, Jack just laughed, smiled, and clapped. Johnson certainly won on points.

L'Intransigeant believed that a more courageous adversary than Moran could have won. Moran gave the impression of being hypnotized. Johnson could not really apply himself in the dull fight, but it wasn't his fault. He was discouraged from following his fleeing adversary around the ring, once even standing still with his hands on his hips, waiting for Moran. Even his 36 years and his time at the café had not destroyed Johnson's athletic qualities. He still was good enough to defeat Moran, even if he no longer was what he once was. Moran had lost the chance of his life.

Le Matin said the exhibition was ridiculous and comedic. The match was nothing for Johnson, but he pretended for an excellent laugh and some fun. He enjoyed moving to the side with a huge smile, eluding blows. While Moran hit him in the body, Jack smiled. When the public booed and whistled, Johnson simply laughed. Americans would call out in anger, "That's the champion?" "[T]he public had to sit there and watch the joy of this child, the infantile joy of this black person. His impudence was unconscious."

Johnson was heavy, fat, and slow. Yet, Moran did not show any of the excellent confidence which he had before the fight. He must have prepared himself too well for the match on paper and in his own imagination.

Moran found himself in the situation of a general who prepared a battle plan which would be excellent, but the response of his enemy was better than what he thought it would be. Close-up, Johnson was big and muscular, and Moran started to re-think, and he thought a long time. He rarely landed anything. The Americans who were sitting at ringside would call out to him, "Go on Frank, hit him." However, Moran seemed more interested in not getting hit.

Both men appeared to be holding themselves back. They smiled at one another amiably. It seemed as if they were apologizing to one another if they landed. Of course, Moran was cut and bleeding, and sometimes the blood blinded him. This writer believed that Moran never would be champion.[1159]

The *New York Herald* ringside reporter said Johnson had no trouble outpointing the white hope, winning with ease. Johnson's superior skill and effective uppercuts wore down his opponent. Toward the end, Johnson had Moran absolutely at his mercy. Moran apparently feared that he would be finished, and clung to Johnson for support, trying at the same time to land, but without success.

Johnson's wife cried out shrilly from time to time: "Hit him daddy!" "Come along, pop." "Now then, Jack, let him have another." The crowd sweltered under the heat.

William Brady was hard on both boxers. He called it a second-rate exhibition, for neither landed damaging blows. The big Paris crowd cried out in disgust, jeering and hissing at the fiasco, for the fight was too friendly and cautious. One said, "Why don't you kiss each other?" Johnson was tired, but Moran's own exhaustion saved the champ. Still, Brady acknowledged, "As a boxer Moran was absolutely outclassed." Moran did not deliver more than a score of really effective blows during the entire fight, while Johnson landed possibly a dozen in each round. A straight left and the old-time right uppercut in the clinches were all that Johnson had to offer, and all that he needed. "It is certain that Johnson was in better general condition than Moran in the last round."

Brady did note that in successfully defending the crown, Johnson had accomplished a feat never before achieved by a man of his age in the history of the ring.

William H. Rocap, the bout's official timekeeper, said the fight was spoiled in the last two rounds because Johnson was not trying. "Johnson affected being tired, and Moran, weak from his own exertions, was quite satisfied to stay the limit."

C. F. Bertelli said at no time did a Moran victory appear possible. Johnson completely outclassed him. It looked as if Johnson was carrying him, and could have punished him more severely had he so desired. Johnson's boxing was superb, particularly with his left. He landed heavy counterpunches, but then was content, and hardly ever followed up his advantages with sufficient keenness.

Moran did nearly all of the clinching, but in the clinches, it was Johnson who landed most of the blows. Blood covered Moran's face. Johnson finished stronger, and was in better general condition than Moran.[1160]

[1159] *L'Humanite* June 28, 1914; *L'Intransigeant*, June 29, 1914; *Le Matin*, June 28, 1914.
[1160] *New York American*, June 28, 1914.

The *London Times* said the event proved that Jeffries eventually would be avenged by age and passing years. Johnson's days as champion were about over, but he still was good enough to beat Moran, who did most of the leading, but rarely landed. The fight was tedious and disappointing.

The spectators suspected the fight was not genuine. "This was a quite excusable, if mistaken, suspicion, and at times it was ludicrous to see Johnson in the middle of the ring revolving on his own axis with Moran strolling round the ring trying unsuccessfully to draw him – indeed, Carpentier once told the men to fight."[1161]

Con Murphy, writing for the British publication, *Mirror of Life and Boxing World*, said Parisians were dissatisfied. Denied a knockout, they hooted with peculiar shrillness, crying, "Fake" and demanding their money back.

There never was a question of fake to capable judges who watched from ringside, though some spectators thought there was an arrangement between the men. The truth was that Johnson was in earnest, showing more aggression than was his custom, willing to do his share of the forcing, but Moran was cautious, and lacking in execution when he was aggressive. His own futile exertions, combined with the punishment he took, left him fatigued, and he could not harm the champ. Despite age, inactivity, and an easy lifestyle creeping up on Johnson, he still possessed his famous boxing ability. He was a classy boxer and sound ring general, and won clearly.

Moran was entitled to credit for being the first challenger to extend Johnson. That said, this writer said the champ's next performance might prove it was nothing remarkable to last rounds with him, for any husky in-shape big man might do so with the champion in his present form.

This writer believed Johnson was nearing the end of his reign, but the question was who was best suited to dethrone him. Many, like Langford, Carpentier, and Gunboat Smith, might give him some trouble, but it was unclear whether they could *beat* him. Johnson had too many advantages in size, strength, speed, and skill to be the underdog against anyone.

Regardless, the contest was the "writing on the wall," so to speak, for Johnson. "He is about finished as an attraction in Paris, and while they would go to see him box Carpentier, in the hope of a victory for the French boy, there would be a very small gate for him against anybody else."

Referee Georges Carpentier said it was one of the best fights he had ever seen. When asked if he would like to fight Johnson, Carpentier responded in the negative. "Johnson is a little bit too heavy for me at present." Carpentier realized that he was not ready for Johnson.[1162]

In interviews, Johnson called attention to the fact that no other champion his age ever defended the title successfully.

> They thought I couldn't last 20 rounds. Well, didn't I? I am satisfied. … Moran? He has a real hard punch with either hand. I know, because I have been there. If they always landed there is not anybody

---

[1161] *London Times*, June 29, 1914.
[1162] Seven years later, Carpentier would fight for the heavyweight crown against Jack Dempsey, giving him the distinction of having both refereed and fought in a heavyweight championship contest.

who could stand up against him. He is a good boy, all right, and I enjoyed the fight. Carpentier was a fine referee. ...

Did I not box all right? I am as strong as ever and I never turned a hair. I'll fight any man in the world, within the next six weeks, too, if he comes along. ... Moran is a big, strong fellow, you know, and I do not know any man in the world able to stop him quickly.

Moran said,

Jack Johnson is a better boxer than I am. The way he got into condition was remarkable and a big surprise to me. ... I have no apologies to make. I put up the best fight I could, but the negro's ring experience was too much to overcome.

A couple days later, Moran said, "I figured I could whip Johnson in view of his age, but I now believe him to be as strong as he ever was."[1163]

The *New York Journal's* Tad Dorgan said many observers simply did not understand or appreciate Johnson, and got their analysis of him and his performance against Moran all wrong. It was the same kind of fight that Johnson had fought for the past ten years, for the "champ is not of the spectacular sort and never was. He fights the same cool, cautious battle every time." Johnson always fought his own way. He was a master at imposing his tactics on everyone, enjoying playing defense and kidding his foes. He outclassed Moran without exerting himself. Regardless of his old age for a boxer, Johnson still would be the betting favorite against anyone.

Some were figuring that Johnson would lay down to Moran. However, he never had done it in his career, and there was no reason why he should do it with Moran when he could have done it with Jeffries and made a lot more. "Our dope here is that when Lil' Artha Johnson lays down it will be on the level. It may not be soon, but it will come."[1164]

In the U.S., there was plenty of action surrounding the fight, and, as sometimes was the case with a Johnson fight, that action included some racial violence. The *Herald* said that during the bout, vast throngs of men, women, and children stood outside newspaper buildings receiving fight bulletins. At least 1,800 swelled Broadway into 36th street in New York's Herald square to receive the *New York Herald's* bulletins.

Any time that the white hope did something positive, there was loud cheering. Although those of Johnson's race kept reasonably quiet, at one point a "dusky" advocate gave vent to a cheer for the "Smoke," shouting, "Go it Jack!" An upset white hoper immediately engaged him with hot words. Sometimes such incidents would lead to violence.

In New York there were some race riots and beatings in the wake of the fight bulletins. The *Herald* reported that there was a race battle between 200 whites and blacks. A black youth named Leon Earley, while riding a street car, uttered a cheer for Jack Johnson. This angered a crowd of white men,

---

[1163] *New York Herald*, June 29, 1914.
[1164] *New York Journal*, June 29, 1914.

who attacked. They dragged him from the street car and gave him a severe beating, breaking his jaw. This brought a score of blacks to his rescue and a general fight took place. Many were beaten severely. It only ended when 50 policemen appeared. A white man named James Walsh charged Earley with slashing him with a razor. Earley was charged with felonious assault, while Walsh was taken into custody on a charge of disorderly conduct.

Another separate battle took place. For several days leading up to the fight, the Johnson–Moran bout had been the subject of bitter argument between white and black factions. Blacks' confidence in their champion and willingness to bet on him served to embitter the members of the white Gopher band, which had pinned its faith on Moran. Word was that the Gophers would wreak vengeance upon black folk if Moran lost. Hence, blacks were warned that if Johnson won, they should not appear in the streets unarmed.

When news of Johnson's victory reached the Gophers, a band of 15 of them appeared in the streets armed with heavy clubs. They gave battle to every black person they met. One of the whites, John Burns, wound up being slashed with a razor by a black man who was acting in self-defense. Burns suffered a ten-inch gash to his shoulder, which required a tourniquet to save his life. He was taken unconscious to Bellevue Hospital.

Blacks were assaulted and badly beaten, overpowered by numbers. Four blacks were beaten into insensibility. Eventually, a dozen police appeared and quelled the riot. The police ordered all blacks off the streets (but not whites). Several lesser riots took place.

In another incident, angered at Johnson's victory, a crowd of white men assaulted a black man. A policeman who came to his rescue was knocked down by the crowd, after which he used his nightstick freely. Several other policemen soon appeared and the trouble was ended.[1165]

Also in New York, a man named Michael Smith was followed down the street by a crowd of hooting children, for he was wearing a woman's dress. He was arrested and taken to the Night Court. He told the judge that he was paying a wager with his wife. He had been so confident in Moran that he agreed that if Johnson won, he would masquerade in an old dress. Smith was released on probation.

Jack Johnson said he would fight Sam Langford in mid-October for a guaranteed $30,000 plus 50% of the motion picture receipts.

Others said that if white heavyweight champion Gunboat Smith defeated Georges Carpentier in their scheduled July 16 bout that he would be the logical candidate for the next crack at Johnson, given that he had beaten Langford.

Unfortunately, the day after Johnson-Moran, on Sunday June 28, 1914 in Sarajevo, Bosnia, a young Bosnian-Serbian student, as part of a nationalist conspiracy, assassinated Archduke Francis-Ferdinand of Austria (heir to the Austro-Hungarian throne and nephew of the Austrian emperor) and his wife, the Duchess of Hohenberg. The anarchist exploded a bomb that failed

---

[1165] *New York Herald*, June 28, 1914.

to kill them, but then he finished them off with a hail of bullets. Eleven others were injured by the bomb. This political assassination would trigger a series of events that led to the outbreak of what later became known as World War I one month later. The "great war," as it was then known, would put big boxing in Europe on hiatus for years.[1166]

For whatever reason, within a couple days of the Moran bout, Jack Adams, one of Johnson's trainers, claimed the Moran fight was faked for the benefit of the moving pictures and insiders who had bet that the fight would go the limit. He said McKetrick proposed Moran to Johnson as a man whom he could handle with the utmost ease. Moran would be built up in movies shown in America, they would fight, Johnson would carry him, and then they could make more with a rematch. Adams said Mrs. Johnson drew her husband's $30,000 the Saturday before the fight.

> I think the plot has been defeated by Johnson himself, who behaved in the ring with consummate folly, as he could have knocked Moran out in the fifth round.
>
> He didn't do so, on account of the movies. Later he spared the white hope in the most obvious way for money-making purposes.
>
> Tom Flanagan, who has been Johnson's adviser through thick and thin, knew the fight would go twenty rounds. Today he declared to me he was thoroughly disgusted and it was the last time he would have anything to do with such a contest. ...
>
> Johnson has now turned against himself the entire sporting public in the country, where he intends to make a permanent home, as the French won't credit him as being a great fighter again.

30,000 people paid over $100,000 to watch the dullest and most wearisome bout that ever masqueraded as a championship fight. "Johnson could probably have won at any time, but he carefully avoided striking Moran in a killing place or with killing strength."

Another claim and theory was that Johnson stood to gain by carrying Moran, because by failing to knock him out, the gullible public now would think that Smith and Carpentier had a chance against him, so he could earn big paydays against them.[1167]

Bill Brady described Jack Adams as a "well known Octoroon sportsman, who was one of the smoke's principal trainers in his last fight." Brady said Johnson was barred in America because of his "escapades with white women," and now, because of his fake fight with Moran, he had turned the entire French sporting public against him.

Brady respected Johnson's ability, and said it was not fair to roast Moran, for he failed as others had. Still, Brady believed there likely would be a new champion the next time Johnson fought a good man, for he was slipping. The concern was that the man who defeated Johnson might be

---

[1166] *New York Herald,* June 29, 1914.
[1167] *New York Journal,* June 29, 1914.

another black man, such as Langford, and the championship would not be restored to the white race.

Based on his boxing knowledge, wisdom, and experience, Brady believed that Jess Willard was the one white man who had a good chance to whip Johnson. Willard was heavier at 235-240 pounds, much taller at 6'6 ½", had a longer reach, and had the punching power and strength to do it. Plus, given his current condition and advanced age, Johnson would not be able to finish off a big man like Willard, and eventually would grow tired and vulnerable to a man of great strength.

Johnson vehemently denied the claims of a fake. "It's an absolute lie. Adams's statement is false from beginning to end." Dan McKetrick also emphatically denied the charge.[1168]

Battling Jim Johnson did not think the Moran bout was a fake. He thought Jack's performance indicated that he was slipping and going back, rather than deliberately attempting to prolong the bout.

Regarding the fight and the decision, Moran said,

> The black completely surprised me. Everybody led me to believe all I had to do was to last ten or fifteen rounds, and I'd be sure to win solely on the bad condition and age of the negro. But Johnson's defense was as good in the nineteenth round as in the first, and when the twentieth round came I was too much all in to be able to notice.[1169]

Several black-owned newspapers offered their perspectives. The *New York Age*'s Lester Walton said Johnson had humorously and easily defended the crown. Responding to those who called the bout second-rate, Walton said the fight was analogous to the recent "battle" at Vera Cruz, Mexico, waged between the American fleet and a handful of Mexicans. "The only difference lies in the fact that our American warriors are given medals of honor for marked bravery; while Johnson is disparaged for participating in the burlesque and dubbed by some American writers as a has-been."

Sportswriters now were nearly unanimous in saying that Moran was the wrong man to go up against Johnson. "And yet many of them before the contest harbored a feeling that Moran was destined to come out victor." Johnson was the first pugilist of modern times to defend his title successfully at the age of 35 and over, and he deserved recognition.

Many were proclaiming loudly that Johnson was all-in because he did not knock out Moran. They said he no longer was the Johnson of old. "But did the champion really and truly want to knock out his opponent?" Walton suspected that Johnson had carried Moran.

Walton noted William Rocap's statement that the bout was spoiled in the last 2 rounds because Johnson was not trying and "affected" being tired. The *New York Sun* said, "It was not a fight. It was not even a near fight. Moran showed absolutely nothing. Johnson was never extended." The *New*

[1168] *Denver Post, New York American*, June 29, 1914.
[1169] *Denver Post*, June 30, 1914.

York Times* wrote, "In the final round Johnson stood still in the center of the ring. Moran circled about Johnson and called out, 'Come on, hit me!' Then the referee forced him to fight, and amid screams from the crowd Johnson landed a left uppercut and the fight was finished as Moran went reeling against the ropes."

On the other hand, William Brady contradicted these reports, claiming that Moran's own fatigue saved Johnson from being knocked out. "Mr. Brady uncorked a sample of race prejudice which afflicts so many of our white Americans…and which renders one totally unable to size up a condition with an open mind and with any degree of fairness." Walton did not believe the champion was the high liver that the hostile white press represented him to be. Jack was a cunning individual.[1170]

Writing for the *Chicago Defender*, Johnson's nephew Gus Rhodes said the boasted white hope was punished at will. Wearing the colors of France, Johnson showed the oldest follower of the game that he still was his old self. Anglo-Saxon supremacy received another crushing blow and was trampled in the dust., as the crafty champion played with him like a cat with a mouse. Owing to the ban on any fight films which traveled in interstate commerce, the motion pictures would not be shown in the U.S.

Rhodes said many French notables, aristocrats, and wealthy Americans who at home would be indignant if the champion's name was mentioned in their presence, all attended the fight.

The *Defender's* Tony Langston lamented the fight descriptions published in some of the daily newspapers, which he called nauseating and the result of personal prejudice. Some reporters gave Moran several rounds, but the detailed round by round descriptions made it clear that Johnson had won every round. "Can you beat it?"

Some falsely claimed that Johnson allowed Moran to stay for the benefit of the pictures, in which he had a 50% interest.

> Now, if that were true, then why didn't the writer, knowing of it, expose the whole thing before the fight? He just naturally prevaricated, and his statement is just another sample of the rotten prejudice taken to Europe by a certain class of white people…who are using every means to instill race hatred among the nations who have always been the race's friends.

The *Defender's* Frank Young said Brady was another Corbett with his bitterness towards Johnson. Young said "the poor whites will never get over it." Johnson retained his title regardless of all the predictions that he was too old, out of form, had dissipated, had failed to train, and was overweight, as the authoritative Brady of the Hearst papers had told all of his readers.

Young said Brady had claimed that it would be the happiest day of his life, for Moran was going to win the crown. It must have been a bitter pill

---

[1170] *New York Age*, July 2, 1914.

for him to swallow, and instead of giving Johnson credit, he and others slurred the fight and Johnson.

Some writers claimed the victory was a signal for a celebration on State street (meaning the black neighborhood) and that the police were called in to quell the disturbance. "Now there was nothing of the sort."

The *Defender* lamented that for many years, every time three or four Afro-American boys and an equal number of white boys got into a row, the daily press termed the incident a race war. Not all friction between hooligans of the races was a race war.

Some accused Johnson of being a disgrace to the race. "Johnson, it is true, may have had troubles and the ever-ready yellow journals that seek to create ill feeling between the two races took this as a matter to inflame the minds of its weak readers." These writers never overlooked any opportunity to slam one in on the dark race, and they went at it with vim.[1171]

The *Freeman's* Billy Lewis said the bout was extremely important for the fight game, notwithstanding the effort by some to belittle it. It was treated like a national pageant in France.

Lewis thought that although some negroes sometimes pushed the race question too much, it was understandable given that white publications did the same. He felt that blacks needed to counter what they saw as the biased white perspective.

Lewis noted that Johnson was a negro with a white wife, which basically was why he could not return to the U.S. Yet, he was in the presence of mighty high society on fight night, and gave an excellent account of himself.

Lewis said the Moran fight helped Johnson greatly in the world's estimation of him. He had proven so infinitely superior to his title challengers that even the most stubborn-hearted finally had given way to admiration. "And it would have been a most perverse generation had it not made an unconditional surrender to Mr. Johnson's greatness."[1172]

The *Freeman* published excerpts from French publications regarding the Moran fight. The *Matin* said, "For Johnson the match was merely the pretext for an excellent joke." The Paris edition of the *New York Herald* said, "It was an easy win for Johnson, the difference in the class of the two men being only too evident from the very beginning of the match."

> Moran, most of the time, was covering his face and trying to ward off the black's deadly uppercuts. ...
>
> Johnson's stomach, indeed, seemed to be made of something harder than mere muscle. Several times when Moran, with a show of energy, tried punching his opponent's abdomen and ribs, the black raised his arms and let him do so without retaliating, turning his head toward the public with a broad grin showing his white teeth, and seemed to say 'He can do that as long as he likes.'

[1171] *Chicago Defender*, July 4, 1914, August 15, 1914.
[1172] *Freeman*, July 4, 11, 1914.

> To most of the spectators it seemed, after the first three rounds, that Johnson could have knocked out his opponent at any moment. Why he did not do so must be a matter of speculation. Certainly, Moran gave him no trouble.
>
> All through the match Johnson never varied his tactics. Standing in the middle of the ring he waited for his opponent to come to him. When Moran got tired of walking round and round, he closed in and it was only then that the black did his fighting, which always turned to the other man's disadvantage.[1173]

The *Defender* said the black race did not forget that Sam Langford viewed the Jeffries fight from Jeff's corner. It was rumored that if he defeated Johnson that Langford then would allow a white man to defeat him for the championship. This persistent rumor made Langford even less popular with some blacks, who saw him as a traitor. Not many believed that Langford could whip Jack, but they had "no particular love for him anyhow."

Johnson had gone to Russia to exhibit there, and then would head to Austria. He planned to fight Langford in October and then retire.[1174]

On July 16, 1914 in London, Georges Carpentier won the white heavyweight championship when Gunboat Smith was disqualified in the 6th round for hitting Georges while he was on the canvas. In the 4th round, Carpentier landed a right on the kidneys that dropped Smith. In the 6th round, Carpentier dropped to his knees, either the result of a right to the jaw or from slipping down when off balance after throwing a blow. There was a mix of opinion. Smith then clearly hit him on the neck while he was down. Referee Eugene Corri immediately disqualified Smith.[1175]

The *Defender* said America had lost its latest white hope. It was a dying American newspaper effort to find a white man able to wrest the title from Johnson. Carpentier had admitted that he was no match for Johnson. Tom Flanagan said, "Take it from me, Johnson can whip any man in the world today, black or white. Anyone sufficiently interested to learn can find out that Johnson is in the best condition and takes better care of himself than any other heavyweight does."[1176]

On July 28, 1914, the Austrian-Hungarian government, backed by Germany, declared war on Serbia. Russia backed Serbia, and Germany declared war on Russia and its ally, France. Great Britain declared war on Germany when German troops invaded Belgium and Luxembourg, violating their official neutrality. Japan and Italy eventually also declared war on Germany. The Ottoman Empire and Bulgaria joined Germany and Austria-Hungary. The U.S. would not declare war on Germany until nearly three years later, on April 6, 1917. This brutal world war, in which over 9 million combatants would be killed, lasted more than four years, not ending

---

[1173] *Freeman*, August 8, 1914.
[1174] *Chicago Defender*, July 11, 1914.
[1175] *Freeman*, July 25, 1914.
[1176] *Chicago Defender*, July 25, 1914.

until November 11, 1918. Naturally, a war which involved most of Europe was going to affect Jack Johnson's boxing career.

It was rumored that Johnson had offered to fight for France in the war. It was claimed that he would be made a colonel of a regiment and given a $500 pension.[1177]

The *Freeman's* Billy Lewis said Jack Johnson was the most widely discussed man who had ever lived, outside of bible characters. Efforts to belittle his significance had failed.[1178]

Some were saying that Johnson was the real promoter of the Moran fight, or a co-promoter. Given that he had a lot of outstanding debts, after the fight, pursuant to a court order, the French authorities seized the gate receipts, pending a decision on the debts owed.[1179]

Startling revelations were made. A Paris newspaper, *L'Echo Des Sports*, printed a facsimile of an offer allegedly made the day of the fight, in which Johnson offered to pay Moran more money if he agreed to lose inside of 8 rounds. Allegedly it read:

> June 27, 1914
>
> I hereby agree to divide my receipts with Frank Moran on June 27 on a basis of 40 per cent to Moran and 60 per cent to me provided that Frank Moran loses inside of eight rounds – Jack Johnson.

Johnson signed the typed document, and then wrote, "After fight must return this receipt."

Apparently, Moran double-crossed Johnson, during the fight deciding not to lie down, or he never agreed. Some said that as a result of the revelations, Johnson never again would be allowed to box in France.[1180]

Allegedly, Dan McKetrick confirmed that Moran had agreed to lie down in the 8th round.

Johnson declared that the fix claims were not true, but simultaneously alleged that he had agreed to allow Moran to last the limit of 20 rounds, and said that he did so in order to get Moran to take the bout. He claimed to have lived up to his end of the bargain.

Folks wondered whether Johnson indeed had held back against Moran, or if he just made the claims to sting Moran and his backers. Many believed Johnson, because heavy money had been wagered on Moran to stay the limit. Others said the two had fought their best, on the merits. Once again, the press and public were not sure exactly what to make of or believe about Jack Johnson.[1181]

[1177] *Chicago Defender*, August 8, 1914.
[1178] *Freeman*, August 29, 1914. On August 12, 1914 in New York, 205-pound Sam Langford and 224-pound Battling Jim Johnson boxed laboriously and perspiringly through 10 rounds of uninteresting milling, with Langford having the better of it. They rested upon each other at every opportunity.
[1179] *El Paso Herald*, August 3, 1914. Some later claimed that Johnson was not paid.
[1180] *Omaha Daily Bee*, August 9, 1914; *Daily Capital Journal*, August 11, 1914.
[1181] *Daily Missoulian*, August 7, 1914.

CHAPTER 47

Something More

In late 1914, Kansas cowboy Jess Willard was being called the best or most logical white hope to dislodge Johnson from his title. Those in the know felt that Johnson was just about ready to be beaten. "In fact, it is the general belief that the first strong young aspirant with a hard punch and a little bit of cleverness to come along will upset him." Most thought Willard matched up better with Johnson than Gunboat Smith. Willard would have height, reach, and weight advantages. And Johnson already was past the age in which all other champions had lost their crowns. Jack Curley said he would back Willard against Johnson.[1182]

Willard had fought a draw with Luther McCarty, and held victories over Arthur Pelkey, Sailor White, Soldier Kearns, 235-pound Carl Morris, and George Rodel (twice). Willard also held a KO11 over John William Young, a.k.a. Bull Young, a huge right uppercut doing the trick. Young remained unconscious and died the next day after surgery to remove a cerebral hemorrhage. Willard was arrested on manslaughter and prize-fighting charges, for which he later was acquitted by a jury.

Johnson was doing a vaudeville stunt at a number of small halls on the outskirts of London. However, to some degree, the world war had broken up the fight game in Europe.[1183]

The *Freeman's* Billy Lewis said when the world was not talking war, it was talking about Jack Johnson. Lewis noted the bias against Johnson, observing how one writer introduced Jack this way:

> Dame Fortune is not only a fickle and flirtatious old girl, but she ain't at all particular on whom she smiles. Witness the case of her outrageous smirking at Jack Johnson, a vain, ignorant immoral negro, who was, 12 years ago, a levee roustabout at Galveston. ...
>
> It's small wonder that men seek fortune in the prize ring today, despite all the drawbacks connected with the game. One glance at the case of John Arthur Johnson and they sidestep the cotton bales and the harvest fields and run for the training camp.

Lewis responded that it was wicked and unjust to talk that way about a man just because he happens to be a Negro. Thousands of whites came up from mean conditions to where they commanded thousands of dollars, yet one Negro was singled out, the only one whose financial success had been phenomenal. "This writer is envious of the 'nigger.' He doubtless is one of

---
[1182] *Freeman*, September 5, 1914.
[1183] *Freeman*, September 12, 1914.

those white men who have decided that the world belongs to them and all that pertains thereto."

Regardless, Lewis also said that Johnson had obtained much consideration recently, owing to his long championship reign even at an advanced age. More whites were throwing down their prejudices and honestly giving him credit. He had not been allowed to fight for the title until he was 30 years old, already an advanced age for a fighter, and yet he still had retained the title for many years.

Regarding Johnson's condition for the Moran fight; one writer believed he actually weighed more than 230 pounds. But still he was the master of his art.

When Johnson was in Moscow filling a theatrical engagement, there was fear of a German bombardment. After he returned home to France, he allegedly was made a colonel in the French army. "The report has not been verified, and probably will not."

One white writer said if Johnson and Willard were matched, once again the rumors of fake would circulate:

> Johnson has absolutely killed all possibility of believing his bouts now are on the level. His written agreement in the Moran affair, by which Moran was to receive a certain increased share of the receipts if he didn't go eight rounds, published in English and French papers, settled that. Johnson has passed his prime as a fighter. Dissipation and easy living have left him a far less effective fighting machine. His endurance has gone, and after boxing a few rounds he loses his strength and hitting power. ...
>
> Personally I'd like to see Willard fight Johnson. He would probably beat the dusky champ. Willard is naturally a defensive fighter like Johnson, and he wouldn't run into anything through over eagerness. When hurt he hits a terrific punch or two before his natural caution returns. He uses a fast and hard left jab, and he has great advantages in height, reach, weight, and strength. Five years ago Willard would have had no chance with Johnson; today it's a different matter, as Johnson is all in.
>
> But it isn't likely Johnson and Willard ever will fight. There'll be no boxing in Europe or England for some time. Even if there were Johnson would be barred because of the Moran agreement in his handwriting, so widely published. He can't fight any one in Australia, as he has been absolutely barred in that country. And he can't come back here and wouldn't be allowed to fight if he did come.

Making a Johnson fight would be difficult, for he could not box in the U.S. or Australia, big-time boxing was on hiatus in Europe owing to the war, and even if it wasn't, many were soured by the Moran fight either because of its dullness or because they thought it was faked to some degree. Billy Lewis said, "Poor old Jack. And his only sin is being a successful Negro pugilist."

A Johnson-Carpentier fight could not take place even if Georges wanted it, because he had joined the French army for a four-year term of service. He would be paid $20.40 per year, or 5.7 cents a day. It would be five years before Carpentier fought again.[1184]

Jack Johnson disputed the stories that he had applied for French naturalization. He visited the American embassy on September 18 to make it known that he still was a U.S. citizen. He showed a passport obtained from the American ambassador in Paris six months earlier. A few weeks ago, he had been in Russia, then Berlin and Paris, after which he came to London. He was going back to Russia to fill more theatrical engagements.

In London, because allegedly he used obscene language to a policeman after refusing to move his *legally* parked automobile, Johnson was called upon to appear before a magistrate. The trouble arose when Jack's auto, parked outside a Leicester square barber shop where he was being shaved, caused a crowd to collect, interfering with traffic. Instead of dispersing the people who were blocking the street, the policeman directed Johnson, who was parked legally, to move his car along, which he refused to do until his shave was finished, accompanying the refusal with a flow of derogatory words for the "ancestors of bobby." Jack told the judge that he could not keep people from staring at him. Nevertheless, the judge fined him $10 for obstructing the street.

The *Freeman* said newspapers continually printed falsehoods about Johnson, on the theory that Jack Johnson fiction was as good as any. All the talk about him becoming a French citizen or joining the French army was a matter of invention.

On October 5, 1914, Federal Judge George Carpenter declared Johnson's $30,000 bond forfeited when he failed to show up to court. The district attorney began a suit against the estate of Matthew Baldwin, the deceased professional bondsman, and Tiny Johnson, Jack's mother.[1185]

Johnson told promoter Jim Coffroth that he would meet *any* man Coffroth selected, black or white, as long as the financial terms were right. There was discussion of a potential bout in Mexico.

Tom Jones, Jess Willard's manager, reported that a Willard-Johnson match likely would be staged on March 7, 1915 in Juarez, Mexico. Cuba also wanted the fight, and officials there said that should any troubles arise in Mexico, the bout could be shifted to their island.[1186]

On October 20, 1914 in Boston, Sam Langford knocked out Gunboat Smith in the 3rd round, avenging his prior 1913 decision loss to Smith. Although many wanted to see Langford fight Johnson, "What the public wants now is a man to whip Johnson, and above all a white man." On

---

[1184] *Freeman*, September 19, 1914. On September 15, 1914 in Boston, Sam Langford and Battling Jim Johnson fought to a 12-round draw.
[1185] *Freeman*, October 3, 1914; *Chicago Day Book*, October 5, 14, 1914. On October 1, 1914 in New York, Sam Langford and Joe Jeannette fought a close 10-round no-decision bout that had a split of opinion regarding who won. Many said it was a draw.
[1186] *Freeman*, October 17, 24, 1914.

October 26, 1914 in Joplin, Missouri, a black fighter named Jeff Clark won a 10-round decision verdict over Langford.[1187]

On November 16, 1914 in London, promoter Jack Curley (who had been involved with the Johnson-Flynn II promotion), secured Johnson's agreement to fight Jess Willard in March 1915 in a fight anywhere from 20 to 45 rounds, the bout's length to be at Curley's discretion. The location had not yet been set. $30,000 was to be paid to Johnson before he entered the ring, plus $1,000 in expense money, plus 50% of the net motion picture proceeds. Willard's end was not disclosed. The bout was financed by a syndicate of sporting men.[1188]

The *Chicago Day Book* said there were rumors that if he fought in Mexico, the U.S. government might kidnap Johnson and bring him back to answer for his white slave violations. However, many whites wanted Johnson to remain at large. "This country is well rid of the black man. As long as a federal court conviction is held over him he will keep out of the United States, and that is all we want. If he returned, took his sentence and served it he would be free at its expiration to come and go as he pleased."

Regarding the upcoming Willard fight, the *Day Book* believed Johnson was due to lose, given that he was out of shape and had dissipated. "Knowing that he is through, Johnson wants to make a final stake."[1189]

The *Rock Island Argus* also noted that the U.S. government was moving to try to capture Johnson, talking with the governments of Mexico and Cuba about his kidnapping, for formal extradition was impossible. One government official said he understood that Johnson was not going to fight in Juarez, Mexico as some suspected, but was heading to Cuba. "Department of justice officials have tried to tempt him back to this country, but the negro declined to bite." Not mentioned was what offer was made in order to tempt him back.[1190]

Some said Johnson stood to make more money if he lost to Willard. If he won, the films would not be worth much, but if he lost, everyone would want to pay to see the fight. In that case, the films would be worth over a million dollars, more than Johnson had made in his entire career combined. Of course, the films could not be shown in the U.S, given the laws against the interstate transport of prizefight films.

Prior to winning the championship, Johnson led a "hand-to-mouth existence, always in debt to his various managers, who succeeded each other in rapid succession." Since then, it was estimated that his fights and exhibitions had generated about $300,000 for him.

Apparently, Johnson had not collected his $35,000 from the Moran fight, for it was tied up in the French courts.[1191]

[1187] *Freeman*, November 7, 1914. On November 10, 1914 in Boston, Joe Jeannette and Battling Jim Johnson fought to a 12-round draw.
[1188] *Freeman*, November 14, 1914; *Harrisburg Telegraph*, December 8, 1914.
[1189] *Chicago Day Book*, November 24, 1914.
[1190] *Rock Island Argus*, November 24, 1914.
[1191] *Ogden Standard*, November 28, 1914. On November 26, 1914 at Vernon, California, despite being dropped four times in the first 2 rounds, Sam Langford came back to score a KO14 over emerging 25-year-old black heavyweight Harry Wills. On December 10, 1914 in New York, Sam McVey won a 10-

On December 19, 1914, California's new law went into effect, limiting all fights to 4 rounds. This law would last for a decade.

Tom Flanagan said Willard might have a good chance to beat Johnson in a long fight, for age was a more formidable rival than man. Folks rarely were able to hit Johnson, except what he allowed for show. He knew how to block, smother, step back or side-step at just the right moment. He was a brilliant counterpuncher, and also could create openings. Still,

> Jack Johnson's next fight will see him 37 years of age. While no prizefighter in the history of the ring has ever taken as good care of himself as Jack Johnson, despite old stories to the contrary, all the same age is age, and there is no elixir for it.

> At 37, Jack Johnson nor no other man can be expected to fight top speed for much over twenty rounds. Decidedly few of them could ever hope to go that distance at even a fair clip. ... If Willard or any other good big man with a punch can hold out for twenty rounds he has a great chance to win a long fight against Johnson.[1192]

Jess Willard would be 27 (listed birthdate of December 29, 1887) (although secondary sources say he actually was 33, born in 1881). Jess was fresh and frisky, having started his pro boxing career in early 1911, yet was sharp and active – with 29 fights under his belt in those four years. Johnson had fought only three times in the last four years.[1193]

During December 1914, Johnson left Great Britain and headed to Buenos Aires, Argentina to give some exhibitions there through January.

Former Kansas cowpuncher Willard revealed his racial motivations, saying the reason he wanted to fight Johnson was to restore the championship back to the white race. "I believe a white heavyweight champion would do more to boost the boxing game than a negro. I believe I will bring the title back to the white race. ... If I never secured a penny for performing the feat, I would feel amply repaid for bringing the title back to the white race." Jack Curley said Willard would make at least $15,000.[1194]

Although initially it was believed that the fight would be held on March 6 in Juarez, Mexico, impediments arose. Mexico was a land of rebellion and revolution. General Francisco "Pancho" Villa was in favor of the fight. However, General Venustiano Carranza of the rival faction said he would prevent Johnson's entry into the country. He was in control of the ports, so it seemed that it would be difficult for Johnson to enter Mexico.[1195]

On January 26, 1915, the 246-pound Willard started training in El Paso, Texas. Willard's reach was 83.5 inches, which exceeded the champ's 78.5-inch reach by 5 inches. Willard stood 6'6 ½" tall to Johnson's 6'1 ½".

---

round newspaper decision over Battling Jim Johnson. Ten days later, on December 20, 1914 in New Orleans, McVey won a 20-round decision over Harry Wills.

[1192] *Chicago Defender*, December 26, 1914.
[1193] *El Paso Herald*, December 29, 1914.
[1194] *El Paso Herald*, January 1, 6, 9, 1915.
[1195] *Day Book*, January 14, 1915.

Willard was confident that he could beat the "shine," for Johnson was not a knockout artist. He was certain that he could withstand any blow the champ could throw, whereas he had sufficient power to score a knockout.[1196]

Having left Buenos Aires on January 21, on February 8, Johnson arrived in Barbados, weighing 245 pounds. Shortly thereafter, he sailed for Cuba.[1197]

When asked why Americans should support a Johnson fight at all, given that he was a fugitive from justice and charged with being a faker, Curley said he saw the Moran fight and it looked square to him. Furthermore,

> It took 25 United States secret service men from the department of justice in Chicago, under the leadership of the chief investigator, five weeks to discover that Johnson, during three years of constant traveling previously, had committed the terrible crime of transporting a woman companion from Pittsburg to Chicago, for which he received one year under the Mann act.

Curley noted that folks were willing to pay Johnson $200,000 to lie down to Jeffries, but he refused and won the fight. He said both Johnson and Willard had too much pride to take a dive.[1198]

On February 8, 1915, D. W. Griffith's film, *The Birth of a Nation*, was released. Based on Thomas Dixon, Jr.'s 1905 bestseller, *The Clansman*, it portrayed the Ku Klux Klan as heroes, and freed blacks as ignorant, rapists, sexually aggressive towards white women, unscrupulous politicians, and hapless idiots. It showed miscegenation as an evil that had to be prevented or avenged. The NAACP's attempts to ban the film only served to advertise it. The film was extremely popular and a huge financial success, generating millions of dollars. Democrat U.S. President Woodrow Wilson even had the film screened at the White House.

Frank Menke said Johnson would defeat Willard with ease if the fight was on the level. He said the negro race could grow old in years, yet retain endurance, and could indulge in wild dissipation yet not lose much physical power. Johnson had dissipated, but the extent had been exaggerated. When he fought Moran, folks had been saying the same thing, and yet he still won, toying with Moran. "He could have knocked out Moran in any round that he chose, but he elected that the white man should stay the limit."

[1196] *El Paso Herald*, January 23, 25, February 2, 1915.
[1197] *Harrisburg Telegraph*, February 5, 1915; *Day Book*, February 8, 1915; *Star-Independent*, March 29, 1915.
[1198] *El Paso Herald*, February 9, 1915. Ticket prices would sell from $5 up to $25.

Menke said Langford and Jeannette were the same way. "And so in the face of what the negro fighters have done – and are doing – in spite of their added years and careless living, it seems to us that it is a bit unsafe to bet on Willard if you are banking on his meeting a physical wreck."[1199]

On February 22, Johnson arrived in Cuba.[1200]

The *Daily Capital Journal* reported that most likely Johnson would not go to Juarez, for he could not secure permission from General Carranza, and he feared capture and deportation to the U.S. Hence, the likely fight location would be Cuba, and the bout would be postponed to late March or early April.[1201]

Johnson began exhibiting in Cuba. Jack Robinson said Johnson was in far better condition than most imagined.

With ease, Willard was handling 220-pound Jim Savage, 208-pound Walter Monahan, 196-pound Jack Hemple, and 220-pound Tex O'Rourke in 50 minutes of the hardest kind of sparring and wrestling. Savage said,

> He's the greatest big man I ever saw. Three rounds is my limit with him at any time. He's so strong, so hard to hit, so like a bear in the clinches that I can do nothing with him. I firmly believe he has an excellent chance of winning. If Johnson isn't in the best of shape Willard will win sure.[1202]

Hugh Fullerton, a Chicago sportswriter, was advising gamblers not to bet a cent on the fight. There were rumors and suspicions that a big job was being pulled off. "Jack Johnson is not now, has not been in the last two years and never will be again in condition to fight a good heavyweight. He has not fought 'on the level' in a long time." Fullerton said the champion's bouts with Jim Johnson and Frank Moran were crosses between a joke and a scandal.

> It is reported in Chicago among negroes and others who have been close to the big cotton-field coon that Jack is broke and needs the money. On that basis, reports have gone out that he has agreed to 'flop' to Willard.

> In justice (or rather, in reason) I must say I do not believe Johnson would lay down to anyone. He is an ignorant, conceited, spoiled negro. His vanity is beyond belief. If anyone could persuade him he would not lose his standing, he would be willing enough to lay down. No moral scruples would hold him.

> I doubt whether money, even, would tempt him to throw away his title.

[1199] *El Paso Herald*, February 17, 1915.
[1200] *El Paso Herald*, February 22, 1915.
[1201] *Daily Capital Journal*, February 24, 1915. *El Paso Herald*, February 25, 1915.
[1202] *El Paso Herald*, February 27, 1915.

> Nothing would be gained by arranging for Willard to lay down. Nine-tenths of the fight fans believe that Johnson, if he is even half way in condition, can whip Willard.
>
> From a sporting standpoint, the fight is a joke. Johnson, in the condition he was when he fought Jeffries, could beat four Willards in an evening. ... [Willard's only chance to win] is to avoid being massacred until the negro gets so weary he cannot hold up his arms or move his legs.[1203]

As had been the case with Moran, the fight would not be the first time that Willard was in the ring with Johnson. Jess said,

> I have fought Johnson before, but only in exhibition bouts. He tried hard to knock me out, but failed utterly. If he couldn't put me away, or even knock me down when I was only a mere novice, it is quite unlikely that he is capable of turning the trick now, so many years after.[1204]

Jim Flynn said Cuba had a rule against bouts between whites and blacks, the same as New York. Hence, the fight could not take place in Havana unless they obtained a special permit from the government.

Yet, as of March 8, it was announced that the fight would be held in Havana, Cuba during the first week of April, likely the 4th.[1205]

Billy Murphy said the fight was not a fake. Many assumed a fake before the Jeffries fight and got fooled. "Johnson is not crazy. If he is beaten he is absolutely through. ... He must win. Not all the money in Juarez could make him throw that fight. He'll lose, but it'll be on the square."

Murphy said Willard would re-draw the color line once he became champion. "Willard will never box another black man, if he can beat the present holder of the title."[1206]

Havana Governor Pedro Bustillo said he would not prevent the battle. He saw no reason for interfering. "I am of the opinion that there does not exist in Cuba such a thing as race hatred."

Cuban President Mario Menocal also declared that he would take no action to prevent the fight.

Johnson said that after the fight, he wanted to remain in Cuba, run a hotel business, and eventually become a citizen. "I've been in the ring nearly twenty years. I know the end must come soon. So this chance of engaging in a legitimate business appeals to me."[1207]

On March 16, Willard arrived in Havana.

[1203] *Tacoma Times*, February 27, 1915.
[1204] *El Paso Herald*, March 1, 1915.
[1205] *El Paso Herald*, March 3, 4, 8, 1915.
[1206] *Ogden Standard*, March 9, 1915.
[1207] *Daily Gate City*, March 15, 1915; *Harrisburg Star-Independent*, March 17, 1915; *El Paso Herald*, March 26, 1915; *Richmond Times-Dispatch*, March 16, 1915.

The fight would take place at the Oriental Racetrack, Mariano, about five miles from the heart of Havana, with easy access by trolley, carriage, and auto. Tickets were priced from $3 up to $25.[1208]

Johnson sent a letter to his mother telling her that he was intending to return to the U.S. "I am getting tired of knocking around. As soon as I have whipped Willard, I will come back to Chicago and take my medicine as the government has fixed it up for me." It is unclear what he meant by this.[1209]

Robert Edgren, who saw Johnson work, wanted to correct some mistaken impressions. Although Johnson was not as good as he was in Reno, he was anything but a dissipated physical wreck. Jack was well trained and still had all of his old skill. He was thicker and burlier, as expected for a man of his age, but appeared to be in better condition than he was for Moran.

In training, the champion smiled and talked as always. He even allowed sparring partners to pound away at his stomach. He said, "I couldn't do that if I'd been doing the drinking they credit me with. If I drank a glass of beer they said I had a hundred." Johnson said he weighed 233, and two weeks ago had weighed 248.

Although the fight had been scheduled for Easter Sunday, April 4, many folks did not like the idea of a fight occurring on the religious holiday, so at President Menocal's request, the bout was moved to Monday April 5 at 12:30 p.m.[1210]

$30,000 in American gold was deposited into a Havana bank, subject to the order of stakeholder Bob Vernon, the amount to be paid to Johnson upon his arrival at the fight. Jack demanded that payment be made before he entered the ring.

Hugh Fullerton said two tipsters had told him that Johnson was going to lose, for he was badly in need of cash and had agreed to lose to clean up on the 2 to 1 odds. However, Fullerton also told readers not to fall for such false tips, which he said were designed to affect the odds for gamblers. Gamblers spread such rumors as a way of dragging money out of their victims. "They know that the 'easiest marks' in the world are those fellows who are anxious to believe everything in sport is crooked." He said Johnson was too insanely egotistical and vain to flop, and even if he had agreed to do so, he would pull the double cross. If Johnson lost, it was because he was old, fat, out of shape, or drugged, not because he took a dive.[1211]

The *Washington Times* said Johnson tried to cover up his distaste for workouts with overindulgence in comedy, smiles, and conversation, but close observers could see that he was not the man who beat Jeffries. Conversely, Willard had not left anything undone in his training. Odds had dropped to 8 to 5, although the champ remained the favorite.[1212]

[1208] *New York Tribune*, March 20, 1915.
[1209] *El Paso Herald*, March 20, 1915.
[1210] *New York World*, March 27, 1915.
[1211] *El Paso Herald, Day Book, New York Tribune, Seattle Star*, March 29, 1915.
[1212] *Washington Times*, April 1, 1915.

Bob Edgren said Johnson was in the best shape a man of his age could be. However, Willard was in better shape.

The confident Johnson said,

> All champions who fight long enough get theirs. I have been fighting over twenty years and my time is about due, but not in this fight. I will not fight again, as I won't risk losing the title. I will retire with it and any time in the next ten years when I want money I can go out and exhibit as the only undefeated champion and get plenty. I am satisfied with my condition and know I can fight forty-five rounds, but I won't have to.[1213]

The champ bet $1,000 at even odds that he would stop Willard within 25 rounds.

Tex O'Rourke said Jess would win by knockout. "A powerful right-hand swing will do the trick."

As of April 1, Willard was weighing 238 pounds. Supposedly Johnson was around 225. The champ said, "I will win before the fight goes twenty rounds, probably before it goes thirteen."[1214]

Gambler Arnold Rothstein said he had a big bet down on Willard.

Robert Edgren said rumors of Johnson being broke were false, for he was quite wealthy. When asked what he would do if beaten, Johnson said,

> Why, I don't think there's much chance of that, although we all get it some time. If Willard beats me he'll have to knock me cold to do it, and if he knocks me out the first thing I'll do when I get over it will be to congratulate him, because he'll be a mighty good man. If any man can beat me I won't hold a grudge against him. I'll show them I can be a sportsman even if they won't let me come home to my own country.

Tom Flanagan said a million dollars wouldn't induce Johnson to throw away his title. One of the promoters attempted to get the champ to take a dive, saying saying, "Jack, you're in pretty soft. If you win you get $32,000 in cash and you make a few thousand more after the fight. If you lose you'll get two or three hundred thousand out of the moving pictures." Johnson replied, "Moving pictures – where'd I get all that money? There's no money in moving pictures now in Europe and they can't be shown in the United States. Don't talk pictures to me. I wouldn't give a nickel for them."[1215]

Those who were trying to get an inside line on Johnson from his 6-round exhibition bout with Sam McVey on April 3, two days before the fight, were disappointed. The champ simply fooled around with McVey, neither man trying to do much.

To dispel all rumors that he would quit to Willard to obtain a fortune from the moving pictures, Johnson put up $10,000 of his own money to bet

---

[1213] *Evening World*, April 1, 1915.
[1214] *El Paso Herald, New York Tribune, Evening Public Ledger, Washington Herald*, April 2, 1915.
[1215] *Evening World*, April 3, 1915.

on himself against $8,000 from Willard's backers. However, his money was not covered, for Willard's supporters wanted better odds.[1216]

The *World* said Johnson had trained well and was anything but a "dead one." He had worked out daily with a cheerful golden smile and was the picture of confidence.

Regardless, Willard had changed the minds of many who originally thought of him as a victim. Cubans were startled by his enormous size. He looked fit enough to have a chance with anyone. His work had been twice as hard as Johnson's. He had hammered his sparring partners and allowed them to hammer away at him. Not once did he show the slightest inclination to avoid work or punishment. He seemed impervious to punches. "In spite of the usual rumors in America, there is no indication here that anything else but a genuine fight is to be expected."[1217]

On April 5, 1915 in Havana, Cuba, 37-year-old Jack Johnson defended his world heavyweight championship against 33-year-old Jess Willard (who then was listed as 27) in a scheduled 45-round bout.[1218]

As early as 6 a.m., vehicles were heading to the battleground, the Miramar race track, nine miles away from Havana. Few Americans spoke Spanish, but making fists like a fighter and pointing in the general direction of Miramar was enough for the taxicab drivers. A large part of the crowd arriving by auto was charged as much as five times the usual taxi rates.

That morning, Johnson was in a playful mood, laughing and kidding with his companions.

Willard was silent and serious. Jess said, "This is more than a personal matter with me. I want to restore the title to the white race."

Willard said he intended to fight cautiously, to go slow and take his time about matters. He expected to take a good deal of punishment during the first 10 rounds, but hoped to wear down Johnson and get an opportunity to land a knockout blow.

Federal district Attorney Clyne had secret service agents at ringside. He said, "Look for sensational developments after the fight. On Jack Johnson's attitude after the fight will depend the actions of the Government's agents." It is unclear what he meant.

At 11 a.m., in accordance with the agreement, Johnson received his money, being paid in full.

A ring was erected on the race track in front of a big steel grandstand. The ring was 18 feet inside the ropes, on a 22-foot platform. The heavy hemp ropes were wrapped twice with black tire tape. Three moving picture machines on tall platforms would capture the fight.

At least 17,000 people were in attendance. The aisles were packed. Americans were all around the ringside. Many boxes were filled with women and even some children. At least 200 women were in attendance,

---

[1216] *Washington Times*, April 4, 1915.
[1217] *New York World*, April 5, 1915.
[1218] The following account is an amalgamation of ringside reports from the *El Paso Herald* and *New York Evening World*, April 5, 1915. Some additional information is from the *Washington Times*, April 5, 1915.

well-dressed in striking colored dresses, which contrasted the duck-suited dandies of Havana or the black suits of the American spectators. Havana's mayor/governor Pedro Bustillo, as well as the speaker of the Cuban House of Representatives, were present.

Hundreds of Cuban army officers were grouped around the ring in full uniform. Many well-armed soldiers guarded the ring and arena, keeping splendid order. They had rifles, bayonets, and revolvers. In fact, soldiers comprised a large portion of the crowd. Two military bands were playing in the grandstand. American and Cuban flags were flying everywhere.

A few minutes after noon, Cuban president Mario Menocal arrived. The Cubans cheered him.

Johnson arrived at the track at 12:23 p.m. Tom Flanagan accompanied Johnson's wife Lucille to the ringside. She said, "Jack told me he is confident of winning and surely will knock out Willard."

At 12:30 p.m., announcer Jim Mace exhibited Johnson's signed receipt for $29,000, the remainder of the money that had been due him on the purse, announcing the facts through a megaphone. Explanations were provided to the crowd in both Spanish and English.

Johnson was the 10 to 6 betting favorite.

At 12:40 p.m., the sun was shining brightly.

There was a rush of automobiles from Havana. Because there were no speed limits or rules of the road, there were several minor collisions.

Shortly after 1 p.m., led by Sam McVey and accompanied by his full staff of trainers, the smiling Johnson appeared, and the enthusiastic Cubans applauded him. He wore a long gray bathrobe. He walked around the ring and looked for his wife's location.

Four or five minutes later, when Willard entered, he received prolonged yelling, cheering, and clapping from both Cubans and Americans.

The fighters shook hands at ring center. Willard towered over Johnson.

They removed their robes. Willard wore dark blue trunks and an American flag as a belt. Johnson wore bright blue trunks and a belt.

Scales were placed inside the ring, and both pugilists weighed in then and there. Most said Willard was 238 pounds, while one said he was 247. Most said Johnson was 227, though one reported 225.

They put on the gloves inside the ring, a tradition utilized to ensure that the gloves were not loaded.

The hot sun was beating down on everyone.

Referee Jack Welch (or Welsh) introduced the principals. At nearly 1:30 p.m., the ring was cleared and time was called to start the fight.

Johnson showed more offensive firepower and output in this contest than he did for most of his championship fights, firing very speedy impressive combinations, particularly for a man of 37 years of age. However, the huge Willard was able to absorb punishment. Plus, he knew how to roll, block, smother, pull away, step back, and clinch. He relied on his height and reach advantages as best he could. Willard was very efficient with his offense, carefully selecting his one or two heavy long punches at a time, utilizing a style that kept him relaxed and fresh, even though he was not landing as often or as many blows. Conversely, Johnson did more work in order to hit Jess. He had to attack more often than usual, because Willard was so tall and long that he could hit Jack from far away, whereas Johnson had to step in to hit him, which Jess made difficult and requiring of more energy by his stepping and leaning back, blocking and clinching.

Quite frankly, it is a testament to how good Johnson was to keep up that type of pace and throw that many quick combinations over so many rounds at his age. He clearly was far ahead on points throughout. It was a fairly entertaining pace for a fight scheduled for such a long distance.

However, in a 45-round bout, it wasn't about points and impression as much as it was about effective punches, pacing, and defense. Johnson was landing, but he was working hard, and Willard was able to take the hard blows and minimize the number of effective punches that got through. Furthermore, the calm Willard maintained a good pace himself, firing quick jabs to the head and solid rights to the body, landing here and there, just often enough to keep Johnson honest and let him know he was there to win and do some damage with his own blows.

Early on, Johnson was landing hard to the head and body, smiling and laughing at Willard. He was landing far more blows, though Jess did manage to land a few good ones of his own. They took turns forcing the fighting. Whenever Jack was hit, he attacked ferociously in order to get payback. He often drove Willard to the ropes when he attacked.

In the 3rd round, after the champ landed several blows to the head and body, Willard asked, "Do you think that can do it?" A hard mix-up followed. Johnson appeared to be trying for a knockout.

In the 4th round, Willard had a small cut on the upper lip that bled.

In the 5th round, Johnson smashed Willard hard to the head and body, forcing him to the ropes. Willard was rattled and distressed. Yet, Willard landed a left to the mouth that drew some blood from Jack's mouth.

In the 6th round, Jess rubbed the cut on his upper lip at every opportunity. He was taking punishment, but apparently was unhurt. Jess smashed a right into Jack's body. Johnson rushed him to the ropes, swinging furiously and landing a right on the cheek, cutting Willard's left cheek bone. At the bell, Johnson was hammering hard on Willard's body.

In the 7th round, a Johnson left to the ribs could be heard throughout the grandstand. Willard's body was covered with red marks. However, Willard's long left landed to the left eye, temporarily blinding Jack. His eye started closing a bit. Johnson came back with a series of swings to the body, though Jess blocked most of them.

In the 8th round, they battered each other across the ring, with Johnson having the better of it. Willard landed a fierce right to the jaw. Jack clutched and held. Another right sent Jack backwards. Jack clinched, spitting blood. He fought back, swinging hard blows to Jess's head.

In the 9th round, Willard landed some hard punches on the mouth and stomach. However, Johnson's blows started one of the cowboy's ears bleeding. The champ landed frequently, but Willard took them well. Willard jabbed Jack's head back and drove in a fierce right to the stomach. The crowd shouted, "Kill the black bear." Johnson immediately rallied, landing hard hooks to the stomach. A Willard left brought blood from Jack's mouth. Johnson then slugged him to the ropes.

Robert Edgren said that despite being outpointed, Jess was laughing at Jack, taking the body blows successfully. This caused the odds on ringside wagering to tighten up, with Willard the 5 to 4 underdog.

In the 10th round, Johnson forced the fighting, driving Willard to the ropes several times. Jess landed some jabs, but a hard right chop to the jaw rocked Willard.

In the 11th round, a bunch of folks around the ring began yelling at Johnson, calling him yellow. Jack replied loudly, "Wish I was, I could pass for white." The crowd derided Johnson, who was fighting and answering the witty remarks at the same time. Johnson's hooking left made Willard's ear bleed more. Jess drove two right smashes to the body. A man in a box seat said to Johnson, "You've got a real fighter in front of you." Jack then tried to rattle Willard by talking. Jess angrily replied in kind. At the bell, Jack tapped Jess's shoulder. The champ sat down, talking to the spectators.

In the 12th round, Johnson kept landing very well and solidly. Jack seemed to have plenty of steam and all of his old skill. However, his blows appeared to have no effect. A furious Willard fired hard jab and drove his heavy right to the body. Jess was bleeding from both cheeks and also his ear, but still seemed spry.

In the 13th round, Willard's body was red from the effects of the punishment. The game man had taken terrific blows without flinching and apparently was not hurt. Jack continued playing for the stomach. There was plenty of snap to his punches. Several rocked Willard's head. However, at the bell, Jess went to his corner laughing.

In 14th round, Willard's jabs were heavy enough to send Jack's head back. Jack missed some of his leads as Jess stepped or jumped back from the rushes. Willard drove a hard right to the ear. Jack smashed a terrific left into the pit of the stomach at the bell.

In the 15th round, both were very cautious. The crowd kidded Johnson, who then rushed Willard to the ropes with five heavy swings to the head. Johnson yelled, "I am a grand old man." Willard responded by driving a right to the body. Jack clinched. The champ was talking while fighting.

In the 16th round, Jess blocked and held. Jack kept up a running conversation with the crowd. He said, "Willard is a good kid," and then rushed Jess to the ropes, scoring two hard punches to the body. Johnson then said, "I must be a great man if this fellow can't lick me." The crowd retorted, "This is the only man you ever fought." At the end of the round, Jack whipped a heavy left to the stomach that hurt Jess a bit.

In the 17th round, both men landed some solid blows to the body and head. Jack rushed and drove Jess to a corner, landing all over. It looked as if Willard had to show some effect from such blows, but instead he ripped into Johnson, forcing the fight, landing rights to the body. Heavy blows had been exchanged in this round.

In the 18th round, Johnson drove Willard back to a corner, landing several blows. The champ picked off the challenger's leads, and occasionally counterattacked. However, Willard landed a straight left jab very hard to the right eye and a right swing to the jaw, putting Johnson over the ropes. It was a terrific punch. Jack slowed up, and Jess jabbed him almost at will. The crowd was delirious with excitement, jumping up and down, yelling Willard's name. He appeared to be the fresher of the two.

Starting in the 18th round, Willard began coming over with at least one solid right to Johnson's head in each round. Mostly, Willard's right went to the body, so when he threw it to the head, he likely caught Johnson off guard, surprising him. When stung by these blows, usually Johnson would attempt to get immediate payback, firing furious combinations.

Willard kept pumping in his metronome jabs to the head, while Johnson's pace slowed, mostly playing defense in between his occasional bursts of speedy combinations.

In the 19th round, both pugilists slowed up, though Willard had become the aggressor. For a long while, Johnson stood in the middle of the ring and blocked blows, mostly jabs. The champ rallied, landing to the body and head. Jess sank a right into the body. Jess jabbed and followed with a heavy right onto the jaw.

In the 20th round, they were fighting very carefully. Jack urged Jess to lead. Willard stabbed and pawed the air until he landed a fearful right on Jack's jaw. Johnson immediately cut loose and mixed desperately, driving Willard back. They battled across the ring. Jess smashed a right into the stomach and Johnson tried to clinch. Jess chopped him on the back of the head. Johnson seemed dazed and distressed. When Willard drove a hard right and left to the body at the bell, the crowd was frantic.

In the 21st round, they waited and feinted for a long while. Johnson hooked his left to the body and sent a right swing to the head. Willard replied with a straight left to the face. When Johnson rushed, Willard blocked his blows, laughing once they were clinched. Ringsiders were applauding Willard uproariously. Jack walked around. Jess missed punches, and they both laughed. Jess jabbed and Johnson swung an overhand right to the jaw. Jess stepped away from Jack's next rush.

By the 22nd round, the fight had degenerated into a slow sparring and clinching battle. Both feinted for a long time. Willard tried setting the pace. Johnson kept holding on while Willard battered away at his stomach. Johnson only grinned at the shrieking crowd. Nevertheless, he was slowing up. Jess did all of the forcing in this round.

In the 23rd, Willard attacked and Jack held on until the referee ordered him to break. Willard walked steadily into Johnson, who retreated. Jack blocked a dozen blows like a fencing master. Willard followed him constantly, but was unable to penetrate his guard. They clinched and wrestled about the ring. Little fighting was done, but most all of the attempts were made by Willard.

In the 24th round, Johnson blocked and wrestled, stalling and making Willard do all of the work. Willard laid his weight on Johnson at every opportunity in the clinches. Johnson pushed him backward in the same manner that he did with Jeffries. Jack landed several light body blows, apparently trying to draw Willard in for a big smash. Jack missed two swings. He kept clinching and wrestling on the inside with the ex-cowboy. The crowd howled its disapproval. Willard smashed him with a left to the face at the bell.

By the 25th round, Johnson had slowed up perceptibly. He was moving back and holding more. The well-conditioned Willard still seemed fresh, outworking Johnson on the inside, digging many body shots as Johnson tried to hold. Johnson appeared to be taking more breaks on the outside as well, not throwing as much, while Willard seemed as frisky as ever.

Johnson's actions seemed to indicate that he did not think he could knock out Willard, and was trying to conserve energy. Johnson was hitting lightly when Willard sunk a right to the heart that shook him. Cries went through the crowd, "Hundred even on Willard." Jess then clipped Johnson on the jaw with a fast left to the mouth, and forced the pace. Jack was conserving every bit of energy. Willard again landed a left to the mouth, and then repeated it. Johnson blocked a right but Willard landed another heavy right to the mouth. Jess landed a heavy left to the nose. At the bell, Johnson dropped heavily onto his seat.

When the bell rang to start the 26th round, Johnson sat still until Referee Welsh called him from his chair. As they met, Willard sunk a right smash into the pit of the stomach and Jack nearly sat down. The referee forced them to break from a clinch. Willard rushed and slammed right and left to the body. In a clinch, Jack looked over his shoulder towards his wife's seat.

Jess smashed his fists into the body. Jess threw a jab and right to the head and Jack clinched for a while. After breaking, they feinted and posed at long range for a bit.

Quickly stepping in off a lead jab, Willard immediately followed with a terrific straight right to the jaw. Johnson's body tottered and went limp, and he went down, unsuccessfully attempting to grab Willard as he fell to the ground. Johnson dropped backwards, with both his back and back of his head hitting the floor with a hard thud.

At first Jack's knees were bent and his hands above and over his face and eyes. Then his knees went limp and he remained motionless as he was counted out. Even after the count was concluded, Johnson remained still on his back, out cold. Jess Willard was the new heavyweight champion of the world.

A large portion of the ringside crowd rushed into the ring. Several squads of soldiers hurried onto the platform and cleared the crowd away to protect the fighters.

Summarizing, the *El Paso Herald* said Johnson led on points all the way up to the 22nd round, when his stamina failed as a result of the hard pace which he had carried throughout the early rounds. When Johnson slowed down, Willard opened up his attack and carried the fighting to the champ. A terrific right to the jaw knocked out Johnson in the 26th round.

A U.S. district attorney revealed the purpose of having secret servicemen at ringside. They were following Johnson. He said if Johnson traveled outside the three-mile limit of Cuban waters, he would be taken into custody.

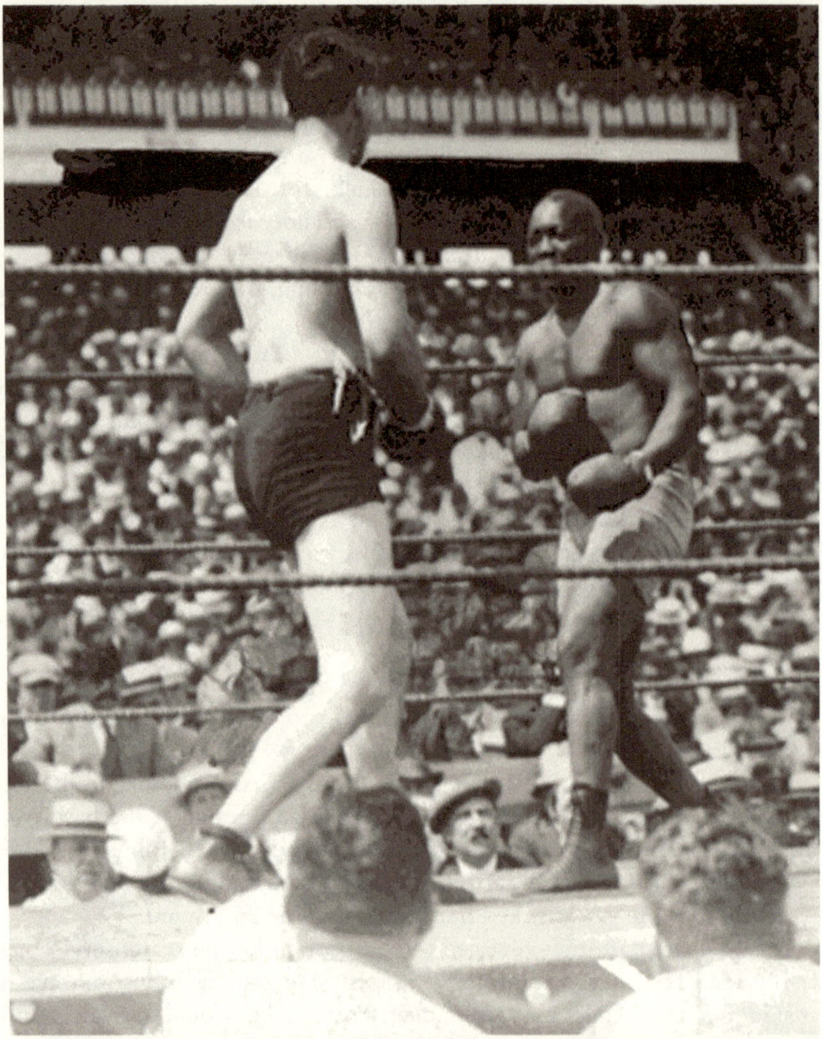

ORIENTAL PARK RACE TRACK
HAVANA CUBA

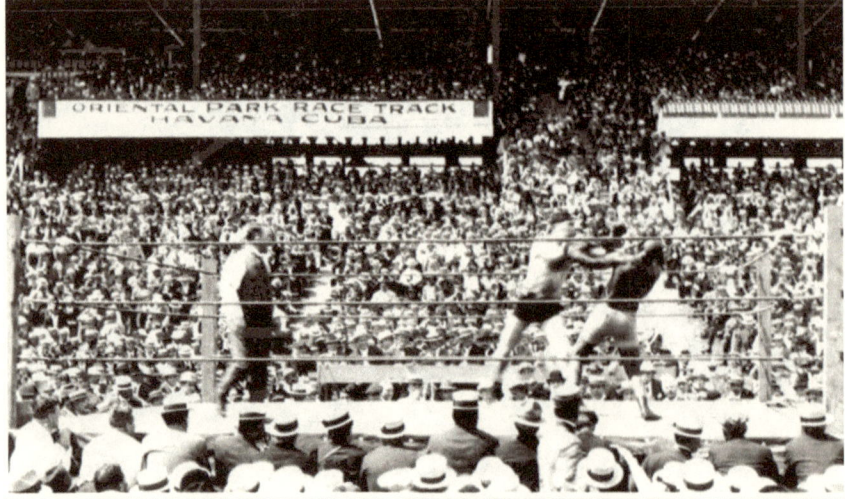

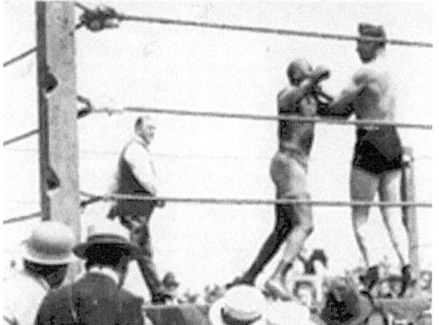

Robert Edgren said it was a great fight. During the first 20 rounds, Willard took punishment that would have knocked out any other man. However, he weathered it all and was as cool as Johnson. He even outwitted Johnson on many occasions, forcing him to lead and then outfighting him. Ultimately, though, youth won for Willard. After the 20th round, it was evident that nature had run its course, for Willard was still fresh, and growing more eager as he felt Johnson weakening.

Just before the knockout, Johnson glanced toward his white wife over Willard's shoulder. He didn't want her to see him knocked out. She was taken away from her box, but on her way out saw the end anyhow.

Edgren said the fight was legitimate, and if it was a fix, Johnson was the greatest actor who ever lived. The end was inevitable, for Johnson's strength was gone and he was lasting on skill alone. When he went down, he was frozen, his arms stiffened rigidly over his head, absolutely out cold. When helped to his corner, his legs and whole body quivered, and still were quivering when he stumbled from the ring ten minutes later. Afterwards, Johnson's quarters were an extremely gloomy place, like a funeral.

Some quoted Sam McVey as claiming that Johnson had laid down. However, Edgren's expert view was that Johnson fought his hardest to knock out Willard, but Jess wore him down and had won fair and square.

The *Sun* said the fight disproved the stories circulated before the bout of a frame-up and fake. Nothing about the fight looked fake. In fact, Johnson had fought like never before, carrying the attack to Willard. Jess replied with counters and allowed Jack to tire himself out. "Johnson beat himself, said many, but it must not be forgotten that the fallen champion taxed his skill to the utmost before his strength began to ebb." Many were shocked and amazed that some of his blows did not deck Willard, for they landed flush on his jaw. Willard's knees sagged a score of times, but he always managed to remain standing. This had a dispiriting effect on Johnson, who had expected to stop him.

The *Day Book* said, "It is a good thing for the fight game that Willard has won." Still, it also said that delirious claims that the white race had triumphed were all bunk. "A big white man, trained to the minute, beat a very fat and leg-weary colored man in a contest between individuals."[1219]

The *Los Angeles Times* reported that the Associated Press hinted that Johnson quit. It said Johnson saw that he could not win, so when he was knocked down, he took the count rather than absorb further punishment. He sent his wife from the arena before the end, and then jumped up after the count was concluded.

For 20 rounds, Johnson punched and pounded Willard at will, but Jess was able to absorb the punishment, and Jack's blows grew perceptibly weaker as the fight progressed, until he was so tired that he seemed unable or unwilling to go on. Jack had realized that he could not stop Jess.

During the 25th round, Willard landed a right smash to the heart that was the beginning of the end. When the round ended, Jack sent word to his wife

---

[1219] *Day Book*, April 6, 1915; *New York Sun*, April 6, 1915; *New York World*, April 10, 1915.

that he was all in, and told her to go home. She was on her way out when the fight ended.

Another AP wire said that well before the end, Johnson was fading and his legs quivered. After he was decked, he never moved. His eyes were glassy and only the whites were visible. Johnson remained stretched on the floor well after the count of ten.

The early rounds were filled with flashes of Johnson's former wonderful speed, raining in rights and lefts, delivering ten blows to the challenger's one, while Willard was on the defensive.

In many ways the fight went as Willard predicted. He said that if it lasted 20 rounds that Johnson could not win. This was based on the belief that he could withstand all of the punishment that Jack could inflict, and also the belief that Johnson's age and condition would be handicaps. Willard said he expected to take a beating for 10 to 15 rounds by a faster and more skilled opponent; had trained to withstand it, and that is just what he did.

Johnson's continual grin during the early rounds changed to a look of wonderment once the battle passed the 20th round. It was evident to the spectators that Johnson came to the conclusion that it was useless to try to knock out the giant. He had fought as if he believed that he could whip Williard within 20 rounds, but was surprised that he had not done so, and realized that he could not. Johnson also seemed to know that he was in no condition to fight for 45 rounds. From the 20th round on he did little, and the fight became slow. Johnson was sparring for time and throwing few punches, trying to conserve energy.

Mike Gibbons said Johnson looked like the Johnson of old up to about the 17th round, but then grew tired. Willard's confidence grew in the 19th round, and he made several rallies. Jack's downfall became evident in the 21st round. He became much more defensive and started stalling. His blows lacked steam. The smile disappeared. Conversely, Willard grew more aggressive.

Jim Jeffries, who had advised Willard to play a defensive waiting game, balked at speculation of a fix. "This talk about it being a fake is ridiculous. The fact that it went twenty-six rounds proves that. If Johnson was going to quit on a frame-up he would have done it long before the twenty-sixth. It's nonsense to think of the fight as being crooked." Jeff said if it had been crooked, he would have been tipped off about it by one of his many friends. He didn't believe Jack ever would take a dive. "Jack Johnson would rather be champion of the world than President of the United States, I really believe, and no amount of money would induce him to part with that title."[1220]

Johnson, now a former champion, said,

> At Reno, after I had beaten Jeffries, I asked you to let the Californian down easy, and you did, but accorded me all the credit I deserved. Now let me down easy.

[1220] *Los Angeles Daily Times*, April 6, 1915.

I was sure my experience and generalship would be too much for Willard, but I was mistaken. There is not another man in the world who could have stood twenty-six rounds with that youngster today. He gave me a beating, but I took his blows without wincing – and he can hit.[1221]

The next day, Johnson said to Edgren, "He's an awfully big fellow, isn't he?" Johnson had tears in his eyes; he was so distraught over losing the title.

Jack Curley said the fight receipts were over $100,000, not the $70,000 originally reported.[1222]

Jess Willard had become heavyweight champion of the world in history's longest Marquis of Queensberry rules heavyweight championship bout, a record in heavyweight championship title fights which still stands to this day.

It actually was a very good and interesting fight, one which should garner more respect for Johnson despite the loss. He certainly showed that he could outpoint a good big tall heavy man in a shorter bout, the likes of which we have today and throughout most of the 20th century. He was very fast and reactive, and his defense still quite good given how huge his foe was. Johnson showed more offense in this fight than he did in most other available fights on film for him. And he proved that he could take some big blows from a big strong man. His performance really is amazing given his advanced age. Perhaps Johnson's biggest mistake was in allowing the bout to be scheduled for more than 20 or 25 rounds. If it had been scheduled for a shorter distance, he would have retained his title on points, and potentially retained his championship for several more years.

Ironically, the Congressional ban on the interstate transportation of fight films also made it illegal to bring into the United States the fight films for purposes of public exhibition. Few U.S citizens would be able to see the fight for many years to come. A law passed in part to prevent whites from seeing Johnson defeat whites also prevented whites from seeing a white man defeat Johnson.

In 1915, the Supreme Court of the United States upheld the constitutionality of the law barring the interstate transportation of fight films in *Weber v. Freed*, 239 U.S. 325 (1915), when the State of New Jersey

---

[1221] *New York Tribune*, April 6, 1915.
[1222] *Washington Times*, April 10, 1915.

refused to allow entry into the country the films of the Johnson vs. Willard fight. However, Johnson and the promoters could make money with the exhibition of the films throughout the rest of the world.

Although many blacks were sad that their champion had been defeated, some were happy, feeling that Johnson had been a menace to the race and had retarded their progress. Others still saw him as a symbol for what blacks could do when given a fair chance.[1223]

Despite the argument that Johnson had hurt the black race, from 1882 to 1908, there was an average of 88 black lynchings per year. There were 89 black lynchings in 1908, even before Jack Johnson won the title in late December. During his reign (1909-1915), there was an average of 59 black lynchings per year. Racism was present before Jack Johnson became champion, it continued during his reign, and after his defeat.

After winning the title, Jess Willard once again publicly re-drew the color line. The *Los Angeles Daily Times* wrote, "He already has announced that if he won he would not fight another negro." For whites, things went back to normal, the way they had been for decades before Johnson, and the way most whites felt things always should be and should have been, with the heavyweight championship being a whites-only position.

For the next 22 years, no black man would be allowed to fight for the heavyweight championship. This was no coincidence. No black fighter was going to be allowed the chance that many believed Johnson never should have had in the first place. Many believed that Willard had "restored pugilistic supremacy to the white race." The caption underneath a photo of Willard in the *Los Angeles Daily Times* stated, "The cowboy pugilist, who yesterday knocked out Jack Johnson and restored the championship to the white race." One article said "the prevailing impression was that Johnson's defeat by the big Kansan would give a stimulus to boxing and make the sport more popular all over the United States. Now that the title is held by an American..."[1224] As a black man, Johnson wasn't even seen as a true American. He most certainly was not going to be allowed to attempt to regain the title, regardless of economics.

One of the more interesting issues surrounding the Willard bout was whether Johnson threw it. In July 1915, a London newspaper reported that Johnson allegedly had sent cables on June 9 (two months after the fight) to New York asking for $50,000 due under an agreement to lay down to Willard. Johnson said, "You signed contract to pay me $50,000 to lay down to Willard, which I did. You never kept your promise. I did. Now you must pay according to contract." Promoters Harry Frazee and Jack Curley vigorously denied that any such agreement existed or that Johnson made any such statement. They said the only wires received by them from Johnson were asking for his end of the Canadian picture returns and a

---

[1223] *Broad Ax*, April 10, 1915.
[1224] *Los Angeles Daily Times*, April 6, 1915.

request to fight Willard again. Neither Johnson nor any newspaper ever produced any such alleged contract.[1225]

The following year, on February 3, 1916, the *New York World* reported an article published by the *People's Journal* in Glasgow, Scotland, with the headline, "Why Johnson 'Faked' His Fight with Willard." In that interview, Johnson said,

> I say now that there is not a man breathing whom I think I could not beat. These may be big words from the boxer who was beaten by Jess Willard at Havana, but those 'in the know' will be able to read between the lines. ...
>
> My fight with Willard was a financial proposition. But the story goes back some little way. ...
>
> Well, they promised me that if I would consent to be defeated by Willard I would no longer be molested and would enjoy the freedom any other man would. I would be allowed to see my old mother, who couldn't travel to see me. I would have my motor cars and other property restored to me. It sounded very attractive, but they played the double cross on me.

The *World*'s Robert Edgren did not believe Johnson's claim of throwing the fight. "Jack Johnson didn't fake the Willard fight and didn't lie down unless he fooled every one around the ring. He surely fought desperately while he lasted and was well knocked out."

However, Edgren conceded that some promises of freedom had been made. The day before the Johnson-Willard fight, promoter Harry Frazee spoke with Edgren. "He said that he had been in communication with the legal authorities here, and that he had assured Johnson that everything had been fixed so that after the fight he could go to America without being arrested." Hence, apparently Johnson was under the belief that a deal had been made.

However, Frazee also told Edgren the day before the fight that he had just received a message from the U.S. legal authorities saying that "it was impossible to square the Johnson matter, and that Johnson would be arrested the moment he set foot on American soil." Frazee and Edgren agreed not to tell Johnson anything about that recent message until after the fight. Hence, Johnson might have been misled and likely was operating under the incorrect belief that a deal was in place, that if he lost that he could return to the U.S. with leniency for his legal troubles.[1226]

In March 1919, while he still was at large and had not yet returned to the United States, Johnson issued a statement saying that the Willard fight was fixed for Willard to win in the 10th round, but Jess made such a poor

---

[1225] *Washington Times, New York Sun,* July 22, 23, 1915.
[1226] *New York World,* February 3, 1916.
Harry Frazee became the owner of the Boston Red Sox in 1916, a team which won the World Series in 1918. After the 1919 season, Frazee sold Babe Ruth to the Yankees. In 1923, Frazee sold the team.

showing and did so little that it was necessary to wait. Of course, that version was contradicted by Johnson's additional statement also claiming that he was waiting for a payment and a signal from his wife that it had been received. Once she signaled that the money had been received, he signaled back to her and then she left with the money.

Johnson also said he threw the fight to straighten out his Mann Act issues and to be able to visit his mother, but that the promise had not been fulfilled.

Some have speculated that perhaps Johnson's motivation for making the claim had to do with the fact that he felt swindled out of payment on the film rights and a copy of the films which had been promised to him, or he might have been trying to save face and generate interest in a rematch.[1227]

In his 1927 autobiography, Johnson claimed to have told Mrs. Johnson a few moments before entering the ring that he was going to lose. Curley had paid him his percentage before he left his home. However, he also told Mrs. Johnson that there was more money due him, and that until the money was paid, he would not take a dive. He claimed that the reason why he did not take a dive sooner was that he was waiting to make sure his wife had been paid the remainder of the money owed, and that once she signaled to him that payment had been made, he then threw the fight.

> Mrs. Johnson was to signal me when she had received the additional money, and I was to signal her so that she might leave the ringside. ... It was nearing the twenty-sixth round when the money was turned over to Mrs. Johnson. ... After examining it she gave me the signal. I replied that everything was O.K. by a pre-arranged sign and she departed.

However, if he had been paid as claimed, it wouldn't make sense for Johnson to be sending telegrams asking for money owed after the fact. Of course, Johnson might say that he was owed additional payments even after the fight.

Johnson also claimed that he did no serious training, and hardly any at all for the fight, which was contradicted by the news reports and his performance.

Johnson said that when he went down he was conscious and was covering his eyes from the sun while on his back. He used the photo with bent knees and hands over his eyes to prove his contention. Some, who only saw that photo, and were not able to see the films, believed him. However, the films show that Jack threw his arms up over his face in a reflex action when he was dropped, and his knees then went limp, and he did not move even after the count concluded. His arms appeared to be paralyzed and frozen in place. It even seemed as if Jack was trying to prevent himself from going down as he was falling, trying to grab Willard. If he was throwing the fight, he would not have tried to stop himself from

---

[1227] *El Paso Herald*, March 13, 1919; *New York Tribune*, March 14, 1919.

going down by grabbing at Willard on the way down, nor would he have gone down as hard as he did.

Johnson also claimed to have thrown the fight in exchange for the ability to return to the United States with leniency for his Mann Act conviction. However, in an earlier part of his autobiography, he didn't exactly say there was a deal for him to throw the fight, but that it was *suggested* that if he lost that things might be easier on him.

> On the day of the fight, my condition was fair and I could have defeated Willard and retained the title, but temptation had come to me and as I was stirred by the irresistible desire to see my mother, I was trying to decide upon a course that would enable me to return to the United States. I still was hesitant about entering prison, but at times had decided that I would return and serve my sentence for the sake of seeing my mother, but never got quite to that point. ... Preceding the Willard fight it was hinted to me in terms which I could not mistake, that if I permitted Willard to win, which would give him the title, much of the prejudice against me would be wiped out. Those who chafed under the disappointment of having a man of my race hold the championship, I was told, would be mollified, and it would be easier to have the charges against me dropped, and I could again be with my folks. ...
>
> As matters turned out, I had cause to regret my action, for after I had permitted the title to pass to Willard, I found that such offers or hints of leniency as had been tendered me were without substantial foundation, and that immediate prospects for my return to my own country without going to prison were so slight that I could not give them serious thought.[1228]

In that same autobiography, Johnson also said that Jack Curley "frankly told me that if I lost the fight to Willard I could return to the United States without being molested."

There is some limited primary source evidence of Johnson's claims. There were rumors of a fix before the fight. However, such rumors had floated around for many of Johnson's fights. Before the fight, some in Johnson's camp claimed that those associated with the promotion had made offers to Johnson to throw the fight. It also was said that government officials had tried unsuccessfully to induce Johnson to return to the U.S. Sam McVey said Jack took a dive. Johnson did look at his wife shortly before the knockout, and she did leave the ringside. However, at the time, the belief was that a fatigued Johnson feared that his end was near, he did not want his wife to see him lose, and she did not want to see it either.

More likely than not, Jess Willard had been at the right place at the right time. Johnson was aging at 37, had fought only once per year for the last four years, and therefore likely was not at his sharpest, and naturally was

---

[1228] Johnson, *In the Ring and Out*, at 100-102; 197-198, 201-203.

fatigued by the 26th round. Johnson had been hitting Willard hard enough to knock him out, and did not appear to be holding back. Even if he had agreed to throw the fight, or even if representations had been made to him that the government might be lenient with him if he lost, which may well be true, the way he attacked Willard so ferociously certainly gives the impression that he was attempting to win. He was knocked out by a right to the jaw by a big 6'6" 238-pound man with a long reach stepping in quickly with full force. The fight and the knockout looked legitimate. The referee believed the fight was legitimate, and said that Johnson had bet on himself to win, he was so confident. Johnson's trainer also believed the fight was on the level. Johnson fought confidently and punched ferociously for most of the fight, as if he expected to win via a knockout. However, fatigue set in against a younger, bigger, stronger, and better conditioned opponent.

It appears that like other champions before him, Johnson's ego did not allow him to concede defeat. He had tried to win, but after losing, used the offers made to him before the fight as an excuse. Years later, Gene Tunney said Johnson preferred to have his fans believe he sold out rather than that he was washed up.[1229]

The fight-film ban helped Johnson make his representations without the public in the U.S. being able to develop its own opinion. However, Europeans, Canadians, and others were able to see the films and draw their own conclusions. Although the preponderance of the evidence does not support a fake, there always will be some lingering doubts.

[1229] Gene Tunney, *A Man Must Fight* (Boston: Houghton Mifflin Co., 1932), 180.

CHAPTER 48

After the Crown

Jack Johnson had reigned as champion for over six years, from December 26, 1908 to April 5, 1915. He held victories over fighters who were skilled, fast, strong, big, small, black, and white. His long resume, with scores of lengthy bouts against the world's best, including 13 bouts that lasted 20 rounds, still stands out today as amongst the best ever career resumes of a heavyweight champion.

Just imagine if Johnson had been granted the title shot that he desired and deserved from 1903 to 1905, an opportunity which he would have obtained but for his race. If he would have won the title back then, he possibly could have been champion for ten or eleven years, which would put his reign's length on par with the likes of Joe Louis and Muhammad Ali. Even with having to wait until late 1908, when he was 30 years old, he still reigned for over six years, nearly as long as Larry Holmes.

If Johnson had scheduled the Willard bout for 25 rounds, which was the greatest distance that James J. Jeffries had defended his title, or 15 rounds, as would be the case for most title bouts throughout the mid-20th century, or 12 rounds as is the case today, he would have successfully retained his title on points with ease. With shorter, limited-rounds bouts, he might very well have reigned for several more years. He quite possibly could have had the longest reign of all time. The fact that he could dominate a big man for so long even at age 37 is a testament to how good Jack Johnson really was.

In fact, Johnson did not lose another fight again for eleven years, until 1926, when he was 48 years old, having won anywhere from thirteen to twenty bouts and exhibitions in a row (depending on what record one consults), although he was not allowed to engage in championship or elite caliber contests during those years.

Some quibble about the fact that he did not defend his title against the best black fighters of his era. However, he defeated them all prior to becoming champion, and was willing to fight them all if his price was met. Economics and race combined were huge factors. When push came to shove, most promoters were willing to put up big money to see a white man attempt to defeat Johnson. Far fewer were willing to bankroll a black versus black championship bout. Also, promoters cancelled scheduled Johnson title bouts with both black and white fighters. At various times, jurisdictions refused to allow Johnson to box for racial, moral, and legal reasons.

One month after the Willard fight, on May 7, 1915, Germany attacked and sunk the *RMS Lusitania* off of the coast of Ireland. It had sailed out of New York, and allegedly there were ammunitions secretly stored on the boat, being sent to the British. The 1,924 passengers aboard the vessel had no knowledge of the cargo being transported. 1,119 passengers perished. However, the United States did not enter World War I formally until two years later.

August 1915 lynching, Temple, Texas. One of the lynchers sent this photo to his parent(s), and wrote, "This is the barbeque we had last night."

From 1916 through 1920, Johnson fought and resided in places like Spain and Mexico. He also lived in France and England.

During 1916, U.S. President Woodrow Wilson signed an executive order designating "The Star-Spangled Banner" by Francis Scott Key as the national anthem. In 1931, the U.S. Congress passed a bill in support, which was signed by President Herbert Hoover. Written in 1814, Key's song, based on his experiences in the War of 1812, included a lesser-known verse criticizing the British for promising freedom to slaves who rebelled against the U.S. and fought on its side. Key was a slave-owner. Key gloated that even the tactical use of mercenaries and rebellious slaves was not enough to secure victory over the United States:

> And where is that band who so vauntingly swore,
> That the havoc of war and the battle's confusion
> A home and a Country should leave us no more?
> Their blood has wash'd out their foul footstep's pollution.
> No refuge could save the hireling and slave
> From the terror of flight or the gloom of the grave,
> And the star-spangled banner in triumph doth wave
> O'er the land of the free and the home of the brave.

Hence, even in 1916 and beyond, U.S. politicians supported a national anthem that was written pre-emancipation and contained such a verse, although it typically was omitted from public performances. It further highlights the inherent American contradiction - a country which supported slavery and segregation while proudly claiming to be a land of freedom.

On March 25, 1916 at New York's Madison Square Garden, just shy of one year after winning the title, Jess Willard defended his championship for the first time, winning a 10-round no-decision bout against Frank Moran. For a mere 10 rounds of work, Willard earned a guaranteed $47,500, and Moran $23,750. The gate receipts were $151,254. Willard did not fight again for over three years.

One year after Willard-Moran, on April 6, 1917, the U.S. declared war on the German Empire and joined the World War. Under the command of General John J. Pershing, several million U.S. soldiers, including black regiments, fought on the battlefields of France and elsewhere on the side of the Allies (United Kingdom, France, Russia, Italy, and Japan).

There still were plenty of race issues in the U.S. The East St. Louis, Illinois riots (a.k.a. the East St. Louis massacres) of May and July 1917 were an outbreak of labor- and race-related violence that caused between 40 and 200 deaths and extensive property damage, amongst the worst riots and worst cases of labor-related violence in 20th-century U.S. history. White unions which had excluded black workers did not appreciate industry owners utilizing blacks as replacements. Whites feared job and wage security due to the competition. Ultimately this led to their attacking blacks. Thousands of blacks were left homeless after their neighborhood had been burned down.

On March 17, 1918, Jack Johnson's mother, Tiny Johnson, died.

World War I ended on November 11, 1918 with the defeat of the Central Powers, which in part consisted of Germany, Austria-Hungary, and Turkey. More than 70 million military personnel had been mobilized in the war, and more than 9 million combatants and 7 million civilians had perished.

On July 4, 1919 in Toledo, Ohio, Jack Dempsey defeated Jess Willard to win the world heavyweight championship. After being decked seven times in the first round, Willard was beaten so badly that he retired after the 3rd round.

During 1919, dozens of race riots erupted throughout the United States, in both the North and South, making it become known as the Red Summer for its hundreds of deaths and massive property damage. Riots occurred in cities such as Bisbee, AZ, Charleston, SC, Chicago, IL, Elaine, AR, Knoxville, TN, Longview, TX, Norfolk, VA, Omaha, NE, Washington, D.C., and many others, in states like Alabama, Arizona, Connecticut, Georgia, Illinois, Louisiana, Maryland, Mississippi, New York, Pennsylvania, South Carolina, Tennessee, Texas, and Virginia.

The following year, on January 17, 1920, the 18th Amendment to the U.S. Constitution went into effect, making the manufacture, sale, and transportation of intoxicating liquors illegal. The amendment would not be repealed until 1933.

On August 18, 1920, the 19th Amendment to the U.S. Constitution was ratified, guaranteeing all American women the right to vote.

Over five years after he lost his title to Jess Willard, on July 20, 1920, a 42-year-old Jack Johnson returned to the U.S., surrendered to federal agents at the Mexican border, and was taken into custody. At his re-sentencing hearing on September 14, 1920, Judge George A. Carpenter once again sentenced Johnson to serve a one year and a day prison sentence at Leavenworth Prison and pay a $1,000 fine.

In January 1921, the Leavenworth Prison's Parole Board (which included former Nevada Governor Denver Dickerson, who had hosted Jeffries-Johnson), held a parole hearing and unanimously recommended that Johnson be paroled.

However, on January 21, 1921, the Justice Department, at the behest of U.S. Attorney General A. Mitchell Palmer, denied parole, and Johnson was required to serve his full one-year term, less any required credits for time previously served. Palmer was the attorney general who in response to strikes, race riots, and fear of communism and anarchism, had created the General Intelligence Unit, which would be led by J. Edgar Hoover.

Interestingly enough, while he was in prison, Johnson applied for and was granted two patents – one for an improved automobile wrench and one for a theft-prevention device for vehicles.

As of May 31, 1921, the segregated Greenwood section of Tulsa, Oklahoma, a district known as Black Wall Street owing to its vibrant, wealthy, and prosperous black community, was one of the most successful flourishing black neighborhoods in the country. However, on that date, the *Tulsa Tribune* published an inflammatory story wherein a white 17-year-old female elevator operator named Sarah Page accused black 19-year-old shoeshiner Dick Rowland of attempting to rape or at least assault her the previous day. In fact, her allegations were that he grabbed her arm. Word quickly spread that a white lynch mob intended to take the law into its own hands and kill Rowland. A group of black men assembled outside the jail to protect Rowland from the approaching lynch mob. A white man attempted to take a gun from a black man, a shot was fired, and violence erupted.

Whites used this incident as an excuse to rampage into the Greenwood district and loot, destroy, and burn down the neighborhood, including black-owned businesses, homes, churches, grocery stores, restaurants, movie theaters, a hospital, bank, post office, libraries, schools, law offices, airplanes, and even buses. The white mob even used some of the black-owned airplanes to launch gasoline and dynamite bombs from the sky. During the riot, the mob, led by the Ku Klux Klan, which included policemen, killed black men, women, and children, shooting and burning them. It was a massacre.

By the time troops were deployed the next day, the town virtually had been obliterated. Instead of arresting whites, the troops arrested thousands of blacks and held them in custody for several days before releasing them. No whites ever were arrested or charged.

Over 600 successful black businesses were ruined. Although the official death toll claimed 26 black deaths and 13 whites, the American Red Cross estimated over 300 deaths (many of whom were buried in mass graves), which is closer to the truth, 8,624 people in need of assistance, and over 1,000 homes and businesses destroyed. 35 square blocks had been torched. Eventually, the charges against Rowland were dismissed.

On July 9, 1921, a 43-year-old Jack Johnson was released from prison.

After his release, Johnson fought and exhibited in places like Cuba, Canada, and Mexico. Johnson later wrote, "I was sincere in challenging Dempsey, or any of the other heavyweights…but I realize that the private regulations and prejudices of boxing commissions prevent me from making a serious effort to arrange such a bout." Johnson was frozen out of big-time bouts. Champion Jack Dempsey never did fight one elite black fighter, either before or during his reign.[1230]

In January 1923, Rosewood, Florida was the scene of yet another racially motivated massacre of blacks and destruction of a black town. A mob of several hundred whites killed at least six blacks (though some report 27, and others 150, which filled mass graves) and burned down the predominantly black town. Members of the mob even kept body parts of a lynched man as souvenirs. The shootings, hangings, and burnings were precipitated by a white woman's claim that a black man had assaulted her, although domestic workers said she had been struck during an argument with the white lover she was seeing while her husband was at work. No arrests were made. The town was abandoned and none of its black residents ever moved back.[1231]

Lucille Cameron divorced Johnson in early 1924, owing to his infidelity. Over a year later, in August 1925, Johnson married Irene Pineau, another white woman, to whom he remained married until his death.

It wasn't until he was 48 years old in 1926 that Jack Johnson again fought on a card in the U.S. It was his first fight in the U.S. since 1912 against Flynn. Some Americans would pay to see Johnson when he was a completely past-it old fighter and more likely to lose.

Johnson continued engaging in occasional bouts and exhibitions throughout the remainder of his life, including charitable exhibitions for war veterans and bonds, and those who suffered from natural disasters.

On June 22, 1937, 22 years after Jack Johnson lost his title, a black man finally was given another chance to fight for the world heavyweight championship, which the phenomenally talented Joe Louis won by knocking out James J. Braddock in the 8th round.

[1230] Johnson, *In the Ring and Out* at 249. Johnson sparred Luis Firpo prior to the 1923 Firpo-Dempsey fight and claimed to have mastered him. "Firpo made such a poor showing in the ring with me that Rickard, the promoter, fearing that publicity of this would injure the gate-receipts, stopped further boxing between Firpo and me." Johnson was willing to fight him. "Firpo would have presented no difficulties for me." Id. at 250.

[1231] In 1994, Florida became the first U.S. state to compensate survivors and their descendants for damages incurred because of racial violence, reacting to an investigation and report regarding the Rosewood massacre which revealed that law enforcement failed to help or protect the residents while the murders and arson of the town was occurring. https://timeline.com/all-black-town-rosewood-wiped-off-the-map-by-white-mob-73ca6630802b; https://en.wikipedia.org/wiki/Rosewood_massacre

60 to 80 million people throughout the world would perish during World War II (September 1, 1939 to September 2, 1945), including soldiers both black and white.

On June 10, 1946, Jack Johnson's driving finally caught up with him, when in Franklinton, North Carolina, he lost control of his vehicle on a curve, struck a telephone pole, and died. He was 68 years old. He was buried in Chicago next to Etta Johnson.

In 1946, when the Rams moved from Cleveland to Los Angeles, they signed two black football stars from UCLA, Kenny Washington and Woody Strode, starting the path for integration in pro football (which had not allowed any black player since 1933). The Cleveland Browns then signed black players Bill Willis and Marion Motley. That fall, pro football began integration on the field.

In 1947, professional baseball finally began the process of gradually allowing some level of racial integration, with black Jackie Robinson entering the professional leagues for the Brooklyn Dodgers.

In 1950, the Boston Celtics of the National Basketball League signed black Chuck Cooper, and the New York Knicks signed Nat "Sweetwater" Clifton, starting pro basketball's path to integration. It would be many years before full integration was allowed.

In 1954, the U.S. Supreme Court decided *Brown v. Board of Education*, overruling the "separate but equal doctrine," holding that legally mandated racial segregation (in that case in the context of schools) was unconstitutional. The Civil Rights Act of 1964 put an end to all state and local laws requiring segregation. It wasn't until 1967, with the U.S. Supreme Court's decision in *Loving v. Virginia*, before all states became legally mandated to recognize marriages between persons of different races.

It would be many years before legalized racial segregation truly would end and be fully enforced, although in many ways, de facto segregation continued. As with the end to slavery, segregation did not end without a fight, nor without the seeds of bitter resentment over its termination being sown, or attempts to thwart its actual application. In 1968, Dr. Martin Luther King, Jr., who for years had advocated civil disobedience and peaceful protest in response to segregation, was assassinated, leading to the worst national race rioting since Johnson vs. Jeffries.

Forty years later, on November 4, 2008, Democrat Barack Obama was elected to be the 44th President of the United States; the first black person to be elected to the U.S. presidency. He served as President from January 20, 2009 to January 20, 2017.

On May 24, 2018, Republican President Donald J. Trump granted a posthumous full pardon to Jack Johnson.

Freedom has progressed greatly, though gradually. The United States of America and the world continues to struggle with issues of race.

Although I have often encountered prejudice on account of my race...I have found no better way of avoiding racial prejudice than to act in my relations with people of other races as if prejudice did not exist. ...

As I look back upon the life I have lived and compare it with the lives of my contemporaries I feel that mine has been a full life and above all a human life.[1232]

- Jack Johnson

[1232] Johnson, *In the Ring and Out*, at 239, 256.

Acknowledgments

Thank you to all who have helped me in some way with this book, be it research, photographs, promotion, editing, or general support:

Tom Seemuth

Clay Moyle

Katy Klinefelter

Dr. Harlan Barbanell

Gregory Speciale

Sergei Yurchenko

Steve Lott/ Boxing Hall of Fame Las Vegas

Thomas Hauser

Evan Grant

Tracy Callis

Derek Mays

University of Iowa / Interlibrary Loan

National Archives at Chicago

Boxrec.com

Eastsideboxing.com

Cyberboxingzone.com

Trufanboxing.com

Index

13th Amendment, 8
14th Amendment, 537
15th Amendment, 19, 96, 337
Abrams, Zeke/Zick, 64, 66, 67, 69, 70, 85, 94, 103, 104, 110, 134
Armstrong, Bob, 15, 26, 27, 38, 45, 51, 60, 69, 120, 125, 162, 314, 334, 357, 366
Austin, Mary, 17, 28, 57, 253
Austin, Sam, 131
Bachrach, Benjamin, 523, 535, 537-539, 541, 542, 544, 545, 547, 549, 553, 554, 555, 556, 557, 559, 561, 562, 565, 588
Baldwin, Matthew, 524, 563, 575, 613
Banks-Davis, Ada, 516, 517
Barber, Jesse Max, 151
Barry, Dave, 43, 103, 180, 281
Barry, Jim, 227, 242, 281, 289, 561
Barry, Richard, 367, 369, 375, 388
Beach, Rex, 360, 363, 400
Beckett, Harry, 166
Beerly, Gustav, 561, 562
Bell, Colin, 535
Benjamin, Ben, 444
Berger, Sam, 152, 153, 154, 160, 194, 244, 247, 252, 273, 280, 281, 292, 316, 322, 323, 334, 335, 336, 342, 359, 376, 377, 388-390, 396, 399
Bernau, Herman, 14, 16, 22
Bertelli, C. F., 601
Bettinson, Arthur, 257
Black Bill, 76, 119, 124, 134, 145, 174, 577
Blackburn, Jack, 145
Blease, Governor Coleman, 529
Brady, William, 592, 593, 601, 605, 607
Brennan, James, 164, 165, 168
Breyer, Victor, 573, 575
Britt, Jimmy, 83, 86, 96, 103, 113
Britt, Willis, 293, 294, 295, 297, 302, 322
Brooks, Charles, 16
Brown, Charles, 501
Brown, Governor Joseph, 505
Brown, William, 486
Burke, Sailor, 178
Burns, Farmer, 374, 398
Burns, Professor Watson, 483, 486
Burns, Tommy, 130, 135, 137-139, 141, 149, 152, 153, 159, 160, 163, 170-172, 175, 176, 179, 180, 182, 185-201, 210, 224, 227-229, 236, 243-245, 248, 254, 255, 259, 268, 270, 278, 289, 297, 330, 334, 346, 352, 354, 359, 366, 391, 392, 416, 469, 474, 560, 561, 576
Bustillo, Pedro, 618, 622
Butler, Joe, 56
Byers, George, 38, 45, 47, 147
Cameron, Lucille, 509, 510, 515, 517, 520, 525, 528, 529, 589, 645
Capone, Al, 589
Caponi, Tony, 270, 292

Carillo, Frank, 30, 41, 43, 45, 47, 48, 50, 66, 67
Carmody, Thomas, 571
Carpenter, Judge George A., 524, 532, 535, 536, 544, 549, 550, 553-561, 613, 644
Carpentier, Georges, 279, 462, 561, 583, 584, 596, 599, 600, 602, 604, 609
Carranza, Venustiano, 615, 617
Carter, Kid, 31, 47, 61, 80, 99, 106, 130, 515, 529
Casey, Jim, 99
Caste, 7, 9, 15, 37, 234, 244, 358, 402, 455, 469, 479
Century Athletic Club, 40, 50, 67, 86
Chanler, William, 581
Childs, Frank, 18, 22, 38, 39, 45, 46, 51, 81, 120
Choynski, Joe, 17, 22-25, 31, 49, 61, 100, 145, 156, 173, 258, 334, 336, 357, 366, 396, 444, 458
Churchill, Winston, 465, 471
Civil War, 8, 9, 10, 12, 148, 150, 176, 321, 463, 519, 569
Clansman, 134, 148, 154, 425, 427, 428, 434, 438, 616
Clark, Jeff, 614
Coffroth, James, 31, 70, 78, 81, 170, 175, 182, 228, 256, 281, 283, 296, 301, 312, 316, 366, 368, 370, 388, 391, 401, 446, 480, 581, 613
Cole, George, 134
Color line, 5, 6, 10-12, 18, 22, 26, 32-38, 49, 54, 55, 59, 60, 66, 67, 69, 72, 74, 76, 78, 81, 83, 84-86, 93, 96-102, 104-107, 109-111, 113-116, 120-124, 127-134, 138, 140, 145, 152-157, 160, 162, 164, 168, 170, 171, 175, 182, 187, 191, 194, 195-199, 201, 202-206, 209, 224-229, 236, 238, 240, 243, 245, 249, 253, 254, 275, 280, 288, 315, 331, 337, 344, 349, 355, 357, 361, 390, 395, 478, 483, 484, 488, 529, 531, 534, 576, 577, 582, 589, 618, 636
Congress, 17, 20, 482, 488, 502, 519, 523, 533, 536, 544, 585, 642
Conroy, Kid, 18
Considine, George, 597, 599
Coon, 26, 42, 46, 50, 53, 60, 62, 69, 72, 73, 92, 94, 98, 103, 109, 110, 111, 118, 122, 134, 155, 184, 185, 191, 208, 212, 241, 245, 250, 262, 274, 290, 298, 316, 323, 349, 359, 369, 371, 374, 375, 390, 397, 442, 445, 617
Corbett, Harry, 78, 103
Corbett, James J., 22, 35, 36, 37, 49, 54, 56, 59, 74, 104, 152, 173, 174, 204, 209, 235, 240, 244, 328, 334, 338, 341, 346, 349, 353, 354, 359, 361, 366, 388, 393, 395, 398, 401, 444, 452, 567, 570, 593, 597
Corbett, Tom, 281, 349
Corbett, W. F., 164, 169, 201, 223, 352
Corri, Eugene, 454, 609

649

Corri, Hugo, 298
Cotton, George, 339, 351, 369
Cotton, Kid, 341
Creedon, Dan, 18
Curley, Jack, 480, 481, 483, 484, 485-489, 498, 508, 611, 614, 615, 616, 635, 636, 638, 639
Cutler, Charles, 177, 255
Cutler, Kid, 177
Cutler, Marty, 338, 486
Dare, Helen, 398, 399
Davidson, Jay, 201
De Forest, James, 14
DeBray, George, 486
Delaney, Bill, 32, 36, 39, 42, 51, 59, 70, 74, 81, 84, 85, 105, 203, 228, 275, 281, 340, 343, 345, 357, 360, 377, 393, 398, 399
Democrat, 11, 17, 29, 30, 36, 37, 74, 195, 426, 488, 521, 530, 581, 590, 616, 646
Dennis, Link, 71
Densham, Jack, 389
DeWoody, Charles, 532, 548, 564, 565
Dickerson, Denver, 344, 346, 351, 355, 365, 644
Dime, Jimmy, 276
Discrimination, 89, 455
Disfranchisement, 19, 27, 89, 151, 176, 463, 534
Dix, Governor John, 476
Dixon, George, 31, 36, 41, 97, 153, 194, 270, 512
Dixon, Jr., Thomas, 134, 148, 425, 616
Dorgan, Tad, 31, 171, 237, 264, 265, 266, 278, 357, 592, 603
Douglas, Aimee, 255
Douglass, Frederick, 236, 255, 256, 362
Drummond, Fred, 576
Du Bois, W. E. B., 56, 244, 463
Due process, 12, 147, 529
Dunning, Billy, 149
Duryea Johnson, Etta, 57, 366, 367, 394, 452, 453, 455, 457, 460, 464, 479, 489, 501, 506, 507, 508, 516, 520, 535, 537-539, 542, 543, 545, 547, 548, 550, 553, 554, 556, 563, 566, 587, 588, 595, 646
Edgren, Robert, 83, 173, 178, 179, 188, 192, 195, 204, 237, 238, 504, 619, 620, 624, 633, 635, 637
Edwards, Harry, 258, 261
Emancipation, 34, 230, 408
Equal Protection, 15
Erbstein, Charles, 510, 513, 525
Everett, Mexican Pete, 27, 28, 58
Eyton, Charles, 65, 91, 92, 137, 170
Eyton, Charlie, 137
Felix, Peter, 155, 162, 164, 165, 167, 196, 198
Fennessey, Tom, 169
Ferguson, Sandy, 55, 58, 60, 69, 71, 73, 74, 75, 100, 125, 147, 194, 257, 276
Fitzpatrick, Sam, 152, 153, 156, 160, 174, 180, 182, 188, 190, 192, 202, 204, 206, 207, 248, 279
Fitzsimmons, Bob, 22, 37, 40, 42, 43, 47, 50, 52, 59, 60, 62, 66, 69, 70, 117, 124, 126, 134, 147, 152, 172, 173, 174, 175, 191, 238, 258, 264, 282, 298, 357, 366, 392, 396, 446, 549
Flanagan, Tom, 344, 359, 464, 486, 497, 527, 532, 564, 593, 605, 609, 615, 620, 622
Floto, Otto, 496, 497, 591, 593
Flynn, Jim, 4, 153, 156, 180, 181, 182, 183, 184, 185, 186, 187, 188, 192, 206, 281, 328, 331, 399, 459, 480-500, 506, 530, 561, 577, 614, 618, 645
Foley, Larry, 213
Fornoff, Captain Fred, 489, 494, 495
Frawley Act, 462
Frawley, James, 462, 476, 503, 504
Furey, Barney, 174, 550, 553
Gans, Joe, 41, 49, 61, 83, 86, 96, 145, 149, 153, 170, 171, 194, 225, 229, 238, 315, 323, 326, 361, 432, 453, 569
Gardner, George, 38, 46, 47, 57, 60, 70, 81, 100, 120, 173, 180, 275, 281
Gibson, Billy, 501
Gillett, Governor James, 336, 338, 339, 340, 342, 343, 417, 420, 451
Gleason, Jack/John, 323, 335, 342, 365, 446
Godfrey, George, 22, 33
Gotch, Frank, 328, 366
Graney, Eddie, 78, 79, 103, 115, 323, 335, 342
Greggains, Alex, 104, 106, 109, 110, 111, 112, 113, 114, 115, 116
Greggains, Alec/Alex, 46, 99, 100, 101, 103, 104, 106, 107, 109, 110, 111, 112, 113, 114, 115, 116, 155
Griffin, Hank, 30, 31, 32, 38, 39, 40, 42, 43, 45, 49, 50, 51, 52, 53, 60, 147, 162, 357
Griffith, D. W., 134, 616
Grim, Joe, 87, 126, 127, 156, 281
Griswold, Sandy, 98, 488, 489, 497
Haghey, Charles, 147
Hague, Ian Iron, 459
Haines, Klondike John, 17, 18, 20, 21, 45, 49, 120
Hall, Frank, 388, 390, 396
Harding, President Warren G., 589
Harlan, Justice John, 15
Harris, Morris, 124, 145, 174
Harrison, Mayor Carter, 515, 517, 529
Hart, Marvin, 45, 83, 99, 100, 101, 108, 111, 116-122, 124, 125, 127, 128, 130, 131, 135, 137, 152, 175, 180, 188, 197, 199, 209, 261, 275, 279, 335, 354, 456, 480
Hart, Sig, 156, 335
Harting, George, 368, 391, 589
Haywards, Jim, 182
Hemple, Jack, 617
Herman, Frank, 390, 397
Houseman, Lou, 18, 351
Hughes, Governor Charles, 292
Hyland, Dick, 175
Ingalls, Senator John, 10
International Boxing Union, 573, 575, 577
Jackson, Peter, 33, 34, 35, 36, 37, 38, 60, 69, 81, 93, 94, 97, 101, 118, 119, 132, 134, 145, 152, 154, 156, 161, 162, 164, 195, 210, 224, 240, 289, 315, 328, 357

650

Jackson, Young Peter, 119, 132, 134, 145, 281, 289, 315
Jacobson, Pauline, 387, 390, 401
Jeannette, Joe, 80, 119, 120, 124, 132, 133, 134, 135, 140, 141, 145, 150, 154, 157, 158, 256, 257, 276, 324, 349, 435, 454, 456, 457, 459, 462, 464, 481, 499, 501, 502, 503, 505, 512, 570, 571, 572, 573, 575, 576, 577, 580, 581, 582, 584, 590, 591, 613, 614, 617
Jeffords, Jim, 118, 119, 154, 155, 156, 177
Jeffries, Alexis, 291
Jeffries, Jack, 40, 41, 42, 66, 153, 334, 348, 359, 360
Jeffries, James J., 3, 22, 26, 30, 32, 37-40, 42, 43, 47, 50, 51, 54, 56, 59, 60, 62-64, 66, 70, 71, 73, 74, 81, 83, 84, 91, 94, 102, 114, 115, 116, 118, 119, 120, 122, 129, 140, 153, 159, 161, 164, 170, 172, 196, 201, 204, 208, 228, 229, 238, 241, 243, 244, 246, 247, 254, 256, 257, 259, 261, 265, 270, 273, 279, 280, 291, 292, 319, 321, 326, 328, 330, 333, 336, 337, 340, 353, 354, 357, 363, 366, 368, 395, 402, 426, 436, 438, 439, 446, 499, 521, 537, 578, 634, 641
Jim Crow, 9, 89, 246, 337, 356, 533
Johnson, Charles, 518
Johnson, Claude, 488, 496
Johnson, Ed, 17
Johnson, Henry, 10, 483, 506
Johnson, Jim, 4, 502, 575, 576, 577, 578, 579, 581, 582, 584, 606, 610, 613, 614, 615, 617
Johnson, Lucy, 454
Johnson, Tina, 8, 232, 322, 324, 408, 448, 457, 517, 524, 550, 563, 613, 643
Johnson, Walter, 119, 120
Jones, Tom, 613
Jordan, Billy, 59, 182, 283, 284, 302, 303, 360, 365, 367, 368
Kaufman, Al, 4, 130, 152, 154, 182, 187, 208, 227, 228, 242, 275, 281, 282, 283, 289, 294, 315, 341, 459, 480, 561
Kelly, Hugo, 156, 292, 297
Kelly, Spider, 66, 80
Kennedy, Joe, 39, 40
Kennedy, Tom, 591
Kenny, Yank, 257
Kerr, Clara, 57
Ketchel, Stanley, 4, 197, 206, 207, 227, 240, 254, 256-259, 261, 263-274, 276, 279, 280, 290, 292-318, 321-323, 327, 334, 342, 361, 366, 391, 414, 445, 447, 449, 454, 473, 537, 539, 542, 555
Kilrain, Jake, 35
Kipling, Rudyard, 17
Kitchen, Jack, 420
Kling, Peter, 169
Ku Klux Klan, 134, 150, 534, 616, 644
Landis, Judge Kenesaw Mountain, 519, 520, 589
Lang, Bill, 166, 192, 196, 198, 352, 366, 457, 474
Langford, Sam, 133, 135, 145, 146, 147, 195, 206, 238, 240, 249, 254, 257, 258, 288, 292, 298, 313, 315, 327, 328, 331, 334, 349, 354,
366, 447, 454, 456, 457, 458, 464, 474, 479, 483, 485, 498, 502, 508, 531, 535, 570, 572-574, 576, 581, 584, 590, 591, 604, 609, 610, 613, 614
Lanigan, W. H., 487
Law, 5, 9, 10, 14, 15, 16, 23-25, 37, 49, 89, 96, 129, 143, 150, 159, 233, 236, 252, 255, 280, 292, 297, 328, 329, 332, 336, 345, 350, 389, 408, 411, 412, 414, 417, 425, 427, 428, 429, 431, 433, 463, 465, 476, 482, 485, 502, 504, 506, 510, 513, 514, 515, 516, 519-523, 525, 527, 529, 530, 534, 539, 548, 549, 557, 558, 560, 562, 564, 569, 570, 585, 615, 635, 644, 645
Lawler, George, 21
Lee, John, 14
Legality, 5, 6, 7, 14, 16, 24, 25, 37, 49, 64, 101, 201, 212, 237, 329, 333, 342, 343, 344, 346, 376, 388, 402, 410, 417, 427, 433, 465, 471, 472, 473, 474, 476, 480, 510, 512, 514, 517, 526, 530, 533, 537, 562, 564, 569, 577, 585, 635, 637, 641, 643
Levinsky, Battling, 583
Levy, Joseph, 514, 550, 564, 566
Lewis, Billy, 499, 559, 562, 569, 582, 608, 610, 611, 612
Lewis, Willie, 120, 190, 593
Lincoln, President Abraham, 8, 9, 34, 195, 567, 576
Little, George, 254, 261, 270, 282, 294, 295, 297, 300, 301, 310, 326, 335, 339, 340, 346, 449, 451, 541, 542, 545, 552
London, Jack, 226, 348, 351, 357, 360, 369, 370, 371, 389, 390, 397, 401, 419, 446
Lynchings, 28, 66, 88, 141, 425, 644
Magilligan, T. P., 349, 358, 445
Maher, Peter, 58, 61, 173, 576
Maitrot, Emile, 590
Malgan, Abdul, 485
Mann Act, 510, 517, 519, 520, 523, 524, 527, 533, 536, 541, 548, 554, 555, 558, 559, 563, 570, 574, 585, 588, 638, 639
Marriage, 54, 134, 247, 451, 508, 509, 513, 520, 525, 528, 530, 531, 533, 537, 545, 553, 560, 570
Martin, Denver Ed, 30, 32, 33, 38, 45, 49, 51, 52, 60, 61, 64, 66, 80, 86, 90, 91, 93, 120, 124, 251, 297, 359
Masterson, Bat, 237, 278, 567, 573
McAuliffe, Jack, 366
McAuliffe, Joe, 33, 34
McCarey, Tom, 40, 42, 49, 63, 64, 66, 86, 90, 93, 135, 161, 170, 289, 290, 323, 366
McCarney, Billy, 534
McCarthy, Charles, 582
McCarthy, Mayor P. H., 396, 417
McCarty, Luther, 530, 531, 532, 534, 535, 560, 561, 611
McClay, Hattie, 248, 253, 259, 324, 451, 453, 538, 540, 542, 548, 549, 554, 555, 556, 563, 587
McCormick/McCormack, Jim/Jack, 19, 20, 83, 103, 125, 129, 147
McCoy, Kid, 47, 57, 86, 91, 152, 267

651

McDonald, Governor William, 482, 485, 489
McGovern, Terry, 262, 345
McGrath, Tim, 85, 323
McGuigan, Jack, 75, 268
McIntosh, Hugh, 195, 196, 198-201, 206-208, 212, 213, 220, 225, 231, 246, 252, 292, 323, 352, 366, 442, 446, 464, 480, 485, 488, 508, 512, 531
McKetrick, Dan, 570, 606, 610
McKinley, President William, 17, 29
McLaglen, Victor, 250, 251, 482
McLean, Alec/Alex, 125, 155, 162, 163, 168, 169, 333
McLoughlin, William, 255, 262, 264
McMahon Brothers, 502, 503
McNeill, William, 20
McReynolds, James C., 561
McVea/McVey, Sam, 49, 52, 53, 54, 55, 59-68, 70, 71, 72, 77-81, 86, 91, 190, 191, 194, 256, 257, 276, 324, 458, 464, 479, 480, 483, 488, 499, 502, 508, 512, 531, 535, 566, 576, 591, 614, 620, 622, 633, 639
McVey, Jim/John, 59, 60, 61
Menocal, President Mario, 618, 619, 622
Meyer, Reverend F. B., 464, 465, 466, 467, 468, 469, 472, 473
Miles Brothers, 295
Mills, Dave, 341, 359
Miscegenation, 7, 54, 252, 559, 616
Mixed-race, 5, 6, 23, 36, 85, 149, 173, 176, 190, 194, 200, 210, 252, 255, 292, 343, 470, 501, 502, 528, 567, 571
Moir, Gunner, 179, 186, 187, 190, 194
Moir, James, 187
Molineaux, Tom, 5, 34
Monahan, Walter, 455, 617
Moran, Frank, 4, 257, 570, 575, 581, 582, 584, 591, 594, 596, 600, 610, 617, 643
Morris, Carl, 456, 458, 480, 561, 611
Morris, Edward, 13, 124, 145, 174, 456, 458, 480, 523, 561, 611
Morris, Jackie, 13
Muldoon, William, 348, 350, 365, 593
Munroe, Jack, 50, 59, 74, 77, 78, 83, 84, 85, 86, 93, 94, 98, 105, 121, 122, 123, 357, 392
Murphy, Con, 602
Murphy, Dan, 18
Murphy, Tim, 71
Murray, Jimmy, 147
National Sporting Club, 154, 191, 193, 195, 249, 257, 459
Naughton, W. W., 72, 73, 80, 83, 98, 104, 110, 111, 116, 137, 188, 228, 244, 282, 290, 291, 309, 310, 315, 316, 370, 373, 388, 389, 399, 457, 478, 486, 488, 496, 502
Neil, Billy, 189
Nelson, Battling, 113, 117, 149, 172, 194, 262, 344, 349, 360, 366, 399
Netherland, Joseph, 256
Nolan, Billy, 340
North, 8, 9, 11, 17, 29, 36, 74, 89, 96, 132, 134, 148, 149, 159, 176, 177, 195, 196, 297, 343, 407, 411, 424, 425, 432, 458, 462, 505, 510, 516, 519, 521, 527, 530, 536, 565, 572, 575, 583, 589, 643, 646
O'Brien, Jack, 4, 99, 103, 104, 133, 134, 137, 138, 147, 152, 153, 155, 158, 159, 163, 166, 170, 179, 187, 254, 257, 258, 261, 264, 265, 268, 270, 275, 281, 292, 366, 392, 464
O'Keefe, Pat, 198
O'Neill, Frank, 481, 504, 595
O'Rourke, Tex, 617, 618, 620
O'Rourke, Tom, 175, 340, 532
Oldfield, Barney, 454, 552
Palmer, Jack, 188
Palzer, Al, 480, 487, 497, 501, 502, 531, 532, 534, 561, 570, 582, 591
Papke, Billy, 279, 292, 334
Paris, George, 249, 251
Parkin, Harry A., 537, 538, 543, 544, 545, 548, 553, 554, 555, 556, 558, 559, 562, 566
Pelkey, Arthur, 560, 561, 576, 581, 591, 611
Perkins, John, 486
Philippine-American War, 17
Pierson, Dave, 13
Pinder, Norman, 326, 329, 330, 331
Plessy, Homer, 15
Police, 7, 9, 15, 17, 18, 22-25, 30, 32, 33, 37-39, 43, 49, 54, 57-61, 64, 67, 69, 70, 77, 81, 82, 85, 86, 94, 96-101, 114, 116-118, 120-123, 127-132, 134, 135, 141, 143, 145, 147, 149, 150, 153, 154, 160, 161, 168, 209, 213, 220-222, 233, 234, 238, 239, 260, 262, 270, 279, 292, 297, 323, 326, 329, 336, 338, 345, 350, 364, 378, 403-412, 420, 428, 429, 435, 436, 441, 442, 450-453, 458, 460, 462, 465, 473, 474, 489, 496-499, 504, 507, 508, 510, 525, 530, 532, 533, 539, 540, 564, 568, 569, 588, 589, 604, 608
Prejudice, 11, 69, 85, 97, 102, 104, 110-113, 128-131, 141, 143, 156, 178, 189, 196, 197, 209, 224, 225, 230, 237-240, 242-244, 253, 255, 267, 271, 278, 279, 282, 288, 292, 315, 321, 322, 326, 336, 340, 343, 344, 353, 355-360, 400, 411, 420, 422, 423, 425, 427, 429, 435, 436, 445, 453, 464, 465, 467, 482, 488, 500, 504, 505, 511, 514-516, 520, 522, 524, 527, 537, 558, 559, 562, 563, 565-567, 569, 572, 586, 588, 594, 607, 639, 647
Race, 5-10, 15-17, 23, 27, 29, 33, 34, 36, 37, 39, 40, 49, 60, 66-72, 74, 82, 83, 85, 89, 96, 97, 102, 106, 110-113, 120, 127-130, 135, 142, 143, 148, 149, 150, 154, 156-159, 161, 170, 173, 176, 177, 180, 189, 190, 194, 196, 200, 204, 209, 210, 222, 224, 225, 227-247, 252-255, 261, 269, 271, 276, 279, 280, 289, 292, 300, 311, 313, 315, 316, 319, 322-328, 331-337, 340, 341, 343, 344, 346, 348-363, 366, 375, 388-392, 395, 396, 398, 400-445, 452, 453, 455, 457, 458, 461, 463, 464, 467-471, 478, 479, 482-488, 497, 498, 500-508, 511-518, 520-530, 532, 533, 537, 552, 559-562, 565-567, 569, 571, 581, 583, 590, 596, 603, 606-609, 615, 616, 618, 621, 633, 636, 639, 641, 643, 644, 646, 647

Race Riot, 17, 20, 56, 71, 143, 151, 195, 196, 242, 339, 362, 403, 406, 411, 450, 498, 515, 574, 604, 644
Ralston, William, 100, 101, 102, 115
Reconstruction, 9, 17, 29, 176
Reliance Athletic Club, 31, 39, 40
Republican, 8, 15, 19, 27, 75, 87, 90, 145, 147, 152, 278, 328, 330, 331, 332, 454, 456, 519, 520, 646
Resspress, Kid Calvin Rastus, 486
Rhodes, Gus, 566, 570, 607
Rhodes, Jennie, 506
Richmond, Bill, 5
Rickard, Tex, 149, 323, 335, 336, 342, 344, 345, 347, 364, 365, 370, 376, 377, 388, 389, 392, 417, 418, 446, 447, 645
Rocap, William, 269, 601, 606
Roche, Billy, 18, 62, 78, 113, 180, 182
Roche, Jem, 189
Roche, William, 18, 62, 78, 113, 180, 182
Rock, William T., 342, 347, 366
Roddenberry, Seaborn, 530
Roosevelt, President Franklin, 502
Roosevelt, Presideent Theodore, 17, 29, 88, 147, 149, 230, 460, 509, 511
Root, Jack, 38, 47, 57, 81, 99, 120, 121, 122, 135, 349
Ross, Tony, 4, 156, 180, 275, 277, 281, 462, 464, 576
Ruhlin, Gus, 30, 32, 39, 58, 59, 60, 73, 74, 76, 100, 118, 124, 129, 152, 173, 297, 392
Russell, Fred, 27, 43, 44, 49, 50, 52, 74, 251, 276, 539
Ryan, Tommy, 97, 156, 187, 268, 331, 333, 484, 485, 487, 496
San Francisco Athletic Club, 103
Savage, Jim, 617
Sayers, Governor Joseph, 22, 23, 24
Scanlan, Jim, 21
Schreck, Mike, 152, 175, 195, 275, 281, 458, 480
Schreiber, Belle, 519, 520, 526, 537-560, 562, 563, 574, 585, 586
Segregation, 5, 9, 17, 51, 56, 134, 642, 646
Sharkey, Tom, 26, 27, 32, 49, 58, 59, 60, 77, 86, 121, 152, 173, 297, 338, 359, 366, 392
Siler, George, 82, 123, 129, 131, 149
Sims Act, 502
Sims, Thetus, 488, 502
Skelly, Kid, 486
Slattery, William, 358, 388
Slavery, 8-11, 23, 34, 74, 88, 90, 148, 319, 400, 426, 458, 514, 519, 523, 526, 527, 530, 534, 536, 614, 642, 646
Smith, Ed, 497
Smith, Ed W., 485, 494
Smith, Eddie, 282, 289
Smith, Gunboat, 299, 300, 314, 315, 570, 574, 576, 581, 583, 591, 602, 604, 609, 611, 613
Smith, Hoke, 151, 463, 516
South, 8-11, 19, 20, 23, 29, 35-37, 87-90, 96, 99, 100, 102, 106, 127-130, 134, 141, 147, 148, 154, 158, 159, 168, 171, 176, 177, 195, 200, 210, 239, 242, 280, 324, 343, 358, 360, 395, 407, 411, 412, 416, 424, 425, 432, 435, 436, 438, 441, 442, 456, 463, 465, 468-472, 476, 478, 496, 505, 515-518, 527-530, 533, 569, 643
Spanish-American War, 17
Squires, Bill, 152, 155, 156, 161, 162, 163, 164, 168, 170-172, 187, 192- 194, 196, 198, 205, 214, 225, 231, 340, 398
Stift, Billy, 26, 28, 40, 99
Stuart, Harry, 41, 42, 43, 50, 52, 53, 54, 78
Sullivan, Jack, 86, 130, 135, 152, 153, 180, 281, 292, 297
Sullivan, John L., 33, 35, 36, 37, 83, 97, 177, 204, 205, 241, 320, 328, 344, 346, 354, 359, 365, 368, 370, 377, 392, 397, 401, 416, 456, 529
Supreme Court of the United States, 15, 252, 292, 413, 523, 524, 530, 531, 533, 534, 561, 574, 588, 635, 646
Sutton, Frank, 506, 549, 550
Taft, President William H., 247, 360, 502, 519
Taylor, Ben, 194
Temple, Larry, 145, 147
The White Man's Burden, 17
Thompson, Bob, 13
Tillman, Senator Ben, 19, 20, 27, 29, 96, 147, 148, 158, 159, 176, 177, 242, 425, 438, 458
Tracy, Tom, 18
Union, 8, 10, 16, 20, 158, 276, 337, 364, 390, 468, 482, 503, 530, 573, 575, 577
Van Court, DeWitt, 326, 354
Van Court, Eugene, 334
Van Loan, C. E., 158, 330, 341
Vancouver Athletic Club, 249, 251
Vardaman, Governor James K., 74, 152, 425, 426, 438
Vienne, Theodore, 575, 590, 595
Villa, Francisco, 615
Vitagraph Company, 414
Walcott, Joe, 13, 15, 31, 41, 45, 47, 55, 61, 83, 97, 119, 125, 130, 133, 134, 145, 146, 147, 153, 194, 486
Walton, Lester, 499, 503, 504, 505, 511, 522, 606
Washington, Booker T., 29, 56, 159, 176, 236, 331, 348, 362, 429, 433, 512
Welch, Jack, 72, 103, 252, 302, 308, 335, 622
Wells, Billy, 4, 454, 459, 462, 464, 472, 487, 561, 584
Wells-Barnett, Ida B., 526
White, Charlie, 445
White, James, 465, 466, 471, 472, 473
Wilkerson, James, 510, 520, 537, 561, 582, 588, 589
Wilkins, Barron, 255, 326
Willard, Jess, 4, 583, 606, 611-627, 633-639, 641, 643, 644
Williams, Al, 481
Willie, John, 77, 100, 119, 190
Wills, Harry, 590, 591, 614
Wilson, President Woodrow, 561, 616, 642
Wilson, Tommy, 17
Woodman, Joe, 240, 327, 359, 461
Woods, Billy, 30

Wren, John/Jack, 162, 163, 164, 166
Yellow streak, 39, 152, 155, 175, 180, 185, 193, 201, 203, 205, 218, 219, 222, 225, 229, 235, 238, 243, 252, 261, 273, 274, 285, 293, 295, 317, 320, 327, 334, 338, 342, 355, 358, 360, 369, 370, 376, 390, 391, 393, 396, 397, 400, 419, 420, 422, 430, 434, 445, 497

Adam J. Pollack is a boxing judge and referee, attorney, and member of the Boxing Writers Association of America.

www.ingramcontent.com/pod-product-compliance
Lightning Source LLC
Chambersburg PA
CBHW030320020526
44117CB00030B/233